No Idle Hands

Anne L. Macdonald

No Idle Hands

The Social History of American Knitting

Ballantine Books
New York

Grateful acknowledgment is made to the following for permission to reprint previously
published material:

The Atlantic Monthly: excerpt from the article "Of Women Knitting" by Esther D.
Hamill. © 1936 by Esther D. Hamill, as first published in The Atlantic Monthly, May
1936.

Little, Brown and Company: excerpt from the poem "Machinery Doesn't Answer, Either,
But You Aren't Married to It," from Verses from 1929 On by Ogden Nash. Copyright
1935 by Odgen Nash. First appeared in the Saturday Evening Post. UK and Open
Market rights controlled by Andre Deutsch, as printed in I Wouldn't Have Missed It
by Ogden Nash. Used by permission of Little, Brown and Company and Andre Deutsch.

Popular Music Publications: excerpt from the song "Knit Two, Purl Two," words by
Eliza Combs Emmons, music by Lee Darnelle. © 1942 by Popular Music Publications.
Reprinted by permission.

Illustration credits may be found at the back of this book.

LIBRARY OF CONGRESS CATALOGING-IN-PUBLICATION DATA

Macdonald, Anne, 1920–
No idle hands.
Bibliography: p.
1. Knitting—Social aspects—United States—
History.   I. Title.
TT819.U6M33   1988   746.43'2'0973   86-92098
ISBN 0-345-33906-1

Design by Beth Tondreau Design

Manufactured in the United States of America

10   9   8   7   6   5   4   3   2

For Peter

In works of labor or of skill
I would be busy too;
For Satan finds some mischief still
For idle hands to do.

Isaac Watts, *Against Idleness*, 1732

Contents

Contents

Acknowledgments

To my late parents, Florence Hite and Walter Franklin Lineberger, whose enthusiastic support of my education enabled me to attend Santa Barbara Girls' School, in whose sunny library I researched my first history paper and was forever hooked.

To Wellesley College, where beloved history professor Barnett Miller advised, "Go to the original sources to catch the voice of the past. Then, and only then, write about it." Hers was the driving force behind my lifelong commitment to the discipline of history.

To National Cathedral School, where I taught American history for many years and honed my research skills through study grants. My special gratitude for the ever-resourceful assistance of librarians Anne Carr, Joan Parker and the late Margaret Keys, who sustained my addition to primary materials.

To legions of my former history students whose research so affected my own, particularly Jennifer Roecklein's study of Amelia Bloomer, Alison Sheehy's examination of women's life on the Overland Trail and Cynthia Paul's exploration of the great bicycle craze of the 1890s. As I write I am conscious of every student's hot breath upon my neck, gleeful that I must punctuate and spell properly, answer to a higher authority (my editor), meet deadlines and vouch for every footnote.

To my treasured friend Patricia Slattery Brand for debunking the myth of helpless southern women and insisting that I include their backbreaking struggles during the Civil War. Discovering records of the Ladies' Aid Society of Greenville, South Carolina, her hometown, was one of my special rewards.

To my professional colleague, fellow author and close friend, Elisabeth Griffith, whose enviously broad background in women's history prompted me to wander from political to social history. Introducing me to the Women's Movement, she assured me that I would lose neither my dignity nor my husband if I identified myself as Anne Macdonald rather than Mrs. Peter Macdonald. When I retired from teaching, she encouraged me to publish the fruits of my research and dispatched me to her literary agent.

To that agent, Leona Schechter, who responded to my original proposal with an encouraging "That's a wonderful idea!" and promptly found a publisher.

To my editors, Joëlle Delbourgo and Michelle Russell, whose respect and encouragement have made writing *No Idle Hands* so rewarding.

To Pat Trexler, without whose help the "modern" parts of this book would have lacked authority and color. Her urging readers of her column, "Pat's Pointers," to respond to my questionnaire brought a Niagara of mail.

To Jane Nylander, formerly of Sturbridge Village, who generously allowed me to take notes from her card file on knitting in early nineteenth-century sources.

To former president Sidney Wasch and current executive vice president Daniel Lowe of the Bucilla Company, who shared their company's history with me through access to their rich files, begun when Bernard Ulmann emigrated to the United States in the mid-nineteenth century. Their permission to reproduce photographs from pattern books and advertising has enriched this publication immeasurably.

To the staff of the Library of Congress, my second home, where materials boggle the mind and assistance from experts is generously given. Bruce Martin in Reader Facilities always had a cheery "How's it going?"; Peggy Coughlin in the Children's Division dispensed hints on children's knitting; Sarah Pritchard shared bibliographies and suggested new sources; Chris Wright borrowed desperately needed materials from other libraries; fellow researchers cheered my luck in landing a contract.

To archivists, curators and librarians of many institutions for their help, especially Doris Bowman of the National Museum of American History; Cynthia Young of the Detroit Historical Museum; Ralph A. Pugh of the Chicago Historical Society; Dale C. Mayer at the Herbert Hoover Library; William G. Allmon, assistant curator of the White House; Carol Downey of the Arizona Department of Library, Archives and Public Records; Helen Matuskowitz of the Valley Forge Historical Society; Linda Baumgarten of the Colonial Williamsburg Foundation; Susan Swan of Winterthur Museum; Cynthia Bertsch of the Oregon Historical Society; Margaret Klapthor of the Divison of Political History of the National Museum of American History; Anne Inglehart of the Schlesinger Library in Cambridge; Polly Mitchell of the Shelburne Museum; Ellice Rowsheim of the Ohio Historical Society; Grant Allen Anderson of the Historical Department of the Church of Jesus Christ of Latter-Day Saints; Terry Geesken of the Museum of Modern Art; Mrs. Marguerite Hubbard of the Franklin Delano Roosevelt Library; Hazel Braugh of the National Red Cross; and the staffs of the Connecticut Historical Society and the Library of the Mount Vernon Ladies' Association of the Union.

To hundreds of knitters, particularly Suzanne Baizerman of the *Weaver's Journal* and Christine Timmons of the Taunton Press, who have shared their stitching histories with me and suggested others to contact.

To our children, Peter, Jan, Lloyd, Roger and Lorrie, who have long since left the nest but applauded my research and massaged my writer's tender ego. To our family's next generation, Vanessa, Jeremy, James, Taylor, Morgan and Paige, I promise that Grandmother will shortly return to her knitting!

ANNE L. MACDONALD
Bethesda, Maryland

Introduction

A social history like this was con-
sidered beyond the pale of "real" history when I was growing up,
and I well remember my father's indignation when his only son, a
Yale history major, enrolled in a distinguished professor's course in
American social history that was irreverently nicknamed "Pots and
Pans" by the prankish students. In those Depression days, my father
equated expenditure on such "twaddle" with money down the drain,
and the message was not lost on his youngest. When I hit the college
big time a few years later, I prudently matriculated in political science
and history, and consorted with kings, presidents, prime ministers
and emperors, with a dash of wars and treaties on the side. The virtual
dearth of women's affairs in historical texts struck me as deplorable,
but in the thirties and forties I was not spurred to demand exhu-
mation of "Herstory." Nor could I have conceived that one day I
would write primarily on women, especially about their *knitting*!

This book grew, not from a decision to "write women into history,"
for knitting is certainly not the vehicle for elevation of their status,
but from curiosity piqued by my own history of unflagging knitting.
With no genetic endowment from a nonknitting mother (an archi-
tectural engineer/homemaker), an indifferent-knitter maternal
grandmother (a proud college graduate whose unsolicited, pro–New
Deal political comments kept the pot boiling in our Republican
household) and a tatting but unapproachable paternal grandmother,
my two sisters and I, impelled by some ancient urge, "took up the

needle" and blossomed into dedicated sewers and knitters. To my knowledge, our brother (the aforementioned pots-and-pans fellow metamorphosed into bank president, horseman and knowledgeable collector of antiques) lifted a needle neither in anger nor in delight but luckily married a gifted and delightful stitcher.

Of my many questions about knitting, I kept returning to "Why don't *men* knit?" I had *heard* that some men knit, but despite maintaining a vigil like an ornithologist scouting a rare species, I never actually spotted one until I had just begun this book—plain as day, right there on the subway! The preppily clad Capitol Hill staffer opened his cordovan briefcase, extracted a magnificent blue sweater on round needles and clicked away. From *my* briefcase, I plucked an article freshly duplicated at the Library of Congress, caught his attention and held up the headline: KNITTING IS GOOD FOR YOUR HEALTH. Bursting with laughter, he held it aloft for craning passengers, and everyone exchanged knitting stories for four stops, parting as old friends at the transfer point—an auspicious beginning.

My research has since validated my previous observations that in America, where knitting has been assigned to woman's domain, adult knitting males are stared at, fussed over, almost petted as daring, even darling, adventurers or avoided for being too "feminine." In a current attempt to obliterate the latter stereotype and to cultivate increasingly unisex markets, knitting publications such as *Knitters*, which devoted eight pages to "Men Who Knit" in its Spring 1987 issue, hope to stiffen the resolve of potential knitting-men who aspire to knit without risking their macho image. Snickerers have always been among us. Even the Greek philosopher Lucretius, who credited men with weaving the first cloth ("[F]or the male sex in general far excels the other [women] in skill and is much more ingenious"), conceded that when "rugged countrymen" upbraided clothmakers for such domestic tasks, the clothiers capitulated and were "glad to give it over into the hands of the women." After the Industrial Revolution, when European textile mills attracted both male and female workers, the exclusively male knitting guilds declined, and *hand* knitting endured as essentially a female household occupation, a tradition exported to America. Though it is generally accepted that knitting is not gender specific, with one sex no more qualified to perform it than the other, an 1888 American needlework writer traced sex differentiation to competition in the Garden of Eden: "Whether he was slower in the work, or made a bad job of it, we are not told; but for some reason he dropped out, and woman is now the admitted queen of needle-work." Many "queens," secure on their domestic thrones, jealously guarded the gates to their needlework sanctuary. One knitting manual editor wrote haughtily, "While it is true that there are men, notably in England, who knit, it is really a woman's job." I thought I'd better look into that!

To broaden and contemporize my research in American knitting, I interviewed dozens of knitting friends and knitters at knitting workshops, conventions and seminars, inserted author's queries in knitting publications and asked for help from Pat Trexler, who generously published my questionnaire in "Pat's Pointers," her weekly column begun in the mid-sixties and nationally syndicated in over eighty newspapers. The response, particularly from Pat's devoted followers, was so monumental that our mailman, exhausted from shoveling fat batches through the slot, rapped on the door and inquired, "Okay, I give up. What *are* you doing?" What I was doing was not very scientific. I was not quantifying responses by entering data in columns and categorizing replies to each question. Into what column would you put instructions for "Granny's bedspread," a "Cape Cod coverlet," a "potato scubber" knit from nylon netting (it really does the job on Idahos!), a scrapbook of forty years of knitting projects, family photographs, a pair of comfy bedroom slippers, several pairs of hardy mittens, an audio tape beginning "Hello there, Anne, let me introduce myself. Of course, you know I knit!"—all contributed by caring knitters to someone they'd never met?

I have a computer, but I don't know how to compute "I spent a total of eighty hours on that rat's sweater, and then he left me for a younger woman!" Nor can I enter on a diskette the interest and consideration that prompts writers to send Christmas and Easter cards, to telephone encouragement in my research ("You are really doing something worthwhile for the knitters; I'm so sick and tired of hearing about *quilters*!"), to dispatch flowers after hearing that my late acknowledgment of a letter was due not to sloth but to a fall on a spiral staircase at the Library of Congress (a good address for a fall—more impressive than the basement stairs), or to determine my favorite colors (to enable a writer to graph her "family" pattern in "my" colors). Knitters' affinity for each other defies description; only their own gestures and words convey that special relationship.

When these hundreds of knitters attacked the "Why do you think more women than men knit?" question, most responded in this vein:

Girls are less fidgety, sit quietly longer and perform small motor tasks like knitting earlier than boys whose inner energy drives them to gross motor skill activity [from an elementary school teacher].

Maybe we women knit more because we're involved in more intimate social interacting—and the tradition of keeping hands busy while talking stuck with us.

Men are too restless to sit still.

They're afraid of being called sissies.

In this part of the country [Wheeling, West Virginia] boys play football; they do not *knit*.

They can't tell their right hands from their left unless they are holding a screwdriver.

In agricultural societies men did the field work and were busy with animals and couldn't take knitting along because it would get dirty while women did housework and had access to running water during free moments between cooking and farm chores.

Women can knit while they nurse their babies—I did it all the time.

Men are more comfortable in their workshops.

They don't really think much about clothes.

We women are more open with our knowledge and share our pleasures more.

I don't know why they don't, but I like it that way; my husband would drive me nutty asking me questions all the time.

The only knitting man I ever knew is my thirty-four-year-old son who has knitted ties and a sweater, but he is in the Navy so doesn't brag about it.

Octogenarian Nellie Dice, of Denver, Indiana, summed it up: "I think men do not generally knit because traditionally it is still as much 'women's work' as it was in my grandmother's day."
Others, however, sensed change:

Perhaps more younger men *are* knitting. They aren't so hung up on sexist roles as in my generation [from a writer in her eighties].

In these changing times all kinds of men are caring for children, doing laundry and housework and are more interested in creative crafts. I believe that with the cost of hand-made sweaters and the change in men's attitudes toward who does what there will soon be an increase in interest in learning to knit.

I'm not so sure that it's fear of being called "sissy" that bothers them but, like my husband, fear that their wives would load them with knitting projects. My husband is sharp enough to realize that it would be curtains for him if he learned how to knit, especially since I work in a yarn shop.

The "sex angle" was only one aspect of my inquiry, and while I didn't specifically ask "Why do you knit?" they told me anyhow, most frequently citing their desire to keep a pleasant companion always at hand ("My knitting bag is my traveling companion and acts as my purse too. I'd be lost without it"). The symbiotic relationship between knitter and knitting is so powerful ("I found that knitting was one activity I couldn't do without—and one worry throughout my childhood was that I'd either go blind or lose my fingers, depriving me of my much loved knitting") that some wags have suggested that knitters, like ancient pharaohs, convey their worldly knitting goods to the great beyond: "My hairdresser says when I go, they should bury me with a bag of yarn and some needles"; "At a family gathering, when we were discussing wills and other legal matters, my daughter asked if I wanted my yarn and needles buried with me!"; "If there is no needlework in Heaven, I may not want to go." A heartfelt summation came from Mary Julius, of Lanham, Maryland: "I knit mainly for the satisfaction of accomplishment. Since, in my thirty-odd years as a full-time homemaker, I expended such an enormous amount of energy merely to maintain the status quo with the same

work still there to be done again the next day that it was so satis-
factory to spend even a few minutes doing something that didn't
need to be done again! I like knitting because it can be enjoyed by
myself or in amiability with friends." Nora Lee of New York tallies
her completed knitting projects with the satisfaction of "never wasting a minute while doing something useful for those I care about."
Alta Shively, of Plymouth, Indiana, reasoned: "My friends call me a
Knit Nut. I find it a real pleasant time consumer. When I got married
my husband was a farmer, coon hunter and trapper. He got up at
4 A.M., did chores, ran his trap line, worked all day, and went coon
hunting every night that was fit and lots when it wasn't. I told him
if he'd keep me in yarn I wouldn't complain. Somehow, we did manage a family, two boys and a girl!"

Other reasons echoed their knitting foremothers and some
forefathers:

To save money
   I wasn't about to pay $350 for a sweater I could make for $30!

To calm nerves
   Knitting has kept me off the shrink's couch.

To make gifts
   I am just an ordinary grandmother knitting ordinary things for
   extraordinary grandchildren.

   I still knit even though true heartbreak is looking out the window
   and seeing your kindergartener dragging his hand-knit sweater
   along the sidewalk by the sleeve and your ten-year-old asks,
   "Mom, can I have a store-bought sweater *just once?*"

To earn money (usually a pittance)
   My friend was shocked that I would ask seven dollars; she
   couldn't grasp how difficult and time consuming it is.

   These classy shops sell sweaters for a fortune, and since my work
   is original, they give me plenty of orders, but it only works out
   to a dollar an hour—slave labor!

   I actually traded knitting a *cashmere* Aran sweater, the yarn for
   which cost $400, to my boss in a jewelry store and got a fabulous
   diamond bracelet out of the deal!

To help others

> We knit sweaters for the National Council of Jewish Women's "Ship-a-Box" project for orphanages in Israel.
>
> Our church group knits caps for children bald from chemotherapy.
>
> We knit for children in Shriners' Hospitals.
>
> We sold our knitting to raise $3,000 for our parson's widow.

To keep busy and/or out of trouble.

> My grandmother always said, "God will never take you as long as you have work to finish."
>
> My strict Quaker mother figured if we knit we'd keep out of mischief.
>
> Every time I wanted to reach for a candy bar, I grabbed knitting instead—lost ten pounds and gained five sweaters!

To be sociable

> When I moved to a new community, a fellow parishioner admired my hand-knit coat and introduced herself after church. We became fast friends and co-founded a neighborhood knitting group.
>
> Our weekly Knit-Wits group of eight was formed twenty-two years ago, and we're like sisters, even knitting for each other's grandchildren as if they were our own. When one of our original members moved to another town, we selfishly made no move to replace her.

To be creative

> On my new zig-zag sewing machine, I found that letting it run without material produced bumpy, bouclé-like cotton which I knit doubled or mixed with yarn for a new texture.

To pursue the Puritan Work Ethic

> Knitting is such a relief from tension for me, but I'd have too much guilt if I just did nothing. This way I can both relax and *produce*.

Isabella Montgomery's recollections of her great-grandmother's last years is illustrative of the "knitting impulse":

My great grandmother was bedridden and senile for the last years of her life, but though alienated from life around her, she still expected (and looked forward to?) her knitting every day. She worked with large needles on thirty to forty stitches of yarn that looked like cotton twine. She produced four or five inches of garter stitch which my grandmother (her daughter) each night, like Penelope, unravelled and rewound into a ball and cast on new stitches for the next day's stint. . . . It seems to me that this illustrated some of the classic attributes of knitting: production, accomplishment (however illusory in this case) and light activity for a person who must remain sedentary after being busy all her life.

To the question "What is the most unusual place or circumstance where you have seen someone knit?" the obvious and often-stated response was "I knit anywhere; so no place is unusual to me!" Knitting during hospital stays is the norm, and dependency has led stitchers to part reluctantly with their work only when being wheeled to delivery or surgical rooms. One knitter wrote: "When I was in intensive care, the doctor told me to exercise my fingers, so I sat propped up in bed and eagerly worked to finish a friend's vest while connected to the monitor, intravenous solutions dripping into my left arm and oxygen tubes spiraling up my nose. The activity prompted a nurse to ask if I'd make her a vest too if she furnished the yarn, and when I checked out of the hospital a week later, I was given enough to make three more vests!" From other sites volunteered, I've selected these few:

> . . . in a boat on a lake while my husband fishes. I love being on the water and enjoy the scenery, but I really care very little about fishing so take my knitting and enjoy it along with the scenery and company.
>
> . . . at my grandmother's one day when I sat knitting in the chicken coop waiting for the hens to hatch their eggs. They finally produced 17 chicks and I did a lot of rows on my knitting!
>
> . . . while pedaling my exercise bike because if I'm not doing something with my hands I feel I'm wasting my time.

. . . during our two and a half years in Guam, with the temperature hovering around ninety degrees year round. My Navy husband was away a lot, I was pregnant with our third child, and I just knit the way some people go to work, eight hours a day!

A teacher at our school makes every minute count by knitting as she walks the ten blocks from the train station to school. When my 8th graders invited all the faculty members to their dance and she decided her casual gear was not formal enough, she pulled out her knitting, finished it right then and appeared, to universal acclaim, in a "dressy evening sweater" pulled over her working clothes.

When I ran seven times for the Colorado State Legislature in a field of thirty-six candidates vying for eighteen slots, I was always knitting sweaters to throw over my shoulders to distinguish me from my rivals. Each sported such eye-catching and identifying insigniae as a flag, my name, "GOP" or an elephant against a white or light blue background and must have helped, for I won all but the first race.

I knit all the time, especially flying to Las Vegas which is four and a half hours each way, and when I get there the casino change girls know me from year to year because I knit when I run out of money. I also knit a lot when bowling, and when our team competed in the state tournament several years in a row, I enjoyed being recognized as the "Redhead who does all that knitting."

When we were married by a Justice of the Peace near Lake Tahoe, his wife sat on the sofa knitting as he performed the ceremony and prompted him when he forgot his lines!

I once knit a bikini bathing suit riding on the back of a motorcycle and worried about losing the ball of yarn!

I'm a Little League Mother who hates baseball, and while I listen to all the other mothers yelling instructions to their kids at bat or in the field, I simply click away serenely. My son really appreciates my silence!

Among my happy memories are the ten years I lived in San Antonio many years ago when I spent *every* Saturday afternoon with a dear friend, an enthusiastic knitter and another opera buff, listening, not talking, to Metropolitan Opera broadcasts on the radio. Now I am here in Washington and she is still in Texas; we are both ninety years old and still knitting and still enjoying lovely music— aren't we lucky!

Curious about nineteenth-century instructions for knitted egg warmers, covers for flatirons, lamp shades, corsets, egg and cracker bags, foot bags, hairpin receivers and whisk broom covers, I asked knitters to describe "the most bizarre objects you've ever seen" and was surprised at the number who reported a "garment I'm sure you won't want to put in your book." I guess I won't! A correspondent I shall not identify wrote, "The most bizarre knitted object I've ever seen was a sweater I made for my first husband. Somehow I misjudged the sleeves so that when he put it on, they reached down past his knees. He looked just like a gorilla! I'm pretty sure this episode had nothing to do with our subsequent divorce!" Then there was the name-embroidered, blue-and-green-plaid horse blanket Amala Derry, of Waterbury, Connecticut, knit from yarn scraps for granddaughter Nancy's horse; a twin-cuffed "Holding Hands" bag into which a lovesick pair could each thrust a sweaty hand, by Elaine Bonney, of Cape Elizabeth, Maine; chain mail for costumes for a community theater performance of *Macbeth* by Kathleen Lancione, of Wheeling, West Virginia; a Monopoly board cover by Lois Dunleavy, of Anaheim, California; a uterus for her daughter's demonstrations with a doll in Lamaze natural childbirth classes, knit by Thelma Muir, of Washington, Kansas; and a sweater for a six-foot boa constrictor to which Ann Ledley of New York City is sole claimant (though she doesn't mention whether she actually knit it or merely viewed it).

Asked about "family patterns," knitters replied as if conversant with an 1891 knitting manual's suggestion: "Would it not be a pleasant occupation for many of our girls to fashion something, the best of its kind, in the style of the days they live in, so well and so prettily, that it would be worth keeping as a reminder of these days when they are past, and we ourselves are among the old-fashioned things?" Debbie McGrath, of Franklinville, New York, who knit her one-of-a-kind wedding gown by cutting silk-lined knitted lace rectangles into construction pieces from a commercial pattern, had just that in mind when she later knit leftover bridal yarn into a "coming-home-from-the-hospital" outfit of cap, kimono and bootees worn by all her children and wrote, "I hope it's a new family tradition!" Cathy Hounshell of Kensington, California, hoping to start her own tradition, plans to assign specific Irish stitches to each family, knitting the current family "name" on the front, the mother's maiden name on the back, the maternal grandmother's on one sleeve and the paternal grandfather's on the other, a knitted genealogical cryptograph for sorting each other out at reunions! Arlene Bauers of Cheektowaga, New York, knits from her mother's notebook of twenty-seven neatly graphed designs placed sequentially one below the other into a "family pattern" ranging from two rows and two colors to nine rows and four colors (the four-strand patterns planned for shoulders and stress points to inhibit sagging). When the entire family assembles, each in his or her color-version of *the pattern*, it's an enviable sight.

After this foreword, I almost succeed in excluding my own experiences from the text, but readers who speculate that in some described scenes I am a participant will probably be right, for I've been knitting for a long time and, like most knitters, also adhere like glue to hidebound techniques. Take the matter of *how* to knit, for instance. I gleaned from interviews that knitters are fiercely loyal to the way *they* learned to knit, whether from grandmother, aunt ("Aunt Bessie gave me sugar string and the straws from a broom for needles"), mother, instruction manual or, in one case, from "our landlady, a little old English lady who survived the *Titanic*'s sinking." To each side claiming superior speed and efficiency, the platoons of "English or American way" yarn-in-the-right-hand knitters or their adversaries, yarn-in-the-left-hand subscribers to the "German" or "Continental" method, I tender the recollection of this knitter:

When I was a child we used to visit two "old maid" sisters, cousins of my mother, who were retired from teaching. They lived together, but there the similarity ended: one was Presbyterian, the other Baptist; one was Republican, the other Democrat; one knitted the 'old country way' of holding yarn in the left hand and "picking" it with the right and the other knitted the "American way" of holding the yarn in the right hand and swinging it around the needle. When they knit for the Red Cross in World War II, they raced to see which one was faster but finally decided there was little difference in speed.

On only one knitting subject is there universal agreement: Knitters relish working with their hands, hands that are *Never Idle*. In tracing that recurrent theme, that idleness approaches sinfulness, I began, as does this book, with the American colonial period.

No
Idle
Hands

1.
Colonial Knitters

The Mayflower foremothers' busily knitting on deck en route to the New World creates a picturesque scene, but there is no recorded proof that it's authentic, a not-surprising omission since knitting was so intrinsic to daily life that few remarked about it in journals, diaries or letters. Pilgrim women were accustomed to spinning and knitting at home, but the Mayflower's cramped quarters precluded stowing spinning wheels, and even water was so severely restricted that leaders Winslow and Bradford reported of the landing, "Our people went on shore to refresh themselves and our women to wash, as they had great need." Yarn, however, was easily transported and undoubtedly knit as needed.

What *is* known is that sponsors of the Massachusetts Bay Colony a few years later supplied voyagers with several knit "peare" of "coarse woolen stockings," cut-and-sew "Irish" stockings ("which if they are good are much more serviceable than knit ones"), "knit hose" (which may have been hand knit) and several "Red knit caps," the latter, when paired with a "Wastecoate of green cotton bound about with red tape," assured a colorful Salem colonist. "Apparrell for 100 men" also included Monmouth caps—thick, warm caps "fulled" by hand- and foot-beating and much favored by seamen.

Once housing and food were assured and plans for home textile production executed, grazing sheep filled verdant pastures, guarded against straying from the common foraging ground by watchful herdsmen and children. To obviate idleness, the unforgivable sin,

"The Old Method."

and to assure that young lookouts performed constructively while keeping their eyes peeled for errant sheep, the township of Andover, Massachusetts, adjudged knitting a productive substitute for "larking about," and decreed in 1642:

> The Court doe hereupon order and decree that in every towne the chosen men are to take care of such as are sett to keep cattle that they sett to some other employment withall as spinning upon the rock, knitting & weaving tape &c that boyes and girls will be not suffered to converse together.

While this ordinance might evoke a pastoral scene of children balancing their wheels on boulders in hilly grazing areas as they spun and knit, "spinning on a rock" meant using a distaff or whorl to hold the flax or wool, not relaxing on a geologic formation.

At home, women and girls hatched, combed and spun flax for

thread, and for woolen yarn they separated, cleaned, oiled, carded, combed and rolled the fleeces in preparation for spinning with locally crafted or prized wheels imported from England on the first few boats. Bleached in the sun and dyed by immersion in broths of herbs, berries or bark, the yarn was knit into coarse stockings or mittens. It was a hand process, just as it had been in England, where knitted caps were in general use for the poorer classes in the fifteenth century and the term *knit* was common by the middle of the sixteenth, when knitting bonnets and hose became a domestic employment.

While colonists probably had heard of machine knitting, it was not an option available to them. In the latter part of the sixteenth century, Englishman William Lee, annoyed by his fiancée's preoccupation with knitting during the courtship but grateful for her financial support (from knitting) during marriage, scrutinized her nimble fingers as she knit stockings in the round, then imitated the operation in a "stocking machine" whose products he called "William Lee hosen." Queen Elizabeth rejected his patent application, rationalizing, "To enjoy the exclusive privilege of making stockings for the whole of my subjects is too important to be granted to any individual. . . . I have too much love for my poor people who gain their bread by the employment of knitting to give my money to forward an invention that will tend to their ruin by depriving them of employment and making them beggars." Though disheartened by his lack of protection from competition, Lee nonetheless constructed his machine for silk stockings, even generously presenting a pair to the delighted but unrepentant queen.

As knowledge of the crude stocking frames leaked out, Britain understandably forbad exporting this technology, forcing colonists to rely upon hand knitting or secure the less desirable "woven" stockings from "stockingers" who wove, cut and pieced fabric into a tolerable but inelastic stocking. Some textile historians mark 1818 as the year when the first stocking machine made it to America secreted in a cargo of salt to escape detection and consequent steep fine, but one ad appeared in the *Virginia Gazette* in 1771 for "a newly invented instrument for knitted, knotted, double looped work, to make Stockings, Breeches Pieces, or Silk Gloves, Cotton or Worsted, together or separated." Colonists were tempted but restrained by the cost. Importing stores conducted a flourishing trade with England for those who could afford British stockings, and a late seventeenth-century invoice of a Boston store listed dozens of "Chil.woll hose"; "Womens woll ditto"; "ditto Mens Woll"; "Womens Worst[ed] ditto"; "Mens Short Worst Mixt," along with other such intriguing necessaries as "4 Snap Mouse Traps"; "4 Double fall Mouse Traps"; "2 Single fall Mouse Traps"; and "4 Wooden Ratt Traps with Springs." Then, as now, there were hazards to "Mail order." One customer who ordered "knitted hose to wear under others" found some of them "damnified in the voyage," and returned them to be dyed, while others proved "too large in the calf."

Despite these imports, credit goes to American "household labor" for meeting requirements for woven and knit fabrics, especially in rural districts, where wives and daughters superintended the family output. When demand escalated to match the spiraling population figures, "clothmakers" converged upon America, particularly upon Germantown, Pennsylvania, where they established such a hosiery center that a traveling British minister noted, "In the year 1759 the women of Germantown sold 60,000 pair of stockings of their own make." While there *were* stocking frame makers (those who wove and cut) in the area, "of their own make" suggests that stockings were hand knit. Dyers, combers, weavers, spinners and knitters were so essential that by the end of the seventeenth century a knitter could receive half a crown for a pair of "coarse yarn stockings." Despite the critical need, one would-be employer lamented that premature matrimony hampered engaging dependable knitters, mostly young women: "Moreover they are usually Marry'd before they are Twenty-Years of Age, and when once in that noose, are for the most part a little uneasie, and make their Husbands so too, till they procure a Maid Servant to bear the burden of the Work, as also in some measure to wait on them too."

With the scarcity of materials dictating the necessity to stimulate textile manufacture, many townships set quotas for spinners ("Selectmen in every towne do consider the condition & capacity of every family, & accordingly to assess them at one or more spinners . . .") or tendered bounties for items woven or knit ("That there shall be paid out of ye Publick Treasury of this Colony . . . for every pair of silk stockings, weighing four ounces, ten shillings."). As early as 1656, Hatfield, Massachusetts, passed an ordinance prescient of the rev-

olution a century hence: "This Court, taking into serious consideration the present streights and necessities that lye uppon the countrie
in respect of cloathing, which is not like to be so plentifully supplied
from forraigne parts as in times past . . . [do order that] weoman,
girles and boyes, shall and hereby are enjoyned to spinn according
to their skills and abilitie." Selectmen studied each family's capacity,
rated it according to its employment in other pursuits, set the standard for its "skills and abilitie" and fined it for noncompliance, an
extraordinary assumption of authority over a family's private affairs.

Virginia's Assembly established a spinning school and agreed to a
premium of ten pounds of tobacco for each dozen pairs of worsted
or woolen stockings knit from yarn spun in the colony. Massachusetts
taxed coaches and carriages to support its spinning school, while
Boston whetted the public appetite for spinning by sponsoring contests on the Common where young and old, rich and poor, flaunted
their skill with the wheels and had a rousing good time.

With all these incentives to colonial textile production, settlers
were outraged by Parliament's threatening 1699 Woolen Act for-
bidding transportation ("loaden in any ship or vessel . . . upon any
horse cart, or other carriage") of wool or wool products between
English plantations in America or "to any other place whatsoever."
Dependent upon colony-wide sheep raising and their singular prosperity in marketing woolen yarn, stockings and fabrics, colonists simply vowed noncompliance, defiantly and surreptitiously shipped over
half their wool crop to continental markets and carried on far from
England's prying eye. An ocean away from the regulators, home industry thus prospered.

Industry won laurels as the most prized colonial virtue, and industrious knitting was a prescribed accomplishment of a "good
dame." A boastful descendant of an early homemaker in Dutch New
Amsterdam exulted, "Placed on a desert island, a Dutch woman . . .
could make everything needed to support life. . . . She instructed
her maids in carding and weaving, and raised flax in her garden for
linen, towels, shirts etc. and knit stockings for the family." Dutch
matrons, who endorsed bright blues, reds and greens for everyday
worsted wool stockings, luxuriated in dainty silk or cotton for dressy
wear, so much so that one bequeathed her special go-to-meeting knit

stockings ("5 pair white cotton stockings . . . [valued at] 9 shillings")
to her legatee.

Knickerbocker author Washington Irving, whose *History of New
York* chronicled early Dutch society, recounted tea parties where
"the young ladies seated themselves demurely in their rush bottom
chairs and knit their own woolen stockings . . . behaving in all things
like decent well-educated damsels" and relished ogling stockings of
"blue worsted, with magnificent red clocks [embroidered embel-
lishments] . . . to display a well-turned ankle" beneath revealing
Dutch petticoats ("Those gallant garments were rather short, scarce
reaching below the knee . . . and, what is more, they were all of their
own manufacture,—of which circumstance, as may well be supposed,
they were not a little vain").

Women in all colonies were paragons of remarkable diligence and
sallied forth with "knitting work" in tow, particularly at town meetings where neighbors could nod in affirmative judgment at their
industry, ever demonstrating the old proverb "A man works from
sun to sun, but a woman's work is never done." Few, however, received the tribute accorded to a Philadelphian whose husband's meticulous diary notations have been mined by historians ever since.
Christopher Marshall's daily recounting so fully enumerated the minutiae of his life that one can imagine his wife's whining, "Why don't
you write about what *I* do?" A bit defensively, he responded, "As I
have, in this Memorandum, taken scarecely any notice of my wife's
employment, it might appear as if her engagements were very trifling,
the which is not the case but the reverse, and to do her that justice
which her services deserve by entering them minutely will take up
most of my time." Something impelled him to *take* the time, and
bestowing upon her the accolade "She looketh well to the ways of
her household, and eateth not the bread of idelness," he limned a
striking portrait of Mrs. Marshall's household efforts, a small part of
which follows:

> Her cleanliness about the house, her attendance in the orchard,
> cutting and drying apples, of which several bushels have been pro-
> cured, add to which her making of cider without tools, for the
> constant fine clothes and my shirts, all of which are smoothed by

her, add to this her making of twenty large cheeses, and that from one cow, and daily using milk and cream, besides her sewing, knitting, &c.

Not all reflections on diligent wives were so complimentary. One exasperated husband griped that his wife "is an irreconcilable enemy of Idleness, and considers every State of life as Idleness, in which the hands are not employed or some art acquired. . . . We have twice as many fire-screens as chimneys and three flourished quilts for every bed. Half the rooms are adorned with a kind of futile pictures which imitate tapestry. . . . She has boxes filled with knit garters." Worse, he trembled at the prospect of further festooning should she transmit her knitting and embroidering skills to their daughters.

Those complaints, however, were exceptions to the rule, and industry, even if misguided, ruled. Young Abigail Foote's daily journal was so replete with the chores of small-town daily life (carding, spinning, weaving, dyeing, knitting, making bonnets, washing, ironing, and cooking) that when she took time and "went a-strawberrying" or "went to town and bought me a pair of gloves," one wants to cheer!

Southward, at her parents' prosperous Virginia plantation, "Hillsborough," industrious, teenaged Frances Baylor Hill chronicled her daily activities for a year, covering such diverse topics as riding horseback to visit friends and meeting on the way "4 gentlemen all strangers one very handsome," attending church to "hear a good sermon preach'd," watching friends ice skating ("[T]hey had a great many falls"), visiting back and forth with family, keeping abreast of local gossip, sewing everything from shirts to quilts and counterpanes, and everlasting and daily knitting. Knitting was usually solitary, while quilting was communal: "[W]e quilt'd a great deal and was very merry . . . we had a number of fine water mellons & Peach's a plenty of Biscuit and Cake fine eating and merry quilting . . . we spent the day agreable eating drinking and quilting . . . we got the quilt out early in the day and then the girls all went to making edging."

The diary is so peppered with "knit a little" that one assumes a daily quota. While she sometimes recorded knitting "a long piece on my stocking" or "knit two inches," her usual stint was one inch, still a creditable accomplishment, given the fine needles and yarn with which she worked. She so often "knit and read" that one might surmise she did both simultaneously, were it not for this entry: "Began a very clever Novel—Evelina it was call'd, knit a short piece for I was reading the best part of the day." Another day she admitted, a bit guiltily, "I dn'd hartily knit a little on my stocking." There was no celebration when she "finish'd my stocking," for there was another to be worked, as shown in this typical week's knitting inventory, tucked into the synopsis of each day's events:

Monday: I knit a long piece on my stocking.
Tuesday: Learnt 3 openwork stitches of Miss Archer knit a little on my stocking. . . .
Wednesday: Did a little openwork. . . . I read a little and knit an inch or two on my stocking, by candlelight.
Thursday: . . . knit a little on my stocking.
Fryday: [no mention of knitting]
Saturday: . . . finish'd the foot of my stocking by candlelight.
Sunday: [no mention of knitting]
Monday: . . . knit 2 inches on my stocking. . . .
Tuesday: . . . knit two inches on my stocking. . . .

She knit at all hours ("got up early knit a little before breakfast"; "got up late knit a little after breakfast"; "knit a little on my stocking got pickle for dinner ate very hearty"; "knit by candlelight") and sometimes knit for others ("I began a stocking for Mr Robt Hill, knit very little on it"). Frances also exchanged sewing for knitting ("Mrs. Tu—ll & myself chang'd work she knit for me and I hem'd her apron"; "I altered Cousin Pollys red sack in[to] a tunick[.] she knit for me"; "Cousin Gwathmey din'd with us, she & I chang'd work I began a bedquilt for her & she knit for me . . . [and] finished my stockings").

While industry was taken for granted, an Englishman evaluating the suitability of the Chesapeake Bay for future immigrants was bowled over by the thrift and productivity of one Irish family: "I never saw four such industrious people before—all sober, and leading a much superior life for industry to most of the people of that or any other country I ever was in. They spun and knitted their own stockings: this I particularly know, because they bought the wool of me."

One historian noted that when German dissenters emigrated, the women were given thread, worsted and knitting needles to employ "their leisure time in making stockings and caps for their family, or in mending their cloaths and linnen" during the voyage. Benjamin Rush, later traveling in Pennsylvania, noted their energy: "Their homes are, moreover, rendered so comfortable, at all times, by large close stoves that the business is done by every branch of the family, in knitting, spinning, and mending farm utensils . . . where every member of the family crowds near to a common fire-place, or shivers at a distance from it,—with hands that move, by reason of the cold, with only half their usual quickness." Those German settlers, usually credited with giving America "domestic women" whose solid home training contributed to the vigor of the population, so struck Rush that he remarked, "When a young man asks the consent of his father to marry a girl of his choice, the latter does not so much inquire whether she be rich or poor, but whether she is industrious and acquainted with the duties of a good housewife."

Martha Ballard's staggering industry transforms her diary into a frontier epic, for in addition to her own housekeeping and child rearing, she acted as midwife, nurse and unofficial physician for her own and neighboring towns. With little time to stay home "combing flax," "collecting herbs," spinning wool, making nightcaps, knitting stockings, binding quilts or making "an undercoat of the blanket the swine tore," she nevertheless discharged those duties in addition to professional attendance at 996 births, a figure easily corroborated by her diary's obstetrical notations such as "Put Mrs. Savage to bed with a daughter"; "I put Mrs. Floid to bed with a daughter at 9 o'clock, evening. . . . [and the next day] . . . came from Floids about day-break. Left her comfortable"; "Ephraim Towne's wife very ill. I removed the obstruction and delivered her safe of a fine daughter about the middle of the night." On her fiftieth birthday she remarked only, "Was at Tilar's. Mrs. Tilar unwell," but threw midwifery to the winds on December 19, 1785: "I have been at home this day. It is the anniversary of my marriage and 31 yrs. since Mr. Ballard and I joined in Wedlock."

The lives of rural women like Ballard differed markedly from those of city women, for a farm family's well-being literally hinged upon active participation of wives and daughters in all the chores, while city girls acquired domestic skills to make them better wives and mothers. If an urban family could afford to buy yarn ready-to-knit, with all the carding, spinning, and dyeing done, it patronized shopkeepers such as Elisha Boardman, of Wethersfield, Connecticut, who advertised "Has a Consignment of Cotton Yarn from Providnce, two and three threaded for knitting, bleached and unbleached, from No. 8 to 20, of a superior quality to any offered in this vicinity, and very cheap for Cash only."

The homemaker, thus released from the tedium of yarn production, occupied her time with ornamental and decorative needlework, purchasing her knitting needles and sewing accessories from advertisers like Joseph Plowman, who specialized in cutlery and metalware: "Joseph Plowman, Pin-Maker in Water-Street, near the Coffee-House, Begs leave to inform the public, That he still continues carrying on that manufactury, and has now for sale the following goods: Pins, brass and iron knitting-needles. . . ."

Some consider "fancy work" a hallmark of upper-class women with leisure for such pursuits, but the class line is not so simply drawn since many who could ill afford needlework as recreation sold fancy knitting and sewing on consignment. Others bartered it for reciprocal services, as shown in a diary notation of Reverend Ebenezer Parkman, "Mr Thos. Warrin & Stephen Maynard cutt up part of ye woodpile today to pay Mrs. Parkman for knitting for ye latter of yarn. They dined. They work till evening."

Penurious needlewomen earned money by teaching elegant stitchery to young women of the community, snobbishly luring their clientele by billing themselves as "lately come from London." Schoolmistresses conducted needlework businesses outside their school hours, like Mrs. Druitt of Boston, who dispatched "with Fidelity . . . All Manner of Needle-works . . . on the most moderate Terms." Others mended or reknit stockings, a job most women hated, and a city woman who listed mending as her specialty, particularly mending waistcoats and breeches by "grafting" worn spots, received avid responses to an advertisement such as: "Also Mending, and all kinds of Sewing Work, by the Widow, Hezekiah Parker. Mrs. Parker has

Particular Recommendations, from Persons of Character, as an honest, industrious woman, and as she has no other means of getting an honest livelihood for herself and family, Begs employment from such Ladies and Gentlemen as wish to have their work done reasonably and expeditiously."

If stocking mending was one hated chore, another was washing them, especially delicate silk, Sunday-best ones boasting ornamental clocks and initials worked into the foot. Here again, the "classifieds" brought succor, such as Mary Callendar's guarantee: "Silk Stockings washed and brought to a proper colour, in the nicest and best Manner; at One Shilling a Pair." Charleston's Mary Corbett washed and ironed "Ladies' Head-Cloaths in the best Manner," and Mrs. Harris cleaned "all Kinds of Laces, particularly Blown Laces . . . as neat as in London."

Plain wool stockings were easier to handle, though dyes were so unstable that stockings were laundered infrequently. Massachusetts Bay Colony women loved bright colors, men usually wore blue or gray, and children preferred red, wearing them out so quickly that knitting them became a childhood requirement. Beginning by knitting long, narrow strips to wind over their "good" stockings to keep them in place, they graduated at four or five to manipulating the four needles needed to make stockings "in the round" and were assigned a daily quota of rounds before they could go out to play. They enjoyed ample opportunities for instruction from more senior family members, from older brothers and sisters to grandmothers. One nonagenarian later remembered the cozy knitting nook so commonplace to the colonial home:

> A low chair, with a seat of twisted osier [willow twigs], covered with some gay material, was generally placed in a corner near a sunny window with a southern exposure. In front of this stood an array of favorite plants—roses, geraniums, stock-lilies. On the back of these chairs hung the bag of knitting, the little red stocking, and the shining steel needles plainly visible, indicating this was the favorite seat of the industrious mother of the family.

With cloth manufacture such an indispensable home function, sharing the more arduous tasks with neighbors substituted conviviality for solitary spinning, sewing, carding, dyeing and knitting, and turned the cooperative social activity, or "bee," into a highly anticipated affair. A participant in such a "tea drinking" visit, when neighbors and friends dropped by to harvest neighborhood gossip, knit socks and swap yarn for "feetings" ("ends" used for lowers obscured by high shoes), remembered, "Out came the sprigged china, the thin silver and the finest linen for the occasion. The guests sat before the fireplace and knit while the hostess and her daughter set forth plates of doughnuts, seed cookies, pound cake and the inevitable pies." She never forgot "how they talked and knit, and knit and talked, with tireless tongues, putting in marks at their narrowings, slowly shaping their socks with oft-repeated measurings. . . . There was a charm in the very click of her needles, which seemed to keep time with the blinking of . . . eyes."

While stockings were the most commonly made articles, second place went to mittens, both utilitarian and decorative. In her book on colonial life, Alice Morse Earle credited a young New Hampshire girl with incorporating not only the entire alphabet but also a verse of poetry into a pair fashioned of fine flaxen yarn, but she conceded suspiciously, "[T]hey must have been long-armed mitts for ladies' wear, to have space enough for the poetry."

Another historian of New England social life, commenting on such workmanship, gasped, "Never am I so glad that I was born in the late nineteenth, instead of the early seventeenth century, as when I contemplate this Colonial accomplishment!" A few years ago Susannah Springer, of Missoula, Montana, purchased at a Shaker sale a similar white wool mitten with rows of tiny red flowers alternating with blue letters. It appears to have " '80" worked into the design, and is attributed to Elizabeth Evans of New Hampshire, who although totally blind learned to knit letters by counting. The verse, a continuation of that on the other mitten, begins at the wrist and reads around and around the mitten: "yours, if others have a share, learn to be contented, then will your troubles cease, and then you may be certain that you will live in peace; for a contented mind is a continual feast."

Intricately beaded bags, their multicolored landscapes, flowers and geometrical shapes first painstakingly sketched on paper, were esteemed tokens to husband or sweetheart since men as well as women

*Mitten made by a
New Hampshire woman,
c. 1780.*

carried them, and tombstones, weeping willows, urns and creped figures were worked into "mourning" bags to memorialize departed ones. By the end of the nineteenth century, a knitter could charge five dollars for knitting one, the high price justified by the laborious process of counting out each row's beads, threading each onto silk thread often spun from home cocoons, easing it forward and holding it carefully while the stitch was slipped from one needle to the other to anchor it in place. These bags, "reticules" or "indispensables," hung from long strings that could be slipped over the back of a chair when a woman seated herself. Though one could reasonably duplicate an existing bag by counting its stitches, carefully diagrammed patterns were closely held secrets, and written rules were divulged only to friends. In a small New England town, leading bag maker Matilda Emerson's affection (and matrimonial intention) toward her widowed parson inspired her to impart to his sister-housekeeper a pattern for a somber mourning bag of funereal willow tree, urn and grave in shaded purples and grays against a black background. Her romantic rival, Ann Green, however, surreptitiously and malevolently changed the penciled cryptographic rules so that what emerged from sister's workbox was a blueprint for a "hodgepodge" rather than funereal symbols. When the exasperated sister imputed to Matilda the scheme for withholding her cherished design and tattled the affair to her brother, he sought connubial solace with a widow from another town and left Matilda literally holding the knitted bag. Only later did the wily Ann's Puritan conscience surface to reveal the misdeed, too late for either of them to snag the vicar.

Since knit silk and bead bags and watch fobs (one with the date and "Remember the Giver" worked in tiny gilt beads) proved more durable than knit garments, many survived as keepsakes. More suitable for children's gift-giving (especially to fathers) were long, narrow watch chains or simple suspenders to which an encouraging mother or grandmother added buttons, attached a backing for stability, and finished the ends with leather buttonholes.

Knit cotton coverlets and counterpanes covering most colonial beds were such protracted undertakings that knitters ran smaller and more portable projects concurrently. Favorite small pieces were sewn on knit "silk day caps" to shield tresses and reduce the frequency of arduous shampoos. One of these caps, knit by Laura Brooks Vosburgh as a child, was exhibited in the Brooklyn Museum's 1924 antique needlework show along with her accompanying note, penned in 1845:

> I wish Elizabeth to keep what is marked with my name and to remember me and my industry by keeping the silk that I have made from the mulberrys which I raised from the seeds sown with my little fingers when quite small, with my father's help and encouragement The feeding of the worms and the reeling of the balls, the knitting and the dyeing, both the yellow and the auburn colors for the head I also did. It has been worn by many and trimmed in various modes and fashions, with ribbons sometimes and sometimes with flowers and sometimes with feathers.

Children less fortunate than Laura Vosburgh ranked knitting more necessity than social accomplishment, and the thousands "bound out" as apprentices in other households acquired it as a marketable skill of "housewifery." Indenture contracts supplied servants for the affluent and furnished young girls, often newly arrived immigrants such as Frances Champion, an opportunity to gain proficiency and experience:

> Indenture, date May 15th, 1693, of Frances Champion, daughter of Frances Champion, with consent of mother, to Anthony Farmer and Elizabeth Farmer, his wife, as an apprentice and servant, for nine years from date. Said Master and Mistress in addition to other Matters "to instruct the said Frances to Reade and to teach and Instruct her in Spinning, Knitting or any other manner of house-wifery etc."

Boston's city fathers considered it their public duty to train children in "labor and other employments which may been profitable to the commonwealth," and if "straitened" parents didn't "dispose of their severall children . . . abroad for servants, to serve by indentures according to their ages and capacities," then the selectmen would discharge the obligation. Some Virginia children of indigent parents unable to meet education costs were selected "to be employed at the public flax houses and be taught carding, knitting, and spinning," and orphan asylum founders in all colonies vowed to provide a religious atmosphere, to teach reading (and sometimes writing) and to promote mastery of useful crafts or trades. Boys received manual training in carpentry and clock-making, for instance, while girls learned sewing, spinning and knitting in the hope that as future family helpers they could exchange work for lodging. A visitor to Orphan House in Bethesda, Georgia, remembered, "After Dinner, they retir'd, the Boys to School and the Girls to their Spinning and Knitting." If a girl could not be placed, at least she had some means of livelihood in her adult years. Orphan Courts could legally "bind out" their wards to petitioners promising "to maintain her decently & see that she be taught to read, sew, spinn, and knitt."

While most children learned needlework at home, prosperous families supplemented that instruction by routing their offspring to neighborhood schools, usually run by penniless but proud widows whose "dame schools" are considered primarily New England institutions but were fixtures in other colonies as well. The youngest children, sent off for a morning or even a day, learned plain knitting, the alphabet and a few simple phrases and maxims from their horn-books. Bostonian Samuel Sewall noted in his diary that son Joseph went "to School to Capt. Townsend's Mothers', his Cousin Jane accompanying him, carried his Horn Book," while daughter Mary "goe to Mrs. Thair's to learn to Read and Knit." In Newport, the Reverend Ellery Channing learned "gaiter knitting" (knitting suspenders) in primary school. Another memorist described the school "where the good dame, as she knits or sews and spins, listens to each child in turn as he calls the letters in their order. She entertains him with stories from the Bible, and strives with moral precepts to bring him up in the nurture and admonition of the Lord." He would not have used the twentieth-century term *day care*, but this part of an eighteenth-century poem he quoted nonetheless portrayed one:

> Where a deaf, poor, patient widow sits
> And awes some thirty infants as she knits—
> Infants of humble busy wives, who pay
> Some trifling price for freedom through the day.

By the time children reached seven or eight and had finished basic reading, spelling, knitting and moral injunctions, they forsook the auspices of the good matron and advanced either to a "town school" established by the more forward-looking communities or to higher-level private school. As one early Rhode Island resident recalled, opportunities for further education for girls were disheartening: "In Winter the distance is too great for them (the girls) to walk, and in Summer they must needs stay at home to help their mothers." The lucky few who did "move up" steadfastly clung to their habit of toting knitting to school, where they harried teachers untrained in needlework. One schoolmaster, irked at a student who consistently interrupted lessons for knitting assistance, shrewdly resolved to employ a knitting phrase he once heard. At her next approach, he signaled her to return to her seat and authoritatively ordered her, "Widen your knitting!" It is no wonder that he was perplexed at the results, a stocking "as wide as a meal bag." Another besieged schoolmaster took the opposite tack and notified his student to "narrow" each time she requested assistance. When she presented the resultant piece for further clarification, he was so nonplussed at the sight of the small, pointed object that he threw up his hands and bellowed, "Go ask your mother!" Intrusions were so recurrent that a few towns contended that knitting in school "taxed the patience of our worthy pedagogues severely," and abolished the practice.

When students ascended the private-school ladder, boys progressed to "Latin Schools" for academic subjects such as "Arithmetick, Geometry, Algebra, Surveying, Gauging, Dialling, Navigation, the Use of Globes, and the other parts of Mathematicks," while girls, relegated to the intricacies of needlework and facing a painfully aborted academic education, must have applauded poetess Anne Bradstreet's succinct

> I am obnoxious to each carping tongue
> Who says my hand a needle better fits.

Despite dissenters such as Bradstreet and Abigail Adams, who regretted "the trifling narrow, contracted education of the females of my own country," agreement was general that the object of a daughter's education was "to make it proper for her sex; to inspire her with the love of those occupations which are their particular province," and knitting so clearly fell within that female province that advertisements for schools carefully delineated the separate sexual spheres. A Hartford schoolmaster indulged himself in ten lines to promote his teaching of scholarly subjects to "young gentlemen" at "Reasonable Rates" and tacked on tersely: "His Wife also teaches Reading, Knitting, and all sorts of Needlework, very cheap." Another couple heralded their arrival in Boston: "A Certain Person and his Wife fit for any Town, to teach School, both Latin, and to Read and Write English, and his Wife for teaching Needle Work." Nathaniel Oliver taught school "in a convenient Chamber, over Mr. People's shop . . . where He endeavors with Fidelity to furnish such Youth as are put under his Tuition, with those Sciences necessary before their Apprenticeship to Business; or qualify them for superior Academies, Purposes, on reasonable Encouragement." So much for the boys. As for the girls, "N.B. Mrs. Oliver teaches Needle Work in most of its Variety, at the dwelling House of Mrs. Hill."

John and Eleanor Druitt, recognizing the necessity for a girls' school and deciding "not [to] take boys" but to devote themselves entirely to the service of females, founded a school in which John instructed "Young Ladies in the Rudiments of English, Epistolary Writing, Writing and Arithmetic" and Eleanor specialized in "French Grammatically, Reading, English and Orthography, likewise following Needleworks, viz." The "viz" was a particularized catalog of embroidery stitches and, of course, knitting:

Point, Brussels, Dresden, Gold, Silver, and Silk Embroidery of every Kind, Tambour, Feather India and Darning, Spriggings, with a Variety of Open-work to each; Tapestry, plain lined and drawn Cat-gut black and white, with a Number of beautiful Stitches, Diaper and plain Darnings, French-quilting, Knitting, various Sorts of Marking, with the Embellishments of Royal-cross, Plain-cross, Queen, Irish and Ten Stitches, Plain-work & Baby-linnen of the newest Taste &c.&c.

The Druitts also scotched rumors that the couple was leaving the province and that "Mrs. Druitt don't teach Plain-work. . . . She does, with equal Care and Assuidity, as she performs the rest of her Undertakings."

In Newport, Elizabeth Allen dispensed with ornamental work and stuck to her knitting (and reading): "Living in the Widow Bristow's house, on the Point, Propose to keep a School for Reading and Knitting, and will be much oblig'd to those who will favor her with the Instruction of their children." In Pittsburgh, "Mrs. Pride" advertised that at her forthcoming day and boarding school for young ladies she would observe "the strictest care to the morals and good breeding" of her charges and teach them "Reading, English and Knitting, if required." "Keeping school," when it entailed sewing and knitting with only a smattering of reading and writing, would not appear too tasking, but a frazzled Mrs. Bowie learned otherwise and grumbled in her local paper:

Stolen, out of Mrs. Bowie's schoolroom, the 9th instant, 2 bodies of shirts, one done, and the other not finished, with the stamp of the linen on each of the bodies; 2 waistcoats, cut out and not begun,

one apron, all done but the gathering; six or seven caps of her own
. . . one ruffled. Any person that can give information on the said
articles, so as they may be brought back to Mrs. Bowie, or the
person convicted who took them, shall receive Ten Pounds reward.

A male teacher in Philadelphia, so spent by the rigors and "sundry
inconveniences [which] result from teaching YOUTH of both sexes"
that he acceded to the "frequent solitications from several socially
respectable families in this city," developed a female academy for
"READING, WRITING, ARITHMETIC AND ACCOMP'TS," the latter a word
readers   of   the   *Pennsylvania   Gazette*   quickly   translated   as
"needlework."

In Charleston, South Carolina, two sisters advertised the opening
of their school for the "tuition of Young Ladies, in the more polite
and useful branches of education, both French and English, writing,
needlework, and dancing &c. . . . They hope to meet with encouragement fruitable, which will be esteemed a particular favor done."
Another teacher, already experienced from tutoring at "Mrs. Howland's School on Broad Street" and "Mrs. Daly's in Elliot Forest,"
welcomed visitors to observe him in his teaching, sweetening the
tuition pot by offering to instruct "gratis" the "first two young ladies
that shall be properly recommended to me." Anything European still
carried such cachet that teachers spiced their ads with promises of
needlework similar to "French Embroidery" or "taught by a method
similar to that of the most approved English Boarding Schools."

In southern homes, where schools were fewer and more widely
scattered, neighborhood women were engaged to teach needlework
and tutors employed for academic instruction of the young of that
plantation and sometimes of neighboring ones. While the latter studies were targeted to the sons, daughters often attended classes and
caught up on needlework on the side. Princeton-trained Philip Fithian at the Carter plantation's Nomini Hall in Virginia recorded the
activities of his "charges," including their games and studies, and
noted that little girls "played house" by imitating their "big house"
knitting elders by working small round stockings, garters and other
small objects with straws instead of needles.

Earle tells of a fourteen-year-old who raised, spun and then knit
silk into elegant stockings as a bridal gift for her older sister. Such

deftness with elaborate stitchery was routinely expected of upper-class girls, who learned to knit lacy stockings or embellish plain ones with fancy clocks, panels and embroidered letters or flowers. A schoolgirl, sent to Boston to live with her aunts to "finish" her education in a richer cultural environment, wrote her parents regularly to apprise them of life in her aunts' houses, her school activities, the contents of Sunday sermons, her clothing needs and her increasing proficiency in knitting. Anna Green Winslow reported, "another ten skein of my yarn was reel'd off today. Aunt says it is very good." She also noted that her inflamed fingernail was improving enough so that "I can knit a little in the evening." A few months later, after including all the obligatory details of church and family, she added, "When I inform you that my needle work at school, and knitting at home, went on *as usual*, I think I have laid before you a pretty full account of the last week."

Quakers concurred with other educators who relied upon segregating the sexes after the early years to thwart "that excess of riot and wickedness that youth is incident to" and to thereby convert fidgety adolescents into "comfort[s] to their tender parents." Thomas Budd, the Quaker leader, drafted instruction for boys in such useful trades as clock-, shoe- or watchmaking and weaving; for girls the menu remained "Spinning of Flax and Wool, the Knitting of Gloves and Stockings, Sewing and all sorts of useful Needle-Work, and the making of Straw-Work &c, or any other useful Art or Mystery that the school is capable of teaching."

The early Quaker school director who confided to a friend that "[g]irls should be taught something of the use of the needle as well as to read and write, if writing should be thought necessary for girls" would have a soul mate in a later historian of Pennsylvania schools who opined magnanimously a century later, "Some things must be set down to the credit of the old schools. As a compensation to girls for the paucity of their instruction in other aspects, provision was made for teaching them needlework."

When the Quaker Westtown School opened in 1799, required equipment was "a pair of Scissors, Thread-case, Thimble, Work-bag, and some plain sewing or knitting to begin with." A mother wrote anxiously to a similar school, where her young Quaker daughter, Priscilla, was a boarding student, about her child's progress:

I long to hear from you both how psila likes being at scool and how the[e] like her and whether she thinks that shee will lern anything worth her while to be kept as [s]cool here. I have sent her some thred to knit me too pares of golves and hjerself on if there be anough to make so much if not one for me and one for her. bid her be a good gerl and larn well and then I shall love her.

With the high maternal death rate depriving young girls of sewing and knitting guidance at the parental knee, other relatives or school-mistresses acted as surrogates. Sarah Todd announced that in addition to her school, where she boarded young gentlewomen and drilled them in "all sorts of needlework," she would also "wait on Gentlemen's children at their House if desired, between School Hours." Employers aspiring to hire full-time, live-in helpers advertised for "a woman who would go into a Gentleman's family to instruct children in Reading, Writing, and Arithmetic, also in the use of their needle" or "a decent middle-aged woman who has been used to the care of Children, she must be able to teach Young Ladies to read, and the use of the Needle." One advertiser hoped to narrow the pool of candidates to someone "under 20 or that has passed her grand climateric."

Of all the advertisements placed to fill the void left by a mother's departure, this one most fully delineated the colonial woman's function and was, perhaps, one man's view of the *perfect* woman:

Wanted at a Seat about half a day's journey from Philadelphia, on which are good improvements and domestics, a Single Woman of unsullied Reputation, an affable, cheerful, and amiable disposition; cleanly, industrious, perfectly qualified to direct and manage the female Concerns of country business, as raising small stock, dairying, marketing, combing, carding, spinning, knitting, pickling, preserving, etc. and occasionally to instruct two Young Ladies in those Branches of Oeconomy, who, with their father, compose the Family. Such person will be treated with respect and esteem, and meet with every encouragement due to such a character.

There is ample evidence that another fount of knitting help remained. Both male and female slaves knit for their masters as well as their own household needs and could sell their work on the outside if it was exceptionally well executed and exceeded their own plantation's requirements. This was done at George Mason's Gunston Hall in Virginia, where, as Mason recalled, "The spinners, weavers and knitters made all the coarse clothes and stockings used by the negroes, and some of the finer texture worn by the white family, nearly all worn by the children of it."

Slave owners, grasping the correlation between knitting skills and inflated prices, stressed knitting aptitude when advertising sales: ". . . an excellent spinner on the flax wheel, a good knitter, can cut and make up linen as well as any servant in Virginia, and is cabable of doing any house business" and "The woman has been used to spin, knit, wash, iron, Needle-Work, and other business in a Family." A faculty for knitting was equally important in advertising for retrieval of a runaway as shown by William Black of Williamsburg, who pledged a reward and "reasonable traveling charges" for recovery of a "Country born Negro woman named Sarah, a very lusty stout maid wench, about two and twenty years of age, very artful, and, though not a Mulatto, may attempt to pass for a free woman. . . . She has been chiefly a House Servant, is a fine Seamstress, Knitter, Washer, and Ironer."

Among 150 slaves accompanying wealthy widow and new bride Martha Custis Washington to Mount Vernon was her personal knitter, listed as "Peter . . . lame Knttr" in the "DOWER" roster of "Mansion House Negroes." As plantation mistress, Mrs. Washington tutored house servants under her supervision in sewing, spinning, weaving and knitting, expending upon these responsibilities, according to her biographer, much "time and thought." With at least one resident knitter and several helpers on hand, most knitting was performed at Mount Vernon, and the products were delivered to the mistress, as noted in one store record: "1 dozen pair stockings delivered to Mrs. W." One should mention here, though out of period, that when the family later relocated to New York after the Revolution, accountability of household servants, sheltered under Mrs. Washington's wing when she was in residence, shifted to the new President of the United States. Conducting plantation affairs by correspondence with his manager, Anthony Whiting, Washington fretted about knitting as well as farming, and once charged, "Doll at the Ferry must be taught to Knit, and MADE to do a sufficient day's work of it, otherwise (if suffered to be idle) many more will walk in her steps. Lame Peter, if no body else will, must teach her, and she must be brought to the house for that purpose."

Despite the fact that the Washingtons, like other wealthy Americans, ordered hosiery from London merchants as well as depending upon local production, stockings remained a presidential burr:

> The deficiency of Stockings is another instance of the villainy of those I have about me, for, as you justly observe, it is impossible for that lame Peter and Sarah's work could amount to no more than 60 pair. The Gardener's Wife must NOW see that there is a just return of all that is given out and taken in, and when the work is handed over by her, to you. I am persuaded it will be safe. Let the Gardener's wife give work to, and receive it from, lame Peter, as well as others; and then the whole will come under one head. Their reports ought to be dated.

Piloting the new nation through the shoals of its new independence only temporarily alleviated anxieties over plantation knitting, and Washington persisted: "And can Lucy find sufficient employment in the Kitchen? It was expected her leisure hours, of which I conceive she must have very many from Cooking, would be employed in knitting, of which Peter and Sarah do too little." Still stewing about the domestic situation at Mount Vernon two days before Christmas, he threatened to dispatch sewers "making less than their allotted number of shirts per week" to another plantation to work as common laborers under an overseer, and delivered this final flourish: "[T]he same attention ought to be given to Peter (and I suppose to Sarah likewise,) or the Stockings will be knit too small for those for whom they are intended; such being the idleness, and deceit of these people." So much for Christmas cheer!

By the end of the Colonial Period, knitting was such a firmly entrenched occupation for women and children that when the subject of separation from the mother country was inevitably broached, knitters, proud that knitting's significance to colonial home industry was as widely and decisively confirmed as cooking, weaving and sewing, stood primed for stitching whatever would enable them to subsist independently.

2.
Knitting
for Liberty

Neighborhood "circles" for spinning, sewing and knitting had only social implications in the early colonial period, but when Britain, driven by the drain on her treasury after decades of foreign wars, stiffened restrictions on formerly laxly governed colonies to require purchasing materials from England, the voices of domestic women fused with those of their husbands in a resounding "NEVER!" Colonists who had masterfully eluded previous restraints but now encountered strict enforcement plotted retaliatory measures such as boycotting British goods and returning to the "old days" of home production. Suddenly the old household virtues of spinning and knitting acquired political overtones, and male colonial leaders, while understandably gratified by the spirit of female cooperation, were soon uneasy over potential abandonment of well-defined roles.

To eighteenth-century American political leaders, political action was not an acceptable or "proper" role for women. Ben Franklin wrote from London that he was proud of his wife's ability to keep out of party disputes because, he chided, "Women never should meddle with them except in Endeavors to reconcile their husbands, Brothers, and Friends, who happen to be of contrary sides." Scouting stores for a token of his "sincere love and affection" for his sister's wedding day, he selected a spinning wheel over a tempting tea table after considering that "the character of a good housewife was far preferable to that of being only a pretty gentlewoman." Concurrence came from Governor Winthrop of Massachusetts, who (despite the fact that all three of his wives were educated women) was so dismayed at the pallor and apparent ill health of a fellow governor's wife that he diagnosed her as suffering from "the loss of her understanding and reason" and ascribed the mutation to husbandly indulgence in permitting too much reading and writing until "too late." Winthrop sermonized that if she "had attended to her household affairs, and such things as belong to women, and not gone out of her way and calling to meddle in such things as are proper for men whose minds are stronger," she might have found umbrage "in the place God had set her."

Thomas Jefferson, too, perceived women as realizing their ultimate felicity in the domestic sphere, and wrote appreciatively from Paris that "our good ladies" should not "wrinkle their foreheads with politics. They are contented to soothe and calm the minds of their husbands returning ruffled with political debate. They have the good sense to value domestic happiness above all others. There is no part of the earth where so much of this is enjoyed as in America."

Scriptural sanctification of woman's sphere was extended by Puritan clergyman, Cotton Mather, who claimed that religious rather than economic grounds bolstered the status quo. When his "vertuous Maid" learned housewifery, needlework, arithmetic, accounts, cooking, preparing medicines and perhaps, if time allowed, some languages and music, she would become the throned monarch in her domestic sphere.

Given the "evidence," it is not surprising that when women did take political action, they accomplished their goals within "domestic" bounds. After increasingly punitive restraints climaxed with the Stamp Act, women ardently supported the boycott of British goods by alleging that "naught but homespun" would cloak their bodies and that spinning wheels and knitting needles would doom "foreign manufactures." Formation of the Daughters of Liberty, the female "auxiliary" to the more radical 1765 Stamp Tax resisters, the Sons of Liberty, presaged an effective instrument for hardening resistance to British measures. An able spokeswoman, Milcah Martha Moore of Philadelphia, hailed such economic clout in lines from her "Patriotic Poesy":

Let the Daughters of Liberty, nobly arise,
And tho' we've no Voice, but a negative here,
The use of the Taxables, let us forbear. . . .
Join mutual in this, and but small as it seems
We may jostle a Grenville and puzzle his Schemes. . . .
Then Merchants import till yr. Stores are all full
May the buyers be few and yr. traffic be dull.

New Englanders, eager to confirm their boldness in dressing only in domestic threads rather than anticipating arrival of modish bolts and bales from England, restructured the social form of the "spinning bee" into a public outcry against British goods. Since spinners regularly spun yarn for knitting as well as for weaving, and many records of the spinning bees specified knitting as well, both crafts were involved.

The assemblages became the rage in New England, and as the Daughters flocked to churches in droves for spinning and knitting bees, many a preacher must have inferred that his sermons were singularly pithy. Clergymen never missed a chance to scoff at the inanity of high fashion and to press for "cloaths of your own make and spinning," and hosting a bee bore welcome compensation to ministers and their families. The *Boston Gazette* noted that after forty-five Daughters of Liberty had spun at a local manse they bestowed "all the yarn they had spun, a very considerable amount . . . to the worthy pastor." The spirit of "Industry and Frugality" also propelled young ladies of Ipswich, Massachusetts, to their vicar's home, where, though some were only thirteen years old and the temperatures soared, they spun steadily from early morning until six that night and scored this accolade from the local paper: "Their Behaviour was decent and they manifested nothing but Pleasure and Satisfaction in their Countenances at their retiring, as well as through the whole proceeding Transactions of the day." The Reverend Mr. Wheeler, whose family gained the bee's bounty, waited until "After the Music of the Wheels was over" before he "entertained them with a sermon," observing that women just might recoup their country's rights, "which is more than the Men have been able to do."

A British writer observed that the ladies spun for six days of the week, while on the seventh the parson "set to work to preach up

Manufactures instead of Gospel . . . [and reaped a] better Profit than the other Spinners, for they generally cloathed the Parson and his Family with the Produce of their Labor. This was a new Species of Enthusiasm, & might be justly termed, the 'Enthusiasm of the Spinning Wheel.' "

The "Enthusiasm" continued unabated, and when a group of seventeen young ladies met in Providence to spin all day at their minister's house, they were so besieged with would-be participants they were forced to move the next day's session into the nearby courthouse, which even then could "barely contain them." Lively spinning and knitting bees spilled over into Newport, where a newspaper writer, "The Rambler," marveled at the "Knot of Misses busy at their Needles . . . [where they] exclude Idleness from their solitary Moments . . . and contribute a Part of the Support of the Families to which they belong." Turning to Newport's other matrons ("Ye Fair"), he urged: "Let the Knitting Needle be your Delight and Wheels and Needles be the Fair One's Theme!" The state of Rhode Island backed the bees to the hilt, and at the first commencement exercises of Rhode Island College (later Brown University), the president proud-spiritedly wore wholly homespun clothing. At Harvard, the faculty and students had all taken to homespun in support of their women spinners, of whom the *Boston Chronicle* had bragged, "[T]hey exhibited a fine example of industry, by spinning from sunrise until dark, and displayed a spirit for saving their sinking country, rarely to be found among persons of more age and experience."

Fierce competition between congregations, between married and unmarried women, between towns and cities and between old and young converted proceedings into such festive social occasions that hundreds of merry spectators milled around the grounds, augmented in the evening by men who joined the spinners and knitters for picnics and boisterous Sons of Liberty ballads. The bees' bountiful harvest of thread and yarn inspired others to imitate their fervor, and newspapers identified patriots by airing individual production records: One man, with the help of his wife and children, completed in one year five hundred yards of linen and woolen cloth from materials raised on his farm; a small country town in Massachusetts produced thirty thousand yards of cloth; epitomizing home industry, a New Hampshire woman, "endowed with such a noble Spirit of

Freedom, Liberty, and Frugality" that she garbed herself in "Cloth of her own Manufacturing from Head to Toe," assembled odds and ends of "foreign pieces" and "compos'd herself a Petticoat out of them, and the Pieces were so small, that it took 45 Pieces for the outside, & 92 for the inside, Quilted them together and wears them to this day."

A patriotic Bostonian confidently dropped off a copy of his haughty letter to an English friend at his local editor's office. The latter, sensing that the author's thrifty, plucky family characterized the industry that would sustain the colonies, distributed the letter to other editors, who reprinted it extensively:

You may keep your goods. . . . Thank God we have a glorious country; we can subsist independent of the whole world. . . . A spirit of economy and industry has wonderfully diffused itself thro' this whole province; and it's scarce credible how many Females of all ranks have in this town learned to spin. . . . I hae ten children, one a daughter 14 years old. . . . This daughter is constantly employed in spinning; both myself and wife, and all my children, wear clothes of her industry alone, all our stockings and gloves. My girl spins, and my wife assists in knitting. . . . I cannot buy 3 pair of English woven stockings here under 6s[hillings] sterling a pair; & I firmly declare, that 1 pair of mine is worth the whole three.

As tales of legendary New England spinning and knitting sped southward, new disciples enlisted. A New York paper reported that Newporter James Nixon's family wove 487 yards of cloth and knit thirty-six pairs of socks within an eighteen-month period, while a neighbor's family was congratulated for yardage spun ("Not a Skein was put out of the House to be spun") and knitting such necessaries as "two Coverlids and two Bedticks, and all the Stocking Yarn for the Family." A New Jerseyite, lest his women's knitting prowess and loyalty be outranked by their northern sisters, wrote to the papers: "I can with Pleasure inform you, that Industry is so prevalent in this Metropolis, that within six months a Lady of Distinction, tho' infirm, and of a very delicate Constitution, has knit thirty-six Pairs of Stockings, besides having the care of a large Family."

So many women emulated the record holders' initiative that what started as a remarkable effort at self-sufficiency, as a morale booster in strenuous times and an omen to England of colonial recalcitrance, grew so commonplace that it surrendered its newsworthiness when most colonists wore clothes "of their own manufacture" as a matter of course. Pitching his appeal to those few who eschewed spinning their own yarn, an enterprising Philadelphia merchant hoped to twist national adversity to personal prosperity by advertising yarn "of the Produce and Manufacture of America only [and hope that] the good People of this and the neighboring Provinces will encourage this, his undertaking, at a time when AMERICA calls for the endeavors of her sons."

With the passage of England's increasingly obstructive measures (such as the Coercive Acts in retaliation to the climactic Boston Tea Party), calls for boycotting tea and wearing homespun and handknit were even more strident. Since women were the purchasers of what was served and worn in their homes, speakers, writers and preachers insisted that the "ultimate power" of saving the country reposed in their hands. Even discounting the hyperbolic prose, women whose previous job descriptions had included little outside the family circle must have been astonished at the new perimeters of their responsibility. Since noncompliance fell on their shoulders, their consequent focus on home production laid the groundwork for clothing their men when war actually came.

On the eve of the Revolution, then, despite the textile industry's great headway, home industry flourished, perhaps leading England to misjudge colonial industrial progress and doze in false security. The New Jersey colonial governor denigrated home products as "coarse Cloathing for themselves or their Servants, but . . . by no means sufficient for their consumption," and Georgia's Governor Wright noted little production: "Some few of the poorer and more industrious make a trifling quantity of coarse homespun cloth for their own families, and knit a few cotton and yarn stockings for their own use." Yet other colonies, such as Maryland in 1760, perceived the gravity of British intimidation and fostered cloth manufacture by endorsing bounties for "those Persons that annually produce to the several County Courts the Best Pieces of Linen manufactured by White inhabitants in the respective Counties." In addition, to stimulate production and guarantee outlets for surplus commodities such as wool and yarn in a country that could no longer bank on outside sales, colonial legislatures promoted regularly scheduled markets or fairs where "everyone [could] turn his own or Families Industry to his own immediate and greatest Gain" and find a social activity to engage all members of the family.

With the outbreak of war, Congress appointed a Clothier-General to estimate the army's needs and apply to state assemblies and executives for funds for supplies, apportioning shares in accordance with each state's population. Short of funds themselves, states usually passed the buck to townships, most of whom agreed to outfit each man serving; others asked the citizenry for specific numbers of blankets, clothing and other supplies; others levied taxes but allowed substitution of clothing for taxes. Citizens who hoarded blankets and clothing in excess of necessary home use incurred penalties and risked confiscation of the "surplus" clothing by local commissioners. Rhode Island's smaller towns couldn't fulfill the 518 pairs of stockings assigned, as shown by only "4 pairs" from Jamestown and Barrington and "6 pairs" from Middletown. Dover, Massachusetts, tried public pressure by listing supplies furnished by each citizen: "Eleazer Allen gave 8 shirts, Joseph Draper a pair of socks, Joseph Haven, two pairs of socks, Ebenezeer Battle, five pairs of socks." The Virginia Assembly advanced stocking knitting by both proposing to buy all the stockings made and bestowing generous premiums for every pair knit. A small New Hampshire town's women's group presented "15 shirts made of good merchantable wool, 20 pairs of good woolen stockings, 20 pairs of good merchantable shoes." By accepting these clothing donations in lieu of taxes, towns killed two birds with one stone by encouraging home industry and keeping the money within the locality.

Most communities enacted resolutions urging women to make a patriotic gesture by spinning thread for soldiers' essentials, flax and wool for sewing, and "doubled" yarn for knitting. A Philadelphia advertisement encouraged each "excellent woman" to sustain her family and "cast your mite into the treasury of the public good." It would, however, take more than individual sewers and knitters to subsidize clothing needs, and there is no argument that the Clothier-General relied heavily on the already well–established stocking and tailoring trades of Germantown for the major portion of supplies, but with limits to what even that thriving town could provide, women were expected to take up the slack.

Wartime wives, mothers, daughters, grandmothers and aunts had to cope in the provider's absence by selling knitting and homespun products, sewing clothes for immediate family and selling surplus to neighbors (wielding thorns as pins when British imports were aborted), assuming backbreaking farm chores, concocting bullets from personal pewterware collections during the lead shortage, soliciting money for soldiers' needs and embroidering "colors" (flags) for fighting units. All this left little material for personal knitting, but South Carolinian Susannah Wells found a solution: "I used to darn my stockings with the ravelings of another, and we flossed out our old silk gowns to spin together with cotton to knit our gloves."

Women tackled their knitting with a vengeance and vaunted their speed and productivity. In Virginia, in 1776, Winifred Carter won wide acclaim for knitting 150 rounds of 185 stitches per row on a stocking. That same year in Charleston, Mrs. Sabina Elliot made socks for the soldiers with the year 1776 knit into them. In Virginia, plantation owner Landon Carter watched his wife's industrious knitting and calculated that she had taken 333,000 stitches in six days of knitting a pair of stockings. In Philadelphia, Sarah Morris Mifflin wrote to a friend in the British army ("though we detest the cause you are fighting for") recounting her personal sacrifices for the cause, decrying British rule and defending America's actions. Her letter, attributed to "A Philadelphia Lady," was so widely published that one wonders at the importance attached to it unless it spoke for thousands of others in her position, women who wanted to do something but were relegated to a domestic role, or, as in her case, to passive activities because of her Quaker background. Boasting of her abdication of tea drinking and resistance to buying a new cap or gown, she added a new skill, "I have learnt to knit, and am now making stockings of American wool for my servants, and this way do I throw in my mite to the public good."

Philadelphia was also headquarters for a knot of matrons classified as "the first large scale women's association in American history" and "George Washington's Sewing Circle," whose president, Esther Reed, entreated members to forward money saved by renouncing "vain ornaments" and extravagant clothing to a fund from which

Martha Washington would disburse funds for soldiers' relief. Going beyond "doing without," they inaugurated door-to-door solicitations, an unheard-of activity for women, and relied on broadsides to justify their political "intrusions" by invoking images of former heroines— "the Elizabeths, the Maries, the Catherines . . . and the Maid of Orleans." Husbands were proud but worried about their wives' stepping out from home and onto city streets for a drive that could hardly sustain the army for long. Undaunted, the persevering women of Philadelphia were soon joined by those in other cities "in the glorious cause of liberty . . . for the relief and encouragement of their brave men in the Continental Army, who . . . have so repeatedly suffered, fought and bled in the cause of virtue and their oppressed country."

When the campaign's president died shortly after the campaign's start, her replacement, Sarah Franklin Bache, daughter of Benjamin Franklin, proceeded enthusiastically despite one loyalist's grumbling: "[T]he ladies going about for money exceeded everything; they were so extremely importunate that people were obliged to give them something to get rid of them." With Philadelphia partitioned into sections, eleven teams embracing Philadelphia's most prominent families ("Women Citizens of the first rank of such as are engaged in the American Cause") canvassed homeowners and businesses like a modern fund-raising campaign and opened the pockets of both philanthropists and the poor, such as the anonymity-cloaked "Miss Humanity" or "Mrs. Worthlittle." A New Jersey fund-raising enthusiast, who industriously knit socks as she circuited the countryside in an ox cart to provoke others to donate funds and knit stockings, collected 133 pairs by the end of a single week.

The ladies considered the money (which averaged to about two dollars per man) an "extraordinary bounty" to ease the soldiers' condition, not intended to replace what Congress or the states were responsible for supplying. They preferred direct distribution to the soldiers, despite lingering fears that the money would be spent for liquor. When "Mistress Washington" returned to Mount Vernon from a camp visit, however, she consigned the money to the general, who broached buying new shirts, or better still, having the ladies *make* them. The shirt plan did not sit well with the ladies, who considered shirts "necessities," but the commander-in-chief persisted

so intractably that Sarah Bache pleaded with her members to ac-
quiesce. The Philadelphia women duly purchased supplies and spent
weeks cutting and stitching 2,200 shirts, to each of which was attached the sewer's name to cement some personal bond with the
wearer. General Washington gallantly deemed their sacrifice proof
"that the love of country is blended with those softer domestic virtues, which have always been allowed to be more peculiarly your
own." They had *hoped* to be recognized for their efforts *outside* their
domestic sphere.

With war at its lowest ebb that winter at Valley Forge, when Washington reported to the Continental Congress that his soldiers were
in truly desperate straits, "[m]any of them absolutely naked," used
clothing was collected and reworked by volunteers. Young Elizabeth
Smith, nine during that "severe and terrible winter when our Army
lay at Valley Forge, enduring almost incredible privations and suffering," remembered that her grandmother, Mary Frazier, of Chester
County, Pennsylvania, already accountable for all domestic production of the clothing of her considerable family ("most of it by her
own hands"), saddled her horse and rounded up blankets, yarn and
half-worn clothing that she

> . . . patched, and darned, and made wearable and comfortable, the
> stockings newly footed, or new ones knit, adding what clothing
> she could give of her own. She often sat up half the night, some-
> times all, to get clothing ready. Then with it, and whatever could
> be obtained for food, she would have packed her horse and set
> out on her cold lonely journey to the camp—which she went to
> repeatedly during the winter, on the same errand. More than 300
> prs of stockings were in this way prepared and taken to the camp
> besides a great deal of clothing and food. While riding she could
> trace the way the foraging parties from the camp had taken by the
> marks of bleeding feet on snow.

Valley farm women rode to the front with saddlebags spilling over
with shirts, breeches, knitted woolen socks by the hundreds and
delicacies for homesick and starving soldiers. Even crossing spy-in-
fested battle areas, the patriots disguised as market women eluded

detection and slipped through the lines with their provisions. William Egle, whose *Some Pennsylvania Women During the War of the Revolution* is a tribute to their activities, sniffs:

> While the dames of the Quaker City [Philadelphia] were lavishing their smiles on the officers of the British Army, those backwoods women were spinning the flax they had raised to make the material to clothe their fathers and brothers, husbands and sons, wintering at Valley Forge. . . . One shudders when reading the story of that winter of suffering, and yet when the self-sacrifice and devotion of a thousand noble women in Pennsylvania is rehearsed, one cannot but thank God that there was a struggle for independence, and that the women of the Revolution assisted to make the Declaration possible.

His encomium for one woman of the valley, Mary Carson O'Hara, who grew to be a "stately, dignified, and beautiful woman," reads: "During the struggle for independence it is said that she greatly assisted her mother and sisters in their handiwork—the making of clothing and other necessities for the soldiers of the Revolution. She was an expert in that almost forgotten art of knitting stockings, and many the pairs which came from her dexterous hands." Egle described many other sewers and knitters, editorializing about housewifely "competitions": "True to her matronly duties, as well as the patriotic inspiration of the times, no one was more diligent in laboring for the relief of the American soldiery"; "Not only a devoted mother but an ardent patriot . . . she vied with her neighbors in preparing clothing and forwarding food to the little Army under Washington"; "She managed carefully a large farm and was enabled not only to assist many of the families of her neighbors . . . but united with the women in the Juniata in making clothing and other necessaries for the soldiers at the front"; "During the most trying part of our history [Mrs. McKee] vied with the women of her neighborhood in their patriotic endeavors to cheer the hearts of the heroes who were gradually achieving the independence of their country." As another historian commented, there was no mistaking the joy of soldiers on the verge of open revolt when sentinels pacing the camp's outer limits spotted an advancing cavalcade of "[t]en women in carts, each cart drawn by ten pairs of oxen, and bearing tons of meal and other supplies, [who] passed through the lines amid cheers that rent the air." Those devoted women, he wrote, "preserved the army, and Independence from that day was assured."

Support flowed from less expected quarters when General Washington set up camp in Whitemarsh, a few miles outside Philadelphia, where "Old Mom Rinker," a local character and loyal informant to the army, picked up scraps of British military information overheard by her tavern-keeping kin. Old Mom Rinker wrote messages for General Washington, encased them inside her ball of knitting yarn and perched on a cliff outside of town. Bestrewing her flax to bleach in the sun and knitting placidly, an image of tranquil industry, she anticipated the general's troops passing on the road below her rocky ledge. When they materialized, she nudged the ball of yarn over the brink, and the soldiers calmly scooped up, pocketed and conveyed to the general her priceless message. Old Mom Rinker never dropped a stitch!

Around army camps local women were not the only knitters, for the circle of officers' wives knit regularly with "Lady Washington" who simply transferred her knitting practice from Mount Vernon to camp, where she spent several months throughout the war. In Mount Vernon records, where every purchase from a favored London establishment was noted, there are frequent references to "Knitting pins of different sizes" or "$\frac{1}{4}$ lb. of Grey's knitting needles." Separated from the general for seven months, Mrs. Washington made her first public appearance at the camp in Cambridge in 1777, the self-described "old fashioned Virginia house-keeper, steady as a clock, busy as a bee, and cheerful as a cricket," promptly organized the other wives to knit socks and caps and make bandages. It was after her first meeting with Martha Washington in Cambridge that the well-known author and patriot, Mercy Warren, wrote her friend Abigail Adams, "I will tell you that I think the complacency of her manners speaks at once of the benevolence of her heart, and her affability, candor, and gentleness qualify her to soften the hours of private life, or to sweeten the cares of the hero, and smooth the rugged paths of war." She was greatly admired, and few begrudged her presence.

While Washington never condoned compensation for his own services to the Continental Army, he regarded his wife's ministrations so significant that he requested payment for her trips, scrupulously documenting each charge, which would eventually total $27,665.30. When his officers once serenaded him at camp, he begged that he had retired for the night but dispatched Mrs. Washington, who good-naturedly heard them out and, in the general's name, bestowed a fifteen-shilling tip, duly recorded as an "expense." Though trips to and from Mount Vernon of the "somewhat dumpy woman with a quick smile" were by "plain chariot," the sight of her scarlet-and-white-liveried servants as she alit from the coach drew an admiring circle of soldiers who knew that her coming immeasurably improved the humor of the general, to whom she jauntily referred as "The Old Man."

Since high officers, taking their leader's cue, also summoned their wives for several months, Mrs. Washington enjoyed a built-in circle of women friends who provided a social life in the camp's spartan quarters and with whom she could sew, mend uniforms and knit socks. The number of women in camp generated amusing camp sidelights, like the sentry's spotting a "startling apparition of a long line of scarlet" in the distance and sprinting into camp to warn, "The British are coming!" Closer inspection revealed the "line" to be red petticoats hung out to dry!

Military couples also formed a social nucleus for the general and his lady when they went into town for special events such as dancing, one of Washington's favorite relaxations. In Philadelphia, he responded to the "I could dance forever" challenge of lively Kitty Greene, the wife of one of his generals, and abandoned his spouse to sideline entertainment by General Greene, who later wrote a friend: "We had a dance at my quarters a few evenings past. His Excellency and Mrs. Greene danced upwards of three hours without once sitting down. Upon the whole, we had a pretty little frisk."

While there was much camaraderie among the women of the camp, the social lines were strictly drawn between Mrs. Washington's clique and those outside her magic circle, making it an awesome experience for the local gentry to meet Mrs. Washington when they visited camp to donate to soldiers' relief. Mrs. Troupe of Morristown was no exception:

Several of us thought we would visit Lady Washington, and as she was said to be so grand a lady we thought we must put on our best bibs and bands. So we dressed ourselves in our most elegant ruffles and silks, and were introduced to her ladyship. And don't you think! We found her *knitting and with an apron on*! She received us very graciously and easily, but after the compliments were over she resumed her knitting. There we were without a stitch of work, and sitting in state, but General Washington's lady with her own hands was knitting stockings for herself and her husband.

Mrs. Troupe further credited Mrs. Washington with observations that prove she was earning every cent required to convey her to the battlefields:

And that was not all. In the afternoon her ladyship took occasion to say, in a way we could not be offended at, that this time it was very important that American ladies should be patterns of industry to their countrywomen, because the separation from the mother country will dry up resources whence many of our conflicts have been derived. We must become independent by our determination to do without what we cannot ourselves make. Whilst our husbands and brothers are examples of patriotism, we must be patterns of industry.

Mrs. Westlake, then a sixteen-year-old Valley Forge "stout girl" who sometimes accompanied Mrs. Washington on her rounds, later related this experience to biographer Benson J. Lossing:

I never in my life knew a woman so busy from early morning until late at night as was Lady Washington, providing comforts for the sick soldiers. Every day, excepting Sundays, the wives of officers in camp, and sometimes other women, were invited to Mr. Pott's— Washington's Valley Forge Headquarters—to assist her in knitting socks, patching garments, and making shirts for the poor soldiers, when materials could be produced. Every fair day she might be seen, with basket in hand, and with a single attendant, going among the huts, seeking the keenest and most needy sufferers, and giving all the comforts to them in her power.

Mrs. Washington, who went home to Mount Vernon during the late spring and summer but always returned to headquarters the following fall, is properly credited with improving the morale of the soldiers as well as of her husband, and the description of her serenity as she "sat day after day knitting socks for the soldiers" certainly qualifies her for the honorary knitter's roll of the Revolution. It is said that in her first weeks as first lady, Martha Washington was begged by a trio of ornately dressed women to conduct her regular Friday afternoon receptions with more pomp and circumstance. Meeting the delegation in simple morning dress, her knitting needles ("the useful companion of many lonely hours") in hand, she gracefully reminded the overdressed group that the very clothes they wore were what the Daughters of Liberty had forsworn. She spoke of her wartime efforts to clothe the soldiers, of accompanying her husband to winter quarters and sharing privations, reminding them that Washington's own mother was a simple woman who "ever looked well to the ways of her household [and] . . . taught him to be industrious in her example, for her spinning-wheel spun the clothes he wore from his earliest days." The storyteller related that Mrs. Washington looked at her needles as she added, "She, like myself, loved the knitting needles." Her simple *American* domesticity confirmed by her knitting, she bade farewell to her visitors, who "impressed, not offended . . . left the presence of this noble matron, bearing her words in their mind . . . and her influence in their hearts; for she gave not merely the precept of her lip, but the example of her life." Her knitting continued long afterward, and a visitor to Mount Vernon described her in the role she loved the most, the homemaker:

[The room] is nicely fixed for all sorts of work. On one side sits the chamber maid, with her knitting; on the other, a little colored pet, learning to sew. A decent old woman is there, with her table and shears, cutting out the negroes' winter clothes, while the good old lady [Mrs. Washington] directs them all, incessantly knitting herself. She points out to me several pairs of nice colored stockings and gloves she has just finished, and presents me with a pair, half done, which she begs I will finish and wear for her sake. It is wonderful, after a life spent as these good people have incessantly spent theirs, to see them in retirement, assume those domestic habits that prevail in our country.

One must acknowledge the proximity of others who pursued their men during the Revolution, some faithful wives functioning as cooks, seamstresses, knitters, menders and laundresses, and other camp followers performing less wholesome services. It is estimated that as many as twenty thousand women endured enormous privations as they slogged along on foot, heavily weighted down with pots, pans, baggage and, often, small children. Though commanders criticized them for clogging the deployment of troops and compromising security, many tendered inestimable nursing care.

Those at home who assumed many male tasks in addition to their own regular domestic duties chafed at the presumption of their inability to comprehend politics and their exclusion from discussions of issues outside their "realms." Young Eliza Wilkinson, of Charleston, who had certainly won her spurs by bravely defying the British and alone maintaining her parents' plantation during the war, seethed at the unjustness of the bias:

> I won't have it thought that because we are the weaker sex as to bodily strength, my dear, we are capable of nothing more than minding the dairy, visiting the poultry houses, and all such domestic concerns; our thoughts can soar aloft, we can form conceptions of things of higher nature; and we have as just a sense of honor, glory, and great actions as these "Lords of Creation". . . . I would not wish that we should meddle in what is unbecoming female delicacy, but surely we have sense enough to give our opinions . . . without being reminded of our Spinning and household affairs, as the only matters we are capable of thinking, or speaking of, with justness or propriety. I won't allow it, I positively won't.

It might sound as if the ladies were about to ask for universal suffrage, but the newly "liberated women" of the Revolution appeared to revert rather quickly to their earlier role. Even Eliza wrote a few days after the above outburst, "Let me read what I have written—my pen is quite unmanageable this morning. . . . What will the men say if they should see this? I am really out of *my sphere* now."

After the war, when the women of Trenton learned of the new president's plan to pass through Trenton en route to his New York inaugural, they planned a triumphal procession second to none to honor their venerable wartime leader. While some had shouldered a gun or two during the fighting, had denied themselves new clothes, had eaten sparingly for months on end, had supervised soldiers' relief organizations, had nursed the wounded, had knit and sewed themselves cross-eyed and had wept for their fallen loved ones, they now, identifying themselves, quite simply, as the "Women of Trenton," conceived an unstinting commemoration. The welcome mat they hung out has long been celebrated in engravings. And well it might be. The tombstone of one "Woman of Trenton" later bore this inscription: "She was what a woman ought to be."

An arch about twenty feet high and twelve feet long was erected on the north side of the bridge. The arch was supported by seven pillars on one side and six on the other for the thirteen new states, each festooned with masses of evergreens and garlanded with long ropes of laurel and early spring flowers. Stretched above was a flower-ornamented banner whose gilt letters proclaimed: THE DE-FENDER OF THE MOTHERS WILL BE THE PROTECTOR OF THE DAUGHTERS. On one side of the arch were posted six little girls in white clutching baskets of flowers; arrayed on the other side were thirteen young ladies representing the states; behind them were banked "matrons" of Trenton and neighboring villages. As the president-elect rode beneath the arch, a chorus of voices swelled in an ode written especially for the event. An onlooker reflected that they performed with "exquisite sweetness," although the following description makes one blanch at the potential for ear-splitting cacophony: "The first four lines were sung by both matrons and young ladies, the young ladies sang the fifth line, the matrons the first part and the young ladies the last part of the sixth line, then both sang the next lines, the matrons the ninth, the young ladies the tenth."

The women of the Revolution were, as one author put it, "the mothers of the men who won the American Revolution." Dedicated knitting was obviously only one small part of their contribution, but it would be soberly and poignantly remembered almost a century later, when, in the midst of another great war, the speaker at the dedication of Boston's Bunker Hill Monument referred to that site's first crude burial during the Revolution, when survivors swiftly dug a grave and lowered the twelve men in their clothes, just as they had fallen. The speaker described what happened when workers re-opened the ground to prepare the new monument to the patriot dead:

> [T]hey found there, mingled with that sacred dust, the remains of socks and garments, which through the long nights of that anxious winter, wives and mothers had been making for those they loved. Little thought those wives and mothers that their work would be treasured as a precious relic.

3.

Knitting in the Circle of Domesticity

The same women who responded patriotically to soldiers' needs in the Revolution discovered ample outlets for their benevolence in the next century. Secure in their organizational skills after shunning tea, wearing homespun, and sewing and knitting for the threadbare army, they transposed those aptitudes into social reform. Their lives still constricted by their domestic responsibilities, they nonetheless resolved to "clean up the nation's house" as competently as they wielded the broom at home, and sought to better the lot of the insane, the criminal, the poor, the widowed, the orphaned, the enslaved, the profane and, especially, the intemperate. Since drinking breadwinners afforded scant comfort and security, financially dependent women and their benefactresses attacked alcohol abuse with special fervor. In ports, where seamen's reputations made them ripe for conversion, societies provided clothing and "comfort bags" for seamen who promised to renounce both drinking and profanity. Descendants of one early 1800s Boston Seamen's group were still morally and financially committed a century later, when they earned this encomium at their centennial celebration: "I doubt if this society would be alive today . . . had it not been for the Women's Seamen's Friend Society. . . . They are the ones, you know who made the wristers and the mufflers, and all those other knitting things."

Fancying themselves their nation's "moral uplifters," women enlisted in the reform crusade with missionary zeal, fueled by exhortations from the pulpit to intermix the Gospel and charitable deeds. Membership in Bible societies blossomed, and knitters learned they could rivet attention on deliberations, sermons and responses while continuing their "work," a breakthrough that has salvaged many a conclave ever since. A female Bible society in Middlebury, Vermont, capitalized on the inclination to knit by scheduling special sewing and knitting sessions to raise a small fund for church philanthropies. Along with Bible groups, antislavery societies appealed to large numbers in the North, and the women's rights movement attracted the truly bold despite admonitions that should a woman "raise her gentle voice amid the storm of debate, or rush into the heat and strife of partizan politics" she would jeopardize her femininity and risk the shame of becoming "madly unsexed." Not many took the gamble.

"Ladies Bountiful" focusing on ameliorating conditions for poor women and children were so worried lest their benefactions encourage pauperism that, despite abysmally low compensation for the products, they substituted instruction in sewing and knitting for outright donations of money. A South Carolina group rationalized: "In dispensing of alms it should be a fundamental rule with us, to contribute nothing to the support of IDLENESS among those that are able to labor. The pecuniary relief given under such circumstances is productive frequently of more evil than good." If, however, society members knit for the poor and no money changed hands, the specter of corruption vanished, and writer Lydia Sigourney noted that knitting was "most appropriate during the severity of Winter [when] The timely gift of a coarse pair of stockings has often relieved the suffering, protected the health of many an ill clad or shivering child." A passel of Boston ladies befriended "a little band of seamen's daughters," and across town the Fragment Society, the oldest continuous sewing circle in the country, undertook a two-pronged attack by contributing needed articles of clothing (made by members) and encouraging their "wards" to equate stitching with a guarantee of their future survival. Salem children whose parents "from poverty, indolence or intemperance . . . or because work calls them from home . . . make it impossible to care for them at home" received knitting and sewing tutelage. A British publication put it bluntly, "The children of the poor should always be taught to knit, and each member of the family ought to have a stocking in hand to take up at idle moments, by which many pairs might be completed in a year."

Men proudly commended their wives' ardent pursuit of "charitable work" as long as it was confined to their "sphere" and concurred with Artemus Muzzey's view that "[t]here is one realm where woman reigns in undisputed supremacy; it is the realm of moral power." As long as "do-gooder" humanitarians acquitted themselves of their "regular" domestic work and served commendable dinners at decent hours, they enjoyed free rein; but they needed more than approbation—they needed money. In an "I'll support your charity if you'll support mine" backscratching technique still much in use, they gravitated to charity fairs to market, or perhaps exchange with each other for an inflated price, products from their "realm" of cooking, sewing, knitting, weaving and painting. A veritable stampede of fair knitters gave their all!

In Boston, after a distinguished committee of city fathers failed to raise sufficient funds for a suitable Bunker Hill memorial in a period disparagingly alluded to as "The Embarrassment," women from a local sewing circle single-handedly ("although with the hearty cooperation and effecient aid of gentlemen") planned and executed the September 1840 "Monument Fair" that drew such crowds it was extended three days. Sarah Hale, editor of *Godey's* and the fair's guiding light, spread the word to women through the middle and New England states, as far west as Ohio and south to the Carolinas, to knit, crochet, cross-stitch, quilt, embroider and send for sale whatever wasn't nailed down, from Grandfather's portrait to Aunt Rachel's imported tea set. The fair's newspaper, *The Monument*, cranked out daily on a miniature hand press, stressed that "each lady will endeavor that the articles on her table should be good of their kind and at fair prices" and featured certain displays: "Ladies in want of any valuable fancy articles can be well supplied on application to the Waltham table, #18"; "At the Taunton table may be found a variety of fancy goods, equal to any in the Hall, for sale cheap." The *Boston Post* judged the scene "bewitching in the extreme"; the *Transcript* rated it "indescribably magnificent" and pronounced booth salesladies "all attention—all smiles—all civility"; the Monument Association's biographer credited its success in raising thirty thousand dol-

lars to the "industry, taste, and spirit of the Ladies of New England."
The fair was so successful in meeting its goals that never again would
anyone treat with disdain women's efforts at fund-raising, quite literally with their own hands. Hale's biographer expansively designated the fair "a symbol of the first concerted effort of American
women to break the hereditary bonds of convention."

Those bonds of convention, the boundaries of woman's traditional
"sphere," had long been confirmed, but by the early nineteenth century domesticity became the emblem of woman's worth. If "Industrious Woman" was the epitome of colonial and revolutionary womanhood, then "Domestic Woman" was all that was good and holy in
the next century. With piety, purity and submissiveness, domesticity
was the pivotal fourth pillar of historian Barbara Welter's "Cult of
True Womanhood," and within that framework, industry was the
yardstick by which woman's value was measured.

Models of such laudable diligence were rural women who bought
their "knitting pins" and "knitting needles" from dry goods stores
but spun their own yarn or obtained it inexpensively from small
stores advertising factory prices ("Knitting Cotton wholesale and retail at the same price as it is sold at the Manufactory") or direct from
the factory itself ("woolen stocking yarn . . . single, or doubled and
twisted for knitting"). Intense pride in their home "manufacture,"
especially their weaving and knitting, prompted rural families to compete for "premiums" at regularly held agricultural fairs, particularly
in upstate New York and New England. In records of the Ontario
County, New York, Agricultural Society for 1822, where pieces
knitted and yardages woven were given, one family listed knitting
of "30 pairs of socks, 7 pairs of stockings, 3 pairs of mittens"; another:
"20 pairs of woolen socks, 14 pairs of woolen stockings, 9 pairs of
mittens for men and boys . . . and 9 runs of worsted stocking yarn";
another: "14 pairs of women's stockings, 10 pairs of socks, 3 pairs
of mittens, 16 runs of worsted yarn for stockings." Items selected
for the competition were "exhibit quality" and therefore only a small
portion of family production.

Knitting for themselves and their families, along with other domestic tasks such as ironing, washing, dyeing, weaving and cooking,
was a routine engagement of homemakers and their daughters. Two
particularly industrious young rural women were Sally and Pamela

"Seventy Years Ago," Thomas Eakins, 1877.

Brown, of Plymouth Notch, Vermont, whose early 1830s diaries record the comings and goings of small-town New England—spinning, weaving, knitting and sewing (either alone or at a bee), teaching in a small school, nursing the sick and noting fluctuations in the weather and maturation of crops. Sally's most frequent diary entry was "worked around the house," with accounts of spinning and knitting projects running close behind: "Spun, doubled, and twisted 20 knots of stocking yarn"; "Began a pair of stockings forty-eight stitches to a needle"; "Finished some stockings I began on the 20th"; "Began a pair of double mittens"; "Finished the mittens begun the 28th." One can almost hear the rustle of paper as she flipped back to corroborate dates.

Younger sister Pamela's diary, with her choice entry being "knit some and read some," recapitulated the housework saga, inventoried her knitting progress ("Knit upon Thomas's mittens"; and the next day, "finished Thomas's mittens") and added a few particulars of daily life. A knitting-toting village schoolmistress ("I expect to commence teaching school tomorrow and to have one dollar and fifty cents per week"), she knit during any hiatus in the day or evening's work. On a blustery March day, she wrote: "Kept school. Snowed and the wind blew very hard. In the evening Mial came in from the mill to play checkers. Knit some and played some." Another day: "Taught school. In the evening knit some and peeled beechnuts." Pamela's knack for merging knitting with other pastimes was unmistakable: "Knit some and Nathan told our fortunes in the book of foreknowledge"; "In the evening knit upon my stocking and listened to the conversation of Mr. Martin and Mr. Homer"; "Taught school. In the evening Mial and I called at Mr. Hall's. I knit, ate apples, and talked with Mial, Homer and Martin"; "Turned the heel to three pairs of stockings . . . and began another pair."

Records of unexceptional daily activities were mingled with knitting operations, including an aggravation despised by all knitters: "Took a pair of the stockings I knit for Lake last winter and pulled out the toes and knit shorter as they were too long." A knitting Good Samaritan, she completed work others commenced: "[F]inished a stocking Marcia had almost done for Dr. Carter"; "Knit on Susan's stocking"; "[K]nit on Susan's stocking what time I had out of school"; "[F]inished Susan's stocking." Her hands never idle, Pamela knit for her father, her brother, her sisters and herself. Still, when knitting was postponed because of a "sore finger . . . so painful . . . [I] could not sleep with it," she was "very lonesome" and couldn't wait to start "a pair of stockings for Thomas," "a stocking for Dr. Carter,"

"George's stocking" and "a pair of mittens for pa." Of even her twenty-first birthday she remarked laconically, "My birthday. Picked Wool and helped mother with the work." Christmas Day drew only, "Washed, sewed. etc. etc." At least once Pamela referred to knitting beyond the family circle by making a pair of stockings for the family doctor, either for sale or perhaps in exchange for his treating the alarming "bunch which is growing in Father's throat."

Knitting during free time (what there was of it) provided needy women an opportunity to earn money. The Reverend Thomas Robbins undoubtedly relied upon such a neighborhood knitter, for his diary indicates that in February 1837 he "[p]aid a woman for knitting, sixty cents" and in April "[p]aid for knitting, seventy-five cents." Since the diary is moot on what he acquired for that price, one cannot decipher the rates, but four years later he still "[p]aid for knitting, etc. seventy-five cents."

Other evidences of knitting for pay exist, among them Mary Barrell's separate account books for her household and her yarn and spinning business, which disclosed both expenses of "new knitting needles at 3c. per pair" and receipts: "fifteen dollars for sock and mittens"; "paid for knitting 9 pairs of socks at 9 p[ence] per pair"; "received of Mrs. Joy for knitting 7.20." Martha Ballard, industrious midwife mentioned in an earlier chapter, noted on March 1800: "I have finished a pair of hose for John Town. It is the seventeenth pair I have knit since this year commenced," which was quite a production figure for three months in which she was also obstetrically engaged! Rural women who looked to village storekeepers for special orders of plain socks for men and ornamental open-worked ones for women also bartered knitted scarves, gloves, tidies and shag mittens (made of leftover warp ends) for other goods. New England knitters depended so heavily upon their home manufactures that when the textile industry's intrusion forecast their dwindling income, they acted together and lobbied against the encroaching mills by inserting this declaration in a prominent farm journal:

INCORPORATING KNITTING

Our industrious dames and daughters of the Commonwealth ought to know that the men are getting the Legislature to incorporate a man company, to do all the knitting in the State. It is too bad, thus to break up almost the last vestige of fire-side industry left to the ladies. We hope they will send in a petition against this infringement on their domestic concerns.

[Signed] Advocate

Other than "domestic concerns," there were so few other occupations open to women that one newspaper queried, "*What* can she do? There are but very few avenues of business in which women are privileged to walk. The wage paid for female labor is very trifling; and when she has others besides herself to provide for, it seems almost impossible that she can succeed." In explanation, the writer described a feisty, frugal, sixty-year-old widow whose only way to finance her walking journey from Virginia to Tennessee was to sell purses she knit en route.

While many early nineteenth-century fortunes were founded almost overnight in frenzied speculations and recklessly lost in the series of "panics" that reduced families to their previous austerity, the country was at peace except for the short-lived War of 1812. There was no large-scale knitting for the troops, but a knitting circle first formed to knit during the Revolution raised about $600 for military uniforms through a stocking-knitting project of their "Ladies' Stocking Society of New York." As a knitting aside, during that war, when future president Zachary Taylor was stationed at Fort Knox, his wife so pined for additional knitting cotton, presumably for personal use, that her husband pointedly asked his brother to bring it when he came to the outpost.

The war influenced knitting in another way. When the Jeffersonian Embargo cut off imports and dry goods prices soared, clicking knitting needles facilitated the reversion to handknit garments. Of that period, Sarah Anna Emery remembered, "Shawls were in great demand. The previous Autumn many ladies had knit or net them from woollen yarn of their own spinning and coloring. . . . Sally Little knit one on large wooden needles for me, which I had colored at Pearson's Fulling Mill. This shawl was very pretty, and most comfortable, being both soft and warm." Emery's recollections are a gold mine of detail of early nineteenth-century domestic life, and one is fascinated that her atypical grandmother eluded the stereotype of those who lived out their lives with a child's family, bent "under heavy burdens," toiling "up rugged steps," weeping through "long nights that seemed as if they would never pass away" and conscientiously setting enviable patterns of industry. Emery's grandmother bypassed the "industrious old lady" route by only pretending to knit along with her daughters; she gabbed instead, leading Sarah to conjecture that if idle hands coupled with hours indulged in "harmless gossip" were sinful then grandmother had much to repent.

Perhaps grannies would be coddled, but younger women, for whom coping with massive quantities of housework was a nonnegotiable condition of domesticity, appealed plaintively, "*How* can we do everything?" To an author, writers of new women's books and magazines cranked out the answer: "PLANNING!" Scheduling each task to a particular hour could convert household management into a "science" and transform harried housewives into well-oiled machines with few "odd moments" of time. To avoid squandering that rare commodity, spare time, one should, said the critics, snatch one's knitting "to employ the fingers with, when listening to others, or when your mind is so preoccupied that you cannot give it to a book." Since businesslike new home "managers" demanded efficient bodies to tackle expanding obligations and thus achieve perfect womanhood, they were persuaded to improve their health through calisthenics ("This hard name is given to a gentler sort of gymnastics, suited to girls"). When their mentor, *Godey's Lady's Book*, published illustrated instructions for acquiring "vigorous muscles, graceful motion, and symmetry of form" within their homes, many ladies expanded their wardrobes to include avant-garde "exercise costumes" of tunic-topped pantaloons.

Magazines, catering to women's pride in their homes and glory in their womanliness by expanding "work departments" with patterns for stitchery of all kinds, bestowed new prestige on "woman's sphere" and swelled their circulation. By the late 1840s, *Godey's Magazine's* first regular needlework department, headed by "Mlle. DuFour" (that revived European touch!) offered instructions for everything from a knitted muff and "Victorine" (a rather large collared object with front panels hanging down to protect the chest) to knitted artificial flowers, holly, berries with fruit, and all shapes and sizes of "chatelaines" (bags hung from the waist or the arm). Mr. Godey's espousal of needle arts was so celebrated that the Ladies' New England Art-Union of Needlework granted him a "certificate of membership" to which he gratefully responded in the next issue: "He will endeavor to make his 'Ladies' Book' worthy of their patronage; then he is sure it will continue to win general approval."

Indeed it did! As editor from 1837 to 1877, Sarah Josepha Hale promoted education for women, urged female writers to cease camouflaging their identities and to publish their full names rather than hiding anonymously beneath "By a Lady" or pseudononymously under "Miss Martin" or "Mrs. Fotheringill," aired the need for women doctors and nurses, highlighted the discrepancies between properties women brought to marriage and amounts under their jurisdiction after the vows, pleaded for better diet and exercise, and caviled for more comfortable clothes. Still, "her" magazine steered clear of national politics and concentrated on recipes, "embellishments" (embroidery and needlework in general) and the famous "fashion plates" that made *Godey's* the ultimate pacesetter. Though other magazines followed, notably *Peterson's*, Frank Leslie's *Lady's Magazine*, *Harper's* and *Atlantic*, Godey's led the pack with about 150,000 copies sold per month. Treasured issues with needlework instructions were exchanged among family and friends so that actual circulation far exceeded paid subscriptions, and women learned not only what was au courant in America's cities but also at the fancier summer resorts such as Saratoga, where ball gowns were required additions to the wardrobe.

Championing the "cult of domesticity" paid handsome dividends to publishers as home products advertisers recognized the perfect medium for tantalizing women in all walks of life who leafed through the magazines searching for innovations in their domestic world. High style was as charismatic to Vermonter Pamela Brown as to her modish city sisters: "I started a pair of mittens for George and read some Ladies Books we borrowed at Esquire Slack's"; "I knit and read in Lady's Book that I borrowed from Carolyn S." By providing women a sense of satisfaction with their role, according to historian Nancy Cott, the canon of domesticity was a bonding force solidifying the entire female sex. She further credits Sarah Hale with making "Womanhood" a vocation in itself by "judiciously directing the at-

tention of females to those subjects which concern them as women
. . . [and] aid[ing] them in their endeavors to perform their duties
as women."

Few questioned that woman's duties included knitting, though
hardworking Maria Brown, well acquainted with the old proverb,
"A man works from sun to sun, but a woman's work is never done,"
speculated: "Mrs. Glazier in Amesville [Iowa] told me that in Ireland
it was the men who did the knitting and the women the sewing. That
seems to me like a fair division of labor. Of course the men were
pretty tired in the evening after a day in the field, but the women
were just as tired after a day of cooking and ironing [and] our work
had to go on after dark by light that was none too good."

Despite questions of sexual division of labor, writer Lydia Sigourney, though ranking women's special realm subordinate to "men's
province," garlanded it with "peculiar privilege" and recommended
knitting as "quiet employment, favourable to reflection . . . a ready
vehicle of charity to the poor . . . [and] well adapted to save those
little fragments of time which might else be lost." Fully agreeing was
a young Iowa farm wife thoroughly fulfilled by familial duties (including knitting to "have 2 good pair of stockings for all"): "It seems
real nice to have the whole control of my house, can say I am monarch
of all I survey and there is none to dispute my right." Surveying even
the special realm of the living room, *Young Ladies' Friend* assured
its readers that "there is more to pouring out tea and coffee than
most young ladies are willing to believe" and clinched the debate by
citing a "very happy match that grew out of the admiration felt by
a gentleman on seeing a young lady preside well at the tea table."

Books of advice to the young proliferated, each bearing the same
message of woman's special role. The Reverend Joseph Mathews, in
his *Letter to School Girls*, inveighed against "[t]hose females who deliver public haranges and desire to be heard in legislative halls and
political contests, [who] are like the meteors that blaze across the
sky, and disappear. . . . God made women for domestic duties, and
her nature must be very much perverted before she can cease to
love such duties." Since gender roles were established early in life,
William Mavor (whose advice on idleness was "Never lie down till
we feel tired [or] . . . remain in bed after we wake in the morning")
dissembled a bit in his *Catechism of Health* when questioned about

equality of education for male and female children: "In their earlier years there ought to be no difference; but there are shades of distinction, and regards to propriety, which judicious and prudent guardians and teachers alone can adjust and apply."

A swarm of "prudent guardians" of femininity eagerly demarcated their domestic role. A widely read British book of 1847 rhapsodized that the needle arts (including knitting) "occupy a distinguished place, and are capable of being made, not only sources of personal gratification, but of high moral benefit, and the means of developing in surpassing loveliness and grace, some of the highest and noblest feelings of the soul." A doyenne of the cult, stressing that "household accomplishment" was fashionable abroad, used that as a wedge to beguile American women into copying their European counterparts who "may be seen in their balconies after dinner, grouped around their work-baskets, while the gentlemen converse with them, or silently watch the progress of their pretty tasks. In the sitting room of every mansion, some one corner is rendered cosier than the rest." It could, she added, happen here! Praying that it would not, young Quakeress Maria Mitchell, later a noted astronomer and the first woman elected to the American Academy of Arts and Sciences, wrote in her diary, "It seems to me that the needle is the chain of woman, and has fettered her more than the laws of the country. . . . I would as soon put a girl alone into a closet to meditate as give her only the society of her needle."

Domesticity was fertile soil for the rash of dexterous knitters who vaulted into print with "how to" and "special patterns" books. The smallest this author has discovered are *The Ladies' Work-Box Companion* of "entirely new receipts" in the Rare Books Division of the Library of Congress, a wee gem about three by four inches easily popped into knitting bag or pocket, and a tiny French knitting *Manuel des Jeunes Demoisels* "presented to Miss Mary T. Don [?] for obtaining the most numbers of marks in French Dialogues, 1 August, 1827" in the Textile Division's collection at the Smithsonian Institution.

Many books appear to have been shamelessly plagiarized. It was exceptional for an author to concede help from another, but Florence Hartley refreshingly prefaced her book: "Nearly all the patterns for needle-work . . . are derived from English, French, and German sources, and these the compiler has freely availed herself." She acknowledged indebtedness to "Miss Lambert's 'Guide' " for some patterns and to Mrs. Pullam's *Lady's Manual of Fancy Work* for "alphabetical arrangement." The latter, however, recently arrived from London to work for *Leslie's*, was not mollified, and complained, "There is not one magazine, in which Fancywork is a feature, that does not, with or without acknowledgement, avail itself of my labors, nor an editor to whom my name is not familiar as a 'household word,' although hitherto it has been, not very justly, withheld from American ladies." In comparing patterns, one is invariably struck by their similarities, and even *Godey's* needlework column helped itself to a Florence Hartley design (of an earlier date) without attribution, but perhaps Florence herself had found it in a "European source."

Miss Lambert's Guide, to which Hartley referred, rewritten and reissued several times in the United States and England, was undoubtedly the best-known needlework book, and in the preface to its 1846 edition, "Miss Lambert" expressed her gratitude to her husband for researching the history of knitting and "allowing my maiden name to appear on the title page, as that by which I am more generally recognized in my avocation." Her given name, Eleanor, never appeared. "Miss Lambert" she remained. With no foreign copyright protection (as Charles Dickens had also learned to his regret), she complained of unauthorized American reprints that even included spurious dedications "to the ladies of the United States." Recognizing that imitation might be considered flattery, she was "fain to accept it . . . as there is no redress for the substantial wrong." In England, however, Eleanor Arnold knew her rights: "To imitators at home, it may be well to hint, that all the designs in this volume are copyright."

Since European patterns and habits still represented luxury and elegance to democratic Americans, authors vaunted their intimacy with European styles and techniques to provide an open sesame to American pocketbooks. An 1844 book promised to deliver "the newest and most fashionable patterns from the latest London edition" and the "foreign excitement of new pattern stitches with which we flatter ourselves they have never been acquainted." German women, though not considered fashion role models, were admittedly the most industrious knitters and therefore worthy of description and emulation:

[It is] customary amongst the German ladies to have some light piece of work, with which they can be employed. When passing the evening in one another's society, even when passing a morning visit, or after dinner at a dinner party, or while sipping coffee, or taking ices at the public garden, they consider their knitting needles an indispensable accompaniment. . . . Our American ladies will undoubtedly find the custom worthy of imitation.

The anonymous author spurred knitters to persevere with their fine-threaded lace patterns on tiny needles even though ambitious projects such as knitting washable cotton lace for petticoat hems would seem interminable. "Patience will soon lead to progress," she cooed. Her glossary of terms puzzles the modern knitter, who effortlessly decodes "[h]ang on" into "cast on" but is stumped by:

Cast over is a term I believe sometimes used by knitters to signify, bring the cotton forward. I have only used it to express, bring the cotton over the needle, quite round.
Round the needle means the same as the last term.
Reversed means quite round the needle, the cotton being passed over the needle and then carried back to its place.

Published only a few years later, *Ladies' Guide in Needlework, A Gift to the Industrious* expectedly promised: "[M]any more stitches are now offered to the ladies of America with which we flatter ourselves they have never been acquainted." The *Guide* embraced typical mid-nineteenth-century knitted patterns for "Baby socks," "Baby Mufflers," "Child's socks," "Knee Caps," "Evening carriage shoes," "Plain mittens," "Lamb's wool Muffattees" ("for driving in cold weather"), "Purses and bags," "D'Oyleys," "Double Blanket," "Shawls," "Kettle Holder," "Night Stockings and caps," "Garters," "Sofa tidy," "Leggings," and "Outdoor caps."

The "Gentleman's Bosom Friend" made a favorite gift, as much for its intimate name as for its temperature-defying comfort. It was a sometimes turtlenecked garment extended to cover the chest and was described as follows in one manual: "The narrow piece is to go at the back of the neck, and the double knitting is to cover the chest.

"Sortie" cap, 1858.

N.B. The narrow part being ribbed is very elastic, and will pass easily over the head and fit pleasantly to the throat." "Muffattees" for ladies and gentlemen were warm mufflers, though some books indicated they were coverings for the wrist and lower arm that could be easily slipped on before donning a coat. The discrepancy in terminology is not explainable. A "Nubian" was usually described as a fleecy woolen scarf about three yards long and about a half yard wide, or sometimes as a triangular shawl. Its use probably defined the term, with one owner calling hers a "most comfortable and graceful wrap for the head and shoulders when exposed to the evening air in a light dress."

In the nineteenth century, fine-denier yarns were increasingly used in popular edgings for linen pillowcases and sheets, larger pieces such as bureau scarves and tablecloths, and rectangular or circular doilies (or "D'Oyleys") to protect table tops from the general wear and tear of lamps, water glasses and pipe racks. With parlors filled with overstuffed chairs, knitters kept busy making fine-cotton replaceable covers or "antimacassars"—circular, rectangular or oval lace "tidies" that could be tacked to the backs and armrests of easy chairs to absorb the liberally applied hair oil fancied by men, women and children. Since Pomade (first made from oils imported from Makasser) was concocted at home by melting together and then beating beef marrow and lard until light and fluffy, housewives wanting their share of the limited supply jockeyed for preferred standing with their butchers and "spoke for" it well ahead.

With bedclothing also needing a buffer against hair dressing, knitters made absorbent cotton nightcaps, usually short, fairly tight-fitting ones. A "French Pattern," however, called for the knitter to shape the crown and then "when your cap is large enough round . . . knit around until the cap is three-fourths of a yard long: make the end like the beginning." Lacking a clarifying sketch, one's imagination soars in ruminating on an object with a cap at each end to double the wear. For the imaginative, old pattern books supply the stuff of conjecture, such as a "save-all bag . . . so called because it may be made with odds and ends of netting silk, or all of one color, at pleasure [which can be worked] until the bag is long enough. The bag looks well with a clasp, and a tassel at the bottom." It must be taken on faith.

The ultimate cotton-knit project was a bedspread or counterpane, and needlework books and magazines abounded with patterns for every imaginable stitch, usually worked in panels or squares and later assembled to avoid supporting heavy pieces during the knitting. The product of endless hours, the surviving counterpanes have been lovingly tended, usually hoarded and judiciously displayed by proud owners. Museums with fine-textile exhibits, such as the Newark Museum and the Sherburne Museum in Vermont, have outstanding examples of the craft, which is recently enjoying a revival of interest as new publications reproduce familiar patterns. Patterns were frequently swapped, and "Anna K" of Amesbury, Massachusetts, seeing a letter to the editor in the March 1858 issue of *Godey's* asking for instructions for a shell counterpane, unselfishly offered her version to Mr. Godey:

Dear Sir: I have been a subscriber and constant reader of your excellent Lady's Book for a number of years. I have received through its columns much valuable information. I have often wished to contribute, if but a mite, to its general stock of instructive and interesting matter; and having seen that a friend of yours wished to be informed as to knitting a quilt in shell pattern, I make bold to send you a specimen, and directions for one, which if you think are of sufficient novelty to introduce to your columns you can do so.

The pattern, calling for five pounds of knitting cotton, sewing together seven to eight hundred shells and finishing "with tassels around the edge on the points of the shells," was duly given. Knowing the influence of *Godey's* and that patterns are handed down from one generation to another, one can assume that many "Anna K" counterpanes still exist. Such a generational pattern is recalled by Barbara McGrann of Sea Island, South Carolina, whose grandmother, Julia, a thrifty German born around 1860, acquired from *her* mother a pattern for a heavy-duty "apple leaf" cotton spread made up of squares, each square in turn divided into quadrants of four leaves at the center of a lovely open-worked design. Her grandmother, like many of her generation, Mrs. McGrann recalled, lived with her daughter's family:

She lived with us in Toronto when I was in grammar school. My earliest memory of her was sitting in her room, in a rocking chair, knitting. In fact, I never saw her hands idle. If she was not knitting she was hooking a rug or piecing a quilt. Her knitting was, I assume, a necessity to keep the children in warm clothing during the cold weather, but even in those very hard days these women wanted to create something beautiful. And she worked incessantly on this spread. The pattern was not written down, but she taught the pattern to my older sister [Emma] who finished the spread when my grandmother died.

Older sister Emma remembers observing her grandmother knitting until shortly before her death in 1934, when she rolled up the spread with a wistful "It was well begun but not half done." Emma many years later retrieved the "not half done" spread from storage, finished it and passed it to *her* daughter. Emma's niece, Julie

McGrann Dougherty, the original knitter's great-granddaughter, picks up the story in 1986:

> When my mother saw that same spread on her niece's bed and noticed how absolutely gorgeous it was, she got the pattern from Aunt Emma. My aunt knew it in her mind but took several tries to get it on a scrap of paper before she got it right. It was from that scrap paper that Mom spent two years working, and now has her own apple leaf spread. It really is beautiful!

Other oversize knitting projects were rugs of wool and cotton "ends" (described in *Godey's* as "soft and downy"), most often knit in strips but sometimes in floral and geometric shapes and later sewn together. For large families, grandmothers, mothers and daughters knit measureless quantities of socks, mufflers, leggings, hoods, wristers, muffs and mittens of every description—cabled, checked, striped, initialed, fancy-stitched and doubled (with one color on the outside and another as lining), all appended to crocheted strings snaking down jacket sleeves to anchor them to their owners. Babies were almost encased in knitwear from ruffled bonnets to embellished bootees. Since small girls wore knit lace-patterned "pelisses" (cloaks) for company visits, *Godey's* November 1848 issue featured a pelisse pattern in its "Work Table" section, advising, "We give in this number a seasonable article for our Work Table. Ladies commencing now can have, before winter sets in, a warm and fashionable cloak finished for a child." With November already well under way and 443 stitches to be cast on for the skirt alone, it would be a hardy and sleepless knitter indeed who finished "before the winter sets in"!

Knitting instructresses recommended "a knitting sheath, &c, to be fastened on the waist of the knitter, toward the right hand, for the purpose of keeping the needle in a steady and proper position," and these fabric, wood, metal or scrimshaw sheaths supported the weight of extra-long needles employed for large projects. Now supplanted by modern, flexible, circular needles even for straight knitting, sheaths are prized collectibles. Since knitters carried their knitting around with them, they were urged to keep it "tidy": "Keep the ball in the pocket, or in a bag hung to the arm, or a basket, and do not allow it to roll on the table or floor, to get dusted."

Early pattern books gave short shrift to gauge (measuring stitches and rows to the inch) despite the availability of several needle gauges such as "Walker's Bell Gauge" and "Chamber's Gauge," which were similar to modern ones into whose graduated holes needles to be measured are inserted. Instead, authors enigmatically prescribed "Use fine knitting needles"; "[K]nit with heavy pins"; "[W]ork with fine, sharp ivory needles"; "[T]ake large bone or wood pins"; "Use steel needles, for they are the best"; "[U]se regular needles." Alerts were posted: "N.B. Do not knit too tight or too loosely"; "The following instructions are for medium knitters." But since garments seldom required a good "fit" of chest or bust, few knitters brooded about final measurements. In children's clothes, if the garment didn't fit, a child was found to fit the garment—a maneuver not confined to nineteenth-century knitters.

Multiplying the potential for sizing disasters were broad variations in nomenclature for yarn types. In general, "German Wool" was similar to today's knitting worsted; "Zephyr" was close to sport or Shetland weight; "knitting silk" dictated fine needles such as zeros or smaller by today's gauges; "knitting cotton" for spreads, doilies, underwear and some stockings varied greatly in degree of fineness; "English Fleecy," "German Fleecy" and "Saxony" were used for gentlemen's stockings; "Merino," often split and knit in single strands, was used for "fancy" knitting or baby clothes. Since sizing was seldom supplied ("for a large man," "for a medium-sized boy," etc.), even competent calculators were stymied in predicting dimensions.

To compound knitting hurdles, ephemeral yarn dyes warranted caution: "Much care is needed, not only in the selection of colors and shades, but also to ascertain if the color has been stained with a permanent dye." Undaunted, Englishwoman Cornelia Mee was so addicted to gradations of color that she suggested twenty-one different shades of "any color that may be approved" for the eighteen-inch border of a "very elegant knitted scarf" and eleven shades for a "shell bag" in German wool. So many patterns called for "scarlet" (especially in knit petticoats) that one deduces that red dye was relatively stable, something a modern knitter would assume to her regret.

Endorsing knitting in their exalted feminine sphere, mothers hoped their daughters' more extensive academic curriculum did nothing to jeopardize needlework's preeminence in "domestic" education. Until 1829, 42 percent of the schools offered plain needlework (including knitting) and 43 percent offered ornamental needlework, but that figure so rapidly dwindled that by 1840 Worcester, Massachusetts, schools had reduced it to two half-days in the primary schools and only one half-day in the "higher female schools." A group of New Jersey Quakers so decried its neglect in schools that they engaged a female needlework teacher for the summer ("when men teachers discontinue") to assure that their girls "learn this art."

Children were chastened to contribute to the family by sewing and knitting, especially during economic crises, which occurred with stunning regularity. During one period of economic depression and consequent westward migration, a small volume, *The Frugal Housewife*, provided practical dosages of homely wisdom for those who traveled and those who stayed behind to cope. Tucking it into apron pockets, women turned to it like their Bibles, unearthing home remedies for described symptoms, simple recipes for inexpensive meals, health maxims, tips on washing clothes ("Woolens should be washed in very hot suds, and not rinsed. Lukewarm water shrinks them"), observations on social issues, criticism of women's education ("Young ladies should be taught that usefulness is happiness, and that all other things are but incidental") and tips on purchasing yarn ("Buy your woolen yarn in quantities from someone in the country, whom you can trust. The thread stores make profits from it of course").

The book's author, Lydia Mary Child, a prominent abolitionist and leading proponent of the new "science" of household economy, "the art of gathering up all the fragments, so that nothing is lost," propounded: "Nothing should be thrown away so long as it is possible to make any use of it, however trifling that use may be; and whatever the size of a family every member should be employed either in earning or saving money." A staunch disciple of the "Time is money" motto, she subscribed to knitting stockings by hand since they "wear twice as long . . . and they can be done at odd minutes of time, which would not be otherwise employed. Where there are children or aged people, it is sufficient to recommend knitting, that is an EMPLOYMENT."

Child revealed little forbearance for dawdling children and upbraided parents for permitting their children to "romp away their existence" rather than inculcating responsibility in them:

BEGIN EARLY is the great maxim for everything in education. A child six years old can be made useful; and should be taught to consider every day lost in which some little thing has not been done to assist others. Children can be very early taught to take care of all their own clothes. They can knit garters, suspenders, and stockings; they can make patchwork and braid straw; they can make mats for the table, and mats for the floor; they can weed the garden, and pick cranberries from the meadow, to be carried to market.

Child appealed directly to children ("Little girls can mend as neatly as women, if they will have patience") in *The Little Girl's Own Book* of 1834, and a well-worn copy in the Rare Books Division of the Library of Congress bears on its flyleaf: "Miss Amanda Hess's Book Presented to her by her Mother for attention to her Recitation and School." The author mingled homespun tidbits such as "Whoever knows how to knit a stocking, cannot help finding out how to knit a mitten, if they look at one" with philosophical reflections on youthful knitting obligations:

The favorite employment of our grandmothers ought not to be forgotten. It enables one to be useful in the discipline of life, when they can no longer be actively useful, and it is a never failing amusement. I never knew an old lady ignorant of it, who did not deeply regret she had never learned. Independent of these considerations, a little girl ought to know how to do EVERYTHING; it may not always be a necessity for her to sew and knit—but she should KNOW HOW.

So many knitting manuals advised planning for old-age needlework projects that female preoccupation with possible disability appears excessive. French visitor Alexis de Tocqueville was struck by women's "delicate health," and statistics corroborated that though women outlived men they still suffered enough "female complaints" to render them more susceptible to debilities. Planning "employments" for old age was not on children's minds, but the elderly grandmother remained a fixture in every home, and despite dim light and clouding vision, knitting was her province. Knitting by touch was always available to the weak-sighted elderly, and Ann Stephens, the author of one of the most popular needlework books of the time, recommended that the young practice "blind knitting . . . and pursue their favorite occupation whilst reading, studying or conversing . . . and not become mere knitting machines," since "none of us can tell how soon sickness or weak sight may compel us to abandon all employment which requires strong light or exertion of thought." She fretted:

> To see young ladies stooping, with rounded shoulders and contracted chest, over a simple piece of knitting, no one would imagine that they were exercising their sense of touch as well as their memory, until the most elaborate pattern is produced in a manner perfectly mechanical; why then should we not be able, in the same manner, to use our fingers, whilst our thoughts, tongues, and eyes are at liberty for the enjoyment of more intellectual pleasures?

Corroborating Stephens and affirming the importance of learning the "mysterious intricacies of toe and heel" and "education of the finger" stood Margaret Maria Brewster's *Household Economy*. Brewster justified knitting for both thrift and preference ("hand knit stockings are far superior to those sold in the shops") and joined in the usual prescription for timely preparation for the "dark day when eyesight begins to fail [when] the stocking wire and nimble fingers will be found a great resource against unwilling idleness."

The other star in domestic economy's firmament was Catherine Beecher, whose purportedly scientific "treatise" on the subject undergirded the prevalent concept of "two clearly distinct lines of action for the two sexes." Beecher rated women's role as lofty as men's, "whether they labor on the foundations, or toil upon the dome" of the temple of the Republic. "Lofty the role might have been, but its functions still lay within the domestic sphere, and to fortify daughters for their position Beecher adjured mothers to train little girls to render "essential aid," even if "the stimulation of the intellect should be very much reduced . . . [and] made altogether secondary in importance."

Keeping youngsters busy and gainfully occupied was such an orthodox doctrine that when the new children's magazine, *Juvenile Key*, debuted in 1830 under the editorship of Oliver Oldwise, whose very name rang with senior authority, parents were comforted to be apprised of his frankly admitted purpose: "to delineate to you, young readers . . . some of the evils of idleness." To the boys he sermonized that learning to use the hammer, hoe or shovel far outweighed "driving hoops, flying kites, playing ball, &c., though these sports may be occasionally indulged in." For girls, the news was no more heartening:

> And if the little girls were indulged in the same manner of training for exercise, instead of jumping the rope or gadding about the streets, it would be much to their improvement in morals & manners; though girls may usually find exercise enough indoors if their mothers would take the trouble to keep them in employ.

Harriet Beecher Stowe's Aunt Harriet complied with the accepted techniques for training her five-year-old niece to become a "lady" and potential homemaker:

> Her ideas of education were those of a vigorous Englishwoman of the old school. . . . According to her views little girls were to be taught to move very gently, to speak softly and prettily, to say 'Yes ma'am' and 'No ma'am,' never to tear their clothes, to sew, to knit at regular hours, to go to church on Sunday and make all the responses, and to come home and be catechised.

Young ladies were to utilize time productively rather than engaging in idle reverie when sewing, embroidering or knitting. Eliza Farrar, Emily Post and Ann Landers rolled into one, urged girls to have at hand something to "provide for the joint occupation of ears and fingers. . . . When engaged with your needle, a younger brother's lesson may be heard, reading aloud can be listened to with advantage, or a sister's practicing can be attended to. . . . [One writer] mentions a highly gifted lady of his acquaintance, who always read whilst she was sewing or knitting, and had so learned to divide her sight between her book and her needle, as to go through many volumes in that way."

In relating her childhood knitting training to her grandchildren many decades later, a memorist who knit and read at the same time ("not so fast, of course, as knitting with my eyes on the work") wrote:

Ma put us girls to work early. It was taken as a matter of fact that we should learn all kinds of housework. . . . You see I had a rather severe course in Domestic Science, but the rest of my education didn't amount to much. . . . At Grandma Foster's school, little girls learned not only to read and write, but to sew and knit also. . . . First we knit our garters, afterwards our stockings. . . . When we were little girls and went some place, we always took our knitting along. We had to knit so many times around before we could play. Children must learn to be useful, they thought in those days. My cousin, Lucinda Gillmore, came to play one day. "My children have done their task," said Ma, "Just give me your knitting and I'll do yours." We went running down to the orchard to the swing while our mother did Cindy's knitting. It made a great impression on me—Ma's doing Cindy's stint for her.

Knitting's practicality was epitomized by *Godey's* short story "Heel and Toe," where the young heroine (who could both knit and "con" her lessons at the same time) earned book money by knitting fancy articles that fetched high prices at the local store where "many a wealthy lady's baby put its tiny hand into the pretty mittens knit by her busy fingers." When Mary's wealthy Prince Charming was captivated as much by her "flying needles" as by her intellect, young girls everywhere swooned and took a leaf from her book by learning to read and knit simultaneously. Mary Elizabeth Maragne of South Carolina manipulated both, as she noted in her diary: "I am very busy copying French exercises, sewing, & knitting—I hold my grammar in my lap and study as I knit till eleven o'clock at night." In New England, Lucy Larcom, an accomplished-enough knitter to shape a stocking "tolerably well" by the age of seven, appreciated knitting because it required so little thought: "I did not need to keep my eyes upon it at all. So I took a book upon my lap and read, and read, while the needles clicked on, comforting me with the reminder that I was not absolutely unemployed, while yet I was having a good time reading."

The expression "tending ["keeping," "sticking" or "minding"] one's knitting" appears to have been well established by the early nineteenth century. In an *Ipswich Register* article of 1837, "Jonathan," protesting the overweening preoccupation of town gossips mulling over the likelihood of his engagement to a young townswoman, recalled his youth in early Vermont, where the mother of Hannah Cooke, "a lazy, shiftless hussy, and an incurable gossip and busy body," was forced to reprove, "Keep your knitting, Hannah! Why don't you keep your knitting?" Jonathan added, "Now, Mr. Editor, I think there is a good deal contained in the commandment of this worthy dame—keep your knitting, Hannah; that is, attend to your own business, Hannah. Would it not be well for us all to pay a little attention to mother Cooke's commandment as well as the ten commandments?"

Since females *were* expected to tend to their knitting, maturing girls such as Caroline Howard carted it along when "visiting": "I shot up into a tall girl, and was allowed to go occasionally with my mother to take tea sociably with her friends at four o'clock, carrying my knitting work for occupation." Bostonian Sarah Anna Emery dropped in on friends "dressed in our best, with our go-abroad knitting work, usually of fine cotton, clocked hose . . . of very elaborate patterns" and clustered about the fire chatting and knitting until after tea, when the "beaux appeared [and] knitting was set aside for games and dancing."

It was a common scene by mid-century, and knitting, whether for personal satisfaction, discipline or money, was solidly enshrined within the protected "circle" of domesticity.

4.
Westward Knit!

At a 1918 reunion of Oregon pioneers, feisty "Aunt Becky," her badge emblazoned with "1848" to mark the year she took the Overland Trail to the West, jauntily summed up her experience:

> We didn't come in automobiles. I can tell you. We came by ox teams. . . . It was a hard, hard trip, hard work, slow progress, and not always dainties to eat. But we got here! We never gave up, never looked back, just kept on the move. And I guess that trip and the tough times we had after getting here were good for us. . . . Look at me! . . . I will race anybody in the crowd who is under fifty if the race is at least four miles, which is about my distance. If you find anybody who wishes to take on such a race, just tell them to . . . ask for Aunt Becky Morris.

That pride and resilience characterized the attitude of most female overland travelers, who carried on as industriously in wagons and carts as at home in their parlors, right down to their knitting. One traveler recalled, "Nancy Morrison's flax-wheel was in the wagon . . . and every woman down the line was knitting for dear life. 'For how can we waste so much time?' cried mothers to whom thrift was a religion." One woman knit so many soft, warm socks on the plains that when she finally reached the Pacific Coast she was importuned by sailors to trade them for Hawaiian curios, sugar, coffee and co-

"Wagon Train on the Prairie."

conuts. Parting from them reluctantly, she remembered, "Dusty days were knit into those socks, and long drowsy days on the train trailing west, ever west, to meet the sea." Another claimed such dexterity that she could both drive oxen and knit, and a young traveler remembered how her mother "knit all the way across . . . [to] keep us all in stockings."

Pioneering was typical of American life from the very beginning, as adventurous souls fanned out from established communities to ensconce their families with a modicum of comfort even in the rudest of huts. In the first vanguard they crossed the Appalachians, then ventured on to the "Trans-Mississippi West" and finally departed for the Far West—Oregon! California! An Iowa settler who thought her moving was behind her commented helplessly that with the contagious "Oregon Fever" raging, "[n]othing seems to stop it but to tear up and take a six months trip across the plains with ox teams to the Pacific Ocean." In the peak year, 1850, emigrants exceeded the numbers who had crossed the plains during the previous decade, and of the 44,000 who went to California, 6,000 to Oregon and 2,500 Mormons to Utah, there were about nine men for every woman. With the frontier moving constantly westward in successive waves, lonely women, separated from the comforts of home, relied on knitting to provide necessary clothing, facilitate relaxation during friendly encounters with other travelers and relieve the tedium of long days on the trail. Without it they felt bereft, as one diarist bemoaned: "Oh what a loss I'm at to know how to amuse myself for tho I have a little sewing yet it's nothing that must be done. . . . I might knit but have only red yarn which I bought for Sis and it's too near Summer to commence woolen socks."

They hiked beside the train when weary of being cooped up inside hot, stuffy wagons, and toted their handwork while visiting other women on the train during stops. California-bound Mary Haun remembered:

> During the day we womenfolk visited from wagon to wagon or congenial friends spent an hour walking, ever westward, and talking over our home life back in "the states"; telling of the loved ones left behind; voicing our hopes for the future in the far west and even whispering a little friendly gossip of emigrant life. High teas were not popular, but tatting, knitting, crocheting, exchanging recipes for cooking beans and dried apples or swapping food for the sake of variety kept us in practice of feminine occupations and diversion.

"Feminine occupations and diversion" notwithstanding, only strong women could manage the responsibilities of frontier life, and the "delicate lady," though still fashionable, had to yield to the healthy woman. By the middle of the nineteenth century, *Godey's Lady's Book* had increasingly emphasized diet, health and exercise, advising women to "go forth into the field and woods, if you live in the country—take long walks in the cool morning and evening hour, if you are in a 'populous cities pent'—let the minimum of these daily excursions average at least two miles." This was scant preparation for the trek many would undertake! Since women of the early nineteenth century were bombarded by the dicta of the "cult of true womanhood," the argument that women were physically inferior, should throw themselves upon the mercy of the more dominant and efficient male and remain in their own women's "sphere," it is especially interesting to note that the strong-willed women who accompanied their men westward in the great migrations of the nineteenth century tried to accommodate to both of their worlds. When celebrating California statehood a few years later, one pioneer woman characterized women's role as "companions" to the toilers, since "our sex forbade further participation." The gender division of work on the trail was well established, just as it was at home. The men drove the oxen, mended the wagon, made all the decisions about provisions, routes and length of time en route. Though the women often shared the backbreaking burdens of shoving reluctant oxen through treacherous currents in rain-swollen streams, and gathering buffalo chips for fuel, they still considered these tasks not their "role" and strived to keep up their personal "toilettes" despite the rigors of the trip. To maintain fair complexions in the blistering sun, they hid under brims stiffened with twigs set into slots like the "stays" on a sail, thus feeding their fondest hope that at their destination someone would gasp, "Lawse, honey, I cain't believe you've been on the trail!"

The impressions recorded by these journeying women both echo their wonder at majestic vistas and articulate their complaints at having exchanged the security and comfort of home for a trip that grew almost too horrible to bear. Outwardly, they tried to appear unruffled, worrying about the same things that pestered them at home—what to have for dinner, how to get the clothes washed and dried, how to find time to knit and sew and mend.

Though trail-women were adventuresome, most were "old-fashioned" and unmoved by the 1844 Seneca Falls Convention's talk of equal rights, of choices and opportunities for daring women. With few exceptions, pioneer women were not women's rights proponents. A few went west to spread the Gospel. Most, influenced by promises of land grants from "Uncle Sam" and the lure of financial rewards (such as the gold), appeased any guilt by viewing themselves as moral missionaries of one of the greatest movements in America, expansion. They were asked to share the planning, but only within their feminine sphere; they were expected to be "fit" for physical tasks, but only on an emergency basis; they were to transfer the felicity and comfort of home to a cramped "prairie schooner" for weeks and months of tortured anxiety, with little control over the trip's execution. It was a noble effort, about which one pioneer's son later philosophized:

I don't know what her feelings were about these constant removals to the border, but I suspect now that each new migration was a greater hardship than those which preceded it. My father's adventurous and restless spirit was never satisfied. The sunset land always allured him, and my mother, being one of those who follow their husband's feet without a complaining word, seemed always ready to take up the trail. . . . I see now that she must have suffered each time the bitter pangs of doubt and unrest which strike through the woman's heart when called upon to leave her snug, safe fire for a ruder cabin in strange lands.

Once a conveyance was determined, the woman cut and sewed the double-cloth wagon tops and sides, sometimes rolled up for better viewing, with muslin on the inside and heavy linen on the outside for extra warmth and protection ("They both have to be sewed real good and strong. I have to spin the thread and sew all those long seams with my fingers") and attached pockets or "pouches" so that items such as knives, firearms, cooking pots, mother's sewing and knitting basket and essential toilet articles could be tucked away safely. Some scrawled slogans or place names on each wagon as perhaps the first transcontinental bumper stickers. Each item—all the food, tools, bedding, clothing, a veritable pharmacopoeia of medicinal roots and herbs, axle grease, spare wagon parts, furniture and so forth—was sharply scrutinized to make certain that it was critical to the survival of the family, the wagon and the animals both on the trail and for the first homestead. Voyagers eagerly solicited advice from experienced wagoners and avidly read dog-eared copies of emigrant guidebooks that cautioned them, "Do not encumber yourselves with anything not absolutely essential to your comfort" and "Never get into trouble with the expectation of getting help; carry nothing but what is absolutely necessary, and mind your own business." Those guides, however, were written by and for men, prompting one twentieth-century historian to write a fictionalized facsimile targeted for women. Women put their own interpretation on "absolutely essential," and many a mother and grandmother lashed her favorite "knitting" rocking chair to the wagon's side and unstrapped it when "nooning" or stopping for the night. Those who insisted upon bringing a stove and tables and chairs for "dining" secured them to the roof or the feed box at the rear. After all, women had always accepted responsibility for "the home," and they set about transmuting ox carts and wagons into as reasonable copies as they could design, wedging into each precious inch of their new household as many comforts as they could wangle. Kitturah Belknap, whose trip preparations included knitting "two good pair" of stockings for each family member, justified taking "four nice little table cloths" to make wagon living "just like at home," and one foresighted family even filled its washtubs with "little peach and cherry trees to set in our Kansas orchard."

Preparations entailed many months of sifting, sorting, bartering and discarding before auctioning off the "truck" of their former lives. Kate Farley, before her trip from Indiana to California with her mother, father and five brothers and sisters, helped her mother spin yarn for socks for the family, sew calico into dresses and pinafores, stitch breeches and woolen shirts for the men and boys and knit socks for all family members. Decades later, Kate remembered her father's verdict on her handiwork: "as fitten socks as ever I wore." Miriam Colt was almost ready to leave on her trip when she wrote in her diary on March 15, 1855: "Have had two sewing bees; one for the old ladies, and one for the young—'united pleasure with business'—my friends visited me for the last time." Another wrote: "Right here I wish to state that many of these emigrants were well equipped for setting up a new home in a far-off land. Whole bolts of sheeting, linsey wool, jean for men's clothing, carpets, home-knit hosiery and mitten of colors, both grave and gay, were stored away by careful hands to circumvent the day of need."

In addition to accoutrements of home and hearth, many women persevered in transporting chickens or cows, though many were abandoned once a few "cow stops" or "chicken flies" had been executed. Wrote one participant,

Mr. Smith has a coop fastened on behind the carriage which curtains some fine white chickens—three hens and a rooster. We let them out every time we camp, and already they seem to know when preparations are made for moving & will fly up to their place in the coop.

Of a cow for whom her wagons had to make regular stops, one woman waxed tenderly, "One luxury we had which other emigrants nearly always lacked—fresh milk. From our gentle 'mulley' cow I never parted. She followed our train across the desert, shared our food and water, and our fortunes, good or ill, and lived in California to a serene old age, in a paradise of green clover and golden stubble-field, full to the last of good works." Butter was another obvious advantage of traveling with cows: "After breakfast, I strain the milk into an old-fashioned churn that is big at the bottom and little at the top, cover closely and fix it in the front of the freight wagon, where it will be churned by the motion of the wagon, and we have a pat of the sweetest, most delicious butter when we stop in the evening. . . . It is wonderful how soon we have learned to live in a wagon."

Fully outfitted, the wagons, usually in family groups, headed west in late winter or early spring to rendezvous along the Missouri or the Platte rivers in time to form "trains" to shove off over well-defined tracks by early May, when the sprouting prairie grasses were at their prime for foraging animals. To secure a semblance of community and discipline, members selected leaders and drafted constitutions and invaluable bylaws ("While I am writing, a public meeting is being held in the area of the corral. There is much speaking and voting upon questions appertaining to the enforcement of the by-laws. . . . We are a pure democracy."). Memories of the vast encampments of emigrants at the "jumping-off places" of Independence, St. Joseph or Council Bluffs were indelibly printed: "I could not begin to tell you how many there [are] in St. Joseph that are going to Oregon and California, but thousands of them. It is a sight to see the tents and wagons on the banks of the river and through the country they are as thick as camp meeting tents. 20 or thirty miles and some say for 50 miles."

Missouri newspapers carried notices of meetings for prospective caravan members, and advertisers announced their wares for travelers who came by steamer and purchased wagons on arrival. Mr. C. W. Stuart, for instance, advertised "200 wagons manufactured expressly for the Salt Lake, Sante Fe, and California trade" at a price far lower than anywhere else in the state, but one can only wonder about their source when he adds, "Emigrants and traders will find it in their interest to examine his wagons, at the Penitentiary in Jefferson City." Knitters needing a few more skeins could buy yarns of the "best Pittsburgh manufacture" in local dry goods stores. Newspapers, beholding large numbers of families and eager to paint encouraging pictures of caravan life, noted the "satisfaction and confidence of the women [who] appeared to be not only indifferent to the hardships and dangers of the way, but to be grateful with their prospects." For single men hoping to join wagons, they bore portentous tidings that among the voyagers were "numerous young girls, just blooming into womanhood and man[y] of them beautiful, neatly dressed, and bound for Oregon and California."

When families separated, exchanging family ties for conjugal bonds, their anguish was poignantly chronicled. Eighteen-year-old Arvazine Angeline Cooper, mother of a sixteen-month-old daughter and pregnant with another child, accompanied her husband and members of his family, leaving behind her own: "[W]hen the day for starting came so quickly, I began to realize that little backwoodsy corner of Southwest Missouri was all the world to me, and I was not only leaving my native land, but every single tie of blood relations, for something so far away and vague that it seemed very unreal, and I had not the remotest idea that I would ever see any of my kindred again."

Melancholy also seized Lavinia Porter, a southern girl whose cooking expertise included "a delicate cake or a fancy pudding" but never an entire meal, as she mounted her California-bound ox cart and bade farewell to her sister:

> I never recall that sad parting from my dear sister on the plains of Kansas without the tears flowing fast and free. . . . It was like tearing our heart strings asunder. But such sorrows are to be endured not described. . . . Climbing into the wagon . . . with everything we possessed piled high behind us, we turned our faces toward the land of golden promise that lay far beyond the Rocky mountains. Little idea had I of the hardships, the perils, the deprivation awaiting me.

Young Mary Ellen Todd, who helped in preparing by spinning, weaving and knitting endless garments, considered the trip a lark:

"I did feel some deep regrets about leaving . . . but I could not have been hired to stay behind, even though we had heard of the harrowing fates and hair breadth escapes of those who had gone before." But all that changed when she looked back through the wagon's rear opening and "beheld that forlorn looking company; with their hands up to their faces; still peering after us; noting their dear familiar forms and longing looks, I just put down my head and wept." Her valiant mother, however, quickly took out her knitting to focus her eyes and thoughts elsewhere. Her daughter recalled, "She always had her knitting or mending at hand. . . . The slow gate of the oxen made this possible. She fully believed and often quoted the old adage that 'a stitch in time saves nine,' " stitches that later kept her family warm when others were reduced to rags. Lodissa Frizzell asked, "Who is there that does not recollect their first night when started on a long journey, the wellknown voices of our friends still ring in our ears, the parting kiss still feels warm upon our lips, and that last seperating word Farewell sinks deeply into the heart?"

Parting over, travelers recorded the startling newness and surpassing beauty of the country their wagons traversed, and it would be hard to say that Lavinia Porter, who had despaired when she left Kansas, regretted her decision to head west: "The aspect of the prairies in the early morning sunshine was most alluring. The air was fresh and bracing, filled with the fragrance of countless Spring flowers, and every little blade of grass hung with drops of dew that scintillated like jewels as they waved in the gentle breeze of the morning. The sweet note of the meadow lark was music to the listening ear. . . . The solitude upon this wide expanse of open plain was absolute." The trauma of the farewell presumably in the past, Sarah Royce was unsettled to relive the numbing pangs of separation as her caravan reached the Great Divide: "In the morning of that day I had taken my last look at the waters that flowed eastward, to mingle with the streams and shores where childhood and early youth had been spent; where all I loved, save so small a number, lived; and now I stood on the most imperceptible elevation that, when passed, would separate me from all these, perhaps forever."

At the height of emigration, the virulent cholera epidemic that swept the entire United States accounted for almost as many deaths on the trail as accidents or sickness. An Oregon-bound bride summarized each day's "grave count" in her journal so consistently that she explained any omission or reduction in number. After consecutively noting "passed 11 graves," "passed 16 graves," "4 graves," "8 graves today," "11 graves," she wrote, "passed 4 graves today we expect the reason that we have not seen more since we struck the river is that we have traveled in the bottom and the graves are on the high land." With so much illness and death, it is small wonder that a sense of foreboding crept into daily entries such as these:

May 7: I have suffered so much from head and toothache that I have scarcely left my couch except when I am compelled to.
May 8: My head and teeth still trouble me.
May 9: Feel some better; have done some sewing and knitting.
May 10: Was too unwell to write yesterday. We passed graves by the roadside. The spot seemed mournful and reminded me that earth is our common burial place; and I reflect that some of us in all probability will find a like burial.

Her despair and resignation were echoed by Amelia Hadley: "They [the wolves] dig up everyone that is buried on the plains as soon as they are left. It looks so cruel I should hate to have my friends or myself buried here, which all may be." Of all tragedies, the death of a child was the greatest, and the letter to her mother from the parent of a child whose head had been crushed by wagon wheels after a fall limned it in anguished detail:

Poor little fellow, we could do nothing for him. He was beyond our reach and Oh, how suddenly, one half hour before we had left him in health as lively as a lark, and then to find him breathless so soon was awful. I cannot describe to you our feelings. We buried him there by the roadside. . . . We had his grave covered with stones to protect it from the wild beasts and a board with his name and age, and if any of our friends come through I wish they would find his grave, and if it needs, repair it.

It is clear that women's diaries were kept not only to register their participation in a great historic movement but to vent boredom, anxiety, despair, homesickness, loneliness and isolation. Since women comprised a company's small minority, observations such as "Mrs. Easton and I get along nicely together we exchange calls every evening" underscore female friendships' weight. Sickness or death of female members left survivors inconsolable. When Sarah Davis's only female friend succumbed to cholera, she inscribed in her diary: "O how lonely I felt to think I was all the woman in company and too small babes left in my care it seems to me as if I would be happy if I only had one woman with me."

Adding to the journey's hurdles were menstruation and childbirth, and bearing both without the comfort and services of another woman seemed an insurmountable task. Lucy Deady recalled the death of one sister and the birth of another: "Three days after my little sister Lettie drank the laudanum and died we stopped for a few hours and my sister Olive was born. We were so late that the men of the party decided we could not tarry a day; so we had to press on. . . . The men walked beside the wagons and tried to ease the wheels down into the rough places, but in spite of this it was a very rough ride for my mother and her new-born babe."

A new family member was matter-of-factly recorded by Marilla Bailey: "Shortly after my brother and I had the cholera we lay over half a day at Chimney Rock, and when we pulled on the next morning we had a new brother. Father and Mother had started across the plains with 12 children, so now with our baby brother, Melvin, there were 13."

Of all the fears besetting the emigrating women, perhaps the starkest terror was an Indian attack on the wagon train and subsequent capture and rape of the women, referred to as "being passed over the prairie." Yarns about "Indian Captivity" had been passed down for generations so that few were immune to anxiety about penetrating Indian territory, and as Adrietta Hixon recalled, "Indian tragedies were folklore stories during my childhood, but father tried to calm our fears." Alerted by travelers to "look out for moccasin tracks," a diarist wrote, "A secret dread and alert watchfulness seemed always necessary. . . . I couldn't go to sleep knowing that some bold prying savage eye might look in at me during the night." Some writers have asserted that colonial and early nineteenth-century captivity narratives provoked fear in meeting savages and exculpated guilt at snatching the lands of the "barbarian predators," who blocked fulfillment of Manifest Destiny's prophecy as stated by Horace Greeley of the New York *Tribune*: "It is the probable destiny of the Anglo-Saxon race to overrun and give laws to the larger portion of our Continent." Probably the most widely known early captivity story was Mary Rowlandson's narrative of her seizure and subsequent "restauration" by the Narragansetts in 1682. Though her wounded child died, she credited her own survival to her Puritan "Godliness," though others patronizingly chalked it up to superiority of white over red. Since Mary had employed her womanly knitting prowess to curry favor with her captors, her tale offered comfort to knitters! Once when she was "asked" to knit white cotton stockings for her masters, the good Puritan woman countered that she didn't work on Sunday but would comply the next day. When "they answered me that they would break my face," she chose to break the Sabbath instead and knit! A squaw who demanded Mary knit a shirt for her husband proffered a "piece of Bear" in payment; another rewarded her with a "quart of Pease." Added Mary, "Then came an Indian to me with a pair of stockings that were too big for him, and he would have me ravel them out and knit them fit for him. I shewed myself willing . . . and he gave me some roasted Ground-Nuts, which did revive my feeble stomach." The wily knitter not only eked out food for her knitting but bartered making three pairs of stockings for a "Hat and a silk Handkerchief."

Though the plucky Mary Rowlandson had been "restaured" to her home, women travelers staunchly maintained that any Indian encounter was essentially threatening, and the stereotype of the Indian Squaw was little improvement over the Cruel Brave ("Some of the squaws looked ugly, and, as I fancied, expressed much malignity in their glances toward us"). Still, one emigrant woman whose party conciliated with the Indians reported, "We visited their wickiups [and] affected as friendly a manner as we could. . . . We asked them to bring their squaws to see us, which they did." While emigrant women admired the squaws' needlework ("I must say that nicer work with a needle I never saw, or anything more beautified, it looked like satin & was finely ornamented with various colored beads"), their responses to the Indians ranged from loftily sneering at their scruffy appearance ("They are the durtyest creatures I ever saw they will pick lice out there head & eat them") to sympathy: "I always felt sorry for the Indians (and do yet), being driven by white people; yes, they are mean and so would I be if driven like they were." Despite admiration for some of "the best looking Indians I ever saw [who] were tall, strongly made, firm featured, light copper color, cleanly in appearance, quite well dressed in red blankets," most agreed with the conclusion of one traveler: "I doubt the savage instinct can ever be eradicated from the wild man's breast." Male travelers responded differently: "I noticed a very beautiful young female, the daughter of one of the chiefs of the party, who sat upon her horse with the ease and grace almost of a fairy. . . . It will be a long time before I forget the cheerful and attractive countenance, graceful figure, and vivacity of feature and language of this untutored child of nature." With little affinity for Indian women, pioneer women longed for their "own kind": "I feel rather lonesome today Oh solitude solitude how I would love it if I had about a dozen of my acquaintances to enjoy it with me."

More than emotional considerations were involved in this yearning for female companionship. Wide, full skirts functioned as "curtains of privacy" or "modesty" by which women could shield each other from men's view when engaged in bodily functions, a "protective" feature that deterred adoption of the more practical short tunic worn over gathered-at-the-ankle pantaloons advanced by "dress reform" advocates. There were other factors. Emigrant women longed to preserve their femininity by clinging to "standards" as long as they could, one noting, "When riding, I always rode astride, with my full skirt pulled well down over my ankles. If we had ridden stride, as they do now, people would have thought we were not lady-like. Mother was always reminding Luvina [her sister] and me to be ladies." Frontier historian Lillian Schlissel attributes this emphasis upon ladylike clothes on the trail to the mixing of the formerly gender-differentiated roles: "Precisely because work roles were blurred on the frontier, and because women were often called upon to do chores recognized as men's work, dress became a primary mode of asserting the delineation of the sexes. Dress was emblematic of the intention of women to restore the domestic sphere as soon as possible." Still, skirts *were* impractical. Even in frontier *cities* such as St. Louis the styles had drawn scorn for "sweeping up the mud or raising clouds of dust."

A few daring women *did* shorten their skirts a few inches to avoid dragging them along wet ground on wash day, thus coining the term "wash dress" for the abbreviated version. Those who opted for variations of the bloomer costume to lessen hemline mud and grime had to deal with taunts. One wearer wrote, "[I]n passing one house the women came out and laughed at me," and an early Kansas settler complained, "I should think that the good people of this town never saw a woman dressed in the short dress before; I seem to attract much notice when I go for water." Despite jibes, many persisted: "My sister and I wear short dresses and bloomers and our foot gear includes a pair of light calf-skin topboots for wading through mud and sand"; "Am wearing the Bloomer dresses now; find they are well suited to a life like mine. Can bound over the prairies like an antelope, and am not in so much danger of setting my clothes on fire, while cooking when those prairie winds blow." The first female climber on Pike's Peak, who boastfully titled the souvenir of her ascent "A Bloomer Girl on Pike's Peak, 1858," discovered she "could not positively enjoy a moment's happiness with long skirts on to confine me to a wagon," while her bloomers provided "freedom to roam at pleasure in search of flowers and other curiosities, while the cattle continued their slow and measured pace."

When skirted women met bloomered women on the trail, some of the former wished they too had the nerve:

> We have been traveling for several days, in company with an old gentleman and his family. The daughter is dressed in a bloomer costume—pants, short skirt and red-top boots. I think it is a very appropriate dress for a trip like this. So many ladies wear it, that I almost wish I was so attired myself. The old lady wears a short skirt and pentletts. She is fifty years old.

Traveler Cora Agatz was likewise impressed with the conversion of "gymnasium costumes" into simple habits that, "compared to the long, slovenly, soiled aprons worn by the other women of the train . . . elicited many commendatory remarks."

But others, sticking to their guns, viewed "The Bloomers" as an attack upon femininity and preferred to ride in the wagon or stride alongside in their long, full dresses. The wife of a physician, en-

countering an "American lady lectress of the most intense description, and a strong minded bloomer of the broadest principles," flailed
out:

How CAN they so far forget the sweet, shy coquetries of shrinking
womanhood as to don those horrid bloomers? As for me, although
a WIFE, I never wear [them] . . . even in the strictest privacy of
life. I confess to an almost religious veneration for trailing drapery,
and I pin my vestural faith with unflinching obstinacy to sweeping
petticoats.

Women were always attentive to their appearance, despite the rav-
aging combination of dusty roads, hard wear on their clothes and
poor washing facilities. When Luzena Wilson met a man in fresh
clothes, she bemoaned her tattered clothes and sunburned face: "My
skirts were worn off in rags above my ankles; my sleeves hung in
tatters above my elbows; my hands brown and hard, were gloveless;
around my neck was tied a cotton square, torn from a discarded dress;
the soles of my leather shoes had long ago parted company with the
uppers. . . ." Her astonishment at "the sight of his white shirt, the
first I had seen for four long months, revived in me the languishing
spark of womanly vanity." She would have preferred a fresh dress
of gingham or seersucker in some inconspicuous shade of brown or
gray since "flaming colors would not have been considered modest
then." In cold weather she would have worn a heavy, hand-knit shawl
in a "practical color" and hand-knit stockings.

In warm weather, she'd have drawn her slatted sunbonnet (the
slats removed for infrequent washing) well over her face, leaving its
matching cape to shelter her neck and upper back. Sunbonnets were
dictated for keeping one's complexion, and a mother's "Now you
don't want to look like that, do you?" as she indicated a shriveled
fellow traveler persuaded daughters to wear them. They stowed away
ruffled "Sunday bonnets" for services ("starched stiff and ironed . . .
packed in a band box and hung from the center of the wagon bow")
along with their calico or linsey dresses. They usually wore "neck-
erchiefs" and aprons when riding, and, to reduce laundry, forswore
"collars and cuffs and fine starched things to do up" in favor of hand-
knit "pretty bead collars made of black and white beads, tied with a

ribbon, that always look nice and do not get soiled." Having executed these changes, one relished the transformation: "I presented a comfortable but neat appearance."

When wagon trains laid over, lonely women who complained "I am so anxious to get someplace to stop that my patience isn't worth much" and "I would have given my interest in California to have been seated around my own fireside, surrounded by friends and relations" grasped the opportunity to visit other companies in the encampment. Dinner over, the preparations for the next day's meals finished and the bedding aired out to prevent mildew, the women swiftly assembled to work on the staples of their housekeeping duties, especially knitting new stockings and mending the old, which could be done by the light of a campfire. Some exchanged harrowing stories of their travels as they knit. "Mrs. Beardsley," who almost drowned when her wagon spilled her into the river during a crossing, complained that though she zealously guarded her knitting after a previous wetting ("It was two days in drying, and in two days I might have knit a stocking"), saved her life but not her knitting: "[T]he color ran so it's spoiled!" Esther Lockart recalled those evening gatherings:

I especially enjoyed the evenings, for it was then that the actual spirit of the company seemed manifested. Campfires burned cheerily in the darkness, groups of congenial people sat around the blaze, the men "swapping yarns," the women usually quiet and serious, sometimes knitting industriously in the half light, the children hiding and playing in the gloom before their early bedtime. The sound of many fiddlers' banjos, flutes and jewsharps made music on the air. Occasionally the gay laughter of some happy young couple would ring out between the pauses in the music and the story-telling and remind us that youth was ever carefree and light-hearted.

Similarly, Mary Haun remembered, "We did not keep late hours but were too engrossed with fear of the red enemy or dread of impending danger around the campfire. The menfolk lolling and smoking their pipes and guessing, or maybe betting, how many miles we had covered during the day. We listened to readings, story-telling, music and songs and the day often ended in laughter and merry-making." Young Laura Brewster had a gay social time: "There were a great many young people, and we had fine times together singing, playing cards and dancing quadrilles, the schottische, polka, and waltz if there happened to be a good, hard, smooth piece of ground to dance on."

The leader of a California-bound company recalled a layover when fifteen wagons drew up alongside, the oxen were released to forage on the prairie grass and he relaxed at the tents of fellow travelers in a scene reminiscent of home: ". . . the ladies busily employed, as if sitting by the fireside which they had recently left for a long and toilsome, if not dangerous journey, and a country of which they knew but little. Mrs. West, a lady of seventy, and her daughter, Mrs. Campbell, were knitting." The more sociable the visit, the more painful the decampment: "Many of them, especially the females, separated from us with much reluctance and regret. When making their adieux, several of them were affected to tears." Noting that many of the young adults had struck up more than mere friendships, he added, "Doubtless tender ties of affection between the young men and young women of the two parties were then sundered, and will never be reunited." As the wagon trains detached, he philosophized, "Such are the stern and inflexible decrees of Fate in the delicate affairs of the heart."

The trail's lack of female companionship was often matched by the isolation of living in outposts of civilization where women labored with no conveniences ("My mother's test for the degrees of heat necessary for baking was her hard bare arm thrust into the oven; If she could hold it there until she could count thirty and no longer, it was all right"). A pioneer who had braved the rigors of the overland route noted little improvement upon reaching Oregon: "I think the most unhappy period of my life was the first year . . . simply for want of something to do. I had no yarn to knit, nothing to sew, not even rags to make patches. One day Mrs. Parrish gave me a sack full of rags and I never received a present before nor since that I so highly appreciated as I did those rags." Another homesick Washington mother, lonely for companionship, finally turned to Indian women, her daughter remembers, and taught many of them to knit, sew and cook so that "the awe they at first had of her, soon changed to love." Another "Indian tale" involved a woman busy with mending and knitting stockings when an Indian burst in and snatched her linefull of stockings drying near the stove. Frantic to save the products of her long hours of knitting, she was at her wit's end, when suddenly her son, just furloughed from the army and still clad in his Civil War blue uniform, walked in the door and surprised his mother. Even more shocked was the Indian, who made tracks—minus the stockings!

Once at their new communities, whether in early frontier territories such as Kentucky, the Middle West or Far West, families craved homes with all the "trimmings" of the homes they had forsaken. In addition to knitting clothing for the family, women clicked away at curtains, bedspreads, tablecloths and tidies for chair arms and headrests. Children of both sexes, a writer for children pointed out, were pressed into service in spinning and knitting, indicating no gender differentiation at the more tender ages: "The women and the girls did the knitting. Some pioneer boys learned how to knit. They knit socks and stockings. They knit caps and mufflers. They knit their own suspenders."

Usually relying on only family help, women such as Kitturah Belknap, who had employed every moment of spare time in the winter to spin flax, invited friends to help pick the wool ("I find the wool very nice and white but I do hate to sit down alone to pick wool so I will invite about a dozen old ladies in and in a day they will do it all up"). The yarn prepared, they could tote their knitting when visiting distant neighbors. Women so cherished their friendships and made the treks so often that one nineteenth-century historian concluded, "[N]ever could one familiar with these associations forget the smooth winding footpaths which led through the deep forest and tall grass or underbrush from the house of one pioneer to another."

Lacking neighbors and stranded in the wilderness with two young children, young widow Mary Carpenter felt an acute sense of isolation. Dreading Indian attacks at night, she pried a timber from the puncheon floor, sequestered her children on a crude cot in the "vegetable cellar" used to protect produce from the frost, and replaced the plank when they dozed off. Positioning her chair above the opening, she knit all night without light since the "smothered embers

[were] not permitted to give out the slightest blaze." She and the children survived.

Many sons have penned tributes to their straining pioneer mothers, and one recalled his mother's buying wool from the salesmen for the woolen mills and then spinning the wool into knitting yarn:

I can see her yet stepping back and forth beside the spinning wheel as she spun the rolls of wool into yarn. . . . Skeins were often taken off the reel and one of us would hold them on our outstretched hands while the other wound it into a ball. Or we would place it over two chairs, turned back to back a little way around, and walking round and round, wind it into a ball. . . . She sat evenings at her knitting, from time to time fitting the mittens to our hands to see if she was getting them the right size. If we were lazy or neglectful of our work or ran away, there was always a little switch called a persuader handy.

Another marveled at the scope of his mother's accomplishments:

Mother bore and cared for the babies, saw that the floor was white and clean, that the beds were made and cared for, the garden tended, the turkeys dressed, the deer flesh cured and the fat prepared for candles or culinary use, that the wild fruits were garnered and preserved and dried, that the spinning and knitting was done and the clothing made. She did her part in all these tasks, made nearly all the clothing and did the thousand things for us a mother only finds to do.

A daughter wrote of her mother's washing and drying wool before the fireplace, then rubbing it with melted lard to make it fluffy and easier to card and form into rolls. When spun into very fine yarn, it was doubled and respun for stronger mitten and sock yarn. Another mother, in addition to her regular routine of "water carrying, cooking, churning, sausage making, berry picking, vegetable drying, sugar and soap boiling, hominy hulling, medicine brewing, washing, nursing, weaving, sewing, straw plaiting, wool spinning, quilting, knitting, gardening and various other tasks," found time to exchange work with other neighbors when they gathered together to spin and knit, skeining yarn for immediate use by simply winding it from hand to elbow and hanging it from her arm while she knit. Reported her daughter, "The buzzing hum of the wheels or the busily flying fingers did not detract from the social enjoyment of the producers of useful material."

In her study of Kansas frontier women, Joanna Stratton cites Mattie Huffman's mother's method of dyeing "clouded yarn" for knitted socks and lap robes for the cold winter. Yarn was first wound on corn shucks before being dipped into the dye bath, so that inner strands next to the shuck would be pale and the succeeding outer layers would have darker hues: ". . . if the dye was red, for instance, next to the shuck would be the natural white color of the yarn, next to that a pink shade, and next or on the outside it would be red."

A settler who had made the long trek to Oregon in the 1850s found that she could make money in spinning wool thread and knitting socks in exchange for fifty cents' worth of groceries. The grocer cannily resold the socks for seventy-five cents a pair to the storekeeper at the nearby mines, who, in turn, exacted double that price from the miners. The settler explained, "Just as beaver pelts and wheat were legal tender at one time, so there was a time in the Willamette Valley when socks were just as good as legal tender. The merchants used to ship bales of them into Eastern Oregon and into Idaho."

Another knitter-for-profit was Oregonian Emiline Himes, who kept her family afloat by spinning fleece obtained "on shares" from neighbors and knitting and selling at least three pairs of men's socks a week, in addition to making socks and stockings for her family of six. When times were so hard that "sometimes the women and girls simply kept out of sight of strangers—their attire was so sketchy," Sheba Hargreaves reported that since a pair of stockings fetched fifty cents and one man's heavy sock could be knit in an evening, "[M]any a mother furnished all the ready cash the family had by knitting by firelight during the long rainy evenings. Every little girl 'did her knitting stint' each day. Idleness was a cardinal sin in pioneer times." Another Washington settler, Mary Ellen Todd, mentioned her assigned knitting ("Louvina and I were doing our alloted knitting") and reminded her children and grandchildren that knitting was more economic necessity than doing something with one's hands: "Mother and I papered good boxes for cupboards, dressers, and other things. She also bought a spinning wheel, and getting some rolls from the woolen mills, we spun them into yarn, and then knit socks, which we sold for a good price. I had to knit one inch most every evening. You see, we just had to keep the wolf from the door." Susanna McFarland remembered: "If we went visiting we went early in the morning to spend the day, and we always took our sewing or knitting along. . . . The older women such as my mother and two aunts carded and spun yarn, and we all knit socks to send to Olympia. There they sold for fifty cents a pair to the loggers and oystermen. This was our means of buying our clothes, shoes, and sometimes groceries. A good knitter in a long day could knit a pair of socks, the legs being six to eight inches long."

In Nebraska, where sand and costly lumber were used only for doorsills and window casings, homesteaders constructed temporary dug-out lodgings of sod with clay-plastered walls. While awaiting money and opportunity to erect more substantial houses, they accommodated themselves to living with dirt floors, evoking this memory from one "Soddy": "Well do I remember the remark my mother and grandmother made. They had gone to visit a neighbor, and one said to another, 'She isn't a very good housekeeper, she has grass growing under her bed!' "

While Nebraska fathers and sons worked the farms, mothers and daughters prepared meals, sewed, carded wool, spun yarn and knit stockings and mittens. It was a spartan existence blighted by natural catastrophes. During the grasshopper plagues of the 1870s a woman who spread sheets over her tomato vines to spare them from "hoppers" discovered by morning that they had ingested not only the tomatoes but also the sheets and had ravaged a hat her husband had hung on a nearby limb. As if skies darkened by ravenous grasshoppers were not enough, Nebraska settlers bore infestations of rattlesnakes and centipedes, "who would crawl in and catch flies at night."

Magnifying their plight were violent storms such as "the blizzard of '88." Lena Knuth needed no prompting many years later to recall that when it howled into Oxford, Nebraska, and buried her small home, "It was one of the most impressive memories of my childhood in the soddy." She was still awestruck at her parents' "fearlessness, courage, and their faith in God" as they struggled to remain calm by knitting by candlelight during the height of the storm.

Wisconsin's cold weather alone called for extra knitting, especially with the advent of a new baby, as Clara Lenroot vividly recalled:

> Mother spent her leisure moments sitting beside it, her hands always occupied with knitting or sewing as her foot on the rocker hogged the cradle at intervals. . . . There I was taught to knit and to sew, sitting by her side in my little chair, carefully overhanding patchwork, or knitting long strips for the garters worn in those days. When I was promoted to knitting stockings, it was understood that I could not go out to play until I had knitted seven times around, and I often retired to sit on the floor under the dining-room table while performing that stunt. I was not allowed to leave the work half way across a needle, but must knit it to the end, and neatly sheathe the needles in the ball of wool.

Knitting for babies called for ingenuity, and a Keokuk, Iowa, settler raveled the tops of old white cotton stockings, reknit the thread into "beautiful gauze-like shirts" and laid claim to being the first woman ("I never knew any other woman who thought of it") to knit babies' underwear. She remembered pioneer life: "When everything else was disposed of, we women always had knitting to do. Everybody's stockings had to be knitted by hand, and so a ball of wool with the knitting needles stuck through it was carried around in one's apron pocket or set up on the kitchen window all ready to be taken up if one had a moment free from more pressing duties."

An Iowa pioneer whose mother first spun the yarn ("We always had white yarn and I never wore colored stockings until after I was married") waited for evenings when, with illumination from a flickering hearth or a "saucer candle" of burning strips of porous cloth in a cup of "coons' oil," she "did all her sewing and knitting by the light from the fireplace, and she sure had a lot to do . . . she made all our stockings and mittens by lamp light." When the Dakota Territory first opened to white settlers in the late 1850s and a railroader's wife with no funds for Christmas presents knit socks, tippets (capes or shawls) and mittens, and cooked molasses candy and cookies, her son labeled it their best holiday: "Everyone was as happy as he would have been with the most conventional and showy gifts characteristic of the Christmas back East." Frontier women understood "making something from nothing."

Of all the groups who settled in the West, none gave greater impetus to domestic production (including home knitting) than the Mormons, who sought to achieve economic independence because of their previous persecution. Their leader's exhortation to "[w]ear the good cloth manufactured in our own mills, and cease to build up the merchant who sends your money out of the Territory for fine clothes made in the East" echoed pre-Revolutionary admonitions against British products.

Within nine years of their arrival in the Great Basin, the Mormons' Deseret Agricultural and Manufacturing Society to promote domestic production of articles from native elements sponsored the Utah State Fair, where the knitter of the "best pair of woolen hose" received a top prize, and exquisite hand-knit lace drew appreciative crowds. A Mormon woman's knitting was regarded so basic a virtue that Brigham Young himself had embraced it in domestic arts training for girls: "Learn them to sew, spin and weave . . . and knit, as well as cakes and preserves, to spin, color, weave and knit, as well as work embroidery. . . . Thus will you and your daughters show yourselves approved, and prove helpmeets in every deed, not only in domestic relations but in building up the kingdom."

Every Mormon mother had the responsibility to pass her "art" on to her daughter. A daughter in a polygamous family of sixteen children, with each of her father's three wives maintaining a separate home but the children "exactly on the same basis as brothers and sisters . . . in one big happy family in one big yard, neatly foot-pathed to each back door," remembered that each mother "gladly taught her arts to all the children. How well I remember when I was but ten years old, Aunt Margaret taught me to knit a pretty pattern of cotton lace." Another recalled of her extended family: "One strong factor in helping us get along so splendidly was that we all kept busy. The girls knit the stockings, and helped with the sewing. Aunt Sally's oldest girl used to spin and weave. We younger ones helped to card the wool bats and to put in quilts. I would take my knitting and run into Aunt Sally's or Aunt Maria's of an afternoon. We did not like to knit alone. We were always neighborly, running back and forth to each other's homes."

President Young urged Mormon women to know everything about the care of their homes and to keep them neat ("Have a place for everything and everything in its place"). To household tasks, or arts, depending on how the sisters perceived them, Young emphasized and pushed the revival of knitting:

If I only had time I would teach you how to knit stockings, for there are few women now-a-days who know how many stitches to set on to knit stockings for their husbands or for themselves; or what size yarn or needles they require; and when their stockings are finished they are like some of these knitted by machinery—a leg six inches long while the foot is a foot or a foot and a half long; or the leg only big enough for a boy ten years old while the foot is big enough for any miner in the country. You know this is extravagant; but it is a fact that the art of knitting stockings is not near so generally understood among the ladies as it should be. I could tell you how it should be done had I time and knew how myself.

Outspoken against the "geegaws" worn by women, he goaded them to eliminate ribbons, laces, bows and extra yardage, warning, "This will do on this subject, for a hint to the wise is sufficient, and enough has been said if the sisters will take counsel." Decrying dresses that made women look as if they were "walking through the streets [with] a long train dragging in the dirt behind," he advised the sisters to "[p]ay no attention to what others do, it is no matter what they do or how they dress." One newspaper article, "Woman and her Mission," put it bluntly:

Give her responsibility, and she will prove that she is capable of great things; but deprive her of opportunities, make a doll of her, leave her nothing to occupy her mind but the reading of novels, gossip, the fashions and all the frivolity of this frivolous age, and her influence is lost, and instead of being a help meet to man, she becomes a drag and an encumbrance. Such women may answer, in other places, and among other people, but they would be out of place here.

It was hard for women to strike the mean between dragging skirts and "those disgustingly short ones extending no lower than boot tops," but try they did. "Retrenchment," the policy of eliminating extravagance in manners, speech and clothing, was soon the byword of Mormon Relief Society Chapters dedicated to diverting Mormon women from the "pride, folly and fashions of the world." There were separate divisions and supervisors for each aspect of the society's work, including knitting, and at society meetings girls were taught to make all their clothes, from straw hats to knit stockings. Like modern co-ops, they helped workers sell their products on commission, and when knitwear was turned into ready cash, workers were praised for keeping the money in the territory. Young had noted, "You will hardly find an old lady in the community who has not been brought up to work; and they would rather knit stockings or do some other useful work than eat the bread of charity." The Mormons intended to remain independent.

Apprehensive that Mormon economy would be undermined by the influx of new settlers brought by transcontinental railroads, their leader hailed members of his own family as models of deportment and dress. When Eliza Snow, one of Young's plural wives and a leader of the Retrenchment Movement, visited Relief Society meetings, she was delighted to behold members garbed in products of their own industry jumping to their feet when the leader shouted "Who is wearing a straw bonnet she made herself?", "Who is wearing a scarf she knit herself?", "Who knit her own stockings?" or "Whose dresses have been completely manufactured at home?" In a show of great restraint, Snow reported quietly, "Home Industries, as the only means of becoming self-sustaining, was everywhere made a prominent subject."

Wool knitting, while it was a main feature of home manufacture in Mormon settlements throughout the nineteenth century, was almost overshadowed by silk knitting when sericulture was introduced. Spurred by the Deseret Silk Association, knitters and sewers raised mulberry trees to nourish their silkworms, reeled hundreds of precious pounds and spent every available moment on embroidery and knitting. Many later labeled silk cocooneries the horrors of their lives, as the prolific worms grew rapidly, took over additional rooms in their homes, demanded a profusion of mulberry leaves and required special temperature control, cleaning and protection from other creeping varmints.

The hard-won products of the Mormon women's silk industry, delicately knit stockings and bags, were later proudly exhibited in the Woman's Building at Chicago's great fair in 1893, where they were seen by hundreds of envious and appreciative viewers who would never forget the beauty of those famous "Mormon Stockings." A proud spinner remembered, "Yarn was spun very fine then doubled and twisted by respinning it. This was used to make ladies' stockings, scarfs and men's socks. . . . The men's socks were made mostly of grey and were purled about six inches at the top with white yarn and the toe and heel would be made white." Mrs. Electa Bullock, chairman of the Woman's Department of the fair's Utah exhibit, summarized the Mormon work ethic:

> While we point with justifiable pride to the proud position of manufactories today, we do know that they are the outgrowth of the hand-card, the old and revered spinning wheel, and the family hand-loom, the knitting and sewing needles. . . . [as a child] When I would get very tired of walking back and forth at the wheel all day my mother would say: "Dear Child, sit down and rest you; there is your knitting-work; you must not be idle. You must alway remember what I have taught you, that industry is the source of wealth."

One can hardly leave the subject of pioneers without including two examples of knitting pioneers of another sort, one the wife of a missionary and the other the wife of a sea captain. Sarah Joiner and her husband established a mission in Hilo, Hawaii, in the 1830s, and her daily struggles in the mission schools were detailed in letters to her family. In one, she added:

I have to-day, been teaching a boy the mysterious art of knitting. Henry [her husband] and I are also knitting a pair of stockings for him, of the yarn sent out by Mrs. Morgan. By the way the stockings sent in the box will be a great comfort to us this Winter. I have so much sewing to do, I scarcely ever knit. I thought I would learn a boy to knit suspenders.

Also in the Pacific, Lucy Vincent Smith, like the overland wagon travelers, tried to convert her husband's whaling ship into home away from home by packing from Edgartown her sewing machine and an organ, the former falling victim to the salt air but the latter surviving to become the property of a missionary whose flock revered it. At sea, Lucy was a typical housewife, interspersing her sewing and ironing with knitting of socks (and reknitting some toes) and "lamp mats." Knitting was not a surprising occupation for a lonely woman at sea, and men on the whalers probably knit as well, though they are best known for whiling away their extra hours carving whalebone into beautiful scrimshaw pieces for loved ones back home. They carved many a pair of knitting needles, but their most elaborate products were "swifts" for winding the yarn, providing the extra pair of arms necessitated by the sailor's absence.

Upon arrival at their final destinations, whether Middle West or Far West, men were not always generous in recognizing the contributions of the women who "fertile in expedients, apt in device, [had] transformed the rude cabin into a cozy habitation." When the president of the Society of California Pioneers delivered his inaugural address in 1863, he greeted his fellow members only as as "Gentlemen" and "Brothers" who were the "earliest Pilgrims to this golden West . . . living types of our State . . . heterogeneous, and yet assimilated, of every nation and clime and every creed and form of belief; of opposing political opinions, and multifarious pursuits, yet united by one common bond of union." Not until after the speeches did the "[f]air ones of our city, [in their] elegant toilettes" appear for the largest celebration in the city's history, remaining "amiable" despite the fact that the crowd was so crushing that "even promenading was restricted" and "terpsichorean entertainment" had to be abandoned.

Perhaps the ladies needed no reminders of their part. Luzena Wilson said upon reaching California, "I remember filling my wash basin three times with fresh water before I had made the slightest change apparent in the color of my face." Perhaps they relished being addressed as the "fair ones" since they had spent enough time under their sunbonnets to have earned the soubriquet. Perhaps they preferred the disbelieving "Lawse, honey, I cain't *believe* you were on the Plains!" Perhaps, after working almost as hired hands in the early years of western settlement, they favored returning to their women's circle of domesticity. Perhaps, as Eleanor Katz and Anita Rapone suggest, the time span of the journey was simply too short to have effected a change in the cultural roles.

Their fortitude under circumstances for which they were poorly prepared led historian William Fowler to laud them as "guardian[s] of our race" without whose presence the whole venture would have failed. While man's work was one of "destruction and subjugation" in leveling the forest, breaking the soil and fighting "all the forces that opposed him in his progress," woman guarded the health and life of the household, hoarded the stores of the family and economized to leave husband, father or son the energy for his task.

Other historians have pointed out that while pioneer women were "deviants" from women's sphere (simply because they agreed to disrupt their home life and move) they nonetheless considered the trip a temporary arrangement, a step toward reigning supreme over an even more comfortable establishment at the end of the trail. It is impossible to pigeonhole frontier women, and knitting experiences are certainly inadequate for drawing conclusions on women's role; but it is nonetheless interesting to note that knitting remained within the previously well-defined perimeter for women, whether home was a wagon or a makeshift lean-to in a first settlement. Frontier life was not easy, remembered one stalwart many decades later: "It was hard, *hard*, hard. The only thing that can make it endurable for a woman is love and plenty of it. . . . I remember one day on the farm [Iowa] when Dan'l was going to Burlington. I remember that before he left he kissed me—kissed me and my little sick baby lying so white on her pillow. I had many things to do that day. But, my! How the work flew under my hands! What a difference a kiss can make!"

5.

Knitting for the Blue

"SEND SOCKS!" pleaded Civil War soldiers, and when their heartrending stories of bleeding, frostbitten and blistered feet reached "the womenfolk," there followed an unprecedented fever of sock-knitting "for the boys" though neither the Union nor Confederate government had asked for help. When complaints such as these filtered back from the front, women at home grabbed their needles and knit even faster: "We were standing in snow up to our knees"; "As I had no stockings and my boots were not a perfect fit, my feet became very sore . . . I could not get my boots on again"; "I took off my boots which had not been off for a number of days [and] in the morning my feet were swollen so badly that I could not get my boots on, and the ground was covered with snow. I had to travel on my bare feet for about two or three miles."

Women on both sides worried about their soldiers' feet, leading one Georgia wife to write, "And I want to know what you done about socks. . . . You must be certain to write for I am anxious to heare, so that I will try again to get some wool to knit your socks; and if you want anything else, if in my power to get, give me word." Similarly, a Philadelphia sister asked her brother if there was "a possibility of going barefoot through Alabama this winter" and assured him that she would knit him stockings: "I have needles and yarn and a heart for any fate. If the stockings Uncle Sam provides are too thin, or too anything, let me know and I will improve them with new ones, and you must tell me whether you want them long or short. I think they would be nice nearly up to the knee, don't you?"

Unusually large numbers of socks were needed because of their obvious vulnerability to wear as soldiers daily slogged through mud, water or snow, seldom laundered them, often discarded them or, when they became soiled or worn beyond redemption, used them as rags. Socks were so treasured that no usable pair could be wasted, as one heartbroken sister poignantly explained in a note attached to her donation: "Three pairs of socks, sent home in the knapsack of a dear brother who fell at Antietam." They would be repacked and sent to comfort another soldier.

When war broke out, women, with no government direction, organized programs for nursing, rolling bandages, scraping lint, sewing and knitting clothing, collecting donations and shipping boxes. The North benefited from already existing women's sewing circles, town meetings and church societies ready for quick conversion to "Soldier's Aid Societies." Southern women were temporarily handicapped by the distances separating their homes and by their inexperience in taking major responsibilities outside their homes, presiding at meetings, giving or taking directions from other women and working in large organizations. Though their own affairs were shrouded with sickness and worry, those inexperienced southern women soon managed to organize remarkably well at local levels, but because their experiences differ from those of northern women, who set up the centralized United States Sanitary Commission, southern efforts will be treated in a separate chapter.

The Union Quartermaster Corps stood ready to compensate states for outfitting their military regiments (ten thousand of whom were actually considered ready to fight) and had purchased socks regularly from "stocking manufacturers" or "stocking weavers" in the Philadelphia area. Military socks, or the longer "stockings," were not hand knit, though records in the National Archives indicate that one producer, Hannah Haws, regularly sent in samples to be judged for army suitability. A knitting historian might hope to have thus discovered an enterprising hand knitter, but Hannah Haws guaranteed delivery of hundreds of pairs of stockings in a time too short for hand knitting, and the historian recognizes her instead as the female proprietor of a thriving hosiery business.

· Despite availability of machine-knit stockings, both families and soldiers considered them poor substitutes for handknits. Members of already existing organizations used the outbreak of hostilities and the general call-up of Union soldiers as springboards for founding new groups dedicated solely to caring for soldiers. In New England alone, 750 were formed within the first year, each with a correspondent to Boston's headquarters at 22 Sumner Street to coordinate efforts so that "not one unneeded stitch" would be sent. Railroads offered the traveling women passes and canceled freight charges for shipping donations.

With Boston's domination of the New England groups, wounded local pride festered among those who longed to maintain their own identity. When church-oriented women proposed a "Christian Commission" to carry the Gospel along with supplies to the soldiers, wiser members asked local groups to subordinate their goals to Union solidarity, cautioning: "Let us, with one voice, claim that our clothes and food shall . . . never once be used as a charm to draw men to listen to the words and the prayers of any." Volunteers throughout the North recognized the mandate for an overall federation to overcome petty rivalries, to redirect overlapping regional efforts to look after their own men, to improve proper distribution of donations and to report conditions of the troops. In search of such leadership, almost four thousand leaders of society gathered at the Cooper Institute in New York on April 21, 1861, to discuss the need for coordination. They established the United States Sanitary Commission (often called the forerunner of the American Red Cross), an umbrella organization to arrange donations and send its own agents to battlefields and hospitals. This meant putting Union over township and state, and the concept had to be sold. The New England Women's Auxiliary Association phrased it compellingly in a bulletin urging every "loving woman in our land" to allow commission agents rather than local agents to aid *any* needy in the battlefields rather than "losing golden moments, in searching here and there for men, who, in a time of peace, gladly brought their identity within the limits of a State boundary, but who, at their country's call, nobly merged all but minor differences in one home, one faith—Liberty and Union."

In trying to "sell" the idea of the commission, newspapers published the New York organizers' plea that existing sewing, knitting, reading, "sociable" and church societies would devote themselves to the "sacred service of the country." Everyone was expected to provide *socks*!: "Every woman in the country can, at least, knit a pair of woolen stockings, or, if not, can purchase them. In each town there should be concert on this subject, taking care that three or four sizes be provided. Fix upon a place for receiving, and a date when the package will be transmitted, and send it as soon as possible to the most convenient of the depots of the commission." Following announcement of the new organization, the New York women's branch responded to the question posed in its own pamphlet, "How Can We Best Help Our Camps and Hospitals?" by advocating support of the Sanitary Commission, which "nationalized the humanity and charity of the whole people." Since it was equally important to alert soldiers that assistance would come impartially from all parts of the country instead of their own town or state, the commission billed itself "the Soldier's Friend" and published a pocket-size explanatory booklet of that name for each man in service.

With organizational kinks smoothed out, women worked with such solidarity and dedication that a veritable flood of knitted socks, mufflers, blankets, mittens and gloves poured into Aid Society workrooms, unleashing a few husbandly complaints that too much time was spent there and not enough on spousal comforts. One anonymous (probably a good thing under the circumstances!) writer did nothing to endear himself with his letter to a national publication: "Tender hearts, if you could have finished the war with your needles, it would have been finished long ago; but the stitching does not crush rebellion, does not annihilate treason, or hew traitors in pieces before the Lord. Excellent as far as it goes, it stops fearfully short of the goal. This ought ye to do, but there are other things which you ought not to leave undone."

Undaunted, the determined women never missed their Aid Society meetings, which filled an important social need. One doubter among them, however, was an Iowa wife who rejected her neighbor's prompting to attend the local meeting and wrote her fighting husband: "I have not attended nor do I intend to. I will work for the soldiers cheerfully but I will do it at home for I do not believe in these societies for they always end in a fuss and I do not want to be in." Despite such isolated protests, meetings were, according to one society's report, "the principal resort of all the young people of the neighborhood," since evening meetings were frequented by the few available young men who "did not aid much with the sewing and knitting but . . . caused the time to pass quickly, while the young ladies plied the needles. The gentlemen were always ready where their services would be of avail—in forwarding boxes, collecting supplies, &c. . . . The first work commenced was mittens for members of the 104th regiment, and before Christmas over 100 pairs of woolen mittens had been knit and forwarded."

Young members anticipated combining work and play, as one soldier learned from his regularly attending sister: "Last Monday Jule and I went to the Sanitary Commission meeting at Church and had a very pleasant time. This time we stayed to tea. They have it handed around; tea and coffee and rolls, split and buttered. The gentlemen come and hand the eatables around and make it very lively. I think you would have shouted to see John A. winding blue yarn, with his great long arms and magnanimous soul intent upon getting the ball in good shape."

Times, places and special announcements about meetings were supplied by the papers. The *Cleveland Leader* donated two columns a week which soon expanded with additional appeals such as the one alerting the public when yarn was available "so that warm socks may be packed in each box—the need is great." In Detroit, where papers also granted free publicity, a plea for "double quick" help with soldiers' clothing was addressed to the "German Ladies," whose knitting skills were universally recognized. German-language papers were requested to copy and reprint the notice.

Women added their "tokens of femininity" to aid rooms where donations were inventoried and packed—bleak church basements, empty schoolrooms, abandoned warehouses and donated storerooms. Into the Cleveland society's small rear "office," where railroad timetables and shipping guides were posted, went a modest carpet, a box of documents "cunningly cushioned" to double as a sofa, a borrowed rocking chair, a bouquet on the table and two or three pictures on the wall. Working-hours routines were interrupted ("when the hive stopped its busy hum") only for special visitors or speakers such as "[l]uminaries of the military firmament" who brought information on the war, officials such as the governor and other state officials who "offered a word of cheer," a recruit who came to the aid room for a blanket or gift to "modify the discomforts of camp life," U.S. Sanitary Commission inspectors who evaluated the society's work with "compliment and approval" or brought news from the camps that spurred workers to even greater activity. When an agent revealed to a Pennsylvania group, "We darn and patch socks that I venture to say even the most careful of your members would think was only fit to be thrown away," they knit with new resolve.

Viewing with admiration women's tenacity of purpose and unrelieved hours of knitting, Albert M. Hubbard composed "The Knitting Song: Dedicated to the Patriotic Ladies of the North," a zesty tribute that quickly became a great favorite with choral groups at fairs and parlor sing-alongs and accounted for even further acceleration of knitting:

> Knit! Knit! Knit!
> For our Northern soldiers brave!
> Knit! Knit! Knit! While the Stars and Stripes they wave!
> While they the rebels in battle meet
> Be yours to fashion with fingers fleet
> The nice warm socks for the weary feet
> Knit! Knit! Knit!
>> For our boys on Southern hills
>> Our boys in Southern vales
>> By the woods and streams of Dixieland
>> Are feeling the wintry gales.
> Knit! Knit! Knit!
> The socks and mittens and gloves!
> Knit! Knit! Knit!
> Each one that her country loves!
> Lay beside the useless, though beautiful toy,
> With which you many an hour employ,
> And knit, instead, for the soldier boy
> Knit! Knit! Knit!
>> Chorus: For our boys &c.

When Sanitary Commission agents visited encampments and hospitals, they carried "miscellaneous niceties . . . showing women's warm hearts and women's skilled hands" to cajole the soldiers into sprucing up for church services. Washing one's feet earned a pair of handknit socks, while an additional clean shirt and drawers went to a soldier who would "perform a general ablution." As one successful agent reported, "In this way we soon brought our cargo of living freight into a more comfortable and presentable condition." It is small wonder that another soldier, astonished by his comrades' squeaky clean appearance, hooted, "It looks as if mother has been here!"

When battle news was worst, headquarters workers stayed at their posts well into the night, sorting, counting, wrapping, stamping "U.S. Sanitary Commission" on each garment to prevent fraudulent use, meticulously filling out report sheets and writing letters of appreciation, determined that their records should bare no hint of sloppiness despite their fatigue.

Stockings topped each separate group's and each region's inventory, but there was no overall Union tally of clothing donations that also included woolen and cotton shirts, woolen and cotton drawers, handkerchiefs, slippers, slings, dressing gowns, pants, overcoats, coats, old clothing and bandages. A group of sympathetic Canadian women, described by a Sanitary Commission manager as "one of the most enthusiastic company of workers I have met," sent their knitted pieces across the Vermont border to help Union soldiers. Like American women, their largest donation was *socks*! In the Boston area, where, for example, the category of knitted goods (which included socks, mittens and shawls) consistently far outnumbered sewn items, famed abolitionist Samuel Gridley Howe recapitulated Boston area Sanitary Commission records and assigned an approximate monetary value to women's sock contributions of $2.63 per pair for the 34,138 pairs of socks. Even his daughter, Florence, added her misshapen mite. Daughter also of Julia Ward Howe (the composer of "The Battle Hymn of the Republic") and encouraged by her minister that Sabbath knitting was permissible since his wife, "ever a saintly character," not only knit on Sunday but whenever she lay down to rest, Florence remembered her sock knitting many years later: "My first pair were by no means mates. As I learned to knit better, and so more loosely, the second stocking bloomed to tremendous size! I could only survey it sadly in the fond hope that shrinking in hot water might reduce it to the size of its companion."

With the sheer number of socks shipped to camps, there were bound to be scandals. Soldiers could buy commercially made socks from the Quartermaster Corps, but Sanitary Commission socks were superior ("softer, more absorbent") and, better still, free. A story that filtered back from the front that some socks purchased from the Quartermaster clearly bore the Sanitary Commission stamp on the toes so justifiably incensed the makers of these socks that they wouldn't knit another stitch until they heard results of an investigation. The president of the Committee on Supplies wrote a mollifying report that the Quartermaster had indeed borrowed "Sanitary Socks" (for sale) when other supplies were exhausted during "a period of dire necessity . . . when the soldiers' feet were naked and half frozen." The commission socks filled a temporary emergency and had since been "repaid." Knitters still refused to calm down until individual soldiers were recompensed for their outlay. No one was going to *buy* their products!

With New England ladies working full tilt in behalf of the soldiers, members of the Fragment Society, Boston's oldest (founded in 1812) and most exclusive sewing circle, with an enviable record of sewing in behalf of the city's poor, agonized over whether to establish a special group to work for soldiers' needs. While "tempted to devote to the soldiers the time formerly given to the poor" and acknowledging their thoughts and sympathies converged on the war, they clung to their original purpose of working for Boston's needy, so that members did war work on their own time. Once the issue was closed, monthly minutes during the war years made no further mention of the national conflict. The Boston Sewing Circle, of around 150 to 200 members, met regularly throughout the war years. Another group, "a large number of ladies of education, refinement, and high social position," paid needy widows with young children to knit and sew for the troops, thus obtaining needed garments and furnishing employment at the same time.

Making soldiers' clothes reinforced the bond between knitters and sewers and the troops, and in lieu of mailing gifts to their *own*, they compensated with verses and notes of cheer to unknown recipients by attaching them to shirts or stuffing them into stockings and mittens. Before adding her socks to the donation barrel, one knitter proudly wrote, "The fortunate owner of these socks is secretly informed that they are the one hundred and ninety-first pair knit for our brave boys by Mrs. Abner Bartlett, of Medford, Massachusetts, now 85 years." Benjamin Franklin's great-granddaughter (whose grandmother, Sarah Bache, chaired "Washington's Sewing Circle" during the Revolution) tucked this note inside her hospital box: "Close by the old battle-ground in Lexington, Massachusetts, the birthplace of the liberty you are fighting so bravely to preserve for us, was this shirt made for you. The young lady who made it hopes that these sleeves will enclose two sound arms, and that no serious wound confines you to a hospital." Even garments sold at fairs and bazaars carried affectionate messages. Philadelphia women who knit dozens of pairs of mittens with flowery messages and verses hidden in the fingers auctioned them off as special talismans and raffled their knitted yellow garters with guarantees-in-a-jingle that lucky wearers would be married within a year: "If you would like to change your state/And Wedlock wish to try/You will no longer hesitate/This article to buy." One can only imagine the giggly meetings where "[p]ens were as busy making verses to go with the garters as were the knitting-needles in their manufacture." Cleveland ladies had their own poets laureate, and one versifying member composed: "Brave Sentry, on your lonely beat/May these blue stockings warm your feet/And when from wars and camps you part/May some fair knitter warm your heart."

More personalizing resulted from piecing together each contributor's separate block into an album quilt, and, though the chance was slight, presenters longed to have a soldier in a remote hospital "cheered by the sight of some such familiar sign on sheet or counterpane, or gladly rest his weary head upon a pillow that bore a dear and well known name." Donors could not have asked for more than this nurse's touching testimonial to a patient's affection for his quilt: "Dixon is very anxious to take his quilt home with him, as it would be a pleasing souvenir in after years. . . . He served his country faithfully until he lost his right leg. In a few weeks he will return home. . . . If the ladies and gentlemen who have ornamented his quilt with their names think he is deserving of it for a keepsake, he would appreciate the gift highly." Unquestionably, Dixon was granted his quilt.

Not all soldiers were the recipients of "women's work," for a few either learned to knit or polished previous skills during prolonged hospital convalescence. Major Charles J. Mills, whose Civil War letters have recently been published privately, knitted a decorative bag "used for carrying personal toilet articles" when recuperating from wounds sustained in the Battle of Antietam, and his descendants have lovingly preserved and proudly photographed it to accompany the letters.

Though socks were the preponderant articles, women carefully logged into the boxes mind-boggling quantities of "comforts"—one Cleveland shipment destined for the front lines even contained "four table cloths" and "four d'Oyley's." The perishables and the fragile bottles were oddly out of place, but workers wished to spare their loved ones nothing. To cushion them during the bouncy ride, they nestled edible goodies such as glasses of jelly, cakes, pastries, meats, bottles of wine and liqueurs into soft mittens, socks, wristers, shirts, underdrawers, linens, bandages and even reading material, of which *The Testament* was always the leader. Such preparation and sending of foodstuffs would be daunting even today, but the Civil War occurred in a day of little refrigeration, uncertain transportation, and constantly moving camps and hospitals. The women of the Hartville, Pennsylvania, Ladies' Aid Society proudly catalogued the contents of the thirty-nine boxes shipped during the last year of the war, which, in addition to the expected articles of clothing, included:

15¼ bushels Apples; 2 barrels Pickles; 1 barrel Crackers; Cheese in quantity; 4 dozen Spoons; 1 dozen Tin Cups; 22¾ lbs. Tea; Eye Shades; Spices, 1 dozen; 22 bushels Onions; 8 dozen [bushels] Potatoes; 1 dozen [bushels] Beets; ½ bushel Strawberries; 24 barrels Rusk; 1 barrel Gingerbread; 44 lbs. Farina; 63½ lbs. Butter; 25 dozen Eggs; 4 cans Concentrated Soup; 160 dozen Fruit; 66 bottles of Wine; 5 gallons Tomatoes; 4 Chickens; 5 gallons Milk; 1 lb. Coffee; 1 gallon of Vinegar; 4 cans of jelly; 3 lbs. Dried Apples; 1 jar Pickled Cabbage; Pins in quantity; Needles in quantity; 23 Comfort Bags; Reading Matter, assorted.

Nor were Cleveland women to be outdone, wrote their historian: "It was not in the hearts of Northern Ohio women to withhold from the soldiers any luxury they themselves enjoyed. To the last, canned fruit crowded the Room shelves and perplexed Aid Room committees." Perplexity about canned fruit was a simple matter compared to the disaster that befell that organization's shipment of its special "stewed down chicken." Doctors had recommended stewed chicken for recovering patients, and the recipe (helpfully printed in the newspaper), calling for condensing the broth and then sealing the whole bird in tin cans, had circulated through the "tributary" societies affiliated with Cleveland in this great endeavor. Society women touted the chicken as an "invaluable article of hospital diet," and as stewing bees flourished, no chicken in Cuyahoga County was safe from the steaming kettles bubbling for the boys in blue. Quickly dispatched, the first shipments arrived in good shape and were served to grateful hospital patients. But trouble ensued. No one knew whether the ladies had "tinned" the chicken too quickly or whether the tins were defective, but the Aid Room soon reeked of "eau de poulette" as broth oozed from leaking, or worse, exploding cans. The chicken broth soaking through much of the knitting and sewing waiting to be boxed was enough to make them throw in the towel—quite literally! It was an altogether nauseous business as society workers cleaned the mess with chloride of lime to forestall the health authorities from closing the workrooms. They were not amused to learn from a surgeon at a nearby hospital that a box recently received was "presumed by the odor to contain condensed chicken."

Families tried to ship requested items to soldiers craving special clothes, food, and "comforts," and Jay Butler recounted both his joy upon receipt of family boxes and letters and his edginess at their lateness when friends had already received theirs: "Lew Smith received his stove packed with splendid apples and clothing"; "Harper Austin received a satchel with clothing." When his own "longed for boxes" finally arrived, he reported:

They were in great deal better order than we expected, nothing spoiled but Charley Dennis's turkey. The bread was somewhat moulded but we cut the outside off and put the rest away. Night before last, we received the package sent by Jacob Camp and today opened Aunty's can of cherry jam. It was splendid like all the rest of the good things from home. You must give a thousand thanks to all the good friends concerned in donating to the box.

When Aid Society members heard such letters read at meetings, they clicked their knitting needles even more industriously. They smiled at one nostalgic letter: "I received the package you sent by Lew Redway. I needed the stockings badly, as well as the other articles. The maple sugar was a treat and reminded me of old times in the sugar camp at home." They could also sympathize with his longing for "just a few things . . . a chicken or two well stuffed and roasted; two or three mince pies well packaged would come through safely, and all the cake you can send would be very acceptable; sponge and jelly cake would come through just as well as fruit cake. . . . One thing more. Some of the boys say, tell them to put in some fried cakes, as many as you are a mind to."

Some soldiers wrote directly to societies to thank them for their handiwork, and Milwaukee members in the throes of a "perfect epidemic of knitting" joyfully read aloud this letter from a "fighting Milwaukee Volunteer" conveying his regiment's excitement upon opening a Milwaukee box:

A box of mittens from the ladies of Milwaukee was distributed by our returned chaplain on Thursday afternoon, and were just in time to do good service. The boys now gladly take the "mitt" from the girls they left behind them. May God prosper the good ladies of Milwaukee in their work of kind deeds. Their gifts touch the rough soldier's heart and call forth many prayerful thanks and thoughts of loved firesides they have left to struggle for union and liberty.

Another wrote that if Wisconsin knitters could "see the caps flying and hear the cheers that are sent up for the ladies of 'Old Grant' upon receipt of these articles, they would feel repaid for their trouble." These boosts to morale so stimulated Milwaukee knitters, who specialized in a "shooting mitten" with forefinger as well as thumb, that young children at home were considered no deterrent to work; chapter members brought even the smallest tots to their meetings and taught them to knit socks as they helped with the "hard parts," toes and heels. One patriotic member, tossing religious scruples to the wind, bragged that she knit until she heard the Sunday church bells peal. Others knit *during* services. To a society in Hartford, Connecticut, a captain wrote of his men's joy at receiving knit gloves and mittens: "We gave three rousing cheers to the ladies of the Hartford Soldiers' Aid Society. In this bleak December snowstorm, their hands and hearts are the warmer for what you sent to them."

Mothers had more to worry about than food and cold feet. Their sons, many of them only teenagers, were thrown in with older, "hardened men," and one cautioned, "Be careful and keep away as much as you can from the hard company you are thrown with at present; I hope it will not last for long. Don't let them entice you to do anything wrong. Never let yourself take the first oath; or if you are tempted once stop there and don't do it again. There is nothing like getting familiar with vice, and I want you to come home as good as when you left us." She then concluded with those age-old mother's questions: "Who washes your clothes now? Do you ever wash in warm water? Be sure to answer all these questions. And who cooks your food?"

Children were eager to be part of the war effort since deaths of family members were common. "Uncle Merry," the kindly editor of their favorite magazine, *Merry's Museum*, who prodded them to bring "cheerfulness and joy" into the family circle and thus raise morale, couldn't resist adding that his own joy would be increased if the children paid their "subscription debts," since making publishing ends meet was almost impossible in wartime. When children were old enough they formed their own knitting groups, such as Cleveland's "Busy Bees" and "Wide Awakes" and Detroit's "Young Girls Stocking and Mitten Society." The latter, to attract new members and taunt men who hadn't signed up for military service, placed an announcement in the *Detroit Daily Advertiser* to urge attendance by the "large number of young gentlemen in our city who, for reasons best known to themselves, have preferred to remain at home rather than volunteer to public service." They hoped those gentlemen would provide the society with woolen yarn at their next meeting, and promised that if "any patriotic bachelor should venture to call in person for the purpose of tendering his aid in liberal donations to the good cause, he need stand in no fear of getting the 'mitten.' "

The "boys" were not always recipients of razzing, and two Indiana scamps tried a little themselves in their local paper: "Wanted! A correspondence wanted, by two gay and festive young gents, with good standing in society. They wish to correspond with any amount of young ladies between the ages of sixteen and twenty, who believe in a vigorous prosecution of the war. No others need apply. Object—fun, and perhaps matrimony."

Cities lauded their young for war knitting, sewing, and fund-raising in general. Brooklyn bragged about her "children of Public School No. 13, under the direction of the principal, Miss Graham, who have knit a considerable supply of yarn into socks." Northern Ohio Juvenile Societies "caught the spirit of good works that incite[d] the efforts of their mothers . . . and sent in many a neatly packed box or snug parcel." Even *fictional* Civil War children such as Beth March in *Little Women* knit for the war. Louisa May Alcott based her book on her own family life, and when Beth heard her father's letter from camp adjuring his girls to "do their duty faithfully . . . [she] said nothing, but wiped away her tears with the long blue army-sock, and began to knit with all her might."

Such huge sums were needed to finance the Sanitary Commission's supervision of the knitting, sewing, nursing and cooking efforts of women and children that local benefits soon gave way to area wide "Sanitary Fairs" in all major cities. Largely staffed by women, these fairs proved to be not only the most important source of income for the commission but also a training ground for women's organizational skills. Public buildings were temporarily converted to showrooms for the thousands of salable donations and to provide space for entertainments. Organizers of the New York Metropolitan Fair announced a two-week "great market. . . . [Where] [n]othing will be declined, however substantial or however perishable, however grand or however trivial." To provide amusements and something for everybody to buy, "something to gratify the sober and please the gay, to win the approval of the serious and the utilitarian, and at the same time to catch the eye and suit the taste of the young, the lighthearted and even the trifling," fair managers worked themselves to the bone. Many years later the secretary of the New York fair re-called the "curious epidemic of unbounded generosity" of donors parting with their most treasured possessions and the extraordinary energy of the leaders: "A great many earnest women killed them-selves by overwork. Mrs. C. P. Kirkland fell dead in the fair building one crowded evening, and Mrs. David Dudley Field died at her own house, just after leaving the fair." Supporting the Metropolitan Fair were neighboring communities such as Passaic, New Jersey, where women who had first worked together as a sewing circle joined hands with New Yorkers to complete sewn, knitted, crocheted, hooked, woven, pieced and embroidered items for sale in the ladies' bazaar. Passaic members enlisted the aid of a "committee of eight gentlemen" to solicit funds door-to-door in the outlying villages, something they considered "improper" for themselves, though their Philadelphia forebears had done just that during the Revolution.

At every fair, knitters displayed their wares in "Women's Bazaars," "Pretty Trifles" or "Cozy Corners." At Rochester's fair, countries were represented in "theme" booths, and with German women's beautiful needlework well recognized, many a Bavarian village sprang up to display knit "tidies," bootees, baby sacques, afghans (one that "surpasses in beauty anything of the kind hitherto produced in the city"), mittens, stockings, "horse reins," boy's harnesses (a knit pair of reins to control an obstreperous lad, very handy for the fair), scarves and "sontags" (shoulder wraps). Cincinnati's German women enthusiastically supported their city's Great Western Sanitary Fair, and donations from such church groups as the German Evangelical Methodist Church, the German Ladies' Society of St. John's and the North German Luthuren [sic] Church helped to swell the coffers and load the tables with elegantly knit pieces. Cleveland's German women gave so much to their fair that to accommodate the out-pouring, organizers had to construct a double-size "German booth," where fairgoers were overwhelmed by such "marvels of knitting . . . [as] breakfast shawls of gossamer texture and brilliant hues."

In Chicago, an observer described the procession when every pos-sible conveyance hauled donated articles to the city's fair and the three-mile-long lines snaked into the city and snarled traffic for four-teen days:

On every road leading to the city there were rickety and lumbering wagons, made of poles, loaded with mixed freight—a few cabbages, a bundle of socks, a coop of tame ducks, a pot of butter, a bag of beans. Mechanics and artisans of the villages and towns came marching, came riding on wagons, came on trains; bringing every kind of product of mechanical skill. Manufacturers shipped every kind of article from pianos to threshing machines. Watchmakers sent watches. Lace, cloth, iron, steel—there was no end to the stuff!

Even Abraham Lincoln contributed to Chicago's fair by forwarding the original draft of the Emancipation Proclamation with this note: "I desire to retain the paper, but if it shall contribute to the relief and comfort of the soldiers, that will be better." An ardent Massachusetts supporter sent a few chips of Plymouth Rock to be sold to "restore the Union." The fair, "a sight such as had never been seen before in the West on any occasion," was organized wholly by women. They soon learned they could not sign contracts without spousal guarantees. When the fair's dynamic leader, Mary Livermore, was apprised of this (and simultaneously discovered that she had control over neither money she herself earned nor over her children), she drew herself up and remarked crisply that once the war was over she knew what cause would get her attention! Prominent Chicago women, acting as salesladies at booths, crowd watchers at cordoned areas surrounding the valuable auction goods and ticket takers at "rides" and special attractions such as "tableaux vivants," plays and concerts, stretched the limits of their "roles." A few husbands, though proud of their wives' loyal efforts, balked at their vendor roles but acceded since all was for "The Commission." Even the doughty Union General William Tecumseh Sherman caved in and wrote his wife, Ellen, "I don't approve of ladies selling things at a table. So far as superintending the management of such things, I don't object, but it merely looks unbecoming for a lady to stand behind a table to sell things. Still, do as you please."

Philadelphia drew upon Chicago's experience by publishing a small daily journal highlighting attractions and directing visitors to special sales. An article in *Our Daily Fare*, featuring items "suitable for a gentleman," sent bargain hunters off to buy hand-knit afghans with this bit of advice: "What is called an 'afghan' would to the uninstructed mind, appear, perhaps, as absurd an article as ever was devised for the use of man. Not so, however, to the few persons of enlightened intelligence. Few things, I am told, are more essential to a gentleman; in fact life is a burden without one." In Rochester, New York, with no items barred for offerings, one enterprising army wife concluded that a lock of General Grant's hair would fetch a fancy price at the fair and enlisted her husband's support in writing his old classmate for a snippet. The general, gratified that the "stock of hair is as abundant as ever," sheared a donation "for the benefit of disabled soldiers and their families," even though its color would "expose to the ladies of Rochester that I am no longer a boy."

Children helped with fairs by sewing and knitting sale items in school, staging "tableaux" as entertainment for fairgoers or helping their mothers staff booths. In Philadelphia, reported that city's *Enquirer*, grammar school children worked so industriously on their fair projects, to the neglect of their studies, that the school's Board of Control was forced to dispense with examinations. Brooklyn and Long Island fairgoers' favorite exhibit (repeated in other fairs) was the "Little Old Woman Who Lived in a Shoe," in which a gray-haired older woman perched at the throat of a huge shoe (constructed of something durable enough to hold her and the children), knitting away madly as children sprawled over the shoe or ran around at the bottom, where dolls and knit clothes were sold. Children who raised money by minifairs or "fair knitting" (with fond mothers and grandmothers gamely buying the output) were publicly acknowledged when they presented the proceeds, and received kudos from the crowd at the "real" fair: "Ten little girls, whose united ages were just one hundred years, arrived in state at the fair one afternoon, having brought to a close an auxiliary fair of their own. They came to bring the proceeds, $16.50 apiece. There are doubtless ten millionaires in the land who have not done as much in proportion, though they may have given thousands."

By bringing together women from neighboring areas to organize projects whose scope would previously have floored them, fairs galvanized workers and raised two and a half million dollars, enough to pay half the Sanitary Commission's operating budget for all the years of the war. Far more than money was involved, however, for the fairs appealed to rich and poor alike by giving all an opportunity to donate. Knitted mufflers and tidies were as valuable as millionaires' valued paintings and family silver. Through it all, in a time of great uncertainty, women's gentle touch and sometimes not-so-gentle management skills steered the fairs to unprecedented heights of fund-raising. At the Patent Office Fair in Washington, D.C., one enthusiast delivered a panegyric to the women:

> The cry of relief for the sick and suffering soldier went through the land; in the answer there was no delay or procrastination, for it came first of all from woman. She hurried to the hospital and the camp; she went everywhere she could do good; she labored for the soldier in her own home; she organized neighborhood societies. . . . No wonder, then, that a stream of bounty began to pour forth from all parts of the country, to all places where that bounty was needed. No wonder that when woman was moved to set on foot such enterprises as this, their success was at once assured.

With the end in sight, there still remained the problem of freedmen who made their way to "contraband camps," staging areas for newly liberated but desperately needy slaves and their families. Northern knitters who had eagerly knit for their own troops but were slow to extend their care to the refugees angered a young Quaker who worked at one of these camps. Castigating abolitionists who had done "so much *talking* and so little *acting*," she asked rhetorically, "Where are the people who have been professing such strong abolition . . . for the last thirty years?" She begged her mother to get Philadelphia groups to "buy yarn and knit some stockings. The government stockings are not large enough for the contraband. Their feet are just exactly like hoofs and cut right through their stockings. It is almost impossible to keep them supplied." Philadelphia's response was to ship quantities of large-size stockings, one of their last projects of the war.

Twelve years after the war, a speaker at a testimonial banquet in Cincinnati toasted the wartime contributions of women: "The American Woman is no doll, no plaything. She is a help meet for the American Man. . . . [To] The Loyal Women at home whom we left!

Lecturer Sojourner Truth, 1864.

Whose hope was always bright! Whose faith never faltered! Whose charity never failed! Whose self-sacrifice never ceased! . . . How their handiwork cheered us!"

The knitters were satisfied.

6.

Knitting for the Gray

Sniffing the winds of war, Baltimore educator Almira Phelps, whose sister, Emma Willard, had founded Troy (New York) Female Seminary, alerted her graduating classes to their coming obligations to rescue their nation even if it meant "wandering out of your sphere." Turning to her "daughters from the South . . . where woman is considered more helpless . . . and not under the necessity of performing household labor," she warned, "You are not excused from a life of usefulness."

She need not have worried about her southern girls! When the break came, they shared the same concerns as their northern counterparts: providing comforts for their men while surviving privations that became commonplace. Gone was the stereotypically fragile antebellum "Southern Lady" described in George Fitzhugh's *Sociology for the South*: "So long as she is nervous, fickle, capricious, delicate, diffident and dependent, man will worship and adore her. Her weakness is her strength. Woman naturally shrinks from public gaze, and from the struggle and competition of life. . . . [She] has but one right and that is the right to protection."

When war summoned their protectors, when meager transportation and communication isolated them from families and friends, when fear for their life's partners or flesh of their flesh shadowed every thought and deed, those "delicate" women administered family business operations, stretched dwindling clothing and food supplies, packed and relocated their children to refugee centers and wept silently at their losses. There was ample cause for grief: the Confederate army lost one in four soldiers, more than half from disease and many from the same families. From the wreckage, the wife of the headmaster of Alexandria's Episcopal School identified new heroines:

> We are weak in resources, but strong in stout hearts, zeal for cause, and enthusiastic devotion to our beloved South; and while men are making a free-will offering of their life's blood on the altar of their country, women must not be idle. We must do what we can for the comfort of our brave men. We must sew for them, knit for them, nurse the sick, keep up the faint-hearted, give them a word of encouragement in season and out of season. There is so much to do, and we must do it.

"Do it" they did. The toughness, commitment and faith of these "gentle" women merited their postwar eulogy: "None can read the simple tales of heroism, suffering and patriotism without loving and honoring the tender mothers, thoughtful sisters, and all the gracious gentlewomen who unfalteringly bade their kinsmen do their duty, and who, for their part, bore unflinchingly mental suffering and physical pain such as no other nation of such women has ever known since the world began."

They started by shipping "delights of home," the jams and jellies for which their men pined, their favorite brandies and spirits, their comfy socks and gloves, their reading material, and their chicken soup. Recalled one worker: "Evenings at home, formerly spent in gayety and social amusement were made pleasant and useful in the labors of love and duty which provided comfortable hose for the soldier, or a warm visor or a fancy colored scarf, which under the patronage of kind old Santa Claus, found their way to the Christmas-bag in the soldier's tent." When, however, the crumbling transportation system offered no guarantee that lovingly crated cartons would reach a designated soldier's "Christmas-bag," it was obvious that personal giving must be sacrificed in favor of packages for the hometown company that was often "adopted" by large-property owners. As in northern cities, women of means hoped to pay needy seamstresses and laundresses for piecework, thus providing them with a livelihood and increasing supplies for the troops, and "Mothers of the Company Boys" compensated others for gathering discarded socks when troops came through town, washing them in steaming tubs, mending or reknitting them if necessary and forwarding them to the front.

When obstacles to specific distribution became insurmountable, donors, still hoping for *some* connection with donees, addressed their boxes to home-state boys. When even that proved futile, generosity was transferred to *all* Confederate soldiers. It was the same lesson northerners had painfully learned, but unfortunately the Confederacy was never able to establish an organization similar to the Sanitary Commission to capitalize on this magnanimity.

Not everything was *shipped* to the front, however, since a good many southern women finagled a way to reach the battlefield themselves, not too difficult a task when the war was carried almost to their doorsteps. Anxious friends and relatives presumed upon their daring sisters to smuggle much-needed drugs and other "comforts" to the fighting men. Lucy Nickolson Lindsay of Missouri, hearing that quinine, morphine and clothing were desperately needed, convinced the local pharmacist to "step out for a few moments" while she "borrowed" what she could fit into her specially tailored skirt, stowing twenty-two pairs of "home-knit socks" into pockets in the hem and wrapping the drugs separately into velvet rolls circling her head ("I put one 'round the coil of my hair and the other 'round the crown of my head . . . since it was then the fashion to wear velvet rolls on the head"). She then navigated the lines with her bounty of stockings and narcotics. Mary Gay, also heading toward enemy lines with a dozen ladies, used her knitting prowess to repay her host's kindness in sheltering them overnight. When he admired her throat warmer ("or, in the parlance of that day, 'a comforter' ") and asked for one, she replied she was willing but had no yarn; she was dumbfounded at the alacrity with which he fetched "soft, pretty lamb's wool thread . . . [which I] put into my already well-filled satchel to await further manipulation." A constantly knitting young wife heading for the front with her infant daughter to see her physician husband was evacuated en route during a heavy raid and spent the anxious night on "a little camp cot, on which I laid my child for the first time out of my arms. I took my knitting and sat by the window. The moon was low in the heavens; yet the tumult continued throughout the town. My child slept peacefully—her father many miles away, yet, I knew, filled with anxiety for our welfare. At dawn we were on our way."

This sacrifice, this knitting and sewing, for that is where most women began, for someone else's husband, son or spouse when one's own fought shivering and hungry on another front, this scraping of lint for bandages that might cover the wound of another while one's own lay bleeding and in need, demanded singular courage bolstered by group activity. As all ages gathered for cooking, sewing and knitting, their chatter served as a safety valve for fear, but deeper than the moral support of collective activity lay the practical consideration of buying knitting yarn and fabric more cheaply and pooling limited spinning wheels, looms and sewing machines.

The nuclei for cooperative effort were church-centered social groups whose chief preoccupation was needlework, from simple knitting projects to working complicated embroidery designs. These sewing circles met in members' homes until war needs outstripped parlors and forced members to scout for potential sites for workrooms for cutting fabric, dispensing yarn, storing materials for packaging and dispatching heavily loaded crates. Having targeted empty schoolrooms and quarters in town halls, courthouses and hospitals, one South Carolinian reported her mission accomplished: "The ladies of our town met at McBee's Hall, and the basement of the Baptist Church, to sew for soldiers. Country neighbors also formed sewing circles, and some of the old ladies were so expert as to be able to knit as they walked or rode along."

Thousands of new "war work" societies sprang up to augment existing sewing, knitting and church circles. One member recalled, "The young ladies established a 'sewing society' and though so young and inexperienced, I attended regularly and vied with the older ones to make as many garments as they did. We were always enthusiastic and harmonious, so we not only sewed but always had on hand a comfort to be quilted and at the same time, socks to be knitted for our brave soldiers." Another recalled, "The ladies knit and kept supplied many companies in socks and gloves, caps, shirts, and comforters. For four years we worked unceasingly, and even at evening parties the knitting needle was a regular attendant. Work for our soldiers was nothing but pleasure, and while the cards were being dealt, our knitting proceeded rapidly—tongues and fingers moved alike."

Societies kept such meticulous records that at the close of the war, when groups such as the United Daughters of the Confederacy and the *Charleston Mercury* wished to memorialize women's wartime benefactions "for all time," they were able to publish the work of even the smallest knitting clubs:

> A Knitting Society was formed and about fifty pairs of socks were sent away every two weeks. (Abbeville, South Carolina)

> The Association shall meet every alternate Saturday, at the residence of one of the members, in regular rotation. Each member to bring to the place of meeting the work done, yarn spun, socks knit, or anything done for the benefit of the cause. (Eutaville, South Carolina)

> Early in 1864 about 24 ladies formed a knitting association for the soldiers, each member to pledge herself to furnish at least one pair of well-knit soldier's socks every four weeks, and as many more as practicable, the yarn being furnished by the Society. (Spartanburg, South Carolina)

Knitting neophytes at war's inception were first-rate stitchers by its end, and during those four long years when their homemade products became their badge of honor, their knitting bees fostered needed camaraderie. Still, the loneliness and ennui remained: "There is nothing to mark one day from another now—always the same, sew knit read. . . . Oh I get so tired of it." Since women worked even while resting, knitting's portability and the fact that it could be done with relatively little light after sewing, spinning or weaving was laid aside at dusk made it particularly suitable. They knit as they walked, relaxed in the parlor, rocked on the veranda, strolled the grounds, visited friends, waited while cakes baked or soothed babies, turning out endless gloves, stockings, underclothes, mufflers and suspenders for soldiers and, with odds and ends of yarn, their own waistcoats, capes, shawls, baby sacques, gloves and stockings. To conceal irregularities in the coarse threads and yarns, they overlaid the knit segments with ornamentation such as "a bordering of vines, with

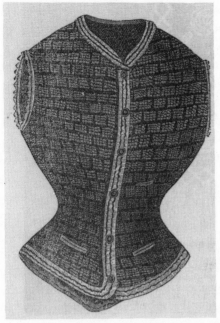

Lady's knitted waistcoat, 1864.

green leaves and rosebuds of bright colors, deftly knitted in [so] that they formed the exact replicas of the copy from which they were taken. . . . A pleasant rivalry arose as to who could form the most unique bordering. . . . There were squares, diamonds, crosses, bats, and designs of flowers formed in knitting and in crocheting."

Plantation owners helped the war effort by converting their homes to manufacturing centers, setting up cutting boards, sewing machines, spinning wheels, yarn distribution centers, knitting instruction alcoves and refreshment tables for visiting workers. One Alabaman remembered such a home "factory":

> In the wide halls within the plantation houses stood tables piled with newly-dyed cloth and hanks of woolen or cotton yarns. The knitting of socks went on incessantly. Ladies walked about in performance of household or plantation duties, sock in hand, "casting on," "heeling," "turning off." By the light of pine knots the elders still knitted far into the night. . . . Young girls moved silently about "helping." Over their pale lips not a ripple of laughter broke. The fire of youth seemed to have died out of their sad eyes, quenched for a time by floods of bitter tears.

The all-consuming needs of the Confederate army left those at home to scrounge for themselves, and wrenching accounts of their plight escalated the risk of soldiers' desertion, especially at seeding and harvest time, when their labor was critically needed. Toward the end, with plundering and burning by the occupying units, the position of those at home became even more pitiful. Still, they held on. Women worked out of pride, necessity, devotion to the Confederacy and the need to keep busy. Recalled one South Carolinian, "We spent all our spare time knitting socks . . . and we never went out to pay a visit without taking our knitting along. It was a common salutation, when we met our friends, to say, 'Come, bring your knitting and spend the day.' " Others remembered: "The few minutes before dinner, and all the time after, I devote to writing, sewing, knitting, etc."; "I do not know when I have seen a woman without knitting in her hand. Socks for the soldiers is the cry. . . . We make a quaint appearance with this twinkling of needles and the everlasting sock dangling below." Later, at a ladies' meeting, this same woman remarked, "No scandal today, no wrangling, all harmonious, everybody knitting. Dare say that soothing occupation helped our perturbed spirits to be calm."

Just as northern sewing and knitting women communicated through newspapers, times and places of meetings and special notices for southern groups were inserted in newspapers through the generosity of southern paper editors. In Savannah, a note read: "Ladies Knitting Society: Having been unable, for sometime past, to supply the demand for thread for Soldiers' socks, we would inform our lady friends, that we have now on hand enough thread for two to three hundred pairs, and they are greatly needed. The cold weather will soon be upon us, and we must not forget our soldiers." Within a month supplies were critically low: "To widows and wives of soldiers, not heretofore supplied, a bunch of yarn. As there is a limited supply, and no more expected, those who apply are requested to come prepared to prove that they really need it, as the list much exceeds the bunches of yarn." A South Carolina woman offered to trade her ninety-dollar "Wheeler and Wilson sewing machine, only in use a year, and uninjured, for one hundred pairs of woolen socks" and added, "Anyone taking up this offer, guaranteeing to deliver the socks by October 1st may get the machine at once. We vouch for the above in every particular. It is needless to add that the socks are for our soldiers in the war."

Newspapers maintaining the crucial link between widely separated sewing and knitting women were especially helpful in Alabama by announcing that Mobile Military Aid Society knitters would knit for any Confederate company, an act of generosity soon suspended when individuals could no longer afford materials and turned to the government for help. Alabama paid the incredibly low price of $4.50 per dozen for the 3,500 pairs of stockings the society delivered until even the state could no longer guarantee financial support. Undaunted, one group boldly announced it would "knit up" whatever the public supplied, and members unraveled old knitwear, blankets and rugs to find enough wool for their mammoth sock project. The ensuing sock knitting craze gripped the state and assured that no Alabama soldier would lack warm socks even though he suffered from other shortages. Attached to a shipment of 1,200 pairs went this note from the knitters: "[M]any willing fingers are diligently plying their needles to furnish much more of the needed socks." Those fingers continued until Alabama's heavy casualties compelled them to produce linen and bandages for hospitals. Fearing that knitting would languish, the governor promised to find the money somewhere to pay fifty cents a pair for heavy cotton socks and seventy-five cents a pair for woolen socks.

Alabama knitters' credentials were not atypical. Southern women's recollections, journals and diaries allude so often to knitting velocity and productivity that even these few excerpts testify to their accomplishment and pride:

Our fingers were never idle. . . . Bone and wooden knitting needles were used when steel failed. . . . Cotton and woolen yarn was used for a hundred different purposes. It was knitted into gloves, caps, jackets, comforters, socks, shirts, and skirts. The click of the needle was heard in every household. My mother knit on an average of three pairs of socks per week for the boys in the field whenever the material could be obtained.

Every woman in town was a miniature knitting machine: knitting sox and comforters for the Army.

I became such an expert knitter I could easily knit a pair of socks in a day.

I recollect, too, to have seen two ladies, each knitting a pair of stockings, at the same time—that is to say, with two feet of the socks set up on the same needles together.

I knitted a sock a day, long and large, and not coarse, many days in succession. At the midnight hour the weird click of the knitting needles . . . was no unusual sound.

The girls knitted hundreds of pairs of socks, mufflers, gloves, wristlets, havelocks [helmets] and were kept busy every moment.

We women spun, wove, and knit thousands of socks and gloves for our soldiers.

Everybody knitted socks. Ladies, negro women, girls, and even little boys learned to knit. Each tried to get ahead as to number and quality.

Miss Ann McCall . . . had inherited a set of gold needles, and I doubt if she could have counted the socks she knit. Her fingers fairly flew, and she never stopped to count. . . . Good knitting is quite an art among the old ladies.

In both North and South, everyone joked about superproductive women who would not stop working even for the Sabbath, and a South Carolina knitter who knit 750 pairs of socks during the war from cotton she herself grew, carded and spun "tasked herself a sock each day, including Sundays." This so horrified even Sherman's soldiers that one rebuked her, "You are a Christian and work on Sunday!" She proudly nodded her assent.

Knitters who were not whizzes were guilt-ridden at their ineptitude. One teenager, called upon to knit for the Confederate troops when they were stationed near her Harpers Ferry home in 1861, was chagrined at the disastrous stocking that emerged from her needles: "[T]he man would have to have had to be deformed to wear it, for it was a succession of bumps all down the leg. Never having the perseverance to knit a companion to it, I one day smuggled it into a box of clothing which was to be sent to camp, hoping it would be a comfort to some poor unfortunate who had one foot amputated."

Similarly, in Charleston, the "cradle of the war," where it was expected that each young woman would "lay aside her books and learn to knit socks for the soldiers, pick lint, and roll bandages," one knitter never forgot her agony and tears trying to knit her first sock:

> My first pair of socks were of coarse woollen yarn, most uneven thread, with sticks and burrs throughout. Diligently I set to work to remove all flaws, but before I had gone very far, being naturally indolent, and like most girls fond of commencing but not finishing work, I got very tired and thought the sticks and burrs knit in would help to "fill up". . . . I have never forgotten the reproof from my mother: "And did you ever think of the poor bleeding feet?" I was conscience stricken!

Young girls who had never learned to knit stockings because advances in the textile industry had improved "store-bought" ones gamely grasped the fundamentals under their elders' tutelage. One student remembered her mentor: "With what delight, after days of toil, she would triumphantly hold up for examination the rude, ill-shapen garment for critical evaluation . . . [my] 'soldier's sock.' Many a merry laugh has been provoked as the grotesque thing was submitted for critical examination."

The war was particularly hard on the young who matured early and forfeited their education as schools closed or they fled enemy advances. One "full fledged young lady," a bride at seventeen, later explained to her granddaughters that her early "turning out and marriage" was simply a sign of the times: "I can only plead as an excuse my early orphanage and the peculiar circumstances surrounding me in times of war. The sight of a young woman was so rare and refreshing that wherever the army encamped they would flock to your houses and every girl was compelled to be a belle."

Not all the young left school, however, and they participated as best they could. Remembered one southern mother: "The children were taught to knit, and their little fingers took many stitches for the dear soldiers who had marched away so brave and happy." Another recalled that a friend's twelve-year-old "housegirl" knit a sock a day with yarn furnished to her by her mistress. In Columbia, South Carolina, it was the same story, with the youngest children learning the simplest projects such as suspenders while older girls who were expert enough to both knit and read gave readings from the few books that reached the South during the war. One knitter read *Great Expectations* and *Les Miserables* to the "absorbed but industrious group."

Other schoolgirls knit "while conning lessons, or reading" and vied to knit socks with the gayest colors and the widest variety of stripes by the light of "Confederate candles," substitutes for expensive tallow-dipped candles, made by twisting sewn-together strips of rags "to the size of lampwicks," dipping them into melted beeswax, cooling them, redipping them and finally winding about two yards around a bottle or corncob, with one end loose for lighting. After the fabric was pressed to the bottle and hardened, it became an ersatz, or "Confederate," candle, provoking jokes about honeybees being "Southern sympathizers" by providing so much beeswax!

North Carolina boasted many special societies for younger women and children such as the "Young Ladies' Knitting Society" and the "Juvenile Knitting Society" in which children from ten to thirteen who reneged on their quota of the minimum fortnightly pair of socks forfeited ten cents. Industrious girls, knitting "with a vengeance," generated hundreds of pairs of socks, mufflers, wristlets and havelocks, and shifted their knitting bees from house to house, where more experienced older women (and those few men who had plumbed the "mystery of the 'turning of the heel' ") corrected the work of less experienced hands. One Richmond knitter described the scene as elders guided those "untutored in this branch of female industry": "It was delightful to watch the busy fingers of our dear old matrons, as they deftly wove the yarn through and through the shining steel needles, making cheerful music by the winter evening's fireside, as the soldiers' socks grew under their skillful manipulation. It was amusing to behold the patient industry with which the young girl who had 'never thought to knit,' caught the manipulations from the dear old hands."

Newspapers, particularly the *Charleston Mercury*, burnished reputations of young knitters. The *Mercury*'s "Dr. Bachman" sprinkled his donation column with such items as: "[F]rom Miss Maggie Horl-beck, six pairs of socks knit by her two little maids ten years old." And a Sumter matron recalled how as a young girl she could scarcely wait to scan her newspaper's column, "The Watchman," to locate her name among the donors of socks for soldiers.

Southern knitters and sewers, like their northern sisters, tucked personal notes and gifts into soldiers' packages. One woman remembered faithfully washing and ironing stockings in one-dozen lots, inserting a "pretty necktie, a pair of gloves, a handkerchief, or a letter" into the socks before "one of our faithful Negro women" folded them for packaging. Workers enclosing memos for soldiers' "spiritual edification, mental improvement, and amusement" targeted soldiers with "Never saw I the righteous forsaken" and "Apples are good but peaches are better; If you love me, will you write me a letter?" Wounded and convalescing soldiers eagerly anticipated plucking these "kindly messages" from their boxes, and one hospital worker reported, "Strange as it may seem, it is perfectly true that I found among them (not once, but several times) the name of one of my patients . . . and watched his delight, the eager grasp, the brightened eyes, the heaving breast of some poor fellow who had thus accidentally received a gift and message from his own home." Such stories breathed hope into the heart of this young knitter: "How faithfully I tried to learn to knit and sew, ever cherishing the secret thought that, perhaps, in time I could send George a gift which would be the work of my own hands."

Receiving a response from a soldier rekindled knitting fervor, and Captain Latham, speaking for his entire regiment, provided just that stimulus in his thanks "for the bountiful and timely supply of clothing" to the ladies of the Grassy Pond (South Carolina) Soldiers Aid Society: "Such acts, while recalling the pleasures of home vividly to the war-torn soldier, also seem to infuse fresh vigor and nerve to meet the despicable foe of our young Confederacy."

Struggling women, rewarded by such outpourings from the soldiers but still apprehensive about their own men's condition, dispatched letters reflecting their grim determination to make do for the "duration." One mother, defending her patriotism and hard work at the Soldier's Aid Society while "stringing my griefs and sorrows along," lamented, "My son, when the twelve months have expired for which you enlisted, you must not leave me alone again. If you remain connected with the army, if I am alive, I must be near you." Perhaps a bit contritely, she concluded with a flourish calculated to verify her allegiance: "We will burn up our houses and sweep the earth literally and die before we give up our fair and beautiful land to the craven wretches who dare to pollute our soil and imbue their hands in noble Southern blood." To his mother's plea that he obtain "home furlough," a soldier replied, "There isn't anything in the world that would please me more . . . [but] a fleshy, healthy looking boy like myself has but a poor chance of obtaining one . . . so I expect I shall have to continue to serve as long as I am blest with a sound body and good health, which I hope may be until the end of the rebellion."

With no alternative, mothers resigned themselves to long, anxious separations by working at Aid Societies, where working and knitting with others helped pass time constructively. While every memorist describes her knitting, most also learned to spin, weave, dye and "make do" with resources even more critically restricted after the South was blockaded. Though yearning for the proscribed rich fabrics and expensive European ornaments, they loyally balked at patronizing blockade-running ships and instead unraveled silk for "new" thread to freshen wardrobes. One avid knitter ("in our isolated corner . . . we knit, knit, knit all the time") raveled black silk and blended it with white cotton yarn for a "very pretty gray for gloves."

Like their Revolutionary forebears, proud women signaled their sacrifice by wearing "homespun" and "homeknit." A Columbia, South Carolina, teenager, savoring the "nice, fine yarn" her father had recently procured for her stocking knitting, smugly wrote in her diary: "It would seem very strange to put on a pair of new store stockings. And I am such an accomplished knitter that I do not look at my work and so can read and study while I knit. My hands are rarely without my knitting except when otherwise employed, and this has been a great resource during the long evenings with the light but dim firelight." Her soldier brother's shortage of drawers inspired another teenager to try knitting them on "big wooden needles" from yarn she had spun: "I am so impatient to get to work on them and see if my plan is feasible. . . . I know the shirts can be knit, for I made some for father last winter which he found quite comfortable, but I am somewhat doubtful as to the drawers. After awhile we learn how to supply most of our needs." Innovators removed worn stocking feet and knit new ones from yarn raveled from the "uppers" of other stockings; they soaked old leather shoes in hot water until they were pliable enough to allow stitches to be snipped out and newly knit slippers to be attached by sewing through the perforations; with no leather for shoes, they improvised by knitting them of dark brown, gray or black cotton or wool homespun, lined them with cloth and bound the upper edges with contrasting or matching cloth strips. For the final touch on women's shoes or slippers they perched a rosette of silk or yarn bits on the instep.

Whatever could be unraveled was. Canvasing their communities "from mansion to hamlet," workers collected blankets; dresses; bed, bath and table linens; window hangings; sofa and chair upholstery; bedspreads and carpets. All eventually found their way to the spinning wheel, where new yarn was spun for sewing, weaving and knitting projects. "Soldier knitting" was always of blue or gray, but knitters were so starved for color for *themselves* that an envious woman who begged her friend for the recipe for home-dyed "solferino" pink received these instructions: "Just take a good, large, ripe pumpkin, have your yarn and pokeberry juice ready, cut out a good piece of the stalk of your pumpkin, scoop out the seeds, leave the threads and juice, mix well in, put back your piece you had cut off the pumpkin and let it soak all night."

To alleviate the thread and yarn shortage, a few women experimented with planting mulberry trees and raising silkworms, but the sericulture project met with limited success, and the small quantities of raw silk harvested were reserved for unique gifts such as elegant open-worked knit gloves or bridal stockings with decorative clocks or initials worked into the stocking foot. In "Ersatz Sewing," few could eclipse one young lady's "most ingenious" black silk dress fashioned from the covers of worn parasols, with the umbrella form preserved in the skirt. The dress, lined with mosquito netting presented to the owner by a young officer and fastened with his battle-seasoned army buttons, was, to say the least, "very much prized."

One of the richest sources on southern women's relief work, both on and off the battlefield, is the matchless record of the Greenville,

South Carolina, Ladies Association in Aid of the Volunteers of the Confederate Army, which germinated from a small sewing circle. Carefully preserved by the daughter and granddaughter of the society's vice president, who permitted publication in 1937, the record chronicles every meeting, from the first organizing session to the poignant disbanding four years later. The Greenville *Minutes* provide a microcosm of southern aid societies, running the gamut from collecting funds, giving out and supervising knitting and sewing projects, logging in and out the work received, recording the contents of each box packed, shipping boxes (often with a society agent in charge), meeting trains, establishing homes and hospitals, writing to other relief organizations and painstakingly copying all letters sent and received long before carbon paper and photocopiers. Closing "with sisterly regard," they corresponded with groups in other states to learn their needs, especially those who had shown "great sympathy and untiring kindness to the sick South Carolina soldiers."

The South lacked resources to compete with the North's almost unlimited advantages in industry, transportation and an organized army, and it was to this disparity that the society addressed itself by determining to supply soldiers with "comforts" of homemade jellies and jams along with favored articles of clothing, medicines, gun cases, canvas tents and flags. They worked until fingers were swollen and bleeding. Because Greenville lay astride a major railway, wounded soldiers who could travel no farther were dropped off at its depot. Greenville women treated these "visitors" as they would their own men and transported the stronger ones to their homes and the more seriously wounded to be "entertained" at their "Soldier's Rest," a building donated by the academy (later the site of Greenville Women's College). All this took money, time and organization. *Everyone* was expected to knit and sew and then specialize in the "depot work" or nursing. Knitters could knit at home, at society meetings, waiting at the train station or in the few moments between packing boxes for the front.

At the first organizational meeting, knitting got off to a good start when "Miss Dean brought the wool she had spun; it was distributed among the members to knit socks." At succeeding meetings sock donations were listed, sometimes with explanations that hint at an unmet quota, such as when "Mrs. Morris" brought one pair along with "some pickles" and Mrs. Burn gave two pairs along with "sage and crackers."

As needs increased (payment of dues was not enforced if members completed assigned work), so too did the frequency of meetings. Members were fined for absences and additional officers were elected to head new committees such as Shopping, Cutting, Giving Out Work, Receiving, Marking, Soliciting Strangers, Packing, Order, and Money Contributions. By running a small hospital in addition to their other activities, members dealt with problems far outside their regular "sphere." For instance, the well problem.

When Mrs. Thompson alerted members to the "inadequacy of the well" for the growing number of patients in the "rest," she, like most who bring up issues, was appointed to "inquire about getting a new rope for the old well" or determine the advisability of digging a new one. Well reports increasingly consumed precious time at each meeting, and Mrs. Thompson was appointed to "continue superintending the workmen . . . when they are ready to blast and wall." Uncompromising well supervisor she might have been, but she had a heart of gold, for the next week's minutes recorded that she had donated $25.00 "from Society funds then in her hands" for a sick soldier's wife. The society moved and resolved that "this case shall be considered exceptional and not regarded as a precedent for the future." Knuckles rapped.

The completion of the well "for the sum of $170" ended the well story until the directresses were apprised that "a well rope is wanting." They requested Mrs. Bolling (a new well chairwoman?) to "buy yarn and have one made," a good move except that cotton was unavailable and the rope had to be bought ready-made. Regarding establishment of a garden to produce fresh food for their Soldier's Rest patients/guests, Miss Johnson of the Garden committee reported that "Captain Davis had kindly lent a horse, and given a load of manure for the garden"; two weeks later he repeated his generosity so that planting could be completed.

Throughout the war, the society's minutes were sprinkled with references to knitting activities—seldom more than a few lines, such as: "27 pairs of socks are on hand"; "Resolved that knitting yarn be procured for socks for the soldiers"; "Moved and Resolved that Knitting yarn be immediately procured for socks." That last resolution (to procure yarn) came a month before the end of the war, when finances were critical in spite of benefits such as a Christmas Supper, a Strawberry Festival and a "theatrical production." The club's discouragement was complete when the replacement for the on-leave hospital steward "got drunk and was carried off to the other hospital," leaving the society's hospital unsupervised while soldiers "stripped and carried away the covering of three beds." That was the last entry, except for this poignant notation added at a later date:

> General Meeting, May 1st [1865]
>   No meeting on account of the Yankee Raiders who stripped the "Rest" of every available article it contained, leaving the Society without the means of carrying on further operations.
>   J. A. Dickson
>   Sec'y Greenville Aid Association

The experiences of the Greenville aid society mirrored those of other such groups throughout the South. While northern ladies harvested General Grant's hair for their fair, an enterprising southerner planned the sale ("for the Cause") of a wreath of floral garlands entwined with snippets of hair from "some of our generals." General Robert E. Lee's wife (who was credited with knitting as conscientiously for the soldiers as did her forebear, Martha Washington) acknowledged the request by culling hair from her husband's staff members and adding it to General Lee's hair, which, she noted, "is so small that I fear the small lock I send will be of little use. You will have to supply all deficiencies from the flowing locks of our very youthful Brigadiers."

Other money-raising schemes to entice prospective donors to swell yarn and knitting coffers were fairs (necessarily local events rather than regional affairs such as the enormous "Sanitary Fairs" of the North), bazaars, "magic lantern" shows and "Tableaux Vivants," skits depicting patriotic themes by young women of the community. As the "high point" of one soiree, eleven young students, each bearing the label of a Confederate state, formed a pyramid at whose apex stood "Alabama" vigorously waving her Confederate flag as the band played "Dixie." When the Soldier's Relief Association of Columbia, Georgia, entreated the "friends of the Southern Cause at Home" by asking for marketable items for its bazaar, sponsors hoped for something fancier than war knitting, of which everyone was sick and tired: "We would especially invite attention to the numberless articles of a useful and fancy kind which the taste and ingenuity of the ladies have developed during the war, as for instance straw and palmetto bonnets and hats, cloth hats, knitting of every description, crochet and tatting, camp bags, tobacco pouches, pins and needles cases. And, in a word, to all the handiwork of the busy fingers of earnest hearths in the cause of our country."

Their "cause" was not to be won, but despite their relentless efforts for their soldiers and their own severe privations, their indomitability was epitomized by this "So, *there!*" advertisement placed in the *Savannah Morning News* after the burning and pillaging of the city: "Miss M. J. Brown respectfully informs the citizens of Savannah that she is now ready to resume her business of Making and Repairing Hoop Skirts, at the corner of James and Montgomery Streets."

7.

Mid-Century Knitters

Not all "fashionable" knitting stopped during the war, and magazines describing modish clothing seldom referred to the conflict for fear of offending subscribers. *Godey's Lady's Book*, whose hundred thousand subscribed readership increased fivefold as its copies circulated to family and friends, lost a third of its subscribers when mail between the Union and the Confederacy stopped. Throughout the war, its "Work Department" continued to offer knitting styles and staples such as cotton "knitted braces" or suspenders with detachable leather straps ("The great charm in these braces is the readiness with which they can be washed; so that they may be changed at least once a week"). Presiding over a similar section in the rival *Peterson's* monthly column on knitting, embroidery and crochet, Jane Weaver attracted war-weary but fashion-conscious women to her patterns for knit bags, undershawls, lace collars and even a "soap bag for toilet," a small hanging bag with foldover soap pocket. Her checkerboard "Sontag" (a triangular shawl) of "crimson zephyr [with] fine bone knitting needles" must have been a welcome relief from socks. And for babies who needed warmth, war or not, there was the infant's shirt of "split zephyr," probably a lightweight shetland using only one of its strands.

Well aware that an elegant knitting bag was "really indispensable [for] going out to spend a sociable afternoon . . . necessary to almost every lady, knitting being now so general," Mrs. Weaver suggested a velvet-covered and bead-encrusted straw bag topped with beaded rosette and dangling beaded tassels to dazzle every woman at the Soldiers' Aid Society. Though a "Knitted Opera Hood" was incongruous in wartime, women who prided themselves on "keeping up" chose it for its adaptability to their coiffures, "so soft that it will not injure the most delicate flowers or curls." Shawls tucked under coats or capes in winter or worn alone in warmer weather were also popular, and *Peterson's* featured one "worked in nearly every kind of wool, and the size varied at pleasure, making it either for a small shawl to wear across the shoulders, or carried out for a large wrapper; if made in strong yarn, it is especially suitable for charitable gifts." Since women "went about" more in increasingly public duties, their eventual choice of comfortably sleeved knit garments whose elasticity was more suitable for room tasks seems foreordained, but to this author's knowledge, the first published endorsement of elasticity was *Peterson's'* 1864 "knitted jacket for wearing under mantles or dresses," described as a "warm and elastic" bodice or jacket to be worn "either over the stays or as an out-door wrap." Within a few decades such jackets would be commonplace.

As members trod rain-soaked lanes or threaded their way through crowded streets, scurrying to meetings, aid rooms and hospitals, they hoisted hooped skirts over curbs, puddles and steps, a task so difficult that *Demorest's Magazine*'s editor, "Mme. Demorest" (also the proprietress of a large emporium of the same name in New York City), invented the "Imperial Dress Elevator," a device promised to be "so easy of application and convenient to raise the Dress and let it down at will [that] no Walking Dress is now considered complete without one." By combining the elevator with "neat dark, durable skirts and thick soled shoes" women could double their exercise without "annoyance or the scare of ugliness or eccentricity." The voluminous skirts created a host of other problems, and it would have taken more than a dress elevator to adapt them for the favorite winter sport, ice skating. Large cities built "Skating Parks," roofed-in gaslit ballrooms, complete with "accommodations for warmth and refreshment [where] . . . [n]o apprehension of drowning can disturb the peace of parents whose children have gone skating." When Mme. Demorest contemplated hooped skirts on skaters, she threw up her hands and warned that their use would "aggravate the unsightliness of a fall, already sufficiently mortifying, and for beginners hardly to be avoided."

Ready for winter with her fitted knit "Hug-me-tight" vest buttoned under her coat, her woolen gloves pulled on tight and her "cloud" wrapped around head and neck, Clara Lenroot was ready for a joyous winter outing of another kind:

A great deal of coquetry was indulged in by the red-cheeked bright-eyed girls in the adjustment of the cloud. It might be bright red in color, or pink, or blue, or white. It was always puckered in at each end, and finished by a fluffy tassel. It was wound around the head two or three times, then around the neck, several times, and the ends, with the swinging tassels, thrown jauntily over the shoulder. A fresh, young face, framed in such fleecy fluffiness, was like a new-blown rose. When 'cutterriding' with one's best beau, in a red cutter drawn by a spirited horse with bells jingling, the two ends of the scarf floating out behind, one's head was in the clouds, sure enough!

Facing the wartime absence of men and sharply decreased resources, most women were compelled to forgo such sporty activities to further prospects for increasing their income, and the advice of women's magazines about the "Sphere of Woman" and the "Mission of Woman" bore scant application to those "thrown upon their exertions." When hard-up knitters tried supplying the exorbitantly expensive and hard-to-find ladies' and gentlemen's handknit hose and stockings, they found a dearth of both customers who could afford custom work and store buyers who appreciated the difference between machine knitting and hand knitting. It was a hopeless prospect, and a book on work opportunities offered little else than advising them to learn machine knitting at nearby factories.

At war's end, the victorious North found more to be grateful for than the South, with its shattered economy, wasted land, higher death toll and remaining population in direst need. For northern women, the eulogies rang out to those whose work was "without parallel in

"The Brown Family," Eastman Johnson, 1867.

the annals of history," whose sacrifices gave "comfort to some poor soldier tossing in agony in some distant hospital," whose steadfast knitting, sewing and nursing had sustained the Union army. As their relief societies disbanded, members glowed with pride at records they had kept, right down to the last quilt, blanket, comfort bag, handkerchief, pair of drawers, wrapper, shirt, sheet, towel, pillow tick, bed tick, muffler, mitten, and thousands of pairs of hand-knit socks. They congratulated themselves, thanked all who had supplied them with the means and expressed gratitude that there was "no further need of their exertion."

Despite sorrow and ruin, remarked *Demorest's Illustrated Monthly*'s editor, "Jenny June," the war had one compensating effect in making women "industrious, self reliant, truthful, and willing to exercise their faculties for the benefit, as well as the pleasure, of mankind. Many have been taught by the severest calamities to place a just estimate upon the trifles which formerly occupied all their atten-

"The Stocking Knitter," 1868.

tion—many have learned to value the lessons taught them by the bitterest experiences." So saying, and even though most knitters could barely contemplate knitting another pair of socks, within a month, *Demorest's* gaily recommended that knitters make stockings for gifts since their price had doubled and sometimes trebled.

Many could not afford to give even inexpensive gifts. Virginia Penny, who had gloomily assessed women's wartime employments, was even more discouraged by the postwar outlook and irked that diehards persisted in their chant, "O, keep women to woman's work!" despite the stark contrast of thousands "tenderly reared and possessed of all the comforts, even the luxuries of life" reduced to poverty. Still appalled at the "pittance" sewers and knitters earned, she summarized: "A Woman may be defined as a creature that receives half price for all she does, and pays full price for all she needs. . . . She earns as a child—she pays as a man."

In the South, penniless but proud upper-class women who preferred payment for performance to outright charity tried to capitalize on their sewing and knitting "accomplishments" but found few customers. Turning to a northern relief association that disbursed money to those in abject need, one supplicant pleaded, "Since my husband's death, I have tried to support myself and children by every kind of honest work in my power. I have kept boarders, taught school, taken in fancy knitting and sewing from the stores. . . . We have been living in almost utter destitution and I have tried everywhere to get some kind of work to support my family, and cannot." A minister upon whom the association relied to locate the neediest reported, "I have been using [the money] very carefully in order to make it last as long as possible. I am using it to pay for work given to the poor such as knitting, spinning, etc. There is no sale for their products, but we do not wish to foster pauperism, & prefer to buy what they offer and give it to those who are more helpless." The outlook was bleak.

Though troubled about their needy sisters, northern women resolved to memorialize the dead and provide nursing for helpless survivors. To solicit funds for their Soldiers' Home, Milwaukee women turned again to a fair and pressured state teachers ("the officers of the line, who are to command and direct the action of the grand army") to elicit fifty-cent contributions from their pupils to "buy" a brick for the home. Their suggestions for children's activities, except for their rurality, echo appeals to children from time immemorial:

> You ask, how can you get the money? We answer, work for it! Earn it with your own hands. Do something for your father and mother or older brothers and sisters, or work for some other persons; work for anybody on the farm, in the shop, at home, at school, in the store, knit, sew, hoe, plough, dig in a garden, drive cows or sheep, tend the baby, get better lessons, make better improvement in writing, be better boys and girls do anything and everything, honest, and right to get articles and money to give to the Soldiers' Home Fair.

Northern and southern women whose loyalties had been riven by the Civil War soon united to support the Women's Building at Philadelphia's Centennial Exposition in 1876. When Elizabeth Duane Gillespie (former chairperson of that city's Sanitary Fair and current head of its Centennial Women's Committee) solicited contributions of women's art or industry for the Women's Pavilion displays, embroiderers, crocheters and knitters dispatched their most impressive products. There, among paintings, tapestries, sculpture, pottery, carvings and sundry inventions such as patented corsets, dustpans, washing machines and alphabet blocks, lay several pairs of old-fashioned mittens, one knit by the seventy-one-year-old granddaughter of a Revolutionary War major, whose accompanying photograph showed her to be, according to one gentleman, "still young in health, if not in years." The Women's Committee's own newspaper, *The New Century for Woman*, cranked out inside the Pavilion, lauded a pair knit by Abigfal Flagg Lovering, an "ancient dame" of one hundred years and four months, and another fairgoer spotted a pair knit by Mrs. Mary Champneys "in her one-hundredth year."

Displayed elsewhere at the exposition were several knitting machines. By the end of the war many knitters had heard of (and some had tried) the hand-cranked, circular Aiken "American Family Knitting Machine." Patented as early as 1855, it was widely advertised in national magazines and sold door-to-door by peddlars who heralded it as a revolutionary replacement for knitting stockings by hand.

A few rural women who knit socks for income bought the portable (39-pound) Aiken machine, but the expected "revolution" never occurred since women preferred hand knitting for reasons other than economy and speed and spoke disdainfully of machine-made products.

Pinning its hopes on this "deepening dislike," the new *Dorcas Magazine* set its sights on two targets, "the delicate daughter of fashion, who occupies her leisure moments weaving some dainty gift for a loved one" and "her less fortunate sister, who must make of the pastime a labor, wherewith to procure food and shelter." Its basic, well-illustrated instructions brought kudos from the press: "It aims to keep as workers those to whom work means bread, and [those] for whom life holds nothing brighter than the gay colors of the silks and wools with which they work"; "There are illustrations of how to knit that even a man might understand"; "It is all very mysterious to us, but doubtless is important and interesting to the gentlewomen." Within a year editors complimented themselves for having rescued their targets from the tentacles of "those books and periodicals which warp our daughters from what is woman's work in the world."

While some writers argued that tending to "woman's work in the world" counteracted "nervousness," an aspect of the widely discussed "hysterical woman" syndrome, others took the opposite tack and attributed "nerves" to the crushing responsibilities of house and home. The replacement of many homemade articles with factory-made products should have lessened rather than multiplied household tasks, but Susan Strasser, in her book *Never Done: A History of American Housework*, points out that as machines simplified housework, women simply performed their tasks more often. Washing machines begat more frequent laundry days. As women grew increasingly preoccupied with the minutiae of homemaking, redoubtable reformer Abba Woolson branded them "worn and jaded" with household work and praised the "giantesses . . . those matrons of that golden age," who wove, spun, knit, churned and quilted with nary a complaint.

Even Catherine Beecher, whose earlier *Treatise on Domestic Economy* preached planning and routine, later admitted (with sister Harriet Beecher Stowe as co-author) that mother and housekeeper, though crowned "sovereign of an empire," suffered "incessant trials of temper, and temptations to be fretful" when forced to deal with "ten thousand little disconnected items." The crown, perhaps hollow, was still not lightly abdicated. A needlework book dedicated to "The Ladies of America" promised instructions for articles by which the "little lady of the house, its mistress," could with her busy little fingers add tasteful touches to "make the Little Realm more enticing."

Withdrawal from the enticing realm was fraught with even more uncertainty. Despite housework's hazard to sanity, intellectual stimulation was, according to Mary Elizabeth Sherwood, an even more insidious culprit: "With some women brain-work is impossible. It produces all sorts of diseases, and makes them at once a nervous wreck. . . . The happiest women are those who can lead the ordinary life, be amused by society, dress, and conventionalities, and who can be early married to the man of their choice, and become in their turn domestic women, good wives and mothers. . . . She has always had a sphere." Sherwood yielded to more education only if a girl "were equal to it," and *Dorcas* certified that reviving "soothing and quieting" knitting, the almost forgotten art of grandmothers, would restore their granddaughters' health: "The quiet, even, regular motion of the needles quiets the nerves and tranquilizes the mind, and lets thought flow free." "Jenny June," pseudonym for author and clubwoman Jane Croly, forwarded her view of knitting serenity: "The little work-tables of women's fingers, are the playground of women's fancies, and their knitting-needles are the fairy-wands by which they transform a whole room into a spirit isle of dreams." Mme. Demorest, the last word in fashion and behavior, chimed in: "Absolute inactivity of the hands gives double play to the thoughts; and the old adage about Satan finding mischief for the fingers of the unemployed is too well understood to necessitate even the quoting of the entire saying. If women thought and worked more, they would gossip and chatter less." The Satan adage was indeed well understood. In speaking of her youth in the 1870s, one Californian remembered, "It was deemed wise to keep me occupied, so far as possible, in order to thwart Satan, ever on the lookout for idle hands. So I was taught to do patchwork and to knit."

Industry, that hallmark of earlier America, was still alive and well in the Victorian Age. "Being without work" remained so unthinkable that knitting was still encouraged to employ "minutes which would otherwise be wasted." Knitting was endorsed for housewives already exhausted from other chores: "A woman who has been at the washtub or at housework all day cannot easily sit down to plain needlework; her hands are 'out of tune'; she cannot, perhaps, even feel the needle, it is too small; but let her be able to knit readily (having been taught at school), and she will add many an inch, at spare moments, to her husband's or her children's stockings, which lies ready to be taken up at any time."

Knitting wasn't confined to the home. A steady knitter, female activist Mrs. Clorinda Nichols, of Kansas, whose portrait was seen by the thousands who flocked to the "woman's room" at the Chicago World's Fair in 1893, firmly planted one foot in politics and the other in her "sphere." A member of Kansas's first state constitutional convention demanding women's rights when its advocates were denounced as "strong minded and unwomanly," she "tended strictly to her knitting, as she finished the sock which she was working at before the convention closed." Feminists hinted that her traditional appearance—knitting—duped male legislators into underestimating her crusade for more liberal property rights for women.

Traveling women packed so much sewing and knitting on vacation trips that baffled husbands puzzled why they "worked" on holiday. *Dorcas* enlightened them: "It is impossible to her to sit absolutely idle (remember, monsieur, she has not the resource of the cigar), and the artistic faculty . . . finds a needed outlet in making pretty things in bright wool and silk." This question of what to do on vacations, which magazines addressed as "Work for Idle Hours" or "Fancy Work at Watering Places," and the conviction that "an idle hand is not a pretty hand" impelled women to cart everything along, packing knitting materials in their fanciest bags. Mme. Demorest advocated donning "coquettish aprons, lace trimmed and be-ribboned, with pockets for balls . . . [to] heighten the effect of the costume of the fair worker" and to excite envy in other ladies wielding their needles on the piazza. Knitting fancy laces ("in as high vogue as ever") in cotton, linen, silk or worsted, she added, was an occupation not only "fascinating to the knitter, but also to the beholders; for certainly no other kind of fancy-work displays a beautiful hand to better advantage." They were further assured that "nothing is more truly feminine than the execution of pretty tasks of fancy work" and that "life at watering places, which is one long whiling away of time is especially suitable to these accomplishments." *Looking* feminine and "right" while knitting was important. Even the popular song "Knitting the Scarf" characterized the knitting woman "daintily plying her needles." Appearance, however, interfered with techniques. An expert who admitted that the German (or Continental) method of holding the yarn in the left hand was speedier and more efficient acknowledged she had an uphill battle in its adoption since it didn't "look so pretty."

Whether on the wide, covered porch at their Saratoga hotels or on their home verandas, women relished chatting and knitting in bamboo or wicker chairs or lazing in ceiling-hung swings. At home, they so treasured this "extra room" that they later enclosed porches with glass and installed hot-air registers for year-round usage. Not all Victorian women were entwined in their knitting, crocheting, embroidering, seaming, tucking and housewifely duties, however, and a few cried out against the obsessed "little woman" whose every tidbit of conversation was focused on "how much embroidery is needed to make a child's dress presentable and volunteers valuable information regarding the newest styles in sashes and yokes . . . on polonaises, braid, flounce, and furbelow." One bemoaned the fact that most needlework (a "trifling pursuit") was produced at the expense of the eyesight, the health and the intelligence of women. A good many women agreed and edged away from home and hearth into higher education and even careers. While many people poohpoohed the newly established female colleges, alleging that most of what they taught would be useless for "young ladies," one of those colleges proudly announced that, in addition to a rigorous curriculum, students operated their own fire department, with a seven-student "company" drilling regularly to handle the pumps, form the lines and pass the pails while another operated the great steam-powered fire engine. Wellesley's foresight and training in "familiarizing students with the best modes of extinguishing fires," a far cry from their "sphere," was instrumental in helping students survive a devastating college fire several decades later. At nearby Radcliffe College (certainly in the forefront of women's liberal arts education), however, the college doctor cautioned career-bent students, "I wish to

"The Winding of the Skein," 1868.

warn those who are sailing or who are about to sail on treacherous
seas. . . . I never saw a professional woman who had not lost some
charm. There comes some hardness. . . ."

Other institutions, especially land grant coeducational colleges established under the Morrill Act, offered newly expanded but separate
curricula to women since, as the report of the commissioner of education for 1871 put it: "There are ineradicable differences between
the sexes which must be taken into account in determining the conditions of a proper culture for each. . . . Care must be taken that in
the ardor for scholastic training domestic education does not decline." As a result, home economics courses were the norm in ag-

ricultural colleges and state universities, and knitting was grouped with sewing in housekeeping studies.

In addition to continuing interest in charities, women established societies and clubs mixing sociability with "moral uplift." One of those, the Sorosis Society, was founded by a group of New York female journalists affronted by the denial of their admission to a banquet honoring Charles Dickens on his return visit to the United States. Vowing to form their *own* club, they assembled in an upstairs room at the famous Delmonico's, but soon quarreled over a suitable name. Most favored "The Women's League" or the more traditional "Women's Circle," but inflexible liberals railroaded adoption of "Sorosis" over objections that it "sounds like a disease." The new president resigned during a particularly acrimonious debate, when "her nervous system was not equal to the strain," an action that fueled opponents' contentions that clubs generated hysteria. Members were soon the butt of jibes from men, who complained that their wives' busy club work obliged them to cope with household responsibilities that rightfully belonged in "woman's domain." Cartoonists had a field day depicting stranded house-husbands juggling babies, laundry, cooking and knitting, and even Grover Cleveland entered the fray by decrying the "restlessness and discontent" of female participants in public affairs and lashing out at clubs that subverted women from their household interests. He drew the line indelibly: "I believe that it should be boldly declared that the best and safest club for a woman to patronize is her home." To which the president of Sorosis retorted spiritedly, "We have tipped the teapot."

To intensify women's interest in the home, where they would presumably knit, *Dorcas* inaugurated the first national knitting contest, in which entrants competed for $100 in prizes for the best six pieces of plain and fancy silk knitting made of Dorcas silk ("The reason for this is obvious, it is the best silk on the market, and its use will insure a uniformity of fabric"). The summer of 1885 was so hot for knitting that editors postponed the deadline for a month. After the judges' eagerly awaited decisions were communicated to the winners, *Dorcas* printed their grateful replies. "The first premium for fancy knitting surprised me in my quiet home," wrote the top ($25) winner. Acknowledged the second-prize winner for fancy knitting, "I appreciate the honor very much, and thank you for your kindness in considering

OLD GENT. *"As Mrs. Nettlerash has gone to the Sorosis Club, I tho't I'd just come over with my Knitting. Baby not well, eh?"*
YOUNG GENT. *"No, poor thing, he requires so much Care that I really don't get time to do my Mending!"*

Cartoon spoofing the Sorosis Society, c. 1870.

my work worthy of such commendation. Perhaps the pleasure your letter gave me was greater from the fact that I am an invalid, and consequently am shut in from some of the enjoyments that other people have." A prize winner for plain knitting found "knitting and crochet work an agreeable change from my literary work"; another was gratified "in that I, a novice in such work, have been able, when pleasantly occupying leisure hours, to produce something in competition with more experienced hands"; another was delighted that "an old lady of three score and ten has successfully competed with many skilled and tasteful among the granddaughters."

Financial "panics" wiped out family stakes with some frequency, and needy women hoping to sell handiwork turned to special publications such as Addie Heron's *Dainty Work for Pleasure and Profit*, which addressed "the great army of women in our country who feel the need of adding their mite to the family exchequer" and suggested salable knit items such as laces, baby clothes and fancy stockings. The business collapses after the "Panic of 1893" left many families penniless in a period that one of the largest dry goods stores in the country, the H. B. Claflin Company, which had long supplied needle-women with their "findings" for sewing and knitting projects, called "the most disastrous of any in twenty years." Heron came to the rescue by building upon her experience as editor of *Home Art*, and her *Dainty Work* was soon followed by *Ladies' Work for Pleasure and Profit*, in which she credited her widespread circle of friends "from Maine to California and from British Columbia to the Gulf Coast, as well as those in England, Scotland, and France" for their "insatiable demands" for more patterns. She urged neophytes to ignore their "deepseated conviction that they cannot learn anything from printed instructions" and to follow her crystal-clear, well-illustrated instruc-

Knitted hood, 1868.

tions. The book was an instant best-seller. *Dorcas*, too, furnished its readers assistance in selling knitting by offering plans for "Women's Exchanges" to put skilled knitters in touch with customers willing to pay good prices for unusual items. Women whose work bore the indelible stamp of "loving hands at home" were coached to sharpen techniques, master "fancy stitches" and create "novelties" not found in shops, since buyers wanted only "garments which cannot be duplicated by the hundred."

Needy knitters were solicited through classified ads to serve as local sales and distribution agents for specialized knitting magazines and booklets. An interesting "give-away" pamphlet in the Library of Congress collection, *The Needle at Home*, is stamped "Compliments of C. F. Maguire and Co., Proprietor, Lion Shoe Store, New Carlisle, Ohio, The Cheapest House in the State for Boots and Shoes." Inside the cover, the publisher advertised: "Lady agents wanted in every town and city in the United States."

As in the past, there was some money in the necessary but tedious tasks of mending, reknitting and darning socks. In her "Over the Mending-Basket" chapter, a housekeeping manual's author folksily addressed her readers: "You will cut out the heel entirely, take up the stitches and knit a new double one in an evening. Or you will have it done by the girls of the Industrial Home, or by old Mrs. Cutter, who earns her missionary money and her liniment by odd jobs at home." If one couldn't afford even this, then full instructions for reknitting of heels, toes and soles were available in instruction books, particularly Mary Louise Kerzman's *How to and What to Knit*, a small twenty-five-cent booklet judged by *The Modern Priscilla*'s editors "The best book on Knitting," their premium to anyone securing three new subscribers.

Women who could "turn a penny" from their knitting were greatly admired, and readers savored sentimental stories of successes such as the young woman who, with her mother and grandmother, first talked the local merchant into selling their mittens and stockings and subsequently branched into knitting fancy items on consignment for summer visitors. She both financed her education and rescued mother and grandmother with her knitting needles!

Grandmothers were great jewels, and the one knitting in the foreground of Eastman Johnson's 1871 portrait *The Hatch Family* in the

"Heel and Toe," 1873.

Metropolitan Museum of Art is characteristic of the Victorian matriarch portrayed in Mary Elizabeth Sherwood's *Amenities of the Home*: "There is no *genre* picture so ornamental to the fireside as an old lady with gray curls. Home should always contain a grandmother. . . . The lovely old lady is a great treasure in a household, has often agreeable accomplishments in the way of needlework and knitting, has a perfect store of excellent recipes for cakes and custards, and knows the most delightful old-fashioned games of cards." Whenever granny was pictured, and she was a standard subject in mail-order art for Victorian walls, she was usually depicted patiently teaching a child to knit, such a fixed role that Lucretia Hale boasted that her explanations and illustrations in *The Art of Knitting* were clear enough to steer a beginner through the shoals of knitting "even if she has not the help of a grandmother or aunt, to show her how it was done in the olden time."

The stereotype was so rigid that should grandmother venture to

camouflage her age, she was rebuked by social and journalistic ar-
biters of dress and custom such as Florence Hall, who put it bluntly:
"One should be very careful to select materials and style of dress
that are suited to one's age, figure, height, and complexion. . . . But,
alas! many people are seized with a sudden desire for youth just as
it is slipping away from them." Similarly, a popular etiquette book
warned "those ladies who have long passed the acknowledged boundaries of youth . . . to avoid adoption of any new fashion until time
has set its seal, and custom in some measure has sanctified its propriety." Gaudy colors, feathers, flowers, a profusion of ornaments,
elaborately dressed hair, short sleeves and low dresses were all considered offenses against good taste guaranteed to "deprive her of the
respect and deference which her age should always command, sub-
jecting her to the ridicule of the thoughtless, and the pity of the
more considerate." Pattern books used no "mature adult" or "senior
citizen" euphemisms to describe clothing for the elderly but frankly
labeled them "cap for an old lady," "old lady's bedroom slipper" and
"shawl for an invalid old lady."

In dozens of odes and poems exalting knitting grandmothers, of
which the following is an example, one metaphor lingers:

> "Life is a stocking," grandma says,
> "And Yours has just begun;
> "But I am knitting the toe of mine,
> "And my work is almost done."

Let grandmother stick to her knitting, helping the young, and all
would be well, for knitting by children was as heavily stressed as
earlier in the century, despite the fact that ready-made socks, stockings, mittens, gloves, scarves and other items were easily obtainable.
Since most parents still wanted knitting taught in schools, Boston
public schools set aside two hours a week for fourth, fifth and sixth
graders. Fearful that other "academic" subjects might encroach, they
remonstrated, "This time shall not be shortened for other studies,
or examinations, or any other purposes, without the consent of the
Committee on Sewing, especially obtained." There would be no idle
hands (and therefore no devil's playgrounds) in Boston classrooms
since "if there be an accidental stop in other work, or the teacher is

"The Learner," 1868.

"Passing on the Tradition," 1868.

engaged with another child" students were to break out their needles and "commence knitting" anything from "blackboard rubbers" to dishcloths and "floor rubbers." Even atrociously knit projects ("the veriest 'waste' of beginners") could be salvaged. Sewing together three long knitted strips, rolling them tightly and fastening them securely, converted projects gone awry into chalk erasers. As children's proficiency increased, they graduated to towels and "personal washing gloves," knit rectangles sewn up the sides and turned inside out to "fit the fingers of the hand like an infant's glove." Legs of stockings without feet ("gaiters") were assigned to girls to whom turning the heel of a sock was still a mystery. These, Boston's Lucretia Hale opined, "are very useful to those who are obliged to walk out in all weathers, as they protect the leg from the wet edge of the petticoat, and are easily pulled off when in school or at home."

Children accompanied mothers and grandmothers to neighborhood stores to shop for needlework supplies until the second half of the century, when horse-drawn buses and streetcars transported them to one-stop marts where they purchased everything in one place. Because of savings in volume sales, these "department stores" undersold specialty shops by as much as 15 to 20 percent, but their main attraction lay less in lower prices than in consolidating an assortment of goods under one roof. Buyers substituted "going shopping" for "running errands" and discovered departments with their own space, buyers, sales forces and, often, separate accounts. By buying most clothing in the new ready-to-wear departments, needlewomen gained additional time for other handwork, and by the late 1800s department stores staffed "art needlework" departments with saleswomen who studied clients' needs and tastes and provided a free instructor so that customers chatted and knit under her practiced eye and also found a nook where they could rest their feet. The introduction of elevators, or "lifts," facilitated shopping even more; Macy's and Wanamakers pioneered with electric lighting; telephones, pneumatic tubes and cash registers followed. With improved glass-manufacturing techniques, enormous street windows permitted sales promotions to lure customers inside and upstairs. They came in droves.

Buyers unable to reach stores for knitting needs relied on well-illustrated mail-order catalogs of "Decorative Art Needlework" to fill the void. One New York house supplied a shopping service for out-of-towners, who had only to state the highest price they would pay and let the store's own "judgment and active experience" make the selections. The proprietress carried *everything* in dry goods, including aprons stamped for embroidery in flowers, birds or such bon mots as "How doth the busy little bee?"; "I don't care what the daisies say"; "When daylight is flitting we take up our knitting." The latter cost forty cents, postage paid.

Within a few years mail order became a source for yarn as well, and needlework magazine advertisements offered it at greatly reduced prices along with premiums of free instructions, knitting needles and crochet hooks. One company advertised its bargain rates for yarn directly from the mill: "[W]e believe that every woman who knits or crochets wants the *best* yarn that can be made at a *fair* price. . . . We deliver LAWRETTE yarn anywhere in the U.S. at the *regular mill price*—full ounce skeins." *Lady's Bazaar* augmented its published patterns by opening a mail-order service for twenty-five-cent instruction booklets. Mail-order giant Sears Roebuck bragged of its knitting materials: "The pleasure of knitting is greatly enhanced by working with good material. The line of yarns we quote is the best, and we take pains to send out such quality that we will have no occasion to apologize, but, on the other hand, are sure to please our customers and gain their future trade." Sears garnered rural customers by stocking a wide variety of yarn weights and colors, giving substantial reductions for quantity orders and promising speedy service.

Whether buying yarn retail or through mail order, knitters who wondered whether weight and consistency matched their patterns received inconsequential help from the latter, which provided little information on specific yarn, needle size or gauge. In her book's introduction, Elvira Corbould, admitting that many readers complained about her patterns' calling for too many (or too few) stitches, attributed this to their use of a different quality of wool from that prescribed, that they knit too loosely—or too tightly, any one of which could spell disaster for stockings, where "a slight thing makes a good deal of difference in the fit." As for yarn, her description of the two most commonly used was not enlightening: "Merino is the thickest and most harsh kind of yarn made"; "Saxony is a trifle less coarse; Saxony is the usual yarn sold for socks and gentlemen's stockings; it ought to be very strong, and to appear about the same size as Berlin [a kind of yarn used in fancy work of the period]. If it looks finer (and some of it does) put on more stitches than are given."

For checking needle size, knitters were directed to Chamber's or Walker's Bell Gauge, similar to modern gauges where the needle is inserted into numbered holes, though one leading instructress remarked that "many do not consider it necessary, especially as gauges are somewhat expensive." Even if the knitter used the "right yarn" and the "right needle" and knit "moderately loosely," she still received all the blame if the garment didn't fit. Corbould weaseled out by giving high points for satisfaction to knitted "couvrettes" (doilies), since size was not a consideration. *Dorcas* increased "knitter guilt" by scolding, "In working these patterns the knitter must have the same degree of faith which is necessary for a cure in taking homeopathic medicine. 'The doctor knows.' Keep this in mind, and remember that each pattern has been worked twice. . . . Remember this, even though it 'may not sound right,' and work on blindly to the end of row or round, and, our word for it, you will find that the 'end justifies the means.' " This was indeed strong medicine, and knitters might have swallowed the dose had not these cautionary words ensued: "Ours is not so well regulated a family but that mistakes occur, even after we have done our best. In locking up his form the printer may unbeknowingly knock off a letter or word, thereby changing the entire meaning of a sentence." To a knitter, readers huffed, "We know about that!"

Since patterns seldom provided stitches or rows to the inch, the knitters were indeed hard-pressed. The first mention of gauge seen by this author, in *Harper's Bazaar* in 1870, was a "Lady's Knitted Under Vest . . . to be worn under high-necked dresses instead of a vest." Instructions called for "heavy wooden Needles in the common patent stitch," the needle size to be determined by whatever produced this result: "Each rib of the design measures about half an inch, 8 rounds in length being 1¼ inches." In 1885, "Jenny June" finally advised knitters to make a swatch (though she didn't use that term): "Knit a few rows, and then measure them carefully. You will see thus how many rows of your work make an inch and can calculate exactly how many stitches will be needed." Other writers studiously avoided the issue.

With sparse stipulations about gauge and a paucity of illustrations, knitters had to visualize the end product. Some terms, such as "muffattee," "pulse warmer," "bosom friend," "flesh scrubber" (washcloth), "fascinator" ("place the end with the bow upon the head, and draw the other gracefully around the neck so as to fall over the shoulders") and "wristers" were common and spoke for themselves. Others, such as "Knitted Cover for a Piano Stool," were self-explanatory since Victorian knitters knew a stool from a bench as they regularly gathered around their pianos.

To assist beleaguered knitters, a profusion of books on knitting and other needle arts flooded the market. Annie Frost noted in her *Ladies' Guide*, "Books of new designs have appeared by the dozens." "Miss Arnold," now the folksier "Nellie Arnold," responded to "the loud call for a new book and new patterns" (her original one had sold more than forty thousand copies) by bringing out fifty-two new patterns, including "a full series of twelve illustrated tidies procured at much expense from London and Paris, and not before made in this country." The old snob appeal of European designs still reigned!

Writers relied upon verbal ingenuity to convey an image and "feel" of the finished product. Corbould wrote of her "Lady's Knitted Woolen Vest, or Jersey" that it was "beautifully warm and comfortable . . . of the greatest comfort to those who suffer from the cold"; of her "Shetland Shawl": "A scarlet or violet crocheted border improves it. It can be finished off with a fringe or not, as suits the taste"; of her "Knee Cap": "These are very comfortable for people who are at all rheumatic." Miss H. Burton, who cited her authorship as "By A Lady Expert," had dozens of patterns but nary an illustration. Her directions for a "Lady's Muffattee (Quick Pattern)" filled only three lines (including "with a bone crochet needle make a very narrow crochet edging lengthwise up and down each rib. This has a very pretty and bright effect"), while another, "Gentleman's Muffattee," on the same page required a half-page of instructions. Without illustrations, the "Lady Expert" fell back upon the printed word:

[Antimacassar] Two stripes of green and purple look very nice.

[Shetland shawl with 320 stitches cast on] Any fancy stitch will do. It had better be a rather simple one.

[Hearth rug] It makes a pretty border to put scarlet stripes at regular intervals.

[Head scarf] It makes the cloud prettier to add a little scarlet crocheted to the tassel.

["A Common Quilt"] This is a quick and neat quilt but is not so pretty as the other patterns.

["A High Bodice"] This pattern is for an ordinary figure, but after one trial the knitter will find it can be altered to any size.

["Round Sofa Cushion"] These cushions used to be very fashionable at one time, although they are seldom seen now. However, fashions change so quickly that they may, perhaps be used again.

["Child's Knitted Reins"] On the ends, sew little bells.

[This Knit 1, Purl 1 pattern was for a "Gentleman's Waist Coat"] When you have knitted it long enough, work up the other side in the same manner, and send it to a tailor to be made up. This knitting will not run when cut.

When Miss Burton added the cautionary "These petticoats pull out several inches longer after being washed" to her instructions for a "Lady's Scarlet and White Petticoat (Worn Inside of a Flannel

One)," she added one more variable for the harassed knitter—laundering. Others, worried more by shrinkage than stretching, advised stitchers to knit "moderately loose." "Home" books and magazines bombarded knitters with laundering and moth-repelling treatments, and even etiquette books provided household remedies, recipes and fabric-care hints, such as these special washing instructions for a "Nubia," a long, knit hood/cape of soft fleecy yarn:

> First braid the tassels, then make a hot suds with fine castile soap, and instead of rubbing or wringing it with the hands, run it through the wringing machine. Then open the nubia as widely as possible and spread it on some clean place to dry. A bed is a good place for this. After it is thoroughly dry take the braid out of the tassels, and the pretty little waves will be in them just as before washing. It is the rubbing and the twisting of a nubia, or any knit article, which damages it, and makes it look old and worn instead of looking light, airy and fleecy, as it does at first.

A novel washing method for knit laces culminated in adding a weak solution of gum arabic to the rinse water, patting the lace around the outside of a large wine bottle and standing the bottle in the sunshine to dry the lace. It was then guaranteed to "wear longer, stay cleaner, and have a rich, new lacy look" if it were peeled off carefully and placed between the "white leaves of a heavy book" for further pressing. Moths were thwarted by placing paper, linen or "blotting paper" moistened with turpentine (or turpentine mixed with camphor and alcohol) in the drawer or wardrobe in which knits were stored.

Since woolen undergarments were notoriously scratchy, silk's lighter weight, lessened bulk and smoother texture soon made it the preferred medium, but knitting the intricately patterned silk stockings that were de rigueur for the well-shod lady called for dexterity and patience since the silk was fine, the needles small and the number of stitches staggering. Major manufacturers, Florence Silk Mills, Corticelli Yarn Company, and Brainerd and Armstrong, produced a wide variety of colors for stockings, underwear, gloves, mittens and vests, and published inexpensive instruction booklets. To protect her precious silk hose when "driving to a ball or an evening party," the knitter drew "leggings" over her stocking and shoe instep. An overall shoe covering (usually called a "knitted overshoe" or "boot") appeared in almost every instruction book or column. One was recommended "for traveling or indoor toilette, and being light and easy, may serve either for a house or overshoe. If it be designed only to keep the dust off other shoes, it must, of course, be made without the heel." *Peterson's'* Jane Weaver showed one "intended to be worn over the boot in cold and frosty weather. It is fastened around the ankle with a bow ribbon." An "Evening carriage shoe" resembled a simple rectangle, but its designer reassured: "When you think the shoe is long enough, cast off. Double it lengthwise, and sew up the ends: put a bit of fringe round it, run in a string, and although it will look like an oblong square, if you put it on, you will find it will fit every well."

The excitement of knitting stockings spilled over into other knit-

Lady's knitted fichu mantilla, 1868.

ting projects, especially afghans in new designs and stitches. Popular again were chatelaine bags and purses, carried in the hand or fitted with a hook to fasten onto the belt of the wearer and "wrought in an intricate pattern in beads . . . [which] are a pretty addition to a lady's toilet, and are dainty and stylish."

While high style was important to most knitters, some grappled with rugged items such as the economical "carpet" Medora Hart knit from narrowly cut strips of old woolen clothes sewn together and dyed. She was so satisfied with hers that she explained her method to *Peterson's'* readers:

> My knitting-needles are wooden ones, made for this purpose. They are about a yard long, and near the size of my little finger. I have a round knob fastened on the end of each needle to prevent the stitches from slipping off, and the other ends are jointed. I commence by casting on sixty stitches just as I would for a stocking; then I take the idle needle and knit across, and as soon as I get the stitches all knit on to this one, I take the other and knit back again, and continue in this way until I get enough to go from one end of the room to the other, then I commence another breadth.

Hart's "plain knitting," however, was the exception to the rule of early Victorian knitting since most workers preferred decorative pieces such as doilies, antimacassars and clothing with complicated, ornate stitchery. Within a few years, when active women joined already eager sportsmen in outdoor recreation, their knitting of choice would become practical yet colorfully stylish sweaters, caps and stockings appropriate to their publicly active lives.

8.

Sporty Victorian Knitters

Though much of late nineteenth-century knitting history parallels that of prior decades, women's new-found interest in active sports subtly effected changes in her domestic role, of which knitting was a part. With increased emphasis on exercise, timidly introduced by "calisthenics" in the earlier decades of the century and bolstered in the Civil War era by female endorsement of ice skating (when they dared to wear the new clocked, scarlet, gray and blue stockings rather than conventional whites), women flocked to archery dressed like delicate, skirted versions of William Tell, with sprightly feathers arching from their caps and color-coordinated dark green stockings peeking out from voluminous skirts. When croquet reached its apex in the seventies and eighties and croquet set manufacturers added candle sockets to wickets to allow nighttime playing, women sheathed themselves in incongruous silk-and-lace raiment for its festive competitions. With "spooning" (spreading the legs to hit the croquet ball between them) considered unladylike, and clothing unsuitable for vigorous movement anyhow, women soon defected to other sports.

Dress reformer Abba Woolson prayed for the day when women would emerge from their "vast, swaying, undefined, and indefinite mass of drapery, into the shape which God gave to his human beings" and to agonize over woman's tendency to "hide and confuse the contours of this common human form, as if they were a disgrace to her." Even the shawls that every woman slavishly knit in the fanciest

"The Convalescent," 1882.

and laciest stitches drew Woolson's scorn for impeding movement in walking, rendering the arms useless and cutting off circulation. She accepted them only for those occasions "when we have a mind to be statuesque at all hazards, or when we rest at ease on carriage cushions, or take a siesta at home." For walking or working, she recommended a "simple, sleeved garment" (later known as a sweater) that would soon outrank all other knitted garments.

With the introduction of tennis into the United States, women who adopted this "genteel" (still untainted by professionalism) sport were cautioned to play "in moderation," something well assured by the prescribed ankle-length, tight-waisted tennis frocks. Eventually, when waists loosened and skirts, though still three yards around at the hemline, rose to just above the ankle, they could pursue the court game more vigorously. After a hot and bracing game, players swaddled themselves in knit "tennis capes." A subscriber, noting that *Dorcas*'s caveat on *the* proper tennis outfit included only "cap, cape, and sash," waggishly queried whether a short skirt was not also al-

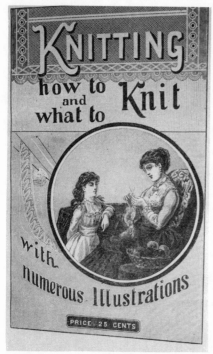
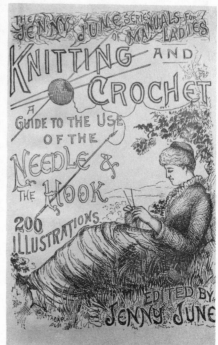

An 1884 instruction manual. *An 1885 instruction manual.*

lowable! *Dorcas* replied airily that it would indeed be allowable, along with "striped stockings, lawn-tennis shoes, and a bodice. We fear you would astonish even the natives if you appeared [only] in the knitted outfit spoken of in *Dorcas*. If you wish to conform to the prevailing style, tie your sash at the left side; but if you are desirous of inaugurating a fashion of your own, tie it behind. You'll undoubtedly soon have many followers." Talk about daring!

American women, conceding the necessity for recreation to build muscle and reduce "surplus avoirdupois," the scourge of the century, also swarmed to golf even though a few swank clubs first excluded them. As golf's necessary freedom of movement required emancipation from tight clothes, knitters hastened to execute warm and stretchy sweaters for impeccable attire, renaming the popular British "jerseys" "golfers" and pairing them with dark serge skirts to achieve a "jaunty, convenient and pretty costume." A fashion writer described them: "Hand knit, in fancy stitches and colors; they come well over the hips and are put on over the head, and fastened with small pearl buttons. Black, red, and navy, either striped or plain, are the colors most worn." Underneath it all, this same modish doyenne of golf recommended a short-on-the-hip-and-not-too-tightly-laced corset, for "[w]ith no corsets at all, a woman has an untidy appearance." After viewing corset advertisements in women's magazines, one is dumbstruck to contemplate a golfer swinging her club while her structured undergirding rearranged pounds of flesh into new and "more desirable" contours.

Sweaters were, of course, knit for men as well as women. The other crucial addition to the golfer's wardrobe, especially for men, were golf stockings, meant to be seen and admired. The term "golf stocking" applied to one knit in a fancy stitch or with a "fancy top," or, better still, *both*, and manuals were crammed with patterns as golf increased in popularity.

Of all the new sports, none had greater impact than bicycle riding. The "Bicycle Craze" endured less than five years, but at its height in the mid-nineties more than three hundred bicycle manufacturers had entered the ring. Specialized newspapers and magazines, chock-full of advertisements of wheels and accessories, catered to the new enthusiasts as armories, roller skating rinks and dance halls were converted to academies where tyros could secure basic instruction. As one social historian wrote, "If its day was brief, it raised the hem, leveled the classes, and widened a generation's horizon." And, it can be added, returned women to feverish sock knitting! Bicycle riding exposed legs, and they had best be stylishly shod.

Men, already riding in the eighties, assembled in local cycling clubs and "wheelmen" associations to improve roads, to publish news of cycle rallies and competitions and to educate their members about new products, safety, riding etiquette and tasteful clothes for their new sport. Quickly accommodating to practicality in dress, they favored somber colors to mask the soil from unpaved roads and short-tailed coats to fall to each side of the saddle-seat, donned long-visored caps for protection from dust and sun and replaced long pants with "knickerbockers." To these, riders added knee-high socks and sturdy, reinforced "bicycle shoes." If they belonged (and most did) to a cycle club, they wore club insignias on jackets or adopted popular

A gentleman of the natty nineties.

"club sweaters." Instructions for knitting the new golf or cycling sweaters filled the "needle magazines," and devoted knitters saw to it that their men were nattily attired.

The "fair sex" didn't cycle in large numbers until the nineties, but when they did, the social revolution was launched. Women who formerly stayed at home didn't! They pedaled in twos and threes, then with clubs, and eventually with *men*. Since women exercised as they cycled, the new sport appeared to be a healthy antidote to "ner-

"The Knitting Circle," 1882.

vousness," leading one doctor, previously alarmed at women's lack of physical exertion ("[H]er chances for physical development outside her household duties are limited to a degree that would be ridiculous if it were not pitiable"), to consider the bicycle heavensent; another extravagantly pronounced cycling "nerve tonic . . . deliverance, revolution, and salvation"; the female author of *Bicycling for Ladies* claimed: "The system is invigorated, the spirit is refreshed, the mind, freed from care, swept of dusty cobwebs, is filled with new and beautiful impressions. You have conquered a new world, and exultingly you take possession of it."

Surprisingly, the liberating bicycle concurrently stimulated an activity within women's "sphere": knitting. The special "affinity for each other" of bicycling and knitting was marked by a writer who noted that although golf stockings were "most stylish on the wheel" for both men and women, the "inartistic patterns and unharmonious colors" of machine-made ones called for corrective action by knitters. She glowed, "[T]he bicycle fad is responsible for the revival of the almost forgotten and homely art of using the knitting needles. . . . Some brainy women, with an eye to possible emolument, inaugurated the knitting fad. Now the women who wish to be thought up-to-date are making substantial golf hose for themselves as well as their male relatives and friends."

Women cyclists may have bred a social revolution, but they weren't sure how to dress for it. For a woman to wear a tight corset and an ankle-length skirt five yards around at the hem was ridiculous, and to restrain the skirt from riding up around her knees or getting caught in the spokes or chain, she sometimes tucked it into her boot tops. To avoid its being caught by the wind, she either inserted weights into pockets along the hemline and removed them after her spin, or attached guards and clips to hoist her skirt enough to foil entanglement with the flying wheel yet maintain decency. She needed wardrobe assistance.

The first specially designed cycling costumes were trim suits of matching skirt and jacket for cooler weather, but when riders doffed their jackets, they preferred smart sweaters with the popular leg o'mutton sleeves and nipped-in waists. Knit in simple ribbed patterns to achieve a form-fitting hourglass effect, they were guaranteed to

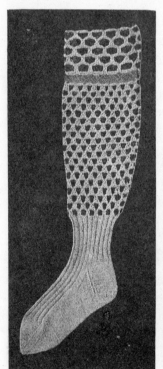

Fancy cycling or golf stockings, 1897.

Woman's cycling sweater, 1897.

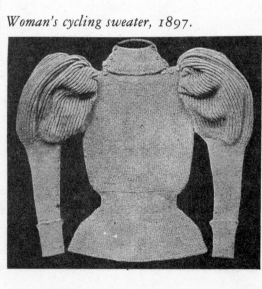

Knitted undervest for the hour-glass figure, 1891.

attract admiring glances. Bicyling arbiter Maria Ward, who cautioned "A corset, if one is worn, should not extend below the waist-line, and should have elastic side-lacing" and recommended carrying on the wheel "an extra change of underwear, with a change of neckwear" when touring, also outlined sweater guidelines:

> The sweater should come well up around the neck, and pull down easily below the saddle; it is better too long than not long enough to cover the large muscular masses that have been at work, and may be turned up if in the way. It should slip on easily, and be soft and wooly, and not so cumbersome that the coat cannot slip on over it and be buttoned up to the throat . . . [and] may be worn for coolness or warmth. As an outside garment, it allows air to pass through its mesh easily; worn under another garment, it is very warm, retaining its heat.

Godey's Magazine, favoring dark colors relieved with white or black stripes or figures, over tasteless "bizarre patterns and startling contrasts," recommended a dark sweater sporting a white shield front and reverse as "an excellent style especially for thin figures, as it gives the appearance of breadth; it consists of a double front in which the 'kerchief' or veil may be tucked away." While *Godey's* spoke of a "kerchief" and most riders tucked one into their pockets for emergencies, knitters opted for simple, quick-to-make mufflers to provide better protection for the throat "when riding against cutting winds" and agreed that "[a] loosely knitted woolen scarf wrapped once around the throat allows plenty of ventilation . . . and by tucking the ends inside the jacket, you have an admirable chest protector."

Headgear generally followed the dictum that "the hat should be close-fitting, in order to present no resistance to the wind," and a knit Scottish "Tam o'Shanter" was considered rakish and snappy, especially when pierced with a "jaunty quill stuck in one side." Not all riders subscribed to knit hats, however, and big favorites were "The Alpine" and "The Sailor," although a strong gust could send the latter spinning.

Even special suits left much to be desired, and women who had previously denigrated dress reform became apostles of the new creed of "rational dress." Some prominent New York women, sick and tired of mud-stained hems, formed the "Rainy Day Club" and shocked staid New Yorkers with skirts elevated three inches above the ground, eliciting this popular joke: "Q: Why does a mother want her daughter vaccinated above the knee? A: Because bare legs may be in fashion before she grows up!" Still disgruntled, even with short- ened skirts, first a few, and then thousands, resurrected the "bloomer" for cycling. The mid-century campaign for bloomers had misfired in most parts of the country despite their acknowledged practicality, and even *Woman's Words*, a new periodical whose avowed purpose was "woman's advancement," editorialized, "We respect what may be termed individualism, but we have no sympathy with those of our sex who persist in habitually wearing those uncouth garments fashioned apparently after bathing suits." Public derision shadowed the "bloomers" until most of their leaders, feeling that the greater cause of women's freedom was lost in antipathy to the cloth- ing, capitulated. Elizabeth Cady Stanton counseled fellow reformer Lucy Stone: "We put it on for greater freedom, but what is physical freedom compared with mental bondage? By all means, have the new dress made long."

Those original bloomers, baggy pants tied close at the calf, gave way to a tighter and shorter version for cycling, and one doctor who recognized their practicality observed that bloomers were becoming

"The Bloomers," 1894.

to the "right woman" and could even "increase and set off the beauty of the wearer while masking her defects." Such a garment could not be all wrong! Bloomers became the "town talk" in every city of America. Tin Pan Alley denizens wrote literally dozens of songs, most with tart lines and innuendos. Crowds gathered at restaurants where patrons were served by waitresses in bloomers; a theater sponsoring a "Bicycle Night" asked the audience to come in knickerbockers and bloomers; fights ensued whenever a bystander made sly comments about a "bloomerette." Somehow, everyone considered lady cyclists fair game, and wags and pundits leaped into the fray with abandon. Columns were set aside in bicycle trade magazines for the latest guffaws about women's newfangled riding costumes. One example will suffice:

> A biker asked a farmer,
> "Has a lady wheeled this way?"
> And the farmer told the biker,
> "It's mighty hard to say,
> From the costumes they are wearing
> From the mountains to the sea,
> If the biker is a she one,
> Or the biker is a he!"

Women responded to the blandishments of most males and the more conservative women until bloomers were finally forsaken in favor of "safer" divided skirts. In 1896, *The Wheelwoman* drove the last nail into the coffin: "No woman can endure contempt long, whether she knows she is right or wrong."

Bicycling, adopted by all classes, wielded a democratizing influence as the camaraderie of the wheel prompted cyclists to strike up conversations with other riders, and upper-class women who had been cautioned to avoid speaking to strangers when going "abroad" from their homes now braved unconventional predicaments. An etiquette advisor allowed gentlemen to talk to a strange "wheelwoman" without an introduction only if she was in trouble ("It is always proper to speak to a wheelwoman who may be in need of assistance—humanity requires it") but not to regard this a "proper introduction." Women still liked chivalry, he reassured, and he, for one, was glad of it: "We prefer the good old-fashioned kind, the gentle woman. In fact, we have mounted her on a pair of wheels. She has broadened her intellect, but we want the same sweet, coquettishly, feminine woman just the same."

This image of the old-time gentlewoman was recalled wistfully by comparing (not too favorably) the woman of the bicycle wheel to her grandmother of the spinning wheel. Each cycling magazine featured nostalgic odes to the spinning wheel (usually with some reference to knitting), such as these verses from "The New Woman and Her Grandam":

"Winding Up the Yarn,"
1897.

My grandam used to turn her wheel,
    And spin the glistening tow;
Or knit a sock as she'd sit and rock
    The cradle to and fro.
And when that sock was worn or torn,
    Oh, then with soft-spun yarn it
Was soon made new all through and through,
    For my grandam she would darn it.

My grandam's daughter's spins
    The wheel with her glistening toe,
The whole day long, for she isn't strong,
    So she daren't work you know.
But when her wheel of polished steel,
    With nothing to forewarn it,
Hits a snag kerplunk and gets a "punk,"
    Why, she's almost sure to "Darn it!"

Many of the "old-fashioned" ladies worried lest young women riding with gentlemen become "coarse," "less refined" and "thoughtless," and were not comforted by a remark in a women's "domestic" magazine that "[i]t does not require uncommon powers of observation to enable a person to see that a young man treats a girl with greater familiarity after having accompanied her on a long bicycle ride." Such incipient "familiarity" was undoubtedly good news to many a sheltered lass on whom the bicycle bestowed not only mobility but privacy, something hard to come by in turn-of-the-century urban areas. To others, fear that privacy would be infringed upon during cycling was so acute that a patent pended for a "curtain screen for women bicyclists" to conceal their identity from the public gaze. Of this, *Godey's* remarked editorially, "Verily, the way of the feminine cyclists is hard enough without imposing further difficulties. Fancy a woman with such an awkward arrangement flapping about her having the courage to wheel at all!" Of more practical use were front-mounted rearview mirrors to compensate for the novice's inability to turn around in the saddle and an ear-splitting warning whistle activated by a foot lever.

As long as style-conscious bloomered or skirted "wheelwomen" were exposed to the public eye, a handsome stocking showing over the top of a specially constructed leather cycling shoe was mandated for high fashion. Maria Ward steadfastly boosted carefully cut knickerbockers ("smooth and tight just over the top of the hips, and fitting easily below; not fulled or gathered; full at the knees, and boxed or finished with a band and button and button-hole; nothing elastic on any count") that could hold stocking tops firmly in place without garters, "which suppress circulation, or pull if attached at the waist." Popular bicycle stockings were footless, with a narrow strap fitting over the side of the foot. Foot and leg sections, being covered by the boot, were knit in dull colors (or leftover scraps), but colorful cuffs were intricately designed with fancy stitches such as cables, openwork, braids, diagonals, ribs, "lightning stripes" or multicolor designs such as "the gayest tartan plaids or checks." When one innovator saved time and energy by capping plain all-purpose stockings with separate knitted cuffs for each outing, pattern books featured these four- or five-inch-wide interchangeable cuffs in a variety of designs. A *New York Daily Tribune* article revealed that an "elaborate top in two, three or even four colors, with a plain heavy ribbed stocking, is the most popular style just now, although many skillful knitters continue a design throughout an entire stocking, with as many as twenty balls or more of different colored yarn." The writer guessed that most knitters, exhausted from the intricacies of the top, would welcome the relief of a plain leg. A special top, or "turnover," was the "basket top," a two-color plaited design "recently sent over from London." Still those vestigial traces of Europeanism!

Taking full advantage of the sock-knitting fad, one popular manual filled over thirty pages with instructions for enough stocking styles to match every sports need and even "elastic hose for invalids" for injured cyclists. A favored stocking was knit in "Railroad Stitch," a pattern caused by dropping alternating stitches to form "ladders" all the way back to the ribbed cuff, resembling, of course, railroad tracks. The very name evoked adventure as the vast network of real railroads crisscrossed the country, and every magazine carried a pattern; even afghans were knit in the stitch, with ribbon run through the ladders. Marcia Watson's *Manual* advised: "Ravel the dropped stitches to the top by putting the finger underneath and pulling the work over it. This will give a pretty, striped open-work appearance, and extend the stocking to be a sufficient length." Since the stockings were made without heels and toes, they were good learning projects for beginners. *Dorcas Magazine* wrote glowingly, "So much time, patience and skill are required to knit and shape a pair of full length stockings, that many ladies who are fond of knitting do not like to attempt so long and tedious a piece of work. All the difficult part is eliminated from the railroad stocking."

The stocking-knitting fad reached such a peak that one set of instructions even appeared in rhyme, beginning:

> To knit a stocking, needles four,
> Cast on three needles, and no more,
> Each needle stitches eight and twenty,
> Then one for seam stitch will be plenty

and plowing relentlessly on for another page and a half before reaching the toe:

Then draw up all to close it tight,
And with a darning needle bright,
Your end of thread securely run,
And then, hurrah! the stocking's done!

When they weren't knitting socks, experienced knitters fashioned lace edgings and insertions. The *Ladies' Home Journal*'s needlework editor presented a "trio of pretty, useful and practical patterns" that turned out to be an insertion for window curtains, a "vine leaf lace suitable for trimming an underskirt," and a necktie, a "useful trifle . . . intended to adorn." She considered knit edgings the ideal task for women under the "spell of knitting needles, whose busy fingers love to ply the magic pins to good purpose" and offered a "Bachelor's Tea Cosy" for that rascal who unreasonably expected his tea and coffee piping hot. A hurrah for the nonsporting knitters!

9.
Old Knitters
in New Roles

By the end of the nineteenth century, advances in industry so lessened the importance of exclusive home production of necessities that women, relying upon their husbands' earnings to finance the outlays, shifted into the "feminine" role of purchaser rather than provider of their family's needs and acquired a new social importance through their "consumerism." Upon the discovery that women spent over 90 percent of the money, some ten million dollars annually, the founder of the National Housewives League of New York concluded that "[M]arriage is a contract by which a man becomes the producer and woman the dispenser" and urged women to acquire training for prudent spending for food, clothing, housing and education. Equating household management (the "New Housekeeping," as some called it) with men's "business" work, reformer Ida Tarbell urged women to demand commensurate business education. Ivory Soap's makers, noting that "the increase of culture and intelligence brings a demand for more highly refined and better articles of home use and consumption," asserted their product was the favorite with "people who choose carefully." The courtship of the housewife had begun.

With many authorities bemoaning that valuable training was lost with the demise of household manufacture, pressure mounted to return "domestic science" and "household arts" to school curricula. Good housekeeping, according to one historian, once meant educating students to "spin, weave, sew, embroider, knit, darn, crochet, patch, do laundry work well, prepare wholesome meals, make butter, cheese, candles, and perform other necessary household duties" as well as fostering such virtues as "cheerfulness, happiness, frugality, independence, diligence, perseverance, skill, and self-reliance." With the demise, grandmothers had to be pressed into service for mending, darning and knitting, a stereotype recaptured in such verse lines as "My Grandma used to sit and knit from morning till the night,/ With her needles glancing, glancing, when the sun was shining bright,/She knitted stockings for us all, and all of us agreed,/That she'd find a satisfaction fitting out a centipede" and "Grandmother knows how a stocking grows,/Ribbing and purling and heels and toes;/Now she is teaching our little Rose." But consumerism demanded more than grandparental help, and "Home Ec" or "Household Arts" entered the curriculum in almost every school system, though some educators considered knitting too "ordinary" for class and better learned at home. At Columbia University's graduate school for teachers, however, knitting was included with sewing, and teachers were apprised of potential donors of free "textile materials" for their classes: Brainerd and Armstrong Company in Connecticut for "raw silk by the skein," the Horstman Company of Philadelphia for Minerva yarn, and Bernard Ulmann of New York for Bear Brand yarns.

"Miss T. M. James"'s course on *Needlework, Knitting and Cutting-Out*, which was published in London, New York and Bombay, became a standard for teaching younger "Home Ec" girls (boys were engaged in their "Manual Arts" classes), relying heavily upon drills "by which numbers of children will act with the precision of an individual." The thimble drill boggles the mind. In this drill, students who had to master needle manipulation before yarn was allowed plodded inexorably through each meticulously illustrated step as instructresses barked left-hand commands: "Left hand—show!"; "Lift knitting needle"; "Turn to the right—hold"; "Push." Then began the drill for the right hand: "Right hand—show!"; "Hold wool"; "Forefinger under—curve," and so on. The knitting class motto, "Line upon line, little by little," spurred bewildered stragglers, as teachers ("bright and cheery, possessing an abundant store of patience") called the signals with the authority of drill sergeants.

Others recommended the young knit useful objects rather than "specimens," squares of plain knitting to show specific "jobs" such as narrowing a stocking back, turning a heel and "chaining" an edge. Ellen and C. A. Claydon's *Knitting Without "Specimens"* provided patterns for successive stages of a girl's knitting, beginning with outfits for her doll ("Doll's Muff Knitted on Bone Needles"; "Doll's Shawl Knitted on Bone Needles"; "Doll's Woolen Shoe"; "Doll's Knitted Petticoat") and graduating to her own garments and accessories such as a "Hug-Me-Tight," "Shawl or Wrap," "Lunch Bag for Child's Own Use," "Boy's Marble Bag" and "Child's Sock." In this way, children learned the rudiments of taking careful measurements, working out new stitches, converting from one size to another, estimating the yarn needs and probable cost, and working in a cooperative effort to produce something useful.

Many rural communities arranged sales for children's class products such as knitted woolen socks, mufflers, woolen squares for "hospital comforts" and knitted washrags, and children in one town used their own ingenuity to organize games and contests for fairgoers: speed in knitting a square, sewing on buttons, tying knots, removing a flat automobile tire and throwing ropes (this was Texas!).

The *New York Daily Tribune*'s "Tribune Sunshine Society" column, which brought news of knitting fads and patterns to its members, responded to the growing number of knitting children by opening its ranks to "Little Sunshiners," who paid a small "initiation fee" of a donation to a charity. *Stitches* began a special "Page for Children" and announced a monthly contest for girls fourteen and under for "the most careful and even work." As an example of a suitable submission, a lace piece knit by a thirteen-year-old was illustrated: "See how evenly she has put in the stitches without ever missing one, and the work is so nice and clean any mother would be proud to have her little angel make a piece of lace as pretty as this." Three prizes would be awarded ("[T]he loveliest wools a little girl ever owned, with crochet and knitting needles, and a book of directions to go with them") plus publication of the winner's name and address and a *picture* of the knitting so that "all your friends will see how much our editor thinks of your work." The first month's winners had knit a piece of diamond lace ("We congratulate Miss Isabel on the evenness of her work, and on the beautiful, fine stitches"), a doll's hood

Spool knitting, 1909.

("Our editor could not find a single mistake") and a pair of "lovely" slippers.

Though their daughters were mastering needle dexterity, mothers who spurned housewifery's exaltation as a science preferred the contest for female suffrage, despite the characterization of them by the "antis" as "a sisterhood of cranks who wear grey woolen underwear and number seven shoes and whose skirt and waist don't meet in the back." Of the hundreds of excuses for denying suffrage, most detractors grounded their arguments on women's perceived penchant for modish garments: ". . . since fig leaves in Eden, they have rushed to don the latest horror, in clothes or conduct. It was hobble skirts last season. . . . This season it's 'Votes For Women'!" Style jokes followed: "If a woman voluntarily puts on a skirt which prevents her from stepping into a street car with safety, what can she know of liberty?"; "Women think too much of clothes to vote intelligently"; "Half the women have long bows and feathers on their hats extending far behind them, and endangering the eyes of their neighbors; such absence of regard for others shows they have no public conscience." Antis ridiculed the "idiocy" of wearing stockings with bathing costumes (*Utopia Yarn Book* gave a pattern for a decorous knit two-piece knee-length dress over matching drawstring bloomers) and concluded that such dimwits were incapable of voting: "[G]irls, just as soon as they reach mature years, always indulge in the nonsensical absurdity of WEARING STOCKINGS IN THE WATER, when ever they have a bathing-dress with a short skirt! Yet no man would ever dream of going into the water with his stockings on."

Wearying of those attacks, antis retreated to: "Women are appointed to be queens of the home"; "Women couldn't qualify because they wouldn't tell their age"; "The men will have to wash the dishes and darn their stockings when women vote"; "My mother was a woman, my wife is a woman, I love them, bless them, and I'd save them from the vote." Others longed for the woman "[i]n whose home

Lady's knitted two-piece bathing suit, 1916.

it is sweet to dwell,/Who believes in raising children, and not in raising h--l!" Further afield, some imputed the "craze" for suffrage to "mental aberration" of a "certain time" in middle age: "Women at such a time ought not to be making fools of themselves on platforms or politics, but retired to the quiet or private life until they are in touch with normal feelings and sympathies again."

Political activity aroused both masculine and feminine suspicion. Grover Cleveland reappeared on the scene and blamed female participation in public affairs for precipitating a "dangerous undermining effect upon the characters of the wives and mothers of our land"; a female anti heartily agreed that women had no place in politics, where "[t]he life is too public, too wearing, and too unfitted to the nature of women"; a politically disenchanted California female voter testified before Congress, "I will not deny that there are some dear, lovable, enthusiastic suffragists, but they know not what they do. . . . Think of the millions of women that have faith in you and that trust their husbands and fathers and brothers and sons to do what is just."

Into the breech bounded the knitting magazines. *Stitches* pledged to revive "the essentially feminine woman . . . the woman womanly" as an antidote to the "strenuous times of 'equal rights' and masculine garb . . . the mannish attire . . . the loud-mouthed girl of heavy tread, equal and ready to fight her own battles." Addressing the "restlessness and discontent" (both synonymous with that old nineteenth-century bugaboo, "nervousness"), the magazine reported ecstatically that physicians suggested that nervous women select a simple piece of knitting, "nothing with an elaborate pattern to tax the brain," and knit with steel needles since "the quick movement and the tiny click of the needles have a soothing, hypnotic influence that is restful to the overwrought women." Advising "every woman whose nerves are breaking under the weight of her complex life [to] try the quieting influence of needlecraft," the editors promised, "It will give her a more calm and rational view of life, it will lead her beside the still waters of simplicity."

Stitches envisioned this Eden of peace and simplicity only if frantic women exchanged knitting for tooting off to golf links, clubs, luncheons and dressing for dinner parties, all of which made them "nerve-wrecked and old." Another knitting magazine chimed in: "Knitting was once every woman's duty. Now it is her pleasure, her relaxation, her nerve-smoothing occupation for leisure moments in a busy life. . . . Knitting has taken on a new dignity." It was not the first time that knitting had been recommended as a palliative for nerves! Nor would it be the last.

"Forward women" such as Haryot Cahoon challenged the contention that knitting was justified for its soothing properties: "Of all nerve-destroying occupations knitting takes the lead. The ceaseless click of the needles and the muscular exertion combine to produce an exhaustion equal to the most vigorous exercise." Singling out lace knitters as engaged in the most time-consuming tasks for reasons of economy, she sniffed:

A vast amount of drudgery is sugar-coated with economy. . . . The world has outgrown knitted lace, just as it did the spinning-wheel long ago. Of course there are still women who make knitted lace, just as women did their own spinning for a long time after the majority of wheels were put away in the garret. Spinning died hard, and so does knitted lace. . . . If you wish to knit lace because you have more time on your hands than you know what to do with, you are the very one the world needs, with your youth and your energy and your industrious spirit. . . . [Don't] puzzle your brain over "knit one, skip one, purl one, drop one." Drop them all! That's best.

Lace knitting, along with the sock and waistcoat knitting of the nineties craze, continued unabated but was almost eclipsed when New York "society" trend setters knit heavy silk cravats in plaid, block or plain designs lined with very thin silk. Available in smart specialty shops for four to six dollars, they could be duplicated for a fraction of the cost; but cost was not the prime factor. Giving a "four-in-hand" knit by *oneself* was the ultimate token to a loved one, especially if the lining was "a bit of an old silk gown which might have been a favorite with her husband or her lover!" This return to femininity ("In our grandmother's day, sentiment ruled supreme") was typical of turn-of-the-century womanhood. As one writer rhapsodized, "All 'girls,' young and old, fiancees, sweethearts, wives, and mothers, love to make something *themselves* that the men whom they adore will wear! It is the womanliness in our nature coming out. To see the man that one is interested in, or that one loves, wearing something worked for *him alone*, appeals to the best side of one's nature." Nonknitters had to console themselves with upholstering plain wooden coat hangers with scented cotton to convert them into popular "shoulder hangers." If the gift was for a man, embroidering his initials on odorless cotton sufficed, "for even a suspicion of cologne, is essentially bad taste." In addition to knitting ties and sewing "shoulder hangers" for their men, women knit decorative open-worked white lisle stockings that showed at the ankle when avant-garde New York men abdicated high-buttoned or laced shoes in favor of low, shiny, patent leather "dancing slippers" fastened at the instep with broad taffeta bows for "full dress wear." One writer admitted, "This all sounds rather effeminate, but when a 'swagger' looking man with well fitting clothes starts such a fad, really anything he chooses 'goes,' and he is willing to hold himself responsible for what might, in another man, be called eccentricity."

Another social leader "started" the fad of knitting her own silk hosiery, something quite common to her foremothers. Another rage was to embroider the loved one's monogram on his golf sweater's cuff. What colonial women knew well appeared as news to an early twentieth-century columnist: "Indeed it seems that to be thoroughly up to date one must be engaged in knitting. . . . It is very pretty work and something which can be engaged in while having a social chat with one's friends." When avid knitter First Lady Edith Roosevelt invited ladies to the White House for knitting and sewing sessions of "woman talk" laced with political discussions, Cabinet members shivered at the prospect of having their reputations "unravelled by their knitting needles." During last-minute preparations for her stepdaughter Alice's White House wedding, Mrs. Roosevelt was reported to have sat alone knitting, an action attributed by gossips to a chilly relationship between them but by knitters to its tranquilizing effect upon jangled mother-of-the-bride nerves.

Knitting was mysteriously "feminine," a bit of sorcery beyond the ken of mere males. One magazine revealed that "all those little embellishments . . . are as mysterious to men as they are bewitching" and explained that a shawl "thrown over the head in a bewitching fashion" formed a graceful hood at the back in some "mysterious

way"; another shoulder wrap was "lacey and bewitching to an extreme"; *Delineator* recommended its "Bewitching Breakfast Cap. . . .
Not just to cover tumbled locks or curl crimpers—no indeed—but
to make one look twice as dainty and bewitching in one's negligee
costumes." These mysterious creatures were the "true" women, not
the orators on suffrage stumps.

Most undergarments, or "intimate wear," were knit of silk into
undervests ("for use beneath a spring gown without a coat when extra
warmth seems desirable . . . adds no ungainly bulk to the figure . . .
is particularly appropriate for use under thin shirtwaists which fashion now decrees may be worn on cold days as well as warm"); "breakfast jackets," close-fitting, waist-length "spencers" with necklines
threaded with silk ribbon; thigh-length "porch jackets" with ribbon
at both sleeves and around the waist (and for an extra-feminine look,
lapels embellished with four roses of "rose silk rope"); and "Ladies'
Chest Protectors" ("arranged to open under each arm and upon one
shoulder, so that it can be worn and removed without in any way
disarranging the bodice"). Knitters also worked dressy bags in silk,
since dangling a beautifully beaded, monogrammed "reticule" of
one's own design, though a regeneration of an earlier fad, afforded
the wearer the latest "look." Every booklet carried instructions for
patient beadwork knitters, from the "Floradora Knitted Purse,"
which could swing equally well from a neck chain or the wrist, to
beaded watch fobs and bookmarks.

Knitters protected their precious pieces with squares of fabric on
the lap that were later wrapped around the knitting when it was set
aside: "A yard of striped or plaided dimity trimmed around with one
of the many pretty imitation laces—Cluny, Valenciennes, or Tor-
chon—will be just the thing . . . especially welcome when engaged
in knitting long shawls, sweaters or golf vests now so popular." There
was keen interest in proper washing, and most agreed with the importance of high-quality yarn and of laundering silk like one's flan-
nels, in cool water with no wringing. Confusingly different, but following the nineteenth-century's Lydia Mary Child's hot-water
dictum, was *Ladies' Fancywork Magazine*'s advice to launder a wool
shawl by plunging it up and down in *hot* suds and when thoroughly
rinsed and dripped, attaching it to a sheet to dry. *Stitches* proposed
a sweater-drying technique: "Place the sweater inside a pillow case

A cape for any weather, 1906.   *Porch or comfy jacket, 1917*

or bag that is no longer than the sweater, and pin the opening of the
pillow case with the shoulders of the sweater to the line. This will
keep the sweater from stretching downward while drying." Laundering laces (and everyone was still knitting them) was said by a writer
who identified herself as "an authority" to be a "labor of love; time
and patience are important requisites to do it well, and it comes
especially within the province of the gentlewoman who possesses it."
The directions, including such cautions as "great delicacy of touch,"
"merely dabbed or patted," "pressed between the hands gently two
[*sic*] and fro in the water" and "water just sweetened with the finest
sugar candy," were enough to make anyone who accomplished the
task proud of her housewife badge.

One instruction book alternated its fashion tidbits, such as "Home
knit vests are now the fad. He'll doubly appreciate one of Utopia
Yarn" and "No cold can strike the chubby legs protected by Utopia
wool leggings," with aphorisms such as "No man was ever wise by

choice" and "The distance is nothing; it is only the first step that counts," a fitting reflection on knitters' endless stitching!

College girls adored cardigans' ease and omitted sleeves to adapt them for indoor vests, each style christened by *Modern Knitting* for one of the "Seven Sisters" colleges: "The Wellesley," "The Vassar," "The Smith," and so forth. With cycling continuing and golfing drawing more and more outdoor enthusiasts ("golf cranks"), knitters kept so busy on the most indispensable part of the athletic wardrobe—a warm, soft and light cardigan sweater prized for its adaptability to temperature changes—that golf, like cycling, was credited with restoring women to their more "feminine" needlework:

> The golf links gave up devotees for a few hours, the short skirt and the severe waistcoat were banished, and the attention turned to knitting a golf sweater—perhaps for the worker, perhaps for a brother, or some other girl's brother. Thousands of these sweaters

Knitted Norfolk jacket, 1904.

were made the past year, and through them the American girl acquired anew a taste for needlework, a taste that is increasing day by day, until the demand for new designs and new work is heard on every hand.

"New" also included "motoring" gear for warding off the chill in breeze-swept cars, where riders snuggled in knit automobile robes and the newer, long-length "motor sweaters" or "Norfolks," knit copies of men's belted jackets with a pocket on each side, combined, for women, with a knit skirt whose separately knit simulated "pleats" were later tacked on. To protect curls in open-air Phaeton models, women knit "automobile hoods" or "fascinators," more loosely knit than nineteenth-century "clouds," edged with fringe and crested with artificial flowers or satin bows. One fascinator's "beautifully unique and clouded effect" was said to suggest "the glowing sunset after the softening shades of night have begun to fall," an altogether "be-witching" illusion. Boating also attracted new devotees, and when the boat captain allowed "the little woman" a turn at the helm, she was nautically garbed in a pert, sailor-collared "yachting" or "outing" sweater.

One of the period's most popular knitting instruction booklets was Alice Maynard's 1903 *What to Knit and How to Do It*. Maynard, whose Madison Avenue shop's potpourri of yarns later attracted hordes of knitting pilgrims, dispensed basic, easy-to-follow instructions, especially for men's and women's golf stockings. Equally well adapted to cycling, they often had fancy, interchangeable, separate cuffs (with a few rows of ribbing at top and bottom to secure them in place) that could be slipped over the top of plain stockings to offer a change of patterns without changing the "lowers." If stockings were expected "to meet with rough wear," knitters were warned to knit the remainder of the sock in two pieces after dividing for the heel so that a new heel and sole could be re-knit if possible, horrible though the thought was to most knitters. Of the many heels recommended, one favorite was the "Balbriggan," named for the footed, cotton long johns of Balbriggan, Ireland, whose heels and gussets lent themselves to re-knitting.

The best-known woman's sweater was "The Maynard," the high-necked, cable-stitched cardigan that became the basic sweater of the

Knitted head scarf or
"fascinator," 1910.

Lady's yachting jacket, 1904.

decade, as much a trendsetter as the "Brooks Sweater" three or four decades later. Maynard's wasp-waisted, full-bosomed woman, her neck awkwardly stretched above the high, cuffed neckline and her rose-bedecked hat at a rakish tilt, appeared uncomfortable but securely garbed in "the right thing." Underneath the "right thing," she bowed to fashion's dictate by trusting her corset to relocate poundage into the coveted "Gibson Girl" silhouette. With the correlation between corsets and good golf as tenuous as "the weight or color of a player's skirt," one is reminded of famed golfer Babe Didrikson Zaharias's comment later in the century, "When I really want to blast one, I just loosen my girdle and let 'er fly." Still, golfers tolerated the corset's inconvenience and discomfort in slavish acquiescence to a fashion counselor's advice that "[a] woman ought to be slender; if that is impossible she must at least look slender." It was to this enviable result, not to reduce size but to improve measurements, that corsets were artfully designed: "If the flesh is loose and flabby they compress it within reasonable limits. If it is hard and firm they push it here and there as skillfully as a masseuse till it is out of harm's

The braided sweater, 1904.   *The Maynard sweater, 1903.*

way. . . . One should always have at least two pairs of corsets—and wear them on alternate days. The day's rest allows the bones to come back into their normal position after they have been somewhat strained by active use." No mention was made of the wearer's bones. No lady, cautioned the stylist, should appear in public (and hardly in private!) without her corset: "It is absolutely impossible for a woman to be well-dressed nowadays unless she is well corseted. The lines of the new fashions demand corresponding lines in the new figure, and even a Paris-made creation will be reduced to the ranks of utter banality if worn by a woman who has failed to acquire the smart silhouette." In view of this necessity, it was de rigueur to build a trusting relationship with one's corsetier, who could gauge with astonishing accuracy one's "amiable weakness in wishing to wear a pair of corsets too small." The body, once "firmed," was ready for emphasis, and to keep hips slim, knitters made black woolen waist-to-ankle tights to provide warmth while participating in outdoor sports.

Custom-made corsets were a luxury few could afford, and thrifty shoppers who also loathed the indignity of trying them on in stores purchased them through mail order. A variety of corsets, lacings and hooks were required to sculpt the prescribed canted, low-slung bust and hand-span waist while preserving "ease and comfort," and one company promised (with no apologies to Abraham Lincoln): "Women of grace may obtain a device for holding all of the clothing in perfect position some of the time; but to find an article which will hold *all* of the clothing in perfect position *all* of the time, is rather difficult." Sears Roebuck's catalog presented its selection: the top-priced ($1.33) "Flexibone, French Model Military Figure, Suitable for Average Shape . . . [to] mold the figure into graceful and well proportioned outlines, at the same time allowing the greatest freedom to the muscles"; the medium-priced ($.90), whose bones and steel ends were enclosed in a protecting covering to prevent "cutting through"; and the cheapest—at $.50. After viewing the wide variety

Knitted petticoat, 1910.   *Russian blouse, 1910.*

Blazer jacket and cap, 1912.   *Knitted "Hug-Me-Tight," 1912.*

of corsets, one is not surprised to learn that a silk "corset cover" to shroud the garment was a favorite knitting item. Sears offered additional aids: a "light as a feather, comfortable, and non-heating" bust form that would neither injure health nor "retard development" and a tempered-steel-wire, shape-retaining, nondetectable bustle "suitable for rainy day skirts." Should corset prices seem low, it is well to note that Sears that year advertised a piano guaranteed for twenty-five years for $98.50, a sewing machine for $10.45, men's "fancy knitted sweaters" for $2.25 to $4.25, a set of five sizes of knitting needles for three cents, shetland wool yarn at seven cents a skein and woolen knitting worsted at sixty-five cents per pound.

For home sewers, one company even advertised a dress form to replicate the "new" hourglass shape, an inflatable "Pneu Woman" of "odorless, air-tight" pure rubber cloth. A customer first made a model by fitting a lining from her bust down past the largest part of her corseted hips, removed it, inserted the "Pneu" woman inside the shaped lining and inflated it ("as easy as breathing"). With a lineup of models, avid sewers and knitters could now inspect fit on projected recipients by simply checking against their "Pneu" women.

Impoverished knitters, with time to be neither "new" nor "pneu" women, still hoped their knitting could augment family income. Cynthia Alden's *Women's Ways of Earning Money* appraised knitting activities as acceptable "feminine avenues for feminine talents" and pointed out that newspapers often ran "help wanted" ads for knitting "piece work" despite abysmally low pay. Still, she added briskly, "Something is always better than nothing, until you can place yourself in a position to demand what you ought to have," and she directed them to local exchanges where "[k]nit or crocheted wash rags always sell . . . and knitted [as well as] crocheted shawls, slippers, scarfs, mittens, wristlets." Should these knitting prospects fail to electrify her readers (she herself abhorred "sweat shop work"), she added gratuitously, "There may not be a thing here that you can do or want to do . . . but if we hunt for [work] systematically it will not take us long to find something that will at least keep the wolf from the door, and meanwhile we will be on the lookout for something better." Knitting, never remunerative, reaped no higher stipends in the twentieth century.

The nineteenth century's reform impetus persevered into the twentieth century, particularly when well-educated women focused on school and settlement house work to ameliorate conditions of the streams of immigrants converging on large cities. The plight of children was especially moving. When a teacher, readying a child for her required weekly bath, tried to snip away the "clothes" of woolen rags literally encasing her small body, the urchin yelped, "Don't do that, my mama's got me sewed up for the winter!" Only about a quarter of those "fresh from the steamer" girls would go beyond eighth grade; the boys stayed on a little longer. To offset the lure of the city, "a veritable ambush of moral danger," neighborhood networks for immigrant adolescent boys and girls were established where volunteers offered something better—in some cases, knitting!

By the turn of the century there were about five hundred settlement houses, among them the North Bennet Street Industrial School, started in the late nineteenth century and located in the predominantly Italian immigrant section of Boston's North End. By

"*Little Betty Sweater,*" 1912.   *Child's derby jacket,* 1915.

offering classes to children through agreements with Boston's schools and supplementing them with afterschool work such as the girls' afternoon knitting classes, the director hoped the girls would be "prepared to earn a livelihood at some skilled work for a few years prior to their marriage . . . and possessing some means of support in case of widowhood or other misfortune after marriage." The two-afternoons-a-week knitting classes were designed to teach the children something that could be continued without supervision at home, a practical industry for making a living and a skill necessary to gaining employment as a "domestic." Notifying teachers that they must require "long and continued washing" to ensure clean hands, administrators outlined sequential programs: "horse reins"; "a white wash cloth, showing the effect of clean hands"; "a skating cap, where the proficiency becomes very marked" and "a pair of baby socks which is the culminating effort and presents all the difficulties over-come." Though conscientious attention was decreed for class dem-onstrations, there were no such strictures during knitting practice, when neighborhood centers stimulated teachers and children to chat, sing, tell stories, recite poetry and plan group activities in what was, for the youngsters, a new language. Classes soon led to recreational knitting clubs whose activities were recorded by the "print shop boys" in the school's publication, *North End Lantern*: "The Knitting Club had a party at Roslindale on Sunday, April 14, and visited the Arboretum"; "The Knitting Club and the Indian Chiefs had Val-entine Parties"; "The Special Knitting Club gave a three-act play Saturday to get money for an outing and netted $6.43"; "Come and see the girls of the afternoon clubs and classes. You will find girls embroidering bureau scarves, crocheting doilies, and knitting scarves, socks, mittens, and sweaters." Similar programs were estab-lished in other settlement houses, where knitting proved a practical as well as recreational facet to immigrant community life.

To support charities of all kinds, twentieth-century women, like

Child's middy sweater, 1917.

their forebears, sponsored church and community fairs to market their products. Marts, which date back to the dawn of civilization and reached their height in Medieval Europe, were, in early nine-teenth-century America, designed to provide farmers an opportunity to exchange information on animal husbandry and agriculture, but as they drew increasingly large numbers of women, new exhibits targeted to "homemaking" skills encouraged competitors and sellers to bring jams, jellies, pies, sewing, weaving and knitting for display or competition. By mid-century the *Minnesota Express* enthusiasti-cally reported that much of the success of the Hennepin County Agriculture Society fairs was due to its "ladies' department." As dis-cussed earlier, Civil War fairs generated support for soldiers' aid; within a few decades "putting on a fair" was so common that skilled specialists emerged to offer advice on organization and presentation.

By sponsoring a fair or bazaar, whether spread over acres of grounds or tucked comfortably inside school gymnasia and church parlors, women identified each other's skills, winnowed the talkers from the doers and generated an "esprit de corps" through group efforts such as weekly knitting meetings that continued long after the affair was over. Entries were normally judged before the opening and winners were proclaimed at the height of attendance so that red- or blue-ribboned exhibits could command higher prices. Tagging objects with prices high enough to flatter donors but low enough to entice buyers required a diplomat's skills. Since larger, time-con-suming items would never fetch their deserved prices, knitters were urged to concentrate on small items such as scarves and baby bootees and include precious knitting instructions in the sale price. Chair-women were advised to bunch together unsalable items into "grab bag" lots at fire sale prices and, one would hope, fervently pray they would be disposed of without the donor's knowledge. Poorly made items were such a problem that two professional organizers en-treated, "Get each person to do the things that she does best. Let the sewers sew, the knitters knit, and the others can stick and paste."

Most early twentieth-century fairs relied upon "themes" to attract customers. At Christmas, for instance, after setting out Christmas trees in pots and hanging holly and ground-pine wreathes with scarlet bows, organizers might suspend from the ceiling a large red ball decorated with red and green streamers to highlight the "Ye Fancy

Work Shop" selling such yuletide ornaments as knitted bells or wee red and green stockings knit with white angora cuffs to be attached to lapels like corsages. Spring fairs featured cycling and golf stockings, knit golf club covers or small knitted Easter baskets in the "Knitting Knook." Most inventive was "The Seven Ages of Woman" Fair, in which decorators arrayed booths in a wide semicircle, festooned them in the seven colors of the rainbow, draped streamers of crepe paper from ceiling to booths or fastened opened barrel hoops ("rainbows") to the top of the uprights at the front corners of each booth. Saleswomen matched booth colors by crossing colored crepe paper sashes diagonally over their white dresses and adding crepe paper bows in their hair. Each "age" had its own booth: The Baby (knit bootees), The Schoolgirl (caps and mittens), The Debutante ("with materials for fancy work including sewing and knitting and crocheting supplies"), The Bride, The Housekeeper, and finally, *The Grandmother*, whose saleswomen ("gray-haired, charming elderly women, wearing pretty gray or black gowns, with little shoulder capes and dainty white caps") sold the accoutrements of old age: footstools, hot-water bags (with knitted covers), sofa cushions, bed slippers, work bags, medicine glasses, knitting and crochet needles, yarns, knit goods and "pretty little lace caps with bows."

Fair arrangers prepared "charming little entertainments" for each "age": schoolgirls "chattering and eating fudge"; debutantes serving tea; "Home Sweet Home" playing softly in the background as "housekeeper" darned stockings amid the mayhem of children and husband making demands on her. The climax, "the prettiest picture of all," presented grandmother in her rocking chair, knitting resting in her lap as she gazed in reverie at the fire ("a light behind piled up wood") while old-fashioned melodies were softly played or sung. Grandmother and her knitting still reigned supreme!

The quietude of such scenes was soon assailed when news of Belgium and northern France's invasion reached America, and knitters responded to the plea for clothing for war-devastated civilians as well as combatants. Of the several organizations that supplemented the Red Cross, one of the most effective was the American Fund for French Wounded, whose heartwrenching descriptions of hospital conditions and pleas "not to fail France in her hour of need" included requests for sweaters ("the dearth of them has become so serious that those organizations who buy their supplies here simply cannot get them") and every other kind of knitted and sewn garment. The fund's forecast was ominous: "The struggle is longer than anyone expected and on a larger scale."

As the magnitude of that scale dawned upon sympathetic Americans, and as their knitting interest was quickened by pictures of Berlin schoolchildren laying aside their schoolwork in favor of sock knitting, they resolved to wield their own needles. As "war knitting" expanded, a *New York Times* writer who complained that most knitting manual sock directions were "calculated to drive the average knitter into an insane asylum" vowed to rescue the amateur with foolproof rules "so rigid that she could not possibly depart from them, so exact that she could not possibly misunderstand them." Maud Nicoll's "How to Knit Socks for Soldiers" in the *Times* fulfilled her promise. Within a year, she expanded the article into a booklet and three years later into a full-fledged book of war patterns.

Other writers followed suit. *War Needlework: Comforts You Can Make for the Suffering Non-Combatants* showed afghans, baby socks, scarves, caps, gloves, mittens, and bed socks. The Allies Special Aid's *Khaki Knitting Book*, with khaki cover appropriately bordered in colored flags of the Allies and priced at fifty cents, ominously warned potentially freeloading knitters: "THE MONEY FOR THE SALE OF THE KHAKI KNITTING BOOK GOES TO THE ALLIES AND ANYONE LENDING THE BOOK TO A FRIEND WHO CAN AFFORD TO BUY ONE, DEFRAUDS THE ALLIES!" Sponsoring yarn companies provided patterns for knitted items from sleeping caps to seamen's helmets, from eye bandages to washcloths, from abdominal bands to hot-water bottle covers. This war knitters' Bible poignantly communicated its heartfelt tribute to "safe" Americans who knit for the less fortunate in these three stanzas of "Knit Your Bit":

> Swiftly, to and fro,
> Let your needles fly!
> Be not yours to know
> Pause, for tear or sigh.

Stitch by stitch they grow
Garments soft and warm
That will keep life's glow
In some shivering form.

Sweater, muffler, sock,
For the soldier's wear!
List to pity's knock—
For those "over there."

Star Needlework Journal's editors had just announced their national knitting, crocheting, tatting and embroidery contest when the war-knitting fever struck. Since only fourteen knitters entered, each won a prize for steadfast knitting if not for skill, with seventy-five dollars, forty dollars and twenty dollars going to the top three and the remaining eleven receiving two dollars each. *Star Needlework* tried to recapture knitters by adding military patterns to subsequent issues.

When the Red Cross surveyed war-zone conditions in the summer of 1917, its special commission cabled home the pressing need for hospital supplies and knitted goods, and begged for a million and a half each of knitted mufflers, sweaters, socks, and wristlets. With a pamphlet to advise how to obtain yarn, knit the garments and pack them for immediate shipment to France, Red Cross National Headquarters provided the necessary coordination by delegating authority to its thirteen divisions to allot to each chapter the numbers of specific items the registrants would knit. Bulletins and newssheets featured letters from grateful recipients, such as one from a surprised but appreciative destroyer fleet commander whose telegraphed request for "knitted outfits for the men, who are going on foreign service" resulted in their delivery two days after the New York and Boston chapters received the order.

Just as Civil War knitters had first designated products for boys from their own communities and then their own states, 1917 knitters first flagged their clothes for "A French soldier," a "fighting Belgian," an "Italian Marine" or "an Englishman of gentle birth in the trenches." Once American seamen shipped out, local Navy League knitters, working under a national Comforts Committee, usually allocated their handwork to men serving on state-named battleships; the Hot Springs, Arkansas, chapter president who galvanized twelve hundred knitters to supply all the men of the battleship *Arkansas* was credited by her state's governor with "reviving what came near to being a lost art—that of knitting." Many authorities contended that such "regionalism" and "sentimentality" should be subordinated to "national" needs, but the Navy League, in a sometimes uneasy knitting alliance with the Red Cross, continued to maintain its identity even after the United States entered the war.

10.
Oh, Say Can You Knit
—For Sammy?

A reporter watched a "pretty young thing" knitting ardently while awaiting her subway train, persevering until she reached her station and then, with her knitting hastily tucked under her arm, scrambling to debark, the needles slithering out and dropping a few stitches in the process. Regarding the departing knitter affectionately, the reporter confided to her companion, "Oh, the stitches may be irregular, and some of them dropped, but some Sammy is going to love that sweater and think of her. The very missing stitches will make his thoughts warm for her." She was right, and "Knitting for Sammy" soon engaged legions of knitters!

Upon America's entrance into the war, Mabel Boardman, the Red Cross Central Commission's only woman member, surveyed the stock of sweaters, helmets, socks, mittens and wristlets. She concluded they could not possibly sustain the soldiers in the coming winter months and pleaded to her countrywomen to knit or at least buy wool for those who couldn't afford the yarn. Responsive knitters snatched up the quarter of a million Red Cross knitting pamphlets hastily dispatched to local chapters and launched a knitting marathon that by war's end had produced six and a half million refugee and almost twenty-four million military garments. Since some sock knitting was done by hand-operated machines and a separate count was not made, it is impossible to know the percentage of handwork, but, by all acounts, it was the majority. Proponents of hand knitting

*Red Cross knitting,
1918.*

claimed their socks outlasted machine-knit ones, but with the need acute, novices were urged to master machines (at Red Cross headquarters) and turn out a "perfectly made pair of socks in forty minutes, [rather] than labor over an indifferently hand-made sock."

Each Red Cross chapter retained a liaison with regional offices, and they, in turn, communicated with "national" offices, so that up-to-date reports of yarn shortages, quotas, most-needed garments, and news of war work such as rolling bandages, sewing, running canteens and sending aides overseas could be speedily disseminated through bulletins and newsletters.

At the sound of war, former Civil War knitters quickly surfaced. One eighty-eight-year-old who had accompanied her husband on Civil War assignments taught knitting to children in a Takoma Park, Maryland, church. Many still-spry United Daughters of the Confederacy who once knit for "Johnny Reb" now contributed over 600,000 knit articles for "Sammy." Instead of gloves or stockings, a grandmother who proudly snapped on her Red Cross button "in place of

Yarn advertisement, 1918.

her accustomed brooch" made "stump socks" to fit over amputated limbs. Seventy-two-year-old Mrs. Mitt Osgood, who lived on a Montana cattle ranch eighty miles from a railroad, knit 18 pairs of socks in twenty days and completed 120 pairs between February and September, 1918. With several grandsons in military service, one of whom was killed in action in France, she had personal grounds for industry. Certainly age was no deterrent. Two other speed knitters, seventy-eight and eighty-four years old, each knit 124 pairs of socks. "Grandma" Parker, acclaimed an "aged though active knitter," completed 27 pairs of socks, three sweaters, two helmets and seven pairs of wristlets; ninety-one-year-old Hannah Eilenberger knit 11 pairs of socks and complained that the twelfth pair was unfinished because her dislocated shoulder slowed her down. Another nonagenarian didn't like Red Cross instructions and huffed that though she knit 8 pairs of socks for the soldiers, she didn't follow them: "I shaped the feet the way Grandma Foster had taught me nearly ninety years before."

As in the Civil War, newspapers broadcast knitting activities through "social coverage" that included such mentions as "The after-luncheon hour will be spent knitting on a quilt for the base hospital" or "The after-luncheon hours were devoted to knitting." Des Moines's Knitting League, founded by fifty Jewish women, asked new recruits to come to the B'Nai B'rith clubrooms for sweater instructions, and its Adelphic Club members were reminded to "make a big effort to finish the work so that articles may be turned in by August 16." Their previous year's work totaled 231 sweaters, two hundred helmets, fifty pairs of wristlets, eighty-seven pairs of sock tops, seventy-four pairs of complete socks and "re-toeing" more than five hundred pairs of poorly made socks contributed to the Red Cross.

So much space was needed for yarn distribution centers; workrooms for sewers, bandage rollers, knitters and packers; and meeting rooms for demonstrations of home canning techniques or lectures on harvesting the most produce from one's "war garden" that church basements, civic centers and donated storefronts were in short supply. To supplement them, owners of large houses converted parts for public use. In Manhattan, for instance, John D. Rockefeller (a recent widower not using his Fifth Avenue mansion) not only opened his basement, dining room and reception room to the workers, supplying chairs, tables, sewing machines and special lighting for their convenience, but also gave kitchen privileges to lunch preparers and his staff for keeping the workroom "in order." Mrs. Joseph Pulitzer pitched in by lending her house and donating yarn for Red Cross "comforts and woolen necessities." Many a nosy knitter who might otherwise have missed viewing the interior of such a mansion was lured for Monday evening instruction. Mrs. Henry Duryea sponsored the Wool Fund, to establish "knitting-rooms" supplied with sock-making machines to supplement the output of hand knitting, and designed "patriotic rings," slender circles of silver to be worn in sets of three, each ring set with red, white or blue stones "of no instrinsic value" but sold for ten dollars a set as an emblem of the fund. When socially prominent leaders offered their homes or sponsored Red Cross events, fashion magazines covered their patriotic wartime activities liberally, with *Vogue*'s formal, full-page photograph of a social doyenne calmly knitting a sock in elegant evening gown being the ultimate coverage.

A vital Red Cross adjunct, the Mormon Relief Society, long committed to thrift, simplicity and beneficence, proffered knitting news and tips through its *Relief Society Magazine*'s "Patriotic Department." One singular item quoted here in its entirety read: "As women's pets in the United States, poodles are giving way to knitting needles, to good purpose"! When knitting needles were too flagrantly clicked in church classes, the general board forbad them, arguing that "active fingers" inhibited concentration, were discourteous to speakers and teachers, and were unnecessary since "[o]ur sisters will have plenty

Chairman of the Free Wool Committee of New York, Mrs. Stephen H. Olin, 1918. (Photo by Charlotte Fairchild.)

Cincinnati Chapter, Daughters of the American Revolution, 1918.

of time at home and in the work meetings to do all the knitting for which they can obtain yarn and thus assist the Red Cross cause." To foster home knitting, the magazine gave pointers for an educational knitting bee: "Provide some good music, a good Victrola will be of use here, or have an interesting story read, or pass papers with a list of famous 'Mormon' women. These may be guessed while the needles click merrily. . . . A simple prize may be given to the one who guesses all the names correctly. Serve sweet apple cider or fruit punch, apple cake, and stock candy."

In other parts of the country, "Knitting Teas" attracted dressed-to-the-nines knitters to patriotic red, white and blue parties. A favorite home magazine, *Delineator*, submitted its suggested invitation in jingle form. Competitive hostesses with no aptitude for rhyme relied instead on trying to concoct other ingenious bids to their "theme parties" and posted invitation cards with hand-decorated facsimilies of military sweaters, wristlets, scarves and socks or knitting paraphernalia. Since rivalry for hosting the most unusual knitting tea didn't stop at the door, party givers also racked their brains for techniques to astonish guests with their distinctive decor and novel activities. After all, they had to restrain nibbling knitters from getting sidetracked. Innovative *Delineator* helpfully contributed a virtual scenario.

On each table for eight, centered with an Allied nation's flag, knitting work was arranged with enough knitting started on socks, wris-

Committee on Convalescent Blankets, Liberty Bell Chapter, DAR, Allentown, Pennsylvania, 1918.

tlets, mufflers and washcloths so that successive guests could pick it up effortlessly. "Uncle Sam" or "Miss Columbia" passed a tray of tally cards with Allied flags to steer guests to the corresponding table. When the Boy Scout bugler blared the call, "sub-deb" knitters in Red Cross uniforms functioning as expediters and judges signaled the start of the first twenty-minute "knit-in." After four such segments were completed, with the "best" at each table progressing to the next, winners were declared and "Hoover Refreshments" served. (Herbert Hoover's economical, food-conserving plans were practiced in every loyal household, and runners-up to the top knitting prize—checks made out to the Red Cross or another war relief organization—were requited with "Hoover recipes or packages of Agricultural Department Bulletins on Gardening, Canning, Food Preserving and Cooking, tied with red-white-and-blue ribbon.")

"Knitting teas" became *the* social rite as former sewing societies metamorphosed into knitting groups much as they had during the Civil War. One attendee explained, "I can make a cap with one hand and with my eyes shut; the only time I don't knit is when I go to church; and it nearly kills me to sit that long and do nothing. So I wish someone would please feed me, while I finish this cap. You wouldn't regard it as an extravagance for me to eat one of grandmother's ginger cakes, would you?" Some, however, disparaged the teas for "frivolity" or for their "dismal tone." Eda Funston, a prominent war widow whose "Family Advice from Mrs. Funston" column in the *Delineator* dubbed them "gloom parties," cited her own ordeal in anticipating a diversionary affair where she could knit patriotically only to have her spirit dampened by war stories and criticism of the armed forces. She vowed not to attend another unless participants pledged not to beef about the war and, for good measure, reproached men who profited from the war but carped at its leaders: "They would be much better engaged in knitting and purling along with the women. They would find less time to criticize." Criticism was out, and cheerfulness was in. In a newspaper article, "If You Worry, Don't Show It in Your Letters," anxious women were advised to bypass shortages and junior's chicken pox and focus on upbeat War Savings Stamps programs, Liberty Loans, rolling bandages and knitting clothes for the boys overseas.

Despite criticism, the popularity of these knitting-cum-eating assemblages was so great that they furnished scenarios for one-act plays suitable for club performances. As the curtains parted for *The Knitting Club Meets or Just Back from France*, the hostess wondered aloud whether more could not be accomplished quietly at home, since "[w]e talk so much—and eat so much—at these meetings!" The playwright described each entering character right down to her knitting bag:

> ELEANOR: dressed smartly but simply in tailored suit; carries cretonne knitting-bag.
> LUCY: She is a rather silly person dressed in the height of fashion, and carries a magnificent knitting-bag.
> MYRA: dressed in uniform of Emergency-Aid or Motor Messenger Service; carries Red Cross knitting-bag.
> GRACE: A cheerful, motherly-looking person, well but comfortably dressed. Carries a capacious, rather shabby knitting-bag.
> JANE: The person cast for this should be very slender and have a spiritual face. She is dressed in a shabby tailor suit, somewhat

out of date, but with neat hat, gloves, and shoes. [No knitting bag, but there is no doubt about who is going to be the heroine here!]

The day's speaker was Red Cross worker Jane (she of the slender form and spiritual face), whose portrayal of the shocking conditions of starving mothers and children recently seen in France made her gag at the lavish spread and sobered the giddier members. Her pleas for contributions elicited generous offerings and a rallying to center stage, where the cast hoisted knitting aloft and trilled the "Marseillaise."

Another skit for wartime thespians, *The Knitting Girls Count One*, introduced similarly stereotyped characters:

MRS. THAYER: a sweet-faced young woman is seated by the table, knitting a soldier's sock. On the table, near her, is a work-basket, containing another sock, only partly completed.

HELEN: a brisk, bright young woman, very much up-to-date as to clothes, is erect at one end of the lounge, knitting a solder's sweater.

KATHLEEN: curled up at the other end of the lounge with her feet under her idly observing the other two . . . a very pretty, fair-haired girl, dressed like a doll.

One was not startled when, a few pages later, "brisk" Helen branded "dressed like a doll" Kathleen a slacker for not knitting a stitch. The rest of the merry knitters chattered about the song, "The Knitting Girl," they'd heard at a Red Cross fund-raiser, and after kicking up their heels to the chorus, solemnly considered their hostess's suggestion to emulate French Revolutionary knitters, who incorporated numbers corresponding to the "heads" that fell to the guillotine, a gruesome thought indeed, but not if one counted each "soul saved by our knitting." When all vowed to "knit as we never did before," even the feckless Kathleen gave her word to knit to "keep some soldier alive," and the hostess saluted Kathleen's redemption by whooping triumphantly, "The Knitting Girls Count One!" The Red Cross got a new recruit as the audience cheered.

Knitting swept not only the country, but a few places outside! In Peking's American enclave, women converted to camel's hair socks

Seattle Red Cross Auxiliary.

and sweaters when sheep's wool was unavailable. Not to be outdone by his loyal Red Cross wife, the Peking International Bank manager extracted his knitting at a dressy dinner party and stunned the guests as he "proceeded to turn the heel with the air of an expert." Nor were members of the diplomatic set the only Asian knitters. In Shanghai, the American founder of the Slave Refuge, a sanctuary for young Chinese slave girls, coached her charges in knitting and dispatched their first contribution (ten pairs of socks) with a memorandum that they wanted to help American boys fight "freedom's battle." The Hawaiian Red Cross's two-thousand-pound wool allotment went like hot cakes to such impatient knitters as Princess Kalanialiole, head of the Hawaiian knitting group, schoolchildren, and scores of knitting clubs embracing thirty-five nationalities. Their project was augmented by women at the Territorial Prison and by firemen whose station house sponsored a contest for the best fireman/knitter, won by a hook-and-ladder man who executed his first sweater in twenty-seven hours.

The Navy League Comforts Committee, independent of the Red

Civil War veteran (right) at the Navy League Knitting Bee in Central Park, 1918.

Cross throughout the war, sponsored a three-day knit-in on Manhattan's Central Park Mall, charging each contestant a fifty-cent entry fee to fund yarn purchases for needy knitters. A benefactor loaned a Fifth Avenue storefront for the selling of wool and the giving of directions, patriotic organizations volunteered enthusiastically, contestants signed up in droves and the resultant publicity gave a fillip to languishing summer knitting. When questioned about their participation, more than one entrant responded, "I can't fight, and I can't make munitions, but I *can* knit!" Shut-ins who couldn't frequent the festival vied for their own special prize, and when one attributed the slowness of her work to needles made from fence wire, the committee dispatched proper ones. A Florida shut-in apologized for the length of time it took to make her sweater, what with temperatures in the hundreds and a weak heart. A semi-invalid in New York State explained, "If it hadn't been for my two little girls, Sallie, aged eight, and Molly, nine, who did all my housework this week and helped with the chickens and farm work, I could not have finished the things

Central Park Knitting Bee,
1918.

I sent yesterday, but they stayed in to help me and, when the package was ready, walked to town together to send it. We wish all the good luck in the world to the boys who get these garments."

Even wet and sweltering weather the first two days deterred neither crowds nor contestants, but on the third day ("a perfect park day") the chairwoman of the event chortled that the knitters were out "in such numbers that the click of the needles could be heard all the way to Berlin." The sight of a sea of knitters was something to behold. As female police officers cordoned off the mall area with red, white and blue bunting, knitters took up stations on folding chairs or park benches drawn up in a circle. Some female contestants simulated their knitting foremothers in colonial dress; others, hatted against the hot August sun, opted for chic, and mercifully cool, voile "lingerie dresses." Supportive caterers contributed lunches, professional entertainers regaled knitters and onlookers; crowds clustered about favorites such as knitting and singing Patrolman Patrick Fitzgibbons, chairman of the Police Glee Club, and rooted loyally for Civil War veteran I. R. Seelye, who manipulated his needles as adroitly as those half his age. "Speed knitting" contests drew the most observers, spellbound at the dexterity of entrants such as Mrs.

Policeman Patrick Fitzgibbons, 1918.

Riggs, who led the pack one afternoon by completing a sweater in less than seven hours. Several women tied for a pair of socks knitted each day of the bee; others finished a sweater, helmet and muffler in three days. Among the winners and runners-up for best muffler, best socks, best wristlets and so forth were four blind women, four children under the age of eleven, two men and an eighty-three-year-old woman. The bee raised four thousand dollars and turned these garments over to the committee: fifty completed sweaters, four dozen mufflers, 224 pairs of socks and forty helmets, in addition to still-unfinished garments which were promised upon completion. *The New York Times* congratulated the Navy League for providing "inspiration to knitters to go on with their war work."

New York hosted another extravaganza when President Wilson marched down Fifth Avenue in the vanguard of a six-mile-long procession of tireless Red Cross workers, including a platoon of members of the elegant Cosmopolitan Club, its phalanx of "drummers" setting the beat by striking tin buckets with knitting needles while rear ranks shouldered poles from which dangled the marchers'

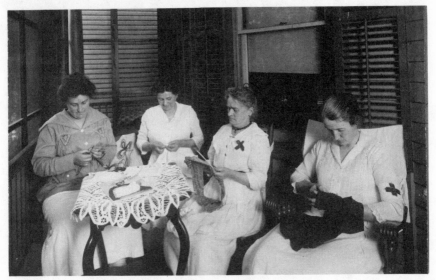

Instruction in knitting for soldiers, World War I.

Instruction in knitting for soldiers, 1918.

Knitting by hand for boys in France, 1917.

Fort Washington Junior Auxiliary #1: Children knitting under the direction of the Red Cross, World War I.

finished products: *socks*! Parades boosted morale across the country, and in the forefront of Ridgewood, New Jersey's, Navy League trooped three leaders in white skirts, middy blouses and caps, yarn skeins draped like bandoleers from shoulder to waist. Falling in behind were three young men, each sporting (among other things!) a "set" of four knitted garments—helmet, vest, gloves and socks. League members carrying knitting bags and fluttering flags chanted their mantra, "Knit, Knit, Knit, Do Your Bit for the Navy League."

Not everyone could be jolted into knitting by watching a parade, so both the Red Cross and the Navy League stoked interest through their publications, crediting groups and individuals for accomplishments. Rivalry in record setting is reminiscent of Civil War knitters' pride in productivity. "Modern" women credited speedy knitters' contributions with being as significant to the war as female railroad-passenger agents, "cow tester" dairy agents for the Department of Agriculture, workers in shipyards and engine shops, and "strong, able-bodied women" who unloaded coal cars. "The Weaker Sex" article in the staunchly feminist *The Woman Citizen* hailed Mrs. Albert Nicolay of Cincinnati for knitting twenty-five hundred pairs of socks for the September quota of the Red Cross in addition to taking care of a grocery, home and family. Not to demean Mrs. Nicolay, but it is well to remember that hand-cranked knitting machines were available at many Red Cross headquarters and in some homes; figures must be examined judiciously.

To assist in developing speed, *Delineator*'s resident needlework instructor, whose monthly columns were faithfully followed by thousands, suggested knitters learn to knit *two* sweaters or two pairs of socks on one pair of needles by "double knitting," with the assurance that "[i]t is not a difficult feat and it does save time. When one becomes efficient, two pairs of socks can be made in the time that three socks take habitually. Of course, when you first attempt this double knitting, you can not make such speed, but it will come with practice."

For sheer velocity and zeal, none could match Mrs. Olivia Kindelberger's record of ten sweaters in less than seven days. These were in addition to the already completed fifty sweaters and other "comforts," feats that led to her coronation by *The New York Times* as "Champion Red Cross Knitter of New York." In an interview granted to an obviously stupefied *Times* reporter, she decried those who carried their knitting on subways and to theaters and other public places "for show" and declared she knit more evenly at home. What advice, the reporter asked, could she give others? "Just sit down quietly and knit," she replied, stressing that she ranked her husband, son and housework ahead of knitting and managed "with only one maid." In revealing her techniques, she explained that, like her Norwegian mother, she carried the yarn in her left hand and leaned back in a pillowed rocking chair, breaking only for "a slight pain on the left side of my neck." She went on:

> The way I work is this: I begin as soon as I have the morning work finished in my apartment—that is, about nine o'clock. I fix myself comfortably in my chair, and I knit right straight ahead all morning until 1. Sometimes after luncheon I go out to market. If not, I knit straight through until 4:30 P.M. In any case, I knit most of the afternoon until that time, when I stop work and lie down. I always lie down for one hour, often for two. Then we have dinner, and after that I knit all evening, almost always until two o'clock. The reason for that is that my husband does not like ever to go to bed early, and enjoys reading aloud. He is 84 years old, but he reads without glasses. He reads to me, and I knit, and so we pass the evening very happily.

Despite national support for knitters such as Mrs. Kindelberger, knitters were criticized for wasting scarce wool by hand knitting soldiers' "comforts" when there was scarcely enough for "necessities." When a writer expressed that position to the Brookline, Massachusetts, *Chronicle*, the paper editorialized that there might be some truth to his argument but doubted that women would stop. *Reader's Digest*, sniffing a national news story, reprinted the letter's taunting conclusion: "For God's sake, wake up and stop this hand-knitting by which at least 20,000 pounds of scoured wool has already been wasted at a time when the Huns are at our gates!" Indignant knitters denounced the author in no uncertain terms. Des Moines women, "not a little disturbed," rejoined that "women who have been spending hour after hour of more or less monotonous knitting do not relish being told in uncouched language that what they have been doing is not only useless but extravagant." How, they asked, could "comforts" be unnecessary when they were besieged with thousands of requests for them? They defended the "earnest desire to be of use" that had steered the Red Cross into the "knitting business." That hit the nail on the head! The issue was not whether hand knitting was most efficient; what mattered was providing women on the home front a means for sustaining their men. Knitting answered that need, and nothing would deter them.

They were acutely sensitive to wool conservation. Hadn't they followed the example of President Wilson, whose flock of sheep grazed on the White House lawn and produced clippings worth a thousand dollars a pound at the Red Cross auction? Hadn't they praised sheep raisers and home spinners for converting wool into "war yarn" by running photographic essays in their Red Cross bulletins? Hadn't they lauded "Grandmother Hegg" for raising her flock of sheep, which had furnished more than four hundred sweaters and seven hundred pairs of socks for the fighting men, and placed her picture with one of its wooly members in the foreground while she spun, her granddaughter carded and her daughter knit—a "three generational team"? It was all in the *Bulletin*.

Wool was not the only shortage, and a rumored needle scarcity caused knitters to panic until manufacturers reassured them that ample numbers were on tap for knitting soldier sweaters if "fair knitters" didn't indulge in luxuries such as "something sweet in pink Shetland wool." They knew better than that! After all, they were disciples of Marie Ashley, who in her *Delineator* column had gamely promised to postpone patterns for making fine lace, crocheting doilies, embroidering linen and knitting fancy gloves: "Until war conditions end and the necessity for great personal sacrifices has passed, we shan't give any more instructions on this page for the unessential pretty things we all love." Instead, Marie had proclaimed: "Mercerized Cotton Takes the Place of Wool in New Sweaters and Collars." Elsa Barsaloux, chatelaine of a fashionable Fifth Avenue knitting shop, knitting book author and scribe for *Modern Priscilla*, supported her by diverting knitters to silk, cotton and angora rather than wool. Carol Lawrence of *Woman's Magazine*, feeling "fashionably patriotic" when knitting with mercerized cotton and silk, added: "I think the slogan, 'Wool will win the war. Don't wear it,' would be a very timely [one] for all fashion pages."

Like Civil War hearsay about abuse of "Sanitary Commission Socks," tales circulated that soldiers discarded army socks after only one wearing, until *Red Cross Magazine* rebutted the canard in "The Saga of the Socks," which related a Red Cross representative's search for sock menders. He corralled refugee women to darn almost six thousand socks the first week, but when the army got wind of his success, it characteristically routed him socks by the sackful, forcing him to enlist almost seven hundred women to reclaim some eighty thousand socks a month. The socks were *not* being thrown away! Thus reassured, women continued to knit! And they knit everywhere, each to her own fashion. One writer commented, "[W]e would seem to instill our own personality into the yarn. Some I see knit phlegmatically; some almost despondently; others patiently and stoically." One woman, who had lost two sons in the war and had a third one on his way to the front, "[made] her needles fly, with the same optimistic cheer with which she does everything." Loessa Coffey, now well up in her eighties, used Red Cross yarn for stockings, caps and sweaters and "thought it was pretty tricky" and patriotic to incorporate a knit stitch on a purl row to emphasize the USA she had emblazoned on her sweater fronts.

One knitter, now in her nineties, still remembers replies she and fellow office workers received from soldiers who found their names and addresses tucked into finished garments sent to the front, and chuckles at this midwestern farm boy's appreciation: "Thanks for the socks 'cause I get nothin' from home. My mother's in bed with the same doctor for a year and won't change." Another soldier sent this brash stanza:

> Thanks, lady, for the socks you knit
> I used one for a hammock and one for a mitt
> And I pause, dear lady, to ask you this
> Where in the hell did you learn to knit??

As months passed, the scarcity of wool became real, and while it was never suggested that knitting stop, the emphasis shifted to socks to the exclusion of other garments. A Red Cross Division that had once begged for *anything* highlighted "Don't Make Sweaters" on its bulletin cover and explained, "Every pound of yarn that can be secured should be used for knitting socks." With a new quota of fifty-five thousand pairs of socks within three months, knitters would have to work "three times as hard." Some *hated* to knit socks and *loved* helmets, mufflers and sweaters, and the Potomac Division promised to let them know if the policy changed. In the meantime, since many knitters were thwarted by the "mystery" of turning a heel, spiral "heel-less" stockings guaranteed to be "knittable by amateurs" appealed to soldiers because of their "close fit without bumps and bulges," and revived interest "among the backward ones." Following wool-saving advice of the Navy League Comforts Committee (to use cotton for the legs and save wool for the feet), both advanced and "backward" knitters continued knitting socks for the rest of the war and deferred other articles until peacetime.

When the War Industries Board chairman, Bernard Baruch, announced yarn rationing, the Red Cross purchased what was still on the market and, recognizing the importance of diplomacy in handling edgy knitters, congratulated them for enabling the Red Cross to have stockpiled sufficient knitwear to offset the wool shortage. The sheer *numbers* of garments already knitted salvaged their pride and reassured them that "their boys" would be warm that winter. Mr. Baruch wrote Red Cross President Davison that he was "confident that all the women of the country would co-operate if they understood the situation and the importance of so doing."

Knitting continued, but not just for soldiers, for as long as they saved wool for "soldier knitting," women knit for their families, often decidedly military fashions such as the "Militaire" coat, promised to "work up handsomely in khaki or brown, with brass buttons and russet leather belt," a "French Aviation Hat" or a trim "Pershing" jacket. For women going overseas for nursing or ambulance services, there were lightweight sleeveless sweaters and vests to wear under uniform jackets, stockings, bed socks for unheated quarters, hats with earflaps, a knitted silk tie and mittens. Those yearning to "look like women," however, jettisoned anything military in favor of the feminine look Marie Ashley recommended to her mavens, particularly her "sports blouse" trimmed with an "adorably soft" angora or brushed-wool collar "rendered even fluffier by determined strokes of a wire hair brush."

Ashley condemned prodigal sweater collectors ("Of course any woman who has a different sweater for each mood should be ostracized") and proclaimed passionately, "One sweater and a great deal of ambition and enthusiasm for olive-drab and gray wool is enough to keep any woman warm." Still, she recognized that a woman could justify at least one warm sweater for house wear when coal became a "variable quantity" and stamped her approval on the "hug-me-tight . . . a good substantial friend when the weather man and thermometer become heartless creatures." Despite wool conservation, a few prewar colored yarns were still obtainable. The *Gentlewoman* introduced its "skating set" instructions by trumpeting "[A]ll the world is skating!" and rationalized knitting a simple pullover as thrifty retaliation to "exorbitant prices asked in shops" and its execution as training for "other more practical things." *Modern Priscilla*'s "Knitted Norfolk Coat for College Girls" required nine hanks of prewar rose-

"Militaire" coat, 1918.

Oversea cap, 1919.

and-white knitting worsted, hardly appropriate for soldiers and a forgivable foray into civilian knitting after official Red Cross work.

With civilians urged to "keep fit," tennis and golf gained official sanction, and knitting sports sweaters and stockings could be reasonably indulged. Despite the crisis, even President Wilson's limousine glided through the White House gates and whisked him across the city to a neighboring country club for an early morning round of golf before government workers swarmed up Pennsylvania Avenue. When "Kid Wonder" Bobby Jones competed at Red Cross tournaments in knickerbockers paired with argyle stockings and coordinated sweaters, modish golfers scurried to clone the master. Pattern companies published throughout the war, injecting sufficient patterns for "civilian knitting" to prevent knitter "burn-out." Women pining for "gimmicks" to relieve the tedium of khaki pounced on "Spiderweb Hats" ("The style sensation of the season"), lacy, weblike contraptions whose yarn-entwined brims matched their sweaters. American Thread capitalized on cotton's unlimited availability by concentrating on "dainty camisole yokes," doilies, and edgings for linens, petticoats and nightdresses.

The "national knitting phenomenon" prompted other businesses to cash in. Articles such as "How to Purchase Clothes on a War-time Allowance," "Three Ways to Conserve Wool," "Suits for Victory in War and Peace," "Coats That Go over the Top on the Winter Dress Line," "Winter Alliance of Blouse and Skirt" and "Fashion Prepares Her Spring Offensive" had their military tie-ins, but advertisers scouted more remunerative leads. When Cabinet members stressed that women should keep not only fit but attractive, admen seized the initiative by advising women of their patriotic *duty* to look their best. Cosmetician Elizabeth Arden warned that "faded, wrinkled and wan" complexions reflected "discouragement and worry." *Harper's Bazaar* contended, "After being aproned for bandage-making most of the day, it is delightful to don a charming hat that by its prettiness brings happiness to all who may be about." If a charming hat and pretty frock were good for women, they were good for the nation, and, heaven knows, they were good for business! "Fair Ladies," cautioned *Vogue*, should scrutinize themselves, for "[a]n external slump bespeaks an internal slump for which there is no place in the world today," particularly slumps into plain or tacky underthings that could even endanger the war effort. The latter wisdom was not wasted upon chic Parisiennes, who luxuriated in "soft and fluffy" undergarments ("a puff of rose silk voile and filet lace in the form of a combination") under briskly serviceable dresses and suits. "The Girls We Left Behind" were advised to take a leaf from their book. After all, remarked *Vogue*, "[I]t is not for the kind of woman who wears ugly lingerie that a man fights!" American women had enough cares without being apprised of competition with Parisian women.

Tie-ins with knitting knew no bounds. One company guaranteed its hand cream would "smooth fingers" and promote more comfortable knitting. Another's ad showing a small can of face powder peeking out from a knitting bag read: "To look her best is part of woman's patriotic duty. . . . The woman, careful of her appearance to the smallest detail, is helping to preserve the *morale* of her country. In thousands of America's busiest knitting bags you will find the little box of Dorine." Abercrombie and Fitch, purveyors of outdoor gear, exhorted women to "look, and act, and feel as our partner at the front would have us look, and act, and feel," and, claiming a woman's courage was "as much reflected in her outdoor tweeds as his in his Sam Browne belt," gushed on: "She is the soldier's pal. She will knit, yes, but she will knit in a trim suit of Irish homespun, between rounds of golf, on the porch of the country club; or in riding habit while she awaits her mount; or in tennis skirt after a set that has made her cheeks tingle—or possibly in her canoe or at the woods camp which brings her nearer the actual life of the soldier."

In an austerity program, everyone felt a bit guilty about attending to "personal" affairs such as vacations or even getting married ("A Spring bride whose war work will not be interrupted by a prolonged wedding trip"). In wartime, one intensely "personal" affair was mourning, and *Vogue*'s model in a "simple frock of black crepe de chine" looked into the camera's lens from beneath her wide-brimmed black hat, her knitting hanging down from her still-working hands. The "Gadabout," *Harper's Bazaar*'s society editor, balanced heading south to cover the Smart Set's winter migration to Palm Beach with a declaration that despite trunks "full of cotton frocks and be-flowered hats . . . we journeyed southward with our knitting bags over our arms." Once there, knitting khaki became a badge of patriotic bustle since, as *Vogue* put it, "Anyone seen knitting a sweater for herself is subject to criticism," and even children with their own knitting bags industriously clicked their needles along with vacationing mothers and grandmothers. Des Moines ladies felt no less guilt than New Yorkers, and for vacations lugged "skein after skein of yarn for the quota of sweaters which must be finished by July 15th, and the allotment of socks which must be ready in August." In Albany, New York's Navy League knitters packed knitting for leisure at summer resorts.

The knitting bag symbolized "We do our bit," and symbols came in all sizes and shapes, from an imitation brass torpedo shell to accommodate knitting and needles to a pastel-enameled wicker pedestal basket for the porch. Caterers to fashion touted knitting bags as "the last word in first aids to patriotic endeavors" and apprised knitters of the importance of carrying bags appropriate to each occasion. Designers went wild: "blue moire . . . [with] gray and silver embroidery"; "a lantern bag, for plaited silk is caught upon rings that slip up and down on silken cords and stretches like an accordion, making it equally simple to accommodate either a bulky sweater or diminutive wristlet"; "ermine combined with woven silks or varied hues, while the needles are carved ivory." *Vogue* coyly suggested pasting a cover of *Vogue* itself on an ordinary paper bag to transform it into a "pretty affair in which that continuous grey or brown knitting may be carried." The editor added somewhat immodestly that the covers were so attractive ("they make the newsstands blossom as the rose") that three thousand extra copies of the next few issues would be patriotically printed in red, white and blue so they could be sold for the Red Cross.

Vogue Patterns could hardly contain itself in passing the word on bags to denizens of surf and sand: "Can't you just imagine what envious things the wild waves will be saying when they see this bathing wrap of white surf satin, lined with navy blue surf satin and trimmed with bands stitched with blue? In addition to her charming sunshade, the fortunate bather has a knitting-bag of grey rubberized satin, with applique of colored rubberized satin in a design of fruit and flowers." Milliners, not to be outdone, matched hats to knitting bags and informed style-conscious readers: "Yesterday a good-looking knitting bag was a possession—today it is merely a requirement

Knitting bag apron, 1918.

of the costume. For morning, noon, and night are bags varying for the hour in fabric and color. When the day begins and the knitting-bag is taken from its peg, one will find that it nearly always accords with the sports hat which its fair owner has donned." To keep home sewers au courant of the new rage, *Delineator* reported, "The head of the wardrobe must keep pace with the knitting bag, so if your new Spring Bonnet is silk or fabric you choose for its trimming the embroidered design of your knitting-bag." In no time, matching scarves transposed duos to trios of "femininity and sportiness," with glamorous combinations of "peacock pongée and purple satin, with a design worked in purple yarn" and "a natural-colored straw hat banded with Chinese red brocaded silk and a parasol-knitting bag of the same gorgeous fabric."

Not all bags were elegant; some were knit of heavy cord or wool, with a service star sewn on for each family member in the armed forces. An inexpensive knitting bag ("a patriotic holiday gift") could be achieved by joining two ordinary, dyed washrags, buttonholing or blanket-stitching the edges, threading worsted or cotton wool through the toweling's open meshes and pulling a drawstring through a casing. *Star Needlework Journal* featured an economical silk-lined bag whose stripes were knit of leftover scraps.

In lieu of bags, some knitters stuffed yarn balls into loose, pocketed pullovers, and *Vogue*'s party-going model was a "shimmering affair of yellow and white changeable silk embroidered in navy blue silk." Its alternative was a knitting bag—apron in drop-dead black taffeta lined with red taffeta, its black velvet cord forming a belt when converted to an apron. But the bag itself won hands down over variations, and knitters clung to them despite this admonition: "Memorize the phrase, 'A bag is a receptacle for objects.' If you can utilize pieces in the house, make yourself an artistic bag, but do not have a very large forty dollar object which contains one small moth-eaten square of gray dangling from your arm. Neither should you load your bag with books, purse, fancy work, a magazine, and your knitting. Be warned in time."

The warning came too late. Knitters were undaunted by published criticism of their elegant bags ("so ornamental and expensive that they might really be a part of the finery with which a lady adorns herself") and their cramming "onions, carrots, and potatoes on top of a half-finished gray sock, with the sharp points of four needles sticking out, all ready to jab some passenger on the crowded trolley car." They sniffed at proposals that "knitters confine their bags to holding knitting and carry suit cases or hire delivery wagons for the other purposes for which the camouflage knitting bag is now used." Already categorizing nonknitters unpatriotic, and therefore somewhat disreputable, knitters shrugged, aware of the futility of explaining that capacious knitting bags were linchpins of their luggage.

11.

Men and Children
for Sammy, Too

So ingrained was the perception of knitting as a facet of woman's sphere that men who knit during the war needed strong male psyches to tolerate jesting busybodies. Ever on the lookout for "features," journalists scented good copy in masculine knitting, but, being part of the male network themselves, characterized the activity with exculpatory masculine adjectives. The caption for a photograph of New York firemen knitting for the Rainbow Division Welfare identified them as "husky firefighters [who are] not idle between alarms." "Husky" men were surely not pantywaists. Similarly, "athletic" trolley conductors who knit "unostentatiously between stations" and "hardy" members of that city's Chauffeurs Union were absolved of effeminacy. Even *The Woman Citizen*, a staunch feminist periodical that archly announced "Men Can Knit Too," buttressed its argument by citing General Custer's Indian fighter whose proficiency in dainty knitting equaled his mastery of "horses that no one else could ride."

When *The New York Times* picked up scuttlebutt that Arizona's governor knit socks for the soldiers, it elucidated, "When not engaged in steering the helm of State," a salty virile portrait. It was an eye-opener for visitors to the executive office to behold the "knitting governor" working on his socks and to hear his unashamed "Of course, I can get more done at home in the evenings, but I find I have quite a lot of spare time that I can use on knitting at the office. No, it isn't very hard to learn, and I've already finished two mufflers

Governor Hunt of Arizona.

and a pair of socks. My mother was a champion knitter, and she taught me how when I was a boy."

Knitting men magnetized observers, and one writer was struck by the placidity of a male commuter "knitting openly and shamelessly, as he might have read a newspaper or smoked a cigar. . . . He slipped the first stitch, knit one, and purled two as nonchalantly as if he were knocking billiard balls about the table or teeing his ball for a long drive . . . and counted his stitches with a veteran's assurance." Other passengers, however, eyed him derisively, "winking at each other, and shaking their heads, as if he were some kind of curious freak." Envying his rhythm and rapidity in knitting the khaki sweater, the writer lamented that most males so concealed their knitting talents that the wife of a "strong, husky, and athletic" comrade who lovingly worked elegant lace patterns for her attributed his work to a "friend"

Fire Department, Cincinnati, Ohio, 1918.

Stenographers instructing in a noon hour knitting session, 1917.

rather than jeopardize his "masculine" label. He reasoned that war might free men from "restrictions and conventions" so that "[E]re long we shall take out our knitting and crocheting with us on the train. . . . We shall sit in our easy chairs in our club-rooms, busy and contented with our weekly darning and mending in our laps, sewing on our missing buttons while we discuss politics and war policies. Instead of rushing out between acts of the theatre to smoke a hasty cigar or to fill our stomachs with some unnecessary drink or refection, we shall knit a few rounds on a sock for Sammy."

His tongue-in-cheek musings are reminiscent of nineteenth-century gags about clubwomen abandoning their men and derogating to them "women's responsibilities." During the war the long-smoldering "Woman Question," and the sight of suffragists marching, demonstrating and going to jail, so raised the hackles of antagonists that they regarded the sight of women knitting ("that least exciting, most old-fashioned, most feminine of occupations") as evidence of rein-

Children's war activities, Plainfield, New Jersey.

statement in the fold, a "soul satisfying reversion to type." One author, having persuaded himself that "high strung females strained by the harrowing newspaper reports of war" were mutated into the "delightful, dependable, tranquilly domestic creature of earlier days," would have been vexed to learn that many White House suffrage demonstrators packed knitting as well as lunch for the Lafayette Park suffrage vigil across from the White House. Nevertheless, it warmed the cockles of his chauvinist heart to note social leaders knitting everywhere, the young promenading the streets "weighted down with enormous and gaily colored work-bags containing embryonic knitted garments for the comfort of the boys at the front," high church clergy condoning knitting during sermons, girls drawing out their knitting when gabbing "with interested young men hanging on the running board," and moviegoers undaunted by subdued light agilely manipulating needles "festooned with loops of grey yarn." Knitting was a glorious thing!

Male residents in almshouses and tubercular, mental and charitable institutions were taught knitting as occupational therapy, and the Needle and Bobbin Club, previously devoted to lace making, assessed its new charitable knitting program as effective in converting once "moody and apathetic" patients into exhilarated workers appreciative of serving their country. Other enrolees for knitting tutelage from local knitters were convicts, petty criminals to "lifers," to whom Red Cross yarn was donated. Unfortunately, not all prisoners were animated with patriotic zeal, and one venture clearly backfired when two inmates braided the yarn into a twenty-five-foot-long rope, scaled the walls of the Idaho State Penitentiary and escaped. The Red Cross aptly titled the story of their escape, "Oh, Lady, Lady, Who Ever Would Have Thunk It?" Such unscrupulous felons were few, and the trustworthy toiled virtuously. A group at Western State Penitentiary in Philadelphia, surmounting "total idleness," dried wood in the prison kiln, fashioned a machine to produce needles in any size, thickness and quantity, and painstakingly hand polished them for the Red Cross. The warden's qualms about allowing pointed "weapons" were allayed as his charges reliably provided free needles.

Recuperating soldiers, particularly those confined to bed, were grateful to knit. When Earl Allmand convalesced from war wounds at Fort McHenry Hospital, he knit an American flag and presented it to Mary Pickford at a Liberty Bond rally in appreciation for her work as top "bond salesman" on behalf of the "Boys Over There." He had declined a one-hundred-dollar offer for his colorful flag (described as a "perfect model"), measuring ninety stitches across with four-row-deep stripes and edged with gold fringe donated by his instructresses from the Maryland section of the Navy League.

Seeing children absorbed in "working their squares" or "stitching their scarves" was as common as seeing mothers, grannies and some daddies frowning over their projects. Youngsters were persuaded to "Make, Save, Give" (the Junior Red Cross motto) and were informed of how to help by a small pamphlet, "What to Do for Uncle Sam":

> [You should] do anything that you can for all the suffering people, and especially for little children. You can collect and make over old clothing, and the boys who are studying manual training will make boxes for packing and shipping these garments. You can collect old toys, knit, make scrapbooks, puzzles, wind yarn, make comfort pillows, bags for hospital use, and make fruit into jellies and jams that getting-well soldiers and children who have not had enough food need.

Red Cross bulletins underscored children's contributions, headlining them in their pint-size uniforms: "Ellarea Baldwin of Minot Knits Afghan Square Every Week"; "Here are two little girls who are spending their spare moments knitting sweaters and scarfs for the Red Cross." A paean to the young was a poem, dedicated to "A Little Red Cross Helper," of which two verses are given:

> I'm awful busy working for
>   The Soldier-men in France;
> I mean to make them a lot of things
>   If once I get a chance.
>
> I've made already one face-cloth,
>   And knitted it myself;
> But Daddy used it by mistake—
>   'Twas laying on the shelf.

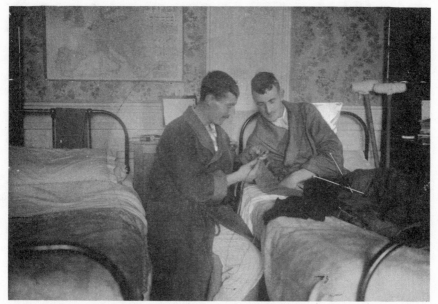

Injured men in a hospital making socks for soldiers.

Eighty-six-year-old Zelpha Gritt proudly recollects her wartime sock project:

> Because of my mother's death when I was four, my Grandmother Clement raised me. She was very handy with the knitting needle and had knit for her husband during the Civil War. When I was fifteen, I accepted a ball of yarn from the Government to make a pair of socks for soldiers in World War I, who were overseas. My grandmother insisted upon washing the yarn, and I never knew exactly why, but it soon dried and I made my first pair of socks and they were sent overseas.

Another wartime teenager, Georgia Vilven, of Wamego, Kansas, remembers:

> The Union Pacific runs through our town; so if we were on the playground and heard a train coming, we would run four or five blocks to wave at the soldiers; since Fort Riley was only thirty-five miles away, there was lots of military activity here. Our high school

Schoolgirls knitting for soldiers.

Domestic Science class went across the street to two large rooms donated by a neighbor to make bandages for war zone hospitals while the older women knit socks (which absorbed moisture better than store ones) and a combination helmet-scarf for the Red Cross. I'll never forget it.

When six-year-old Nancy McClure grew restless while waiting for the adults who sewed, knit, made bandages and packed boxes in the Red Cross rooms in Spring City, Tennessee, the ladies cast olive drab yarn onto tiny sock needles and taught her to knit a simple garter-stitch sweater for her doll—just a back, two fronts, a tie neck and no sleeves, an outfit she still treasures sixty years later.

"Home" magazines, such as *Delineator* and *Woman's Magazine*, both published by Butterick Company, lured young readers through monthly columns on Junior Red Cross chapters, hitting the jackpot with a contest for "best record of war work" for the month of April 1918. The prize was "Pershing," every child's dream "police dog," whose father was at that very moment serving with the Red Cross in France! The winning club could elect to keep Pershing or send him to France "to serve with his father," and panicky leaders were heartened to learn that he was already housebroken! The deliriously happy winners were members of the Maplewood, New Jersey, chapter, whose volume of knitted garments stunned the judges, especially when they were apprised of the large number made by boys: 354 knitted articles including thirty-one sweaters, eight scarfs, one helmet, thirty-one pairs of wristlets, seventy-five pairs of socks, and 208 washcloths. In awarding the prize, however, contest sponsors were pained to explain that Pershing's skin disease had not responded to his trainer's ministrations and that a substitute would be supplied. When the princely Sonny was gratefully embraced by the Juniors who proudly marched with him in the local Fourth of July parade, there was no further talk of sending him "over there."

A photograph captioned "Indian boys vie with their sisters in knitting for our soldiers" illustrated *Delineator*'s report on "True American" southwestern Indian children, "doing everything in their power to win the war" by selling war bonds, making surgical garments, raising money through benefits with sales of Indian handicrafts, and knitting "work of the highest caliber" for the Red Cross and individual soldiers. Citing the diversity of young helpers, *Delineator* also commended the "little natives" of the Southeastern Alaska Indian children of the Government School, the "Juneau Juniors": "You ought to watch the speed with which knitting needles fly in their deft brown hands. They are alert and quick to learn, taking an eager place among our most patriotic and useful juniors. . . . Geographically, they are remote from the scenes of distress and suffering, but in thought and sympathy they are very close to the little unfortunate war victims."

When time was set aside for knitting in schoolrooms across the country, teachers with rusty skills enlisted help from agile mothers. A writer for *Vogue* characteristically inventoried what New York private school girls were doing for the war effort and concluded that patriotic knitting not only reduced mindless chattering "over the chocolate cups" but stimulated the double activity of hand and brain as students knit during lectures and some lessons. A New York teacher with boys in her class was apprehensive that they would be galled at engaging in "some effeminate thing" but was astonished at their absorption and proficiency: "When a geometry lesson is over, and there is a wait for geography hour, they immediately draw out their knitting and work tremendously. Right after turning a beautiful heel in a sock they go out and play the roughest game of football imaginable."

When Des Moines summer playgrounds included juvenile knitting classes, everyone gathered leftover yarn or unraveled old sweaters so that children could knit squares for "convalescent blankets" for the nearby Camp Dodge base hospital. Knitting squares of assorted colors that were later assembled by adults was so commonplace that one young Baltimore lad remembered decades afterward that others envied his wide array of bright yarns while they were stuck with blues and grays. His father owned a five-and-ten-cent store and supplied him liberally! Lillian Lunny of Staten Island brought two lollypop sticks and a ball of any cotton knitting yarn to school, where her kindergarten teacher helped her knit squares for warm afghans for soldiers recuperating in nearby Halloran Hospital. Without her Aunt Blanche's help in straightening out her piece "when stitches got too mixed up," she would never have been able to contribute her finished squares. Octogenarian Lewella Francis recalls her fourth-grade knitting project in Winsted, Connecticut:

> Our boys were in the trenches in France and even nine and ten year olds got involved in the war effort. Besides making "trench candles" of rolled newspapers dipped in paraffin, we also learned to knit. Inspired by our lively, young red-headed teacher, Miss Frances Glynn, we knit blocks for afghans to keep our boys warm.
>
> Money to buy knitting needles was scarce and with no needles I could not participate in the project. My grandfather, sensitive to my disappointment, *whittled* me two knitting needles from some hardwood twigs. Sanded though they were, they were rough and 'snaggy'; also the points were too long so it was hard to keep even stitches. Nonetheless I was delighted. I learned to knit on these home-made needles and was permitted to choose a favorite color from the yarn bin and sat at my desk clicking away and very proud for a small part in the war effort.

The "Rocky Mountain Knitter Boys" of Mapleton, Colorado, achieved national prominence by telling their story in the leading children's magazine, *Saint Nicholas*. Their savvy school principal had explained the lack of warm clothing for the "brave Sammies . . .

fighting to save our homes, to save our schools, to keep back the zeppelins that any day might be coming over Mapleton Hill and drop bombs on our school-house," and he taunted the boys, "Would it be patriotic for only girls to do the knitting and the boys just sit back and look on? . . . Why shouldn't the boys learn to knit and prove themselves as patriotic as the girls?" The boys, after retorting "Do you think we are sissies?" and "Let the girls knit—it's women's work," galvanized and embarked upon washcloths and scarves until the entire class knit during oral reports and recess, after lunch and after school, whenever they could grab a moment. Reported one of the "Knitter Boys":

> Knitting's the best thing ever to steady your nerves. The boys in our room that used to sit and fumble their ink-wells, or tap their pencils, or tinker with their rulers, or maybe flip bits of art-gum at you when somebody was reciting, are so busy with their knitting that they never fidget or misbehave. And the girls—my, how their knitting does count up! Pauline and Esther each knit a sweater a week and keep up with their lessons as well as ever while Guy's the champion boy-knitter of the school. He has finished three sweaters and four pairs of wristlets, and is knitting a helmet now. Helmets are hard, too, but we've got half a dozen boys well started on them.

Though there were many such "boy-knitters," girls far outnumbered them, patterning their behavior after female family members. One aunt remarked proudly of her nieces: "Their knitting bags go with them everywhere. The older girl of fifteen is on her fourth pair of big gray socks; she has knit two sleeveless sweaters and two helmets. She knit while we were waiting for dinner; we went to the theater; she knit between the acts. The youngest is knitting washcloths and hot-water bag covers."

Girl Scouts cultivated gardens, canned fruit and vegetables, helped at rehabilitation centers, rolled bandages, sewed and knit. Their national magazine's "News of the Troops" reported scout troop activities: "The Narcissus Troop of Memphis made an afghan with an American eagle knit in the center"; "The War Service Award went to a girl who, though deaf and dumb persuaded ten persons to buy Liberty bonds and her nimble fingers have knitted two pounds of wool for the Red Cross"; "The Iris troop #13 of Brooklyn knit slumber slippers as well as an afghan." With yarn purchases financed by bake sales of their special, low-sugar "War Bread," most scouts knit two-pound "sets" of sweater, muffler, a pair of wristlets and a pair of socks. But those who could manage only the simplest afghan squares were encouraged to use scraps of bright yarn ("If you want to combine the soft gray wool left from Brother Bob's sweater with the lavender from grandma's slippers, go right ahead") to enliven soldiers' quarters. Following the Civil War custom of their grand-mothers and great-grandmothers, scouts added "Made By a Girl Scout of Troop Number . . ." tags to finished products and enclosed warmhearted notes.

Knitters always hoped for letter exchanges with appreciative re-cipients, but *Red Cross Magazine* told of one soldier's finding a dead comrade ("a mere slip of a boy who had been killed while trying to assist his wounded pal to a place of safety") still carrying this message penned in a "clear, childish hand": "Dear Soldier Boy: This scarf was made by a little girl ten years old. I would like to hear from you if you have time to write." The soldier wrote back: "You are only a little girl, but you have cause to feel proud because your contribution to the boys who fought on a foreign battlefield found its way to one who fought well and died well. . . . I hope that you will find comfort in knowing you heard from 'Dear Soldier Boy' even though he writes by proxy."

This personal identification with "Sammies" coaxed wartime chil-dren to knit military wardrobes for their dolls, following instruction books targeted to their age group. One of the most interesting of these is the charmingly illustrated *The Mary Frances Knitting and Crocheting Book or Adventures Among the Knitting People*, which was not originally intended as a wartime book but was converted to one by an appendix added at publication. As its characters—"Crow Shay," the twins "Knit and Knack," "Wooly Ball," "Yarn Baby," "Hookey," and "Fairly Flew" (a sort of knitting instructor fairy!)—tutored young Mary Frances in knitting, one is reminded of "Miss Lambert"'s 1846 observation, "It is said that knitting should be taught to children, when young. It is curious to observe how much more easily those persons handle the needle, who have learnt it in childhood." Like Mary Frances, who followed advice from "Aunt Maria" and Fairly Flew and thus "learnt in her childhood," 1918's children transposed those "learnings" into soldier knitting and spawned a new generation of knitters.

Carol, the teenage heroine of the popular novel for girls *A Girl Scout of Red Rose Troop*, published in 1918, and once an indifferent knitter, took it up when apprised of the needs of the boys at camp and declared to her mother, "Some of the girls are doing trench caps; some are doing mufflers; some are doing sleeveless sweaters; and I believe I could do those, for I am getting to knit faster and more evenly." Joining her was teenage Rilla, daughter of "Anne of Green Gables," who knit to ease "frayed nerves." As Rilla's friend Susan put it, "Knitting is something you can do even when your heart is going like a trip-hammer and the pit of your stomach feels all gone and your thoughts are catawampus." Rilla was delighted with her progress: "I finished my sixth pair of socks today. With the first three I got Susan to set the heel for me. Then I thought that was a bit of shirking, so I learned to do it myself. I hate it. But I have done so many things I hate . . . that one more or less doesn't matter."

While men and children also knit, it was to women (who represented home and all it stood for) to whom sentimental songs and poems paid tribute. The "Knitting Song," dedicated "To the Soldier Girls Back Home," arranged for part-singing, featured at patriotic meetings and sung around the piano that graced almost every parlor, was part of a collection of such patriotic songs as "A Song of Liberty," "Hymn of Freedom," "Peace with a Sword" and "America Triumphant." Audiences loved to chime in on the tag lines, "It isn't hard to cast a stitch; the work goes on without a hitch," "For everybody's doing it; You can't persuade the girls to quit. . . . Knitting! Knitting! Knitting!"

The last stanza of novelist Kathleen Norris's "The Knitting Women" best expressed the symbiosis between knitting women and their "Sammies":

> We are the knitting women, weaving swift
> Our webs of olive drab and navy gray
> We are the women, keeping thought away

DAR Nifty Knitters Club, 1918.

> By this new work of love, this eager gift
> Through which our men, facing bitter flight
> Under the stars of foreign lands,
> Shall know that still a million women's hands
> Uphold them in the darkness and the night.

Fighting "Sammies," warmed both by their garments and the love that prompted them, would relate to grandchildren their elation at receiving those consecrated offerings.

12.

Flappers Versus the "Old-Fashioned Knitters"

When the armistice was finally signed in 1919 and families welcomed home their "soldier boys," war-weary knitters discovered far-reaching cultural changes had occurred during the emergency. Young and newly independent women, their sisterhood sparked by entrance into the wartime work force, proselytized those whose chief objection to universal female suffrage was grounded in the "home is the place for women" canon by insisting that women's wartime experience of combining home and business, of turning women's "pink teas and frittering needlework" into war organizations committed to essential work, had brought about changes so profound that it was "hard to remember what it was like before." Sharing this view, Mabel Potter Daggett, who had studied and written of women's war work, exulted in *Pictorial Review*: "Have the American Women Made Good? Well, I guess Yes! . . . Every girl worth her salt today wants to earn her own living. . . . The strongest possible social force has been set operating and actively cooperating toward the economic independence for the

New Woman." Another feminist writer roused the New Women: "Now That We've Got to Reconstruct the World, Let's Do It Right!"

At war's end, hems rested innocuously six inches above the ankle, short-haired women were still associated with radicalism, cosmetic wearers were labeled "not well brought up," garters attached to corsets securely held up black or tan stockings and ladies wore veiled hats for shopping trips. Within months of the peace, hems crept steadily upward and necklines plunged relentlessly downward. The *Woman's Home Companion's* editor smugly held last rites over the dress reform issue ("as dead as suffrage") since in postwar fashion "[t]he neck of our dress is not extended up under our ears; and even the smartest blue serge from Saks Fifth Avenue's most exclusive shop allows the waist of the wearer to take its rightful place in breathing." Twenties women, like those of previous generations, hooted at visions of their grandmothers in trailing, dirty street dresses and congratulated themselves for replacing thick, shapeless sweaters ("a vulgar garment with a vulgar name") with smart and "eminently comfortable" sports garments.

Despite many of the young's denigration of knitting as "woman's work," those who had rallied their knitting needles for the war effort were called upon again by the Red Cross to knit for war refugees, to "express with your knitting needles that sympathetic love for those who suffer." One chapter, recognizing that some faithful and industrious knitters were simply "knit out," emphasized that knitting warm, sleeved sweaters, shoulder shawls, scarves and stockings for destitute women and children provided "a little variety" from soldier knitting. The Red Cross had considered sending yarn and needles abroad to give employment to refugee women but feared it might deter American women from knitting support. Throughout the twenties Red Cross magazines featured knitters such as octogenarian Lucy MacKenzie, of Portland, Oregon, who, though she kept house for four, finished her fortieth sweater in one year and vowed to "keep knitting as long as the wool lasts," and others who knit for everyone from disabled exservicemen in hospitals to Bulgarian refugees.

The American Committee for the Devastated French pleaded for two thousand pairs of socks: "Don't stop knitting. Khaki and gray wool are almost impossible to buy, but white or colored wools are still obtainable and there is an urgent need for stockings . . . [with]

The Smart Set, 1926.

longer legs and smaller feet so that the little children who are without foot covering in lands where fuel and shelter are scarce may be saved from the curse of frozen feet." Sighed a knitting manual's author, "The revival of knitting seems to be the one and only benefit derived from the War . . . [and] provides just enough movement for those who are too nervous to sit quite still and rest [since] there are many war-wrecked constitutions, in these days, alas!"·

War-wrecked or not, knitters longing for new colors and designs were heartened by the opening words of Fleisher Yarns' advertisements, "Now that the shadow of war has passed . . ." Fleisher proposed color changes, but when it enumerated its new shades for summer wardrobes ("Consider the possibilities of such colors as henna, pumpkin, reindeer, burgundy. There is a charming new olive . . .") expectant buyers recoiled in horror. "A charming new olive"? To jaded knitters, olive was synonymous with khaki, and they speculated that old dye pots had not yet been dismantled. Fleisher appeared to combine dark colors from the old stock with new, bright highlights ("Many of the most fascinating knitted things of our grandmother's time were gay with little flecks of full color, against a sombre background") until they were mercifully exhausted, then bragged with relief that its new line included "Every Color in the Rainbow." *Delineator*'s Marie Ashley, who had renounced fancy needlework during the "emergency," crowed, "Back to Our Needlework: Released War Knitters Take Up the Thread of New Embroideries," and treated her readers to butterflies, flowers, beads, embroideries, filet crochet and decorations for "lingerie dresses." War knitting was officially over!

The *Star Needlework Journal*, whose ill-starred wartime contest had backfired, optimistically tried again, but seasoned knitting veterans filled in few entry blanks. Filet Crochet, with tatting a close second, so swamped New York's Hotel McAlpin that only a portion could be displayed at the five-day exhibition. Cotton manufacturers, especially those such as American Thread Company, rejoiced that customers were at least doing some kind of needlework and stepped up crochet patterns. The younger "liberated" girls who cheerfully knit in their Junior Red Cross groups but now balked at a craft "meant for grannies" were the bane of the yarn industry.

To recapture defecting "knit-out" and "put-off" knitters, Fleisher launched a nine-week national knitting-only contest in April 1923 that made American Thread's *Star Needlework*'s $1,500 prize money appear miserly compared to their $11,000, the top prize alone being $2,000. Local groups sponsored warm-up sessions for the big contest. The Drop Stitch Knitting Club in Atlantic City staged a "Knitting Marathon" at the Ambassador Hotel, where twenty-three entrants began knitting at four o'clock in the afternoon. The lone male participant, a veteran who had learned to knit while recuperating from shell shock in a French hospital, dropped out after five hours. By midnight, only thirteen, including a seventy-five-year-old great-grandmother and a twelve-year-old grammar school student, still knit. After twelve hours, doctors initiated hourly five-minute rest periods, but, sustained by hot soup delivered by waiters and stimulated by the phonograph's blaring the wildest jazz anyone could find, the remaining contestants managed to stay awake, though the great-grandmother called it quits a little after four in the morning. By four the next afternoon, though the remaining eight were still blithely knitting, fatigued officials called a halt before contestants persisted to the point of exhaustion, and admiringly awarded them joint custody of the record for unprecedented staying power. The knitters were indignant, but the contest was officially over. Each "survivor" received a prize and was singled out for "having the best work," and together they made twenty articles during the marathon, including five sweaters and assorted baby wear. Today, the Bucilla Company of Secaucus, New Jersey (marketers of Fleisher yarns), still cherishes its crumbling special Photogravure section showing scenes from those preliminary contests.

The main contest attracted the wives of two prominent politicians, the first lady of the land, Mrs. Calvin Coolidge, and the first lady of New York, Mrs. Alfred E. Smith (as well as the latter's daughter). Grace Coolidge had always found solace in vigorous knitting, observing once on the presidential yacht, the *Mayflower*, "Many a time when I have to hold myself firmly, I have taken up my needle. It might be a sewing needle, knitting needles, or a crochet hook—whatever its form or purposes, it often proved to be the needle of the compass, keeping me to the course." Spurred by the Coolidge publicity and generous prize money, thousands entered the contest, from a woman who knit a lavishly designed fly swatter to convalescing war veterans who had mastered knitting in hospital wards. Since makers' names were removed from garments before submission, the panel of five needlework editors of the major women's magazines and the fashion editor of *Vogue* never knew the identity of the knitter of the white, yard-square baby carriage robe of old-fashioned four-fold Germantown yarn ("the sturdy opposite of the fluffy fibres dear to the flappers"), with stripes of plain knitting alternating with three panels of yarn "lace" and lined with pink crepe de Chine.

So much excitement was generated over the contest that *The New York Times* complained editorially that knitting for prizes was as old as the hills, that women had been competing at fairs for generations and recommended that anyone wanting to see a knitting contest should visit the "Three County Fair" in Northampton, Massachusetts, where the Coolidges had a modest home. Though prizes amounted to $15 rather than $2,000, the blue ribbon alone was adequate compensation. Mrs. Coolidge had to wait through the summer to learn if she was the first lady of knitting. She was not—though she won an honorable mention. Mrs. E. C. Wyman of Jamestown, Rhode Island, carried home the top prize for her "most beautiful and original" sweater and scarf; the second-prize winner had knit a dress, the third, a beach robe. Coolidge's baby carriage robe ("Slumberland Afghan"), when displayed at an Atlantic City exhibit tucked around a nine-month-old resident of that city, brought a rash of offers that were politely rejected in favor of saving it for her first grandchild. Today, however, the parents of that first grandchild, the daughter of John Coolidge, her only surviving child, and his wife, have no recollection of the "Slumberland Afghan," though Mr. Coolidge does remember the many "sweaters, scarves, mittens, socks, helmets and toques" she knit for him and his brother. It was common for her to donate small knit objects for bazaar and benefit raffles, such as powder puff bags, knit coverings for balls of yarn, and cardboards covered with knit hoods for a pocket mirror and comb. For herself and close friends she undertook such elegant silk stockings that the press reported, "So expert is the president's wife in knitting silk hose that she can work in the daintiest clocking and even insert a monogram without undue trouble."

Mrs. Coolidge knit a counterpane that achieved some renown when, as "Mrs. Coolidge's Great Grandmother's spread," it was shown in a well-known knitting instruction booklet. The pattern, however, was *not* her grandmother's, but had been given to her by a Virginia congressman's wife who saw the original on a bed in the Home for Needy Confederate Women in Richmond. When a newswoman interviewing Mrs. Coolidge admired the counterpane, she sold her the pattern for $250 and turned the money over to the home. The Smithsonian Institution has a replica knit from that pattern, since it does have historic interest, but John Coolidge has no knowledge of the disposition of his mother's spread.

Knitter Grace Coolidge epitomized the steady, "old fashioned" (and that included knitting!) woman almost engulfed by the rising tide of "New Women" bent on changing the mores of the decade. Skirts ascended until one writer ho-hummed, "The modern male has seen so much that there is really very little left to see. . . . Men still cover the body from chin to soles, but women are (or were) rolling up from below, down from above, and in from the sides." A Fifth Avenue bus conductor, noting the nervous descent of a rider from the upper deck, called to her, "Come right down, lady. Legs ain't no treat to me!" Shocked elders, including solons in some state legislatures, translated "dress reform," which once meant delivering women from the bondage of impractical and constricting clothing, into attempts to ban dresses more than three inches from the ankles, limit decolletage to two inches, proscribe diaphanous fabrics and outlaw garments unduly outlining the female form. The principal of a Santa Rosa, California, school, asked to resign for wearing skirts eight inches from the floor *and* powdering her nose, sought a student referendum on the board's decree. When students signaled endorsement of their teacher, three trustees retired in a snit. *The American Journal of Public Health* warned that unprotected lower legs ("there being no skirt to cover them and thin silk stockings being often the only covering") were subject to a disease producing a reddened thickening of the skin and hoped that the fashion would not remain in vogue long enough to cause additional damage. New York University's student newspaper, alarmed at "cobwebby" evening fabrics, deplored coeds in a "minimum of clothes and a maximum of cosmetics." Another college group was aghast at "toddle" or "shimmy" dancing: "To jig and hop around like a chicken on a red-hot stove, at the same time shaking the body until it quivers, like a disturbed glass of jell-o, is not only tremendously suggestive but it is an offense against common decency that would not be permitted in a semirespectable roadhouse."

Ohio's Catholic archbishop warned against "bare female shoulders"; the pope appealed to fathers, husbands and brothers to check women's increased immodesty; the Hebrew Union of Orthodox Congregations condemned women's scant garb, particularly when attending services; Georgia's Baptist *Christian Convention* inveighed against clothing "calculated to do great violence to the sanctities of womanhood"; *The Methodist Protestant Herald* warned that though evil might be in the eye of the beholder, a woman should realize the effect of abbreviated garb and exposed legs upon a male "not so virtuous as she." *That* ignited an Arkansas respondent, who shot back, "Why should men be permitted to tell us how to dress? . . . Why should the fact that a girl has legs arouse the wrong kind of impulses in a man? Does he think we travel around on wheels?" Tennis great Helen Wills staunchly asserted, "Emancipated Legs Mean Better Sports"; a middle-aged respondent to the *Literary Digest*'s query about new styles and mores contended, "Skirts can't get too short for me, now that at this age I am climbing in and out of automobiles . . . and playing golf in all weathers." Another seconded the motion: "The girl of to-day is not going bad. She is in a fair way to make a finer, healthier wife and mother and to produce a cleaner stronger generation than ever before." Short-skirt protagonists elicited welcome support from almost four hundred "Rainy Daisies" marking the silver jubilee of their Rainy Day Club's formation in 1896 when, despite stout opposition, they courageously donned full, circular skirts a shocking four inches from the floor and faced the derision always due innovators. One pioneer remarked, "You know, any reform has to develop and grow and pass through many phases before the public will have confidence in it." Still, Rainy Daisies were now in their fifties and hoped that abbreviated and "immodest" skirts would be short-lived and that hemlines would settle at a "sanitary, artistic and useful" ten inches from the floor. Uneasy at the burgeoning movement toward lengthening skirts, the club resolved that "their clothes, including panels or other draperies be no nearer the ground than seven inches; and that they be cut in such a manner . . . to permit perfect freedom of the limbs."

Most men feared the extinction of the sweet, modest, innocent, old-fashioned girl who knit. As flappers elevated skirts to thighs, rolled gossamer silk stockings (in a color shockingly called "nude") below knees, discarded corsets, razored their legs, boyishly flattened their chests, lowered belts to the hips (acquiring the "proportions of a goddess above and a pigmy below"), covered foreheads with "headache bands," applied rouge and powder, shaped mouths into small, puckered, "bee stung" lips like "It Girl" Clara Bow's, tweezed eyebrows, drank in speakeasies, smoked, swore and dieted away their curves, alarm spread. Bobbed hair was the final straw!

This badge of "flapperhood" was attributed by its detractors to famed dancer Irene Castle, whose clipped tresses were blamed for everything from broken engagements to wrecked homes. When she secured her hair with a flat, seed pearl forehead band, devotees sallied forth with their own "Castle Bands." Her *Ladies' Home Journal* explanation, "I Bobbed My Hair and Then—," yielded a rich harvest of bob-and-tell stories such as Mary Garden's "Why I Bobbed My Hair" and Mary Pickford's rejoinder, "Why I Have Not Bobbed Mine." Bobbed hair, credited with taking "ten years off a woman's looks and at least fifteen off her leaden-footed mind," couldn't be

Fleisher's Knitting and Crocheting Manual, 1926.

all bad, though sleeping on it without a small cap "like babies wear to keep their ears flat" produced disastrous results. Knitters simply worked boudoir caps on smaller needles and hoped for the best.

An innovative but anxious woman who couldn't bring herself to sacrifice her own tresses for the coveted bob attached artificial curls and puffs such as the "American Girl Cluster Bob" to mask long hair "without detection." If she *had* bobbed and hated it, she could shroud the calamitous results with the Cluster Bob until her own locks grew back. Hairdressers would win either way, for, in addition to cutting, they offered the permanent wave, which, one stylist noted, seemed to have swept over the country like the "high tide up the Bay of Fundy."

For those who resorted to curling irons, whose temperatures were not easily regulated ("If it scorches paper ever so little, it will also scorch your hair and cause it to break"), the frizzed look was unavoidable. For protection of bobbed coiffures, pull-down cloche hats were ideal since one could tuck ends under with invisible hairpins and fluff them out upon removing the hat. Some were made of felt, but many handicrafters crocheted or knit them, one of knitted silk being hailed as "the caprice of Spring fashions." A writer in the *Atlantic Monthly* recognized the little "knitted hat with hardly any brim" as one of the signposts of that new breed "Flapper Americana Novissima," while another explained, "They have a delightful 'come hither' quality that hints at beauty, but they keep their secret well, for they keep the hair well hidden from the careless or unappreciative eye." When curly bobs were declared passé, liberated women switched to the shingle cut and the "wind-blown," the latter a flat, forward-brushed, face-framing coiffure that led fashion authorities to announce "Ears are in!"

At home, millions had telephones, electric lights, indoor plumbing, radios (encroaching on pianos and phonographs for entertainment) and most of the housekeeping conveniences, such as electric flat-irons, vacuum cleaners, washing machines, fans, toasters, heaters and refrigerators. "Home," however, had changed, as one-room-with-kitchenette-and-folding-bed apartments increased faster than the national income. Who wanted to stay home when the twenty-five million automobiles that hit the road by the end of the decade offered the elation of speed and the promise of romance, adventure and escape with a "Jump in it, step on it, all are yours." Where would all this freedom lead?

One disgruntled commentator groused that freedom-seeking women were "dressed for a formal ball from the waist up and for a tennis game from the waist down," while another implored in a letter to *The New York Times*, "Dear God, give us back our women!" "Our women" stayed home and "stuck to their knitting." They were the long-haired, busty, broad-hipped, wasp-waisted, domestic Gibson Girls of yesteryear and not the scrawny results of intemperate dieting. With waistlines and bosoms smoothed and flattened (the lowered belt line "straightens out the waistline and makes hips and bust appear smaller"), derrieres rolling free of restraint and dresses pared to the minimum, women were left to battle fatty bulges without long-trusted corsets to rearrange problem areas. Despite corsetiers' arguments that corsets were "sound, physical aid[s] in helping women to keep the upright posture," the corset was so equated with the subjugation of women that one commentator concluded that suffrage demonstrators "might well have carried a tattered corset as evidence of their emancipation." The depth of the corset industry's depression was publicized when the will of the previously prosperous Warner Corset Company's president was probated in 1927, indicating that half the value of his estate had been written off because of the business decline. With the "Iron Maiden" a symbol rather than a garment, some would-be flappers, eager to achieve the boyishly uncontoured look, encased their entire bodies or "selected parts of bust, chin, neck etc." in rubber "reducing" garments to process them for slimmer knits that cast every fault into bold relief. Of those who resorted to diet crazes, one concluded smugly, "I guess dieting is making us girls what we are today." What they were were toothpicks, and though the term "anorexia nervosa" was not used in the twenties, doctors were appalled at the abuse to women's bodies.

"Our women" were knitters, for not all of them had renounced "silly domestic work." "Real" ladies were still knitting beaded bags, updating designs to conform to the newly popular stripes and tubes, and bead fringing and tasseling the bases so that they could swing

The tubular look, 1926.

the bags with graceful abandon to complement handkerchief-hem-lined tea gowns. To the faithful, once "olive" and "reindeer" were exhausted, vivid color and high style were passwords, especially shades found on hieroglyphics when King Tutankhamen's tomb was unsealed. Trendsetter Irene Castle's "smart afternoon frock" bore embroidered Egyptian motifs; entrants in Fleisher's knitting contest reflected the "King Tut" influence in their designs; others encrusted simple hand-knit silk sweaters with Egyptian embroidery. Color was so vivid that an etiquette author gushed, "Women's sports clothes are like spot-lights bringing the individual sharply out against the landscape like a tree of beautiful foliage or a patch of gay flowering on the hillside." Men, lamentably, were relegated to somber tones to match the "shrubbery and undergrowth through which they hunt and fish."

With color, the second component was *style*. Fleisher stressed that ambitious knitters aspiring to community leadership could no longer "rest content with just a 'hand-knitted' sweater . . . [for] Dame Fash-ion has learned to Knit!" "Dame Fashion" held court in Europe or at "smart" country clubs, the hub of sports enthusiasts' lives. Knitting manuals were aimed at upper-class, sports-minded knitters who spent more and more time outside the city at clubs or exclusive resorts. While it was reported that "trousered ladies" credited their new garb with paring their games by at least ten shots, most women stuck to skirts with their sweaters. Peace Dale Company's pattern book hyped its knitted-in designs for sweaters with the imprimatur of "the fash-ionable resorts." Fleisher, adding winter Alpine and Mediterranean resorts to inspirations from Parisian sweaters, delineated categories: "Sport sweaters" for active sports and "country club sweaters" for general outdoor wear. All bore names of well-known eastern country clubs. "The Pinehurst," named for North Carolina's great golf capital, was a "sports sweater," while "The Chevy Chase," named for Wash-ington's "Cave Dwellers" club, was respectfully berthed in the "country club sweater" slot. The softly colored "Chevy Chase," worn with a sheer blouse and skirt in a soft fabric such as satin or crepe de chine, was accessorized by a "wide-brimmed, flower trimmed hat," perfect for promenading the lush, green sward stretching out from the clubhouse. For variety, Fleisher suggested adapting the "country club sweater" for active sports by knitting it in such appropriate

Skating costume, 1921.

colors as "black, dark reindeer, pigskin, camel, heather, and natural mixtures." A few dye lots survived!

Sweaters were prescribed for stay-at-homes as well, and many entered those ranks when they became addicted to bridge, crossword puzzles or mah-jongg. Women's magazines ran columns on what to serve at bridge luncheons, where, as "dummy," a knitter could work a few stitches and annoy the rest of the foursome by finishing "just this row" as the next hand was dealt. A mah-jongg player, once ivory and bamboo tiles were arranged on her Wall, could knit as she contemplated "Plum Blossom from the Roof," "Earthly Peace," "The Hand from Heaven," "Invisible Dragons" and "Flowers" and opponents plotted strategic collections for "Pung," "Chow" and "Kung" victories.

While older knitters stuck to traditional patterns, the young approved of slim, tubular knits with horizontal banding that would have "cut in half" their fleshier counterparts. De rigueur wardrobes for college girls consisted of dark, durable serge dresses for the classroom, "best" dark dresses with interchangeable collars and cuffs (many knit or crocheted to avoid ironing) for "constant Sunday wear," plenty of low shoes and woolen stockings knit in "softly variegated colors" to match dresses, and garters for rolling athletic stockings below the knee. Up-to-the-minute twenties students required an absolute minimum of one sweater, perferably a handknit one "to suit individual fancy and size even better than ones displayed in the stores." To be truly au courant, that sweater should be an Argyle with matching stockings. For basic sweaters, *Ladies' Home Journal* favored a snowy white, scarf-collared sweater with the "smart vestee effect" for skating, skiing and coasting, and an all-purpose practical gray sweater whose "gay Roman-striped border, collar and cuffs keep it from being at all somber. It has so many colors that it will match whatever sports togs you may possess." Paris had decreed that "stripes go roundabout more than ever even if the effect is to make the wearer look like a barrel." The barrel look was an obvious consequence of attending dorm "fudge parties," to which "shindigs" a fashion writer considered it compulsory to wear becoming negligees and boudoir caps in summer and warm bathrobes and cozy worsted knee-length knit slippers in winter. Finished with an elastic band to fit just over the knees, the slippers were guaranteed to arouse envy "if the party lasts after the heat has gone out of the radiator."

The heat went out of more than the radiator. Home Economics knitting enthusiasts who had successfully overseen inclusion of knitting in prewar school sewing programs and observed wartime school knitting regarded as a "definite value to the community" now shuddered at knitting's demotion to little more than a "mechanical process" unworthy of a place in school curricula.

The hand yarn industry, despite its championship of color revolution and "high style" knitting, knew a slump when it saw it but continued publishing instruction pamphlets despite sagging interest. When older, burned-out, wartime knitters shifted to other needlework (including rug making) and younger women, "liberated" from domestic pursuits, turned thumbs-down, the industry took action. To the rescue came the enterprising Ulmann (owner of Fleisher and Bear Brand labels) representative, Clair Wolf, who managed to penetrate the screen around the royal House of Windsor to suggest that the empire's sales of Australian wool would rebound if the popular princes, Albert and George, espoused knitting. To her astonishment, the endorsement came when they actually *knit* the scarves their doting mother showed off at Queen Mary's Needlework Guild in 1929. As news spread that the world's most eligible bachelor (and his brother) actually *knit*, needles as well as tongues clicked. A revival would, however, require more than a combined royal boost and the blandishments of *Vogue* and *Harper's Bazaar* that knitting was "fashionable." Though hand knitting languished, the machine knitting industry boomed as new technology facilitated copying fancy handwear. Appetites were whetted by trade publications portraying "society" persons at prominent resorts and clubs in classic "veddy British" knits. In *Sweater News*, prestigious bankers posed in knickers "on the links," their Argyle sweaters twinned with Argyle stockings; a couple well known in social and philanthropic circles, she in her Argyle sweater, appeared "relaxing at Hot Springs, Virginia"; tennis champion Helen Wills wore *her* Argyle sweater, "one of the outfits in her tennis collection," at an exclusive club on Long Island. Golf great Bobby Jones's Argyle socks were conspicuously snappy above cleated shoes.

Men's Argyle hosiery grew so popular that, according to *Men's Wear*, the "Scotch wave" soon spread to Argyle-patterned neckwear

A quartet of stylish golfers, c. 1925.

such as silk ascots, ties, and then, of course, to sweaters. *Men's Wear* wondered why this "hereditary and natural . . . urge to wear brilliant trappings [and] artificial plumage" should be restricted to women, "the courageous sex," when brilliant colors should rightly be worn by *all* "those who dare!" Plenty dared!

This American penchant for British fashions emerged from an age-old fascination with Europe, especially Britain. *Harper's Bazaar* illustrated its "What the Smart English Sportswoman Wears for Golf" with models posing in Scottish knit "Jumpers" in all over, yoked, or collared-and-cuffed Fair Isle designs, and inaugurated a passion for Fair Isle and Argyle designs in both ready-made and hand-knit garments. If knitters were too squeamish to undertake a complicated "full Argyle" sock, they knit a ribbed "lower" and added an Argyle cuff as they had for cycling stockings in the 1890s. Since 1920s Argyle patterns were not graphed and color changes were indicated

Man's sweater, 1920.

stitch by stitch and row by row, knitters familiarized themselves with instructions such as: "9th Row: 4 tan, *5 natural, 1 brown, 5 natural, 1 brown, 5 natural, 7 tan, 5 brown, 1 natural, 5 brown, 1 natural, 5 brown,* 7 tan. Repeat between *'s ending with 3 tan." It was no wonder that most dodged Argyle vests and knit plain jumpers to accompany knickers for men and tweed or knitted skirts for women. As to the latter, however, American golfer Glenna Collett noted that the knit skirt's initial advantage ("It stretches to fit the widest stance and falls back into place") spelled defeat for a Canadian opponent whose play was interrupted by a downpour: "Miss Mackenzie was wearing a knitted suit that reached just below her knees. But as the rain fell harder, the soaked skirt grew longer, and finally reached her shoe-tops. It is no simple matter to drive with a soaked skirt clinging to your legs."

Miss Mackenzie's fate aside, *Knits are in* (whether handmade or by machine) was further hammered home when industry reporters covered Paris shows and encountered designers only too happy to cater to America's ripening interest in sportswear. Vionnet rated his models "eminently practical and smart at the same time." Monsieur Lelong judged his collection "the happy combination of style and suitability that shall fill a long felt want." Drecoll, sensitive to the "Scotch Wave," spotlighted four Argyle designs; others quickly followed suit. Children's patterns reflected the French influence as slavishly as did their elders', from the hand-knit "Marcel Suit" (a "jaunty French sailor outfit"), knit middy blouse and skirt (perfect for the hoop-rolling miss who modeled it), striped sweaters in the longer, leaner look favored by mothers, and delicately lacy open-worked mesh caps and coats to horizontally banded, long-waisted, belted cardigans.

As reports of Parisian knitwear reached American shores, not only style-conscious city women but rural buyers as well demanded copies or patterns. The Scranton, Pennsylvania, Dry Goods Store's manager related his experience in establishing a full-size knitwear department:

The women demonstrated at once that they weren't waiting for any fashion decree to wear sweaters; and our big department demonstrated that it didn't have to wait for the flapper in order to sell its handsome knitted garments. The flapper's mother, and her aunt,

Man's golf sweater, 1922.

Woman's golf vest, 1919.

Lady's golf sweater and skirt, 1920.

*The Marcel (jaunty
French sailor suit), 1921.*

her older sister and her sister-in-law turned up promptly for sweaters they could wear and be more comfortable in. The more they [sweaters] appeared, the more they were pleased.

By the end of the decade—when helmet-shaped hats sprouted brims, when sun-tanned legs replaced silk-stockinged limbs, when parvenu "talkies" threatened "silents," when the Graf Zeppelin's globe-circling trip grabbed headlines, when golf (with over five thousand courses and two million players) remained the businessman's game, when Babe Ruth reigned as top man of the diamond and Bill Tilden ruled the Forest Hills courts, when listeners swooned to the strains of "Pagan Love Song" and "Vagabond Lover," when Amos and Andy moved to prime-time radio, and when Herbert and Lou Henry Hoover (another knitting first lady) had served in the White House for only six months—the bull market reached its peak and the wave of postwar prosperity crested and broke.

Fashionable women still wanted new sweaters, whatever the cost, but by the end of the decade when cost became the prime consideration in whether to purchase them ready-made or re-create them at home by hand knitting at a fraction of the cost, long-idle knitters seized their needles and launched a knitting "craze" unmatched in peacetime.

Striped twosome, 1926.

13.
The Thirties Knitting Craze

Within months life changed, and the vaunted prosperity was not "just around the corner," after all. As the economy worsened, families slashed spending—and, apparently, marrying, procreating and divorcing—since marriage, birth and divorce rates dropped precipitously. When fewer people could afford country clubs, the havens of the twenties, the number of clubs participating in the U.S. Golf Association was almost halved, as golfers turned to municipal courses or even the overnight sensation, "miniature" golf, an easily constructed and inexpensive amusement. Bank night at the movies, lotteries such as Bingo and Keno, and marathon anything, especially dancing and flagpole sitting, furnished exciting and inexpensive diversion. Daytime hemlines dropped along with the stock market, to within nine or ten inches from the floor, and waists returned to midsections. When *Vogue* announced that curves had returned to fashion, brassiere companies advertised the means for acquiring the youthful, pointed "uplift bust." Depression or not, *some* figures could point up.

When cash-pressed customers hankered for prohibitively priced European-designed sweaters, knitters logically copied them "for peanuts." Some knitters voiced concern about assigning the term *sweater* to the European "Jersey" (button-front) or "Guernsey" (pullover) since "the name is not a nice one and the garment is not used to induce perspiration," but the name stuck. Waiting in the wings for the rebirth of knitting was the Bernard Ulmann Company, whose publicist, Clair Wolf, was credited with having planted the seed at Buckingham Palace. Scanning a 1920 market survey, Ulmann isolated three key ingredients for success: convincing knitters that hand knitting saved money, designing high-style patterns and encouraging art needlework departments to dispense reliable fashion advice. The first was easy: Everyone was interested in economy, and magazines such as *McCall's* declared that with handmade sportswear in vogue and thrift such a "fashionable virtue," women were again knitting their own sportswear. No one wanted to appear "chintzy," so making one's own needed the imprimatur of the cognoscenti. *McCall's*, in effect, elevated penny-pinching hand knitters above their profligate sisters buying expensive store models. Said *McCall's*, "A gaily becoming sweater blouse always makes us feel like conquering the world. The new handmade sweaters are not only recommended for the superiority complex they give their owner but for the ease with which they are made and laundered." Home sewers, too, waxed enthusiastic: "One thing the depression did for me. It taught me to *make* my own clothes and I *know* they look smart. Think of it, my dear, I have prettier clothes than ever before and I'm spending only *half as much*—I never had the courage to try making them when Bob could give me plenty of money to buy clothes at the shops." In 1932, Bernat agreed: "What better way is there for you to be in style than wearing a garment that is knitted with your hands and designed in the current fashion?" Making it oneself was one thing. Making it according to high fashion was another. Bernat, reading the tea leaves on knitting's resurgence, added more and more knitting patterns for boleros, sweaters and suits in "glow crinkle" to its *Handicrafter* until it finally took the plunge by moving knitting to its front cover in the 1933 Winter/Spring issue.

With Ulmann taking the lead and others quickly following suit, companies trained college girls to model in knitwear fashion shows and dispense knitting suggestions to captivated spectators. Temporary schools for instructors in New York, Chicago and San Francisco demonstrated knitting techniques and styles to their pupils, briefed them on local fashion show promotions and outlined procedures for sponsoring knitting contests. Ulmann even diagrammed a comprehensive plan for style promotions, including mannequins, accesso-

The favorite knit suit, 1934.

ries, music, appropriate show times, choice store locations, advertising and window display concepts and general organization.

Style shows were needed not only for the ultimate customers, the knitters, but also for art needlework buyers. Clair Wolf staged one at the Waldorf-Astoria Hotel in New York for nearly three hundred buyers, who raved over the table decorations, twelve-inch figurines clad in hand-knit replicas of the company's fall pattern collection. The show's commentator, *Vogue*'s merchandising manager, asserted that fads had relatively little effect upon knitting yarn sales since hand-knit garments formed "a basic part of the well-selected wardrobe. . . . Knitting appeals to a feminine instinct which many merchants overlook—the desire for individuality."

With instructors essential to successful promotions, the search was on for suitably proficient knitters, and since most families preferred to have more members work to reduce their high level of consumption established during the palmier 1920s, a new female work force waited to be tapped. With the bias against women still strong, full-time Depression jobs were reserved for male heads of families, but sales or demonstration work of this kind offered married women part-time or temporary work for a few hours each day, on peak days and during holidays. While in 1920 only slightly over a fifth of sales-women were married, the figure jumped to a third in 1930 and up another 10 percent by the end of the decade. When job seekers read that expert knitters could practically write their own salary tickets for the hundreds of jobs available to instruct novices in the art, they jammed personnel offices. They were hired in droves, since nothing would sabotage the industry more than clumsily knit garments on knitters who bragged "I knit this myself." The industry, previously hampered by fuddy-duddyism, swallowed the costs and found that when style was coupled with smartness and competency, 1935 department store yarn sales increased by 50 percent over the previous year and doubled 1932 figures (some stores even reporting a quadrupling). Knitters not only flocked to the department stores

The "Northwestern,"
1934.

but patronized the hundreds of tiny knitting shops that had sprung up, leading one commentator to remark: "Fad nothing! It's a profession. . . . The country has broken out like a bad case of measles with Knit-a-Bit Shops, Wield-a-Needle Dens and Yarn Emporiums by the dozens."

College adult education departments were pressured into offering courses in knitting, and the introduction to a successful 1940 book still popular today attributes its author's expertise to experience in teaching in just such a department in the thirties: "For the last four years Mrs. Duncan has been successfully teaching the art of knitting to women in the metropolitan area of Detroit. More than 3,000 mothers and homemakers have completed from 12–24 intensive weeks of study under her guidance. These adults have participated in classes sponsored by the Adult Homemaking non-credit unit operating out of the College of Education, Wayne University, and the homemaking program in the Detroit Public Evening Schools." Another instructress "yielded to the urgent request of pupils, knitting teachers and yarn representatives . . . for a practical handbook based on her vast experience in teaching," and in the resultant *Knitting and Fitting* listed herself on the title page as "Knitting Consultant and Dean of Women Knitters" to place the stamp of academic authority on her pronouncements.

Those who once knit to enjoy hearing envious "oh's" and "ah's" from country club friends realized that with a bit more effort and initiative they could embark upon knitting careers and manage tidy little businesses. To the homebound who hoped to cash in on the prevailing handknit obsession, Bernat's *Handicrafter* offered encouragement that home knitting or instructing could be profitable since "many of your acquaintances would like hand-knitted creations [and] there is a source of good profits in selling yarns with good instructions." Expert hand knitters could also sell through retail outlets. In early 1939 Saks Fifth Avenue staged an elaborate promotion of the biggest Palm Beach success, an elegant cardigan "remarkably priced at $29.50 and the central motif of practically every smart costume—with slacks and tea frocks as well." If Saks could do it, so could others, and knitters were contacted to make garments on special order instead of being forced to rely on consignment sales. While knitting as a livelihood had always been fraught with low pay, one woman with broad teaching experience in adult education classes in the thirties foresaw multiple opportunities: art needlework department employment gave a knitter with creative and artistic ability an opportunity to move from a $15-a-week sales job to head buyer at $5,000 annually; owning one's own knit shop (a "clean business with that added touch of pride") demanded business acumen and obeying the "first commandment" of knit shops, "Know Your Yarns"; blocking and repairing hand-knit garments was another "clean comfortable business of one's own"; custom knitting by fast, expert knitters was narrowed to those talented few who kept abreast of fashion and revealed individuality in design and color; knitters with writing skills could author knitting columns in women's periodicals and women's pages of newspapers or write instructions for yarn company manuals; those with both teaching and knitting skills could work in recreation departments, schools, community colleges, universities and in occupational therapy. Eager to certify that knitting was now "associated with modern art," a far cry from "Grandma's heel-turning stage," she deplored American veneration of imports ("By So and So, Paris," "Imported from England" and "Copied from the original by So and So, London") and charged designers to wrest designing laurels from their European sanctuary: "Are we to sit back and proclaim these people of the old world superior in creative ability? . . . Let our star of creative ability shine in the salons of Paris, London and other smart centers of the world."

To attract a steady stream of future knitters, stores launched Saturday morning classes for the young with simpler patterns for beginners who would soon weary of small gauges. Great favorites were doll clothes and "Jiffy" outfits of heavy yarn knit on jumbo knitting needles to hasten completion before youngsters ran out of steam. These "knit in a few hours" patterns, or "KwiKnits" as one company called them, were also adopted by adult knitters looking for speedier results. Nancy McClure, of Chattanooga, remembers the summer of 1935, when she could hardly wait to try Jiffy Knits for her fall wardrobe. She bought the best buttons and belts ("the accessories really made the outfits") and knit three separate skirt-and-long-sleeved-top outfits in three days, including finishing and blocking.

"Jiffy Knits" were somewhat of a fad, and as such, anathema to the industry, since yarn companies could ill afford fads and bent every

Junior Miss of the thirties.

effort to assure the longevity of knitting's popularity. *Vogue* had taken pains to say in its instruction book, "Knitting is no longer a fad—it's a national institution." Still, companies wanted to ride the wave, and capitalizing on the public's joint preoccupation with the movies and knitting, Ulmann and Fleisher (a company Ulmann later bought out) teamed with Motion Picture Publications, Inc. to produce the blockbuster *The Motion Picture Movie Classic Hand Knit Fashions as Worn by Warner Brothers Stars*, the "First of Its Kind—a Hollywood Knitting Book!" where movie-attending, star-struck knitters could see their heroines in hand-knits and aspire to "dress like the stars" at a fraction of the price. Twenty-three patterns such as "Tailored Town Coat" or "Suits Herself" modeled by Bette Davis, Joan Blondell in "Spider Web Dress" and Olivia de Havilland in "Correctly Casual" entranced needlewomen. While no one promised that the stars had actually knit the garments themselves, the magazine guaranteed that, "The vogue is sweeping Hollywood and on every lot the busy click-click-click of knitting needles is heard." Women devoured their movie magazines, memorized the inside "dope" on stars' off-screen lives and were not surprised to hear that Joan Crawford "startled more than one studio assistant and mannequin when, at

Motion Pictures Movies Classic
Hand-knit Fashions, 1936.

Bette Davis in "Suits Herself,"
1936.

every breathing spell between poses and fittings, she fell upon her knitting as though her salary depended upon it." That was enough for the knitters.

According to *Motion Picture Classic*, readers who wanted to be in style and wear the same garments as the stars had only to follow simple Hollywood-inspired instructions. Each issue (and movie magazines *Motion Picture* and *Movie Classic*) carried slip-out rules and entry blanks for a knitting contest for knitters with "pride in knitting carefully and well." To participate in the four-month contest each entrant sent in the application blank to "reserve space" for the garment, fortuitous advice since the over three thousand garments received could have swamped receiving rooms; enclosed all the yarn wrappers to prove that the garment was knit with a sponsor's yarn (after all, this was a yarn sales promotion); and shipped the dress or suit to the knitting editor in New York, where it would be assessed on quality of workmanship by a panel of nationally famous women.

Joan Blondell in "Spider Web
Dress," 1936.

Anita Louise in "Lacy Loveliness,"
1936.

For a company that had "contacted" the crown, recruiting a notable
panel was elementary, and judges included Mrs. James Roosevelt,
mother of the president of the United States, a "fashion authority,"
a "society leader," a "newspaper feature writer" and (trumpets!)
Grand Duchess Marie, for the customary European touch, preferably
ermine.

Top prizes were a round-trip, all-expenses-paid, railroad junket to
Hollywood or a one-way airplane trip from New York to Hollywood
or Hollywood to New York (value $288). Among the fourteen prizes
were a handknit afghan, a $100 "Mendoza beaver coat," a $50 matching pearl necklace and bracelet "evening ensemble," a $50 year's
supply of "Vogue à Paris" perfume by Corday and a $50 "one year's
supply of Maiden Form brassieres and girdles." The fourteenth-place
(the Corday perfume) winner was a sixteen-year-old boy, and one
hopes that he swapped with the winner of a Gruen wristwatch of the
same value. Grand Duchess Marie pronounced knitting a wonderful

Katharine Hepburn, 1938.

escape from life's problems: "When the needles slip through the fingers, your imagination takes flight."

More than imagination took flight. Soaring sales heartened an industry whose bleak prospects only ten years before were now rosy. William Bernat, whose grandfather, Emil, founded Emil Bernat and Sons Co., recalls:

> My grandfather started out in Budapest as a master dyer because he worked on reproducing colors in the world's great tapestries. Here in the United States he continued his work restoring priceless tapestries such as in Boston's Museum of Fine Arts and for private collectors such as Marshall Field and the Vanderbilts. Eventually people came to his company because they found greatest range of colors in threads and yarns.
>
> When we first started publishing *The Handicrafter*, we devoted most of the space to weaving and other crafts; thus the title. But

ALPINE

SKI SUIT (Electra)

This appropriate winter sport costume modeled by Maureen O'Sullivan.

Instructions Page 52

*Maureen O'Sullivan
in Alpine ski suit,
1936.*

by 1934 we realized that the interest lay in knitting, and for the first time we brought out an all knitting issue in 1934. The lady on the cover of that first issue is my Aunt Helen, the wife of my Uncle Paul Bernat!

Companies expanded their pattern lines and, by charging from ten to twenty-five cents per copy, developed lucrative publishing departments for everything from beginner's projects such as knit potholders, place mats and coasters to copies of the latest Paris-designed fashions. They watched fashion trends carefully, and when Paris designers showed short sweaters giving way to knit tunics ("New excitement . . . the tunic style is giving the Little Sweater a Run For Its Glory. . . . [That's] enough to keep your little brains in a whirl"), American manufacturers snapped up tunic patterns for their manuals. Fleisher's accentuated Parisian fashions by instruction sheets for single French designs, "One of Fleisher's French Fashions in Hand Knits" by Alix, Lanvin and Lelong.

While Bernat concentrated on fairly classic designs (with special issues devoted to knitting for men, babies, afghans and so forth), others struck a balance between reliable classics and "high fashion" styles. Though college girls faithfully clung to Brooks's sweaters, varying them only to combine pullovers and cardigans into popular "twin sets," other women knit dresses and suits demanding not only infinite patience and stamina but also, to the absolute jubilation of manufacturers, skeins and skeins and *skeins* of yarn. While a typical woman's sweater required six or seven skeins, a dress or suit called for twenty-eight to thirty. Ulmann's joy spilled over: "Something's happening. Something important to your smartness. The craze for hand-knitting is growing daily. Along Park Avenue in New York, in Newport, out in Hollywood, at Palm Beach, Southampton—in all the places where fashionable people gather, hand-knits are the big news." All this was to reassure knitters that Ulmann was not asleep at the switch but would quickly bring to its readers instructions for "the very models sighted at places that set the country's fashions" (and appropriate Bear Brand or Bucilla yarns with which to duplicate them).

The "places that set the country's fashions" were chic resorts, and Bucilla's "Frappe" yarn ("a frosted look . . . exquisitely boilproof") was destined for cruise and resort wear. In the 1920s, models for the "country club set" were named after old, eastern and highly exclusive country clubs; the 1930s list more democratically included Del Monte, Lido Beach, Arrowhead, Beverly Hills and Cannes. The population's westward shift, particularly to the Pacific Coast, "where folks live longer distances from the urban centers and think nothing of driving fifty miles for an afternoon at the country club, followed by dinner and an evening at the show," made smartly tailored woolen

or silk two-piece knit suits with fancy blouses more "eminently sat-
isfactory" than regular dinner or evening clothes.

Customers insisted upon a broad selection of styles and yarns to
give them a wide choice when they opened their drawers to select
that day's knit (laid flat rather than hung). Shops with the broadest
selection enjoyed the most loyal clientele, and one shop's inventory
revealed 135 varieties of yarn, not counting different colors of the
same yarn. Knitters raised on Germantown worsted marveled at displays ranging from lace-weight yarns for bed jackets to fingering yarn
for Argyle socks, but usually picked wrinkle-resistant bouclé, whose
crinkly texture masked a beginner's uneven tension and maintained
its shape through repeated washings, a key consideration since knit
skirts tended to sag. Knit on small gauges of seven or eight stitches
to the inch, bouclé knitting called for daunting instructions such as
"Cast on 600 stitches for the bottom of the skirt." This formidable
number precluded speedy progress, but would lessen as the skirt
inched slowly but inexorably toward (one would hope) the narrower
waistline. It was in a "gray mixture" with highlights of red and white
Boucle de Laine (as Bernat called it) that "Aunt Helen" Bernat debuted on *Handicrafter*'s cover.

Knitters who undertook bouclé garments still grit their teeth at
the recollection. Fifty years later, Peg Gorman, of West Simsbury,
Connecticut, remembers making a knit bouclé tie on quadruple-zero
needles "perhaps not as large in diameter as toothpicks with yarn
only slightly heavier than sewing thread. Others must have been
making similar projects. I couldn't have thought up that form of
torture all by myself. I never finished it. I chucked it when I realized
it would take many *years* to complete!" Irene Steptoe, of Chevy
Chase, Maryland, who cast on 800 stitches on tiny circular needles
to make a flared skirt and knit "round and round and *round*," wonders
if anyone would do it today, and if so, "What would she charge? It
couldn't be enough!" Time was no hindrance to Elizabeth Dorshimer,
of Whiting, New Jersey, who first knit nine-inch squares for the Red
Cross in World War I: "Of course, during the 1930's I knit bouclé
dresses. What else could one do? It was the depression, and there
was little money for entertainment. The radio was free, and a person
could knit and listen." Alyce Misner, of Big River, California, remembers "Hand-knit bouclé suits were in fashion. They were beau-

tiful but expensive. . . . I knit a brown skirt and green jacket which I wore at my typing job at the World's Fair on Treasure Island in San Francisco Bay." Nancy McClure slaved for days and days on several two-piece bouclé dresses, using one of the "new metal cabled needles for circular knitting" for her gored skirts. She made a variety of tops, her favorite a light gray cowl-necked top with butterfly sleeves and tight, unribbed cuffs, accessorized by a belt with a silver buckle and a matching silver clip in the fold of the cowl neck. She still wears the belt and clip.

To sell more yarn, manufacturers persuaded knitters that truly distinctive, ultrasophisticated women needed different knits for each mood, need and hour: "In the early morning she dons a dainty bed jacket . . . soon after she wears a smart golf costume or a trim dress for town wear . . . in fact, any time of the day or for any occasion you'll find her impeccably correct in a hand knit." Viewing 1930s pattern books loaded with bed jacket instructions, one might worry about the health of half the nation, but most women of that time remained in bed after childbirth, dangled their legs over the edge only after ten days and remained upstairs until the third week had passed. Bed jackets were a necessity. For "occasions of dignity," the model for a two-piece "Nubbly Cobble Crepe" ribbed dress posed before a group with pen in hand. Woman executive? Secretary? Club-woman taking minutes at the annual meeting? All bases were covered. For sheer *chic*, another company posed its (knit) chenille-jacketed and chiffon-skirted model in front of the Eiffel Tower to punch home the identity of "Tower Brand Yarns" and accentuate Parisian styling.

Bear Brand, heeding its own advice of knits for every occasion and hoping customers would adapt them for all seasons, introduced two new cottons for "smart knitters." "Tweed-Knit," in a wide palette of colors, was guaranteed "BOILPROOF so that you can tub it as often as you want." "Magic-Print," a cotton and rayon blended to create a "lovely illusion of a soft pastel blend," carried the same guarantee: "BOILPROOF, so that no matter how often you launder it, the delicate soft tones are always captivatingly fresh." It is hard to picture a knitter relentlessly *boiling* her garments, but the company made its point that what was made stayed made, and in a depression that counted!

There was no limit to *what* could be knit, including bathing suits or "swimwear." One garment was even modeled in the luxurious below-decks pool of the Cunard Steamship Line's fashionable *Berengaria*. Some knitters reported disastrous bathing suit experiences. Naugatuck, Connecticut, knitter Ruth Mead who had long been a prize-winning knitter was pictured in her bank's 1938 newsletter in a "handsome one-piece black wool topped with a white angora sweater, an outfit she knitted in a couple of months," but the dextrous stitcher suffered one painful episode: "That Winter I knit a lovely two-piece red and beige bathing suit with a coverall top (no bikinis in those days!) and eagerly took it with me on my trip South. I couldn't wait for my dip in the ocean, but once the water hit the underpants they just wouldn't stay on. I couldn't get out fast enough! I clutched them to me and struggled to emerge without too much embarrassment. I was lucky I brought an extra suit. That may be forty-nine years ago, but I remember it vividly!" Echoing that experience, Jean Olmstead, of Browns Summit, North Carolina, re-

Bathing on the Berengaria, 1934.

Beach cape, 1935.

Handknit for Shirley too, 1934.

called *her* knit-suit-meets-ocean nightmare: "I had taught myself to knit in my teens and everyone admired my beautiful lavender knit swim suit when I proudly wore it to the beach one day. After my sister and some friends [and I] had swum around a while, they got cold and came out, but I didn't dare because the suit had absorbed most of the water in sight until its weight pulled it down around my knees. I squeezed out as much as I could and crawled crabwise out on the beach to dry. You can imagine the hilarity that greeted my emergence!"

Equally popular were knit hats ("Lots of young ladies lately are going quite heady and producing smart little hats"), simple face-framing stocking caps, "pert and saucy" berets, or long, intricately wrapped, twisted and draped turbans. The procedures for arranging one turban were so complicated that it was suggested the wearer should "[s]tart draping by placing one square end on top of your head pointing forward; then fold the remaining part of the band around the head into the most becoming shape. Pin into place and later tack. This process may be made easier by slipping a fitted lining on the head before draping, and pinning to that."

A revival of interest in the fine arts of pioneer life sparked knitting cotton bedspreads and doilies from the new "mercerized, gassed, double-A quality" cotton that was vastly superior to the cruder material of the nineteenth century. After all: "Handcrafters of today who are busy fashioning heirlooms of tomorrow will leave a precious heritage. Their work may be admired, their patterns may be copied, but added to the mellowness of years . . . will be the blessed sanction of quality." The new "boilable string" was also knit into fancy collars, dresses, blouses, bedspreads and luncheon sets.

Alert soap manufacturers capitalized on the knitting craze, and Lever Brothers (makers of Lux), pitching its ads to thrifty housewives who could ill afford washing disasters, coined the word *luxables* to refer to women's intimate undergarments, her precious woolen sweaters (which would wash "like lambs") and her beautiful knit suits. Saving pennies was good news for thrifty housewives, and Lux had just the jingle for that:

> Sing a Song of New Quick Lux
> Of Sweaters Large and Small
> One Big Box of These Fast Flakes
> Washed TWENTY-NINE in all.

Lux explained that to keep sweaters soft and new-looking one should first pencil an outline of the garment on heavy paper and then "Lux"—rinse, towel-roll and pat out to dry by pinning it within the outline. Another ad, a harbinger of "Which Twin has the Toni?", showed two identical sweaters, one new and one "Luxed" five times. Next came the now-familiar traced sweater outline, but the sweater has been cut in half, the "Luxed" side fluffily contained within its proper boundaries and the other shrunken, matted, felted and misshapen side missing the perimeters by a mile. "Lux Laboratories" intoned that improper washing and rough handling had tolled the knell for the bad side. Within a month Lux announced that wool was not only "temperamental" and "sensitive" but "firmly resents hot water, rubbing, or needless agitation. In protest, it shrinks and mats."

Should the complaining lamb fail to redeem errant laudresses, admen butchered an entire dress to show the havoc wrought by the wrong soap: "This charming two-piece model, beautifully knit after one of the season's smartest designs was sacrificed to help YOU avoid washing mistakes." This sacrifice of the knitted virgins to the Temple of Lux would not be in vain if knitters tossed out "harsh soaps containing harmful alkali and rubbing with cake soap."

If bad washing, blocking and alkali soaps didn't devastate precious knitting, *moths* did, and a company that christened its permanently mothproofed yarn "Nomotta" illustrated how a doll's knit trousers and cap, made of mothproofed yarn, were miraculously spared the ravages of "the destructive attack of moths" while the loved one's jacket and bootees were tattered indeed. Certainly no knitter could countenance devouring demons feasting on her handiwork.

Columbia Yarns hoped to enlist new knitters ("Needles will be clicking more feverishly than ever now") by demonstrating that knitters could simply create fabric pieces. They marketed life-size

Stylish sportman, 1931.

diagrammed patterns, with each part showing every stitch of the knitted garment. The paper patterns also provided handy outlines for blocking the parts.

The knitting craze appeared to have ten million adherents at its peak. Knitting, once considered too ordinary to be chic ("a little distance from the fringe of society") had made it at last. As one writer concluded, "It took a long time to make the grade, but it's in now, and sitting pretty. More power to knitting and knitters." By the mid-thirties the National Dry Goods Association estimated that one twelfth of the population knit, a statistic not very startling until one contemplated one out of twelve persons knitting in the same place—say, the subway. They did—in subways, trains, buses, airplanes, motorcars, boats and every other form of conveyance. Women were so busy counting stitches they could barely converse with long-suffering husbands, prompting humorist Ogden Nash to comment poetically that men whose wives knit were forced to talk to themselves:

Life will teach you many things, chief of which is that every man
    who talks to himself isn't necessarily out of his wits;
He may have a wife who knits.
Probably only he and his Maker
Know how many evenings he has spent trying to raise a conversation while his beloved created sweaters by the acre.
Ah, my inquiring offspring, you must learn that life can be very
    bitter,
But never quite so much so as when trying to pry a word out of
    a knitter.

Knitting was so prevalent in public places that Ottawa's Speaker of the House of Commons banned "gallery knitting" during the sessions, an act for which he was roundly abused by the Canadian yarn industry. In Washington a woman knit as she listened to the Supreme Court justices deliver their decisions until an attendant whispered in her ear and her needles disappeared. Across the street at the houses of Congress, knitting was allowed if it did not disturb others.

College students were among the most avid knitters. Elizabeth Hart of Baltimore, a 1931 graduate of Wellesley, remembers:

By my Senior year most of us were knitting Brooks sweaters, and I still have the typed instructions on Alice Maynard paper around here somewhere. Maynard's was *Mecca* for yarn lovers, and a trip to her establishment on Madison Avenue was a rare treat. I made so many of those sweaters, I still don't need to look at the directions. I cast on 232 stitches on a #2 circular needle, knit for 3 inches and then changed to #4. Of course, everything we made was exactly the same—just different colors. And *we* probably all looked the same; but I suppose that was the whole point!

Sometimes we changed the pattern and added "an inch worth" of stitches to the front and then bravely *cut* up the front, trimmed with grosgrain ribbon and turned a pullover into a cardigan. Making buttonholes was a real pain, but since I was a pretty fair sewer, I made them well and was in great demand.

She was typical of the composite student of a mid-decade survey of women's college students, who was healthy, liked to knit and, according to *Harper's Bazaar*'s 1935 college issue, washed her sweaters in the approved Lever Brothers procedure: "She's a collector of sweaters . . . favors hand knits . . . pushes the sleeves up over her elbows, buttons her cardigans down the back, contrasts her dark sweater with light skirts, and enlivens the neck with a strand of pearls, a printed silk square, or a scarf of tie silk. If you should spy her in her room after nine P.M., you might find her playing bridge or knitting . . . or sticking pins in the sweater she has just washed, patting it out on a Turkish towel to dry overnight."

Delineator had its stereotype, too, a collegienne whose looks ("so soft and fragrant you wouldn't believe she knew how to boil an egg") belied her efficiency and hardheadedness and whose "femininity" allowed her to swoon at the sight of a handsome young man and be a whiz at sewing and knitting ("She made the outfit she is wearing and made it like an expert . . . and is pleased with the 'figger' the football shoulder and unbelted waistline give her"). In winter she could look cuddly ("as if she had handfuls of snow") in hand-knit mittens of heavy, long-haired Polar Angora De Luxe. *Delineator*'s "College Winners" monthly column broadcast late-breaking campus fads: Smith girls succumbed to what one company called "soft as a bunny—yours for a little money" angora mittens and scarves in white

Angora kerchief and muff, 1938.

or pastels, and Ohio State coeds replaced buttons with corks on their hand-knit sweaters, sewing them on with shanks of matching yarn.

Knitting college students quickly identified professors who tolerated the click of needles in class; they knit when dummy at bridge (an occupation losing its top favorite status to knitting though many did both at the same time); they knit on the way to the library and often in the stacks when they got there; true addicts dangled from their wrists a small, flexible gadget (like a miniature bird cage with drawstring top) encasing the yarn ball so that they could knit standing or in transit, handy for dormitory visiting or lurching along to the club car on transcontinental trains. They knit for themselves and for the men in their lives. Should a romance falter before the beloved's garment was complete, the knitter drowned her sorrow and persevered expectantly as she scouted replacements with the canny eye of an engineer with a blueprint: wrist-to-shoulder, waistline-to-underarm, chest circumference, shoulder-to-shoulder, underarm-to-wrist. Sock knitters had to "eyeball" foot dimensions. Once socks, especially Argyles, were made, few trusted their precious products to careless laundering by collegiate bachelors, so more than one knitter included personal "washing and stretching" services with her gift rather than see socks fall into shrunken neglect or early death in the ragbag. A few knitters kept *several* sock stretchers in use, laundering for more than one "favorite," an awesome sign of popularity much coveted by knitters with no such backlog. Some knitters judiciously decreed that Argyles would be tendered only in return for a similar token from the other party—preferably an engagement ring!

The New York Times called the knitting craze an "enthusiasm" unequaled since wartime. Everyone talked and wrote about it, but few could explain it. One paper likened it to other fads: "The click, click of the knitting needles is again heard in the land; which proves, like the present renaissance of the bicycle, that there is nothing new under the sun." Priscilla Page, of *Gentlewoman* magazine, reminded her readers: "These are knitting days. Everywhere we go we see women knitting, old ladies, middle-aged mothers, young brides and 16 year olds"; "Women are all divided into 2 classes these days— those who sew and those who knit. There are no idlers nowadays who sit and do nothing"; "If you do not have at least one knitted costume in your wardrobe today, something is wrong. If you can hold up your head with pride and brag that you knitted a dress your-self, then you are indeed a woman of achievement. Knitting is the order of the time, and smart women are accomplished with their knitting needles."

At women's club meetings parliamentary order was mixed with "knit one, purl one"; at tea, young ladies gulped their brew to leave time to finish their knitting. In Cleveland, a reporter noted, "Along with the New Deal, alphabetical bureaus and the return of slit skirts and bicycles, there comes a revival of knitting . . . a regular tidal wave. . . . What was once a need to keep people clothed, becomes a fad, and women everywhere are making berets, sweaters, coats, and even dresses. I haven't heard that they are going to make men wear wristlets again so they can knit them as Christmas gifts, but that may come later."

True aficionados knit during the movies and swore they didn't miss a stitch; women lugged knitting to family picnics, parties, beach clubs, and tennis courts—even to the courtroom. One such avid knitter attended a lengthy Abington, Massachusetts, trial where a motorist was charged with negligence in an accident fatal to her friend's mother. Passing the time knitting a bouclé dress on circular steel needles, she angered the defendant's attorney, in a scene recently recalled by her daughter:

Being a close friend, Mum sat directly behind her friend and his attorney. As the trial progressed, Mum would knit. The attorneys were carrying on and waving their arms and shouting to make their points—and Mum was really going like crazy with her steel needles. Suddenly, she was startled when the defense attorney shouted, "I object, Your Honor, to the prosecuting attorney's tactics. He is harassing me." The opposing attorney denied any wrongdoing and the trial proceeded.

Well, things got started again and it was getting back to the excitement of before. Mum got her knitting going at a good clip once more. Again the walls resounded with the attorney's, "I object! He's doing it again!!! All the time I am trying to make my point, my worthy opponent is harassing me. He is sitting there making clicking sounds behind my back." As the prosecuting attorney, shocked, denied making any sounds at all, Mum unobtrusively slipped her knitting in her bag and kept it out of sight through the remainder of the trial.

Even Sanka Coffee's ad showed grandma dozing off in her chair, her knitting on her lap: "Knit one, Purl Two . . . ZZZ What wouldn't some people give to be able to doze off as easily as Grandma." Knitters communicated with each other in special "exchange" newspaper columns, such as the *Boston Globe*'s "Household Department" where knitters employed "handles" like current CB motorists: "Dear Lucky Seven: Will you please send in the two-piece knitted suit pattern for a three year old that you mentioned in your letter to Sandy's Pal? I have never knitted anything before, but would like to try this suit. [signed] George's Sister." "Dundlestilskin" elaborated to "A Reader" on her previously perplexing instructions in a letter worthy of preservation for its pure "knitterese": "The f in the knitted lace stands for fagot, a shorter direction for 'once over twice and purl two together,' one of the overs making an extra stitch to replace the one narrowed, the other is the usual over made before purling. Have I made it clear?" Well, er, no.

Knitting was a shot in the arm to knitting accessory companies such as the largest needle company, Boye of Chicago, which cornered 75 percent of the needle market in 1934 and allowed only salesmen with knowledge of fundamental knitting stitches to represent the company. Boye recognized the potential for circular needles in skirt knitting and took out a series of patents on the most promising model, hailing its final version as the greatest advance since a circular bone needle that was unearthed in Pompeii. Marie Madsen, now of Ocala, Florida, a Boye employee from 1927 to 1972, who recalled of the period, "Don't forget that knitting as a recreation helped to ease the tension of those very trying times, and people knitted everywhere, even on street cars going to work," points out that most knitting needles made before the Depression were very fine sized, and when Boye developed new needles in a time when many women could not afford the yarn, its salespersons suggested raveling old garments rather than buying new yarn, something that didn't endear them to the yarn industry. Following that advice, Arlene Bauers, of Cheektowaga, New York, remembers: "When we ripped out the yarn, we tried to work in the knots, but when the sweaters were done, we had to undo them and use a crochet hook to work them in the end, up, down and sideways. Ma was a perfectionist. If she could feel the lump, you had to redo it until you had it *right*, which meant *perfect*, and that was that. One didn't argue with Ma!"

Patent office records show that independent inventors deluged the office, hoping for patents before the public tired of knitting. There were needles with inch measurements along the side and a circular needle with one end conventionally pointed and the other with a crochet hook to avoid time wasted "throwing the yarn with the right hand." Another inventor, aware that knitters "do such work in street cars, subways, buses, etc.," patented a transparent workbox to hold yarn in a "visible yet unsoiled condition . . . [so that] work may be readily packed or unpacked from the box and the unused yarn cannot become tangled or knocked to the floor, etc." Among the slew of other patent applications during the decade, one inventor wrote in behalf of his needle protector: "The revival of knitting has created a demand for devices that can be placed on the pointed end of the knitting needle for the purpose of protecting the points of the needles and preventing them from sticking out through the knitting bags . . . and to prevent the stitches [from] sliding off the needles when the work is laid aside or being carried from place to place as is now so common."

Checking "New Aids to Knitting," *Delineator* apprised its readers of the "Whirley" gadget, a wire cone on a stand for winding skeins of yarn: "You carry it around with you in your knitting bag. The advantage is that it keeps yarn from rolling around on the floor, snarling, or breaking. The Whirley can accommodate two balls, a help when you're using two colors." Another "temptation" was the "divinely easy to work with" Universal circular steel knitting needle with hinges where the points began to ease the strain of holding a heavy skirt. *Popular Science* instructed home handymen and women how to fashion a "Roomy Knitting Bag Designed to Stand Beside a Chair" by fastening a bag large enough to hold yarn, needles and knitted fabric to a folding, trestle-legged wooden frame "for any woman who has been attracted to the present vogue for knitting." Thrifty knitters with no carpentry skills could convert an old camp stool by adding custom-sized pockets along the sides for scissors, needle protectors, stitch holders, needle gauges, rulers, and note pads for measurements. For those who wanted to make their own bags, wooden bag handles were widely available.

At the height of the craze, a few stitchers suffered "knitter burn-out," like this anonymous writer to *Atlantic Monthly*'s "Contributor's Column":

Once I was a knitter. Sweaters and mittens, scarves, bonnets, dresses, and shawls budded, grew, and dropped from my assiduous fingers as leaves from a tree. One day, quite unexpectedly, I found that knitting exasperated me. Perhaps, just as everyone has an al-lotted number of words to speak during the course of his life, every woman has her quota of stitches she can knit. Evidently I had reached mine.

The clean-smelling wool, fresh-dyed, and coiled in virgin hanks, did not entice me. The glossy pages of the pattern books lured me no more. I gave away my collection of needles—the ivory ones with the long points polished by use, end blunted in flat ebony knobs, the double-pointed needles of aluminum bent into flexible hoops for knitting around and around in an endless circle; my beloved set of tiny tri-colored needles, sharp as Spanish stilettos at both ends. I gave away my knitting bags, the green one with the wooden handles for the beach, the trim tapestry bag I took out to dinner with me, the capacious cotton damask, the newly fashionable gay cardboard cylinders.

Then I settled back to enjoy the quiet of my idle hands or the relaxation of fixing my gaze on nothing more substantial than the gauzy unfolding of my cigarette smoke. But I found myself a keen and ever-developing sympathy for the dislike some men have for women knitting. . . . When a man watches a woman knitting he feels shut out. She is absorbed by an occupation he cannot share. She is in a sanctuary where he cannot follow. And her knitting folds her in solidarity with other women. The whole character of a group changes when after dinner women fetch their bags, pregnant with colored wools, like squaws bringing out their papooses.

While the ten million thirties knitters were primarily women, females were by no means alone in their addiction. Every knitting contest drew male contestants, and some female entrants admitted their submissions were fashioned with spousal help. A forty-seven-year-old man who as a child of three had learned to knit at his mother's knee beat out a hundred perspiring women and a few men knitting a huge American flag at the Boston Common's August 1935 commemoration of its early significance to New England's wool industry by recalling its eighteenth-century bees. "Olden days" were reenacted, like those in 1720, when "[s]pinning wheels were brought into the Common and worked by females of the town, all vying with each other to attain the greatest speed," and like the August 13, 1753, fourth anniversary celebration of the "Society for Encouraging Industry and Employing the Poor," when, as that day's *Boston Post* reported, "about three hundred spinners, all neatly dressed, and many of 'em Daughters of the best Families in Town, appeared on the common and being placed orderly in Rows, at Work, made a most delightful appearance and spectators walked in procession to view the spinners."

In 1935, the Civic Chorus sang "The Old Spinning Wheel," a gong rang and knitters began the red, white and blue squares they sub-

Knitting bee on the Boston Common, 1935.

sequently tacked on a huge board to form a complete American flag. One prize-winning contributor attributed his prowess to early training: "Someone had to help mother out because I had five other brothers who were very hard on their knitted stockings. I've knit ever since, and find it helpful in supporting my invalid wife in New Hampshire." Another male contestant quipped to a reporter who worried lest his interview disturb the sixty-six-year-old Back Bay guest house proprietor, "You can't rattle me, young man [drawing from the yarn ball in his straw hat]. I'm an old hand at this. I'm just binding off my first square. I was late starting and I'm afraid I won't get as many squares done as some. I have been knitting since I was sixteen, although there have been years when I have not done any knitting at all. I knitted all through the World War for the soldiers and since then have knitted articles for disabled veterans. . . . Yes, I have a wife, but I knew how to knit long before I met her." The admiring reporter headlined his article MAN CAN KNIT AS GOOD AS WOMAN. The flag, then believed to be the first knit in the country, was, according to the press, to be sewed by the "Boston Historical

Society," but no such society then existed, and the Bostonian Society surmises today that the flag may have been auctioned off for a local cause.

Men from all walks of life like to recall how they were taught as children. Samuel MacDonald, of Sun City West, Arizona, credits the Depression for his learning since there was no money for a baby-sitter when his mother's Girl Scout troop started their knitting badge. Only five when he mingled with the Brownies and picked up rudiments of knitting, he has knit ever since. Male streetcar conductors knit waiting at the turnaround; a Dorchester, Massachusetts, hockey player ran a knitting shop and conducted classes; Columbia University male students in their newly constituted "Nita Nata Nu Fraternity" posed prankishly with needles "at full tilt" for a newspaper story; among the "most proficient pupils" in a Syracuse Salvation Army knitting class, the building's janitor, Aagie Henson, saw "no reason why men should not knit"; and Elmer Hartin, who previously had mastered "fancy work," took his knitting with him almost everywhere he went. What was the fuss?

If no one knew quite why the knitting fad had returned, everyone agreed with one economist's conclusion, "Let the needles click. It

Columbia undergrads take up knitting, c. 1930.

helps recovery." Was there anything harmful about all this knitting? Was there anything crazy in the craze? "Heavens, no," chorused the psychologists who applauded knitting as a means for avoiding tension while producing something of utility and style. What stimulated the economy benefited health. Using handcrafts in treatment of mental illness was a time-honored practice, and the stressful thirties surely required an outlet. As a *New York Times* writer stated, "In a period of worry and uncertainty not only do we need relief from tension and a new channel for pent-up energy, but we need to see concrete results from our efforts. Needlework has filled the need for women ever since Penelope sat at her web." A California college graduate of the thirties remembers that many people knit "because the craft was recommended therapy for recovery from nervous breakdowns," and she herself, a psychiatrist's receptionist who had little to do but oversee patients coming and going on the hour, knit in office slack time.

In the closing weeks of New York's World's Fair, as part of a "blitzkrieg of promotion" designed to attract everyone who had planned a trip but not yet paid their visit to the fair, managers sponsored "America Through the Needle's Eye," the world's largest needlework show and contest, to demonstrate women's achievement in making things for the home. While three thousand dollars was to be awarded for "every phase of knitting and crocheting," to knitters' disgust the two top prizes went to crocheters of a bed quilt and lunch cloth.

Throughout the thirties, knitters had knitting role models in the White House. Like her predecessor, Grace Coolidge, Lou Henry Hoover was importuned for samples for raffles and "recipes" for favorite pieces. Writing to one friend, she ascribed her switch from needlepoint to knitting to new bifocals that blurred everything when she looked up: "I have resigned myself entirely to knitting—which can be accomplished without the aid of eyesight." When sending instructions for her double-knit reversible blanket, she sighed that it was easier to demonstrate than write the steps but gamely contributed five pages of meticulously detailed directions. Mrs. Hoover's stitches were somewhat unorthodox, since she had taught herself knitting, and when a friend spotted an error in her work and started to rip out the entire row, Mrs. Hoover's reply would have endeared

Lou Henry Hoover, c. 1930.

her to other knitters: "Don't rip it. You and I are too busy to rip. Make the same mistake in the next row and make a pattern of it." Her successor as First Lady, Eleanor Roosevelt, an inveterate knitter whose bulging knitting bag was a familiar sight on the campaign trail and then as she traveled the country as her husband's "eyes and ears," posed for an early White House Christmas card sitting at a table, knitting at hand, beside the president. She would later turn her interest and knitting competence into a cry for help for war-torn Europe.

As the thirties drew to a close with the invasion of Poland in late 1939, knitting continued with a new, but still old, goal. As reports of another war in Europe reached America, women who first learned to knit during World War I quickly responded to their instinctive longing to knit for soldiers and sailors of the Allied forces and the injured and homeless civilian populations of war-devastated European countries. A craze was recast as a necessity, and like their knitting forebears in other wars, they welcomed their role.

14.

The Forties: Knitting in War and Peace

In arguments reminiscent of those heard in World War I, some commentators pointed out that women should be knitting for their own less fortunate rather than knitting free for Britain and paying high prices for British imports. The stalwart members of Boston's Fragment Society, who had resisted "soldier" knitting and sewing in the Civil War and World War I, stood firm again in 1940 and recorded in their annual meeting's minutes: "Our deep sympathy goes out to the suffering poor in many countries, but in our great desire to help those in foreign lands, remember that charity begins at home. We must help our own, of course doing our bit for others." Vetoing financial aid to Britain, they rationalized forwarding layettes through the English Speaking Union because chaotic conditions brought the war "to our very doors." Still, the society clung to local charities except when "[M]embers knitted as they listened to the reports."

Relief knitting spelled a comeback to the yarn companies, who, despite slim profits, foresaw that the millions learning to knit would continue after the crisis. Business leaders beamed at the effort "where hardly a woman—from the Park Avenue debutante sunning herself at Palm Beach to the hard-working farmer's wife in her Iowa kitchen—feels comfortable about sitting down without an R.A.F. helmet or a refugee's sweater to work on" and at the fact that movie actresses recognized that cheesecake combined with a bit of war knitting doubled the publicity value of the shot.

As the ever-increasing flow of volunteers poured into Red Cross rooms to furnish material for relief, they divulged their incentive. An older woman, hands nimble from experience, made clothing "[f]or someone over there. You see, I lost two sons in that other war, and somehow, doing this, I feel that I am helping to keep them warm." The wife of a ranking embassy official, apprised by a frantic telephone call that her country was suddenly at war, tearfully continued knitting her sweater: "No fanfare; no eulogies, just a job that needs doing. And women doing it as they always have; thoroughly, efficiently—knowing war." Prompted by sympathy for British victims, many towns "adopted" English cities for which they raised money and sent garments, and in Saginaw, Michigan, the "Bundles for Britain" coordinator, a septuagenarian amateur pilot, barnstormed the countryside exhorting apple growers to knit for the fighters. From Winston Churchill and the king came grateful acknowledgments, Mrs. Churchill appending urgent requests for navy blue pullovers with long sleeves, sea boot stockings, gloves with fingers, and socks.

To ensure that knitters had proper instructions, the British Voluntary Organizations circulated their official *Knitting for the Army*, prefacing the guide with the call that "[k]nitting is no longer a pleasant hobby. No one makes jokes about knitters now, for knitting is no joke. It is a great war industry, run by an unnumbered host of workers who ask no pay, and expect no profits. . . . The woman who knits, like her sisters in the munitions factories, and in the hospitals, is doing important war work." In America, British actress Gertrude Lawrence, appearing on Broadway in *Susan and God* and chairman of English workers in the American Theater Wing of the Allied Relief Fund, crammed her New York apartment with wool, knit to fill in "chinks of her time" and inspired others on Broadway to follow suit. The clicking army of pro-British knitters might not have needed commemoration in song, but by 1941 five songs titled "Knittin' for Britain" flooded the airwaves. One, inspired by the work of film star Madeleine Carroll, opened with "I'm knittin' for Britain to help a worthy cause, I'm knittin' for Britain but listen while I pause. The British fight with all their might so freedom long may live. A moment lent is well worth spent so hurry now and give." Knitters hastened to craft top-priority items: oiled wool "Gum-Boot Stockings" to protect against cold and wet, mittens with ribbing long enough to extend over battle-dress cuffs, sleeveless pullovers to wear underneath for extra warmth for chest, back and lumbar regions, and two-in-one cap-mufflers to wear along with or under steel helmets to replace earlier "Balaclava helmets" that prevented quick adjustment of earphones.

Jane Alencewiz, of Colonia, New Jersey, still treasures her "Official Patterns from the War Office and the Air Ministry for Knitted Garments for His Majesty's Forces" and remembers responding to her high school English teacher's call for volunteers to "Knit for Britain":

> Our teacher started the item, about 1 inch of a cuff on a glove and then showed us what to do with four needles. Our next semester part of our sewing class was knitting garter stitch maroon and gray squares, sewing them into blankets with the maroon making a cross. We took turns holding and winding the hanks of wool onto a knitting needle, so the beginning came from the center of the ball. We also knitted socks, chest protectors, hats and gloves with only the thumb or forefinger; the other fingers were one section like a mitten for handling a rifle.

The hand-yarn industry worried about losing sales to relief organizations, but rather than wring hands, companies like Ulmann cooperated by lowering prices to stores that carried its yarn, acted as representatives of relief organizations and offered their customers discounts, free instruction leaflets for specialized garments and consultation with knitting experts.

Catherine Nearing, of Gales Ferry, Connecticut, remembers: "I feel I contributed to the war effort even though I was only about twelve when my mother and I went to the local Bundles for Britain headquarters in a store where they gave us beautiful wool and the dimensions. I learned to knit young and practiced by knitting enormous scarves for the RAF." In Birmingham, Alabama, volunteer knitters swamped the store asking for help in knitting helmets, scarves and socks for a "worthy cause," but some, remembers the needlework department chairman, "were terrible knitters, a lot like the thirties knitters who came in and knit all day long." Lillian Lunny, of Staten Island, remembers receiving Royal Air Force wool some years after the war from a friend who had planned to knit a sweater for her son, who left college to join the Canadian forces: "She never made it because he was killed on one of his early flying missions. His grieving mother put this wool away for years. I have made myself a sweater and treasure it not for its beauty but for the history of the wool."

While the United States didn't enter the war until December 1941, knitters made garments for reserves who had been called up and sent to training camps months before. A knitter now in her seventies, Rebecca Cripe Allen, of Goshen, Indiana, remembers knitting a khaki vest for her brother, who was stationed with the infantry in Georgia: "The evenings, when they went into town on a pass, were too cool for just their Blouses, but too warm for an overcoat. The knitted vest under the shirt was just the right thing. A couple of his buddies kept wanting to borrow his vest, so he wrote and asked me to please make each of them one too, so he could wear his own when he wanted to. As a result, one vest went through the Battle of the Bulge—and the other went through the Italian campaign." Theresa Konen, of East Brunswick, New Jersey, also knit wool hats, sweaters and scarves for her serviceman brother, who to this day continues to wear the nylon socks she made him and clung to his favorite sleeveless turtleneck sweater for twenty-five years before asking her to camouflage holes with pockets.

A few soldiers knit to pass the time in camp, but the brother of Beverley Royce, of Langdon, Kansas, a downed American flyer held prisoner of war in Germany, demonstrated his youthful knitting experience by showing fellow prisoners how to unravel Red Cross sweaters for yarn to reknit into desperately needed socks. That done, they scouted unsuccessfully for needle substitutes until they learned to straighten pointed barbed wire pieces into implements.

Such knitting was rare if not unique, and Bernat devoted an entire issue to "Hand Knits for the Boys in the Service"; Columbia Minerva used almost the same title, but upgraded boys to men and sprinkled the issue with amusing cartoons from *Punch*, such as the one of the older woman looking up from the newspaper and remarking, "Whenever I think I've done enough knitting for a bit they go and call up another age-group." Another pattern book charted service insignia such as "Gunner's Mate," "Fire Controlman," "Ship's Fitter," "Turret Captain" and "Signal Mate" on graph paper for sweater sleeves, socks, mittens or scarves.

The cover of Bernat's *Handicrafter*'s "Hand Knits for the Boys in the Service" portrayed four bombers breaking through the clouds while inside were such injunctions as: "The Navy Department makes it official by voting this turtleneck pullover the most wanted sweater by every mariner"; "Give a sailor a set like the above—gloves, watch cap, and scarf . . . and he's gale-proof"; "A sailor will be at home in any port when he wears this specially designed sailor sweater with big pockets"; "It will be 'Thanks a million' from the one you send this [turtle necked chest protector] to in any branch of the service"; "[A]ctual war duties proved that abdominal belts kept many men out of the sick wards by protecting the body against sudden chills"; "[F]ingerless gloves will keep his hands warm and his fingers free for active duty"; "To a sailor on the cold seas long sea stockings are a priceless possession"; "A knitted helmet is a must for every fighting

Patterns for servicemen, 1941.

Soldier's chest and back protector, 1941.

man. He wears it in his plane, under his steel helmet, and to protect him against the cold on guard duty. He'll thank you many times over for your effort."

Servicemen prized hand knits as reminders of home, and a home knitter's morale escalated when a soldier wrote of his sweater, "It kinda laughs at the wind trying to get through. I've appreciated it a million times." Bernat's *Handicrafter* capitalized on the personal bond: "The practical way to show that you love him is by knitting something especially for him . . . socks to keep his feet comfortable on long hikes . . . sweaters for chilly days and nights . . . gloves and mittens to keep his fingers warm." Bucilla, delighted that women were knitting for the Red Cross and other groups, but still worrying about lost business, assured each woman that knitting for her boy in military training assured not only his warmth and comfort but, since garments were made to his specific measurements, they were "visible evidence that someone at home has been thinking about him—a lot." A knitting book advertised, "Nothing warms the hearts of the boys away from home like the articles knitted by the loving hands of those they hold near and dear." Since army, navy and marine *women* were not in the *"fighting* forces," few knitters thought to endow them with their largesse. As one knitter interviewed for this book explained, "Well, the girls could certainly knit for themselves, couldn't they?" For women engaged in war time activities of air raid wardens, first aid workers and war bond campaigners, Bear Brand and Bucilla's "Victory Fashions in Hand Knits"'s cover showed a snappily vested and smiling civilian defense worker beaming her flashlight.

When Ulmann issued its official army and navy regulation patterns, it announced to retailers, "There'll be lots of knitting for Service Men. . . . Go After This Business!" Macy's aggressively responded with this newspaper advertisement:

Are you knitting for Bundles for Britain, American-French War Relief, Finnish Relief, Polish Women's Relief Committee, A Bit for Belgium? If you are, Macy's will help you knit socks, sweaters, mufflers, mittens and helmets for Europe's unfortunate. Macy's offers you two types of all-purpose yarns at special prices, our instructress will be glad to help you . . . and when your knitting is finished *Macy's will send it to the organization you designate!*

In addition, a window display on 34th Street showed a huge American eagle against a gold foil background overlooking red, white and blue wallboard shields displaying mittens, socks and sweaters, boxes of "regulation" yarns and overflowing barrels of packages ready to be shipped to camps to punch home the message that if the knitters returned finished garments to the store, Macy's would forward them to any camp at no cost to knitters. As an additional lure, some stores sponsored speed knitting contests where at the sound of a gong each contestant started knitting a simple Red Cross scarf that, upon completion, was rated for quality as well as speed. If knitters were slow, the gong rang after an hour (the scarf could be finished later) and prizes were awarded for "most progress."

Knitting needles were activated even though the Red Cross and service chiefs, to avoid the impression that the government couldn't meet its own clothing requirements, labeled handknit sweaters "comforts" rather than "necessities." Many women knit because women had *always* knit in wartime. As one writer put it, "The womenfolk

Open knitting marathon for war relief, New York City.

are at it again. . . . [They] can't be stopped"; another added, "The men have hardly time to grab their guns before their wives and sweethearts grab needles and yarn." When the secretaries of the war and navy became privy to women's unquenchable appetite for knitting, they capitulated by allowing sweaters for hospitalized servicemen or those garrisoned at island defense bases. To meet the sweater needs of soldiers stationed in Alaska, for example, the New York chapter of the Citizens Committee for the Army and Navy relied upon its six thousand regular knitters to respond. As critical needs multiplied, that group's Knit for Defense Committee kicked off what *The New York Times* called "the greatest mass knitting movement . . . since the first World War" at New York's Waldorf-Astoria Hotel, where Eleanor Roosevelt, introduced as "first knitter of the land" to the audience of two thousand, knit a row in the first sweater of the expected landslide. Soberly telling her listeners at the "Defense Tea," "There is no such thing today as business as usual, life as usual, or play as usual," and referring to the sweaters that had had to be raveled and reknit in World War I, she added candidly, "I hope you will do better than we did twenty years ago." She urged knitters to procure regulation khaki yarn (for $1.85) and official directions from the nine thousand participating stores and knit the proposed million sweaters by Christmas, two months hence.

New York's "Knit for Defense" Tea, 1941.

Sloppily knit sweaters were the bane of the services. Helping to corroborate the message that knitters should follow directions precisely was *Punch*'s 1940 cartoon of a soldier poured into a short, tight, slim-waisted, high-necked, puffed-sleeve sweater mournfully excusing it to his buddy: "She says she can't knit any other kind." *Life* answered what it called the great American question, "What can I do to help the war effort?" with one word, "Knit!" and put on its November 24, 1941, cover young Notre Dame college student Peggy Tippet furrowing her brow over her knitting to feature the "How to Knit" article inside. Before the *Life* photographer flashed her picture, Peggy, despite her scant knitting experience, vowed to make the new V-neck standard army sweaters for which the Citizens Committee appealed, and the committee, recognizing that women savored the sociability of group knitting, opened a special Madison Avenue knitting shop where knitters could meet informally, purchase yarn, obtain instruction and donate finished products.

Life Magazine, 1941.

Knitting at Red Cross chapters became so intense that when a distraught lad charged in to ask "Do you darn socks here?" the volunteer countered calmly that workers knit only for servicemen and refugees. Exasperated, he wailed, "You ought to mend socks too! Since my mother has been knitting for the Red Cross, I've had to mend my own!" His plaintive cry in no way deterred what one writer called "slaves-to-the-habit-knitters," upon whom knitting had about the same effect as marijuana cigarettes: "They get satisfaction from the orderly row of stitches falling into patterns of accomplishment. In times like these there are few occupations that have that sort of effect. It is quite possible that women in wartime knit as much for the knitting as for what their knitting accomplished."

Knitting women, who conversed in "yarn overs," "yarn to the front of cable needle" and "pass the slip stitch over the knit stitch" as if knitting lingo were their native tongue, chuckled when they heard that FBI agents, ever on the lookout for agents of unfriendly powers with subversive pamphlets, apprehended a woman passenger on an incoming liner whose papers included such scribbled notations as "K2.p.4.k.6" and demanded a translation of the code to which the vast State Department library had no key. They were duly embarrassed to learn their "agent" was simply a patriotic knitter. Knitting instructions in another code were given to a car pool friend by an aircraft company worker who always worked on mitten cuffs while riding to work: "Set up 42 stitches and k.1, p.1 from Red Bank to Linden."

The new magazine *Calling All Girls* urged young girls to help the war effort by helping at home, taking part in community activities, studying nutrition, writing letters, baking food for the soldiers, giving benefits, buying defense bonds and stamps, and *knitting* for women and children in war-torn countries through Bundles for Britain. Parents of teenagers must have been gratified by this further advice: "If you whine and complain about your selfish problems, you make everyone around you nervous and unhappy, and that's not fair, now is it?"

Teaching the young to knit was a good investment in future buyers, and Lincoln, Nebraska's, Rudge and Guenzel department store conducted a successful ten-lesson children's knitting class for boys and girls between six and fourteen, bestowing a knitting bag embroidered with his or her own first name and the store's monogram to each child with an unsullied attendance record. Children in Manitowac, Wisconsin, near a navy submarine construction site, learned knitting from their playground handicraft teacher, who carried her Red Cross knitting to work and in daily sessions converted the most eager and adept of her charges into knitting instructors. Working with donated Red Cross yarn, seven- to fifteen-year-old girl knitters elicited support from the boys, who rolled skeined yarn into balls and braided "idiot's delight" cords for sweater neck closures in a project so successful that they founded knitting clubs to continue through the school year. In Greenville, South Carolina, children who knit caps and helmets for airmen combined learning with giving by converting their Bundles for Britain donation box to a depository for coins required to atone for each grammatical error.

Barbara Moeller, of Charlotte, North Carolina, recalls that when her eighth-grade teacher gave the class a choice of airplane spotting, first aid or knitting for war relief, she chose knitting. Then came another choice, knitting for Bundles for Britain or Russian War Relief? She chose the Russians and "loved every minute of it and made a number of scarves, not quite so many helmets and one other garment, but I can't remember what it was. Later, when the Cold War started, I was very bitter and said I hoped the Russians choked on the scarves I knit!" A promising correspondence loomed between a young wartime knitter who made squares for her class afghan project and a soldier who found her name included in the Red Cross package. Thrilled at his invitation to be a pen pal, she promptly replied, but followed her parents' advice to alert him that she was only eight years old: "I'm certain that came as a great surprise to him because that's the end of the story. No more letters arrived."

Gloria Witherow, of Houtzdale, Pennsylvania, remembers watching her elders knitting:

> We lived in a small backwoods town in the coal fields of central Pennsylvania where my grandparents owned and operated a general store where people came to talk and relax in the early evenings. The men sat around the potbelly stove and argued politics, talked of hunting and discussed their work in the mines while the women sat towards the store front chatting and tatting, knitting, crocheting or darning socks. My grandmother taught me to knit and crochet

on those long winter evenings at the store—some 42 years ago. She was a lovely soul who possessed that rare quality—patience. At that time the ladies were knitting sweaters for the men in the service with yarn supplied by the Red Cross. I was too young to participate but I remember it as if it were yesterday.

Nancy McClure, with her new graduate degree in progressive education, soon combined educational and community activities at a consolidated county school in western North Carolina to which students either walked or traveled by bus from remote mountain areas. Allowed by a lenient principal to teach her eighth-grade girls knitting during her study hall periods, she obtained olive drab yarn, needles and instructions for seventy-two-inch mufflers from the tiny Red Cross headquarters and soon had her girls knitting them. Their mothers, eager to contribute to soldiers in that area, begged for knitting, too, and, with student couriers delivering yarn to and bringing finished products from these isolated "mountain ladies," Nancy McClure soon realized her goal of integrating "home and school" and helping the war effort.

As in the previous war, knitting appeared in children's literature, and one of the most charming books was *Rufus M.*, relating young, left-handed Rufus's difficulties with the class project, knitting string washcloths for soldiers ("He knit the way he wrote, with large loose generous stitches"). Poor Rufus's washcloth widened perceptibly as it lengthened, despite ministrations from his sister, who decreased stitches to fill in the larger holes. When Rufus learned of his school's contemplated depot field trip to visit a passing troop train, he surreptitiously retrieved his "Rufus M., room three" washcloth from the Red Cross pile, pocketed it and scurried along with his class to the station, where he pressed it into the hand of a friendly soldier, explaining proudly, "I knit it myself." Neither teacher nor principal was amused by his breach of school rules but relented when Rufus received this note from the soldier: "The washcloth you knitted sure comes in handy. My buddies and I all take turns. Al."

When wartime marriages upped the two and a quarter million annual birth rate, yarn companies saluted the Baby Boom with gimmicks such as having stores advertise free sweater-set wool for the first baby born in their city in the new year. When National Baby

Week was announced in early May 1943, stores jumped on the baby bandwagon with hundreds of new patterns. The high birth rate, the need for extra warmth in fuel-rationed homes and the shortage of rubber (enough only for elasticized waistlines and pant legs of "waterproof" panties) led women to knit "soakers" of four-ply, absorbent wool or boilproof cotton to drain the moisture from babies' diapers. No mother had enough, since they took days to dry! Bucilla sold "Wonder Knit" kits for fifty cents (sixty-nine cents for wool), and every company featured patterns for these simple drawstring staples of every layette. A picture of soakers is enough either to warm the cockles of 1940s mothers' hearts or curdle their blood.

Vivian Filipak, of Mansfield, Ohio, remembers:

I had four children between 1938 and 1946 and during the intervening years whenever I had any slack time I knitted only one article, SOAKERS, but I did it two hundred times. They guaranteed a more contented baby, one without diaper rash or winter chills that seemed the precursor of all those sniffles. "Modern" mothers bought the latex pants at a dollar a pair, but their babies

Soakered babies, 1951.

suffered sore bottoms, often severe enough to require medical attention, a problem during doctor shortage of the war years. Another plus for soaker knitting was that mothers developed strength of character to counter the ridicule of those who espoused the "why bother?" school of mothering.

In general, mothers rated ventilation in soakers superior to that in plastic pants, but complained: "They don't soak very much"; "[T]hey turned yellow from too much washing—or worse"; "[T]hey were draped to dry over every available piece of furniture in our tiny apartment"; "My mother told me they *had* to be made of wool so I couldn't throw them in the washing machine"; "I never want to HEAR that word again!" Mothers heaved a collective sigh of relief when "breathing" panties were introduced.

As in World War I, knitting clubs again became the rage, and *Popular Science* magazine featured "It's more fun to knit in company, as every woman knows," "[K]nitters and knitting are everywhere! everywhere!" and "Knitting has become an almost universal pastime among women" to inspire home craftsmen to make knitting accessories. One inventor sprang forward with the perfect tool for the knitting club, an umbrellalike stand whose separate cylindrical compartments made from cardboard tubes ("such as the new linoleum is rolled up in") could be reached by each club member.

In Akron, Ohio, twelve young women, who moved in with parents or in-laws when husbands went overseas, gave their elders a free night once a week (so to speak, since they parked their children there!) to attend "Stitch and Bitch Club" meetings. Loaded with sewing and knitting, stuffed on supposedly "light refreshments" provided by the evening's hostess, voicing opinions on everything from parenting to politics and exchanging news from each war zone represented, they met until each member's husband returned home—all but one. The sensitivity of the others to that member's sorrow has bound them for life, but none could face continuing the club after the war.

A knitting club was even the impetus for a wartime musical hit:

> Floss joined a knitting group with just
> An hour each day to spare,

And noted as the needles sped,
    The girls all hummed an air.
Thought she: "I'm sure a knitting song
    With an appealing swing
Would make a smashing wartime hit
    That everyone would sing."

When the resultant "Knit One, Purl Two" was recorded by band leader Glenn Miller, whose "White Cliffs of Dover," "When the Roses Bloom Again," "She'll Always Remember" and "Don't Sit Under the Apple Tree" had already established him as a wartime music leader, it caught the eye of *American Weekly*'s editor, whose Sunday supplement plugged it nationwide. While other songs, such as "Knit, Sister, Knit," "Knittin' on a Mitten," "Knit a Kiss, Purl a Prayer," "Knit Wit Me," "Knit, Sister Sue," "Knit for Victory," "Stick to Your Knittin', Kitten" and endless combinations of knitting and purling, competed, none caught the public's fancy, including one with a chorus that went:

"Knit One, Purl Two"
for the Boys!

First I Knit 2, Purl 2, Then I stop and think of you
This token of my love must keep you warm
Again I Knit 2, Purl 2, One to drop, then carry through,
While praying it will keep my love from harm.

When forties women, like the knitters of the late "teens," carted work to lectures and concerts, syndicated etiquette arbiter Emily Post advised knitters to defer hauling out knitting until they ascertained from the speakers that it would not be distracting. Assuming that speakers would not dare to confront wartime knitting women, she proffered etiquette rules: "Do not wave long or shiny needles about in the air; Do not flap your elbows as though you were a bird learning to fly; Do not leave your wool in a bag at your feet and keep hauling it up every so often with a thrust higher than your head." *The New York Times*, applauding Post's "healthy vigor and common sense," joshed that perhaps speakers, too often given to "fruitless oratory," should not be permitted to interrupt the knitting!

While women recognized that Red Cross and baby knitting were laudable, they needed assurance that knitting warm, practical, long-lasting, all-occasion civilian garments would conserve other clothes, that it was more economical to knit than to purchase, and that knitting, since it "soothes the nerves and is a splendid outlet for pent up war emotions," was an acceptable morale builder. Even good old grandmother was trotted out to reassure knitters that they were simply recapturing their grandmothers' craft. New York's Wanamakers, remarking that the Machine Age had rekindled the joys of creative work, clad its saleswomen in mid-Victorian costumes to focus attention on its afghan exhibit: "Grandma's afghan has the place of honor on the back of the sofa now. The whole family is proud of it, to the last dropped stitch. Father proudly sports the knitted tie Aunt Aggie did for him . . . but the joy of all these was in the *making*! It can be fun." Granny always came through in a pinch.

Knitters were soon engrossed with their own projects. Peck and Peck endorsed "That Hand-Knit Look"; Saks Fifth Avenue called 1941 "The Year of the Hand-Knit Fever," a fever so high that "women are refusing to doff their knits for practically any occasion short of an embassy ball"; *Vogue* coined the term *tailorknit* for its handknit, "full-fledged jacket, tailored as a wool or tweed one." Matching knit hats heightened the sophisticated "citified" look of tailorknits that ranged from "reefers" and fingertip jackets to a "knitted chauffeur's jacket, trim shouldered, trim waisted, lined with red and buttoned with gilt." Those who yearned for these latest fashion crazes and handknit suits and dresses from European designers commanding $75 to $150 in small shops could reproduce them for only $10 to $30.

Interest in knitting for nonservicemen was honed when the Hollywood connection with Warner Brothers stars, so profitable to Bernard Ulmann Company in the thirties, was plugged in again. Aware that many knitters were drafting sweaters for bodies now given to girth and paunch, Ulmann added heftier character actors such as Guy Kibbee and Victor McLaglen to the roster of slimly sweater-clad Tim Holt, Lyle Talbot, Otto Kruger, Jackie Cooper and young singer Bobby Breen. *Movie Star Hand Knits for Men*, with its all-star, all-contours, all-age cast, sold like hotcakes. It purred:

Knit your way to his heart! What a thrill for any man to receive a sweater you have knitted with your own hands, especially if it's a style like one worn by a popular screen personality. Show him this book and let him pick the sweater he likes best. Watch his face light up with satisfaction as he chooses his favorite style. And when he wears the finished garment . . . he'll be pleased as punch because you made it for him . . . whether he's the outdoor type, the sports enthusiast, or the man who loves to stay home and enjoy his comfort in leisure.

The company released stars' pictures to three thousand newspapers, who reproduced them in women's and fashion pages. Not a movie fan? How about radio? Ulmann had a special book for those star chasers, too, and Rudy Vallee, Fred Allen, Dick Powell and others posed in their broadcasting sweaters.

Knitting was so prevalent that both *The New York Times* and the *Herald Tribune* ran center-page spreads in photogravure sections showing twin sets, fitted jackets, college pullovers and wool-and-

Movie Star Hand Knits for Men,
1940.

Victor McLaglen in sleeveless
pullover, 1940.

Jackie Cooper in turtleneck
sweater, 1940.

angora Argyle patterns in both sweaters and socks with yarns from leading stores such as McCreery's, Alice Maynard, Abraham and Straus, Bloomingdale's, Macy's and Frederick Losser's in Brooklyn. A newspaper advertisement, headlined KNITTING IS PATRIOTIC-FASH-IONABLE-THRIFTY, advised: "From shop-girl to socialite, practically *every* woman is interested in knitting for National Defense in buses, train cars, in the smartest women's clubs; everywhere knitting and crocheting needles are doing their stint for America. . . . With our country at war, it's the patriotic duty of every woman to knit—not only for men in the service but for those at home as well." Quite simply, the forties' "perfect woman" took her cue from the faithful Red Cross heroine of a woman's magazine story: "Mary knits helmets steadily; she has knitted more than a hundred altogether. The yarn is given her, but she does the knitting."

Given the wartime shortages, it took some doing for the perfect woman to *look* perfect for her role, but ingenuity beat out restrictions. With leather rationed and full skirts, patch pockets, knife pleats, padded shoulders and large, fancy hats proscribed, along came low-heeled shoes (especially ballet slippers), "ballerina-length" evening skirts, natural shoulders, bare arms, accessories to triple the effect of each outfit, and soaring hats, especially turbans, though film star Carmen Miranda carried the latter to ludicrous heights and weights by festooning hers with "victory gardens" and avian plumage. With rubber forbidden in girdles, women had either to eat wisely to prevent bulges or opt for adjustable waistbanded attire to camouflage them; even zippers "went to war." When sophisticated, shorter skirts revealed more knee, ingenious cosmeticians countered the hosiery slack (nylon, too, had "gone to war") by introducing leg makeup. Women daubed their legs with "Suntan," "Rosy Beige" and "Pale Camellia," penciled seams on faux "stockings," wrought patchup jobs in ladies' rooms with terry cloth leg mitts and carefully deleted the excess from skirt and slip hems. It was a different story, however, when the War Production Board planned to limit face powder, lipstick and rouge. The women attacked: "Don't you understand that our make-up is vital to our morale? Don't you realize that our men want us to look good for them?" The board hurriedly bowed to the fury and reclassified facial cosmetics "essential" to the war effort.

Among the home front garments knit, sweaters were touted as

Campus favorite, 1940.

basic to the college wardrobe. Surveying their college mates, students in a statistics course at Wellesley College discovered each student owned ten and one-half sweaters, "with variations arising from the strength of the urge to knit." College girls from all over the country serving as guest editors for the college issue of *Mademoiselle* were enthusiastic about handknit sweaters, especially the Brooks type, with scattered pockets of support for the "long sloppy type." Knitting members of department store "College Boards" were asked to knit in any free moments. Bucilla, eager to garner college knitters, tested its "Campus Classics" patterns with a "fashion jury" of college girls, and offered free copies of plans to "get the students to become loyal customers."

After Pearl Harbor it was reported that more knitting was begun in the two days following Japan's attack on Hawaii than during the first three months of the college year; at New Jersey College for Women, the knitting center ran out of wool before the second day passed; colleges across the country reported students taking up their knitting with similar zeal. On the home front, everyone wanted to participate, to *do something*! Advertisers capitalized in their advertisements. Dr. West's toothbrushes ordered: "Take good care of yourself. . . . You belong to the U.S.A." Kleenex remonstrated with sneezers to use tissues lest they be "public enemies" by spreading colds. The need for silence on war information spawned "Loose Lips Sink Ships," "Idle Words Make Busy Subs" and "The Less Said; The Less Dead." An imaginative hat maker warned: "Keep it under your Stetson!" It might be hard to keep their mouths shut, but no one suggested they couldn't *knit*! They responded as if trumpets had blared.

Jean H. Coe, of Maiden, North Carolina, recalls that when she finished high school in Abington, Massachusetts, she and a group of friends earned college money by working on Martha's Vineyard: "All of the waitresses decided to knit sweaters and got permission to knit while waiting for our assigned people to come in to dine as long as we stood in our designated spot. At first it was fine, but as the sweaters got larger, it was quite a sight to see girls in every corner of the dining room with various colored sweaters hanging down." Josephine Zillian, of McLean, Virginia, remembers the stretch bandages she knit for the New York Red Cross so well that she was still able to reproduce one for the author: "I made mine while riding to and from work on the New York City subways by using either Clark's Knit-Cro-Sheen or Bedspread yarn in four hundred yard length spools. I'd put fifteen to twenty stitches on a number four or five needle and knit to the end of the ball in garter stitch. The fifteen to twenty feet long roll could be sterilized since it was made of 100% cotton." Nationally syndicated knitting columnist Pat Trexler, of North Myrtle Beach, South Carolina, recalled,

As a sophomore in high school in 1942, I was again taught to knit by volunteer ladies from the Florence, South Carolina Red Cross Chapter. This time it was olive drab (ugh) scarves made on size one needles. The people who were most surprised when I started writing a knitting column several years later were my high school friends as we all vowed we would never knit again if we could just get through that one interminably long scarf! One friend just knitted to the end of the war and stopped.

Eager teens scouring the fashion pages in search of the latest "make-do" fad were rewarded with directions for "Socks with a Sock," made by drilling holes in the top of two empty walnut shells, running a string of yarn through, and then—"What gives? Why, a pair of castenets; attach them to the top of your socks and you'll sound like a gay senorita!" *ole!* Tired of old buttons? A simple ruler cut into inch-long pieces (or less, depending upon the size of the buttonholes) could be drilled with two holes and sewn onto one's school sweater, justifying the claim that it was "made to measure." "Simple and snazzy" reversible knitted belts added new life to old skirts, and knits, "popular with the Coke crowd," were described as "Beau Catcher," "feminine" and "trimmed with coquettish bows."

Since teens wanted to knit for themselves as well as soldiers and prized handknits as dearly as their college-bound siblings, stores gave out free pencil cases and other school paraphernalia to mothers who purchased yarn for children's sweaters. Surveys showed that the great majority of teenage girls knit or were learning to, and the editor of *Calling All Girls* prated, "So you're crooning for a V-neck sleeveless job like the boys wear? Well, as that radio comic would say, 'Tell you what I'm gonna do'. . . . I'm going to send you instructions. . . ." Along came the "Bluey Woozy" sweater, with sailor boys on the yoke, and an invitation to "Male-Robbery" by matching their own cable vests to those of their "T.D.&G.s" (Tall, Dark, and Gruesomes!). Wow!

Life's article on "Dressed-Up Sweaters" vindicated sweaters for dressy occasions since fuel-rationed cold rooms made them "fitting apparel for day and night, at work and at play, with one exception. In factories where men and women work together sweaters are discouraged. They are considered unsafe and distracting." Not so, rejoined "Oomph girl" Ann Sheridan, who contended that sweaters were bad only if a small girl's too-big sweater caught in the machinery or a big girl's too-small sweater caught the eye of nearby male workers and constituted a "moral hazard." Vought-Sikorsky Aircraft Corporation, subscribing to the latter argument, sent home fifty-three girls on "moral grounds" for wearing sweaters on the job, and edgy Sperry Gyroscope commissioned Vera Maxwell to design decorous coveralls for its "Sperry Girls." Outside the workplace, however, sweaters were so ornamented—so patched and doctored, so camouflaged by beads, braid, buttons, embroidery and ribbon, belying their earlier lives as sloppy college gear or movie starlets' skimpy and revealing little favorites—that, according to *Life*, they flustered even the Hays office's wiliest inspector.

The "Hays office inspector," that sentry of American morals, gained notoriety in scuffles that delighted both press and public, and nothing did more for sweaters or vice versa than starlet Lana Turner, whom columnist and radio announcer Walter Winchell dubbed "America's Sweater Girl Sweetheart." Hollywood, defending itself against charges from vigilant organizations such as the Catholic church's Legion of Decency, had established a Motion Picture Producers' Code (enforced by Will Hays) to forbid expressly "indecent or undue" exposure, but since there was no stricture against skin-tight, bosom-outlining knits, Lana's sex queen crown was won without code violation. Her bouncy saunter in the aptly titled 1937 movie *They Won't Forget* with Claude Rains and Otto Kruger was photographed from every angle, all of them good. Director Mervyn LeRoy savored the memory: "I figured that a tight sweater on a beautiful young girl would convey to the audience everything we couldn't say outright. . . . When Lana walked down the street, her bosom seemed to move in a rhythm all its own. Later, when I added the musical score to the picture, I made sure that the composer emphasized that rhythm with his music." As one panting movie magazine noted, "One of those bright wardrobe boys who infest studios took a second look at her, beat it for the wardrobe department, got the sweater, and told her to don it. . . . It revealed a startling amount of Lana to the public." The Hays office's retaliatory ban on pictures of stars in sweaters merely helped sweaters ascend the rating ladder to the top rung as "*The* glamor garment" of the younger set. More girls than ever clicked away at their shorter, form-fitting "sweater-blouses," with what dreams of glory one can only surmise.

At the close of the war, there was still plenty to do for the thousands of war refugees, and *Smart Knitting* sponsored a "Knit for Needy Children" contest in conjunction with several yarn manufacturers, the Red Cross, Catholic Welfare Conference, Church World Service and American Women's Voluntary Services. News of the contest was broadcast on "The Guiding Light" radio program, which was "an inspiring dramatic serial of a hard-working clergyman and his unselfish devotion to the problems of his parishioners." Appliance-starved knitters could salivate at the prizes: an Emerson *television*-radio, a Launderall refrigerator, a Dishamatic dish washing machine, and assorted cameras and watches, but their hearts were moved by the plight of suffering children.

By the end of the war, knitting was still so ascendant that the New York School of Knitting and Handcraft on Fifth Avenue headlined "There's Money in Knitting" for the graduates of its home study course and advertised a "knitting swatch book album . . . and work kit with needles, accessories and enough yarn to complete every lesson" to new enrolees. At the end of the rainbow lay the dream of one's own career, armed with the "certificate of graduation" from founder Sonna Noble, an expert knitter and author. Some years later, in 1961, Ms. Noble wrote *How to Successfully Operate a Knitting Shop*; so she must have taken her own advice.

On the practical side, major yarn companies united in the National Hand Yarn Association and its related Institute of Hand Knitting to upgrade knitting teachers' skills, shrewdly counting on their expertise to "liberate the art of knitting from the rocking chair set and introduce it to the just-out-of-the-cradle one." To their delight, they heard that four hundred young people were knitting identical Syracuse school sweaters in their school colors. Requests for instructions for long-torso sweaters and knee socks to go with the new Bermuda shorts swamped the institute, whose director, counting hives of activity, shaded her United States map to highlight availability of courses and instructresses. According to Bucilla, the sporty "hand-knitted bare-knee ensemble" consisted of "pull-over sweater, flared skirt, panties [assumed!] and knee-length socks." With the new "jiffy-knit sweaters," knitters would save enough time to turn heels, something everyone hated. Within a few years the institute taught thousands of teachers and sponsored locally judged contests to spur yarn sales, and when asked if mothers were shirking their duties in teaching children to knit, its director replied, "Well, no, but mothers may not know too much beyond the elementary steps. Today's high-style knit fashions call for high-powered skills." Granny wouldn't have liked hearing that about her daughter.

By the end of 1945, stylists rushed to create postwar "looks." *Esquire*'s "Bold Look" for the "Dominant Male" called for socks as "potent as punch." What better foil than Argyles, bold enough for anyone's blood, including the knitter struggling with tangled strands to give her man his bold image. She was prodded: "Knock His Socks Off"; "Rate Tops with the Top Man in Your Life"; "Knit for Him"; "Want to impress the man in your life? Here's a sweater-and-socks set that really will take his eye. He'll be contender for the best-dressed man on the campus, and you'll be the smartest gal he knows. You may start a fad, and you'll be ahead of the game. Knit this set for him, and he'll call it a labor of love, but you'll know it was fun"; "Knit him a pair of socks with the BOLD LOOK and watch him zoom with pride."

When the bold ones aired their preference for longer-wearing and easier-washing nylon socks, *Men's Wear* promised, "Nylon They Want, Nylon They Get." While nylon was acceptable for *manufactured* stockings and a few knitters bought it for Argyle knitting, die hards snapped, "Who on earth would knit with something made from *coal?*" and worked in nylon only for toe and heel reinforcement. Jane Snibbe, of Pebble Beach, California, cast her lot with the old-timers:

> Imagine, a beginning knitter working on argyle socks, one of the hardest kinds of projects, but that's what I did. My father was kept in argyles for years because I would start a pair for the current boyfriend, and by the time the socks were done, the romance would be over, and my father would get the socks. He treasured them enough to hand wash them himself as he lived away during the week and was home only on week-ends. That hand knit turned heel certainly outwears anything that can be bought, and the socks lasted for years. I knit only with pure wool, as I don't, even today, care for acrylic yarns.

For knitters too rushed to wind or too thrifty to buy a whole skein of yarn when only a portion was needed, companies countered with Argyle "sock pack" assortments of premeasured lots for background, contrasting diamonds and diagonals, some of it already wound on "Bob-O-Wool" cards. The son of Bernat's founder recalls that at the height of the four-year Argyle "hot fad" promotion, their company marketed twenty-one different Argyle styles in socks, mittens and sweaters, with packs for each. Knitters who were embroiled in the forties and fifties Argyle craze respond to their recollections with feeling. Doris Walton Epner, of Brooklyn Heights, relives the experience: "In order to earn some pocket money I knit argyle socks (in my sleep, practically), for my schoolmates. I also finished a lot that were started by well-intentioned souls and somehow got shoved to the back of the drawer. I can't tell you how many pair I made or completed, but by the time I got out of college, I didn't want to see another argyle *anything*!" Maria Robertson, of Annandale, Virginia, born a Hollander but married to a Scot and therefore knowledgeable about Scottish patterns and primed for the craze, gamely manipulated bobbins and needles, eternally grateful that the luscious colors provided a welcome respite from tedious war time navy blue and khaki.

Phyllis Treloar, of Garden Grove, California, remembers: "I made every pattern of argyles I could find during the 40's and 50's. I bought frames to stretch socks on and knitted nylon thread into the heels and toes to make them more durable. The argyle sweater I knit for my daughter turned out to be 5 feet long and 1½ feet across! It discouraged me so much I never tried again. I sent it to the cleaners and it came back the same. I didn't know you had to measure and improvise etc. I still don't know how—so I mostly knit bedroom slippers and scarves!" Shirley Cannon, of Sandy, Utah, learned to turn a heel to make Argyle socks, "But after I married the man I gave the socks to and discovered that they had to be washed by hand (they were wool, of course) I didn't make any more! In college since none of us had much money we'd knit 'mukluks' for Christmas presents, using a contrasting color for the top and the cable up the front middle. We bought furry-lined leather bottoms and sewed the knit sections to those. They were a lot easier than argyles!"

Ruth Folsom, of Charlotte, North Carolina, who started Argyle socks in the forties, never understood the directions about bobbins: "I just kept on knitting the colors they told me to, pulling each yarn across the back until my sock had so many cross yarns that it was getting narrower. I wondered how a foot would get into it without the toes getting tangled but went ahead undaunted until my friend's sister, a proficient knitter, showed me how to use bobbins. We all had a good laugh at my project!" Edith Anne O'Brien, now of Mount Vernon, Washington, whose English neighbor lured her into knitting for Bundles for Britain by helping her with cables and Argyles, knit many for a high school Italian boyfriend whose gift of a taffeta, rollup needle container she never returned when the romance soured. She added, "In college I did special order patterned and argyle socks to earn extra money. I did the top part at night in the dorm after studying and the feet part, round and round, in classes. I can remember only one or two who were disconcerted by this and even they gave in when I explained how much I needed the extra money because my Dad had just died."

Home from boarding school for the holidays, young Sam MacDonald, now of Sun City West, Arizona (who learned to knit as a youngster), was so irked by his girlfriend's inattention when she stitched away at her Argyle socks that he bought himself yarn and "sock needles," knit madly all day to ready *his* stocking for heel turning by evening and waited with delicious anticipation for the moment she reached for her knitting. It came. With a flourish, he brandished his own project and settled back to count stitches. She got the picture and postponed the Argyles until after he returned to school. Sam MacDonald, a lifelong serious knitter, still enjoys the raised eyebrows as he advises stewardesses that he will need his "knitting bag" (a fancy European shopping bag) during flights, extracts his knitting and sits there "in my three-button suit trying to look casual while other passengers stretch and crane necks." An active member of the Clan Donald, he has proudly knit his own Argyle stockings with the cuff doubled over to achieve the "manly calf" look to which a Scot aspires.

Many people sought to extract the agony from Argyle knitting, but knitters somehow felt the challenge itself guaranteed deeper appreciation. Despite mountains of gadgets such as the "Line Reel," "Yarn O'Bobbin," "Stitchex" and "Rispindle" (to dispense yarn from the wrist), the task remained daunting. An ingenious approach was "Colorplus," yarn *dyed* in premeasured lengths and guaranteed to "knit up" into diamonds and diagonals if knitters ruthlessly maintained a steady, predetermined gauge in "plain stockinette" stitch. When fashion-crazy, bobbin-weary knitters strayed from gauge, truly grotesque patterns emerged from their needles. Florence Polens, of Stafford, Connecticut, not only recalls making those socks but still has the evidence: "My husband still has a forty year old pair. My beloved mother was the *Great Shrinker* when it came to hand knits, so that each family member inherited knitwear made for older siblings. When I married in 1953, even my husband got the argyles I had knit for my brother's larger feet. I can remember doing some fancy, private cussing when my tension strayed and I had to rip back and re-knit. I finally discovered that if I wrapped the yarn around my finger twice, it helped the tension but slowed my progress." Before long, Colorplus yarn exited the market, but not before dashing the hopes of embattled Argylers.

A covey of Argylers was saved by this author's teenage ingenuity. On the long transcontinental train trip from Santa Barbara to Boston, she had plenty of time to ponder solutions to the "Argyle mess." Speculating that trapping yarn bobbins or balls in their sequential positions might circumvent snarls, she adhesive-taped (this was before Scotch tape!) them to her skirt and took up her needles. Resolute in the face of the first row's tangled wreckage, she purled back and ecstatically discovered that the strands resumed their parallel position. Hobbling around with yarn taped to one's skirt, however, was not a better mousetrap. During her Chicago stopover, she wheedled an empty shoe box from a bewildered shoe clerk and modified it to separate the yarn in compartments while permitting the strands to stick out through holes punched in the lid. She hopped the next train, purposefully positioned the box on her lap and serenely Argyled her way to Boston with nary a knot. "Argyle Boxes" became a standard knitting accessory to that generation of Wellesley Argylers, but it was not until the eighties that she applied for and received a patent. Receiving it, she founded a company to market her invention, aptly named the Great Scot Argyler.

Knitters became true connoisseurs of "proper" Argyling techniques and looked askance at those who made *knots* ("Oh, I see you didn't bury the ends of the yarn on the diagonal") even though the condemnatory practice was endorsed by a former teacher from Alice Maynard's hallowed showrooms: "When tying one color to another, after completion of diamonds, tie the two ends together with a square knot right up against the needle, leaving about three inches of free end to thread through a needle later on." To this day that practice would separate the girls from the women of needledom! That writer should, however, be credited with introducing charts showing the

The Argyle look, 1949.

numbers of stitches of each color for varying sizes, a long way from graphs, but still a beginning. *Doreen Two Needle Argyles* offered a ray of hope by promising a patented method of making Argyles "without bobbins" by picking up stitches for contrasting diamonds along the edges of previously worked ones, but it did not provide the smooth color-block transition prized by intarsia knitters. If weary of knitting diamonds, one could try the new "chicken wire" socks with contrasting lines outlining interlocking hexagons, a new if not classy look.

Eileen Hasselwood, of Pacific Grove, California, who had little time to knit as a wartime riveter in Boeing Aircraft's Seattle plant, later worked in Carmel, California, as an "All-Nite" relief girl to two telephone company employees, both avid knitters, and recalls:

> We had to count and check the day's long distance calls, clean the switchboards and be available to answer customer calls, but otherwise had plenty of extra time. Each took turns reading aloud, never dropping a stitch in the process, and one's college husband must have been the best dressed man there because she made at least thirty sweaters for him and her mother completed the outfits with matching socks! Needless to say, it was not long before I had my needles out making sweaters and caps for my son! Over the years I have taught a lot of gals to knit and enjoyed seeing how delighted they were to finish an item and say "See what I made myself."

Late forties knitters revived angora. In 1903, *Stitches* had noted that an "average person" would think it was fur "so closely does it resemble it," and later generations either embellished other garments with the furry yarn or made boleros, jackets, mittens, caps and scarves of it. A college student, Eleanor Holland, of Holden, Massachusetts, even decorated her sweaters with knit-in beer mugs brimming with angora foam. Angora was so popular that Bernard Ulmann enlightened its dealers: "Angora rabbit hair continues to grow after it is plucked from the animal and made into finished yarn sometimes as much as half an inch." That was indeed startling news to many a knitter who kept a close watch on her mittens, caps and gloves. It would surely have surprised Shirley Cannon: "I first started to knit in the fall of 1949, when I went off to college in California, my home state. The rage was angora sock tops/cuffs. They were expensive to buy so we knit them ourselves. We put them in the refrigerator just before wearing them to make the angora stick out and look fuzzier." At Annapolis, squeaky-clean, dark-suited midshipmen, fearing fall out from angora accessories, allowed precious airspace to separate them from their furry "drags."

Ribbon was the next fad, either knit separately or combined with wool for sweaters, skirts and dresses or added to update short sweaters. To lower skirts from the waist to conform to the postwar "New Look," knitters covered the unsightly gap where a new piece of fabric had been inserted to give an extra six or eight inches at the top with a long-torsoed sweater ("Wear this blouse five to nine inches below the waist, or even longer if you like the style and your figure can stand it").

Undaunted forties knitters still carried their knitting "about" as had their forebears; but one carried hers "about" to a spot more remote than others dared contemplate. Edith (Jackie) Ronne of Bethesda, Maryland, accompanied her husband's Antarctic expedition to Punta Arenas, Chile, the southernmost tip of South America, for a last farewell before their months-long separation and to help with final preparations as the ship's stores were provisioned for wintering over on the continent some two thousand miles farther south. Captain Finn Ronne, son of a famous Norwegian explorer and himself a participant in an earlier Byrd Antarctic expedition, led his own privately financed expedition in 1948 and, as leader, made all final decisions, among them a last-minute inspiration to have his wife accompany the expedition. At first considering the proposition outrageous, she entertained the possibility if a woman friend could be

Like mother, like daughter,
1945.

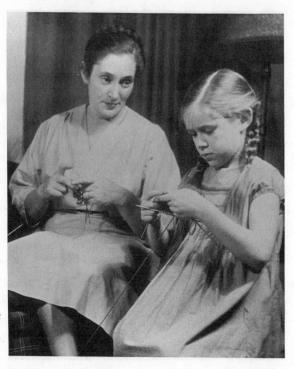

*Elizabeth Zimmermann
and her daughter,
Meg, c. 1949.*

included. She could. They went. Jackie Ronne became the first American woman to spend a winter there, and maps of the Palmer Peninsula memorialize her stay with Edith Ronne Land. She still remembers vividly the panicky preparation for those long months, dependent upon the limited supplies of the embarkation town. Frantic for knitting, she followed a knitting townswoman's directions to a small back-alley store that carried hanks and hanks of yarn but no needles. Her guide, sensing her dismay, left the crestfallen explorer at the shop and returned shortly with needles she had scooped up from her own supply, pressing them upon Jackie with an expression that said "Lady, you're going to need these more than I will!" In the long Antarctic winter, knitting became a salvation, and specimens of Jackie Ronne's socks and gloves are now in the Navy Museum's polar exploration hall in Washington, D.C.

15.

Knitting from A to Z: Argyles to Zimmermann

Feminist novelist Fannie Hurst, who predicted that women's wartime focus on community and factory work presaged their postwar economic independence and widening opportunities, soon reported dejectedly, "A sleeping sickness is spreading among the women of the land. . . . They are retrogressing into . . . that thing known as The Home." The retreat was blatantly apparent as middle-class and working-class families migrated to their identical housing units in mushrooming bedroom communities. To expedite a down payment on that "house in the suburbs" and thus warrant the newly popular Ph.T. ("Putting Hubby Through") degree, many women temporarily held on to their "until Johnny comes home" jobs unless those jobs were as "domestics," for, as CIO spokesman Maurice O'Connell inelegantly explained to the Los Angeles Chamber of Commerce, "People have become accustomed to new conditions, new wage scales, new ways of being treated. Rosie the Riveter isn't going back to emptying slop jars."

Most women in the work force, now almost a third, were not young, for the young hungered for connubial rather than job security. By the 1950s, the average age for marrying dropped to twenty; fourteen million girls were engaged by seventeen (with younger teens describing their circumstances as "pre-engaged" or "engaged to be engaged"); declining female college enrollment indicated matrimony and babies triumphed over careers in forward planning; 60 percent of already matriculating collegiennes (many of whom candidly confessed they were there to "find a man") dropped out to marry or, at least, to scout prospects. *Mademoiselle* justified their preference for motherhood: "Marriage and children are part of a very ambitious woman's ambitions. . . . When you marry and have children the whole family pools brains, looks, activities . . . like an army platoon that competes against other platoons in the neighborhood." Somebody obviously bought the platoon concept, for when the postwar baby boom peaked at the end of the decade, the nation's birth rate almost surpassed India's.

Savvy American advertisers, no neophytes to motivational research, appreciated the back-to-the-home movement's potential and not too subtly fanned the flames of domestic preoccupation by redefining woman's "feminine" nature as unequivocally as had their predecessors a century before. As a result, a woman "ready to be a woman" viewed ensnaring and maintaining a firm grip on her man ("every girl wants to be a man-trap") to be life's primary mission. To heighten allure by revitalizing sagging bodies, they ingested chalky Metrecal in lieu of "fattening meals," lightened their tresses to comply with an ad campaign's "If I have only one life to live, let me live it as a blonde," greedily acquired appliances to alleviate housework and provide more time for personal improvement, transformed kitchen workstations into family centers, designed houses with "open" floor plans in place of private retreats, fretted about their clothes' whiteness, their tile's gleam and their hardwood floors' shine, pitied their working sisters and smugly responded "Housewife" to every query about occupation. As it had during earlier sanctifications of women's household role, knitting enjoyed the fruits of the revival, and yarn manufacturers could be forgiven for parlaying the domestic syndrome into "Knit for the Man in Your Life"; "Knit to Make Him Proud of You"; "He'll love you more if you knit for him"; "Put Those Adorable Babies into Knits!"; "Make Matching Outfits for You and Your Little Charmer"; "Stitchers are Bewitchers." Knitting was synonymous with home and motherhood, and if not too swamped with the latter (like one mother whose seven children in the eleven years following her 1950 marriage allowed little time for knitting), knitters worked nonstop.

While fifties women hankered for and produced babies, the war years had exacted such a toll in social isolation that wives anticipated combining domesticity and freedom, incompatible goals for young mothers "trapped in a squirrel cage" of modern appliance-packed, plate-glass-and-broadloomed split level or ranch houses or modern apartments, which feminist writer Betty Friedan described some years later as "comfortable concentration camp[s]." The problem, concluded a Nebraska mother of four with a doctorate in anthropology, was just as painful as when her grandmother "sat over an embroidery hoop in her gilt-and-plush parlor and muttered angrily about women's rights." A Pittsburgh housewife lamented, "I feel like a pie being cut into six pieces and served to a dinner party of ten!" Emancipation, especially for those far removed from parental and grandparental support systems, hinged upon a jealously guarded baby-sitter roster posted by the phone. War-absent husbands, ready to nest after catching up on missed education through the G.I. Bill and struggling to gain a toe-hold in business, grumpily cooperated with social plans but relished hours in home do-it-yourself workshops, a commitment so widespread that insurance statistics reflected the extent of their injuries: well over half a million sawed fingers, burns from spray paint and shock from electrical tools.

Even with labor saving devices, housewifery expanded to exalt performance rather than escalate freedom, until one young wife, her energies sapped, sniveled that though her washer and dryer made possible clean sheets twice a week, her family came to expect them: "Last week, when my dryer broke down, the sheets didn't get changed for eight days. Everyone complained. We all felt dirty. I felt guilty. Isn't that silly?" Disquieted by the specter of failed marriages hitting divorce courts, women who struggled to preserve their super-little-woman reputation brooded: "I've been married ten years and I still feel that my husband expects me to be a combination of Fanny Farmer and Marilyn Monroe"; "I get terribly defensive if I serve dinner late or he comes home early and finds my hair's still in curlers"; "I spend all day Saturday rehearsing so I can serve an effort-free Sunday-morning breakfast"; "I don't know how I can stand it! It's just too much!" When women compounded complaints of exhaustion with boredom in the suburbs ("We hardly ever do anything that's fun. . . . The men talk about real estate. The women talk about their children and their husbands"), McCall's conceded that those whose intelligence exceeded job requirements might well be frustrated by isolation, monotony and lack of stimulation, but reprovingly suggested they focus on *some* interesting aspect such as "cooking or an incentive such as a party in the offing." Should that not avail, the author ardently championed "male praise" as a fitting antidote to "domestic boredom."

Women's magazines admonished in voices of tradition blended with Freudian sophistication that readers could consummate their greatest destiny through glorification of their femininity—ever young (like the mother who could rock and roll as dervishly as her teenage youngsters), ever frivolous, ever slim (by reducing the way the models did), ever charming, ever serving the needs of their men and their children. Women's magazines hewed strictly to that party line, but Betty Friedan learned from questionnaires compiled from Smith College classmates out there in presumed Gloryland that a schizophrenic split separated the images to which they tried to conform from the reality of their lives. Friedan named the disparity between the "I don't know what's wrong with me" lack of satisfaction and life as it was supposed to be fulfilled the "Feminine Mystique." Women retreated to the home, but home wasn't what it was cracked up to be.

When the at-home decade opened with the United States in the United Nations "police action" to restrain North Koreans from incursions below the treaty-set 38th parallel, "Knit for Korea" and "Korean War Orphans" campaigns drew knitters' expectedly sympathetic response. A member of the General Federation of Women's Clubs who had spent a year in Korea with the USO after World War II inspired its six million members to join forces with the American Legion Auxiliary in "Operation Winter" to knit fourteen thousand children's sweaters and afghans from scraps and reclaimed wool. With ten million homeless in Korea, particularly orphans, knitting groups formed nationwide, with seventy-eight in St. Louis alone. To hasten delivery, groups shipped yarn with the unassembled squares so that children themselves could sew them together.

With so many young men again in uniform, *Smart Knitting*'s "Serviceman's Section" announced, "We've surveyed the boys themselves to find out what they actually want and would find most useful," and posed models in smart vests and sweaters against army trucks. Teens, always reliable wartime knitters, were reminded, "Let's not forget those fellows who are doing their bit for us in the service of our country. It may be your brother, a school friend, or the love of your life, but don't forget to let him know you remember. He's the one who's trying to make a better world for you and me. Here's the 'G.I.' turtle-neck sweater. For this one he'll be grateful to you forevermore."

War knitting was not widespread, however, and Argylers were still in full cry, elaborating on "traditional" Scottish patterns by knitting diamonds within diamonds and combining diamonds with plaids and stripes. Argyles were so popular for high school cheerleaders that the going rate was $20 a pair for handknit ones. They were equally popular on college campuses, and Virginia Williams, of Omaha, Nebraska, who earlier made them in high school, bargained with matriculating G.I.s to knit two pairs of socks in exchange for the loan of a full set of textbooks. As one writer commented, "As every woman who has done it knows, knitting colors into your own design, watching it grow, is a pleasure more than worth the bother of keeping all those yarns from tangling as badly as they do." Argyle-knitting teenagers were humored by one authoress's jaunty introduction: "You all know what I'm doing! Knitting. And I love it . . . knitting all the time. Right now I'm turning the heel of a pair of argyles— they're gray, red and navy. I'm sure he'll like these. . . . Socks, socks and more socks! He just can't get enough of them. Socks prove that a little goes a long way. Probably he clings to precious wool, but maybe he's taken up nylon, and if that's his liking, nylon's your meat. It's a great advertisement, too, with socks so easy to carry around, and knit."

She never clarified *what* was being advertised, but with nylon as "meat," someone's trap was baited! Swains were eager to be caught and savored crossing their legs "just so" to expose a few inches of Argyle handiwork. Some male knitters might have attacked Argyles themselves had not one of their sex, who denigrated knitting as "just tying knots with the help of two pointed sticks," cautioned, "Under no circumstances learn how to knit argyle socks. They are very boring. All those needles and bobbins and different colored yarn. Plenty of women will knit them for you. Leave the drudgery to them."

Catherine Niering, of Gales Ferry, Connecticut, voluntarily saddled herself with that drudgery when she met her future husband:

Big Boy-Little Boy Argyles, 1952.

"I remember making him a dozen pairs of socks the year before we were married, and he still has a few pairs. In those days you could buy cards of reinforcing nylon thread for the heels and toes. How I miss it! Now I buy something as near to it as possible for reinforcement, but it isn't the same." Wanting to be part of the knitting crowd, beginning knitter Anne Shoe, of China Grove, North Carolina, bought Argyle kits from Sears and knitted three pairs for her boyfriend: "What fun! I still have the little plastic bobbins. I also still have the boyfriend, for I married him, but the wool socks haven't lasted as long as he has!" At Joan Newton's Downey, California, high school, where it was the rage to knit Argyle socks for boyfriends, she knit her first pair for her father: "They were a horrible, black-red-yellow color. I had no help from anybody on how to *turn a heel*, and I knit those instructions every night for three weeks until one night it finally dawned on me what they wanted me to do. To this date, I still know the exact amount of stitches and think I can recite the turning of the heel backwards!"

Argyles for teenagers, 1953.

Argyle designs decorated far more than socks and vests. *McCall's*, with its "many argyle enthusiasts" in mind, offered a quartet of winter accessories "keyed to young tastes and active lives," matching Argyle stocking cap with jaunty tassel, drawstring bag, mittens and knee socks, de rigueur with the "new" Bermuda shorts. When teens, converging on high school and college gyms for "sock hops" instead of sedate proms, coveted socks personalized right down to their faddishly visible toes, knitters, long experienced in substituting scraps for "feetings," strategically mapped out striped, diagonaled, fancy-stitched and often initialed insigniae for pedal extremities. A teenage military school cadet, whose mother knit black socks until she sensed his loathing for uniforms, became the envy of the corps when, shielded from the inspecting officer's probing eye, stocking toes sprouted initials, pumpkins in October and November, Christmas trees for the holidays, red hearts for Valentine's Day and eggs for Easter.

When not wrapped up with socks, knitters worked to clad their baby boomers, and the Knitting Committee of the Woman's Auxiliary of St. Paul's Church in Chestnut Hill, Pennsylvania, after two years of "frayed nerves, neglected families, and untilled gardens," published the charming *Knit One for the Crib Kids*. The delightfully hand-illustrated booklet, with patterns for every conceivable garment for baby and small child, updated the ubiquitous soakers of the 1940s to "Bikinis" that were "good up to six months. From then on, they are hopeless. Switch to pants or panties." Truer words were never spoken!

Emily Kimbrough, co-author with Cornelia Otis Skinner of *Our Hearts Were Young and Gay*, wrote an introduction guaranteed to evoke sympathy from survivors of similarly botched projects:

> Recently I read a book about some natives in New Guinea. They are called Papus. One of their distinguishing characteristics is the extraordinary length of their arms. I have a surprise for the Papus. They are going to receive from me a large box of sweaters. The sweaters are in a variety of colors and sizes, but they have one physical characteristic in common: the extraordinary length of arms on each of them. I knitted these garments myself. They were made with love and with meticulous attention to the directions in knitting patterns. . . . Turning back enough of a sleeve to make a cuff is one thing, and an acceptable one; doubling back an entire sleeve length turns the little creation into an oddity. I hope the Papus will like their present.

Luxuriating in knitting aplomb since the auxiliary's foolproof, tested patterns had curbed her "waywardness," she certified, "The Papus will not hear from me again."

In addition to baby clothes, stockings, Argyle anything and classic sweaters such as the popular "Letter Sweaters" for college he-men, fifties knitters created fluffy pullovers to top felt "poodle skirts" for Hula-Hooping teenagers; "Toppits," short jackets like earlier "Hug-Me-Tights," for the neighborhood barbecue, where everyone was trying the new sour-cream-and-dried-onion-soup dip; "cover-up" shoulder warmers to wear over strapless evening gowns; belts; bags; eyeglass and cosmetic kits; cotton, angora or beaded collars such as Victorian "detachables"; and improved, machine-safe soakers attached to plastic panties. "Darlan," the new miracle yarn guaranteed not to pill, shrink, stretch, thin out or lose its shape even in the washing machine and dryer, promised: "It dries soft, fast, and fluffy, and it's moth proof forever!" Old-fashioned knitters complained they didn't like its feel and would stick to wool!

As knitting drew more enthusiasts, magazines such as *Woman's Day* committed additional pages to patterns. *The New York Times* entered the field with "Patterns of the Times," mail-order instructions and photographs of "winter knitting projects for the busy needles of women who seek the smart handmade look." Fashion notes described the elegance and popularity of cashmere pullovers and cardigans (a term honoring British General Cardigan, who outfitted his soldiers with heavy knit garments during the Crimean War), but the distinctive Scottish machine-knit sweaters were so finely gauged that few knitters attempted duplication.

The Institute for Hand Knitting, founded in the immediate postwar years to assure a steady flow of new knitters by training teachers and wooing the young through enticements such as knitting contests, took aim at male knitters by designating special prizes for boys. 1950's prize-winner of the all-expenses trip to New York, fourteen-year-old David McGee, of Randolph, Vermont, who knit a ski sweater for his father in three months while listening to the radio, had been inspired by the knitting proficiency of the Duke of Windsor and the late king of Sweden. Girls, of course, were expected to knit because they had *always* knit. Betty Cornell, the author of *Betty Cornell's Glamour Guide for Teens* and therefore "in tune" with teens, was enlisted by the institute to draft a knitting book just for them. Her folksy approach ("Hi! Oh, pardon me for just a minute. . . . There, I've finished the row"; "Be patient, and stick to your knitting . . . remember, Rome wasn't built in a day!") and chapters on everything from gift giving to money raising by knitting clubs ("What fellow wouldn't buy a pair of hand-made argyles?") urged girls to knit for fashion and economy and evangelized: "A few rows every night knitted on a stole means having that stole for the big luncheon party at Sue's house. Carrying your knitting on the school bus means having that new sweater for the big dance two months from now"; "Your list of musts definitely includes your bobby socks in white wool. You just can't own enough of them"; "Does your Dad like to putter around in the garden? Take off early in the morning for the golf course? . . . If so, he'll love an easy pullover like this one, knitted by his darling daughter." Dad would also welcome Bernat's long- or short-sleeved, pocketed, V-necked cardigan "Saturday Night TV Sweater" as he smoked his pipe, mesmerized by his black-and-white tube.

The author of *The* Seventeen *Book of Quick Things to Make and Wear* scoffed at "poor workmanship" and "standardization of clothing" as huffily as late nineteenth-century women had derided products of the new industrialization; another begged the young to assure that their garments bore their own personal, creative stamp in "this plastic, manufactured world"; still another, echoing advice dispensed by an instructor over a hundred years before that "friendship . . . will always accept with delight various produce of the knitting needle, as mementos at once of the skill which wrought, and the affection that gave them," pushed teenagers to knit for others, especially boyfriends: "I hope you'll not just sit and think about how nice he is. Do something! Go out and get that wool today, and cast on, you'll know knitting for him can be, and is, *fun*. It not only whiles away your idle hours, but reaps heaps of results—gifts that stand up and say, 'Knitted with Love.' And what could be better?"; another quipped, "You can knit that man right out of your life or—better advice, you can knit one right in."

Accompanying buoyant espousal of everything "natural" and "craftsy," a swell of nostalgia for the halcyon thirties and forties seized trendsetters. William Unger revived and expanded ribbon knits by manufacturing them in every color and weight so that knitters, fortified with large needles, could quickly fashion the lightweight, easily packed dresses, suits or blouses. When Unger's styling director introduced an iridescent silk-and-acrylic yarn, with each thread a different color, knitters stormed the shops to lay in supplies for "evening blouse" projects. Unger wasn't alone in casting a long, lingering look behind; an earlier 1942 book, reissued "with some corrections and additions" and retitled *Knitting and Crocheting Your Own Fashions of the Forties*, heralded the return of "[t]he fabulous '40's" of platform shoes, cardigans, jerkins, crocheted blouses, pleated skirts, waistcoats, crew necks and plaid socks.

Something other than styles seemed the same—abysmally low compensation for custom knitting. One avid knitter, who started photographing all her projects in 1979 and has since filled five albums, sold four beautiful jackets with knit-in designs to a customer who paid her handsomely, but a woman she scarcely knew asked her to duplicate one for her nephew and then balked at the forty-dollar price, snapping, "Forty dollars for *what?*" The knitter, patiently explaining that the price included yarn and labor, found the would-be purchaser "irate that I would charge her. She was not a friend for whom I'd make the sweater free. I could not believe she could be that stupid; I had to pay for the yarn and the zipper, and my time was certainly worth something!" It was an age-old but no less heartfelt complaint.

By the sixties, the descended hems of the postwar "New Look" rose to such startling heights that long sweaters could double as thigh-length "minis." With less to cover, one would infer that women had more time to knit, but harried knitters were ripe for another innovation, "quick-knitting" with giant needles. Freelance knitwear designer Jeanne Damon used whittled-down broomsticks as needles to kindle emotionally disturbed children's interest in knitting and discovered that other knitters were electrified at the possibility of making a garment in "under six hours." Reynolds Yarn Company's hollow, inch-wide aluminum "Jumbo Jets" needles at $2.50 per pair (or in a kit with yarn and pattern for from $18 to $50) were an immediate sensation, with Chicago's Marshall Field selling three thousand pairs in a single month. A nearby Highland Park knit shop owner exulted, "They've gotten us a lot of new customers, and old customers who haven't knitted for ages are taking it up again." Though the resultant garments were of such revealing transparency that they necessitated firm reliance upon "body stockings" to mold contours and camouflage off-limits zones, others jumped on the broomstick bandwagon. Susan Bates promised, "Jiffy Jumbos are huge almost weightless Luxite needles that won't catch your wool or click while you knit." Joan Rattner Heilman introduced *The Official Knit-a-Dress-a-Day Knitting Book*, and Damon cashed in by writing the *Quick Knit Book*, both rich sources of "the big stitch" fad. Damon dedicated her knit-today-and-wear-tomorrow patterns to those who "lead fast-moving lives . . . busy, modern women-on-the-go, career girls, college girls, young mothers, anyone who loves the look of a good knit and has learned to do just a few simple stitches." With hems high, shapes simple and coverage minimal, busy knitters who quickly doubled the number of skimpy dresses in their closets could slip into chic knits and dash "when the phone rings, opportunity knocks, or your husband calls you for lunch in town." Or all of the above! Big-needle patterns were a godsend for teaching knitting to the restless young since they propagated instant wardrobes "chock-full of clothes for every teen-age occasion." The former director of a New York knitting school cannily advised shop owners of the stimulating effect of quick-knits upon yarn sales since knitters would speedily replenish supplies to indulge their habit. At least one knitter, Joyce Goetz, of Charlotte, North Carolina, embraced but soon abandoned the new procedure: "One project using those huge needles in the 60's was more than enough for me. When I wore the garment made from double four-ply yarn, I decided I looked like a house, promptly unravelled it and knit more suitable children's sweaters."

Some knitters refused to succumb, not only to the "knit-kwik" fever but to any interest in knitting at all, causing such a marked decline that *Vogue* discontinued its handsome knitting book inaugurated in 1932. So few young people knit in the sixties that one who persevered recalled, "Sometimes I felt I was the only young knitter in the world. For a while in high school I never even picked up my knitting needles because absolutely no one else did and only resumed in college when I wanted knits for myself and didn't care what others did. . . . Now I live in Niagara Falls, a big tourist attraction, and when I take my knitting to a park at the Falls, people stop to admire my work and say they wish they could learn. Then there are the other people who look you straight in the eye and say, 'I hate creative people like you.' I have yet to discover a squelching response to *that*!"

Those a little older, however, lavished the same skillful, painstaking efforts as had their knitting foremothers. Mrs. Irene Steptoe, of Chevy Chase, Maryland, describes one of her sixties projects, a sequin-covered shell knit of fine baby yarn:

It is like a shimmery sheath, and it has been washed by hand many times, and it is still pretty. It took patience, for the sequins came 1,000 on a string and it took 10 strings to cover my shell. I can't bear to throw it away, remembering all the fun I had making it. It had an evening skirt to match, but no sequins on that! The young people of today seem to want to dump everything in the washing machine which is a pity, for caring for good sweaters is not too hard.

The fifties mother-of-seven-children-in-eleven-years resumed knitting in the mid-sixties, following a generations-old regimen:

> I always carried my work everywhere and made a lot of items sitting in the car waiting to pick up one of the children, when I waited for them in dentist's, doctor's and orthodontist's offices, at little league games and on trips to the beach. It got so bad that the very few times I didn't have my knitting, people questioned me if I were ill or something. PTA got to be a laugh. If someone were asking about me and didn't know my name, they simply identified me as "the lady who's always knitting!"

Of her college years in the sixties, Sharron Freeman, of West Hartford, Connecticut, recalls, "I knit my way through college, probably driving my professors crazy, but I took knitting whenever I talked and interacted with people, and when I knit through all those anti-war meetings in the sixties, I felt I was watched warily as if I were a possible Madame Defarge or informant." Another constant knitter (who first learned to knit "rope" on a wooden spool with nails) who also took her knitting with her everywhere, recalls knitting at her husband's side during his fatal illness. Minutes after his death, when his doctor urged her to take a tranquilizer, she replied firmly, "No, my tranquility is my knitting." In all her years of knitting, she reports, "I have found over the years that knitting has a more calming effect than any medication. . . . My knitting bag has become like an extra arm. Wherever I go, it's there with me. . . . One time a group of people were talking about a part of the body they would hate to lose the use of most, and my reply was my hands. As long as I can keep my hands busy, I can be content."

Remaining content while queued up at service stations during the *Great Gasoline Shortage* of the early seventies, knitters saw nothing unusual about stitching to pass the time. Commuting daily to work, Myrna Lippman, of Scotch Plains, New Jersey, logged at least an hour waiting in the dark every other day before or after work and still treasures her rust mohair-and-wool long-sleeved, V-necked sweater in a raised criss crossed pattern, made "totally behind the steering wheel." Other fuel-seeking, thermos-toting knitters tucked flashlights and sweet rolls into knitting bags, confident the delay would not find them unproductive. Idleness, after all, was a sin, gas shortage or not!

William Unger, now in his nineties, gleefully recalls when his company, despite warnings that he would lose his shirt, imported light, fluffy, gloriously colorful and eminently suitable for larger needles "Mohair de Luxe" and turned it into the biggest seller in company history. So many cheap imitations followed, however (such as the Italian "pure" mohair forced off retailers' shelves by the government because of its low mohair percentage), that fickle and suspicious buyers mistrusted all mohair and ended the "craze" within only a few years. But affection for mohair products lingers. Ida Lloyd, of Indianapolis, whose father taught her to knit as a child with pointed wooden sucker sticks or butchers' skewers, combined strands of wool and mohair to knit a fully lined hooded coat to rate the Purple Medallion for champion knitter in Indiana's State Fair.

When hems replunged in the seventies, Myrna Lippman recycled her classic sixties knit "Chesterfield" into a three-quarter-length jacket, and favorite above-knee tunics were reincarnated as trendier hip-length sweaters. She became so adept at restyling that when her seventies floor-length light weight Aran Island skirt was outmoded a decade later, she fearlessly whacked off ten inches. Unabashed, she contemplates future fashion forecasts.

In honor of the Bicentennial, the Long Island chapter of the Telephone Pioneers of America (a national organization of telephone employees with many years of service) opened a contest to employees, friends and community groups to knit, crochet, quilt, appliqué or embroider a thirty-six-inch by forty-inch "Lap Robe" depicting a Bicentennial theme in red, white and blue to go afterward to retired telephone people, veterans hospitals and nursing homes. Lillian Meade, of Toms River, won second prize out of nine hundred entries for knitting a blanket with the cracked Liberty Bell centered on a blue background with the dates 1776 and 1976, surrounded by red-and-white borders with stars in each corner. Later displayed in Philadelphia at the Bicentennial celebration, it is now on display at the Telephone Pioneers Museum in Jamaica, Queens.

In that same decade, a males-only group met weekly under the tutelage of Mindy Nix, described by a *New York Times* writer as a "leggy blonde" in her mid-twenties with a master's degree in social work from Columbia University who had already taught her father and two brothers to knit. Her upscale pupils, who included an engineer, a lawyer, two United Nations translators, a graduate student in economics, a social worker, a writer and a real estate man, rationalized their participation: "If a woman can change a tire, a man can knit"; "My wife [was] a great knitter, and it looked so relaxing [from a recent widower]"; "Anything a woman can do, I can do better, I told her. My wife can't knit at all [after an argument with his wife about women's liberation]"; "I just might become the first knitting-school drop-out"; "She doesn't know I'm here, she thinks I'm out with the guys, shooting pool [from someone knitting a hat for his wife]"; "Hey, if we get any good, we can challenge Vassar." Mindy Nix tutored gamely on, collecting twenty dollars (including fees for yarn, needles and instruction booklet) for five two-hour lessons.

With the sixties and seventies back-to-nature movement heightening interest in natural fibers and crafts, *Mademoiselle* eschewed high-style clothes in favor of sturdy, rustic, traditional, "Primal" and "cottage craft as anything" handknit inspirations from Colombia, Bolivia, Ireland, Iceland and Peru to achieve the long, slouchy look to accompany either "neats or jeans." Knitters could, of course, duplicate them. In *Mother Earth News*, the icon of the disaffected, dedicated to "alternative energy and life styles, ecology, working with nature and doing more with less," a writer asked prankishly, "Why Not Knit a Nosewarmer?" and outlined construction of a "snout stocking" by sewing together two edges of a knit triangle, stretching the third side over the nose and securing the glorious contraption with crocheted-chain ear loops. "Then," she summarized smartly, "if your friends make jokes about your new eagle-beaked profile, you can knit nosewarmers for them too. After all, a few hours of your time is a small price to pay for 'equality before the thaw.' " Oh, dear!

Toward the end of the seventies, and within a few years of each other, three women wrote books that would influence American knitters for decades to come. Barbara Walker's two "treasuries" of knitting patterns culled hundreds of knitting stitches from the Library of Congress's knitting pamphlets and magazines dating from the middle of the nineteenth century, and when she described her quest, itchy researchers envied her task: "[W]hen you go to the Library of Congress' stacks, you end up in this sort of catacomb—little tiny dark aisles, with bare light bulbs way up high in the ceiling, no desks, no chairs, no nothing. Just books and books and books, and it is like being lost in the bowels of the pyramids."

Mary Walker Phillips's *Creative Knitting: A New Art Form* not only detailed the history of knitting but through illustrations of objects other than garments (such as covers, pillows, wall hangings and rugs) boosted interest in experimenting with color, texture, stitchery and design of projects that need not "fit." Phillips, called by a leading knitting magazine the "Doyenne of Art Knitting" and by a prominent textile designer "the transition between old-fashioned pattern book knitting and the extraordinary things going on . . . today," came to knitting via weaving and has built such a reputation through her books, exhibits, workshops, speaking and teaching that at a recent knitting convention, where her two twelve-hour classes in techniques (each spread out over two days) drew eager sycophants, one of them, exhausted but inspired, reported, "She is still going strong!" Phillips underscores the need to comprehend the structure of stitches: "I'm trying to get people to learn what knitting is all about, and how doing something one way may be more expedient than another or more traditional way. . . . There are tricks, too, that can make production not only faster but more interesting."

The third member of the triumvirate, the twentieth century's answer to the nineteenth century's Miss Lambert, is Elizabeth Zimmermann, whose slim, saucy, advice-packed 1971 *Knitting Without Tears* has never since been out of print and has transformed its author into the foremost "guru" of knitting. She is the one knitter most often cited by current knitters as their paragon and savior, their light at the end of the tunnel, their intellectually stimulating, delightfully amusing and proudly opinionated mentor, who claims, "Properly practiced, knitting soothes the troubled spirit, and it doesn't hurt the untroubled spirit either. . . . The main thing about knitting is, keep it simple and enjoy it." Zimmermann's first break in publishing

Mary Walker Phillips, Elizabeth Zimmermann, and Barbara Walker, 1980.

came from selling an Aran pattern to *Vogue*, which paid nothing for the design but furnished her name and address as the source for the yarn. She was in business. With her lucid illustrations (though British, she studied art in Munich) and "EPS" ("Elizabeth's Percentage System"), she has turned math-anxiety-prone, totally-dependent-upon-printed-instructions knitters ("blind followers") into creatively confident knit-by-the-percentages artists who forsake stitch-by-stitch instructions to design their own garments. Her firmly avowed likes and dislikes have trickled down to her legions of followers, who knit *only* on round needles, won't touch any yarn but wool, won't pat sweaters out on brown paper (no matter what Lever Brothers said about "Luxables"), won't tolerate seams or zippers in their sweaters and won't knit without first determining gauge, all because "Elizabeth says so."

It is not surprising that the faithful wanted, quite literally, to knit at her feet, and by the end of the seventies it became a reality when she opened her first "knitting camp" near her home in Wisconsin. An attendee at that first session, Joan Schrouder, of Eugene, Oregon, who knew Zimmermann only by reputation but read of camp plans in a knitting magazine, stationed her children with her supportive husband, took her first plane trip to Minneapolis and bused for three hours to small Shell Lake, Wisconsin, for her "exhilarating but exhausting" session. She has returned every summer since, and reports of her experiences:

> [The first time] [t]here were about twenty-five campers in a dormitory belonging to the University of Wisconsin and taking classes Monday through Friday in a nearby high school. It wasn't very expensive since we weren't in some snappy resort, our room and board and knitting lessons coming to only about two hundred dollars. The whole thing was certainly a lot cheaper than going to a shrink! We were so absorbed that even when a tornado passed close, we knitters never dropped a stitch. After dinner, we sat around stuffing ourselves on Wisconsin cheeses, telling jokes and *knitting*!
>
> While I've used my "learnings" from the workshops to enhance my own teaching of knitting, my main joy has been the camaraderie and sharing of ideas with other expert knitters. The friendships we forged there have been renewed almost annually since most of us have returned so often.

When Zimmermann's "repeaters" or "old girl" campers, most of them now leaders in the knitting field themselves, intimidated newcomers by their expertise and giggling camaraderie, the groups were separated into shifts. One student calls Elizabeth Zimmermann the "Queen of the Knitters," and another says, "Elizabeth's knitting hands have forgotten more than mine will ever learn. We knitters learn things the pattern books don't tell you not only from Elizabeth and Meg [Swansen, Zimmermann's daughter] but from each other. If Elizabeth is the Queen, Meg is certainly the Princess!" Both Zimmermann and Swansen manage a thriving mail-order business in which customers feel like the "in" crowd of knitting, write for national knitting magazines, teach camp classes that have moved from Shell Lake to Marshfield, about twenty minutes from Zimmermann's home, license and sell "Knitting Workshop" video tapes for those who can't come in person, and conduct workshops across the country.

Zimmermann's television work began when a friend asked her to talk about knitting on a Milwaukee show, an appearance that drew so many spirited letters that she successfully proposed a series on knitting to the public broadcasting station. It was taped in a studio mock-up of her living room, complete with fireplace and cat, the latter ferried to the studio daily in Zimmermann's knitting basket. Of the week's filming she recalls, "It nearly killed me. Then the mail poured in." Moving into television work with a showwoman's aplomb, she and Swansen later created their own "Knitting Workshop," about which more than one home viewer sighed nostalgically, "It was like having my patient grandmother there to help me. If I didn't catch on at first, I simply replayed it until I got it right!"

16.

Knitting Now and WhitherKnit?

Though the fifties' soaring birth rate declined by the end of that decade, within twenty years the baby boomers themselves, in what Census Director Bruce Chapman called the "echo effect," produced babies who, by the time they reach their mid-thirties and forties in the 1990s, will be knitting consumers. They aren't, however, there yet, and yarn marketers, smarting from the sixties' and seventies' needlepoint mania but detecting a cyclical upswing in knitting, warily count their eggs and pray for chickens. Responding to the earlier decline, urban department stores have discontinued art needlework departments, once Meccas for needlewomen, and ceded prized clientele to suburban yarn stores. As rental rates skyrocket, many of the latter have "gone under," prompting some owners who studied demographic changes and could afford relocation to pull up stakes and trail the customers to Sunbelt states.

With twice as many women working in the eighties as in the sixties, the market altered in other ways. Those who juggle husbands, children, households and careers now rate quick completion ahead of other criteria for selecting knitting projects, and one designer, attuned to the "fast-paced modern life style," suggested "Weekender" projects of bulky yarn on large needles: "Start a project on Friday and have a great looking sweater, jacket, or hat and scarf to wear on Monday." A yarn shop owner interviewed for *Yarn Market News* reasoned that working women with only a few hours to devote to knitting preferred top-quality yarn, whatever the cost, and *Vogue*

Knitting's senior editor, Lola Ehrlich, agreed: "People don't knit to be thrifty anymore. Now knitting is the fashionable thing to do." It was obvious, too, that in addition to cutting production time to several days, stylishly oversized sweaters of bulky yarn knit with large needles masked technical flaws and eliminated fitting problems. Atlanta writer Maggie Righetti, whose forthright *Knitting in Plain English* encourages students to "make a unique statement of their own personality" by resolving the mysteries of designing and charting their own garments, concurs: "Hand knitting is not cost effective when articles can be bought more cheaply. The only reason for hand knitting is recreation and creation." *Boston Globe* writer Linda Weltner also discounted economy's incentive to knitting:

> . . . [I]t hardly pays to knit anymore. The baby will spit up on his hand-washable sweater and, in exasperation, his mother will most likely sentence grandmother's handiwork to death in her washing machine. The price of yarn, especially imported wool, is so high that hand-knitted sweaters in discount stores are cheaper than anything you can make, and more dependable, too. Anyone who knits for a teenager knows that somehow the finished project will not resemble the picture in the magazine closely enough or the wool will itch and the sweater will be tucked into the back of the drawer for the rest of its life. Knitting, even for the most skillful, is part guesswork and part prayer, the triumph of hope over certainty.

The tidings that knitters pursue their craft for reasons other than economy is not earth-shattering, for knitters have long waxed eloquent over the sensual satisfaction of rhythmically clicking needles ("The quiet, even, regular motion of the needles quiets the nerves and tranquilizes the mind, and lets thought flow free," said *Dorcas* in 1888), the restorative power of mindless but productive stitching when the world seems out of kilter, the freedom from guilt by putting to use the "odd moments" of one's life, the release from stress and the pleasure of participating in a chain begun long ago. Bryna Millman, of New York City, says, "Maybe it has something to do with a longing for simpler times and traditional values. I have been knitting since I was 14. I was very much a loner and spent most of my time reading and biting my nails to the quick. My mother hauled me to a knitting store to find something to keep my fingers out of my mouth, and thus began my almost obsessive hobby. I don't think I've been without a project for more than a couple of months in all these years and surely stopped biting my nails right away!"

The actions of a woman who knit daily on the bus and then, like Penelope, raveled it only to begin anew the next day brought an offer of help from a sympathetic knitter onlooker who asked if she could help. Replied the resolute ripper, "No, my doctor told me to do this just for therapy." Daisy Burka, of Berwyn, Pennsylvania, declares, "Knitting keeps me out of psychiatry!" and Betty Peacock, of Reston, Virginia, plans ahead to avoid tension build up: "I always have several things going at once (my husband says it is my 'grand passion' and I think he is right) as some are more portable than others so I wouldn't dream of leaving the house without my knitting in case of an emergency, a long wait in a doctor's office, or getting stuck in an elevator."

Knitting was a lifesaver when Connie Ferdinandson, of Santa Barbara, struggled to overcome agoraphobia so severe that after quitting her job, avoiding supermarkets, movie theaters, church and driving, she simply stayed home for two years. With a therapist's help, she finally summoned the courage to drive again—at first only a block from home. She explains:

> I had to practice *staying* somewhere instead of running home in fear; so I'd park my car a block away and pull out my knitting. Knitting, because it is rhythmic, soothing and creative, was just the diversion I needed to distract me from my self-defeating panic at being away from home.
>
> In our self-help group, we used the phrase, "Bring your knitting," to mean planning to *stay* somewhere. It was a *positive* action, and, while it took many sessions of knitting in the car or some other "new" place for me to recover, I now drive to and from a full-time job—still with my knitting, but not as a crutch. I simply enjoy doing it. Maybe my experience can help someone else. Ironically, now that I am cured, I have very little time to knit!

In 1902, *Stitches* recommended knitting, whose gentle action has the "same beneficial effect as a massage," for rheumatism of the hands, advice now seconded by arthritis specialist Dr. Morris Bowie, who lauds knitting's twin benefits of relaxing finger joint tissues while helping sufferers to forget pain in the excitement of the creative process. Blanche Matyerniak, who has arthritic hands, agrees: "You really push through the chores because you're looking forward to getting back to your knitting. It takes away from the boredom of your day and gives you a real sense of accomplishment. Time doesn't hang heavy." Rebecca Newman also notes its therapy: "Knitting to me is just a part of my early morning schedule, the same as reading my Bible. It calms me—also gets my old Mr. Arthur (arthritis) out of my fingers and ready for the day."

In suburban Philadelphia, Ona Bloom's Upper Darby Yarn shop prominently displays a large Knit Your Way to Health sign. Bloom attributes to knitting not only healing but a sense of belonging: "When you work and you're creating, you haven't got time to think of your problems. Worries just melt away. . . . [Customers] can meet other people here and know that they are not alone in their problems." One of her pupils agrees: "I have become much calmer in the four or five years I've been coming here." In West Hartford, Connecticut, Sharron Freeman is aware of an unusual camaraderie: "I am instantly drawn to other knitters—it's almost as if we're possessors of different chromosomes than non-knitters, and I get such pleasure from talking with them; we seem to share the same vocabularies, even though we may be absolute strangers."

Other knitting market changes reflect the economically elevated status of "Senior Citizens." With the "frankly fifty" and over crowd (whose mortality rates declined at twice the rate of the general population) now composing one fifth of the population and controlling 28 percent of discretionary income, stereotypes of the aged barely eking out an existence no longer pertain. Older men and women enjoy leisure for handwork, decline to adjure style with advancing age, insist upon quality yarns and willingly spend to get them, but with more grandmothers living in Sunbelt climes or retirement communities than with grandchildren, fewer have time or opportunity to pass on knitting traditions. As a *Wall Street Journal* writer recently remarked, "The frail old lady knitting in the rocking chair has been replaced by the well-coiffed matron selling real estate." Patterns for "Maine Mittens," twin-layered and often lined with tufts of fleece for additional warmth, which were handed down orally for almost three centuries, are now meticulously illustrated and described in *Fox and Geese and Fences* "to bring an old warm tradition into the reach of young women and men who prefer to knit from a pattern, or who have no grandmother or great aunt to teach them directly." After its publication, so many knitters inundated the author with requests for additional patterns and techniques that she and her co-author published a supplement to pass them on in the "new tradition—by book":

> They [the patterns] have been unearthed not by us but by people who make them or remember them and want the techniques remembered too and passed down. We have been a clearing house to receive and pass on information that other knitters have developed over generations. . . . We do hope you will choose one or two to make on your own, ones that you'll come to know inside out, to which you'll add your own little fillips and improvements. And we hope you will knit these one or two patterns for everyone in your family for a hundred years and teach them to your granddaughters. In this way, you will become part of the folk process, and the good, warm patterns of our grandmothers will be carried on in new generations.

With fewer grandmothers, aunts and mothers bequeathing their skills to the next generation, prospective knitters, thrown upon their own resources, converged upon knitting classes at local shops, adult education programs, regional workshops, camps and conventions. Since patently incompetent teachers are the bane of the yarn industry and a thorn in the side of eager novices, the American Professional Needlework Retailers and the National Needlework Association introduced a knitting teacher certification program in 1977 that has now expanded into a prestigious educational procedure whose graduates, confident of the credibility bestowed upon them by their training, conduct classes with enviable expertise. Its new "Key Program" inspires instructors to complete fifty additional hours in approved courses at markets and seminars to gain the coveted gold key pin, designed to display a ruby for an additional seventy-five hours and a diamond for an overall total of two hundred and twenty-five hours of special instruction. Lest garden variety knitters aspire to such bejeweled recognition, it should be pointed out that the program is restricted to retailers and their employees, the true "professionals" of the knitting world.

Since even these board-certified retailers—whom one yarn company executive calls "alert, smart, aggressive, knowledgeable [and] businesslike" managers who no longer run their "Sittin' Knittin'" corners without inventory control, advertising, special sales and high quality instruction—are not necessarily teachers who foster an environment of camaraderie, warmth, sharing and enjoyment as well as technical assistance, planners of conventions and seminars screen potential instructors for classroom presence as well as skill and carefully pore over student evaluations before rehiring. Evie Rosen, a gifted and "well-papered" instructor who owns a retail store in Wausau, Wisconsin, serves on the board of the professional association and teaches at national conventions, laughs when she says, "I have to keep in mind that students haven't traveled hundreds of miles to hear me drone on about buttonholes and bindings but want to chat and have a good time while picking up new tricks. I aim to have a good time myself; so we all have fun together."

Enjoying one another's knitting company has been responsible for converting many local knitting groups into members of national organizations such as The Knitting Guild of America (TKGA), founded in 1985 as an umbrella organization for the rapidly growing number of groups open to anyone interested in sharing fellowship and knowledge with other knitters. The first group to affiliate was the Western Reserve Guild of Canfield, Ohio, about sixty-five miles east of Cleveland. No group succeeds without able leadership, and Canfield knitters chose Marlyn Ibele as their first president. Having first taught knitting in a converted second story of a local hardware store before moving to a more elegant site, the Knitting Corner yarn store, Ibele knew Canfield's knitters well, and when she heard of the formation of The Knitting Guild of America, convinced knitting shops to offer members a 10 percent discount, placed posters in local shops announcing an organizational meeting and happily greeted forty-seven interested knitters. The paperwork done, Mrs. Ibele located a room in the Odd Fellows Hall for meetings, cranked out monthly newsletters and made certain that the national guild magazine, *Cast On*, featured the Western Reserve knitters as the *first* guild. The *Youngstown Vindicator* widened the range of potential members by providing dates, places and agendas of meetings to readers beyond Canfield: "[November] Members are reminded to take size two and three needles for a poinsettia workshop and demonstration. . . . Kits will also be available at the meeting. There is a display of afghans made by members at Knitting Corners until November 12"; "[December] As early darkness and cold weather keep us housebound, knitting for oneself or others is far more satisfying than watching something worthless on television"; "A 'show-and-tell' program is planned. Each member is limited to one item for the program"; "The method of casting on invisible stitches and tubular binding off will be featured at the January 14th meeting. Members are asked to take sizes seven and eight needles and worsted weight yarn for the workshop"; "A special demonstration of how to cut fabric for knitting. . . . Also members will have a 'knit-in' with members and guests asked to take their own knitting projects"; "Area-wide knit-ins will be scattered throughout the area, a wide radius geographically, day and night to accommodate everyone's schedules"; "Members' daughters interested in knitting are welcome to join the guild at half the membership fee." The guild's scrapbook and photograph album record all monthly activities, from displays of new yarns by local shops to an outdoor picnic with a birthday cake to celebrate the guild's incorporation.

Through the Knitting Guild's quarterly *Cast On*, knitters can practice the "Stitch of the Season" in Shirley MacNulty's column, read reviews of new knitting books, study patterns from outstanding designers, learn of activities of other guilds, enter knitting design competitions at the annual conventions and rent sample "stitch kits" and slide shows. In its "Needles and Purls" section, guild members express interest or ask for help: "I have only been knitting a little over a year now, but I am totally hooked and suffer withdrawal symptoms (general crankiness and an itchy knitting finger) if I don't get in at *least* half an hour of knitting a day (usually a lot more). As a matter of fact, I sold the first sweater I designed myself, the first time I wore it in public"; "I need help in locating a pattern for a large dog sweater . . . Doberman size! Any assistance would be greatly appreciated"; "I am looking for a way to knit the profile of a Belgian Sheepdog on the front of a sweater. I do great with instructions in front of me—from Deer to Rainbows but I do not have a clue as to how to draw my graph for knitting a sweater"; "I am searching for knitted dress patterns from the 30's, 40's and 50's. Does anyone know where I can find such patterns? I would be interested in original patterns or copies." The rapidly growing guild held its fourth national convention in the spring of 1988.

Not all local guilds, however, choose to ally themselves with the national organization. In Atlanta, where the original membership of fifty-two doubled in three years, founder Whit Robbins notes a favorite program is a pattern exchange, where members can swap their own used patterns for knitting shop leftovers or other members' donations. Like most guilds that sponsor knitting projects for others, Atlanta members knit slippers and caps for "street people" and contribute to the national "Caps for Kids" drive.

The Creative Fiber Guild, of Sheridan, Wyoming, started in the mid-seventies by women interested in all aspects of fiber arts, meets monthly and offers workshops on everything from basketry to furs. Janet Mysse, author of *Affordable Furs*, who has conducted five-day workshops on combining knitted pieces with furs at her sheep ranch in Ingomar, Montana, has conducted a fur jacket session for the Sheridan guild, and members who have attended workshops elsewhere return to pass on their new expertise. Marcia Spracklen, who demonstrates so well that her tips are now considered "annual" workshops, explains why she doesn't charge a fee: "I only do it for Guild members, and it has brought in some new members. I don't feel right about charging for someone else's workshop, and it's a way to repay the Guild for the many things it's done for me." She adds of her guild: "You would have to meet our members to appreciate the bond that has developed within this group where there seems to be an unspoken agreement that our guild is too precious to all of us to let anything ruin what we have."

A spin-off of the Creative Fiber Guild is the group called the Tuesday Threaders, which meets *every* Tuesday all year, in town in the winter but car-pooling to ranches or mountain cabins in the summer. Marcia Spracklen joked, "When Christmas, Thanksgiving or other holidays fall on Tuesday, we seriously consider postponing them—but not the Threaders!" Member Victoria Legerski added, "We are like a closely knit family. Anyone can join and many of us bring a new friend from time to time. If the friend doesn't accept us—they just don't continue to come. Everyone is welcome and the group seems to get excited about what a new member knows and can teach us. Most of our members say they wouldn't belong to a 'women's group,' but what makes our group so compatible is that we respect each other and actually accomplish things!" "Knottie Nannies" who can't make daytime meetings reserve Thursday night.

Knitting clubs and guilds proliferate, and though members thirst for new designs and methods, they also act as preservers of an earlier culture, curators of old techniques, safeguards of bygone styles and protectors of traditional patterns. Publishers respond to this lingering backward look by including the word *traditional* in many book titles (especially those on European crafts such as Fair Isle and Aran knitting), and by duplicating patterns of earlier periods. Old *Vogue Knitting* patterns reappear in color; the twenties, thirties and forties enjoy a revival; an author titles her book *Knitting in the Old Way*. "Traditional" knitting even made news when Linda Chavez, then the highest ranking female White House appointee, irked at White House Chief of Staff Donald Regan's remark that most women didn't understand such summit issues as Afghanistan and missile throw weights, parried: "I'm going to throw my weight around and knit him an afghan for Christmas."

Aficionados of Victorian needlework can read the paperback reprint of Mrs. Warren and Mrs. Pullan's well-known 1870 *Treasures in Needlework* or they can select patterns from *Godey's Lady's Book*, now edited and compiled into another "treasury." Even the "reticule" is scheduled for revival, as readers of *Knitters* are treated to instructions for the "Floradora Bag" from a 1902 needlework magazine. Knitters hoping to emulate their knitting forebears found instructions for *Godey's'* famous "fan" counterpane reproduced in a recent magazine and will soon have access to an entire book of counterpane patterns by Mary Walker Phillips. Knitting a spread is only for the hardy, as Yolanda Thompson, of Washington, D.C., found out when she had finished ten four-inch-wide panels: "I was a veteran of bouclé knitting and thought nothing could be harder, but since I was using Coats and Clark thread and #1 needles, just ten panels consumed almost a year. I was exhausted, decided it was a little much, cut it up into strips for a skirt, spent another year making a top but was rewarded by having a great summer or 'winter white' dress!"

Knitters may fancy traditional crafts, but "modern" women must cram knitting into already loaded schedules. Sensing this, Wild and Wooly Needlecrafts, a chain of shops in the Washington, D.C., metropolitan area, targeted its press and radio campaign to a stereotypical customer, the career-oriented "Wild and Wooly Woman" whose knitting competes for time with such contemporary activities as windsurfing, scuba diving, karate and skydiving. Epitomizing this "new knitter" was this thirty-three-year-old dentist:

> Describe myself? That's easy. Busy! Between my job (which I love), my friends (whom I never see enough of), my exercise classes, week-end adventures, traveling, shopping, museum going and everything . . . my life feels like a tornado, and I love it all. For me the secret of happiness is balance. I'm a juggler of time. And I'm a knitter! That's right . . . I love needlecrafts. It's funny, I used to watch my grandmother knit, crochet, and do needlepoint. She made the most fantastic things (very often for me) but I never took the time to learn. And then last year I found out that Wild and Wooly has great knitting classes. So I signed up. The classes were great and today I love to knit. My friends tease me because wherever I go, doing all that I do . . . I'm always knitting. To me, it's creative, fun, and it's an accomplishment I can wear! You know knitting and juggling make an interesting balancing act. I get a lot out of life . . . I'm a Wild and Wooly woman!

Wild and Wooly Woman's ability to juggle career and knitting is reminiscent of Joan Crawford or Katharine Hepburn knitting between "takes" in the thirties and forties. Despite some theatrical superstitions that "crossed needles" in onstage or backstage knitting might "knot" or entangle the production, current musical comedy actress Cheri Butcher knit her boyfriend's sweater to relax during short breaks because, as she said, "It makes me feel I'm not wasting time. I come back sometimes and knit maybe five stitches before I have to go on again." A chorine's knitting helped her to "relax and think about my life," and a wardrobe assistant, working on a mohair-and-silk bedspread, added, "It's something to do, instead of having to go out in the cold before coming back for the evening show."

Though today's career women and "better fixed" older women have more to spend, they still draw the line at exorbitantly priced handknit sweaters, memorize their design and construction, snip haughtily to clerks, "No, that isn't at all what I had in mind" and dash to sketch patterns and stitches while images are still fresh. Well worth copying were products of thirty knitters on the payroll of an enterprising twenty-five-year-old graduate of the Parsons School of Design, whose sweaters of angora, cashmere or mohair blended with suede, fur, marabou or guinea hen feathers were carried by New York's East Side boutiques and such gilt-edged caterers of chic to the limousine set as Bergdorf-Goodman, Saks Fifth Avenue, Elizabeth Arden, I. Magnin and Beverly Hills's Rodeo Drive establishments for prices beginning at $500 and ascending quickly to $1,850.

Other collectibles and copyables are "Estelles," from the fertile brain of Phoenix knitter/designer Estelle Gracer, a homemaker, mother and professional volunteer who experimented with a middle-of-the-night brainstorm, knitting and crocheting fabric strips into colorful sweaters. Gracer began modestly, by bundling off her cottage industry's one-of-a-kind "Glad Rags," sometimes accompanied by matching skirts, to a local fashion store. When she discovered several customers fighting for the same "unusual but not kooky" jacket, she concluded, "Wait a minute; we can make some more!" With her daughter's help, she was soon marketing nationally and moved her business to a factory/studio of her own where home knitters pick up supplies and deliver finished garments, products are shipped to retailers, samples are sold in a small salesroom and new designs are developed. When Gracer supplied patterns for "fabric knitting" to magazines such as *Good Housekeeping* and *Family Circle* ("I was dumb about the fashion business then and told everybody about what I had discovered"), other entrepreneurs entered the competition, many to supply home knitters with spools of bias-cut fabrics or ribbon. With "Estelles" still selling briskly because of their distinctive lines, color and workmanship, however, Gracer concludes, "I have made wearable works of art. I took the rag, literally, and made it into high fashion. . . . Everyone should try. All this happened after I was fifty years old."

Observing customers' appetites for copying expensive models, Macy's in 1981 inaugurated a "Knit Works" department where knitters could scrutinize high-priced sweater samples and secure patterns, yarn and trimmings to copy them. The department director explained airily, "Yarn shops sell yarn; Knit Works sells fashion," by which she

meant swank imported yarn at up to forty dollars a skein and a soup-
çon of extras—foxtails woven through knitted strips, knit-in sequin
strips and garnishes of feathers and plumes that could easily run the
total sweater cost to several hundred dollars. The department's out-
of-the-way location, she commented, was no deterrent: "I don't think
it matters where a store puts you, knitters will find you."

In Washington, D.C., where avant-garde designers purvey their
sweaters in Georgetown's expensively trendy shops, Charles Higginbotham holds court in his Woolgatherer shop near Dupont Circle
and supplies knitters with the means to design their own creations
or copy his Washington collection of a green "National Cathedral"
cardigan; a striped, multicolored "Phillips Collection" sweater; a "Library of Congress" jacket of oxidized copper and pigeon gray colors;
or a sobering puffed-sleeve cardigan, the "National Debt." Testy at
knitters who say they are too impatient to knit, Higginbotham rebuts,
"[T]hey ought to say, I should learn to knit because I'm impatient."

Reacting to the recent knitting revival and paralleling the grievance
of Ogden Nash decades before, a beleaguered husband who anticipated quiet, conversational evenings at home, those "golden hours
reserved for the scraping of barnacles off the great barrier reef of
marriage," instead found his wife's delight in him replaced by a passion for knitting that left her lap and environs "fortified" with yarn
balls and a "menacing battery of knitting needles." Unable to break
into her concentration, he complained bitterly of the box score, "Knit
2, Purl 1, Hubby 0," and added, "When that woman begins purling
and dropping, neither rain nor sleet nor gloom of husband can keep
her from her appointed rounds."

It is not only women who make their "appointed rounds," and the
increasing number of male knitters can be traced to the gradual blur-
ring of gender roles as men tend babies, cook, clean and perform
duties once deemed exclusively feminine. Knitting men who produce
as prodigiously as women expect more deference from designers,
and one, noting that of the forty-five patterns in a recent issue of
Vogue Knitting only three were for men, importuned the editors,
"Please, there are legions of us out there; increase the number of
patterns for Men!" Editors, hoping to placate everyone, soothingly
indicated that male readers were a very small segment of their audience ("[W]e don't want to disappoint our women") and directed

the complainant to *Vogue*'s his/her sweaters and the many patterns that were so well proportioned as to be "perfectly appropriate for menswear."

Male knitters tell their knitting history proudly. James Phelan, of Fayetteville, North Carolina, whose wife suggested knitting when he exhausted wall space to display his needlepoint projects, knit with such a vengeance that within a two-year period he completed sixty garments, their patterns, yarns, sizes, names of recipients and brief comments all carefully noted in his journal. Knitting mainly while watching TV at home, he was uncomfortable about knitting in public until, on a recent plane trip, he boldly opened his canvas carryall ("Like an L. L. Bean bag") and broke out his needles despite stares of disbelief. He has found knitting helps strike up conversation, and adds: "I've also had some interesting experiences while browsing in yarn shops where edgy owners finger alarm buttons when males browse their shelves—as if we couldn't possibly be looking for our next project. I've managed to solve that problem by patronizing one particular shop in my community where I get the red carpet treatment, especially when I bring in new customers."

Sam Miller, of Fairfield, Indiana, also began knitting in the early eighties when the class in which his wife, Dolly, enrolled needed more students. After volunteering to boost the head count, he hasn't stopped knitting since, including several sweaters and a lady's suit, and remarked, "Yesterday a lady brought me another pattern and some ribbon yarn. My first for ribbon. I enjoy it, it's relaxing and fun, and I'd recommend it to anyone." A septuagenarian, who as a young Boy Scout knit squares for soldiers' blankets in World War I, he rediscovered the craft years later when, as a traveling salesman, he knit to while away lonely hours in hotel rooms. In those days, so few men knit that he felt compelled to slink in to buy supplies, but today he talks easily and proudly of his one-of-a-kind Scandinavian mittens and his "hunter's socks" of baby wool reinforced with double knitting at the heel. Along with his wife, who is an ardent craftswoman, he supplements knitting with making canoes, salmon fly kits and sturdy pack baskets, and attests, "There are no idle hands in this house."

"No idle hands" is still the watchword. *Mother Earth News*, enviously citing the conventional wisdom that knitters could indulge their habit during any spare moments, sighed, "Who hasn't envied a needle clicker during a long, boring town meeting, political speech, or other obligatory function? That person's twiddling up something useful while many other folks are twiddling their thumbs!" Jane Snibbe, of Pebble Beach, California, is the perfect example: "As a school librarian, I have numerous meetings to attend and knit shamelessly during them. Two years ago, after finishing my term as President of our teachers' association, when I not only had to attend those meetings but also every school board meeting, a board member asked how many sweaters I had knit in a year and was astonished that I had made twenty-one. And I was working full time and not sitting around home knitting!"

Such passion is not unusual. A knitter, foresworn of knitting after making her first boyfriend a pair of socks, gravitated to knitting again a few years later to help herself stop smoking and then simply traded one obsession for another, knitting fourteen sweaters the first year, tapering off to eight the second and eventually curbing her new addiction by knitting only when she was "nervous." Another compulsive knitter reported: "My husband and I made a bet once. Could I stop knitting for two days? I lost! Couldn't do it. . . . Busy hands keep me thin." The busy hands of industrious knitter Jane Alencewiz, of Colonia, New Jersey, produced within a recent six-month period a quantity of items to match the output of an early eighteenth-century worker: three sleeveless vests, a long-sleeved turtleneck sweater, two dozen miniature sweaters as Christmas decorations, fifteen ascot scarves, two fan-and-feather afghans as wedding gifts, *plus* two large crocheted afghans for bridal shower gifts, a dozen pairs of slippers in assorted sizes, eight Christmas tree pot holders and piece-quilting a double bed quilt as an ordination gift for her priest and a crib-size quilt.

An eighties knitter, more practical than passionate, is Lynnette Timko, of Clearfield, Pennsylvania, whose knitting resourcefulness is worthy of inclusion in this history:

I'm your typical modern 80's mother—the story book middle class family complete with dog! I'm self-employed in my home as a hairdresser, active member in two churches, Girl Scout Leader and advisor and delegate for Girl Scout Assembly, member of a Girl

Scout Service team, room mother for both my children's classes, visitor to patients in our hospital and, with my husband, interested in a YMCA swim team and the Pennsylvania Association for Gifted Children and so on. When my children were younger, I needed help, especially keeping the hardwood floors clean and waxed, so I'd move everything out of the rooms and put the wax on.

Here is where knitting came into the picture because I knit bootee slippers in an array of sizes from left-over scraps of wool or wool-blend yarn and invited my children's friends (we live in a housing development so there are plenty) over for "skating parties." I'd join in and swish into the corners and along the baseboards while the slippered children had a raucous time slithering around the room for as long as they liked. I served refreshments afterwards, and had a gleaming floor. I later bought an electric buffer, but it certainly isn't as much fun!

Current knitters are no less generous with products of their needles than those of earlier generations, working locally on such projects as supplying a bank's or a church's "mitten tree" or "warm tree" with knit clothing for needy children, "preemie caps" for maternity hospitals, cotton-knit bandages for leprosaria and clothing for children in Shriners' hospitals. Marcia Freeman, of West Caldwell, New Jersey, knit mittens in assorted sizes and colors for children of the rural Vermont two-room schoolhouse she and her siblings had attended as a one-room school many years before. These letters were reward enough: [spelling is preserved] "Thank you for the mittens you gave to us. I liked your letter too. The tree you carved your names in has been cut down. I got yellow mittens"; "Thank you for those great mittens. They are rellely warm and I woude like to tell you that they added another room in the school"; "Thank you for the mitins they fit good"; "Thank you for the mittens. The tree that you were talking about fell in a bad storm. There are two houses where the brook was where you used to get water. I have been in Woodford school for 5 years. I'm in the fith grade and I turned 10 on Thansgiving day." Hallie White, of Rutherfordton, North Carolina, knits "tobaggans" (caps) for children of Crossmore School, a mountain school for youngsters of little or no means, and through the "Parson of the Hills" program for Appalachian Mountains children.

The scope of such projects is as broad as it is generous. When Bonnie Greene, owner of Yarn Country in Danville, California, and the spirit behind "Caps for Kids," wanted to increase donations, she turned to knitters, who always "give of themselves":

My customers always seemed to have an extra ball of yarn left over from projects, and the idea of using it to make a cap for a child was the perfect solution. The resultant 'Caps for Kids' program has spread all over the country and abroad, helped along by the big needlework companies who donate yarn to stores who participate in the program. I have been speaking to various needlework groups and getting announcements placed in knitting magazines so I know that our 1985 figure of 11,000 caps will soon be eclipsed by the knitters who are marching forward to help children across America.

Knitters eager to apply their knitting energies toward international projects knit scarves and mittens from Soviet and American wool spun together into "peace fleece" as symbols of peaceful cooperation. Others participate in the "We Can Knit the World Together!" plan by knitting individual sections to be assembled into an enormous tapestry for the United Nations made by over seven thousand world-wide knitters. Eighty-six-year-old Nellie Dice, of Denver, Indiana, contributes scarves, caps (usually twenty-five or thirty), mittens and novelties to a bazaar raising money for a Haitian children's hospital. As a member of the National Council of Catholic Women, Audrey Calligy, of Hoboken, New Jersey, knits bandages for hospital patients in underdeveloped areas and Third World nations.

Large numbers of knitters assist Church World Service, founded in 1946 to provide emergency/disaster service in more than seventy countries, mostly in refugee camps. Nellie Dice remembers her first contact with the organization: "One day in the sixties a woman waiting to speak at a missionary convention knit busily while waiting for her turn. When I asked what she was making and she explained that it was a ten foot stretch bandage for Church World Service, I decided that was something I could do and get others interested in. We never kept track of how many we made over the years, but it was a lot!" The organization's clothing appeals have spurred knitters to establish "yarn banks" for donations of leftover pieces, and many make the functional "Remsen Baby Blanket" (a pattern contributed by Mrs. John Remsen) because it's easy, can be made of any weight yarn and accommodates scrap yarn in a rainbow of colors. When the organization's truck made its annual pickup from churches in Manchester, Connecticut, in 1986, Mary Warren was happy to report that her Center Congregational Church, which had been sewing, crocheting and knitting all kinds of baby garments for years and started making "Remsens" about ten years ago, contributed 174 blankets.

Historically, one of the most interesting groups for which devoted women and men knit is the Seamen's Church Institute of New York and New Jersey, originally founded in 1834 to improve treatment of merchant seamen entering the Port of New York. Within a decade, the founders brought the influence of the church directly to the seamen by mooring a floating chapel in the heart of Ship's Row on Manhattan's East River. By World War I the institute's broad social services included a "Christmas-at-Sea" program that almost seventy years later attracted three thousand volunteer knitters in two hundred groups who hand knit sixteen thousand scarves, watch caps and sweaters for seafarers away from port on Christmas Day. In a totally ecumenical fashion, knit goods plus stationery kits, luggage tags, pocket atlases and handwritten Christmas cards are packed, laden onto departing ships and stowed away until Christmas.

The institute, asking only that knitters use the standard patterns, provides yarn for those unable to buy their own but allows other variations. In a national knitting magazine, volunteer Charlotte Stafford suggested adding "racing stripes" to the institute's "Easy Sleeveless Pullover" not only to help a seaman identify his own sweater but to recruit new knitters who hated drab colors. Many faithful knitters, quite a few of them elderly and homebound, have contributed for years. One, who knit more than a thousand pairs of socks in twenty-five years, explained simply, "I like to knit"; another, with thirty years' participation, added, "It's so good to know that even at my age you can make a contribution. They are lonely men out there at sea and their wonderful letters of appreciation make it all so worthwhile." The *Newsletter* binds together volunteers throughout the country: "My mother, Cornelia Lattin, knitted for you some twenty plus years ago and my aunt, Edith Newcomb, did also. My daughter, Becky, likewise knit from Montana for you. Although I'm the only one currently knitting for the SCI, it's a family tradition with us, too." Another, who wrote, "I will not go into detail but knitting these sets has been a 'God-send' for me," bought so much variegated yarn at a store's big sale she hoped the seamen "would appreciate the change." Irene Graessle, of Maplewood, New Jersey, who knit the standard pattern in whatever color she liked, said of her Seamen's knitting, "I couldn't believe I'd derive so much satisfaction from helping people I don't even know." In Washington, D.C., active army widows, many of them in their eighties, gather to knit regularly and enjoy the friendship of their "circle" as much as the satisfaction of sending the garments. Now in his late seventies, William Pickslay, of Carson City, Nevada, explains how he became involved in the Christmas-at-Sea knitting program:

> After my cousin, the former director of the Seamen's Church Institute of N.Y. officiated at my father's interment in 1966, I made a donation to the Institute and got on their mailing list and learned about their Christmas At Sea project. After I retired and had moved to Reno, my wife suggested I try knitting. I had a vague recollection of knitting balaclava helmets during World War I; so I agreed to try. I found it so satisfactory a way to pass idle time, that we have been knitting ever since for SCI and we must be approaching the 1,000 garment mark. I knit as a boy when confined to bed by two mastoid operations and had no problems in starting in knitting again. EASY!

This loving concern is matched by recipients' pleasure: "I would like to kiss the hands of the one who knitted the beautiful pullover. This gift gives me not only material warmth, but also spiritual comfort"; "I put a big Christmas tree up in the foremast with fifty lights on it"; "Thanks, again, for what you are doing for us. We do not feel alone—even in the middle of the Pacific—with such friends as you around"; "As we are coming back to New York now in the wintertime, we can sure use your knitted caps, shawls and sweaters. Thank you and we wish you all a peaceful 1986 in good health"; "It was obvious that a lot of time was spent by your volunteers . . . and it was special to receive something handmade."

"Handmade" has a special ring to it in the eighties, with the spread of the knitting machine—a savior or a devil, depending upon one's point of view. When a local group modeled its machine-knit outfits and a knitting machine distributor demonstrated in the exhibits hall of the Knitting Guild of America's first convention in Dallas in 1985, diehard hand knitters sniffed disdainfully, "They aren't *knitters*; they just push that lever back and forth!" One brave hand knitter admitted that while she always did the "fancy stitches" by hand, she secretly did the backs of sweaters and "other boring parts" by machine to accelerate completion of a project, and added, "But I still feel guilty about it!" Others chimed in that machines didn't fulfill the urge to hand knit, no matter how efficient they were. With punchcard electronic machines that can, according to their makers, "knit two hundred stitches in the time it takes to hand-knit one" and duplicate stitches once possible only in hand knitting, home workers feel their machines pay for themselves in time reduced and number of products made, a sound investment for housebound women who need to make money from their labors. The owner of Ramsey, New Jersey's, Knitting Corner prognosticated, "One day knitting machines will be as common as the sewing machine in the average home." "Not so," says the proprietress of Needleworks, in Springfield, Vermont, who wrote, "We had a knitting machine in the store, but it's like *ironing*, and who wants to do that?"

In many New England homes, however, particularly in Vermont, knitting machines became such staple appliances and provided homebound workers such opportunities for additional income that knitters implored the Labor Department to rescind the 1943 ban on industrial homework in the apparel industry. The ban was ostensibly passed to uphold the minimum wage laws but was quite obviously in response to pressure from the highly organized, politically oriented International Ladies' Garment Workers Union. For decades, home knitters argued that they were not victimized by exploitive bosses and they should be allowed to work on their own terms. Car decals bumptiously demanded LET KNITTERS DO IT AT HOME, and when the Secretary of Labor finally rescinded the ban, they went into business in earnest. Two years later, after resurgent union pressure to protect factory wages from undercutting by competition from "sweatshop" workers (a loaded term referring to isolated and hapless workers who could be gulled by unscrupulous jobbers) the ban was reproposed. Cartoons showed irate knitters armed with knitting needles to repel troopers who ordered them to desist, and the legacy of those staunch New England ladies who fought encroachment by factories a century and half before sprang to mind. *Who* was cruel enough to go after a dear little old knitting lady? Cried the *Washington Post*, "No Knitting at Home"; the *Wall Street Journal* reported the argument was only "The Tip of the Ski Cap." The picture wasn't quite that simple, however, because the ladies were operating machines rather than knitting by hand, and the ingrained nostalgia about grandmotherly knitting didn't transfer to their modern counterparts. It was not until the knitters agreed to keep logs of hours and output to show that a minimum wage was being paid that the issue was temporarily settled.

Even hand knitting can benefit from modern technology when a computer, programmed with new gauge and size data, recalculates and prints an individualized pattern, an accomplishment only math-savvy knitters have previously engineered; math illiterates who have nonetheless mastered computers find these programs handy. Instructional video tapes, whether used in shops or at home, allow knitters to replay or freeze-frame difficult exercises. While Zimmermann pioneered, others have joined the market. The Knitting Fever Company's "Watch and Learn—Basic Knitting" is advertised to give "fashion independence forever" by providing instruction sheets to accompany the lessons; Maggie Righetti, Atlanta designer, teacher and writer, recognized the medium's advantage: "I thought of it as teaching a class of one person and that one person was the camera which could zoom in for closeups by peering over my shoulder in a way impossible to a person without breathing down my neck." Many school Home Ec classes use "Knitting: A Simplified Approach to Basics," a set of two filmstrips with accompanying cassettes to demonstrate everything from selecting yarn to finishing projects. A reviewer in an educational journal pointed out the advantage of holding one frame while students practice the visualized demonstrations and then added the ultimate clincher: "A young man is shown knitting!" A young *man*? Well, now! What will they think of next?

Needlework shop owners necessarily observe cyclical swings and try to keep abreast of change. Looking back over her knitting years, the last seventeen as a shop owner in a suburban mall, Barbara Moody, of Washington, D.C., sums up her experiences:

When I went into business in the late sixties, everyone was into needlepoint, but how many pillows and glasses cases can you make? When needlepointers burned out, they took up knitting. If current knitters overdose, they'll move back to needlepoint or some other craft; it's a cyclical thing. Knitting isn't the home craft it used to be. Even in my family, it skipped a generation.

I *have* seen some changes. Knitters increasingly combine contrasting fibers for distinctive textures, work with several colors, adapt patterns by varying sleeves, neckline, length etc., experiment with higher style, knit more for themselves than others, knit less when the economy is good because they stay home less, knit less for men who are pickier and won't tolerate that "loving hands at home look," knit less for children since most modern mothers want to throw everything into the washing machine and dryer, count on knitting to keep their hands busy and *out of food* or *off cigarettes*, enjoy knitting's "social image" that attracts conversation, knit to reduce travel tensions over late departures, late arrivals, late room check-ins, late meals and gridlocked traffic and still perceive European designs more stylish than American ones.

While the pace of life has quickened and fashions change with great regularity, actual knitting techniques remain virtually the same. As one knitter sitting beside the author on the subway remarked, "Well, knitting is still just taking long pieces of cotton, wool, string or what-have-you, forming loops and getting them on the needle, making more loops from those, switching them back and forth from one needle to the other, all the while praying they don't skid off the needles before you finish what you're making—which could take from a week to a couple of years!" Still, there *are* tricks to be learned, and most knitters want to pass them on. Grandmothers such as Pat Coukos, of Richmond, California, still hope their granddaughters will be knitters: "Two years ago, when my granddaughter was eight, I started teaching her to knit, never pressuring her and doing it only when she's in the mood. If she drops a stitch, I simply say, 'No problem' and pick it up so that she won't associate anxiety or tension with knitting. Knitting has been a delight to me and kept me from wasting time. I want to pass this wonderful craft on to her."

As incentives for knitting, pleasure has prevailed over duty; fashion has triumphed over thrift; relaxation has edged out industry; creativity has outranked knitting-by-the-book; "working with my hands" long ago nosed out "fear of the devil." The old saw of idle hands becoming the devil's playground fades to a memory, revived with a chuckle by this stanza from "Grandma Says," a 1986 poem:

> When Satan moves in with his Cohorts of Sin
> Say, "You'll never find me submittin'
> You irk me, I find
> So get thee behind
> And please don't disturb me—I'm knittin'."

Notes

The notes that follow contain shortened bibliographical references. For full publication information please see the bibliography at the end of the book.

Introduction

page

xvi   "[F]or the male sex . . .": Lucretius, "The Nature of Things," in Oates, *Stoic and Epicurean Philosophers,* vol. 1, p 189.

xvii   "Whether he was slower . . .": *Art Needlework* (1889), introduction.

xvii   "While it is true . . .":Barnes, *Manual of Knitting and Crocheting* (1936), introduction.

xviii   "Girls are less fidgety . . .": All quotations taken from a discussion at the March, 1986 Convention of the Knitting Guild of America in Milwaukee, Wisc., and taped by the author.

xix   "I think men do . . .": Nellie Dice, of Denver, Ind., to ALM, June 16, 1986. The other quotations are extracted from group discussions, oral interviews, questionnaires and letters and are not separately cited to protect my sources!

xix   CHANGES: "Perhaps more younger men . . .": Lillian Lunny, of Staten Island, N.Y., to ALM, July 2, 1986; "In these changing times . . .": He-

lene R. Angevine, East Aurora, N.Y., to ALM, June 12, 1986; "I'm not
so sure . . .": Deb Lipinski, Freemont, Nebr., to ALM, June 17, 1986.

xix–xxi   REASONS: "My knitting bag is . . .": Arlene Bauers, of Cheektowaga, N.Y.,
to ALM, June 23, 1986; "I found that knitting . . .": Lois Fuller, of Bing-
hamton, N.Y., to ALM, June 16, 1986; "My hairdresser says when . . .":
Beulah Dicovitsky, of Brick, N.J., to ALM, June 24, 1986; "At a family
gathering . . .": Sharron Freeman, West Hartford, Conn., to ALM, June
15, 1986; "If there is no . . .": Martha Branden, of Dover, Fla., to ALM,
August 1, 1986; "I knit mainly for . . .": Mary J. Julius, Lanham, Md.,
to ALM, August 1, 1986; ". . . never wasting a minute . . ."; Nora Lee
of New York, to ALM, June 4, 1986; "My friends call me . . .": Alta
Shively, of Plymouth, Ind., to ALM, June 22, 1986; "I wasn't about to
. . ." and other quotations are listed alphabetically to preserve anonymity:
Arlene Bauers, of Cheektowaga, N.Y.; Ruth Bluestone, of Roselle Park,
N.J.; Daisy Burka, of Berwick, Pa.; Anne Crawford, of Ocala, Fla.; Catherine Dodd, of Waterbury, Conn.; Ida L. Lloyd, of Indianapolis, Ind.;
Joan McGowan, of San Clemente, Calif.; Diana Parker, of Washington,
D.C.; Virginia Phillips, of Denver, Colo.; Charlotte Stafford, of Ches-
terland, Ohio; Hallie White, of Rutherfordton, N.C.

xxi   "My great grandmother was . . .": Isabella Nutt Montgomery, of Chevy
Chase, Md., telling of her great-grandmother, Martha Gale Turner
Nichols (1836–1932), of Royalston, Mass., to ALM, January 10, 1986.

xxii   "When I was in . . .": Rebecca Cripe Allen, of Goshen, Ind., to ALM,
June 17, 1986.

xxii–xxiv   WHERE TO KNIT: ". . . in a boat on . . .": Helene R. Angevine, of East
Aurora, N.Y., to ALM, June 18, 1986; ". . . at my grandmother's one
. . .": Joan Kinghorn, Fort Erie, Ont., to ALM, September 11, 1986;
". . . while pedaling my exercise . . .": Deb Lipinski, of Freemont, Nebr.,
to ALM, June 18, 1986; ". . . during our two and . . .": Sherry Ann
Masser, of Scotia, N.Y., to ALM, May 22, 1986; "A teacher at our . . .":
Related by Audrey Callighy, of Hoboken, N.J., to ALM, July 1, 1986;
"When I ran seven . . .": Jean Bain, of Denver, Colo., to ALM, June 22,
1986; "I knit all the . . .": Arlene Bauers, of Cheektowaga, N.Y., to ALM,
June 23, 1986; "When we were married . . .": Patricia Brown, of Stanton,
Calif., to ALM, July 12, 1986; "I once knit a . . .": Joan Newton, of
Stanton, Calif., to ALM, July 13, 1986; "I'm a Little League . . .": A
knitter whose sentiments I wrote down but whose name I lost. Since so
many later told me the same thing, they may all recognize themselves;
"Among my happy memories . . .": Marie Laflamme, of Washington,
D.C., to ALM, September 15, 1986.

xxiv   UNUSUAL OBJECTS IN KNITTING MAGAZINES: Knitted egg warmer, a limp
rectangular piece with sewn-on pockets to hold the eggs: *Godey's Lady's
Book*, January 1882, p. 83; Knitted cover for a flatiron: *Harper's Bazaar*,

January 18, 1868, p. 180; Knitted lamp shade: Ibid., p. 180; Knitted corset: Ibid., February 1, 1868, pp. 215–6; Knitted egg and cracker bag: Ibid., March 21, 1886, p. 333; Foot bag: Ibid., p. 321; Knitted cover for a whisk broom: *Fancy and Practical Knitting*, vol. 3, no. 2 (1887), p. 81; Hairpin receiver: Ibid., p. 8.

xxiv   BIZARRE: Horse blanket: Amala Derry, of Waterbury, Conn., to ALM, July 2, 1986; "Holding Hands" bag: Elaine Bonney, of Cape Elizabeth, Maine, to ALM, August 4, 1986; Chain mail: Kathleen Lancione, of Wheeling, W.Va., to ALM, July 5, 1986; Monopoly board cover: Lois Dunleavy, of Anaheim, Calif., to ALM, August 15, 1986; Uterus: Thelma Muir, of Washington, Kans., to ALM, June 30, 1986; Boa constrictor's sweater: Ann Ledley, N.Y.C., to ALM, June 18, 1986.

xxiv–xxv   FAMILY PATTERNS: "Would it not be . . .": *The Last and Best Book of Knitting* (1918), p. 14; Wedding gown: Debbie McGrath, of Franklinville, N.Y., to ALM, July 10, 1986; Irish sweaters: Cathy Hounshell, of Kensington, Calif., as related to ALM by Jean Y. Haley, of Moundsville, W.Va., August 15, 1986; Rows of "family pattern": Arlene Bauers, Cheektowaga, N.Y., to ALM, June 23, 1986.

xxv–xxvi   LEARNING TO KNIT: "Aunt Bessie gave me . . .": Marjorie Tackitt, of Indianapolis, Ind., to ALM, June 19, 1986; "our landlady, a little . . .": Sherry Masser, of Scotia, N.Y., to ALM, June 3, 1986; "When I was a . . .": Ruth Anne Schoen, of Weston, Nebr., to ALM, September 22, 1986.

Chapter 1:
Colonial Knitters

page

3   "Our people went on . . .": Cited in Marble, *The Women Who Came in the Mayflower*, p. 6.

3   "which if they are . . .": *The Record of the Governor and Company of the Massachusetts Bay in New England*, cited in Earle, *Two Centuries of Costume in America*, vol. 1, pp. 28–30.

3   MONMOUTH CAPS: Ibid., pp. 219–20.

4   "The Court doe hereupon . . .": Cited in Bailey, *Historical Sketches of Andover*, p. 34.

4   "spinning on a rock": Bailey herself calls this a "scene for the painter . . . tended by boys and girls with knitting-work in hand, or spinning wheel on the rock, themselves watched by the sharp-eyed herdsmen," p. 36.

5   "To enjoy the exclusive . . .": Osborne, *The Story of the Stocking* p. 14.

5   "a newly invented instrument . . .": *Williamsburg Virginia Gazette*, September 12, 1771.

5–6   IMPORTED HOSIERY: "An Invoice of English Goods Shipped to New England about 1690," in Dow, *Domestic Life in New England in the Seventeenth Century*, pp. 37–38; "knitted hose to wear . . .": Order of Colonel Thomas Jones in 1726, as cited in Grass, *History of Hosiery*, p. 162.

6   "In the year 1759 . . .": Burnaby, *Travels Thru the Middle Settlements in North America*, n.p., cited in Grass, p. 166.

6   PRICE OF STOCKING: Bishop, *A History of American Manufactures from 1608 to 1860*, vol 1, p. 319.

6   "Moreover they are usually . . .": Thomas, *An Account of Pennsylvania and West New Jersey*, p. 3.

6–7   SPINNING QUOTAS: "Selectmen in every towne . . .": Bagnall, *The Textile Industries of the United States*, vol. 1, p. 105; "That there shall be . . .": Act passed by the General Assembly of Connecticut, May session, 1734, ibid., p. 23; "This Court, taking into . . .": General Court, May 14, 1656, in Wells and Wells, *A History of Hatfield, Massachusetts*, p. 146.

7   STATES ENCOURAGE SPINNING AND KNITTING: Virginia: Bishop, p. 321; Massachusetts: Ibid., vol. 1, p. 333; A contest on Boston Common was reenacted two hundred years later in celebrating the role of wool in New England's textile industry. See chapter 13.

7   "loaden in any ship . . .": Woolen Act, cited in Green and Green, *The Pioneer Mothers of America*, p. 60.

7–8   DUTCH HOUSEWIVES: "Placed on a desert . . .": Van Rensselaer, *The Goede Vrouw of Mana-ha-ta at Home and in Society, 1609–1760*, p. 12; "5 pair white cotton . . .": Inventory of Madame Jacob de Lange, cited by Earle, *Two Centuries of Costume*, vol 1, p. 100. "the young ladies seated . . .": Irving cited by Earle, vol. 1, p. 105. "As I have, in this . . .": Duane, ed., *Extracts From the Diary of Christopher Marshall*, p. 158.

9   "is an irreconcilable enemy . . .": *The New-York Mercury*, October 16, 1758.

9   "went to town and . . .": *Abigail Foote's Journal*, pp. 1, 3.

9   "4 gentlemen all strangers . . .": "The Diary of Frances Baylor Hill of 'Hillsborough,' King and Queen County, Virginia, 1797," Bottorff and Flannagan, *Early American Literature Newsletter*, Special Issue, vol. 2, no. 3, Winter 1967, p. 38. Other special passages are found on pp. 7, 12, 13, 23, 45, 47. Though this diary was written in 1797, it is included in the colonial section since her daily life mirrored that of previous decades.

10–11 IMMIGRANT FAMILIES: "I never saw four such . . .": Parkinson, *A Tour in America in 1798, 1799, and 1800*, vol. 2, p. 389. "their leisure time in making . . .": Quoted in Calhoun, *A Social History of the American Family*, vol. 1, p. 225. "Their homes are, moreover . . .": Rush, *An Account of the Manners of the German Inhabitants of Pennsylvania*, p. 6; "When a young man asks . . .": Rush, cited in Kuhns, *The German and Swiss Settlements of Colonial Pennsylvania*, p. 101.

11   "an undercoat of the blanket . . .": *Diary of Martha Moore Ballard*, 1785,

in Nash, *History of Augusta*, p. 24. Other citations are from pp. 235, 242, 244. Again, a slightly later diary is included for its relevance to the colonial period.

12   SHOPKEEPERS: "Has a Consignment of . . .": *Hartford Connecticut Courant*, November 6, 1797, from research done by Grace Nylander; "Joseph Plowman, Pin-Maker . . .": *New York Constitutional Gazette*, June 22, 1776.

12   "Mr Thos. Warrin & . . .": Forbes, ed. *Diary of Ebenezer Parkman*, entry for February 12, 1779, pp. 97–98.

12–13   NEEDLEWORK SERVICES: "with Fidelity . . .": *Massachusetts Gazette*, April 15, 1774; "Also Mending, and all . . .": *The New York Journal and Weekly Register*, 1788, cited in Matthaei, *An Economic History of Women in America*, p. 62; "Silk Stockings washed and . . .": *The New-York Gazette or the Weekly Post-Boy*, May 21, 1759; "Ladies' Head-Cloaths in . . .": *Charleston South Carolina Gazette*, April 10–17, 1762; "all Kinds of Laces . . .": Ibid., March 6–13, 1762.

13   "A low chair, with . . .": Mrs. Vanderbilt (not further identified), cited in Bowles, *Homespun Handicrafts* (1931), p. 89.

14   "Out came the sprigged . . .": Anonymous, cited in Bowles, pp. 83, 87.

14   MITTENS: "[T]hey must have been . . .": Earle, *Home Life in Colonial Days*, p. 262; "Never am I so glad . . .": Crawford, *Social Life in Old New England*, pp. 34–35; Susannah Springer to ALM, July 16, 1987.

15   STORY OF MATILDA EMERSON: Earle, *Two Centuries of Costume*, vol. 1, pp. 593–4.

16   "I wish Elizabeth to . . .": Item no. 61, circa 1780, lent by Mrs. John V. B. Thayer, in *Brooklyn Museum Catalogue of Early American Handicraft*, n.p.

16–17   TRAINING CHILDREN OF THE POOR: "Indenture, date May 15th . . .": Cited in Brownlee and Brownlee, *Women in the American Economy*, p. 73; "labor and other employments . . .": Calhoun, *A Social History*, vol. 1, p. 125; "to be employed at . . .": Henning's *Statutes of Virginia*, vol. 2, pp. 336–37, cited in Cubberly, *Readings in Public Education*, p. 223; "After Dinner, they retir'd . . .": "Itinerant Observations in America," reprinted from *London Magazine*, 1745–46, Georgia Historical Society, Collection IV, 17, cited in Spruill, *Women's Life and Work in the Southern Colonies* p. 192; "to maintain her decently . . .": Contract for Grace Griswold of the Isle of Wight County in Virginia, in "Education in Colonial Virginia," Part I: "Poor Children and Orphans," *William and Mary Quarterly*, April 1897, p. 223.

17–18   DAME SCHOOLS: "To School to Capt. Townsend's . . .": *Diary of Samuel Sewell*, in the Letter Book of Samuel Sewell, in 6 Coll. Massachusetts Historical Society, II, 135, cited in Seybolt, *The Private Schools of Colonial Boston*, entry of November 10, 1686, pp. 5–6; "gaiter knitting": Reverend George C. Channing, "Early Recollection of Newport," in Higginson, *A History of the Public School System of Rhode Island*, p. 345; "where the good dame . . .": Martin, *The Evolution of the Massachusetts Public School System*, pp. 56, 54; "Where a deaf, poor . . .": Higginson, p. 347.

18–19 GIRLS IN SCHOOL: "In Winter the distance . . .": Small, *Early New England Schools*, p. 288; "Widen your knitting!": Runnels, *History of Sanbornton, N.H.*, vol. 1, p. 104; "taxed the patience of . . .": Small, p. 288; "Arithmetick, Geometry, Algebra, Surveying . . .": Advertisement of Royse and Williams, *Boston Evening Post*, May 3, 1762.

19 PHILOSOPHY OF EDUCATING FEMALES: "I am obnoxious to each . . .": Anne Bradstreet in 1642, quoted in Smith, "Feminism in Philadelphia, 1790–1850," *Pennsylvania Magazine of History and Biography*, July 1944, p. 24; "the trifling narrow, contracted . . .": Abigail Adams, cited by Calhoun, I, 85; "to make it proper . . .": Hitchcock, *Memoirs of the Bloomsgrove Family*, vol. 2, p. 29.

19–20 ADVERTISEMENTS FOR SCHOOLS: "His Wife also teaches . . .": *Hartford Mercury*, March 19, 1750; "A Certain Person and . . .": *Boston News-Letter*, July 28–August 4, 1718; "in a convenient Chamber . . .": *Boston Gazette or Country Journal*, October 1, 8, 15, 1764. (Some years later the *widow* Oliver still advertised stitchery classes); "Young Ladies in the Rudiments . . .": *Massachusetts Gazette*, April 15, 1774; "Living in the Widow . . .": *Newport Mercury*, June 27, 1768; "the strictest care to . . .": *Pittsburgh Gazette*, November 11, 1786.

20–21 "Stolen, out of Mrs. Bowie's . . .": *Charleston Gazette*, January 26, 1765.

21 SCHOOL SOLICITATIONS: "sundry inconveniences [which] result . . .": *Philadelphia Pennsylvania Gazette*, October 25, 1770; "tuition of Young Ladies . . .": *Charleston Mercury*, October 22, 1764; "Mrs. Howland's School on . . .": Ibid., February 25, 1764; "taught by a method similar . . .": J. and M. Tanner, Advertisement, *New York Gazeteer*, April 7, 1774.

21 FITHIAN: Fithian, *Journal and Letters, 1767–1774*, p. 252.

22 YOUTHFUL STITCHERY: Earle, *Home Life*, p. 27; "another ten skein of . . .": Earle, ed., *Diary of Anna Green Winslow*, p. 27; "When I inform you . . .": Ibid., p. 28.

22–23 QUAKER EDUCATION: "that excess of riot . . .": Budd, *Good Order Established in Pennsylvania and New Jersey in America*, pp. 43, 44; "girls should be taught . . .": William Parsons, of Easton, to Richard Peters, October 19, 1754, in Wickersham, *A History of Education in Pennsylvania*, p. 70; "Some things must be set . . .": Wickersham himself, p. 206; "a pair of Scissors . . .": Quoted in DePauw and Hunt, *Remember the Ladies*, p. 102; "I long to hear . . .": Letter of December 20, 1702, in Pemberton Mss., vol. 3, p. 2, History Society of Pennsylvania, cited in Woody, *Early Quaker Education in Pennsylvania*, p. 182. The original spelling has been kept.

23 MOTHERLESS HOUSEHOLDS: "wait on Gentlemen's children . . .": *Boston Gazette*, May 24, 1736; "A woman who would . . .": *New York Gazette*, April

25, 1765; "a decent middle-aged . . .": *New York Mercury*, April 27, 1767; "under 20 or that . . .": *South Carolina Gazette*, September 11, 1755; "Wanted at a Seat . . .": *Philadelphia Pennsylvania Packet*, September 23, 1780.

24   SLAVES: "The spinners, weavers and . . .": George Mason, quoted in Morgan, *Virginians at Home*, p. 53; Sales: ". . . an excellent spinner on . . .": *Williamsburg Virginia Gazette*, October 25, 1776, and "The woman has been . . .": Ibid., August 6, 1775; Runaway: "Country born Negro woman . . .": Ibid., May, 6, 1773.

24   MOUNT VERNON SLAVES: Mansion house slaves: Fitzpatrick, ed., *The Writings of George Washington* (1970), vol. 32, pp. 256–57. Washington property, listed in two columns, "GW" and DOWER"; Martha Washington and slaves: Wharton, *Martha Washington*, p. 62; "Doll at the Ferry . . .": George Washington to Anthony Whiting, Philadelphia, November 4, 1792, Fitzpatrick, ibid., p. 205.

25   "1 dozen pair stockings . . .": *Mount Vernon Store Book*, January 1, 1787–December 31, 1787, Mount Vernon Ladies' Association of the Union Library.

25   GEORGE WASHINGTON AND SLAVE KNITTING: "The deficiency of Stockings . . .": Letter of November 18, 1792, Fitzpatrick, ibid., p. 232; "And can Lucy find . . .": Letter of December 9, 1792, ibid., pp. 256–57; "making less than their . . .": Letter of December 23, 1792, ibid., p. 258.

Chapter 2:
Knitting for Liberty

page
26   "Women never should meddle . . .": Franklin 1756 letter, in Smyth, ed., *Writings of Franklin*, vol. 3, p. 438.

26–27   "the character of . . .": cited in Ulrich, *Good Wives*, p. 68.

27   "the loss of her . . .": Cited in Crawford, *Social Life in Old New England*, p. 17.

27   "wrinkle their foreheads with . . .": Cited in Holiday, *Woman's Life in Colonial Days*, p. 143.

28   "Let the Daughters of . . .": Moore, "Patriotic Poesy," *William and Mary Quarterly*, XXXIV, April 1977, pp. 307–8.

28   "all the yarn they . . .": *Boston Gazette*, May 21, 1766.

28   "Their Behaviour was decent . . .": *Ipswich Essex Gazette*, June 27, 1769.

28–29   "set to work to . . .": Cited in Adair and Schultz, eds., *Peter Oliver's Origin and Progress of the American Revolution*, p. 63.

29   ENTHUSIASM: Crawford, p. 266.

29   "Knot of Misses busy . . .": Reprinted in the *Portsmouth New Hampshire Gazette*, January 22, 1678.

29   "[T]hey exhibited a fine . . .": *Boston Chronicle*, April 7, 1766.

29   CLOTH PRODUCTION: *Boston News-Letter*, July 6, 1769; Ibid., January 7, 1768; *Boston Evening Post*, November 2, 1767; "endowed with such a . . .": *Portsmouth New Hampshire Gazette*, March 17, 1769.

30   "You may keep your . . .": *Portsmouth New Hampshire Gazette*, May 25, 1770.

30   PRODUCTION IN OTHER AREAS: "Not a Skein was put . . .": *The New-York Gazette and the Weekly Mercury*. February 1, 1768; "I can with Pleasure . . .": *The New England Gazette or the Weekly Post-Boy*, February 29, 1768.

31   "of the Produce and Manufacture . . .": *Philadelphia Pennsylvania Gazette*, May 1, 1766.

31   "coarse Cloathing for themselves . . .": Governor Franklin of New Jersey, n.d., in *Pa. Archives*, 4th ser., III, 332, cited in Tryon, *Household Manufactures in the United States, 1640–1860*, p. 102.

31   "Some few of the poorer . . .": Governor Tryon of North Carolina, January 30, 1767, in *Col. Rec. of N.C.* VII, 429, cited by Tryon, p. 103.

31   "those Persons that annually . . .": *Archives of Md.* XIV, 496, f., cited in Tryon, p. 102. This is interesting in that only "White" inhabitants were to benefit from this bounty.

32   "everyone [could] turn his . . .": "The Committee of Observation and Correspondence for the County of Somerset, in the Province of New Jersey, at their Meeting at Hillsborough, on Wednesday the 14th Instant [1775], took into their Consideration the great Importance of promoting Manufactures in America at this time. . . .": Introduction to a newspaper extract, cited by William S. Stryker, *Archives of the State of New Jersey*, vol. 1 [no others mentioned], in *Documents Relevant to the Revolutionary History of the State of New Jersey* (1901), pp. 45–47.

32   SOLICITATIONS: Ford, ed., *Journals of the Continental Congress*, vol. 8, p. 611.

32   TOWN DONATIONS: Rhode Island: *Records of Rhode Island and Providence Plantation* (1789–83), cited in vol. 9, p. 534. Tryon, p. 115; Dover, Massachusetts: Smith, *A Narrative History of Dover, Massachusetts*, p. 108; New Hampshire women: Meyer, *Petticoat Patriots of the American Revolution*, p. 135; Virginia laws: Grass, *History of Hosiery*, p. 160.

32   "cast your mite into . . .": "To the Spinners in the City and County," August 1775, as cited in Duane, ed., *Extracts from the Diary of Christopher Marshall . . . During the American Revolution*, p. 40.

33   "I used to darn . . .": Williams, *Demeter's Daughters*, p. 258.

33   WINIFRED CARTER: Information supplied to the author through research done by Grace Nylander in Gibbs, *Cloth Production in Virginia to 1800*, unpublished Colonial Williamsburg Research Report, 1978.

33   KNITTERS ELLIOTT AND CARTER: Elliott cited in Engle, *Women in the American*

Revolution, Introduction, p. xiv; Carter cited in Cometti, *Social Life in Virginia,* p. 56. Since Cometti gives no citation, this *may* be the afore-mentioned Winifred Carter.

33   "I have learnt to knit . . .": The Mifflin "Philadelphia Lady" letter appears in virtually every book on Revolutionary War women and was widely published in colonial newspapers. The source cited is: *Williamsburg Virginia Gazette,* January 13, 1776.

34   "the Elizabeths, the Maries . . .": *The Sentiments of an American Woman.* Another broadside was printed in New Jersey.

34   "in the glorious cause . . .": *Philadelphia Pennsylvania Packet and General Advertiser,* July 4, 1780.

34   "[T]he ladies going about . . .": Anna Rawle to Rebecca Rawle Shoe-maker, June 30, 1780, in William Brooke Rawle, "Laurel Hill and Some Colonial Dames Who Once Lived There," *Pennsylvania Magazine of History and Biography* XXX (1911):398.

34   "Women Citizens of the . . .": Anna Wharton Morris, contributor, "The Journal of Samuel Rowland Fisher," *Pennsylvania Magazine of History and Biography* 41 (1917):296.

34   "Miss Humanity" or "Mrs. Worthlittle": Lyman Butterfield, "George Washington's Sewing Circle," *American Heritage,* Summer 1951, p. 8.

34   WOMAN IN OX CART: Mrs. Rhoda Smith Farrand, described in Meyer, p. 135.

35   "that the love of country . . .": Butterfield, p. 68.

35   "[m]any of them absolutely . . .": Ford, ed., *Journals of the Continental Congress,* vol. 14, p. 884.

35   "severe and terrible winter . . .": Smith, "A Reminiscence," *Pennsylvania Magazine of History and Biography* XLVI (January 1922):55.

36   "While the dames of . . .": Egle, *Some American Women During the War of the American Revolution,* p. 118; "One shudders when reading . . .": Sarah Harris Irvine, described by Egle, p. 93.

36   PENNSYLVANIA WOMEN: "stately, dignified . . .": Egle, p. 145; "True to her matronly . . .": Ibid., pp. 148–49; "Not only a devoted . . .": Ibid., p. 169; "She managed carefully . . .": Ibid., p. 201; "During the most trying . . .": Ibid., p. 118.

36–37   "[t]en women in carts . . .": Fowler, *Women on the American Frontier,* pp. 136–37.

37   OLD MOM RINKER: Meyer, pp. 86–87.

37   "Knitting pins of different . . .": *Invoices and Letters,* 1775–6, references from 1773, Mount Vernon Ladies' Association of the Union Library.

37   "old fashioned Virginia house-keeper . . .": Cited in Booth, *The Women of '76,* p. 165.

37   "I will tell you . . .": Cited by Egle, p. 222.

38   WASHINGTON'S EXPENSE ACCOUNT: Booth, p. 162.

38   "somewhat dumpy woman with . . .": Chidsey, *Valley Forge,* p. 110.

38   "startling apparition of a . . .": Meyer, p. 106.

38   "We had a dance at . . .": Cited by Egle, p. 252.

39   "Several of us thought . . .": Bruce, *Women in the Making of America*, pp. 100–101. Bruce reports that Mrs. Troupe was "relating her experience to the wife of the Reverend Joseph P. Tuttle, to whom the present generation owes this interesting side-light on Revolutionary history," but he does not mention whether it was in letter form or not. This particular story is found in many other works on women in the Revolution, but Bruce is the only author who identifies "Mrs. Troupe."

39   "I never in my life . . .": Ibid., pp. 98–99.

40   "ever looked well to . . .": "Lady Washington's Rebuke," *Harper's Bazaar*, August 20, 1870, p. 538.

40–41   "[The room] is nicely fixed . . .": Thane, *Washington's Lady*, pp. 22–23. The writer is identified only as "Mrs. Colonel Carrington."

41   "I won't have it . . .": Gilman, ed., "Eliza Wilkinson to Miss M— P—," n.d., *Letters of Eliza Wilkinson*, p. 61.

41–42   "Let me read what . . .": Ibid., p. 66.

42   TRENTON RECEPTION: "She was what a woman . . .": Stryker, *Washington's Reception by the People of New Jersey in 1789*, p. 13; "The first four lines . . .": Ibid., pp. 6–7.

42   "the mothers of the men . . .": Bruce, p. 80.

43   "[T]hey found there, mingled . . .": Smith, *An Address Delivered in Behalf of the Soldiers of West Cambridge*, p. 53.

Chapter 3:
Knitting in the Circle of
Domesticity

page

44   "I doubt if this society . . .": Mervin M. Deems, *A Home Away from Home*, p. 138.

45   VERMONT KNITTERS: in Katz and Rapone, *Women's Experiences in America*, p. 106.

45   "raise her gentle voice . . .": Muzzey, *The Young Maiden*, p. 23.

45–46   LADIES BOUNTIFUL: "In dispensing of alms . . .": "Address to the Members of the Ladies' Society," *The Constitution of the Ladies' of Columbia*, p. 11; "most appropriate during the . . .": Sigourney, *Letters to Young Ladies*, p. 80; "a little band of seamen's . . .": *Tenth Annual Report of Seamen's Aid Society for the City of Boston*, p. 9; "from poverty, indolence or . . .": *Circular and Constitution of the Salem Children's Friend Society*, p. 5; "The children of the poor . . .": ["By a Lady"], *The Workwoman's Guide* (1838), p. 253.

46   "[t]here is one realm . . .": Muzzey, p. 8.

46–47   MONUMENT FAIR: "although with the hearty . . .": Alpheus S. Packard, *History of the Bunker Hill Monument*, p. 31; "each lady will endeavor . . .": *The Monument*, Boston, February 8; "Ladies in want of . . .": Ibid., September 10; "At the Taunton table . . .": Ibid., September 11; General coverage: *Boston Evening Transcript*, September 8, 9, 1840; "bewitching in the extreme": *Boston Post* coverage referred to in *Boston Transcript*, September 9; "industry, taste, and spirit . . .": Packard, p. 32; "a symbol of the first . . .": Ruth E. Finley, *The Lady of Godey's*, p. 72.

47   Barbara Welter, "The Cult of True Womanhood: 1820–1860," *American Quarterly* XVIII (Summer 1966):152.

47   FACTORY PRICES: "Knitting Cotton wholesale and . . .": *Hartford Courant*, February 2, 1797; "woolen stocking yarn . . .": Ibid., February 14, 1810.

47   "30 pairs of socks . . .": *Niles Weekly Register*, November 23, 1822.

49–50   "Spun, doubled, and twisted . . .": Brown and Bryant, eds., *The Diaries of Sally and Pamela Brown, 1832–1838*, p. 11; subsequent citations from pp. 17, 21, 24–25, 27, 30–34, 38, 44–48, 83, 91.

50   ROBBINS DIARY: "[p]aid a woman for . . .": Tarbox, ed. and annotator, *Diary of Reverend Thomas Robbins, D.D.* vols., vol. 2, p. 443; "[p]aid for knitting, seventy-five . . .": Ibid., p. 730.

50–51   KNITTING FOR PAY: "new knitting needles at . . .": and other diary citations: Mary Salward Barrell, of York, Me., *Detailed Household Accounts & Separate Yarn and Spinning Account*, January 20, 1844; August 7, 1844; December [n.d.], 1840; January 27, 1840; from research done by Jane Nylander; "I have finished . . .": "Diary of Martha Ballard," in Charles E. Nash, *History of Augusta {Maine}*, entry of March 29, 1800, p. 390; Bartering: Carolyn Sherwin Bailey, *Boys and Girls of Pioneer Days from Washington to Lincoln*, pp. 127–28. "Our industrious dames and . . .": "Incorporating Knitting," *New England Farmer and Gardener's Journal*, January 27, 1836, p. 229; "WHAT can she do?": *Petersburg* [Virginia] *American Constellation*, August 12, 1834, cited by Suzanne Lebsock, *The Free Women of Petersburg: Status and Culture in a Southern Town, 1784–1860*, pp. 164–65.

51   "Ladies' Stocking Society . . .": Linda K. Kerber, *Women of the Republic*, p. 111.

51   ZACHARY TAYLOR: Letter to Hancock Taylor, December 22, 1813, Zachary Taylor Papers, R, Alexander Bate Collection, Louisville, Ky., in Holman Hamilton, *Zachary Taylor, Soldier of the Republic*, vol. 1, p. 68.

51   "Shawls were in great . . .": Emery, *Reminiscences of a Nonagenarian*, pp. 277, 280.

52   GRANDMOTHERS: T. R. Arthur, "The Dear Old Grandmother," *Godey's*, May 1858, p. 435; Emery's grandmother: Emery, p. 8.

52   "to employ the fingers . . .": Farrar, *The Young Lady's Friend*, p. 14.

52   "This hard name is . . .": "Calisthenics," *The Lady's Book*, May 1836, p. 209. These articles ran in serial form.

53   "He will endeavor to . . .": Ibid., May 1852, p. 405.

53   BALL GOWNS: *The Ladies' National Magazine* used its May 1846 issue to report: "Ladies will soon begin to make up ball dresses for their sojourn at Saratoga and elsewhere," p. 179.

53   "I started a pair . . .": Brown and Bryant, p. 65; "I knit and read . . .": Ibid., p. 94.

53–54   SARAH HALE ON WOMANHOOD: "judiciously directing the attention . . .": and "aiding them in their . . .": "Cordelia," *Ladies' Magazine*, October 1830, p. 458, and June 1829, p. 282, cited by Nancy F. Cott, *The Bonds of Womanhood*, p. 100.

54   "Mrs. Glazier in Amesville . . .": Maria Foster Brown, cited in Harriet Connor Brown, ed. *Grandmother Brown's Hundred Years*, p. 124.

54–55   WOMAN'S SPECIAL REALM: "quiet employment, favourable to . . .": Sigourney, pp. 90, 80; "It seems real nice . . .": Riley, ed., "Family Life on the Frontier: The Diary of Kitturah Penton Belknap," *Annals of Iowa*, Summer 1977, p. 41; "there is more to pouring . . .": Farrar, pp. 45–46; "[t]hose females who deliver . . .": Mathews, *Letters to School Girls*, p. 224; "Never lie down till . . .": Mavor, *The Catechism of Health*, pp. 21, 42.

55   KNITTING RECOMMENDED: "occupy a distinguished place . . .": *The Ladies' Work Table Book* (1847), Introduction, p. x. The Smithsonian Institution's copy was inscribed "A present from her mother"; "may be seen in . . .": Stephens, *Ladies' Complete Guide to Crochet* (1854), pp. 7, 8; "It seems to me . . .": Maria Mitchell, cited in Merriam, *Growing Up Female in America*, p. 77.

55   SMALL BOOKS: *Ladies' Work-Box Companion* (1850).

55–56   PLAGIARISM: "Nearly all the patterns . . .": Florence Hartley, *The Ladies' Hand Book of Fancy and Ornamental Work* (1859), Introduction, p. 5; "There is not one magazine . . .": Mrs. Pullam's *Lady's Manual of Fancy Work* (1859), Introduction; "allowing my maiden name . . .": Miss Lambert, *Hand-Book of Needlework* (1846), Preface, pp. ix–x. The first edition published in the United States appears to be the one of 1842 published by Wiley and Putnam in New York.

56   "the newest and most . . .": *Knitting, Netting, and Crochet Work* (1844), p. A2. This reference to knitting by German women reminds one of an 1842 English traveller:

> At home and abroad, Sundays and week-days, in private parties and at public out-of-door concerts and in public gardens, the dear, good, industrious souls sit knitting and smiling and gossiping in the seventh heaven of delight. It is to be hoped that there is a German heaven where knitting is one of the appointed rewards of virtue; for without the idea of eternity

of knitting-needles, what German lady could look forward with any comfort. (William Howitt, *The Rural and Domestic Life of Germany*, p. 233.)

57   "Patience will soon lead . . .": *Knitting, Netting . . .* , p. A6; *"Cast over is a term . . .":* Ibid., Glossary, p. x.

57   "[M]any more stitches are . . .": *The Ladies' Guide in Needlework* (1859), p. 149.

57–58   "The narrow piece is . . .": Mrs. Henry Owen, *The Illuminated Book of Needlework* (1847), pp. 93–94.

58   "most comfortable and graceful . . .": Quoted without citation by Ella Shannon Bowles, *Homespun Handicrafts* (1933), p. 90.

59   "when your cap is . . .": *Knitting, Netting, and Crochet Work*, p. 51.

59   "save-all bag . . .": Ibid., p. 28.

59–60   "Dear Sir: I have been . . .": "Godey's Arm Chair," *Godey's Lady's Book*, May 8, 1858, p. 475.

60–61   MCGRANN COUNTERPANE: Julie McGrann Dougherty, of Bethesda, Md., to ALM, enclosing letters from her mother, Barbara McMillan McGrann, of Hilton Head, S.C., and her aunt, Emma McMillan Heighton, of Colborne, Ont., May 18, 1986.

61   RUG OF COTTON ENDS: *Godey's Lady's Book*, n. mo., 1864, n.p., cited by Bowles, p. 91.

61   "We give in this number . . .": *Godey's Lady's Book*, November 1848, p. 34.

61   "a knitting sheath, &c . . .": *The Seamstress* (1848), p. 247.

61   "Keep the ball in . . .": *The Workwoman's Guide*, p. 238.

62   DYES: "Much care is needed . . .": *The Workwoman's Guide*, p. 245; "any color that may . . .": Mee, *A Manual of Knitting, Netting and Crochet* (1844), p. 66 and shell bag, p. 13.

63   KNITTING IN SCHOOL: Woody, *A History of Women's Education in the United States, Report of the Worcester, Massachusetts, Schools* cited by Thornton D. Appolonio, *Boston Public Schools, Past and Present* (1923), p. 7; *Minutes of the East Branch School Trustees*, 1801, cited in Woody, *Quaker Education in the Colony and State of New Jersey*, p. 189.

63   "Woolens should be washed . . .": and subsequent quotations: Child, *The Frugal Housewife*, (1829), pp. 14, 92, 11, Introduction, 1, 3.

64   "Little girls can mend . . .": and subsequent quotations: Child, *The Little Girl's Own Book* (1834), pp. 207, 228, 226.

65   "blind knitting . . .": and subsequent quotation: Stephens, *Ladies' Complete Guide* (1854), pp. 86–87.

65   "mysterious intricacies of toe . . .": and subsequent quotations: Brewster, *Household Economy* (1858), pp. 59–60.

65–66   "two clearly distinct lines . . .": Beecher, *A Treatise on Domestic Economy* (1841), pp. 14, 26.

66   "to delineate to you . . .": *Juvenile Key*, vol. I, September 18, 1830, introductory page.

66   "Her ideas of education . . .": Cited by Ida M. Tarbell, "The American Woman," Part II, *American Magazine*, December 1909, p. 207.

66   "provide for the joint . . .": Farrar, p. 24.

67   "not so fast, of course . . ." and subsequent quotations: Brown, *Grandmother Brown*, pp. 62, 59, 61, 47.

67   "many a wealthy lady's . . .": Virginia De Forrest, "Heel and Toe," *Godey's Lady's Book*, September 1857, pp. 217–18.

67–68   READING AND STUDYING: "I am very busy . . .": Entry for June 9, 1837, in Davis, *The Neglected Thread*, p. 40; "tolerably well" and "I did not need . . .": Larcom, *A New England Girlhood*, pp. 124, 126.

68   "a lazy, shiftless hussy . . .": *Ipswich Register*, January 29, 1837.

68   KNITTING WHILE VISITING: "I shot up into . . .": *Recollections of a Housekeeper*, p. 8; "dressed in our best . . .": Emery, pp. 55, 77.

Chapter 4: Westward Knit!

page

69   "We didn't come in . . .": Oregon Pioneer Association, *Transactions of the 46th Annual Reunion in Portland of June, 1918 and of the 47th Reunion of June, 1919*, v, p. 17, of 46th Convention.

69   "Nancy Morrison's flax-wheel . . .": Herndon, *Days on the Road Crossing the Plains in 1865*, p. 39.

70   "Dusty days were knit . . .": Dye, *The Soul of America*, pp. 19, 56.

70   KNITTING ON THE TRAIL: "knit all the way . . .": Hall, *The Story of Maggie*, manuscript in the Bancroft Library of the University of California at Berkeley, cited by Myres, *Westering Women and the Frontier Experience*, p. 133; Driving oxen and knitting: Hively, *Journal, 1863–64*, in the Denver Public Library, cited in Ibid.

70   "[n]othing seems to stop . . .": Riley, ed., "Family Life on the Frontier: The Diary of Kitturah Penton Belknap," *Annals of Iowa*, Summer 1977, p. 44.

70   EMIGRATION FIGURES: Holmes, ed. and comp., *Covered Wagon Women*: vol. 3, Introduction, p. 9. Owing to cholera reports, the loss of cattle and wagons and the lessening of the hysteria for gold, those figures dropped the following year.

71   "Oh what a loss I'm at . . .": Lucy Rutledge Cooke, in a letter to her sister, in Holmes, II, 294.

71   "During the day we . . .": Catherine M. Haun, "A Woman's Trip Across the Plains," manuscript at the Huntington Library and Art Gallery, San

Marino, Calif., cited in Faragher, *Women and Men on the Overland Trail*, p. 84.

71   "go forth into . . .": *Godey's Lady's Book*, June 1941, p. 281.

72   "our sex forbade further . . .": *Address of Miss Elizabeth Burnham (of San Jose) on the Presentation of the Flag by the Pioneer Ladies of the Society of California Pioneers, Sept. 9, 1853*, p. 1.

73   "I don't know what . . .": Hamlin Garland, *A Pioneer Mother*, p. 9.

73   "They both have to be . . .": Riley, ed., Belknap Diary, p. 48.

73   EMIGRANT GUIDES: "Do not encumber yourselves . . .": Ware, *The Emigrant's Guide to California*, p. 9; "Never get into trouble . . .": Clark, "Overland to the Gold Fields in California in 1852," in Barry, ed., *Kansas Historical Quarterly*, August 1942, p. 240. Other good sources are: Marcy, *The Prairie Traveler*; Hastings, *The Emigrants' Guide to Oregon and California*; Kroll, "Books That Enlightened the Emigrants," *Oregon Historical Quarterly*, June 1944, pp. 103–23. FICTIONALIZED FACSIMILE: Brown, "An Emigrant's Guide for Women," *American West*, September 1970, pp. 13–17, 63.

74   PACKING THE WAGON: Horack, "In Quest of a Prairie Home," *The Palimpset*, July 1924, p. 252, ff.; "four nice little tables . . .": Riley, ed., Belknap Diary, pp. 41, 50; "little peach and cherry . . .": Colt, *Went to Kansas*, p. 40.

74   "as fitten socks as . . .": Waite, *Kate Farley, Pioneer*, p. 13.

74   "Have had two sewing . . .": Colt, p. 23.

74   "Right here I wish . . .": Cummins, *Autobiography and Reminiscences*, pp. 26–27.

74   "Mr. Smith has a coop . . .": Harriet Talcott Buckingham, in Holmes, III, 19.

75   "One luxury we had . . .": Wilson, *Luzena Stanley Wilson, '49er*, p. 2.

75   "After breakfast, I strain . . .": Herndon, p. 17.

75   "While I am writing . . .": Bryant, *Rocky Mountain Adventures*, p. 60.

75   "I could not begin . . .": Mary M. Colby in Holmes, II, 48.

75   "Emigrants and traders will . . .": "WAGONS," *Weston Weekly Platte Argus*, December 26, 1856.

75–76 "best Pittsburgh manufacture": *St. Louis Reveille*, November 19, 1844, and *St. Louis the Osage Yoeman*, November 28, 1844.

76   NEWSPAPER DESCRIPTIONS: "satisfaction and confidence of . . .": *St. Louis Missouri Republican*, May 2, 1846, in Morgan, ed., *Overland in 1846*, vol. 2, p. 512; "young girls, just . . .": *St. Louis Missouri Republican*, May 15, 1846, in Ibid, p. 530.

76–77 FAREWELLS: "[W]hen the day for starting . . .": Arvazine Angeline Cooper reminiscences, "Our Journey Across the Plains from Missouri to Oregon, 1863," in Manuscript Collection 1508, Overland Journeys to the Pacific, Oregon Historical Society, Portland; "I never recall that . . .": Porter, *By Ox Team to California*, pp. 6–7; "I did feel some . . .": Todd, in Hixon,

On to Oregon, pp. 9, 15; "Who is there that . . .": Frizzell, *Across the Plains to California in 1852*, Paltsis, ed., p. 5.

77   DESCRIPTIONS: "The aspect of the prairies . . .": Porter, pp. 14–15; "In the morning of . . .": Royce, *A Frontier Lady*, p. 23.

77–79   DEATH AND ILLNESS: Susan Amelia Cranston, in Holmes, *Covered Wagon Women*, vol. 3, p. 103; "I have suffered so much . . .": Mrs. Velina A. Williams, "Diary of a Trip Across the Plains," in Oregon Pioneer Association, *Transactions*, p. 188. Edwin Bryant wrote feelingly of another interment, "The grave was then closed and carefully sodded with the green turf of the prairie, from whence, annually will spring and bloom its brilliant and many-colored flowers," p. 64; "They [the wolves] dig up . . .": Amelia Hadley, in Holmes, vol. 3, p. 76; "Poor little fellow, we . . .": Lucia Loraine Williams, in Holmes, vol. 3, pp. 131–32; "Mrs. Easton and I . . .": Anna Maria Morris, in Holmes, vol. 2, p. 22; "O how lonely I . . .": Sarah Davis, in Holmes, vol. 2, p. 179.

79   "Three days after my . . .": Lucy Henderson Deady, in Lockley, *The Lockley Files*, p. 86.

79   "Shortly after my brother . . .": Marilla R. Washburn Bailey, in Lockley, pp. 165–66.

79   FEAR OF INDIANS: "Indian tragedies were folklore . . .": Hixon, p. 21; "look out for moccasin tracks . . .": Letter of George L. Curry, printed in the *Reveille*, May 14, 1846, cited by Morgan, II, 518; "A secret dread and . . .": Haun, cited by Lillian Schlissel, *Women's Diaries of the Westward Journey*, pp. 175–76; Captivity Narratives: Glenda Riley, *Women and Indians on the Frontier*, passim;

80   MANIFEST DESTINY: *New York Tribune*, July 19, 1843. "they answered me that . . .": and other quotations: F. Franklin Jameson, ed., "A Narrative of the Captivity and Restauration of Mrs. Mary Rowlandson," *Original Narratives of Early American History*, pp. 131, 135, 144, 151.

80–81   REACTIONS TO MEETING INDIAN WOMEN: "Some of the squaws . . .": Ferris, *The Mormons at Home*, p. 14; "We visited their wickiups . . .": Boquist, *Crossing the Plains with Ox Teams, 1862*, pp. 7, 10. "I must say that . . .": Frizzell, p. 25; "They are the durtyest . . .": Stewart, *Diary of Helen Stewart, 1853*, p. 25; "I always felt sorry . . .": Margaret Archer Murray, "Memoir of William Archer Family," *Annals of Iowa*, Summer 1968, p. 371; "the best looking Indians . . .": Frizzell, p. 18; "I doubt the savage . . .": Hecox, *California Caravans*, pp. 33–34; Male traveler: "I noticed a very . . .": Bryant, p. 137.

81   "I feel rather lonesome . . .": Stewart, p. 2.

81   "When riding, I always rode . . .": Hixon, p. 21.

81   "Precisely because work roles . . .": Schlissel, p. 85.

81   "sweeping up the mud . . .": "Women and Fashion," St. Louis *Reveille*, March 30, 1856.

82   ABBREVIATED ATTIRE: "[I]n passing one house . . .": Harriet Foster Cum-

mings, in Holmes, *Covered Wagon Women*, vol. 4, p. 120, "I should think that . . .": Colt, p. 156; "My sister and I . . .": Ann McAuley, in Holmes, vol. 4, p. 37; "Am wearing the Bloomer . . .": Colt, p. 65; Mountain Climber: Holmes, *A Bloomer Girl on Pike's Peak, 1858*, Spring, ed., pp. 16–17.

82   "We have been traveling . . .": Frances Sawyer, in Holmes, *Bloomer Girl*, p. 90.

82   "compared to the long . . .": Agatz, "A Journey Across the Plains," *Pacific Northwest Quarterly*, April 1936, p. 172.

83   "American lady lectress . . .": Clappe, *The Daily Letters from California Mines in 1851–1852*, pp. 142–43.

83   "My skirts were worn . . .": Wilson, p. 9.

83–84   TRAVEL CLOTHES: "flaming colors would not . . .": Esther M. Lockhart, in Holmes, *Covered Wagon Women*, vol. 3, p. 155; "practical color": Nelson, *My Sister and I* (1973), p. 7; "Starched stiff and ironed . . .": Herndon, p. 39; "I presented a comfortable . . .": Haun, cited by Schlissel, p. 168.

84   LONELINESS: "I am so anxious . . .": Lydia Allen Rudd, cited by Schlissel, p. 198; "I would have given . . .": Frizzell, p. 29.

84   "It was two days . . .": Ward, *The Mormon Wife*, p. 175.

84–85   WAGON TRAIN LAYOVERS: "I especially enjoyed the . . .": Esther Lockart, in Kenneth Holmes, *Covered Wagon Women*, vol. 3, p. 153; "We did not keep . . .": Haun diary, cited by Faragher, p. 9; "There were a great . . .": Boquist, p. 18; ". . . the ladies busily employed . . .": Bryant, pp. 23, 69. Bryant later recalled nearing another encampment at night: "The tents and wagon-covers at the distance of a mile, appeared in the moonlight like a cluster of small white cottages comprising a country village. . . . The scene was peaceful and pleasing, awakening such emotions as are felt when revisiting some favorite haunt of boyhood, engraven upon the memory and consecrated by juvenile affection" (p. 77).

85   "My mother's test for . . .": Case, *Hudson of Long Ago*, p. 3.

85   "I think the most unhappy . . .": Bethinia Owens Adair, cited by Vuolvo in "Lost Women: Pioneer Diaries, the Untold Story of the West," *Ms. Magazine*, May 1975, p. 34.

85–86   "the awe they at first . . .": Memoirs of Mrs. Harriet Low Holbrook as told to her daughter, in *Told by the Pioneers*, p. 150.

86   INDIAN TALE: Mrs. Eva M. Hamilton, as told in Bauersfield, *Tales of the Early Days*, p. 12.

86   "The women and the girls . . .": Adams, *Pioneer Life for Little Children*, p. 24.

86   "I find the wool . . .": Riley, ed., Belknap Diary, p. 40.

86   "[N]ever could one familiar . . .": Ellet, *Pioneer Women of the West*, p. 233.

86–87   "smothered embers [were] not . . .": Story of Mary Craig Carpenter Dunlevy, related by Ellet, pp. 229–29.

87   PRAISE FROM SONS: "I can see her yet . . .": Orr, *Reminiscences of a Pioneer Boy*, reprinted from *Annals of Iowa*, no. 7, Winter 1971, and no. 8, Spring 1971, pp. 30–31; "Mother bore and cared . . .": George C. Duffield, "An Iowa Settler's Homestead," *Annals of Iowa*, October 1903, p. 210.

87–88   PRAISE FROM DAUGHTERS: Elizabeth Lotz Treat Longmire, in *Told by the Pioneers*, p. 71; "The buzzing hum of . . .": Closz, *Reminiscences of Newcastle, Iowa, 1848*, descriptions and quotation: pp. 195, 167, 192; ". . . if the dye was red . . .": Huffman, quoted in Stratton, *Pioneer Women*, pp. 66–67.

88   "Just as beaver pelts . . .": Harriet Elizabeth Tuctness Bailey, in Lockley, p. 148.

88   FLEECE: Douthit, *The Souvenir of Western Women*, p. 81.

88   "sometimes the women . . .": "Pioneer Home-Makers of the 1840's," unpublished manuscript, Sheba Hargreaves, Sheba Manuscript Collection, Mss 375, Oregon Historical Society, p. 16.

88   "Louvina and I were doing . . .": Hixon, pp. 46, 45.

89   "If we went visiting": Susannah McFarland quoted in Zimmerman and Carstonsen, "Pioneer Women in Southwestern Washington Territory," *Pacific Northwestern Quarterly* (October, 1976), p. 141.

89   SOD HOUSES: "Well do I remember . . .": and experiences: Mrs. Jane Shellhase, of Kearney, Neb., in *Sod House Memories*, vol. 2, pp. 163–64; "who would crawl in . . .": Mrs. Lottie Gilmore, ibid., p. 154; "It was one of the most . . .": Ibid., p. 137.

90   "Mother spent her leisure . . .": Lenroot, *Long, Long, Ago*, p. 7.

90   "beautiful gauze-like shirts": Maria Fost Brown, cited in Brown, ed., *Grandmother Brown's Hundred Years, 1827–1927*, pp. 123–24.

90   "We always had white . . .": Murray, pp. 360–61.

91   "Everyone was as happy . . .": Towne, *Old Pioneer Days*, p. 122.

91   "[w]ear the good cloth . . .": Brigham Young, quoted in Gates, *History of the Young Ladies' Mutual Improvement Association*, p. 9.

91   UTAH STATE FAIR: Carter, comp., *Heart Throbs of the West*, pp. 310–11.

91   "Learn them to sew . . .": Brigham Young and Heber C. Kimball, "The Fourteenth General Epistle to the Latter-day Saints," *Journal History of the Church* (December 10, 1856), p. 4.

91   "exactly on the same basis . . .": Tributes to "The Other Mother: Early Utah Pioneer Homes of More Than One Mother," in Carter, p. 273; "One strong factor in . . .": Ibid., p. 282.

92   BRIGHAM YOUNG: "Have a place for everything . . .": Discourse of Brigham Young, reported in *Journal History of the Church*, pp. 5, 6; "This will do on . . .": Remarks of President Brigham Young on Sunday, August 18, 1872, printed in *Deseret News*, August 28, 1872; "walking through the streets . . .": Discourse by President Brigham Young, reprinted in *Deseret News*, October 23, 1872, pp. 568–69.

92–93   "Give her responsibility . . .": *Deseret Evening News*, May 19, 1869. Interestingly, the Relief Society organization has continued into the twentieth century, focusing on economic activities rather than dress reform.

93 RETRENCHMENT: "those disgustingly short ones . . .": From the ARTICLES of the Young Ladies' Department of the Co-Operative Retrenchment Association, organized in Salt Lake City, 1869, cited by Gates, p. 12; "pride, folly and fashions . . .": Gates, p. 11; "You will hardly find . . .": Brigham Young, in John A. Wildtsoe, sel. and arr., *Discourses of Brigham Young* (1925), cited as "14:101," p. 336; Young's wives as role models: Leonard J. Arrington, "The Economic Role of Pioneer Mormon Women," *The Western Humanities Review*, Spring 1955, pp. 148–49; Relief Society: Eliza Snow, in *The Woman's Exponent*, September 1, 1875, p. 62.

93–94 SERICULTURE: Arrington, pp. 153–54.

94 CHICAGO FAIR: "Yarn was spun very": "Yarn Making as told by Mrs. James Crawford, Jr.," in Carter, pp. 296–297. "While we point with": Electa Bullock, "Industrial Women," in *The Congress of Women*, p. 510.

95 "Story of Lucy Vincent Smith on the Nautilus," in Whiting and Hough, *Whaling Wives*, p. 163.

95 "fertile in expedients . . .": Fowler, *Women on the American Frontier*, p. 193.

95 "earliest Pilgrims to this . . .": Society of California Pioneers, *Transactions, January 12–May 7th, 1863*, part I, vol. 2, pp. 42, 45.

96 "I remember filling my . . .": Luzena Stanley Wilson, quoted by Schlissel, p. 61.

96 CULTURAL ROLE CHANGE: Katz and Rapone, *Women's Experiences in America*, p. 308.

96 "guardian[s] of our race": Fowler, p. 489.

96 FRONTIERSWOMEN "DEVIANTS" FROM WOMEN'S SPHERE: Riley, *Frontierswoman: The Iowa Experience*, p. 52.

96 "It was hard, *hard* . . .": Brown, ed., p. 127.

Chapter 5:
Knitting for the Blue

page

97 COMPLAINTS: *Personal Reminiscences and Experiences by Members of the 103rd Volunteer Infantry*, pp. 246, 271, 298.

97 "And I want to know . . .": Letter written from Franklin, Ga, November 10, 1861, in Peddy, *Saddle Bag and Spinning Wheels*, p. 14.

97 "a possibility of going . . .": Delia Colton, to Matthias Baldwin Colton, cited in Colton, *The Civil War Correspondence of Matthias Baldwin Colton*, p. 71.

98   "Three pairs of socks . . .": Quoted in Brayton and Terry, *Our Acre and Its Harvest*, p. 63.

98–99   HANNAH HAWS: Office of the Quartermaster General, Consolidated Correspondence Files, 1794–1915, National Archives, R.G. 92, Box 389, entry 225.

99   "not one unneeded stitch": New England Auxiliary Association Branch of the Sanitary Commission, *First Annual Report* (1862), p. 11.

99   "Let us, with one voice . . .": New England Executive Auxiliary Association Branch of the Sanitary Commission, *Third Annual Report* (1864), Report of the Executive Committee, p. 13.

99   "loving woman in our land": Ibid., *Second Annual Report* (1864), p. 9.

100   "Every woman in the country . . .": *Detroit Free Press*, October 10, 1861. This same announcement appeared in all northern newspapers.

100   SELLING THE COMMISSION: "nationalized the humanity and . . .": Women's Central Association of Relief, "How Can We Best Help Our Camps and Hospitals?", p. 15; U.S. Sanitary Commission, *The Soldier's Friend*, pp. 10–11.

100   "Tender hearts, if you . . .": "A Call to My Country-Women," *Atlantic Monthly*, March 1863, p. 346.

100   "I have not attended . . .": Glenda Riley, ed., "Civil War Letters of Harriet Jane Thompson," *Annals of Iowa*, Spring 1970, pp. 311–12.

101   "the principal resort of . . .": *History of the Hartville {PA} Ladies' Aid Society*, pp. 4–5.

101   "Last Monday Jule and I . . .": Delia Colton, to Matthias Baldwin Colton, Philadelphia, September 21, 1862, in Colton, pp. 134–35.

101   NEWSPAPER APPEALS: "so that warm socks . . .": *Cleveland Leader*, January 31, 1863; appeal to German ladies: *Detroit Free Press*, August 25, 1861.

101–2   "when the hive stopped . . .": and subsequent Cleveland descriptions: Brayton and Terry, pp. 72, 73, 41; "We darn and patch . . .": Hartville Ladies' Aid, p. 6.

102   "Knit! Knit! Knit! . . .": Hubbard, *The Knitting Song*. Only two of four verses are given here.

103   "In this way we soon . . .": Soldiers' Aid Society of Northern Ohio, *First Annual Report to the United States Sanitary Commission of the Soldiers' Aid Society of Northern Ohio* (1862), pp. 88–89.

103   "one of the most enthusiastic . . .": *Report Concerning the Special Relief Service of the U.S. Sanitary Commission* (1864), p. 8.

103–4   BOSTON KNITTING: New England Woman's Auxiliary, *Second Annual Report*, p. 11; G. J. Howe, *List of Contributions Received*, passim.; "My first pair were . . .": Hall, *Memories Grave and Gay*, p. 141.

104   "a period of dire . . .": Report of Henry W. Bellows, in Women's Central Relief Association [NY], *Second Annual Report*, p. 8.

104   BOSTON LADIES: "tempted to devote to . . .": *Annual Report of the Fragment Society* [Boston, Mass.], December 1862, Schlesinger Library, Radcliffe

College, MC 338 12V, Series II, Box 2; "a large number of ladies . . .": "New England Women's Auxiliary Association," in L. P. Brockett and Mrs. Mary C. Vaughan. *Woman's Work in the Civil War*, pp. 557, 588.

105 NOTES ENCLOSED: "The fortunate owner of . . .": Mrs. Bartlett, cited in Bruce, *Woman in the Making of America*, p. 193; "Close by the old . . .": and other Philadelphia verse quotations: Gillespie, *A Book of Remembrance*, pp. 101, 119 (Gillespie was Franklin's great-granddaughter); "Brave Sentry, on your . . .": Brayton and Terry, p. 62.

105–6 BLANKETS AND QUILTS: "cheered by the sight . . .": Brayton and Terry, p. 62; "Dixon is very anxious . . .": *Hartville Ladies' Aid*, p. 14.

106 SOLDIER KNITTING: Coco, comp. and ed., *Through Blood and Fire*, p. 107.

106 SHIPMENT TO THE FRONT: *Hartville Ladies' Aid*, pp. 25–26.

107–8 CLEVELAND AID SOCIETY: "It was not in the hearts . . .": and subsequent descriptions: Brayton and Terry, pp. 63, 66–67, "Harper Austin received a . . .": and subsequent references: Butler, *Letters Home*, pp. 33, 34, 40, 42, 45.

108 "I received the package . . .": Mason, in *Personal Reminiscences*, pp. 339–40.

108 MILWAUKEE WOMEN: "A box of mittens . . .": and other references: Hurn, *Wisconsin Women in the War Between the States*, p. 29.

109 "We gave three rousing . . .": Captain Trumbull, 10th C.V., to Mrs. Cowen of the Hartford Soldiers' Aid Society, reprinted in the supplement to the *Hartford Courant*, January 14, 1865.

109 "Be careful and keep . . .": Colton, pp. 122–23.

109–10 CHILDREN AND YOUNG ADULTS: "Merry's Monthly Chat with His Friends," *Merry's Museum*, November 1862, p. 153; September 1862, p. 90; "large number of young . . .": *Detroit Daily Advertiser*, December 30, 1861; "Wanted! A correspondence wanted . . .": *Rochester {Ind.} Chronicle*, January 12, 1865.

110 SCHOOLCHILDREN: "children of Public School . . .": Woman's Relief Association of the City of Brooklyn, *Report* (1863), p. 10; "caught the spirit of . . .": Soldiers' Aid Society of Northern Ohio, p. 15; "do their duty faithfully . . .": Alcott, *Little Women*, pp. 8–9.

110–11 NEW YORK FAIR: "great market . . .": *Metropolitan Fair in Aid of the United States* (1864), p. 4; "A great many earnest . . .": Sherwood, *An Epistle to Posterity*, p. 89; Passaic Fund-raising: Ladies' Relief Society of Passaic, N.J., *Report of the Ladies' Relief Society* (1865), p. 3.

111 ROCHESTER FAIR: "surpasses in beauty anything . . .": [Rochester] Ladies' Hospital Relief Association, *Report of the Christmas Bazaar, Held Under the Auspices of the Ladies' Hospital Relief Association* (1864), p. 47.

111 CINCINNATI FAIR: *Great Western Sanitary Fair Papers*, U.S. Sanitary Commission, Cincinnati Branch, Financial Records, Cincinnati Historical Society, Box 37, Folders 21, 24, 32.

111 CLEVELAND FAIR: "marvels of knitting . . .": Brayton and Terry, pp. 172–73.

111–12 CHICAGO FAIR: "On every road leading . . .": Greenbie, *Lincoln's Daughters of Mercy*, p. 186; "I desire to retain . . .": Cited in Young, *The Women and the Crisis*, p. 311; "a sight such as . . .": *Our Daily Fare*, June 9, 1863, referring to the Great Northwestern Fair held in Chicago in September 1863; "I don't approve of . . .": Young, p. 310.

112–13 PHILADELPHIA FAIR: "What is called an . . .": *Our Daily Fare*, June 9, 1863.

113 ROCHESTER FAIR: "stock of hair is . . .": [Rochester] *Christmas Bazaar*, p. 47.

113 SCHOOLCHILDREN AT FAIRS: *Philadelphia Enquirer*, July 11, 1864; "Ten little girls, whose . . .": Goodrich, *The Tribute Book*, p. 89.

113–14 MONEY RAISED: Greenbie, p. 187.

114 "The cry of relief . . .": Ladies' Relief Association of the District of Columbia, *Proceedings on Opening of the Patent Office Fair*, p. 21.

114 "so much *talking* and . . .": and subsequent citations: Cornelia Hancock, *The South After Gettysburg*, pp. 34, 35, 36, 40.

115 "The American Woman is . . .": and "[To] The Loyal Women . . .": Mussey, "Response," {a response to a toast to} "The Loyal Women of 1861–1865", pp. 6, 3.

Chapter 6:
Knitting for the Gray

page
116 "wandering out of your . . .": and subsequent quotations: Phelps, *Hours with My Pupils*, pp. 299, 37, 47.

116 "So long as she . . .": Fitzhugh, *Sociology for the South*, pp. 214–15.

117 "We are weak in . . .": Diary of Judith Brockenbrough McGuire, in Andrews, *The Women of the South in War Times*, pp. 76–77.

117 "None can read the . . .": *Our Women in the War*, Introductory page to the series of sketches.

117 "Evenings at home, formerly . . .": Putnam, *Richmond During the Civil War*, p. 88.

118 "Mothers of the Company Boys . . .": Anderson, *North Carolina Women of the Confederacy*, p. 95.

118 "I put one 'round . . .": Missouri Division, United Daughters of the Confederacy, *Reminiscences of the Women of Missouri During the Sixties*, pp. 106–7.

118 "soft, pretty lamb's wool . . .": Gay, *Life in Dixie During the War*, pp. 200–1.

118 "a little camp cot . . .": Mary Ann Webster Loughborough, whose letters

and journals were published in New York in 1864, cited in Merriam, *Growing Up Female*, pp. 93–94.

119   "The ladies of our town . . .": Mrs. Brunson on War Work in Greenville, S.C., in South Carolina State Division, United Daughters of the Confederacy, *South Carolina Women in the Confederacy*, Taylor, ed., vol. 2, p. 26.

119–20   WAR WORK SOCIETIES: "The young ladies established . . .": Mrs. Samuel M. Meek, in United Daughters of the Confederacy, West Point, Miss., *War Reminiscences of Columbus, Mississippi, and Elsewhere, 1861–1865*, p. 24; "The ladies knit and . . .": Miss C. Waring, of Black Oak, S.C., in *South Carolina Women*, vol. 1, pp. 58–59.

120   REPORTS OF SMALL GROUPS: "A Knitting Society was . . .": Report from the town of Abbeville, in *South Carolina Women*, vol. 1, p. 70; "The Association shall meet . . .": Minutes of the Eutaville [SC] Aid Association, in Ibid., 59; "Early in 1864 about . . .": Report on Spartanburg, in Ibid., vol. 2, p. 44.

120   "There is nothing to . . .": Massey, *Refugee Life in the Confederacy*, p. 127.

120–21   "a bordering of vines . . .": Hague, *A Blockaded Family*, pp. 50–51.

121   "In the wide halls . . .": Beers, *Memories*, pp. 54–55.

122   "We spent all our . . .": Cited in Wiley, *Confederate Women*, p. 145.

122   "The few minutes before . . .": Sarah Morgan Dawson, in Robertson, ed., *A Confederate Girl's Diary*, p. 88; "I do not know . . .": Chestnut, *Diary from Dixie*, Ben Ames Williams, ed., pp. 121, 128.

122–23   NEWSPAPER ANNOUNCEMENTS: "Ladies Knitting Society: Having . . .": *Savannah Daily Morning News*, August 18, 1864; "To widows and wives . . .": Ibid., advertising section, September 1, 1864; "Wheeler and Wilson sewing . . .": *Edgerfield {South Carolina} Advertiser*, August 29, 1861.

123   ALABAMA KNITTERS: *Greensboro Alabama Beacon*, August 9, 1862, cited in Sterkx, *Partners in Rebellion*, p. 99.; "[M]any willing fingers are . . .": Report of the Military Aid Society of Mobile, Statement of Work from May 4, 1861 to November 1, 1861, in Caroline Hausman to Governor Gill Shorter, October 1862, Executive Papers, cited by Sterkx, p. 99; Governor's statement cited by Sterkx, p. 107.

123–24   KNITTING VELOCITY AND PRODUCTIVITY: "Our fingers were never . . .": Rose W. Fry, of Bowling Green, Ky., in *Our Women in the War*, p. 427; "Every woman in town . . .": Helen R. Garner, in *War Reminiscences of Columbus*, p. 14; "I became such an . . .": Mrs. George Butler, in *South Carolina Women*, vol. 2, p. 136. "I recollect, too, to . . .": Mrs. Virginia C. Tarr, Ibid., vol. 1, p. 29. "I knitted a sock . . .": Gay, p. 29; "The girls knitted hundreds . . .": Anderson, p. 15; "We women spun, wove . . .": Alice Campbell, president of the Young Woman's Knitting Society of Fayetteville, N.C., in Anderson, p. 15 (Anderson adds that Campbell used "the same large needles for the boys of the World War that she used for the boys in Gray"); "Everybody knitted socks . . .": Beers, p.

56; "Miss Ann McCall . . .": Mrs. Brunson, on war work in Greenville, S.C., in *South Carolina Women*, vol. 2, p. 26; "tasked herself a sock . . .": John Singleton's 1899 recollections of Mrs. John Brown, of Wedgerfield, S.C., in *South Carolina Women*, vol. 1, p. 100.

124   "[T]he man would have . . .": Macon and Conway, *Reminiscences of the Civil War*, pp. 10–11.

124   "lay aside her books . . .": "By a Charleston Woman," in *Our Women in the War*, p. 281.

125   "With what delight, after . . .": Putnam, p. 87.

125   "I can only plead . . .": Macon and Conway, p. 10.

125–26   CHILDREN: "The children were taught . . .": Mrs. T. C. Albergotti, of Orangeburg, S.C., in *South Carolina Women*, vol. 2, pp. 36–37; "house-girl": Z. E. C. Fleming, of Abbeville District, Ibid., vol. 2, p. 31; "absorbed but . . .": Ibid., vol. 1, p. 80.

126   CONFEDERATE CANDLES: Mrs. Ruth McLaurin, Historian of Sumter County, S.C., in *South Carolina Women*, vol. 2, pp. 172–73; "Southern sympathizers": Beers, p. 117.

126   OLD AND YOUNG KNITTING TOGETHER: "with a vengeance": *Our Women in the War*, p. 454; "mystery of the 'turning . . .": Anderson, pp. 23–24, 15; "untutored in this branch . . .": Putnam, pp. 87–88.

126–27   CHILDREN IN NEWSPAPERS: "[F]rom Miss Maggie Horlbeck. . .": *Charleston Mercury*, November 9, 1864; Sumter matron: Mrs. Ruth McLaurin, in *South Carolina Women*, vol. 2, p. 172.

127   PACKAGE: "pretty necktie, a pair . . .": Gay, p. 43; "Strange as it may . . .": Beers, p. 50; "How faithfully I tried . . .": "By an Old Southern Girl" in United Daughters of the Confederacy, Arkansas Division, Elliott, comp., *The Garden of Memories*, p. 24.

127   "for the bountiful and . . .": Cited in *South Carolina Women in the Confederacy*, vol. 2, p. 48.

127   "stringing my griefs and . . .": Beers, p. 25.

128   "There isn't anything in . . .": Butler, *Letters Home*, p. 92.

128   "in our isolated corner . . .": Pringle, *Chronicles of "Chicora Wood"*, pp. 196, 198.

128   "It would seem very . . .": LeConte, *When the World Ended*, p. 84.

128–29   SHORTAGES: "I am so impatient . . .": Diary of Susan Bradford, of Pine Hill Plantation, Leon County, Fla., September 1, 1863, cited in Jones, *Heroines of Dixie*, p. 259; Parthenia Hague remembered needles of "seasoned hickory or oakwood a foot long, or even longer" and described other improvisations, pp. 50, 52.

129   MAKING AND DYEING NEW YARN: "from mansion to hamlet": *Our Women in the War*, vol. 1, p. 454; "Just take a good . . .": "Mrs. W. A.," Ibid., p. 401.

129   SERICULTURE: Finger, "Some Womanly Recollections of the War Between the States," *Carolina and the Southern Cross*, February 1914, p. 17.

129   PARASOL SKIRT: Mrs. J. V. Franklin, of Augusta, Ga., in *Our Women in the War*, vol. 1, p. 62.

129–30 GREENVILLE LADIES' ASSOCIATION: "great sympathy and untiring . . .": Letter to Culpepper, Va., in *Minutes of the Proceedings of the Greenville Ladies' Association*, Patton, ed., *Historical Papers of Trinity College Historical Society* (1937), Series XX, p. 67. Subsequent citations will be to *Minutes*.

130–32 MINUTES: The sequence of material used appears on pp. 21,38–39, 58–59, 64, 56, 57, 60, 61, 67, 69, 70. After the society disbanded, those who formed the nucleus of the organization turned their efforts in the postwar years toward building a Confederate Monument in Greenville, a project that was completed in 1892.

132   "is so small that . . .": Letter to Miss Jeanette Emily Conrad, of Harrisonburg, in Mary Custis Lee Papers, Confederate Museum, Richmond, cited in Jones, *Ladies of Richmond, the Confederate Capital*, p. 153.

132   TABLEAUX VIVANTS: Sterkx, pp. 56–57.

133   "We would especially invite ...": Soldier's Relief Association, *To the Friends of the Southern Cause at Home*, p. 2.

133   "Miss M. J. Brown respectfully . . .": *Savannah Morning News*, February 1, 1865.

Chapter 7:
Mid-Century Knitters

page
134   GODEY'S MAGAZINE: Finley, *The Lady of Godey's*, p. 177; "The great charm in . . .": "Work Department," *Godey's Lady's Book*, August 1861, p. 161.

134–35 JANE WEAVER PATTERNS: "crimson zephyr [with] fine . . .": *Peterson's*, May 1862, p. 142; "really indispensable [for] going . . .": *Peterson's*, September 1865, p. 208; beaded bag: Ibid., September 1862, pp. 145–46; "knitted Opera Hood": Ibid., October 1865, p. 28; "knitted jacket": Ibid., May 1864, p. 381.

135   IMPERIAL DRESS ELEVATOR: "so easy of application . . .": *Demorest's Magazine*, April 1865, advertisement opposite p. 193; "neat dark, durable skirts . . .": Ibid., p. 203.

135   ICE SKATING: "accommodations for warmth and . . .": *Demorest's Magazine*, April 1865, p. 203.

136   "A great deal of . . .": Lenroot, *Long, Long, Ago*, p. 21.

136   ECONOMIC SITUATION: Penny, *The Employments of Women*, pp. 454, 447.

136–37 "without parallel in the . . .": Brockett, *The Philanthropic Results of the War in America*, pp. 119, 122.

137   "no further need of . . .": *Report of the Ladies' Relief Society* (1865), p. 7.

137–39 SELF-RELIANT WOMEN: "industrious, self reliant, truthful . . .": Croly ["Jennie June"], "Amiability," *Demorest's Illustrated Monthly*, April 1865, pp. 186–87; "Holiday Gifts": Ibid., January 1866, p. 5.

139   "O, keep women to . . .": Penny, *Think and Act*, pp. 20, 21.

139   NEEDY SOUTHERN WOMEN: "Since my husband's death . . .": Letter from a resident of Prince Edward County, Va., in Anne Middleton Holmes, *The New York Ladies' Southern Relief Association 1866–1867*, p. 35; "I have been using . . .": Letter from John D. Easter, Ibid., p. 41.

139–40   "the officers of . . .": *Home Fair Journal*, May 20, 1865, cited in Hurn, *Wisconsin Women in the War Between the States*, p. 171.

140   MITTENS: "still young in health . . .": Ingram, *The Centennial Exposition, Described and Illustrated*, p. 368; Mrs. Lovering: *The New Century for Women* (May 27, 1876), p. 1; Mrs. Champneys: McCabe, *The Illustrated History of the Centennial Exhibition*, p. 219.

140–41   Aiken "American Family Knitting Machine": Advertisement in *Harper's Weekly*, January 7, 1871.

141   DORCAS MAGAZINE: "the delicate daughter of . . .": *Dorcas Magazine*, January 1884, p. 1; Press kudos: *Harrisburg {Pa.} Daily Patriot, Lowell {Mass.} Daily Courier* and *Wilmington {Del.} Morning News*, cited by *Dorcas Magazine*, March 1884, p. 115; "those books and periodicals . . .": Ibid., December 1884, p. 1.

141–42   HOUSEWORK: Strasser, *Never Done*, passim.; "giantesses . . . those matrons of that . . .": Woolson, *Women in Modern Society*, p. 258; "incessant trials of temper . . .": Beecher and Stowe, *The American Woman's Home*, pp. 2–3; "little lady of the . . .": Jones and Williams, *Ladies' Fancy Work*, vol. 3, *Williams' Household Series* (1875), Preface.

142   WOMAN'S SPHERE AND KNITTING: "With some women brain-work . . .": Sherwood, *Amenities of Home*, pp. 41, 75; "The quiet, even, regular . . .": *Dorcas Magazine*, March 1844, p. 1; "The little work-tables of . . .": Jane Croly, *Knitting and Crochet* (1885), quoting from "Richter," title page.; "Absolute inactivity of the . . .": "Work for Idle Hours," *Mme. Demorest's Semi-Annual What to Wear and How to Make It for the Spring and Summer of 1883*, p. 44; "It was deemed wise . . .": Bixby-Smith, *Adobe Days*, p. 14.

143   "A woman who has . . .": Hale, ed., *Plain Needlework, Knitting, and Mending*, Tilton's Needlework Series, no. 4 (1879), p. 22.

143   "tended strictly to her . . .": *Report of the Kansas Board of World's Fair Managers*, p. 43.

143–44   VACATION KNITTING: "It is impossible to . . .": *Dorcas Magazine*, June 1884, p. 174; "coquettish aprons, lace trimmed . . .": "Work for Idle Hours," *Mme. Demorest's Semi-Annual {etc}*, p. 47; "nothing is more truly . . .": "Fancy Work at Watering Places," *Demorest's*, Spring and Summer of 1880, p. 38; "daintily plying her needles": George L. Osgood, *"Knitting the Scarf"* (song) (1880); Continental knitting: Elvina Corbould, ["E.M.C."] *The Lady's Knitting Book* (1879), Introduction, p. x.

144 ARGUMENTS AGAINST TOO MUCH NEEDLEWORK: "how much embroidery is . . .": Patterson, *The American Girl of the Period*, p. 143; needlework a "trifling pursuit": Woolson, *Woman in American Society*, p. 53; Wellesley: *Godey's Lady's Book*, November 18, 1876, p. 474.

144-45 "I wish to warn . . .": S. Weir Mitchell, M.D., "When the College is Hurtful to a Girl" [an address to the students four years before publication], *The Ladies' Home Journal*, June 1901, p. 14.

145 "There are ineradicable differences . . .": Bevier and Usher, *The Home Economics Movement*, I, 23.

146 WOMEN'S CLUBS: "her nervous system was . . .": Croly, *Sorosis* (1868), p. 13; "I believe that it . . .": Grover Cleveland, "Woman's Mission and Woman's Clubs," *The Ladies' Home Journal*, May 1905, pp. 3-4; "We have tipped the . . .": Ross, *Taste in America*, p. 51.

146-47 DORCAS CONTEST: "The reason for this . . .": *Dorcas Magazine*, February 1885, p. 1; "The first premium for . . .": Ibid., October 1885, p. 1; Other responses: Ibid., January 1886, pp. 2-3.

147-49 FINANCIAL CRISES: "the great army of . . .": Heron, *Dainty Work for Pleasure and Profit* (1891), pp. 399-400; "the most disastrous of . . .": H. B. Claflin Company, *Report for the Season Ending December 31st, 1893*, p. 1; "from Maine to California . . .": Heron, *Ladies Work for Pleasure and Profit* (1894), p. 326; Women's exchanges: *Dorcas Magazine*, April 1884, p. 1; "garments which cannot be . . .": Ibid., April 1886, p. 1.

149 "Lady agents wanted in . . .": *The Needle at Home* (1885).

149 MENDING AND REKNITTING: "You will cut out . . .": Power, *Anna Maria's House-Keeping* (1884), p. 179; Kerzman, *How to and What to Knit* (1884), pp. 14-17; "The best book on . . .": *Modern Priscilla*, December 1887, p. 5.

149 SENTIMENTAL STORY: "The Knitting-Needles," *Dorcas Magazine*, January 1884, pp. 159-60.

150-51 GRANDMOTHERS: "There is no *genre* . . .": Sherwood, *Amenities of the Home*, vol. 5, *Appleton's Home Books* (1884), pp. 79-80; "even if she has . . .": Hale, *The Art of Knitting* (1881), Preface, p. iv.; "One should be very . . .": Hall, *Social Customs* (1887), pp. 252-53; "those ladies who have . . .": *Ladies' and Gentlemen's Book of Etiquette* (1882), p. 8; "Life is a . . .": Hale, ed., *Plain Needlework*, p. 59.

151 "This time shall not . . .": Ibid., pp. 37-39.

152-53 SHOPPING: Pasdermadjian, *The Department Store*, pp. 10, 25.

153-54 MAIL ORDER: "How doth the busy . . .": Farnham, *Home Beautiful* (1883), pp. 20, 28; "[W]e believe that every . . .": *Home Needlework Magazine*, March 1905, p. 383; Instruction books: *Lady's Bazaar*, September 1879, p. 415, and December 1879, p. 94; "The pleasure of knitting . . .": Sears Roebuck & Co., *Catalogue*, no. 104, 1897, p. 332.

154 YARNS: "a slight thing makes . . .": Corbould, Introduction, p. ix; "Merino is the thickest . . .": Ibid., p. x.

154–55   GAUGE: "many do not consider . . .": Croly, *Knitting and Crochet*, p. 13; Corbould on "couvrettes": Introduction, pp. ix, x; "In working these patterns . . .": *Dorcas Magazine*, November 1884, p. 1; "Each rib of the design . . .": *Harper's Bazaar*, December 10, 1879, p. 789. This same issue featured a "Netted Ball Bag to hold balls of yarn or worsted while working"; "Knit a few rows . . .": Croly, p. 14.

155   FASCINATOR: "place the end with . . .": *Rules and Designs for Silk Knitting* (1888), p. 46. Another pattern for a "fascinator" describes it as suitable in "summer evenings when a light covering is needed for the head" and is made by gathering the ends together with a tassel or bow on each end, pleating the straight side across the forehead and "there placing a cream-white satin bow" (*Knitting and Crochet* (1889), p. 25).

155–56   NEW NEEDLE ARTS BOOKS: "Books of new designs . . .": Shields, *The Ladies' Guide to Needlework, Embroidery, etc.* (1877), p. 73; "the loud call for . . .": Arnold, *Miss Arnold's Book of Crocheting, Knitting, and Drawn Work* (1880), Introduction, [n.p.].

156   DESCRIPTIONS OF KNITTED GOODS: Corbould, pp. 32, 34, 59; Burton, *The Lady's Book of Knitting and Crochet* (1874), pp. 69, 70, 73, 77, 78, 83, 92, 96, 103.

156   WASHING: "These petticoats pull out . . .": Burton, p. 78; Shrinkage: Corbould, Introduction, p. ix; "First braid the tassels . . .": Kernan, *Perfect Etiquette* (1877), p. 88; "wear longer, stay cleaner . . .": Ibid., pp. 88–90.

157–58   CARRIAGE SHOES: "driving to a ball . . .": *Godey's Lady's Book*, February 1882, p. 178; "for traveling or indoor . . .": *Harper's Bazaar*, May 22, 1869, p. 341; "intended to be worn . . .": *Peterson's*, December 1874, p. 435; "When you think the . . .": *Knitting, Netting, and Crochet Work* (1847), p. 18.

159   "My knitting-needles are wooden . . .": *The Lady's Friend*, Peterson, ed., February 1873, p. 165.

Chapter 8:
Sporty Victorian Knitters

page

160   CALISTHENICS AND ARCHERY: *Harper's Bazaar*, February 27, 1869, p. 72; Ibid., December 3, 1870, p. 771.

160–61   DRESS REFORM: "vast, swaying, undefined, and . . .": Woolson, ed., *Dress Reform* (1874), p. 231; "when we have a . . .": Ibid., pp. 248–49.

162   "striped stockings, lawn-tennis shoes . . .": *Dorcas Magazine*, August 1884, p. 234.

162   "jaunty, convenient and pretty . . .": "Golfing and Golfers," *Domestic Monthly*, August 1895, pp. 21–22.

163   "If its day was . . .": Fred C. Kelly, "The Great Bicycle Craze," *American Heritage*, December 1956, p. 69.

163–65   BICYCLING FOR HEALTH: "[H]er chances for physical . . .": R. L. Dickinson, M.D., "Bicycling for Women, the Puzzling Question of Costume," *Outlook*, April 25, 1896, p. 751; "nerve tonic . . . deliverance, revolution . . .": *Scribner's Magazine*, June 1895, pp. 700–701; "The system is invigorated . . .": Maria E. Ward, *Bicycling for Ladies*, p. 12.

165   "[T]he bicycle fad is . . .": "Fancy Work: Knitting," *Woman and Home*, May 1897, p. 555.

167–68   BICYCLING CLOTHING: "A corset, if one . . .": Ward, p. 95; "an extra change of . . .": Ibid., p. 98; "The sweater should come . . .": Ibid., p. 98; "bizarre patterns and startling . . .": "Sweaters," *Godey's Magazine*, September 1897, p. 442; "when riding against cutting . . .": *The Wheelwoman*, February 1897, p. 222; "the hat should be . . .": *Godey's*, September, 1897, p. 442.

168   BLOOMERS: "We respect what may . . .": "Dress Reform," *Woman's Words*, April 1877, p. 1; "We put it on . . .": Stanton's words are quoted from memory and may not be exact.

168–70   RESPONSE TO BLOOMERS: "increase and set off . . .": Dickinson, p. 752; comments on: Smith, *The Social History of the Bicycle*, p. 107; "A biker asked a farmer . . .": *The Wheelwoman*, January 1897, p. 212; "No woman can endure . . .": Ibid., August 1896, p. 5.

170   "It is always proper . . .": Hanson, *Etiquette and Bicycling* (1896), p. 362.

171   "My grandam used to . . .": Nixon Waterman, "The New Woman and Her Grandam," *The Wheelwoman*, July 1897, p. 341.

172   CYCLING AND MODESTY: "[i]t does not require . . .": "The Woman's World," *Home Comfort*, March 1898, p. 9; "curtain screen for women . . .": "Current Comment," *Godey's Lady's Book and Magazine*, July 1896, p. 111; "Verily, the way of . . .": "Wheel-Whirls," *Godey's Magazine*, October 1896, p. 446.

172–74   LADIES' BICYCLE STOCKINGS: "smooth and tight just . . .": Ward, p. 83; "the gayest tartan plaids . . .": Mrs. Reginald DeKoven, "Bicycling for Women," *Cosmopolitan Magazine*, June 1895, p. 692; "elaborate top in two . . .": "A Fad of the Day," *New York Daily Tribune*, October 20, 1895; "elastic hose for invalids", *Fancy and Practical Knitting*, vol. III, no. 2 (1897), p. 159; Railroad stitch stockings: "ravel the dropped stitches . . .": Watson, comp., *The Ladies' Manual of Knitting and Crocheting*, Central Squares Series, vol. I, no. 1, n.p.; "So much time, patience . . .": *Dorcas Magazine*, January 1884, p. 31; "To knit a stocking . . .": Croly, *Knitting and Crochet: Guide to the Use of the Needle and Hook*, pp. 55, 57.

174   FANCY NEEDLEWORK: "trio of pretty, useful . . .": Margaret Sims, "The Art of Knitting," *Ladies' Home Journal*, March 1894, p. 21; "vine leaf lace

suitable . . .": Sims, "Dainty Knitting and Crocheting," Ibid., April 1894, p. 32; "Bachelor's Tea Cosy," Ibid., August 1895, p. 21.

Chapter 9:
Old Knitters in New Roles

page

175   WOMEN AS CONSUMERS: Matthaei, *An Economic History of Women in America*, p. 165; Statistics: Helen Louise Johnson, "The Gospel of the New House-keeping," *Harper's Bazaar*, March 1913, p. 122.; "[M]arriage is a contract . . .": Mrs. Julian Heath, "The Work of the Housewives League," *Annals of the Academy of Political and Social Sciences*, July 1913, p. 121; Ida M. Tarbell, "The Cost of Living and Household Management," Ibid., p. 130; Ivory soap: *Ladies' Fancywork Magazine*, April 1902, inside front cover.

175–76   KNITTING, STEREOTYPE OF HOMEMAKER: "spin, weave, sew, embroider . . .": Tryon, *Household Manufactures in the United States, 1640–1860*, p. 9; "My Grandma used to . . .": Alfred J. Waterhouse, "Just Keep Knitting, Knitting," *New York Times*, n.d., reprinted in *Stitches*, April 1903, p. 5; "Grandmother knows how a . . .": Mary J. Jacques, "The Knitting Lesson," *Saint Nicholas*, November 1903, p. 23.

176   HOME ECONOMICS CLASSES: "raw silk by the . . .": *Teachers' College Bulletin* (1915), p. 24; "by which numbers of . . .": James, *Longman's Complete Course of Needlework, Knitting and Cutting-Out* (1901), pp. 4, 261–63; Claydon, *Knitting Without "Specimens"* (1916), preface, pp. v, vi; table of contents, passim; Patterns, passim.

177   FAIRS: Amanda Stoltfus, *How to Organize and Conduct a School and Community Fair*, University of Texas Bulletin no. 2409 (Austin, Tex., March 1, 1924), p. 34.

177–78   SPECIAL COLUMNS FOR CHILDREN: "Little Sunshiners Entitled to Membership," *New York Daily Tribune*, March 20, 1900; "the most careful . . .": *Stitches*, January 1903, p. 17: "See how evenly she . . .": Ibid., February 1903, p. 19.

178–80   OBJECTIONS TO SUFFRAGE: "a sisterhood of cranks . . .": *Votes for Men*, pamphlet, "antis' file in National Woman's Party Collection, Manuscript Division, Library of Congress, cited in Macdonald, *Documentary Case Studies in American History*, "The Antis" chapter, Document no. 6, p. 6; ". . . since fig leaves in . . .": Ibid; "If a woman voluntarily . . ." and others: *Objections* [to Woman Suffrage], an undated, mimeographed list of reasons for withholding suffrage from women, "antis" file in Ibid., Document no. 36, p. 35; Bathing suit pattern in *Utopia Yarn Book* (1916), pp. 221–23; "[G]irls, just as soon . . .": *Woman Suffrage a Menace to Male Population*, leaflet distributed in 1916 by Herbert N. Carleton, West

Newbury, Mass., in "antis" files in Macdonald, Document no. 24, p. 23; "Women are appointed to . . .": and additional quotations in *Objections*; "[i]n whose home it . . .": Verse from a 1915 calendar sold by antisuffrage organizations, in "antis" file of National Woman's Party, in Macdonald, Document no. 12, p. 11; "Women at such a . . .": *Votes for Men*.

180   WOMEN IN PUBLIC LIFE: "dangerous undermining effect upon . . .": Grover Cleveland, "Woman's Mission and Woman's Clubs," *The Ladies' Home Journal*, May 1905, p. 3; "[t]he life is too . . .": Gilder, *Why I Am Opposed to Woman Suffrage*, pamphlet issued by the Massachusetts Association Opposed to the Further Extension of Suffrage to Women, "antis" file of National Woman's Party, in Macdonald, Document no. 9, p. 9; "I will not deny . . .": Address of Miss Anne Bock, of Los Angeles, Ca., before the Committee on Woman Suffrage, United States Senate, August 9, 1913, in Macdonald, Document no. 10, p. 10.

180–81   CALMING INFLUENCE OF KNITTING: "the essentially feminine woman . . .": *Stitches*, December 1902, pp. 4, 17; "every woman whose nerves . . .": Ibid., March 1903, p. 6; "nerve-wrecked and old": *Stitches*, March 1903, p. 6; "Knitting was once every . . .": *Columbia Book of the Use of Yarns* (1904), p. 5.

181   KNITTING AS PALLIATIVE/ECONOMY: "Of all nerve-destroying . . .": Cahoon, *What One Woman Thinks*, p. 196.

181–82   KNITTING FOR A MAN: "a bit of an . . .": Patty DePeyster, "Society Fads," *New Ideas Woman's Magazine*, July 1902, p. 84; "This all sounds rather . . .": "Society Fads," Patty DePeyster, Ibid., January 1902, p. 84; "Indeed it seems that . . .": Patty DePeyster, Ibid., July 1902, p. 84.

182   EDITH ROOSEVELT: Parks, *My Thirty Years Backstage at the White House*, p. 211.

182–83   BEWITCHING PIECES: "all those little embellishments . . .": *Stitches*, December 1902, p. 4; "thrown over the . . .": Ibid., September 1903, p. 6; "lacy and bewitching to . . .": Ibid., January 1904, p. 6; "Bewitching Breakfast Cap," *Delineator*, May 1912, p. 68.

183   ELEGANT KNITTING: Knitted undervest, *Stitches*, March 1903, p. 11.; breakfast, spencer and breakfast jackets in *Utopia Yarn Book* (1916); "Ladies' Chest Protectors," *Stitches*, September 1903, p. 7; All three beaded patterns are in *Home Needlework Magazine*, October 1902, pp. 306, 362.

183–84   CARE OF KNITTING: "A yard of striped . . .": *Home Needlework Magazine*, May 1902, p. 307; "How to Launder Shetland Shawls," *Ladies' Fancywork Magazine*, October 1901, p. 58; "Place the sweater inside . . .": *Stitches*, January 1904, p. 8; "labor of love; time . . .": "To Wash Laces," *Ladies' Fancywork Magazine*, January 1902, p. 106.

184   "Home knit vests are . . .": etc.: *Utopia Yarn Book*, passim.

185–86   SWEATERS: "golf cranks," in Genevieve Hecker, *Golf for Women* p. 30; "The Columbia Sweater," *Home Needlework Magazine*, October 1902, p.

368; College sweaters, in Alice Simon Chundelah, *Modern Knitting*, vol. I (1916), pp. 12 ff.; "The golf links gave . . .": *Stitches*, December 1902, p. 4.

186   KNITS FOR OUTDOOR WEAR: A good motoring sweater may be found in "Lady's Motor and Golf Sweater," *The Delineator*, February 1910, p. 32; "beautifully unique and clouded . . .": *Stitches*, June 1903, p. 5 and *Minerva Book for Knit and Crochet*, vol. 3 (1919), color drawing; Boating: *Columbia Book of Yarns* (1907), p. 132 and *Stitches*, June 1903, cover.

186–87   Maynard, ed., *What to Knit and Crochet* (1903), pp. 86–89; Balbriggan heel: *Manual of Handiwork*, (1916), pp. 168–69.

187–88   CORSETS AND SPORTS: "[a] woman ought to . . .": Helen Berkeley-Loyd, "You and Your Corset-Maker," *The Delineator*, October 1910, p. 293; Tights: *Stitches*, February 1904, p. 4.

189   "Women of grace may . . .": Advertisement of Merrill Novelty Co., *Stitches*, April 1903, p. 22.

189   CORSETS BY MAIL: *Sears Roebuck and Company Catalogue*, no. 111, 1902, p. 942; prices, passim.

190–91   "Pneu Woman" advertisements appeared in many women's magazines. This was from *Home Needlework Magazine*, April 1905, p. 376.

191   "feminine avenues for feminine . . .": Alden, *Women's Ways of Earning Money*, pp. 9, 35.

191–92   IMMIGRANT CHILDREN: Woods, ed., *Americans in Progress*: pp. 293, 298; Robert A. Woods, *The Neighborhood in Nation-Building*, pp. 120–21, 156–57.

192   "prepared to earn a . . .": George C. Gruner, *Report of the Director of the North Bennet Street Industrial School on the Industrial Work of the Special Class from the Hancock School, April 14, 1909*, Schlesinger Library, Radcliffe College, MC 269, North Bennet Street Industrial School papers, Series II, Box 54, Folder 14, pp. 1, 3.

192–93   KNITTING CLASSES AND CLUBS [Circa 1903–1910]: *Afternoon Classes— Neighborhood Work: Knitting*, Ibid., one page of descriptions; Reports of clubs: "The Knitting Club had . . .": *The North End Lantern*, North Bennet Street papers, Series II, Box 57, Folder 48, May 1819, p. 4; "The Knitting Club and . . .": Ibid., February 1919, p. 5; "The Special Knitting Club": Ibid., April 1919, p. 7; "Come and see the . . .": Ibid., March 1920, p. 7.

194   Hennepin County Agriculture Society: Cited without date in Morrish, *A History of Fairs*, p. 42.

194   RUNNING A FAIR: *Proceedings of the First Annual School in Fair Management*, p. 120; "Get each person to . . .": Seranne and Gaden, *The Church and Club Woman's Companion*, p. 198.

194–95   THEMES FOR FAIRS: Christmas, etc., and Seven Ages of Woman: Burrell, *Benton's Book of Needlework* (1912), pp. 67–68, 21–22, 17, 28.

195   "not to fail France . . .": American Fund for French Wounded, *Monthly*

Report, vol. II, September-October 1917; "The struggle is longer . . .": report of November 17, 1917, n.p.

196   BERLIN CHILDREN: Rotogravure section, *New York Times*, December 13, 1914.

196   "calculated to drive the . . .": Maud Churchill Nicoll, "How to Knit Socks for Soldiers," *New York Times*, December 13, 1914; Nicoll followed with *How to Knit Socks* (1915) and *Knitting and Sewing for Men in the Army and Navy* (1918).

196–97   WARTIME INSTRUCTIONS: *War Needlework* (1914); "THE MONEY FOR THE . . .": and poem: Whiting, ed., *The Khaki Knitting Book* (1917), inside front cover.

197   CONTEST: *Star Needlework Journal*, vol. 3, no. 1, 1918.

197   *The Red Cross Bulletin*, Washington, D.C.: National Red Cross, August 17, 1917, p. 1.

197   "knitted outfits for the . . .": Letter from J. B. Will, Lieutenant, USN, commanding USS *Cahill*, to American Red Cross National Headquarters, published in *Red Cross Bulletin*, August 23, 1917, p. 3.

Chapter 10:
Oh, Say Can You Knit—
For Sammy?

page

199   "Oh, the stitches may . . .": "The Woman Who Saw," *Gentlewoman*, January 1918, p. 7.

199   MABEL BOARDMAN LETTER: quoted in "Work! Work! Work! All Around America with War Activities," *The Delineator*, April 1918, p. 10.

199   WARTIME KNITTING FIGURES: *The Work of the American Red Cross During the War, July 1, 1917–February 28, 1919*, p. 23.

200   "perfectly made pair of . . .": "The Call to Knit," *Vogue*, July 1, 1918, p. 100.

200–202 CIVIL WAR WOMEN: "Woman of Civil War Times Now Instructs Knitting Class," *Gentlewoman*, August 1918, p. 13; "in place of her accustomed . . .": Andrews, *The Women of the South in War Times*, p. 457; Mrs. Mitt Osgood: "The Farm," *Atlantic*, February 1919, p. 288; Speed knitters: American Red Cross, Northern Division, *Bulletin*, September 5, 1918, pp. 1, 2, and July, 18, 1918, p. 2; Hannah Eilenberger: "The Work of the Comforts Committee," *Sea Power*, October 1918, p. 61; "I shaped the feet . . .": Maria Foster Brown, in Brown, ed., *Grandmother Brown's Hundred Years, 1927–1927*, p. 47.

202   DES MOINES: "The after-luncheon hour will . . .": *Des Moines Register*, July 5, 6, 7, 1918; "make a big effort . . .": Ibid., July 21, 1918.

202–3   SOCIETY LEADERS: *Gentlewoman*, February 1918, p. 2; "A War Charity Established by a New York Woman," *Vogue*, April 15, 1918, p. 49; *Vogue*, August 1, 1918, p. 30.

203–4   MORMONS: "As women's pets in . . .": *Relief Society Magazine*, February 1918, p. 146; "[o]ur sisters will have . . .": Ibid., October 1918, p. 599; "Provide some good music . . .": Ibid., February 1918, p. 85.

204–6   WOMEN'S TEAS: *Scenario*: Winifred, Leonghridge, "Suggestions for a War Tea," *The Delineator*, March 1918, p. 44; "I can make a . . .": "A Tea Party at Molly's," *Gentlewoman*, May 1918, p. 33; "They would be much . . .": Eda B. Funston, "Family Advice from Mrs. Funston," *The Delineator*, July 1918, p. 23; "If You Worry, Don't . . .": *The Newark Evening News*, July 18, 1918.

206–7   ONE-ACT PLAYS: Helen S. Griffith, *The Knitting Club Meets*, pp. 4, 7–9, 17; Elise West Quaife, *The Knitting Girls Count One*, pp. 5–8, 19–20. The song referred to was "To the Soldier Girls at Home: The Knitting Song," by Anna Priscilla Risher (with words by Frank L. Armstrong), first published in 1917 by Arthur P. Schmidt Co. in Boston and later included in *Part-Songs for Patriotic Occasions*, published by the same company in 1918.

207–8   OUTSIDE THE U.S.: "proceeded to turn the . . .": "From Camel to Sock," *Vogue*, November 1, 1918, p. 94; Shanghai slave girls: "Work of the Comforts Committee," *Sea Power*, March 1918, p. 208; Hawaii: American Red Cross, [Fourteenth] Territorial, Insular, and Foreign Division, *Bulletin*, May 1918, p. 2.

208–11   NAVY LEAGUE KNITTING BEE: "I can't fight, and . . .": "The Work of the Comforts Committee: Old Fashioned Knitting Bee in Central Park," *Sea Power*, September 1918, p. 204; "If it hadn't been . . .": "New York's Enviable Record," Ibid., December 1918, p. 374; "in such numbers that . . .": *New York Times*, August 1, 1918; "inspiration to knitters to . . .": Ibid., April 1, 2, 1918.

211–14   PARADES: "Red Cross Parade," *Vogue*, July 1, 1918, p. 53. It is interesting to note that in other reading I came across a description of knitting machines being used at the Cosmopolitan Club. A club member remarked, "I have just forty minutes before the lecture; that will give me time to make a pair of socks!" In "Women's Clubs and War Work," *Vogue*, April 1, 1918, p. 128. Perhaps club members knit both ways; New Jersey Navy League: "The Work of the Comforts Committee," *Sea Power*, January 1918, p. 60.

214   "The Weaker Sex," *The Woman Citizen*, October 19, 1918, p. 419.

214–15   SPEED: "[i]t is not a . . .": Marie Ashley, "Saving Precious Moments," *The Delineator*, November 1918, p. 92; MRS. KINDELBERGER: "Champion Red Cross Knitter of New York," *New York Times*, August 23, 1918.

215   CRITICISM: "For God's sake, wake . . .": Samuel E. Dale, "Why Not to Knit," *Literary Digest*, July 16, 1918, p. 31; "not a little disturbed": *Des Moines Register*, July 14, 1918.

216   SHORTAGES: White House sheep: *Pictorial Review*, November 1918, p. 15; Mrs. Hegg: American Red Cross, Northwestern Division, *Bulletin*, November 16, 1918, p. 1; "something sweet in pink . . .": "Plenty of Knitting Needles," *Literary Digest*, November 10, 1917, p. 89; "Until war conditions end . . .": Marie Ashley, "For the Period of the Emergency," *The Delineator*, January 1919, p. 55; "Mercerized Cotton Takes the . . .": Ashley, Ibid., May 1918, p. 84; Elsa Barsaloux, "Silk and Yarn are Both Used for Knitting," *Pictorial Review*, February 1919, p. 76;" I think the slogan . . .": Carol Lawrence, "Woolless Ways for Warm Days," *Woman's Magazine*, June 1918, p. 53.

217   SOCKS: Melville Chater, "The Saga of the Socks," *Red Cross Magazine*, February 1919, pp. 77–80.

217   KNITTERS' RESPONSE: "[W]e would seem to . . .": "The Woman Who Saw," *Gentlewoman*, March 1918, p. 8; "thought it was pretty . . .": Loessa F. Coffey, of Washington, D.C., to ALM, September 8, 1986; Replies from soldiers contributed by Grace Hudkins of Springfield, Vt. (who has talked with the knitter about her wartime knitting), to ALM, June 13, 1986.

218   NEED FOR SOCKS: "Every pound of yarn . . .": Red Cross, Northern Division, *Bulletin*, May 20, 1918, cover; "three times as hard": Ibid., June 27, 1918, p. 1; Concentrate on socks: American Red Cross, Potomac Division, *Bulletin*, September 27, 1918, p. 2; "close fit without bumps . . .": "A Sock Anyone Can Knit," *Illustrated World*, March 1919, pp. 112–13.

218   STOCKPILING KNITWEAR: Insertion in Potomac Division *Bulletin*, February 2, 1918; "confident that all the . . .": Bernard M. Baruch, Chairman, War Industries Board, to Henry P. Davison, Chairman of the Red Cross War Council, inserted in Ibid., August, 30, 1918.

218–19   CIVILIAN KNITTING: "work up handsomely in . . .": *Corticelli Yarn Book* (1918) no. 8, p. 2; "Knitted Comforts for the Woman Going Abroad to do War Work," *Pictorial Review*, October 1918, p. 32; "rendered even fluffier by . . .": Marie Ashley, "New Versions of an Old Yarn," *The Delineator*, February 1917, p. 69; "Of course any woman . . .": Marie Ashley, "New Work for Your Needles," Ibid., April 1918, p. 92; "hug-me-tight . . . a good substantial friend . . .": Marie Ashley, "Crochet and Knitting Needles Lead an Infinitely Useful Life," Ibid., October 1918, p. 92; "exorbitant prices asked in . . .": "How to Make a Skating Set," *Gentlewoman*, January 1917, p. 33; Norfolk sweater: Elsa Barsaloux, "A Knitted Norfolk Coat for College Girls," Ibid., September 1917, p. 1; "Mr. Wilson Believes in Plenty of Play," *New York Times*, April 14, 1918; "Spiderweb Hats," *The Delineator*, September 1918, p. 39; A particularly attractive knit camisole appeared in *Modern Priscilla*, February 1918, p. 17.

220–21   BUSINESS TIE-INS WITH KNITTING: "faded, wrinkled and wan": *Vogue*, October 15, 1918, p. 112; "After being aproned for . . .": *Harper's Bazaar*, April 1918, p. 68; "[a]n external slump bespeaks . . .": "What War Has Done to Clothes," *Vogue*, October 15, 1918, p. 62; "a puff of rose . . .": "Keeping Up the Morale of French Lingerie," *Vogue*, November 15, 1918, p. 57; "To look her best . . .": *Harper's Bazaar*, March 1918, p. 83. The ad appeared in many other women's magazines; "look, and act, and . . .": Abercrombie's: *Harper's Bazaar*, May 1918, p. 15; "She is the soldier's . . .": Ibid., April 1918, p. 86.

221–22   PATRIOTIC: "A Spring bride whose . . .": *Harper's Bazaar*, June 1918, p. 37; "simple frock of black . . .": *Vogue*, June 15, 1918; "full of cotton frocks . . .": *Harper's Bazaar*, April 1918, p. 70; "Anyone seen knitting a . . .": "Pleasure, Patriotism, and Palm Beach," *Vogue*, March 1, 1918, p. 47; Children: "Palm Beach Balances Its Work and Its Play," Ibid., March 15, 1918, p. 12; "skein after skein of . . .": *Des Moines Register*, July 7, 1918; Albany knitters: "The Work of the Comforts Committee," *Sea Power*, September 1918, p. 208.

222–23   KNITTING BAGS: Torpedo shell: *Sea Power*, June 1918, p. 428; pedestal basket: *Harper's Bazaar*, June 1918, p. 75; "the last word in . . .": Ibid., June 1918, p. 73; "blue moire . . .": [with] gray . . .": Ibid., May 1918, pp. 80–81; "pretty affair in which . . .": "Vogue Covers Join the Ranks," *Vogue*, August 1, 1918, p. 29; "Can't you just imagine . . .": *Vogue*, May 15, 1918, p. 7; "Yesterday a good-looking knitting . . .": Ibid., February 1918, p. 65; "The head of the . . .": Marie Ashley, "The Knitting-Bag Embroidery Goes to One's Hat," *The Delineator*, April 1918, p. 91; "peacock pongee and purple . . .": Ibid.; "a natural-colored straw hat . . .": *Vogue*, May 1, 1918, p. 73; Bag with service star: Marie Ashley, "The Flight of the Needle Keeps Step with the Times," *The Delineator*, March 1918, p. 82; "a patriotic holiday gift": *Pictorial Review*, December 1918, p. 68; Bag made of toweling: *Star Needlework Journal*, vol. 3, no. 2, 1918, p. 12.

224   GARMENTS AND BAGS: "shimmering affair of yellow . . .": *Vogue*, May 1, 1918, p. 73; Knitting bag–apron: Ibid., December 1, 1918, p. 68; "Memorize the phrase . . .": Eleanor Gehan, "When You Come to the End of a Perfect Row," *Catholic World*, July 1918, p. 528; "so ornamental and expensive . . .": "Knitting Bags: A Great Convenience to Owners Perhaps, Not to Others," *New York Times*, March 2, 1918.

Chapter 11:
Men and Children for
Sammy, Too

page
225–26   KNITTING MEN: "husky firefighters [who are] . . .": *Gentlewoman*, March 1918, p. 8; "unostentatiously between stations": "Of Women Knitting,"

Atlantic Monthly, May 1936, p. 250; "horses that no one . . .": "Men Can Knit Too," *The Woman Citizen*, June 8, 1918, p. 32; "When not engaged in . . .": "Governor of Arizona Knits," *New York Times*, March 10, 1918.

226–28 "knitting openly and shamelessly . . .": "Emancipation of Man," *The Atlantic Monthly*, January 1919, p. 141.

228 "that least exciting, most . . .": "The Recrudescence of Knitting," *Scribner's*, February 1918, pp. 249–50.

229 TEACHING OTHERS TO KNIT: Patients: *Bulletin of the Needle and Bobbin Club*, vol. 1, no. 3 [n.p.], December 1917, pp. 29–30; Prisoners: "Oh, Lady, Lady, Who Ever Would Have Thunk It?" Northwestern Division, American Red Cross, *Bulletin*, December 1918, p. 3, and Pennsylvania and Delaware divisions, *Red Cross Clippings*, March 1918, p. 3.

229–30 RECUPERATING SOLDIER: "Mary Pickford Flag," *Sea Power*, May 1918, pp. 350–51.

230 "[You should] do anything . . .": Bailey, *What to Do for Uncle Sam*, p. 195.

230 CHILDREN: "Ellarea Baldwin of Minot . . .": Northern Division, American Red Cross, *Bulletin*, May 20, 1918, p. 3; "Here are two little . . .": Northwestern Division, American Red Cross, *Bulletin*, February 9, 1918, p. 3; "I'm awful busy working . . .": This was credited to the children's magazine, *St. Nicholas*, and appeared in the Northwest Division *Bulletin*, February 9, 1918, p. 2.

231–32 RECOLLECTIONS: "Because of my mother's . . .": Zelpha M. Gritt, of Black Creek, Wis., to ALM, June 16, 1986; "The Union Pacific runs . . .": Georgia C. Vilven, of Wamego, Kans., to ALM, February 4, 1987; Nancy C. McClure, of Chattanooga, Tenn., to ALM, March 9, 1987.

232–33 WIN-THE-DOG CONTEST: "Win a Red Cross Dog!" *The Delineator*, April 1918, p. 44; "The Red Cross Dog Is Won," *The Delineator*, October 1918, p. 42; "How They Won the Red Cross Dog," *Woman's Magazine*, October 1918, p. 33.

233 FEATURES ON CHILDREN: "Indian boys vie with . . .": "Indian Children Work for the Junior Red Cross," *The Delineator*, June 1918, p. 41; "You ought to watch . . .": "Work in Far-Off Alaska for the Junior Red Cross," Ibid., May 1918, p. 59.

233–35 KNITTING IN SCHOOL AND CAMP: "over the chocolate cups": Ruth deRochemont, "The School Girl in War Relief," *Vogue*, March 15, 1918, p. 32; "When a geometry lesson . . .": "What We Can Do to Help," *Gentlewoman*, December 1917, p. 4; Camp: *Des Moines Register*, July 11, 1918; Bright yarns: Dorothy Smith Schlosser, of Baltimore, related this to Elizabeth L. Hart, who passed it on to the author in April 1986; "when stitches got too . . .": Lillian Lunny, of Staten Island, to ALM, July 2, 1986; "Our boys were in . . .": Lewella Francis, of Winsted, Conn., to

ALM, June 13, 1986; "Brave Sammies . . . fighting to . . .": "The Rocky Mountain Knitter-Boys," *St. Nicholas*, May 1918, pp. 605, 609.

235   "Their knitting bags go . . .": "What We Can Do to Help," p. 4.

235–36   GIRL SCOUTS: "The Narcissus Troop of . . .": "The News of the Troops," *The Rally*, May 1918, p. 11; "The War Service Award . . .": Ibid., June 1918, p. 13; "The Iris troop no. 13 . . .": Ibid., May 1918, p. 11; "If you want to . . .": Anne Hyde Choate, "Girl Scout Knitting of Sammie's Sweater Sets," Ibid., October 1917, p. 7; "Made By a Girl . . .": "Our Own Win the War Page," Ibid., October 1917, p. 12.

236   "a mere slip of . . .": "The Scarf with the Bullet Hole," *Red Cross Magazine*, April 1919, p. 1.

236   Fryer, *The Mary Frances Knitting and Crocheting Book* (1918).

236–37   "It is said that . . .": "Miss Lambert," *The Hand-Book of Needlework* (1846), p. 221.

237   FICTION: "Some of the girls . . .": Blanchard, *A Girl Scout of Red Rose Troop*, p. 119; "Knitting is something you . . .": Montgomery, *Rilla of Ingleside*, pp. 84, 94.

237   "It isn't hard to . . .": Anna Priscilla Risher, music, and Frank L. Armstrong, words, "Knitting," in *Part-Songs for Patriotic Occasions*.

237–38   "We are the knitting . . .": Kathleen Norris, "Knitting Women," reprinted in the *Bulletin*, Mid American-Chapter, American Red Cross, May 17, 1918, p. 24.

Chapter 12:
Flappers Versus the
"Old-Fashioned Knitters"

page

239–40   NEW ROLES FOR WOMEN: "hard to remember what . . .": "Women and the War," *Des Moines Register*, July 21, 1918; "Have the American Women . . .": Mabel Daggett, "Your Part in Rebuilding the World," *Pictorial Review*, January 1919, p. 17; "Now That We've Got . . .": Charlotte Perkins Gilman, Ibid., March 1919, p. 31.

240   "[t]he neck of our dress . . .": "Dress Reform Again," *Woman's Home Companion*, May 1921, p. 2.

240   RED CROSS REQUESTS: "express with your knitting . . .": *Potomac Division Bulletin*, Supplement (February 21, 1919), n.p.; "a little variety": *Northwestern Division Bulletin* (February 15, 1919), p. 3; "keep knitting as long . . .": *Red Cross Bulletin* (March 24, 1919), p. 1; Refugee knitting: *Red Cross Courier* (July 15, 1926), p. 1.

240–41   "Don't stop knitting . . .": Clarke, "Your Part in Rebuilding the World," *Pictorial Review*, February 1919, p. 16.

241 "The revival of knitting . . .": Klickman, *The Popular Knitting Book* (1923), p. 1.

241 FLEISHER ADS: "Now that the shadow . . .": *The Delineator*, April 1919, pp. 86, 117; "Consider the possibilities of . . .": *Harper's Bazaar*, April 1919, p. 115; "Many of the most . . .": *Ladies' Home Journal*, October 1921, p. 125.

242 "Back to our Needlework . . .": Ashley, "Back to Our Needlework: Released War Knitters Take Up the Thread of New Embroideries," *The Delineator*, June 1919, p. 111.

242–44 NEEDLEWORK CONTESTS: *Star Needlework Journal*, vol. 5, no. 2, 1920, p. 1; Atlantic City marathon: *New York Times*, April 28, 29, 1923; "Many a time when . . .": Quoted in Ross, *Grace Coolidge and Her Era*, p. 95; "the sturdy opposite of . . .": "Mrs. Coolidge Knits a Baby Carriage Robe in National Competition for $2,000 Prize," *New York Times*, August 17, 1923; "Three County Fair": "New England Knitters," *New York Times*, August 20, 1923; Contest winners: "Wins Prize of $2,000 in Knitting Contest," *New York Times*, August 23, 1923; "Slumberland Afghan": "For a Coolidge Grandchild," *New York Times*, September 27, 1923; "sweaters, scarves, mittens, socks . . .": John Coolidge to ALM, July 15, 1986.

244 GRACE COOLIDGE: "So expert is the president's . . .": July 24, 1924, clipping supplied by the White House Historical Society does not identify the source—probably the Washington *Times Herald*; Coolidge counterpane: "Mrs. Coolidge Earns $250 and Gives It Away," *New York Times*, December 30, 1926; John Coolidge To ALM, July 15, 1986.

244–45 SHORT SKIRTS: "The modern male has . . .": Chase, *Prosperity Fact or Myth*, p. 66; "Come right down, lady . . .": "To-day's Morals and Manners—the Side of 'The Girls,'" *Reader's Digest*, July 9, 1921, p. 34: Schoolteacher: *New York Times*, May 13, 1922; "there being no skirt . . .": "Fashion and Disease," *The American Journal of Public Health*, September 1925, p. 790; "minimum of clothes and . . .": and "To jig and hop around . . .": "Is the Younger Generation in Peril?" *Reader's Digest*, May 17, 1921, p. 12; Church views: "The Pope's Appeal to Men to Reform Dress," *Literary Digest*, January 29, 1927, pp. 27–28; "Church Decrees on Women's Dress," Ibid., November 21, 1925, p. 32.

245–46 WOMEN'S REPLIES: "Why should men be . . .": "To-Day's Morals," p. 36; "Emancipated Legs Mean Better . . .": Helen Wills, "Emancipated Legs Mean Better Sports," *Ladies' Home Journal*, April 1923, p. 33; "Skirts can't get too short for me . . .": and "The girl of to-day . . .": "To-Day's Morals," pp. 34, 36, 39. This article appeared in response to the earlier "Is the Younger Generation in Peril?"; Rainy Daisies: "Rainy Daisies' Triumph," *New York Times*, October 30, 1921; "their clothes, including panels . . .": "Women Renew Fight Against Long Skirts," *New York Times*, September 30, 1922.

246–47 BOBBED HAIR: Irene Castle Treman, "I Bobbed My Hair and Then—,"
Ladies' Home Journal, October 1921, p. 124; Mary Garden, "Why I
Bobbed My Hair," *Pictorial Review*, April 1927, p. 8; Mary Pickford,
"Why I Have Not Bobbed Mine," Ibid., p. 9; "ten years off a woman's
looks . . .": Hazel Rawson Cades, "Good Looks: Your Hair—the Long
and the Short of It," *Woman's Home Companion*, September 1924, p. 75;
"American Girl Cluster Bob": *American Hairdresser*, May 1922, p. 15
(additional ads for "The National Bob" and "The Natural Curly Bob"
are on pp. 32, 38); "high tide up the Bay . . .": Elsie Waterbury Morris,
"As Your Hair Is Arranged," *The Delineator*, July 1921, p. 42; "If it
scorches paper . . .": Celia Caroline Cole, "When You Bob Your Hair,"
The Delineator, January 1923, p. 57.

248 HATS: "the caprice of Spring fashions": Isabel De Nyse Conover, "In the
Pink of Fashion," *Woman's Home Companion*, March 1927, p. 89; "knitted
hat with hardly . . .": G. Stanley Hall, "Flapper Americana Novissima,"
Atlantic Monthly, June 1922, p. 771; "They have a delightful . . .": Marise
de Fleur, "What's Under Your Hat?" *Sunset Magazine*, October 1928,
p. 78; "Ears are in!": *Woman's Home Companion*, November 1920, p. 102.
"Jump in it, step on it . . .": Chase, p. 63.

248 "Dressed for a formal ball . . .": "The Girl of To-Day," *Woman Citizen*,
January 26, 1924, p. 16.

248 "Dear God, give us . . .": Andrew J. Haire of New York, letter to the
editor, *New York Times*, February 25, 1922.

248–49 LIBERATED BODIES: "straightens out the waistline . . .": Helen Rawson
Cades, "Here, There, and Nowhere," *Woman's Home Companion*, December 1924, p. 108; "sound, physical . . .": "The Renaissance of the
C-r-s-t," *The Independent*, July 25, 1925, p. 88; "might well have carried
. . .": Carrie Chapman Catt, "How Many Yards in Your Skirt?" *Woman
Citizen*, August 1926, p. 11; An example of De Walter's Reducing Rubber Garments may be found in *Harper's Bazaar*, April 1923, p. 169; "I
guess dieting is . . .": Hugh Grant Rowell, "Father Discourses on Dieting," *Hygeia*, July 1927, p. 340.

249 BEADED BAGS: the "Alice," the "Daytona," the "Sunshine," the "Castil-
lian," the "Florida Starlight" and the "Agnes" in *New Simplified Instructions* (1925), pp. 3, 10, 11, 12, 13.

250 EGYPTIAN MOTIFS AND COLOR: "Marathon," *New York Times*, April 29,
1923; Examples: *Harper's Bazaar*, January 1923, p. 66, and April 1923,
pp. 116, 129; "Women's sports clothes are like . . .": Lutes, *The Gracious
Hostess* (1923), p. 479.

250–51 STYLE: "rest content with just . . .": *Blue Book of Dresses, Sweaters, Scarfs,
Tams Etc. for Women and Children* (1920), vol. 33, inside front cover;
"trousered ladies": William D. Richardson, "The Call to Colors," *Country
Life*, August 1927, p. 9; Knitted-in designs: *Peace Dale Knitting Book*

(1922), vol. 4, p. 3; "country club sweaters": *Fleisher's Knit and Crochet Manual* (1920), pp. 1, 9, 10, 71.

251   BRIDGE: Field, "Bridge Luncheon and No Regrets," *Pictorial Review*, September 1928, pp. 108–9; "Mid-Winter Bridge Luncheons," *Woman's Home Companion*, March 1926, pp. 152–55.

251–52   COLLEGE CLOTHES: "to suit individual fancy . . .": "No College Wardrobe Is Complete Without a Sweater," *Ladies' Home Journal*, September 1924, p. 178; Argyle outfit: "'Merry Christmas'—1921 Model," *Woman's Home Companion*, December 1921, p. 55; "gay Roman-striped border . . .": "No College Wardrobe," Ibid.; "stripes go roundabout more . . .": *Sweater News and Knitted Outerwear*, June 1926, p. 36; "if the party lasts . . .": Helen Woodbury, "The College Girl's Trunk," *Woman's Home Companion*, September 1921, p. 66.

252   "definite value to the community": Hanna, *Home Economics in the Elementary Schools*, p. 125.

252–54   BRITISH INFLUENCE: "Knitting Revival," *Business Week*, March 24, 1936, p. 31; "veddy British" knits: *Sweater News and Knitted Outerwear*, 1926, passim, pp. 44–46; Bobby Jones's Argyles: "Dramatic Scenes on the Links at Muirfield During the British Amateur Championship," *Town and Country*, July 1, 1926, p. 31; "hereditary and natural . . . urge . . .": *Men's Wear*, August 7, 1924, p. 65.

254–55   GOLF CLOTHES: "What the Smart English Sportswoman Wears for Golf," *Harper's Bazaar*, April, 1923, p. 75; "Miss MacKenzie was wearing . . .": Glenna Collett, *Ladies in the Rough* (1928), p. 88.

255–57   PARIS STYLES: Designers: *Sweater News and Knitted Outerwear*, 1927, p. 70; Patterns for children: "Outfitting the Youngsters," *McCall's Embroidery Book*, Summer 1921, p. 9; "Middy Blouse and Skirt," *Peace Dale Knitting Book* (1922), vol. 4, p. 36; other period designs: *Fleisher's Knitting and Crocheting Manual* (1921), p. 90; "The women demonstrated . . .": *Sweater News and Knitted Outerwear*, 1928, p. 52.

Chapter 13:
The Thirties Craze

page

259   "the name is not a nice one . . .": "Names: that Jar," *New York Times*, October 17, 1937.

259–60   ULMANN SURVEY: "1935's First Boom," *Forbes Magazine*, February 15, 1935, p. 14.

260   FASHION ADVICE: "fashionable virtue . . .": *McCall's Decorative Arts and Needlework*, Summer 1932, p. 14; Women taking up their needles: "From

the Editor's Notebook," Ibid., Winter 1932–1933, p. 2; "A gaily becoming sweater . . .": Ibid., Spring 1932.

260 "One thing the depression . . .": Advertisement for correspondence course from Woman's Institute, Ibid., Summer 1931, p. 43.

260 "What better way . . .": "Boleros, Sweaters and Suits," *The Handicrafter*, July, August 1932, back cover.

260–61 ULMANN'S PROMOTIONS: "Current Knit and Purl Craze Puts New Techniques into Yarn Selling," *Sales Management*, January 1, 1935, p. 19; "a basic part of . . .": "B. Ulmann Co., Inc. Fashion Show," *New York Times*, July 23, 1937.

261–63 WOMEN IN THE WORK FORCE: Wandersee, *Women's Work and Family Values, 1920–1940*, p. 100; "Jobs for Knitters," *New York Times*, November 25, 1934; "Current Knit and Purl Craze," p. 18; "Knitters Persist," *Business Week*, March 30, 1935, pp. 25–26; "Fad nothing! It's a profession . . .": Barnwell, "Fad Aids Yarn Sales," *Textile World*, July 1935, p. 64.

263 "For the last four . . .": Grant and Capps, Introduction to Duncan, *The Complete Book of Progressive Knitting* (1940).

263 "yielded to the urgent . . .": Wood, *Knitting and Fitting* (1936), introduction and title page.

263 "many of your acquaintances . . .": *Handicrafter*, Winter/Spring 1935, inside front cover.

263–64 KNITTING ON CONSIGNMENT: At Saks: "Popularity of Hand-Knits: Sales to Major Stores," *Sportswear Review*, January 1939, p. 15; "Are we to sit back . . .": Duncan, pp. 378–84.

264 "accessories really made . . .": Nancy C. McClure, of Chattanooga, Tenn., to ALM, March 9, 1987.

265 "Knitting is no longer . . .": *Vogue's Third Book of Knitting and Crochet* (1936), p. 1.

265–66 HOLLYWOOD: "The vogue is sweeping . . .": *The Motion Picture Movie Classic Hand Knit Fashions* (1936), inside front cover; "startled more than one . . .": Gladys Weston Ryan, "Eventually, Why Not Now?" *American Home*, August 1932, p. 194; Prizes: *Motion Picture Classic* entry form.

266–67 CONTEST WINNERS AND GRAND DUCHESS: "National Knitting Contest Winners Announced," *New York Times*, May 12, 1936.

268–69 "My grandfather started out . . .": William Bernat, interview with the author at the EBSCO (Emil Bernat and Sons Company), Uxbridge, Mass., October 15, 1985.

270 "New excitement . . .": Carleen Davenport, "First Sketches of Paris Collections Show High Hats," *Boston Evening Transcript*, August 14, 1935.

270 PARISIAN FASHIONS: *One of Fleisher's French Fashions in Hand Knits* (1934), Alix: no. C2168; Lanvin: no. C2167; Lelong: no. C2166.

270 "Something's happening . . .": *Bear Brand* (1939), no. 1568, p. 49.

270 RESORT SWEATERS: *Bear Brand* (1937) no. 118, passim.

270 "where folks live longer . . .": Sarah Barnes, ed., *Manual of Knitting and Crocheting* (1936), p. 7.

271 SHOP INVENTORIES: Ruth Seinfel, "Snarls of Joy," *Colliers'*, December 7, 1935, p. 26.

271–72 BOUCLÉ KNITTING: "perhaps not as large . . .": Peg Gorman, West Simsbury, Conn., to ALM, June 29, 1986; "What would she charge . . .": Irene Steptoe, of Chevy Chase, Md., to ALM, June 21, 1986; "Of course, during the thirties . . .": Elizabeth Dorshimer, of Whiting, N.J., to ALM, July 23, 1987; "Hand-knit boucle suits . . .": Alyce Misner, of Big River, Calif., to ALM, September 12, 1985; "new metal cable needles . . .": Nancy McClure, of Chattanooga, Tenn., to ALM, March 9, 1987.

272 MOODS: "In the early morning . . .": *Bear Brand* (1938), no. 1356, inside cover and p. 3; "occasions of dignity": *Bear Brand* (1939), no. 1356, p. 47.

272 CHENILLE JACKET: *Boucle and Venet Fashions of Tower Brand Yarns* (1935), cover.

272 "Tweed Knit" and "Magic-Print": *Bear Brand* (1939), no. 1568, inside cover.

273 "handsome one-piece black . . .": Ruth Mead, of Naugatuck, Conn., to ALM, June 23, 1986.

274 "I had taught myself . . .": Jean Olmstead, of Browns Summit, N.C., to ALM, June 25, 1986.

274 "Lots of young ladies . . .": Ryan, p. 194.

275 MERCERIZED COTTON: "Handcrafters of today who are . . .": Barnwell, "From Horse and Buggy Days," *Textile World*, January 1936, p. 92; "boilable string": *Bucilla Handcraft Publication* (1936), no. 108, inside front cover.

275 LUX AD: This advertisement and subsequent ones were on many back covers of Bernat's *Handicrafter* and *Bear Brand* books in the 1930s and are not separately cited.

276 NOMOTTA ADS: ran regularly in 1930s instruction books published by Nun's NOMOTTA.

276 "Needles will be clicking . . .": "And Sew On," *The Delineator*, January 1937, p. 49.

277 "a little distance from . . .": [by an "Onlooker"], "As the Parade Passes By," *Cleveland Plain Dealer*, January 27, 1935.

277 "Life will teach you . . .": Nash, "Machinery Doesn't Answer, Either, But You Aren't Married to It," in *Not Many Years Ago*, pp. 265–67.

277 GALLERY KNITTING: "Canadian Yarn Making Firms Resent Ban on Knitting in House of Commons Gallery," *New York Times*, February 8, 1934; "Knitting Barred in U.S. Supreme Court," *New York Times*, February 5, 1933. The Supreme Court Public Information office still advises that an attendant would ask a knitter to "put her work away."

277–79 COLLEGE STUDENTS: "By my Senior year . . .": Elizabeth Lineberger Hart,

Ruxton, Md., interview with ALM, October 22, 1985; Typical student: Catherine Mackenzie, "They All Knit, One Row Plain, One Purl," *New York Times Magazine*, January 6, 1935, p. 8; "She's a collector of . . .": "The Smile of America," *Harper's Bazaar*, August 1935, p. 39; "so soft and fragrant . . .": "College Angle of the Girl Who Knows Clothes," *The Delineator*, August 1936, p. 30; "soft as a bunny . . .": in *New Cardigans for You to Knit* (1939), vol. 4, no. 116, p. 6 [Ulmann also published a complete angora pattern book in 1938: *Angora Accessories for Day and Evening*, vol. 2]; Fads: "College Winners," *The Delineator*, February 1937, p. 33.

280   PRESS COMMENTS: An "enthusiasm": "Back to Knitting Gains," *New York Times*, April 28, 1935; "the click, click of the needles . . .": "See the Knitters Knit," *Cleveland Plain Dealer*, May 4, 1935. An official of the National Dry Goods Association calculated that there were ten million women knitters.

280   COMMENTS BY PRISCILLA PAGE: "These are knitting days . . .": "Smart Women Are Knitting," *Gentlewoman*, December 1934, p. 11; "Women are all divided . . .": "Towels and Top Knots," Ibid., February 1935, p. 8; "If you do not have . . .": "Did You Make It Yourself?" Ibid., February 1936, p. 10.

280   "Along with the New Deal . . .": "As the Parade Passes By," *Cleveland Plain Dealer*, January 27, 1936.

281   "Being a close friend . . .": Pauline Taylor Hendrick's story, as written by her daughter, Jean H. Coe, of Maiden, N.C., to ALM, June 16, 1986.

281   SANKA COFFEE AD: *New York Times*, November 12, 1939; "EXCHANGE" NEWSPAPER COLUMNS: "Household Department," *Boston Globe*, August 9, 1935.

282   BOYE NEEDLES: "Knitting Needles," *Fortune*, July 1935, p. 14; "Don't forget that knitting . . .": Marie H. Madsen, of Ocala, Fla., to ALM, August 10, 1986.

282   "When we ripped out . . .": Arlene Bauers, of Cheektowaga, N.Y., to ALM, June 12, 1986.

282–83   PATENTS: U.S. Patent no. 2,102,600 for "Flexible Knitting Needle," granted by the United States Patent Office to L. M. Miller on January 27, 1937; U.S. Patent no. 2,169,297 for a "Workbox," granted to Harry E. Smith, August 15, 1939; U.S. Patent no. 2,040,289 for "Needle Protector," granted to John H. Adams, May 12, 1936.

283   NEW GADGETS: The "Whirley," in "And Sew On: New Aids to Knitting," *The Delineator*, July 1936, p. 61; Standing bag, in "Roomy Knitting Bag Designed to Stand Beside a Chair," *Popular Science*, July 1935, p. 78; Wooden handles, in *Our Drummer* (Fall 1939), p. 32. Butler Brothers sold its full line of "Fast Selling Knitting Needs" mainly to department stores.

283–84 "Once I was a knitter . . .": "Of Women Knitting," *Atlantic Monthly,* May 1936, pp. 639–40.

284–86 BOSTON: "[s]pinning wheels were brought . . .": Barber, *Boston Common,* p. 69; "Someone had to help . . .": *Boston Globe,* August 14, 1935; "You can't rattle me . . .": "Man Wins Knitting Prize," *New York Times,* August 5, 1935; "Man Can Knit as Good as Woman," *Boston Post,* August 14, 1935; *Boston Herald,* August 13, 1935; Knitted flag: Philip Bergen, Librarian, The Bostonian Society, to ALM, June 24, 1986.

286 MEN KNITTING: Samuel E. MacDonald, of Sun City West, Ariz., in a telephone conversation with ALM, March 16, 1986; conductors, hockey player and Columbia students in Mackenzie, p. 8; "no reason why men . . .": "Two Men Lead Knitting Class," *New York Times,* October 6, 1936.

287 "In a period of . . .": Mackenzie, p. 8.

287 "because the craft was . . .": Alyce Misner, of Big River, Calif., to ALM, September 12, 1985.

287 WORLD'S FAIR: "Crowded Series of Varied Events Announced in Plan to Spur Attendance," *New York Times,* August 14, 1940; The disgruntled response, not mentioned in the *Times,* was reported to the author by someone present when awards were made.

287–88 LOU HENRY HOOVER: "I have resigned myself . . .": Lou Henry Hoover to Mrs. Theodore Roosevelt, Jr., circa May 2, 1935, in Lou Henry Hoover Papers, Personal Correspondence, Herbert Hoover Presidential Library, West Branch, Iowa; Blanket instructions: Lou Henry Hoover to Therina Pearson, December 4, 1939, in Ibid.; "Don't rip it . . .": Etna M. Kelly, "The Many-Sided Mrs. Herbert Hoover," an unpublished manuscript, p. 11, Lou Henry Hoover Papers, Subject File Series: Hoover, Lou Henry: Articles and Books About, Herbert Hoover Presidential Library.

Chapter 14: The Forties: Knitting in War and Peace

page

289 KNITTING FOR BRITAIN: Hugo L. Smith, "On the Matter of Knitting," Letter to the Editor, *New York Times,* September 17, 1940; Fragment Society, Schlesinger Library, Radcliffe College, MC 338, Box 3, Folder 15; *Minutes of the Annual Meeting,* December 3, 1940; Ibid., Report of meeting of February 2, 1941; Ibid., Report of meeting at the end of the year, 1940–41; Box 2: *Society Scrapbook,* n.p.

289 "where hardly a woman . . .": "U.S. Knits Again," *Business Week,* February 22, 1941, p. 49.

290 RED CROSS KNITTING FOR ALLIES: "Hands and Materials," *Red Cross Courier,*

July 1940, p. 15; British victims: Dorothy Bobbe, "Bundles for Britain," *New York Times Magazine*, December 1, 1940, pp. 12, 21.

290   "[k]nitting is no longer . . .": Director of Voluntary Organizations, *Knitting for the Army: Official Guide* (1941), Introduction.

290   AMERICAN THEATER WING: "Gertrude Lawrence," *Vogue*, July 15, 1940, p. 60.

290   MUSIC: Jo Cobello (words and music), *"Knittin' for Britain"* (1941).

291–92   KNITTING RECOLLECTIONS: "Our teacher started the item . . .": Jane Alencewiz, of Colonia, N.J., To ALM, June 13, 1986; "I feel I contributed . . .": Catherine Nearing, of Gales Ferry, Conn., to ALM, January 21, 1986; "[some] were terrible knitters . . .": anonymous contributor, telephone interview by ALM, July 1986; "She never made it . . .": Lillian C. Lunny, Staten Island, N.Y., to ALM, July 2, 1986. "The evenings, when they went . . .": Rebecca Cripe Allen, Goshen, Ind., to ALM, June 14, 1986; nylon socks and turtleneck sweater: Theresa Konen, East Brunswick, N.J., to ALM, June 12, 1986.

292   DOWNED PILOT: Beverley Royce, Langdon, Kans., to ALM, March 19, 1986.

292–94   SERVICE KNITTING: *Bernat Handicrafter* (1943), vol. XIII, no. 4; *Minerva Hand Knits for Men in the Service* (1941), vol. 62, p. 14; Insigniae: Bernat Handicrafter (September 1941), vol. XII, no. 4, pp. 40, 42, 44; "Give a sailor a set . . .": "Hand Knits for the Boys in the Service," *Bernat Handicrafter* (1942) vol. XIII, no. 3, passim; "It kinda laughs at the wind . . .": Mary Hornaday, "Knit Two, Purl Two—Fingers Fly," *Christian Science Monitor Magazine*, November 11, 1941, p. 12; "The practical way to show . . .": Bernat *Handicrafter* (November 1941), vol. III, no. 3, inside front cover; "visible evidence that someone . . .": "'Knit for Your Boy at Camp'—A New Bear Brand–Bucilla Yarn Promotion," Bernard Ulmann Co., *Bucilla Art Needlework Bulletin*, August 1941; "Nothing warms the hearts . . .": Advertisement for Alice Carroll, ed., *Complete Guide to Modern Knitting and Crocheting* (1942), in *American Weekly*, April 14, 1942, back cover.

294   "Victory Fashions in Hand Knits": I have not seen the entire pamphlet, but the cover was shown in Bernard Ulmann Co.'s *Bucilla Art Needlework Bulletin*, August 1942, n.p.

294–95   "Are you knitting for Bundles . . .": Quoted by Bucilla Art Needlework Bulletin, June 1940.

295   CONTEST: *Bucilla Art Needlework Bulletin*, September 1940, p. 1; Ibid., January 1941, p. 4.

295–96   WOMEN'S RESPONSE: "The womenfolk are at it . . .": Hornaday, p. 12; "The men have hardly time . . .": Jane Cobb, "Knitters—Plain, and Fancy and Otherwise," *New York Times Magazine*, July 21, 1940, p. 8.

296   ALASKAN TROOPS: "Troops in Alaska Need Sweaters," *New York Times*, June 26, 1941.

296   CITIZEN'S COMMITTEE FOR THE ARMY AND NAVY: "the greatest mass knitting . . .": "'Knit for Defense' Tea," *New York Times*, September 15, 1941; "Mass Knitting Movement to Be Launched Tuesday," Ibid., September 28, 1941; "Mrs. Roosevelt Urges All Women to Knit for Soldiers and Sailors," Ibid., October 1, 1941; "Defense Knitting Pushed" Ibid., October 10, 1941; "200 More Enroll to Knit for Troops," Ibid., October 30, 1941; "Christmas Knitting for Soldiers Pushed," Ibid., December 10, 1941; Hornaday, p. 12.

297   "She says she can't knit . . .": Douglas Low cartoon in *Punch*, December 1940, reproduced in *The Pick of "Punch": An Annual Selection*, July 1939—June 1940 (1940), p. 83.

297   "How to Knit: A Million Sweaters Wanted by Christmas," *Life*, November 24, 1941, pp. 110–15, 26.

298   "Do you darn socks here?": Hornaday, p. 12.

298   "They get satisfaction . . .": Cobb, p. 19.

298   FBI STORY: *Bucilla Art Needlework Bulletin*, January 1942, p. 3.

298   "Set up 42 stitches . . .": Elizabeth Ward, "The Mittens That Multiplied Like Rabbits," *Atlantic Monthly*, August 1945, p. 125.

298   GIRLS CAN HELP: George J. Hecht, "Ways Girls Can Help in the National Defense," *Calling All Girls*, June 1944, p. 20; "If you whine and complain . . .": Margaret E. Jessup, "Girls Can Help Win the War," Ibid., March 1942, inside front cover.

298–99   CHILDREN ORGANIZED: Classes in department stores: *Bucilla Art Needlework Bulletin*, December 1940; Playground instruction: Leslie J. Mangin, "Playgrounds Aid National Defense," *Recreation*, September 1941, pp. 389, 402; Greenville, S.C., children: Dorothy Bobbe, "Bundles for Britain," *New York Times Magazine*, December 1, 1940, p. 21.

299–300   RECOLLECTIONS OF WARTIME KNITTING: "loved every minute . . .": Barbara Moeller, of Charlotte, N.C., to ALM, July 4, 1986; "I'm certain that came . . .": Margaret A. Teney, of Fayetteville, N.C., to ALM, June 25, 1986; "We lived in a small . . .": Gloria Witherow, of Hourtzdale, Pa., to ALM, June 17, 1986; Country school: Nancy C. McClure, Chattanooga, Tenn., to ALM, March 9, 1987.

300   "The washcloth you knitted . . .": Eleanor Estes, *Rufus M.* (1943), pp. 36, 45–55, 56.

300–301   BABY BOOM AND SOAKERS: 1940 census figures; Preliminary estimates of twenty thousand more births in the first four months of 1941 than in the comparable period of 1940, in *Bucilla Art Needlework Bulletin*, December 1941, p. 2.; Two good soakers patterns are in Ulmann's *Bear Brand* (no. 329), 1941, p. 7; "I had four children . . .": Vivian Filipak, of Mansfield, Ohio, to ALM, July 1, 1986.

302   Random quotations from interviews with 1940s knitters.

302   KNITTING ACCESSORIES: "It's more fun to knit . . .": *Popular Science*, January

1941, p. 174; "Knitting has become an almost . . .": Ibid., December 1941, pp. 183; Umbrella stand: Ibid., May 1942, p. 193.

302–3 "Floss joined a knitting group . . .": Percy Shaw, first verse of an illustrated poem on the inside cover of "Knit One, Purl Two," lyrics and music by Flossy Frills and Ben Lorre (1942).

304 "First I Knit 2, Purl 2 . . .": Eliza Combs Evans, words, and Lee Darnelle, music, *"Knit 2, Purl 2"* (1942), chorus.

304 EMILY POST: "Etiquette and the War," *New York Times*, May 17, 1943.

304 "Grandma's afghan has the place . . .": "Grab Bag of Ideas," *Bucilla Art Needlework Bulletin*, June 1940.

304 PECK AND PECK AND SAKS: *Bucilla Art Needlework Bulletin*, June 1941, p. 1.

304–5 TAILORKNITS: "Knits in Fashion," *Vogue*, January 1941, pp. 56–60.

305 SWEATERS FOR MEN: "Knit your way to his heart! . . .": *Movie Star Hand Knits for Men* (1940), vol. 316, inside front cover; Broadcasting sweaters: *Fleisher Book of Men's Hand Knits* (1940), vol. 62.

305–7 RHOTOGRAVURE SECTIONS: New York *Herald Tribune*, December 22, 1940; *New York Times*, January 8, 1941.

307 "From shop-girl to socialite . . .": Advertisement for a book edited by Alice Carroll, *American Weekly*, April 14, 1942, back cover.

307 "Mary knits helmets steadily . . .": Kathleen Norris, "Woman's Share of War Is Service," *Woman's Life*, Fall 1942, p. 86.

308 WELLESLEY STUDY: Dorothy Jane Hendrickson and Doris Mosher of the class of 1941's study was reported by Rosalie Goldstein, "Wellesley Wardrobe Contains 10 Sweaters, Six Skirts, .7 Fur Coats," *Wellesley College News*, February 13, 1941.

308 CAMPUS KNITTING: *Mademoiselle* poll; *Bucilla Art Needlework Bulletin*, August 1942, p. 4; "get the students to become . . .": Ibid.; College Boards: Ibid.; October 1940, n.p.; New Jersey colleges: Ibid.; January 1942, p. 3.

308–9 WARTIME ADVERTISING: Lingeman, *Don't You Know There's a War On?*, p. 292.

309 MEMOIRS: "All of the waitresses . . .": Jean H. Coe, Maiden, N.C., to ALM, June 16, 1986; "I made mine while riding . . .": Josephine Kaiser Zillian, of McLean, Va., to ALM, May 13, 1986; "As a sophomore in . . .": Pat Trexler, of North Myrtle Beach, S.C., to ALM, May 17, 1986.

310 TEEN KNITTING FADS: "Socks with a Sock" in "Gadgets for Girls," *Calling All Girls*, June 1942, p. 41; Ruler buttons: Ibid., October 1942, p. 34; Belt: Ibid., July 1942, p. 9; Reversible belt: "Keep Yourself in Stitches," Ibid., September 1942, p. 42.

310 "So you're crooning for . . .": "Teen Agers Urged to Knit Ahead for School," Ibid., June 1944, p. 44.

310 STORE PROMOTIONS: *Bucilla Art Needlework Bulletin*, July 1941, p. 4.

310   "fitting apparel for day . . .": "Dressed-Up Sweaters," *Life*, January 25, 1943, p. 45.

310   SWEATERS ON THE, JOB: Lingeman, pp. 150, 157–58.

310   SWEATERS OFF THE JOB: "Dressed-Up Sweaters," p. 45.

311   LANA TURNER: The picture: Schumach, *The Face on the Cutting Room Floor*, p. 169; "I figured that a tight sweater . . .": Mervyn LeRoy, quoted in Valentino, *The Films of Lana Turner*, p. 59; "One of those bright . . .": "Life and Loves, of Lana Turner," *Movie Mirror*, June 9, 1940, p. 91.

311–12   "KNIT FOR NEEDY CHILDREN" CONTEST: *Smart Knitting*, 1st ed., August 1947, center spread. The first-prize winner, Mrs. Wayne Block, of Washington, Okla., was announced in Ibid., 5th ed., 1948, p. 49.

312   HOME STUDY COURSE: Advertisements in *Smart Knitting*, August 16, 1948, p. 66; Ibid., Winter 1946–47, p. 80.

312   "liberate the art of knitting . . .": Elizabeth Harrison, "Knitting Skill is Now Taught to Youngsters," *New York Times*, April 19, 1951.

312   "hand-knitted bare-knee ensemble": *The Bucilla Bulletin*, January 1940, n.p.

312   "Well, no, but mothers . . .": Harrison, ibid.

313   "Knit for your man" exhortations were chosen at random from advertisements and magazine articles in late 1940s women's and knitting magazines; "Knit for Him," *Good Housekeeping*, April 1948, p. 229.

313   NYLON: "Nylon They Want, Nylon They Get," *Men's Wear*, July 22, 1949, p. 130; "Imagine, a beginning knitter . . .": Jane Snibbe, of Pebble Beach, Calif., to ALM, April 8, 1986.

313–16   ARGYLE FAD: Interview with William Bernat in Uxbridge, Mass., October 15, 1985; "In order to earn . . .": Doris Walton Epner, of Brooklyn Heights, N.Y., to ALM, May 6, 1986; Maria Robertson, of Annandale, Va., telephone interview with ALM, March 16, 1986; "I made every pattern . . .": Phyllis Trelaor, of Garden Grove, Calif., to ALM, July 24, 1986; "But after I married . . .": Shirley Cannon, of Sandy, Utah, to ALM, June 18, 1986; "I just kept on knitting . . .": Ruth Folsom, Charlotte, N.C., to ALM, September 27, 1986; "In college I did special . . .": Edith Anne O'Brien, Mount Vernon, Wash., to ALM, November 10, 1986; "in my three-button suit . . .": Samuel E. MacDonald, Sun City West, Ariz., telephone conversation with ALM, March 16, 1986.

316   COLORPLUS PATTERNS: Good examples of Colorplus patterns can be found in *Smart Knitting*, 5th ed., 1948, pp. 34, 53; "My husband still has . . .": Florence Polens, Stafford Springs, Conn., to ALM, June 30, 1986.

316   INVENTING THE "ARGYLE BOX": United States Patent no. 4,548,055 granted to Anne L. Macdonald, 1985.

316–17   ARGYLE INSTRUCTIONS: "When tying one color . . .": Abbey, *Susan Bates Presents 101 Ways to Improve Your Knitting* (1949), pp. 58–60; Nell Armstrong, *Doreen Two Needle Argyles*, vol. 96, Lowell, Mass.: Doreen Knitting Books, 1947 (the original of this leaflet is at the Detroit Historical

Museum); Patent no. 2,416,040 granted to N. M. Armstrong for *Method of Knitting Socks on Two Needles*, February 1947; "chicken wire" socks: *Smart Knitting*, 4th Ed., 1948, pp. 35, 52.

318   "We had to count and check . . .": Eileen Hasselwood, of Pacific Grove, Calif., to ALM, May 5, 1986.

318   "so closely does it resemble . . .": *Stitches*, September 1903, p. 6.

318   ANGORA: Foam on beer mugs decoration: Eleanor M. Holland, of Holden, Mass., to ALM, July 4, 1986; "Angora rabbit hair continues . . .": *Bucilla Art Needlework Bulletin*, May 1942, n.p.; "I first started to knit . . .": Shirley Cannon, of Sandy, Utah, to ALM, June 18, 1986.

319   "Wear this blouse five . . .": *Smart Knitting*, 3rd ed., 1947, p. 2.

319-20   Edith (Jackie) Ronne, of Bethesda, Md., interviewed August 5, 1986.

Chapter 15:
Knitting from A to Z:
Argyles to Zimmermann

page

321   "A sleeping sickness is . . .": Fannie Hurst quoted in Goldman, *The Crucial Decade*, p. 47.

321   "People have become accustomed . . .": Maurice O'Brien quoted in Goldman, p. 13.

322   "Marriage and children are . . .": Polly Weaver, "What's Wrong with Ambition?" *Mademoiselle*, September 1956, p. 191.

322   MOTHER OF SEVEN: Jane Alencewiz, of Colonia, N.J., to ALM, June 13, 1986.

323   "comfortable concentration camp[s]": Friedan, *It Changed My Life*, p. 16.

323   "sat over an embroidery . . .": Jhan and June Robbins, "Why Young Mothers Feel Trapped," *Redbook*, September 1960, pp. 28-29, 94.

323   INSURANCE STATISTICS: Goldman, p. 262.

323   "Last week, when my . . .": Robbins and Robbins, pp. 83-85.

323   "We hardly ever do . . .": Weaver, p. 191.

324   "cooking or an incentive . . .": Judith Churchill, "Is Boredom Bad for You?" *McCall's*, April 1957, pp. 51, 53.

324   KNITTING FOR KOREAN CHILDREN: "Warmth for the Orphans of Korea," *McCall's*, October 1953, pp. 15-16.

324   "We've surveyed the boys . . .": "Serviceman's Section," *Smart Knitting*, 1951, 8th ed., p. 24.

324-25   "Let's not forget . . .": Betty Cornell, *Betty Cornell's Teen-Age Knitting Book* (1953), p. 99.

325   Virginia Williams, of Omaha, Nebr., to ALM, June 11, 1986.

325 "As every woman who . . .": Rose Wilder Lane, *Woman's Day Book of American Needlework* (1963), p. 165.

325 "You all know what . . .": Betty Cornell, *Betty Cornell's Teen-Age Knitting Book* (1953), introduction, p. 1, and p. 102.

325 "just tying knots . . .": Thomas E. Doremus, "The Uses of Knitting," *Atlantic Monthly*, April 1958, pp. 97–98.

326 "I remember making him . . .": Catherine Niering, of Gales Ferry, Conn., to ALM, January 21, 1986.

326 "What fun! I still . . .": Anne Shoe, of China Grove, N.C., to ALM, June 18, 1986.

326 "They were a horrible . . .": Joan Newton, of Stanton, Calif., to ALM, July 13, 1986.

327 "keyed to young tastes . . .": "Argyle Knits for Teens," *McCall's Needlework and Crafts*, vol. 6, 1956, pp. 34–35. *McCall's* previously showed caps, socks and mittens in "New Plaids Have a Young Appeal," Ibid., vol. 2, 1951, pp. 36–38.

327 CADET: Story related to ALM by Jean Y. Haley, Moundsville, W.Va., August 8, 1986.

328 "frayed nerves, neglected families . . .": The Woman's Auxiliary of St. Paul's Church, Chestnut Hill, Pa., *Knit One for the Crib Kids—The Carriage Trade—and the High Chair Set* (1953), introduction, pp. iv, v; p. 88.

328 "Recently I read a book . . .": Ibid., pp. 1–2.

328–29 OTHER NEW STYLES: *Book of Toppits-Stoles-Jackets* (1954), no. 168; *Bernat Book of Collars* (1954), no. 16; Cover-up: *Handicrafter* (1951), no. 154 and no. 169; Darlan: *Handicrafter* (1957), no. 179, p. 1.

329 INSTITUTE FOR HAND KNITTING: "California Girl, 16, Wins Knitting Prize," *New York Times*, October 4, 1950; "2 Teen-age Knitters Visit City as Award," ibid., December 6, 1950.

329 "Hi! Oh, pardon me . . .": Cornell, *Teen-Age Knitting*, pp. 3, 63, 115, 131.

330 TV SWEATER: *Saturday Night TV Sweater* ([c. 1950]). Original pamphlet is in the collection of the Detroit Historical Museum.

330 "poor workmanship": Schulte, *The Seventeen Book of Quick Things to Make and Wear* (1973), p. 1.

330 "this plastic, manufactured world": Cornell, p. 106.

330 "friendship . . . will always accept . . .": Owen, *The Illuminated Book of Needlework* (1847), p. 56.

330 "You can knit that . . .": McElwaine, *Knitting with Stop and Go Needles* (1968), p. 8.

330 William Unger: Interview with ALM in Queens, N.Y., July 2, 1986.

330 FORTIES' KNITTING: Carroll, *Complete Guide to Modern Knitting and Crocheting* (1942).

331   "Forty dollars for *what*?": Jane Alencewiz, of Colonia, N.J., to ALM, June 13, 1986.

331   "They've gotten us . . .": "The Big Stitch," *Time*, October 13, 1967, p. 74.

331   "Jiffy Jumbos are huge . . .": *Vogue Knitting*, Spring/Summer 1968, p. 82.

331   "lead fast-moving lives . . .": Jeanne Damon, *Jeanne Damon's Quick Knits*, Jane Bedford, ed., (1968), no. 1, Introduction and pp. 11, 40, 41, 101.

332   KNITTING SCHOOL DIRECTOR: Noble and Levin, *How to Successfully Operate a Knitting Shop* (1961), p. 87.

332   "One project using those . . .": Joyce Goetz, of Charlotte, N.C., to ALM, July 15, 1986.

332   "Sometimes I felt I . . .": Mary Ellen D'Aurezio, of Niagara Falls, N.Y., to ALM, June 16, 1986.

332–33   "It is like a shimmery . . .": Mrs. Irene Steptoe, of Chevy Chase, Md., to ALM, June 21, 1986.

333   "I always carried my . . .": Alencewiz, ibid.

333   "I knit my way . . .": Sharron Freeman, West Hartford, Conn., to ALM, June 1986.

333   "No, my tranquility is . . .": Vivian Russell, of Morganfield, Ky., to ALM, June 15, 1986.

334   "totally behind the steering . . .": Myrna Lippman, of Scotch Plains, N.J., to ALM, February 5, 1987.

334   WILLIAM UNGER: Interview, July 2, 1986.

334   Ida L. Lloyd, of Indianapolis, Ind., to ALM, June 26, 1986.

334–35   BICENTENNIAL LAP ROBE: Lillian Meade, of Toms River, N.J., to ALM, June 9, 23, 1986.

335   KNITTING CLASS: Angela Taylor, "Out with the Boys? Yes, But for a Knitting Lesson," *New York Times*, February 14, 1971.

335   NATURAL FIBERS: "The Primal Knits," *Mademoiselle*, July 1973, pp. 102–105.

335   "if your friends make . . .": Lynn Spaulding, "Why Not Knit a Nosewarmer?" *Mother Earth News*, January/February 1979, p. 165.

336   BARBARA WALKER: "[W]hen you go to the Library . . .": Quoted by Alexander Xenakis, "The Barbara Walker Mosaic," *Knitters*, Fall/Winter 1985, p. 12; Walker, *A Treasury of Knitting Patterns* (1968); Walker, *A Second Treasury of Knitting Patterns* (1970).

336   MARY WALKER PHILLIPS: Phillips, *Creative Knitting* (1971); "the transition between old-fashioned . . .": quoted in "Mary Walker Phillips: Doyenne of Art Knitting [Interview]," *Knitters*, Spring/Summer 1985, pp. 15, 17; ALM's conversation with Phillips at the Knitting Guild of America Convention in New Orleans, March 5, 1987.

336–37   ELIZABETH ZIMMERMANN: ALM conducted background telephone interviews with Elizabeth Zimmermann on February 2, 1986, and with Meg

Swansen on March 27, 1986. Other materials are cited herewith: "Properly practiced, knitting soothes . . .": Zimmermann, *Knitting Without Tears* (1971), p. 2; "The main thing about knitting . . .": Robin Hansen's interview with Zimmermann, in "Elizabeth Zimmermann," *Vogue Knitting*, Spring/Summer 1985, p. 14; "Elizabeth says so": Ellen Burton, of Nacogdoches, Tex., interview with ALM on March 3, 1986.

338   "[The first time] [t]here . . .": Joan Schrouder, telephone conversation with ALM, February 2, 1986.

338   "Queen of the Knitters": Jean Krebs, Saulk Centre, Minn., telephone conversation with ALM, February, 1986.

338   "Elizabeth's knitting hands have . . .": Beverly Royce, of Langdon, Kans., to ALM, February 24, 1986.

339   "It nearly killed me . . .": Editor's interview with Elizabeth Zimmermann, "An Afternoon with Elizabeth," *Knitters*, premier issue, 1984, p. 12.

Chapter 16: Knitting Now and WhitherKnit?

page

340   MERCHANDISING: Duane Newcomb, "Merchandising for Today's Decade of Change," *Yarn Market News*, March/April 1985, pp. 26–27, 35, passim.

340–41   CURRENT TRENDS: "fast-paced modern life style": Margaret Hubert and Dorothy Dean Gusick, *Weekend Knitting Projects* (1979), Introduction, p. 5; Bruce Goodpasture, "In the Crannied Wall," *Yarn Market News*, March/April 1985, p. 25; "People don't knit to . . .": Elizabeth Sporkin, "We're Tangled Up Again in Knitting," *USA Today* [c. October 1985] (this clipping was given me without a date); "Hand knitting is not . . .": Maggie Righetti, of Atlanta, Ga., to ALM, April 23, 1986; "[I]t hardly pays to . . .": Linda Weltner, "Stitches in Time," in "Ever So Humble," *Boston Globe*, January 17, 1986.

341–42   KNITTING FOR TRANQUILITY: "The quiet, even, regular . . .": *Dorcas Magazine*, March 1884, p. 1; "Maybe it has something . . .": Bryna Millman, of New York City, to ALM, June 6, 1986; "No, my doctor told . . .": Esther Willard, of Glastonbury, Conn., to ALM, June 18, 1986; "Knitting keeps me out . . .": Daisy Burka, of Berwin, Pa., in an interview with ALM in Milwaukee, March 5, 1986; "I always have several . . .": Betty Peacock, of Reston, Va., to ALM, March 17, 1986.

342   "I had to practice . . .": Connie Ferdinandson, Santa Barbara, Calif., to ALM, August 16, 1987.

342–43   KNITTING FOR HEALTH: "same beneficial effect . . .": *Stitches*, December 1902 [premier issue], p. 17; "You really push through . . .": Quoted in

Jody Kolodzey, "Knit Your Way to Health," *Prevention*, June 1981, pp. 104, 106; "Knitting to me is . . .": Rebecca Newman, of Point Pleasant, N.J., to ALM, June 18, 1986; "When you work and . . .": Kolodzey, p. 102; "I have become . . .": Ibid., pp. 104–106; "I am instantly drawn . . .": Sharron Freeman, West Hartford, Conn., to ALM, June 12, 1986.

343–44   NEED FOR GRANDMOTHERS: "The frail old lady . . .": Alan A. Otten, "Grandparents Today Are Sprier, Sharper, Richer and Plentiful," *Wall Street Journal*, May 11, 1987; "to bring an old . . .": Robin Hansen, *Fox and Geese and Fences* (1983), p. 7; "They [the patterns] have . . .": Hansen with Dexter, *Flying Geese & Partridge Feet* (1986), Introduction.

344–45   CERTIFICATION: Evie Rosen, "The APNR/TNNA National Certification and Education Program," *Yarn Market News*, January/February 1986, pp. 24, 43–45; Interview with Evie Rosen by ALM at Milwaukee convention of Knitting Guild of America, April 5, 1986.

345   "alert, smart, aggressive . . .": Irving Nacht, "Recollections of the Early Days in the Yarn Industry," *Yarn Market News*, January/February 1986, p. 40; "I have to keep . . .": The author took Mrs. Rosen's "buttonholes" class at the Knitting Guild of America's convention in New Orleans in March 1987, and talked with her afterward.

346   "[November] Members are reminded . . .": These are excerpts from *Youngstown Vindicator* clippings covering several months in 1985 and are preserved in a scrapbook kept by the Western Reserve Knitting Guild. Janie S. Jenkins wrote of the December 10 meeting when the guild made fifty-seven caps in "Bits 'n Pieces."

346–47   "I have only been . . .": Margaret Chasalow, Maplewood, N.J., in "Needles and Purls," *Cast On*, Fall 1985, p. 4; "I need help in . . .": Gloria Strayer, North Lima, Ohio, Ibid., Summer 1986, p. 4; "I am looking for . . .": Elinor Elligott, of Wynantskill, N.Y., Ibid., Spring 1985; p. 7; "I am searching for . . .": Charlotte Miller, of Harrison, Ariz., Ibid., Spring 1987, p. 6. Regarding the latter's query about patterns for those decades, the author met Ms. Miller at the national convention of the Knitting Guild of America in New Orleans in March 1987 and arranged to show her where yards and yards of Library of Congress shelves house just what she is searching for!

347   ATLANTA: Whit Robbins reported on the Atlanta Guild at Dallas, Milwaukee and New Orleans TKGA conventions.

347–48   SHERIDAN, WYOMING: "I only do it . . .": Marcia Spracklen, Sheridan, Wyo., to ALM, June 6, 1986; "We are like a . . .": Victoria Legerski, Birney, Mont., to ALM, May 5, 1986.

348–49   "TRADITIONAL" KNITTING: Probert, *Knitting in* Vogue (1982); Probert, *More Knitting in* Vogue (1983); Probert, *Great Knitting in* Vogue (1985) [Probert has several other books based on *Vogue*'s patterns]; Waller, *Classic Knitting Patterns from the British Isles* (1985); Waller, *A Stitch in Time* (1973); Carroll, *Knitting and Crocheting Your Own Fashions of the Forties*

(1973) [This is actually a reprint of *The Complete Guide of Modern Knitting and Crocheting*, originally published in 1942 and 1949]; Bradley, *Stitches in Time* (1986); Gibson-Roberts, *Knitting in the Old Way* (1985); "I'm going to throw . . .": Linda Chavez, in "Washington Wire," *Wall Street Journal*, November 22, 1985; Warren and Pullan, *Treasures in Needlework* (1870); Wiczyk, ed. and comp., *A Treasury of Needlework Projects from Godey's Lady's Book* (1972); Lizbeth Upitis, "Return of the Reticule," *Knitters*, Spring/Summer 1986, pp. 44–47; "A Knitted Counterpane," circa 1860, reproduced from *Godey's Lady's Book*, in Grace Nylander, "Counterpanes," *Early American Life*, April 1986, p. 64; Mary Walker Phillips has a book in progress on counterpanes; "I was a veteran . . .": Yolanda Thompson, of Washington, D.C., to ALM, June 19, 1986.

349   "Describe myself? That's easy . . .": Advertisements for the *Washington Post* and radio scripts were furnished to the author by Mr. Peter Schlossberg, president of Wild and Wooly Needlecrafts, of Falls Church, Va.

349   THEATER: The superstition was brought to the author's attention by Cindy Weeks, of Sparta, N.J., in a letter of June 24, 1986. Weeks also heard of conductors' going into a rage if anyone knit during rehearsals, perhaps because of the noise rather than the taboo; "It makes me feel . . .": quoted in Susan Heller Anderson and David Bird, "Without Dropping a Stitch," *New York Times*, January 9, 1986.

349–50   SWEATER COSTS: "Susan Beebe's Sweaters Are Warm, but Can Cost a Cool $1,850 Each," *People*, November 16, 1981, p. 144.

350   COTTAGE INDUSTRY: *Arizona Republican*, May 15, 1979; Quotations from "Rags to Riches," *Greater Phoenix Jewish News*, March 20, 1985, and Julia Jones, "Knitting Pretty," *Phoenix Gazette*, November 1, 1985; ALM's interview with Estelle Gracer, February, 12, 1986.

350–51   "Yarn shops sell yarn . . .": "Macy's New Knit Works: Everything for the Hand-knitter Who Wants Designer Sweaters," *Stores*, January 1982, pp. 34–35.

351   HIGGINBOTHAM: Susan Davidson, "Knit One, Purl One," *Washingtonian*, December 1982, pp. 241, 244; L. Lanier Cooper, "Craftsman Has Knit His Niche Selling Yarn," *Washington Post*, September 8, 1983.

351   "golden hours reserved for . . .": Maynard Good Stoddard, "Knit 2, Purl 1, Hubby 0," *Saturday Evening Post*, April 1982, pp. 62–63.

351–52   MALE KNITTERS: "Please, there are legions . . .": Jim Pitzer, of Seattle, Wash., in "The Write Word," *Vogue Knitting*, Spring/Summer 1985, p. 6; "I've also had some . . .": James J. Phelan, of Fayetteville, N.C., to ALM, June 19, 1986; "Yesterday a lady brought . . .": Sam Miller, of Fairfield, Ind., to ALM, June 17, 1986.

352   "There are no idle . . .": Quoted in Jan Oblinger, "Knitting know-how a knockout," *Bangor Daily News*, March 2, 1982.

353   BUSY KNITTING: "Who hasn't envied a . . .": "A Gallery of Winter Craft Projects," *Mother Earth News*, January/February 1984, p. 37; "As a school

librarian . . .": Jane Snibbe, of Pebble Beach, Calif., to ALM, April 8, 1986.

353   PRODUCTIVENESS: Enid Nemy, "Quitters: Two 'smoked' food, another knitted," *New York Times*, February 22, 1987; "My husband and I . . .": Lynn M. Hardy, New Bedford, Mass., in "The Write Word," *Vogue Knitting*, Spring/Summer 1985, p. 6; Jane Alencewiz, of Colonia, N.J., to ALM, June 13, 1986.

353–54   "I'm your typical modern . . .": Lynnette Timko of Clearfield, Pa., to ALM, March 10, 1987.

354   PHILANTHROPY: "Thank you for the . . .": Related by Marcia Freeman, West Caldwell, N.J., to ALM, June 12, 1986; Hallie White, of Rutherfordton, N.C., to ALM, June 16, 1986, and April 17, 1987.

355   CAPS FOR KIDS: "My customers always seemed . . .": Bonnie Greene, of Danville, Calif., to ALM, January 10, 1986; Help from Bernat, Bucilla, Brunswick and Boye: "News and Notes," *Yarn Market News*, November/December 1986, p. 50.

355   INTERNATIONAL PROJECTS: Peace fleece, project of Peter and Marty Hardy, of Kezar Falls, Maine; "Peaceful Yarn," *Washington Post*, February 8, 1986; "We Can Knit the World Together," advertisement in *Cast On*, Summer 1986, p. 18; Haitian children: Nellie Dice, of Denver, Ind., to ALM, June 6, 1986; Third world hospital patients: Audrey Calligy, of Hoboken, N.J., to ALM, June 1, 1986.

355–56   CHURCH WORLD SERVICE: "One day in the . . .": Dice, ibid.; *Church World Service*, n.p.; *Highways of Service* (Church World Service: Elkhart, Ind; n.d.), passim.; *Forget-Me-Knots*, Church World Service Clothing Appeal; Elkhart, Ind., n.d., p. 8; Mary Warren, South Lyme, Conn., to ALM, June 30, 1986.

356–58   SEAMEN'S CHURCH INSTITUTE: *Seamen's Church Institute of New York and New Jersey*, published by the institute; "I like to knit . . .": and other quotations: *The Lookout*, Summer 1986, p. 27; Charlotte Stafford, *Knitting World*, April 1986, pp. 22–23; "They Make Sailors' Christmas Seasonal," *Modern Maturity*, December 1983–January 1984, pp. 60–61; *Christmas-at-Sea Newsletter*, December 1986, n.p.; "I couldn't believe I'd . . .": Irene Graessle, Maplewood, N.J., to ALM, June 24, 1986; Knitters from the Army Distaff Hall in Washington have been active knitters and have generously drawn from their storehouses of knitting memories; "After my cousin, the . . .": William Pickslay, Jr., of Carson City, Nev., to ALM, July 6, 1987; "I would like to . . .": "Christmas at Sea 1985," *The Lookout*, Spring 1986, p. 10; "I put a big . . .": *Christmas-at-Sea Newsletter*, Spring 1986, p. 3.

358   KNITTING MACHINES: "One day knitting machines . . .": "Knit One, Purl Two, But with a Twist," *New York Times*, April 17, 1986; "We had a knitting . . .": Grace Hudkins, of Springfield, Vt., to ALM, June 12, 1986.

358–59   VERMONT KNITTERS: Toby Kahn, "A Controversial Labor Law Has Vermont Home Knitters Outraged but Tied up in Knots," *People*, March 19, 1984; "No Knitting at Home," *Washington Post*, December 12, 1983; "Tip of the Ski Cap," *Wall Street Journal*, November 12, 1984.

359   KNITTING AND AUDIO-VISUALS: "I thought of it . . .": Maggie Righetti, Atlanta, Ga., to ALM, April 23, 1986. Righetti's tape was done for Jeanette Crews Designs; "A young man is . . .": *Knitting: A Simplified Approach to Basics* (1983), reviewed in *School Library Journal*, January 1984, p. 54.

360   "When I went into . . .": Barbara Moody, of Washington, D.C., owner of The Yellow Binding in suburban Bethesda, Md., interview with ALM, April 14, 1987.

360   "Two years ago, when . . .": Pat Coukos, of Richmond, Calif., to ALM, July 16, 1986.

361   "When Satan moves in . . .": *The Quiet Hour Echoes*, March 1986, p. 13, reprinted in *News from Frazee Retirement Center*, 1986, and submitted June 6, 1986, to ALM by Madeline Andress, of Silvis, Ill.

Bibliography

Secondary Sources

Adair, Douglas, and Schultz, John A., eds. *Peter Oliver's Origin and Progress of the American Revolution: a Tory View.* San Marino, Calif.: The Huntington Library, 1961.

Adams, Estella. *Pioneer Life for Little Children.* Indianapolis: Bobbs-Merrill Co., 1916.

Alden, Cynthia Westover. *Women's Ways of Earning Money.* New York: A. S. Barnes and Co., 1904.

Allen, Eleanor. *Canvas Caravans.* Portland, Oreg.: Binford and Mort, Publishers, 1946.

Allen, Frederick Lewis. *Only Yesterday: An Informal History of the 1920's.* New York: Harper and Row, 1931.

————. *Since Yesterday: The 1930's in America.* New York: Harper and Row, 1940.

Anderson, Lucy L. *North Carolina Women of the Confederacy.* Charlotte, N.C.: The United Daughters of the Confederacy, 1926.

Andrews, Charles M. *The Boston Merchants and the Non-Importation Movement.* Cambridge, Mass.: John Wilson and Company, 1917.

Andrews, Matthew Page. *The Women of the South in War Times.* Baltimore: The Northern, Remington Co., 1920.

Appolonio, Thornton D. *Boston Public Schools, Past and Present.* Boston: Wright and Potter, 1923.

Arrington, Leonard J. *Orderville, Utah: Pioneer Mormon Experiment in Economic Organization.* [Salt Lake City, Utah]: Utah State Agricultural College, March, 1954.

Ayer, Mary Falwell. *Early Days on Boston Common.* Boston: privately printed, 1910.

Bagnall, William R. *The Textile Industries of the United States.* 2 vols. Cambridge, Mass.: Riverside Press, 1893; Reprint. New York: Augustus M. Kelley, Publishers, 1971.

Bailey, Carolyn Sherwin. *Boys and Girls of Pioneer Days from Lincoln to Washington.* Chicago: A. Flanagan Company, 1924.

———. *What to Do for Uncle Sam: A First Book of Citizenship.* Chicago: A. Flanagan Company, 19[18?].

Bailey, Sarah Loring. *Historical Sketches of Andover {Mass.}.* Boston: Houghton Mifflin, 1880.

Baldwin, Alice M. *The New England Clergy and the American Revolution.* Durham, N.C.: Duke University Press, 1928.

Banner, Lois A. *American Beauty.* New York: Alfred A. Knopf, 1983.

Barber, Samuel. *Boston Common: A Diary of Notable Events, Incidents, and Neighboring Occurrences.* 2d ed. Boston: Christopher Publishing House, 1916.

Barrows, Esther G. *Neighbors All: A Settlement Notebook.* Boston: Houghton Mifflin, 1929.

Bauersfield, Marjorie Edith [O'Neil]. *Tales of the Early Days.* Hollywood, Calif.: Oxford Press, 1938.

Beard, Mary R., ed. *America Through Women's Eyes.* New York: Macmillan Company, 1933.

Beecher, Catherine E. *A Treatise on Domestic Economy.* Boston: Marsh, Capen, Lyon and Webb, 1841.

———, and Stowe, Harriet Beecher. *The American Woman's Home, or Principles of Domestic Science.* Boston: J.B. Ford and Company, 1869.

Beilenson, Evelyn L., and Tenenbaum, Ann. *Wit and Wisdom of Famous American Women.* White Plains, N.Y.: Peter Pauper Press, 1986.

Benson, Mary Sumner. *Women in Eighteenth-Century America: A Study of Opinion and Social Usage.* New York: Columbia University Press, 1935.

Bevier, Isabel, and Susannah Usher. *The Home Economics Movement.* Part 1 of 2. Boston: Whitcom and Barrows, 1906.

Bishop, John Leander. *A History of American Manufactures from 1608 to 1860.* 3 vols. Philadelphia: Edward Young and Company, 1868.

Blake, Frances Everett. *History of the Town of Princeton.* 2 vols. Princeton, Mass.: Published by the town, 1915.

Blumenthal, Walter H. *Women Camp Followers of the American Revolution.* Philadelphia: George S. MacManus Company, 1952.

Booth, Sally Smith. *The Women of '76.* New York: Hastings House Publishers, 1973.

Bowles, Ella Shannon. *Homespun Handicrafts.* Philadelphia: J. B. Lippincott, 1931.

Boynton, Charles B. *History of the Great Western Sanitary Fair.* Cincinnati: C. F. Vent and Co., 1864.

Braeman, John. *The Road to Independence: A Documentary History of the Causes of the American Revolution, 1763–1776.* New York: G. P. Putnam's Sons, 1963.

Britton, Dorothea S. *The Complete Book of Bazars.* New York: Coward, McCann and Geoghegan, 1973.

Brownlee, W. Elliot, and Brownlee, Mary M. *Women in the American Economy: A Documentary History, 1675–1929.* New Haven: Yale University Press, 1976.

Bruce, H. Addington. *Woman in the Making of America.* Boston: Little, Brown, and Co., 1912.

Budd, Thomas. *Good Order Established in Pennsylvania and New Jersey in America.* New York: Burt Franklin, 1685; Reprint. New York: Burt Franklin, 1971. Burt Franklin Research and Source Works Series.

Burt, Emily Rose. *Make Your Bazar Pay.* New York: Harper and Brothers, 1925.

Bushman, Claudia L., ed. *Mormon Sisters: Women In Early Utah.* Cambridge, Mass.: Emmeline Press, Ltd., 1976.

Cahoon, Haryot Holt. *What One Woman Thinks.* New York: Tait, Sons & Company, 1893.

Calhoun, Arthur Wallace. *The Colonial Period.* A Social History of the American Family, vol. 1. n.p., 1917. Reprint (3 vols. in 1). New York: Barnes and Noble, Inc., 1945.

Case, Lora. *Hudson of Long Ago.* Hudson, Ohio: Hudson Library and Historical Society, 1963.

Chase, Stuart. *Prosperity Fact or Myth.* New York: Charles Boni, 1929.

Chidsey, Donald Barr. *Valley Forge.* New York: Crown Publishers, Inc., 1959.

Clinton, Catherine. *The Other Civil War: American Women in the Nineteenth Century.* New York: Hill and Wang, 1984.

Cole, Arthur Harrison. *The American Wool Manufacture.* 2 vols. Cambridge, Mass.: Harvard University Press, 1926.

Collett, Glenna. *Ladies in the Rough.* New York: Alfred A. Knopf, 1928.

Cometti, Elizabeth. *Social Life in Virginia During the War for Independence.* Williamsburg, Va.: Virginia Bicentennial Commission, 1978.

Cooper, Patricia, and Buford, Norma Bradley. *The Quilters: Women and Domestic Art.* New York: Doubleday, 1977.

Cott, Nancy F. *The Bonds of Womanhood: "Woman's Sphere" in New England, 1780–1835.* New Haven.: Yale University Press, 1977.

Cowan, Ruth Scwartz. *More Work for Mother: The Ironies of Household Technology from the Open Hearth to the Microwave.* New York: Basic Books, Inc., 1983.

Crawford, Mary Caroline. *Social Life in Old New England.* Boston: Little, Brown and Co., 1914.

Creekmore, Betsey B. *Traditional American Crafts.* [n.p.]: Hearthside Press, Inc., 1968.

Croly, Jane C. *Sorosis: Its Origin and History.* New York: Press of J. J. Little and Co., 1868.

Cruzic, Kathleen. *Disabled? Yes. Defeated? No : Resources for the Disabled and Their Families, Friends, and Therapists.* Englewood Cliffs, N.J.: Prentice-Hall, Inc., 1982.

Cubberly, Ellwood P. *Readings in Public Education.* Boston: Houghton Mifflin, 1936. Reprint. Westport, Conn.: Greenwood Press, 1970.

Dannett, Sylvia, and Jones, Katharine. *Our Women of the Sixties.* Washington, D.C.: U.S. Civil War Bicentennial Commission, 1963.

Deems, Mervin, M. *A Home Away from Home: The Boston Seamen's Friend Society, Inc., 1827–1975*. Bangor, Maine: Fursburg-Roberts Printing Co., 1974.

Degler, Carl N. *At Odds: Women and the Family in America from the Revolution to the Present*. New York: Oxford University Press, 1980.

DePauw, Linda Grant. *Founding Mothers: Women in America in the Revolutionary Era*. Boston: Houghton Mifflin Co., 1975.

———. *Fortunes of War: New Jersey Women and the American Revolution*. Trenton, N.J.: New Jersey Historical Commission, 1975.

———, and Hunt, Conover. *Remember the Ladies: Women in America 1759–1815*. New York: Viking Press, 1976.

Dexter, Elisabeth D. *Colonial Women of Affairs*. Boston: Houghton Mifflin, 1924.

Dickens, Charles. *American Notes*. New York: John W. Lovell Co., 1883.

Douthit, Mary Osborn. *The Souvenir of Western Women*. Portland, Oreg.: Anderson and Duniway Co., 1915.

Dow, George Francis. *Domestic Life in New England in the Seventeenth Century*. Topsfield, Mass.: Perkins Press, 1925.

Drake, Daniel, M.D. *Pioneer Life in Kentucky*. Cincinnati, Ohio: Robert Clarke and Company, 1870.

Draper, Mabel Hobson. *Though Long the Trail*. New York: Rinehart and Co., Inc., 1946.

Earle, Alice Morse. *Colonial Days in Old New York*. Detroit: Singing Tree Press, 1968.

———. *Customs and Fashions in Old New England*. Williamstown, Mass.: Corner House Publishers, 1969.

———. *Home Life in Colonial Days*. New York: Macmillan, 1898.

———. *Home Life and Children's Life in Colonial Days*. New York: Macmillan, 1899. Reprint. *Child Life in Colonial Days*. New York: Macmillan, 1969.

———. *Two Centuries of Costume in America, 1620–1820*. 2 vols. New York: Macmillan, 1903. Reprint. New York: Dover Publications, 1970.

Earle, Walter A. *Scrimshaw: Folk Art of the Whalers*. Cold Spring Harbor, N.Y.: Whaling Museum, Inc., 1957.

Egle, William Henry. *Some American Women During the War of the American Revolution*. Harrisburg, Pa.: Harrisburg Publishing Co., 1898.

Ellet, Elizabeth Fries. *Pioneer Women of the West*. n.p., 1852. Reprint. Freeport, N.Y.: Books for Libraries Press, 1973.

———. [Mrs. Ellet]. *Domestic History of the American Revolution*. New York: Baker and Scribner, 1850.

Engle, Paul. *Women in the American Revolution*. Chicago: Follett Publishing Company, 1976.

Entrikin, Isabelle Webb. *Sarah Josepha Hale and Godey's Lady's Book*. Philadelphia: University of Pennsylvania, 1946.

Evans, Elizabeth. *Weathering the Storm: Women of the American Revolution*. New York: Charles Scribner's Sons, 1975.

Faragher, John Mack. *Women and Men on the Overland Trail.* New Haven: Yale University Press, 1979.

Finley, Ruth E. *The Lady of Godey's: Sarah Josepha Hale.* Philadelphia: J. B. Lippincott, 1931.

Fitzhugh, George. *Sociology for the South.* Richmond, Va.: A. Morris, 1854.

Fowler, William M. *Women on the American Frontier.* Hartford, Conn.: S. S. Scranton and Company, 1879.

Friedan, Betty. *It Changed My Life: Writings on the Women's Movement.* New York: Random House, 1963–76.

————. *The Feminine Mystique.* New York: W. W. Norton & Co., Inc., 1963.

Garland, Hamlin. *A Pioneer Mother.* Chicago: Thee Bookfellows, 1972.

Gates, Susa Young. *History of the Young Ladies' Mutual Improvement Association.* Salt Lake City: Deseret News, 1911.

Gillum, Lulu W. *Program Suggestions for Home Economics Entertainments.* Kirksville, Mo.: Jewell Printing Co., 1929.

Girl Scout Program Activities, Ranks, and Badges. New York: Girl Scouts Inc., 1933.

Goldman, Eric. *The Crucial Decade and After: America, 1945–1960.* New York: Alfred A. Knopf, 1966.

Grass, Milton N. *History of Hosiery.* New York: Fairchild Publications, Inc., 1955.

Green, Constance McL., and Hutcheson, Harold R. *The History of the Volunteer Special Services, 1916–1947. The History of the American Red Cross,* vol. 3. Washington, D.C.: American Red Cross, 1950.

Green, Harry Clinton, and Green, Mary Wolcott. *The Pioneer Mothers of America.* New York: G. P. Putnam's Sons, 1912.

Green, Harvey. *The Light of the Home.* New York: Pantheon Books, 1983.

Greenbie, Marjorie Bristow. *Lincoln's Daughters of Mercy.* New York: G. P. Putnam's Sons, 1944.

Groves, Sylvia. *The History of Needlework Tools and Accessories.* London: Country Life Ltd., 1966.

Hale, Lucretia. *Manners: Or Happy Homes and Good Society All the Year Round.* Boston: William F. Gill and Company, 1874.

Hall, Florence Marian Howe. *Social Customs.* Boston: Estes and Lauriat, 1887.

Hamer, Sarah S. [Phyllis Brown]. *What Girls Can Do: A Book for Mothers and Daughters.* New York: Cassell, Petter, Galpin Co., N. Y. [1880?].

Hamilton, Holman. *Zachary Taylor, Soldier of the Republic.* 2 vols. Indianapolis: Bobbs-Merrill, 1941. Reprint. Hamden, Conn.: Archon Books, 1966.

Hanna, Agnes K. *Home Economics in the Elementary Schools.* Boston: Whitcomb and Barrows, 1922.

Hanson, John Wesley, Jr. *Etiquette and Bicycling.* Chicago: American Publishing House, 1896.

Haskell, Ira J. *Hosiery Through the Years.* Lynn, MA: Carole Mailing Service, 1956.

Hawes, Harriet, and Edelman, Eleanor. *McCall's Complete Book of Bazaars.* New York: Simon and Schuster, 1955.

Hecker, Genevieve. *Golf for Women.* New York: Harper and Brothers, 1902.

Higginson, Thomas W. *A History of the Public School System of Rhode Island from 1636 to 1876.* Edited by Thomas B. Stockwell. Providence: Providence Press Co., 1876.

Holiday, Carl. *Woman's Life in Colonial Days.* Detroit: Gale Research Company, 1970.

Home Decorative Work. Minneapolis: Buckeye Publishing Co., 1891.

Howitt, William. *The Rural and Domestic Life of Germany.* London: Brown, Green, and Longmans, 1842.

Huntington, Emily. *The Little Housekeeper.* New York: Anson Randolph and Co., 1897.

Inge, Thomas. *American Popular Culture.* 2 vols. Westport, Conn.: Greenwood Press, 1978.

Ingram, J. S. *The Centennial Exposition, Described and Illustrated.* Philadelphia: Hubbard Brothers, 1876.

Jeffrey, Julie Ray. *Frontier Women.* New York: Hill and Wang, 1979.

Jensen, Oliver. *The Revolt of American Women.* New York: Harcourt, Brace and Company, 1952.

Jones, Katharine. *Ladies of Richmond, the Confederate Capital.* Indianapolis: Bobbs-Merrill, 1962.

Katz, Eleanor, and Rapone, Anita. *Women's Experience in America.* New Brunswick, N.J.: Transaction Books, 1980.

Kerber, Linda K. *Women of the Republic: Intellect and Ideology in Revolutionary America.* Chapel Hill, N.C.: University of North Carolina Press, 1980.

Kernan, James. *Perfect Etiquette.* New York: Albert Coswell, Publisher, 1877.

Kidwell, Claudia B., and Christian, Margaret C. *Suiting Everyone: The Democratization of Clothing in America.* Washington, D.C.: Smithsonian Institution Press, 1974.

Kuhns, Levi Oscar. *The German and Swiss Settlements of Colonial Pennsylvania.* New York: Eaton & Maines, 1901. Reprint. Ann Arbor, Mich.: Gryphon Books, 1971.

Ladies' and Gentlemen's Book of Etiquette. New York: Popular Publishing Co., 1882.

Leech, Margaret. *Reveille in Washington, 1861–1865.* New York: Harper and Brothers, 1941.

Leuchtenburg, William. *The Perils of Prosperity, 1917–1942.* Chicago: University of Chicago Press, 1958.

Lingeman, Richard G. *Don't You Know There's a War On?* New York: G. P. Putnam's Sons, 1970.

Loose, John W. *The Military Market Basket.* Lancaster, Pa.: Lancaster Historical Society, 1976.

Lutes, Della Thompson. *My Boy in Khaki: A Mother's Story.* New York: Harper and Brothers., 1918.

———. *The Gracious Hostess, A Book of Etiquette.* Indianapolis, Bobbs-Merrill, 1923.

Lynes, Russell. *The Tastemakers.* New York: Harper and Brothers, 1949.

MacArthur, Burke. *United Littles: The Story of the Needlework Guild of America.* New York: Coward McCann, Inc., 1955.

Malone, Anne Paton. *Women on the Texas Frontier*. El Paso: Texas Western Press, 1983.

Marble, Annie Russell. *The Women Who Came in the Mayflower*. Boston: Pilgrim Press, 1920.

Martin, George H. *The Evolution of the Massachusetts Public School System*. New York: D. Appleton and Co., 1923.

Massey, Mary Elizabeth. *Bonnet Brigade*. New York: Alfred A. Knopf, 1966.

———. *Ersatz in the Confederacy*. Columbia, S.C.: University of South Carolina Press, 1952.

———. *Refugee Life in the Confederacy*. Baton Rouge: Louisiana State Press, 1964.

Mathews, Rev. Joseph D. *Letters to School Girls*. Cincinnati: Swormstedt and Poe, 1853.

Matthaei, Julie A.. *An Economic History of Women in America*. New York: Shocken Books, 1982.

Mavor, William. *The Catechism of Health: Containing Simple and Easy Rules and Directions for the Management of Children, and Observatons on the Conduct of Health in General*. New York: Samuel Wood and Sons, 1819.

McCabe, James Dabney. *The Illustrated History of the Centennial Exhibition*. Philadelphia: National Publishing Company, 1876.

McCall's Bazaar Book by the Editors of *McCall's Needlework and Crafts Magazine*. New York: McCall's Corp., 1954–9.

Merriam, Eve. *Growing Up Female in America*. Garden City, N.Y.: Doubleday and Co., Inc., 1971.

Meyer, Edith Patterson. *Petticoat Patriots of the American Revolution*. New York: Vanguard Press, Inc., 1976.

Montross, Lynn. *Rag, Tag, and Bobtail: The Story of the Continental Army*. New York: Harper and Brothers, 1952.

Morrish, R. W. *A History of Fairs*. Books and Bulletins, #4. New York: International Association of Fairs and Expositions, 1929.

Muzzey, Artemus S. *The Young Maiden*. Boston: Wm. Crosby and H. P. Nichols, 1847.

Myerson, Abraham. *The Nervous Housewife*. Boston: Little Brown and Co., 1920.

Nash, Ogden. *Many Long Years Ago*. Boston: Little, Brown and Co., 1945.

Noble, Sonna, and Levin, Theodore. *How to Successfully Operate a Knitting Shop*. Washington, D.C.: Public Affairs Association, 1961.

Norton, Mary Beth. *Liberty's Daughters: The Revolutionary Experience of American Women, 1750–1800*. Boston: Little, Brown and Co., 1980.

Oates, Whitney J., ed. *The Stoic and Epicurean Philosophers*. New York: Random House, 1940.

Ohio Newspapers: A Living Record. Ohio State Archeological and Historical Society. Columbus, Ohio: Ohio History Press, 1950.

Osborne, Owen. *The Story of the Stocking*. Philadelphia: Owen Osborne, Inc., 1927.

Packard, Alpheus S. *History of the Bunker Hill Monument*. Portland, Maine: Brown Thurston, Printer, 1853.

Parkinson, Richard. *A Tour in America in 1798, 1799, and 1800 Exhibiting Sketches of Society and Manners*. 2 vols. London: J. Harding, 1805.

Parks, Lillian R. *My Thirty Years Backstage at the White House*. New York: Fleet Publishing Co., 1961.

Pasdermadjian, Hrant. *The Department Store*. London: Newman Books, 1954.

Penny, Virginia. *The Employments of Women: A Cyclopedia of Woman's Work*. Boston: Walker, Wise, and Company, 1863.

———. *Think and Act: A Series of Articles Pertaining to Men and Women, Work and Wages*. Philadelphia: Claxton, Remson, and Haffelfinger, 1869. Reprint. New York: Arno Press and *The New York Times*, 1971.

Perica, Esther. *The American Woman: Her Role During the Revolutionary War*. Monroe, N.Y.: Library Research Associates, 1981.

Phelps, Almira Hart. *Hours with My Pupils*. New York: Charles Scribner, 1859.

The Pick of "Punch": An Annual Selection (July, 1939–June, 1940). London: Chatto and Windus, 1940.

Power, Mrs. S. D. *Anna Maria's House-Keeping*. Boston: D. Lothrop and Co., 1884.

Pruette, Lorine. *Women and Leisure: A Study of Social Waste*. New York: E. P. Dutton and Co., 1924.

Pulliam, John D. *History of Education in America*, Columbus, Ohio: Charles E. Merrill Publishing Co., 1982.

Riley, Glenda. *Frontierswoman: The Iowa Experience*. Ames, Iowa: Iowa State University Press, 1981.

———. *Women and Indians on the Frontier*. Albuquerque: University of New Mexico Press, 1984.

Ross, Ishbel. *Grace Coolidge and Her Era*. New York: Dodd, Mead and Co., 1962.

———. *Taste in America*. New York: Thomas Y. Crowell Co., 1967.

Ross, Nancy Wilson. *Westward the Women*. New York: Alfred A. Knopf, 1944.

Runnels, Moses T. *History of Sanbornton, N.H.* 2 vols. Boston: Alfred Mudge and Sons, 1882.

Rush, Benjamin. *An Account of the Manners of the German Inhabitants of Pennsylvania*. n.p., 1789. Reprint. Collegeville, Pa.: Institute on Dutch Studies, 1974.

Ryan, Mary P. *Womanhood in America: From Colonial Times to the Present*. New York: New Viewpoints, 1979.

Sangster, Margaret E. *Winsome Womanhood*. New York: Fleming H. Revell Co., 1900.

Schumach, Murry. *The Face on the Cutting Room Floor*. New York: DeCapo Press, 1964.

Scott, Anne Firor. *The Southern Lady: From Pedestal to Politics 1830–1930*. Chicago: University of Chicago Press, 1970.

Seranne, Ann, and Gaden, Eileen. *The Church and Club Woman's Companion*. Garden City, N.Y.: Doubleday and Co., 1964.

Seybolt, Robert Francis. *The Private Schools of Colonial Boston*. Cambridge, Mass.: Harvard University Press, 1934.

————. *The Public Schoolmasters of Colonial Boston*. Cambridge, Mass.: Harvard University Press, 1939.

————. *The Public Schools of Colonial Boston, 1635–1775*. Cambridge, Mass.: Harvard University Press, 1935.

Sickles, Eleanor. *In Calico and Crinoline*. New York: Viking Press, 1935.

Simkins, Francis Butler, and Patton, James Welch. *The Women of the Confederacy*. Richmond, Va.: Garrett and Massie, Inc., 1936.

Sinclair, Andrew. *The Better Half: The Emancipation of American Women*. New York: Harper and Row, 1965.

Sklar, Kathryn Kish. *Catharine Beecher: A Study in American Domesticity*. New Haven, Conn.: Yale University Press, 1973.

Small, Herbert Walter. *Early New England Schools*. Boston: Ginn and Co., 1914. Reprint. New York: Arno Press and *The New York Times*, 1969.

Smith, Frank. *A Narrative History of Dover, Massachusetts*. Dover: The Town, 1897.

Smith, Robert A. *The Social History of the Bicycle*. New York: American Heritage Press, 1972.

Spruill, Julia C. *Women's Life and Work in the Southern Colonies*. New York: Norton and Co. Inc., 1972.

Sterkx, H. E. *Partners in Rebellion: Alabama Women in the Civil War*. Rutherford, N.J.: Fairleigh Dickinson University Press, 1970.

Stoltfus, Amanda. *How to Organize and Conduct a School and Community Fair*. Bulletin #2409, March 1. [Austin], Tex.: 1924.

Strasser, Susan. *Never Done: A History of American Housework*. New York: Pantheon Books, 1948.

Stratton, Joanna L. *Pioneer Women: Voices from the Kansas Frontier*. New York: Simon and Schuster, 1981.

Stryker, William S. *Extracts from American Newspapers*. Documents Relating to the Revolutionary History of the State of New Jersey. 2 vols. Trenton, N.J.: The John L. Murphy Publishing Co., 1901.

————. *Washington's Reception by the People of New Jersey in 1789*. Trenton, N.J.: Naar, Day & Naar, 1882.

Svejda, Dr. George J. *Quartering, Disciplining, and Supplying the Army at Morristown, 1779–1780*. Washington, D.C.: U.S. Department of the Interior, 1970.

Swan, Susan Burrows. *Plain and Fancy: American Women and Their Needlework, 1700–1850*. New York: Holt, Rhinehart, Winston, 1977.

————. *A Winterthur Guide to American Needlework*. Wilmington, Del.: Henry Francis duPont Winterthur Museum, 1976.

Thane, Elswyth. *Washington's Lady*. New York: Dodd, Mead, 1960.

Thomas, Gabriel. *An Account of Pennsylvania and West New Jersey*. London: n.p., 1698. Reprint with an introduction by Cyrus Townsend Bradley. Cleveland: Burrows Brothers Company, 1903.

Towne, Arthur E. *Old Pioneer Days*. Otsego, Mich.: Otsego Union Press, 1941.

Tryon, Rolla M. *Household Manufactures in the United States, 1640–1860*. Chicago: University of Chicago Press, 1917.

Ulrich, Laurel Thatcher. *Good Wives: Image and Reality in the Lives of Women in Northern New England, 1650–1750.* New York: Oxford University Press, 1982.

Unruh, John D., Jr., ed. *The Plains Across: The Overland Emmigrants and the Trans-Mississippi West, 1840–1860.* Urbana, Ill.: University of Illinois Press, 1979.

Valentino, Lou. *The Films of Lana Turner.* Secaucus, N.J.: Citadel Press, 1976.

Van Rensselaer, Mary [King]. *The Goede Vrouw of Mana-ha-ta at Home and in Society, 1609–1760.* New York: Charles Scribner and Sons, 1898. Reprint. New York: Arno Press, 1972.

Walton, Perry. *The Story of Textiles.* n.p., n.d. Reprint. Boston: Walton Advertising and Printing Co., 1925.

Wandersee, Winifred D. *Women's Work and Family Values, 1920–1940.* Cambridge, Mass.: Harvard University Press, 1981.

Ward, Maria. *The Mormon Wife.* Harford, Conn: Hartford Publishing Co., 1873.

Ward, Maria E. *Bicycling for Ladies.* New York: Brentano's, 1896.

Warren, Ruth. *A Pictorial History of Women in America.* New York: Crown Publishers, 1975.

Waters, Thomas Franklin. *Ipswich in the Massachusetts Bay Colony.* 2 vols. Vol. 2: *A History of the Town from 1700 to 1917.* Ipswich, Mass.: Ipswich Historial Society, 1919.

Wells, Daniel White and Wells, Reuben Field. *A History of Hatfield, Massachusetts.* Springfield, Mass.: F. C. H. Gibbons, 1910.

Wharton, Anne Hollingsworth. *Martha Washington.* New York: Charles Scribner's Sons, 1897.

Whiting, Emma Mayhew, and Hough, Henry Beetle. *Whaling Wives.* Boston: Houghton Mifflin, 1953.

Wickersham, James Pyle. *A History of Education in Pennsylvania.* Lancaster, Pa.: Inquirer Publishing Co., 1886.

Williams, Selma R. *Demeter's Daughters: The Women Who Founded America 1587–1787.* New York: Atheneum, 1976.

Wiley, Bell Irwin. *Confederate Women.* Westport, Conn.: Greenwood Press, 1975.

Woods, Robert A., ed. *Americans in Progress: A Settlement Study by Residents and Associates of the South End House.* Boston: Houghton Mifflin, 1903.

———. *The Neighborhood in Nation-Building: The Running Comment of Twenty Years at the South End House {Boston}.* Boston: Houghton Mifflin, 1923.

Woody, Thomas. *A History of Women's Education in the United States.* 2 vols. New York: Science Press, 1929.

———. *Early Quaker Education in Pennsylvania.* New York: Teachers' College, Columbia University, 1920. Reprint. New York: Arno Press and *The New York Times*, 1969.

———. *Quaker Education in the Colony and State of New Jersey.* Philadelphia: University of Pennsylvania, 1923.

Woolson, Abba Goold, ed. *Dress Reform: A Series of Lectures Delivered in Boston, on Dress as It Affects the Health of Women.* Boston: Roberts Brothers, 1874.

———. *Women in Modern Society.* Boston: Roberts Brothers, 1873.

Young, Agatha. *The Women and the Crisis: Women of the North in the Civil War.* Obolenski, N.Y.: McDowell Co., 1959.

Young, John H. *Our Deportment, or the Manners, Conduct, and Dress of the Most Refined American Society.* New York: F. B. Dickerson and Co., 1879.

Nineteenth-Century Instruction Books, Manuals and Leaflets

Arnold, Miss [Eleanor]. *Miss Arnold's Book of Crocheting, Knitting and Drawn Work.* Glascow, Conn.: Glascow Lace Thread Co., 1890.

Art Needlework: Knitting, Crocheting and Embroidery. New London, Conn.: Brainerd and Armstrong, 1881, 1891, 1899.

Beeton's Book of Needlework. London: Ward, Lock and Company, 1870.

Burton, Miss H. ["By a Lady Expert"]. *The Lady's Book of Knitting and Crochet.* Boston: J. Henry Symonds, Publisher, 1874.

Corticelli Home Needlework, a Quarterly Magazine of Art Needlework, Crocheting, Knitting, and Home Decoration, vol. 1, no. 2. Florence, Mass.: Corticelli Silk Mills, January 1899.

Corbould, Elvina ["E.M.C."]. *The Lady's Knitting Book.* New York: Anson D. F. Randolph and Co., 1879.

Croly, Jane C. ["Jenny June"]. *Knitting and Crochet: A Guide to the Use of the Needle and the Hook.* New York: A. L. Burt, 1885.

Cupples, Mrs. George. *A Knitting Book of Counterpanes.* Edinburgh: Johnstone, Hunter & Co., 1871.

———. *The Stocking Knitter's Manual.* Edinburgh: Johnstone, Hunter & Co., 1878.

de Dillmont, Therese. *Encyclopedia of Needlework.* English language ed. Alsace: Brustlein and Co., 1890.

Fancy and Practical Knitting, vol.3, no. 2. New York: Butterick Publishing Co., 1897.

Florence Home Needle-Work. Florence, Mass.: Nonotuck Silk Company, 1877, 1888.

Frank Leslie's Illustrated Needlework. Edited by Mrs. Ann S. Stephens. New York: Stringer and Townsend, 1885.

Goaman, Muriel. *Judy's Book of Sewing and Knitting.* London: Faber and Faber, Ltd., 1851.

Gaubaud, Madame. *Madame Gaubaud's Knitting and Netting Book.* London: Ward, Locke & Co., [1881].

Gaugain, Mrs. *The Lady's Assistant in Knitting, Netting, and Crochet Work.* 4 vols. Edinburgh, I. J. Gaugain, 1857.

Hale, Lucretia P., ed. *Plain Needlework, Knitting and Mending for All at Home and in Schools.* Boston: S. W. Tilton and Company, 1897.

———. *The Art of Knitting.* Boston: S. W. Tilton and Company, 1881.

Hall, [Mrs.] Mary E. *The Starlight Manual of Knitting and Crocheting*. Boston: Non-antum Worsted Co., and J. A. Lowell & Co., 1887.

Hartley, Miss Florence. *The Ladies' Hand Book of Fancy and Ornamental Work*. Philadelphia: G. G. Evans, Publishing, 1859.

Heron, Addie E. *Dainty Work for Pleasure and Profit*. Chicago: Danks and Co., 1891.

———. *Ladies' Work for Pleasure and Profit*. Chicago: Home Manual Company, 1894.

Home Decorative Work. Minneapolis: Buckeye Publishing Co., 1891.

Household Leaves: A Manual of Knitting and Crocheting. Lynn, Mass.: Household Publishing Co., 1887.

Illustrated Manual of Knit and Crochet. New York: M. Hemingway & Sons' Silk Co., 1889.

Jones, Mrs. C. S. and Williams, Mrs. Henry T. *Ladies' Fancy Work*. Williams' Household Series, vol. 3. New York: Henry T. Williams, Publisher, 1876.

Kerzman, Marie Louise. *How to and What to Knit*. Brooklyn, N.Y.: Henry Bristow, 1884.

Knitting and Crocheting: An Illustrated Manual for Home Workers. New York Tribune Extra, no. 87. New York: New York Tribune, 1889.

Knitting, Netting, and Crochet Work: A Winter Gift for Ladies. New York: Burgess and Stringer, 1844. Reprint, "Revised and Enlarged by an American Lady." Philadelphia: G. B. Zieber and Co., 1847.

The Ladies' Guide in Needlework, A Gift to the Industrious. Philadelphia: J. and J. Gilion, 1850.

The Ladies' Work Book. London: John Cassell, Ludgate Hill, 1853.

Ladies' Work-Box Companion: A Handbook of Knitting, Netting, Tatting and Berlin Work. Philadelphia: George S. Appleton, 1850.

The Ladies' Work Table Book. London: Darton and Co., 1847.

The Lady's Keepsake or Treasures of the Needle. London: Darton and Co., 1851.

Lambert, Miss. *The Handbook of Needlework*. New York: Wiley and Putnam, 1846.

The Last and Best Book of Knitting, Crocheting, Embroidery, and Art Needlework. New York: Brainerd and Armstrong Co., 1891.

Manual of Needlework, Embroidery, Knitting, Crochet, Lace-Making, Etc. New York: Patten Publishing Co., 1883.

Mee, Cornelia. *A Manual of Knitting, Netting and Crochet*. London: David Braque, 1844.

Needle and Hook. n.p.: Belding Brothers, 1895.

The Needle at Home: A Complete Instructor in All Branches of Plain and Fancy Needlework. Springfield, Ohio: Franklin W. Fromme, Publisher, 1885.

Niles, Eva M. ["En Experienced Knitter"], comp. and arr. *The Ladies' Guide to Elegant Lace Patterns, Etc. Done with Common Steel Needles*. Gloucester, Mass.: Proctor Bros., Publishers, 1884.

Owen, Mrs. Henry. *The Illuminated Book of Needlework*. London: Henry D. Bohm, 1847.

Pullman, Mrs. *Lady's Manual of Fancy Work*. New York: Dick and Fitzgerald Publishing Company, 1859.

Rettberg, Mrs. Lina, ed. *Penelope Knitting and Crochet Series, books* 1–2. Brooklyn, N.Y.: The Misses Stock, 1885.

Ryder, H. P. *Cycling and Shooting Knickerbocker Stockings: How to Knit Them with Plan and Fancy Turnover Cuffs.* London: Macmillan and Co. Ltd., 1896.

The Seamstress: A Guide to Plain and Fancy Needlework, Baby Linen, Millinery and Dressmaking, Embroidery and Lacework, Knitting, Netting, Crochet-work, and Tatting. New York: J. S. Redfield, Clinton Hall, 1848.

The Self-Instructor in Silk Knitting, Crocheting, and Embroidery. New York: Belding Brothers and Co., 1886, 1887, 1889, 1891.

Shields, S. Annie [S. Annie Frost]. *The Ladies' Guide to Needlework, Embroidery, Etc.* New York: Henry T. Williams, 1877.

Stephens, Ann S. *Ladies' Complete Guide to Crochet, Fancy Knitting, and Needlework.* New York: Garret and Company, 1854.

Swett, [Mrs.] Henrietta, comp. *Household Leaves: A Manual of Knit and Crochet Compiled from "The Household Leaves" Monthly.* Lynn, Mass.: Household Publishing Co., 1887.

Warren, Mrs. and Pullan, Mrs. *Treasures in Needlework.* n.p., 1870. Reprint. New York: LancerBooks, Inc., 1973.

Watson, Marcia L., comp. *The Ladies' Manual of Knitting and Crocheting.* Central Square Series. vol. 1, no. 1. Lynn, Mass.: W. N. Swett and Co., 1889.

———, comp. *Needles and Hooks, and What Is Made with Them.* Central Square Series, part II. Lynn, Mass.: Home Cheer Company, 1891.

Workman's Guide ["By a Lady"]. London: Simkin, Marshall, and Co., 1838.

The Young Ladies' Journal: Containing Instructions in Berlin Work, Crochet, Drawn Thread Work, Embroidery, Knitting, Knotting or Macrame, Lace, Netting, Poonah Painting, and Tatting. London: Merton House, 1885.

Twentieth-Century Instruction Books, Manuals and Leaflets

Abbey, Barbara. *Susan Bates Presents 101 Ways to Improve Your Knitting.* New York: Studio Publications, Inc., 1949.

Angora Accessories for Day and Evening, vol. 2. New York: Bernard Ulmann Co., 1938.

Barnes, Sarah, ed. *Columbia Book of Water Wear for Women,* vol. 62. Philadelphia: William H. Horstman Co., 1934.

———. *Manual of Knitting and Crocheting.* Philadelphia: William H. Horstman Company, 1936.

———. *Manual of Knitting and Crocheting: Infants' and Children's Wear,* vol. 34. Philadelphia: William H. Horstman Co., 1931.

———. *Styled Spring Hand Knits for Misses and Women.* Philadelphia: William H. Horstman Co., 1934.

Barsaloux, Elsa, designer. *Good Shepherd Fingering Yarns and Their Uses: Infants' Wear*. Newton, Mass.: Good Shepherd Worsted Mills, 1917.

———. *Priscilla War Work Book: Comforts for Soldiers and Sailors*. Boston: Priscilla Publishing Co., 1917.

———. *Utopia Yarn Book: Being a Practical Treatise on Knitting and Crocheting*. 14th ed. New York: H. E. Frankenberg Co., 1916, 1919.

Bear Brand Blue Book of Yarncraft, vol. 29. New York: Bernard Ulmann Co., 1921.

Bear Brand Manual of Handiwork. New York: Bernard Ulmann Co., 1902, 1904, 1910, 1911, 1912, 1915, 1916.

Bellamy, Virginia Woods. *Number Knitting*. New York: Crown Publishers, Inc., 1952.

Bernat's Handicrafter. Jamaica Plain, Mass.: Emil Bernat and Sons, 1928–85. Special attention has been given to: *Baby Handknits*, #27, 1951; *Fashion Handknits*, #28, 1951; *Sweaters, Cardigans, Blouses*, #33, 1952; *Socks and Accessories*, #36, 1953.

Blue Book of Dresses, Sweaters, Scarfs, Tams Etc. for Women and Children, vol. 33. New York: Bernard Ulmann Bucilla Manufacturing Company, 1920.

Boucle and Velnet Fashions of Tower Brand Yarn. New York: Albert and Broder, Inc., 1935.

Bradley, Sue. *Stitches in Time*. New York: Holt, 1986.

Bucilla Nubby-Knit Fashions, vol. 108. New York: Bernard Ulmann Co., 1936.

Burrell, Caroline French [Mrs. Caroline French Benton]. *Benton's Book of Needlework*. Boston: Dana Estes and Company, 1912.

Campus Classics for Knitters. New York: Bernard Ulmann Co., 1940.

Carroll, Alice. *Complete Guide to Modern Knitting and Crocheting*. New York: Wm. Wise and Co., 1942. Republished as *Knitting and Crocheting Your Own Fashions of the Forties*. New York: Dover Publishing, Inc., 1973.

Chundelah, Alice Simon. *Modern Knitting*. Portland, Oreg.: A. S. Chundelah, 1916.

Claydon, Ellen P. and Claydon, C. A. *Knitting Without "Specimens."* New York: E. P. Dutton and Co., 1916.

Columbia Book of the Use of Yarns. 5th ed. Philadelphia: William H. Horstman Co., 1904.

Cone, Ferne Geller. *Knutty Knitting for Kids*. Chicago: Follett Publishing Co., 1977.

Cornell, Betty. *Betty Cornell's Teen-Age Knitting Book*. New York: Prentice Hall, 1953.

Cro-Knitting. New York: Bernard Ulmann Co., 1914.

Damon, Jeanne. *Jeanne Damon's Quick Knits*, no. 1. Edited by Jane Bedford. New York: Cowles Education Corporation, 1968.

Duncan, Ida Riley. *The Complete Book of Progressive Knitting*. New York: Liveright Publishing Corp., 1940.

Fleisher Angora Creations for All Occasions, vol. 54. New York: Fleisher Yarns, Inc., 1940.

Fleisher's Children's Book, vol. 33. New York: Fleisher Yarns, Inc., 1935.

Fleisher's Classic Hand Knits for Men and Women, vol. 43. New York: Fleisher Yarns, Inc., 1936.

Fleisher's Crochet and Knitting Book, no. 103. Philadelphia: S. B. and B. W. Fleisher, Inc., 1919.

Fleisher's Knitting and Crochet Manual. Philadelphia: S. B. and B. W. Fleisher, Inc., 1918–20.

Fleisher's New Showing of Handknits: Beachwear, Sweaters, Scarves and Vestees, no. 28. New York: Fleisher Yarns, Inc., 1935.

Fryer, Jane Eayre. *The Mary Frances Knitting and Crocheting Book or Adventures Among the Knitting People*. Philadelphia: John C. Winston Company, 1918.

Gibson-Roberts, Priscilla A. *Knitting in the Old Way*. Loveland, Colo.: Interweave Press, 1985.

Good Shepherd Fingering Yarns and Their Use: Infants' Wear. Newton, Mass.: Shepherd Worsted Mills, 1917.

Gray, Adelaide J., ed. *The Sunlight Book of Knitting and Crocheting*. Chicago: W. G. Perry, 1912.

Great Britain Directorate of Voluntary Organizations. *Knitting for the Army: Official Guide*. London: Her Majesty's Stationery Office, 1941.

Hand Knits by Beehive: Socks for Men, Women and Children, no. 18. New York: Patons and Baldwins, Inc., 1941.

Hansen, Robin. *Fox and Geese: A Collection of Traditional Maine Mittens*. Camden, Maine: Down East Books, 1983.

———with Dexter, Janetta. *Flying Geese & Partridge Feet: More Mittens from Up North and Down East*. Camden, Maine: Down East Books, 1986.

Heilman, Joan Rattner. *The Official Knit-a-Dress-a-Day Knitting Book*. New York: Grosset and Dunlap, 1968.

Hubert, Margaret and Gusick, Dorothy Dean. *Weekend Knitting Projects*. New York: Van Nostrand Reinhold Co., 1979.

Jack Frost Blouse Book. New York: Gottlieb Bros., 1940.

James, Miss T. M. *Longman's Complete Course of Needlework, Knitting and Cutting-Out*. New York: Longmans, Green, and Co., 1901.

Khaki Knitting Book. Edited by Olive Whiting. New York: Allies Special Aid, 1917.

Klickman, Flora. *The Popular Knitting Book*. New York: Frederick A. Stokes, Publishing Co., 1923.

Knit-Knacks. New York: World Editions, Inc., December 1949, and May 1950.

The Ladies' Home Journal *Fashion {department} Leaflets*. Philadelphia: Curtis Publishing Co., 1937.

Lane, Rose Wilder. *Woman's Day Book of American Needlework*. New York: Simon and Schuster, 1963.

Last Minute Fashions in Hand Knits, vol. 9. New York: Bernard Ulmann Co., 1940.

Lessons in Knit and Crochet, book 10. Florence, Mass.: Corticelli Silk Mills, 1919.

Manual of Handiwork. New York: Bear Brand Yarns, Mfgrs., 1902, 1916.

Maynard, Alice, ed. *What to Knit and Crochet and How to Do It* [The Lion Yarn Book]. New York: Calhoun Robbins and Co., 1903.

McCormack, Mary A. *Spool Knitting*. New York: A. S. Barnes and Co., 1909.

McElwaine, Charlotte. *Knitting with Stop and Go Needles*. New York: Rheinhold Book Corp., 1968.

Minerva Book for Knit and Crochet, vol. 3. Bridgeport, Pa.: James Lees and Sons Co., 1919.

Minerva Hand Knits for Men in the Service, vol. 62. New York: James Lees and Sons Co., 1941.

Minerva Men's Book, vol. 34. New York: James Lees and Sons Co., 1934.

Minerva Style Book, vol. 30. New York: James Lees and Sons Co., 1935.

Motion Picture Movie Classic Hand Knit Fashions as Worn by Warner Brothers Stars. New York: Bernard Ulmann Co., 1940.

Movie Star Hand Knits for Men. Bear Brand and Bucilla Yarn, vol. 316. New York: Bernard Ulmann Co., 1940.

Mysse, Janet Whitney. *Affordable Furs*. Helena and Billings, Mont.: Falcon Press Publishing Co., 1983.

———. *The Classics: Fisherman Knits*. Helena and Billings, Mont.: Falcon Press Publishing Co., 1983.

Needlework. The Woman's Library, II. London: Chapman and Hall Ltd., 1903.

New Cardigans for You to Knit, vol. 4, no. 116. New York: Bernard Ulmann Co., 1939.

New Simplified Instructions for Making Crocheted and Knitted Beaded Bags and Chains of Exclusive Design. New York: Julian Roberts, 1925. (Original is in the collection of the Detroit Historical Museum.)

Nicoll, Maud Churchill. *How to Knit Socks*. New York: Brentano's, 1915.

———. *Knitting and Sewing for Men in the Army and Navy*. New York: Doran Company, 1918.

Nun's Variety in Knitting and Crochet Stitches. Chicago: T. Buettner and Co. Inc., (#830) July 1935, (#842) July 1937.

One of Fleisher's French Fashions in Hand-Knits. New York: Fleisher Yarns, Inc., 1934. Alix: #C2168; Lanvin: #C2167; Lelong: #C2166.

Orr, Anne. *Decorative Bedspreads: Knitting*. Nashville, Tenn.: Anne Orr Publications, 1936.

———. *Star Book of Knitted and Crocheted Bedspreads*. New York: American Thread Co., 1936.

Peace Dale Knitting Book, vol. 4. New York: Peace Dale Mills, 1922.

Phillips, Mary Walker. *Creative Knitting*. New York: Van Nostrand Reinhold Co, 1971.

Priscilla War Work Book. Boston: Priscilla Publishing Co., 1917.

Probert, Christina. *Great Knitting in* Vogue. New York: St. Martin's Press, 1985.

———. *Knitting in* Vogue. New York: Viking Press, 1982.

———. *More Knitting in* Vogue. New York: Viking Press, 1983.

Righetti, Maggie. *Knitting in Plain English*. New York: St. Martin's Press, 1986.

Schulte, Sarah. *The* Seventeen *Book of Quick Things to Make and Wear*. New York: David McKay Co., 1973.

Shields, Emma L. and Wemple, Helen D. *Knit One, Purl One: A Little Girl's Knitting and Crochet Book*. New York: Frederick A. Stokes Co., 1938.

Thomas, Mary. *Mary Thomas's Book of Knitting Patterns*. New York: Macmillan, 1945. Reprint. New York: Dover Publications, 1972.

Von Wartburg, Ursula. *The Workshop of Knitting*. New York: Atheneum, 1973.

Vogue's *Knitting Book*. New York: Conde Nast Publications, 1939.

Vogue's *Third Book of Knitting and Crochet*. New York: Conde Nast Publications, 1936.

Walker, Barbara G. *A Second Treasury of Knitting Patterns*. New York: Charles Scribner's Sons, 1970.

———. *A Treasury of Knitting Patterns*. New York: Charles Scribner's Sons, 1968.

Waller, Jane. *A Stitch in Time: Knitting and Crochet Patterns of the 1920's, 1930's & 1940's*. Radnor, Pa.: Chilton Book Co., 1973.

———. *Classic Knitting Patterns from the British Isles: Men's Hand-Knits from the 20's to the 50's*. New York: Thames and Hudson, 1985.

War Needlework: Comforts You Can Make for the Suffering Non-Combatants. Philadelphia: Needlework Department of the *Ladies' Home Journal*, 1914.

Wiczyk, Arlene Zeger, ed. and comp. *A Treasury of Needlework Projects from* Godey's Lady's Book. New York: Arco Publishing Co., 1972.

Widdeke, Mary, collaborator. *Worth's Hand Knit Creations*, vol. 23. Los Angeles: Worth Brothers, Inc., 1936.

The Woman's Auxiliary of St. Paul's Church, Chestnut Hill, Pa. *Knit One for the Crib Kids—the Carriage Trade—and the High Chair Set*. Chestnut Hill, Pa.: n.p., 1953.

Woman's Day Knitting Annual. New York: Woman's Day, Inc., 1949.

Woman's Day Teen-Age Knitting. New York: Woman's Day, Inc., 1950.

Wood, Irene Tutt. *Knitting and Fitting*. Chicago: Maestro Co., 1936.

Zimmermann, Elizabeth. *Knitting Without Tears*. New York: Charles Scribner's Sons, 1971.

———. *Knitting Workshop*. Pittsville, Wis.: Schoolhouse Press, 1981.

Eighteenth-Century and Nineteenth-Century Newspapers

Boston Chronicle, April 7, 1766.

Boston Evening Post, May 3, 1762; November 2, 1767.

Boston Evening Transcript, September 8, 9, 1840.

Boston Gazette, May 24, 1736; May 21, 1766.

Boston News-Letter, July 28–August 4, 1718; January 7, 1768; July 6, 1769.

Boston Gazette or Country Journal, October 1, 8, 15, 1764.

Charleston Mercury, October 22, 1764; November 9, 1864.

Charleston South Carolina Gazette, March 6–13, 1762; April 10–17, 1762; January 26, 1765.

Cleveland Leader, January 31, 1863.

Detroit Daily Advertiser, December 30, 1861.

Detroit Free Press, August 25, October 10, 1861.

Edgerfield {South Carolina} Advertiser, August 29, 1861.

Greensboro Alabama Beacon, August 9, 1862.

Hartford Connecticut Courant, February 2, November 6, 1797; February 14, 1810.

Hartford Mercury, March 19, 1750.

Ipswich Essex Gazette, June 27, 1769.

Ipswich Register, January 29, 1837.

Massachusetts Gazette, April 15, 1774.

The New England Gazette or the Weekly Post-Boy, February 29, 1768.

Newport Mercury, June 27–July 4, 1768.

New York Constitutional Gazette, June 22, 1776.

The New-York Gazette or the Weekly Post-Boy, May 21, 1759.

The New York Journal and Weekly Register, 1788

New York Gazette, April 25, 1765.

The New-York Gazette and the Weekly Mercury, February 1, 1768.

New York Gazeteer, April 7, 1774.

New York Mercury, October 16, 1758; April 27, 1767; November 9, 1864.

Niles Weekly Register, November 23, 1822.

Philadelphia Enquirer, July 11, 1864.

Philadelphia Pennsylvania Gazette, February 25, 1764; May 1, 1766; October 25, 1770.

Philadelphia Pennsylvania Packet, September 23, 1780.

Philadelphia Pennsylvania Packet and General Advertiser, July 4, 1780.

Portsmouth New Hampshire Gazette, January 22, 1768; March 17, 1769; May 25, 1770.

Rochester {Indiana} Chronicle, January 12, 1865.

Savannah Daily Morning News, August 18, 1864; September 1, 1864.

Savannah Morning News, February 1, 1865.

South Carolina Gazette, September 11, 1755.

Williamsburg Virginia Gazette, September 24, 1767; September 12, 1771; May 6, 1773; August 6, 1775; January 13, 1776; October 25, 1776.

Newspaper Articles

Anderson, Susan Heller and Bird, David. "Without Dropping a Stitch." *New York Times*, January 9, 1986.

"As the Parade Passes By" [by an "Onlooker"]. *Cleveland Plain Dealer*, January 27, 1935.

"Back to Knitting Gains." *New York Times*, April 28, 1935.

"B. Ulmann Co., Inc. Fashion Show." *New York Times*, July 23, 1937.

Bobbe, Dorothy. "Bundles for Britain." *New York Times Magazine*, December 1, 1940, pp. 12, 21.

"Canadian Yarn Making Firms Resent Ban on Knitting in House of Commons Gallery." *New York Times*, February 8, 1934.

"Cashmere Becomes a Fashion Favorite; Dior-Designed Sweaters Now Available." *New York Times*, November 15, 1954.

"Champion Red Cross Knitter of New York." *New York Times*, August 23, 1918.

"Christmas Knitting for Soldiers Pushed." *New York Times*, December 10, 1941.

Cobb, Jane. "Knitters—Plain, Fancy and Otherwise." *New York Times Magazine*, July 21, 1940, pp. 8, 19.

Cooper, L. Lanier. "Craftsman Has Knit His Niche Selling Yarn." *Washington Post*, September 8, 1983.

"Crowded Series of Varied Events Announced in Plan to Spur Attendance." *New York Times*, August 14, 1940.

Davenport, Carleen. "First Sketches of Paris Collections Show High Hats." *Boston Evening Transcript*, August 14, 1935.

"Defense Knitting Pushed." *New York Times*, October 10, 1941.

"Etiquette and the War." *New York Times*, May 17, 1943.

"A Fad of the Day." *New York Daily Tribune*, October 20, 1895.

"For a Coolidge Grandchild." *New York Times*, September 27, 1923.

Goldstein, Rosalie. "Wellesley Wardrobe Contains 10 Sweaters, Six Skirts, .7 Fur Coats." *Wellesley College News*, February 13, 1941.

"Governor of Arizona Knits." *New York Times*, March 10, 1918.

Harrison, Elizabeth. "Knitting Skill Is Now Taught to Youngsters." *New York Times*, April 19, 1951.

Holob, Dorothy M. "Knit Pickers Are More Than Just Busybodies." *Coronado Journal*, May [6?], 1987.

Hornaday, Mary. "Knit Two, Purl Two—Fingers Fly." *Christian Science Monitor Magazine*, November 15, 1941, p. 12.

"Household Department." *Boston Globe*, August 9, 14, 1935.

"If You Worry, Don't Show It in Your Letters." *The Newark Evening News*, July 18, 1918.

"Incorporating Knitting." *New England Farmer and Gardener's Journal*, January 27, 1836, p. 229.

"Jobs for Knitters." *New York Times*, November 25, 1934.

Jones, Julia. "Sitting Pretty." *Phoenix Gazette*, November 1, 1985.

" 'Knit for Defense' Tea." *New York Times*, September 15, 1941.

"Knit One, Purl Two, but With a Twist." *New York Times*, April 17, 1986.

"Letter to the Hartford Ladies' Aid Society." *Hartford Courant {supplement}*, January 14, 1865.

"Knit One, Purl Two." Sanka Coffee advertisement. *New York Times*, November 12, 1939.

"Knitting Bags: A Great Convenience to Owners Perhaps, Not to Others." *New York Times*, March 2, 1918.

"Knitting Barred in U.S. Supreme Court." *New York Times*, February 5, 1933.

"Little Sunshiners Entitled to Membership." *New York Daily Tribune*, March 20, 1900.

Mackenzie, Catherine. "They All Knit, one row plain, one purl." *New York Times Magazine*, January, 6, 1935, p. 8.

"Man Wins Knitting Prize." *New York Times*, August 5, 1935.

"Man Can Knit as Good as Woman." *Boston Post*, August 14, 1935.

"Mass Knitting Movement to Be Launched Tuesday." *New York Times*, September 28, 1941.

"Mr. Wilson Believes in Plenty of Play." *New York Times*, April 14, 1918.

"Mrs. Coolidge Earns $250 and Gives It Away." *New York Times*, December 30, 1926.

"Mrs. Coolidge Knits a Baby Carriage Robe in National Competition for $2,000 Prize." *New York Times*, August 17, 1923.

"Mrs. Roosevelt Urges All Women to Knit for Soldiers and Sailors." *New York Times*, October 1, 1941.

"Names: that Jar." *New York Times*, October 17, 1937.

"National Knitting Contest Winners Announced." *New York Times*, May 12, 1936.

Nemy, Enid. "Quitters: Two 'smoked' food, another knitted." *New York Times*, February 22, 1987.

"New England Knitters." *New York Times*, August 20, 1923.

Nicoll, Maud Churchill. "How to Knit Socks for Soldiers." *New York Times*, December 13, 1914.

"No Knitting at Home." *Washington Post*, December 21, 1983.

Oblinger, Jan. "Knitting know-how a knockout." *Bangor Daily News*, March 2, 1982.

Otten, Alan A. "Grandparents Today Are Sprier, Sharper, Richer and Plentiful." *Wall Street Journal*, May 11, 1987.

"Peaceful Yarn." *Washington Post*, February 8, 1986.

"Rags to Riches." *Greater Phoenix Jewish News*, March 20, 1985.

"Rainy Daisies' Triumph." *New York Times*, October 30, 1921.

"See the Knitters Knit." *Cleveland Plain Dealer*, May 4, 1935.

Smith, Hugo L. "On the Matter of Knitting." Letter to the Editor. *New York Times*, September 17, 1940.

Taylor, Angela. "Out with the Boys? Yes, but for a Knitting Lesson." *New York Times*, February 14, 1971.

"Tip of the Ski Cap." *Wall Street Journal*, November 12, 1984.

"Troops in Alaska Need Sweaters." *New York Times*, June 26, 1941.

"Try it 7 Days Free! Alice Carroll's New Complete Knitting Guide!" Advertisement. *American Weekly*, April 14, 1942.

"200 More Enroll to Knit for Troops." *New York Times*, October 30, 1941.

"Two Men Lead Knitting Class." *New York Times*, October 6, 1936.

"Washington Wire." *Wall Street Journal*, November 22, 1985.

Weltner, Linda. "Stitches in Time," in "Ever So Humble." *Boston Globe.* January 17, 1986.

"Wins Prize of $2,000 in Knitting Contest." *New York Times,* August 23, 1923.

"Winter Homework." *New York Herald Tribune,* December 22, 1940.

"Woman and Her Mission." *Deseret Evening News,* May 19, 1869.

"Women Renew Fight Against Long Skirts." *New York Times,* September 30, 1922.

"Women and the War." *Des Moines Register,* July 21, 1918.

Young, Brigham. "Discourse." *Deseret News* (Weekly), October 23, 1872.

———. "Discourse of Sunday, August 18, 1872." *Deseret News,* August 28, 1872.

Magazines Carrying Knitting Instructions and Designs

Cast On, 1984–

Delineator, 1873–1937

Demorest's Magazine [title varies], 1865–99

Dorcas Magazine, 1884–86

Domestic Monthly, 1873–95

Gentlewoman, 1890–1926

Godey's Lady's Book and Magazine [title varies], 1830–98

Good Housekeeping, 1885–

Handmade, 1979–1985

Harper's Bazaar [title varies slightly], 1867–

Home Needlework Magazine, 1899–1917

Knitters, 1984–

Ladies' Home Journal, 1883–

Ladies' Fancy Work, 1900–1904

Leslie's Illustrated Magazine [title varies slightly], 1855–1922

McCall's Needlework and Crafts, 1923–

Modern Priscilla, 1887–1930

New Idea Home Magazine, 1896–1912

Peterson's Magazine, 1842–98

Pictorial Review, 1899–1939

Smart Knitting, 1946–47

Star Needlework Journal, 1916–25

Stitches, 1902–1904

Threads, 1986–

Vogue Knitting [published irregularly until 1982, published regularly since 1982.]

Woman and Home [sometimes published as *Home Magazine*], 1900–1935

Woman's Day, 1937–

Woman's Home Companion [originally published as *Ladies' Home Companion*], 1873–1957

Articles in Journals and Magazines

Adams, Elizabeth. "The Girl of To-Day." *Woman Citizen*, January 26, 1924, pp. 15–17.

"A Gallery of Winter Craft Projects." *Mother Earth News*, January/February 1984, pp. 37–50.

Agatz, Cora Wilson. "A Journey Across the Plains." *Pacific Northwest Quarterly*, April 1936, pp. 171–74.

"A Knitting Machine." *Ladies' Own Advertiser* [supplement to *Ladies' Own Magazine*], December 1872, p. 1.

"And Sew On." *The Delineator*, January 1937, p. 49; July 1936, p. 61.

"Argyle Knits for Teens." *McCall's Needlework and Crafts* 6 (1956):34–35.

Arrington, Leonard. "The Economic Role of Pioneer Mormon Women." *The Western Humanities Review*, Spring 1955, pp. 145–64.

"As the Parade Passes By." *Cleveland Plain Dealer*, January 27, 1935.

Ashley, Marie. "Back to Our Needlework: Released War Knitters Take Up the Thread of New Embroideries." *The Delineator*, June 1919, p. 111.

———. "Cotton Takes the Place of Wool in New Sweaters and Collars." *The Delineator*, May 1918, p. 111.

———. "Crochet and Knitting Needles Lead an Infinitely Useful Life." *The Delineator*, October 1918, p. 92.

———. "The Day of the Sweater is at Hand." *The Delineator*, May 1919, p. 118.

———. "The Flight of the Needle Keeps Step with the Times." *The Delineator*, December 1918, p. 82.

———. "For the Period of the Emergency." *The Delineator*, January 1919, p. 55.

———. "The Knitting-Bag Embroidery Goes to One's Hat." *The Delineator*, April 1918, p. 91.

———. "New Versions of an Old Yarn." *The Delineator*, February 1917, p. 69.

———. "Saving Precious Moments." *The Delineator*, November 1918, pp. 92–93.

Barnwell, Mildred G. "Fad Aids Yarn Sales." *Textile World*, July 1935, p. 64.

Barsaloux, Elsa. "A Knitted Norfolk Coat for College Girls." *Gentlewoman*, September 1917, p. 1.

———. "Silk and Yarn Are Both Used for Knitting." *Pictorial Review*, February 1919, p. 76.

Berkeley-Loyd, Helen. "You and Your Corset-Maker." *The Delineator*, October 1910, pp. 293–94.

"The Bewitching Breakfast Cap." *The Delineator*, May 1912, p. 68.

"The Big Stitch." *Time*, October 13, 1967, p. 74.

Blake, Minnie E. "The Rocky Mountain Knitter Boys." *St. Nicholas Magazine*, May 1918, pp. 603–10.

Brown, Terry. "An Emigrant's Guide for Women." *American West*, September 1970, pp. 12–17, 63.

Burton, Richard. "Knitting," in "The Bellman's Notebook." *The Bellman*, September 8, 1917, p. 261.

Cades, Hazel Rawson. "Good Looks: Your Hair—the long and the short of it." *Woman's Home Companion*, September 1924, p. 75.

———. "Here, There, and Nowhere." *Woman's Home Companion*, December 1924, p. 108.

"Calisthenics." *The Lady's Book*, May 1836, p. 9.

"A Call to My Country-Women." *Atlantic Monthly*, March 1863, pp. 345–49.

"The Call to Knit." *Vogue*, July 1, 1918, p. 100.

"Can'ts." *Time*, June 16, 1941, p. 8.

Catt, Carrie Chapman. "How Many Yards in Your Skirt?" *Woman Citizen*, August 1926, pp. 10–11.

Chater, Melville. "The Saga of the Socks." *Red Cross Magazine* XIV, no.2 (February 1919):77–80.

Choate, Anne Hyde. "Girl Scout Knitting of Sammie's Sweater Sets." *The {Girl Scout} Rally*, October 1917, p. 7.

"Church Decrees on Women's Dress." *Literary Digest*, November 21, 1925, p. 32.

Churchill, Judith. "Is Boredom Bad for You?" *McCall's*, April 1927, pp. 51, 53.

Clark, John Hawkins. "Overland to the Gold Fields of California in 1852." Edited by Louise Berry. *Kansas Historical Quarterly*, August 1942, pp. 227–96.

Clarke, Ida Clyde. "Your Part in Rebuilding the World." *Pictorial Review*, February 1919, p. 16.

Cleveland, Grover. "Woman's Mission and Woman's Clubs." *The Ladies' Home Journal*, May 1905, pp. 3–4.

Cole, Celia Caroline. "When You Bob Your Hair." *Delineator*, January 1923, p. 57.

"College Angle of the Girl Who Knows Clothes." *The Delineator*, August 1936, pp. 30–31.

"College Winners." *The Delineator*, February 1937, p. 33.

Conover, Isabel De Nyse. "In the Pink of Fashion." *Woman's Home Companion*, December 1927, p. 89.

"The Constitutional Degeneracy of American Women." *Young Lady's Friend*, May 1866, p. 376.

Croly, Jane C. ["Jenny June," pseud.]. "Amiability." *Demorest's Illustrated Monthly*, April 1865, pp. 186–87.

"Current Comment." *Godey's Lady's Book and Magazine*, July 1896, p. 111.

"Current Knit and Purl Craze Puts New Technique into Yarn Selling." *Sales Management*, January 1, 1935, pp. 18–19.

Dale, Samuel E. "Why Not to Knit." *Literary Digest*, July 6, 1918, p. 31.

Davidson, Susan. "Knit One, Purl One." *Washingtonian*, December 1982, pp. 241–44.

Davies, Maria Thompson. "From Bayonet to Knitting-Needles." *The Delineator*, February 1919, p. 7.

"The Dear Old Grandmother." *Godey's*, May 1858, p. 435.

de Fleur, Marise. "What's under Your Hat?" *Sunset Magazine*, October 1928, pp. 78–79.

De Forrest, Virginia. "Heel and Toe." *Godey's Lady's Book*, September 1857, pp. 217–19.

De Koven, Mrs. Reginald. "Bicycling for Women." *Cosmopolitan*, August 1895, p. 386.

DePeyster, Patty. "Society Fads." *New Idea Woman's Magazine*, July 1902, p. 84; January 1902, p. 84.

deRochemont, Ruth. "The School Girl in War Relief." *Vogue*, March 15, 1918, pp. 32, 74, 76.

Dickinson, R. L., M.D. "Bicycling for Women, the Puzzling Question of Costume." *Outlook*, April 25, 1896, pp. 751–52.

Dobie, Charles Caldwell. "Gray Socks." *Harper's Monthly*, April 1919, pp. 590–96.

"Dramatic Scenes on the Links at Muirfield During the British Amateur Championship." *Town and Country*, July 1, 1926, p. 31.

"Dress Reform Again," *Woman's Home Companion*, May 1921, p. 2.

"Dress Reform." *Woman's Words*, April 1877, p. 1.

"Dressed-Up Sweaters." *Life*, January 25, 1943, pp. 44–46.

Duffield, George C. "An Iowa Settler's Homestead." *Annals of Iowa*, October 1903, pp. 206–215.

"Education in Colonial Virginia." Part I: "Poor Children and Orphans." *William and Mary Quarterly*, April 1897, pp. 219–25.

"The Emancipation of Man." *Atlantic Monthly*, January 1919, pp. 141–42.

Engle, Jennie. "New York Gossip." *The Ladies' Own Magazine*, December 1872, pp. 217–18.

"Fancy Work: Knitting." *Woman and Home*, May 1897, p. 555.

"Fancy Work at Watering Places." *Mme. Demorest's Semi-Annual What to Wear and How to Make It*, Spring and Summer 1880, pp. 38–39.

"The Farm." *Atlantic*, February 1919, p. 288.

"Fashion and Disease." *The American Journal of Public Health*, September 1925, p. 790.

"Fashionable Hosiery." *Mme. Demorest's Semi-Annual What to Wear and How to Make It*, Spring and Summer 1884, pp. 86–88.

Field, M. "Bridge Luncheon and No Regrets." *Pictorial Review*, September 1928, pp. 108–109.

Frazer, Sarah [Elizabeth W. Smith]. "A Reminiscence." *Pennsylvania Magazine of History and Biography* XLVI (January 1922):39–56.

"From Camel to Socks." *Vogue*, November 1, 1918, p. 94.

Funston, Eda B. "Family Advice from Mrs. Funston." *The Delineator*, July 1918, p. 23.

Garden, Mary. "Why I Bobbed My Hair." *Pictorial Review*, April 1927, p. 8.

Gehan, Eleanor. "When You Come to the End of a Perfect Row." *Catholic World*, July 1918, pp. 526–30.

"Gertrude Lawrence." *Vogue*, July 15, 1940, p. 60.

"Godey's Arm Chair," *Godey's Lady's Book and Magazine*, May 8, 1858, p. 475.

"Golfing and Golfers." *The Domestic Monthly*, August 1895, pp. 21–22.

Goodpasture, Bruce. "In the Crannied Wall." *Yarn Market News*, March/April 1985, p. 25.

Graham, Janet. "Don't Be a Knitwit." *Good Housekeeping*, January 1948, p. 20.

Gray, Virginia G. "Activities of Southern Women, 1840–1860." *The South Atlantic Quarterly* 27 (July 1928):264–79.

"Great Needlework Contest." *Harper's Bazaar*, June 1913, pp. 284–85.

Hall, G. Stanley. "Flapper Americana Novissima." *Atlantic Monthly*, June 1922, pp. 771–80.

Hansen, Robin. "Elizabeth Zimmermann." *Vogue Knitting*, Spring/Summer 1985, pp. 14, 140.

Heath, Mrs. Julian. "The Work of the Housewives League." *Annals of the American Academy of Political and Social Sciences*, July 1913, pp. 121–23.

Hecht, George J. "Ways Girls Can Help in the National Defense." *Calling All Girls* I (June 1944):20–21.

Hill, Frances Baylor. "The Diary of Frances Baylor Hill of 'Queensborough,' King and Queen County, Virginia, 1797." Edited by William K. Bottorff and Roy C. Flannagan. *Early American Literature Newsletter*, special issue, vol. 2, no.3 (Winter 1967):1–53.

"Holiday Gifts." *Demorest's Monthly Magazine*, January 1866, p. 5.

"Hooked Rugs—The Decorative Vogue of the Day." *Woman's Home Companion*, March 1926, p. 61.

Horak, Katherine. "In Quest of a Prairie Home." *The Palimpset*, July 1924, pp. 249–57.

"How They Won the Red Cross Dog." *The Delineator*, October 1918, p. 42.

"How to Knit." *Life*, November 24, 1941, cover and pp. 110–15.

"How to Make a Skating Set." *Gentlewoman*, January, 1917, p. 33.

"How to Pose Like Lana Turner." *Life*, December 23, 1940, p. 62.

Hubert, Philip. "The Bicycle: The Wheel of To-Day." *Scribner's Magazine*, June 1895, pp. 700–705.

"Indian Children Work for the Junior Red Cross." *The Delineator*, June 1918, p. 41.

"Insidious Mah Jong." *Literary Digest*, March 29, 1924, pp. 54–58.

"Is the Younger Generation in Peril?" *Literary Digest*, May 17, 1921, pp. 9–12.

Jacques, Mary J. "The Knitting Lesson." *Saint Nicholas*, November 1903, p. 23.

Johnson, Helen Louise. "The Gospel of the New Housekeeping." *Harper's Bazaar*, March 1913, p. 122.

Kahn, Toby. "A Controversial Labor Law Has Vermont Home Knitters Outraged but Tied up in Knots." *People*, March 19, 1984.

"Keeping Up the Morale of French Lingerie." *Vogue*, November 15, 1918, p. 57.

Kelly, Fred C. "The Great Bicycle Craze." *American Heritage*, vol. 3, no. 1 (December 1956):69–73.

"Knitted Comforts for the Woman Going Abroad to Do War Work." *Pictorial Review*, October 1918, p. 32.

"Knitters Persist." *Business Week*, March 30, 1935, pp. 25–26.

"Knitting Needles." *Dorcas Magazine*, June 1884, pp. 159–60.

"Knitting in Vogue." *Publishers' Weekly*, July 16, 1982, p. 33.

"Knitting Revival." *Business Week*, March 24, 1936, pp. 31–32.

Kolodzey, Jody. "Knit Your Way to Health." *Prevention*, June 1981, pp. 102–107.

Helen B. Kroll. "The Books That Enlightened the Emigrants." *Oregon Historical Quarterly*, June 1944, pp. 102–123.

"Lady Washington's Rebuke." *Harper's Bazaar*, August 20, 1870, p. 538.

Lawrence, Carol. "Wool-less Ways for Warm Days." *Woman's Magazine*, June 1918, p. 53

Leonghridge, Winifred. "Suggestions for a War Tea." *The Delineator*, March 1918, p. 44.

"A Letter: The Scarf with the Bullet Hole." *Red Cross Magazine* XIV, no. 4 (April 1919):1.

"Life and Love of Lana Turner." *Movie Mirror*, June 9, 1940, p. 91.

Lyman, Lila Parrish. "Knitting: A Little Known Field for Collectors." *Antiques*, April 1942, pp. 240–42.

"Macy's New Knit Works: Everything for the Hand-knitter Who Wants Designer Sweaters." *Stores*, January 1982, pp. 34–35.

Mangin, Leslie J. "Playgrounds Aid National Defense." *Recreation*, September 1941, pp. 389–90.

Marquis, Kathleen. "Diamond Cut Diamond: Mormon Women and the Cult of Domesticity." *University of Michigan Papers in Women's Studies*, 2 (1974):105–123.

"Mary Pickford Flag." *Sea Power*, May 1918, pp. 350–51.

"Mary Walker Phillips: Doyenne of Art Knitting." *Knitters*, Spring/Summer 1985, pp. 15–17.

Mather, Frederick G. "Work and Play for Young Folk: The Playthings and Amusements of an Old-Fashioned Boy." *Merry's Museum for Boys and Girls*, September 1883, p. 404.

Mathews, Gertrude S. "Tell Them to Knit." *Good Housekeeping*, September 1917, p. 35.

"Men Can Knit Too." *Woman Citizen*, June 8, 1918, p. 32.

"Merry Christmas—1921 Model." *Woman's Home Companion*, December 1921, p. 53.

"Merry's Monthly Chat with His Friends." *Merry's Museum for Boys and Girls*, September 1862, p. 90; November 1862, p. 153; December 1862, p. 185.

"Mid-Winter Bridge Luncheons." *Woman's Home Companion*, March 1926, pp. 152–55.

Mitchell, S. Weir. "When the College Is Hurtful to a Girl." *The Ladies' Home Journal*, June 1901, p. 14.

Moore, Milcah Martha. *Commonplace Book*, in "Patriotic Poesy." *William and Mary Quarterly* XXXIV, no. 2 (April 1977):307–308.

Morris, Anne Wharton, contributor. "The Journal of Samuel Rowland Fisher." *Pennsylvania Magazine of History and Biography* 41 (1917): 145–97, 274–333.

Morris, Elsie Waterbury. "As Your Hair Is Arranged." *The Delineator*, July 1921, p. 42.

Moynihan, Ruth Barnes. "Children and Young People on the Overland Trail." *Western Historical Quarterly*, July 1975, pp. 279–94.

Munkres, Robert L. "Wives, Mothers, Daughters: Women's Life on the Road West." *Annals of Wyoming* 42, no. 2 (October 1970):191–224.

Murray, Margaret E. Archer. "Memoir of William Archer Family." *Annals of Iowa*, Summer 1968, pp. 357–71.

Nacht, Irving. "Recollections of the Early Days in the Yarn Industry." *Yarn Market News*, January/February 1986, pp. 15, 40.

"New Coiffures Announce That Ears Are Back in Favor." *Woman's Home Companion*, November 1920, p. 102.

"The New Coiffures Are Wearable." *Woman's Home Companion*, December 1921, p. 53.

"New Plaids Have a Young Appeal." *McCall's Needlework and Crafts* 2 (1951):36–38.

Newcomb, Duane. "Merchandising for Today's Decade of Change." *Yarn Market News*, March/April 1985, pp. 26–27, 35.

"The News of the Troops." *The {Girl Scout} Rally*, May 1918, p. 11; June 1918, p. 13; May 1918, p. 11.

"1935's First Boom." *Forbes Magazine*, February 15, 1935, p. 14.

"No College Wardrobe Is Complete Without a Sweater." *The Ladies' Home Journal*, September 1924, p. 178.

Norris, Kathleen. "Woman's Share in War Is Service." *Woman's Life*, Fall 1942, pp. 95–96.

———. "Knitting Women." Reprinted in Mid-American Chapter, American Red Cross. *Bulletin*, May 17, 1918, p. 24.

Nylander, Grace. "Counterpanes." *Early American Life*, April 1986, pp. 62–65.

"Of Women Knitting." *Atlantic Monthly*, May 1936, pp. 639–40.

"Our Own Win the War Page." *The {Girl Scout} Rally*, October 1917, p. 12.

Page, Priscilla. "Smart Women Are Knitting." *Gentlewoman*, December 1934, p. 11.

———. "Towels and Top Knots." *Gentlewoman*, February 1935, p. 8.

———. "Did You Make It Yourself?" *Gentlewoman*, February 1936, p. 10.

"Palm Beach Balances Its Work and Its Play." *Vogue*, March 15, 1918, pp. 18, 92.

Pickford, Mary. "Why I Have Not Bobbed Mine." *Pictorial Review*, April 1927, p. 9.

"Pleasure, Patriotism, and Palm Beach." *Vogue*, March 1, 1918, pp. 47, 128.

"Plenty of Knitting Needles." *Literary Digest*, November 10, 1917, p. 89.

"The Pope's Appeal to Men to Reform Dress." *Literary Digest*, January 29, 1927, pp. 27–28.

"Popularity and Possibilities of the Bob." *American Hairdresser*, May 1922, pp. 62–63.

"Popularity of Hand-Knits: Sales to Major Stores." *Sportswear Review*, January 1939, p. 15.

"The Primal Knits." *Mademoiselle*, July 1973, pp. 102–105.

Rawle, William Brooke. "Laurel Hill and Some Colonial Dames Who Once Lived There." *Pennsylvania Magazine of History and Biography* XXXV (1911):385–414.

Read, Georgia Willis. "Women and Children on the Oregon-California Trail in the Gold Rush Years." *Missouri Historical Review* 39, no. 1 (October 1944):1–23.

"The Recrudescence of Knitting." *Scribner's*, February 1918, p. 249.

"The Red Cross Dog Is Won." *The Delineator*, October 1918, p. 42.

"Red Cross Parade." *Vogue*, July 1, 1918, p. 53.

"The Renaissance of the C-r-s-t." *The Independent*, July 25, 1925, p. 88.

Richardson, William D. "The Call to Colors." *Country Life*, August 1927, pp. 9–10.

Riley, Glenda, ed. "Civil War Letters: The Letters of Harriet Jane Thompson." *Annals of Iowa*, Spring 1970, pp. 296–314.

———. "Family Life on the Frontier: The Diary of Kitturah Penton Belknap." *Annals of Iowa*, Summer 1977, pp. 31–51.

Robbins, Jhan and Robbins, June. "Why Young Mothers Feel Trapped." *Redbook*, September 1960, pp. 28–29, 84.

Rosen, Evie. "The APNR/TNNA National Certification and Education Program." *Yarn Market News*, January/February 1986, pp. 24, 43–45.

Rosenberg, Carrol Smith. "Beauty, the Beast and the Militant Woman: A Case Study in Sex Roles and Social Stress in Jacksonian America." *American Quarterly*, October 1971, pp. 562–84.

"Roomy Knitting Bag Designed to Stand Beside Chair." *Popular Science Monthly*, July 1935, p. 78.

Rowell, Hugh Grant. "Father Discourses on Dieting." *Hygeia*, July 1927, pp. 340–41.

Ryan, Gladys Weston. "Eventually, Why Not Now?" *American Home* 8 (August 1932):194.

Schlissel, Lillian. "Mothers and Daughters on the Western Frontier." *Frontiers* 3 (1978):29–33.

Seinfel, Ruth. "Snarls of Joy." *Colliers*, December 7, 1935, pp. 26–30.

Sims, Margaret. "The Art of Knitting." *Ladies' Home Journal*, March 1894, p. 21.

———. "A Bachelor's Tea Cosy." *Ladies' Home Journal*, August 1895, p. 21.

———. "Dainty Knitting and Crocheting." *Ladies' Home Journal*, April 1894, p. 32.

"Skating Parks." *Young Lady's Friend*, January 1886, p. 84.

Slater, Sarah. "What Girls Are Wearing." *New Ideas Woman's Magazine*, March 1902, p. 92.

"Slip-over Sweater." *Gentlewoman*, August 1917, p. 7.

"The Smart and the Young Knit Sweaters Like These." *Life*, December 23, 1940, pp. 46–47.

"Smile of America." *Harper's Bazaar*, August 1935, p. 39.

Smith, Thelma M. "Feminism in Philadelphia, 1790–1850." *Pennsylvania Magazine of History and Biography*, July 1944, pp. 243–68.

Snow, Eliza. "Report." *The Woman's Exponent*, September 1, 1875, p. 62.

"A Sock Anyone Can Knit." *Illustrated World*, March 1919, pp. 112–13.

Spaulding, Lynn. "Why Not Knit a Nose Warmer?" *Mother Earth News*, January/February 1979, p. 165.

"Spiderweb Hats." *The Delineator*, September 1918, p. 39.

Sporkin, Elizabeth. "We're Tangled Up Again in Knitting." *USA Today* [c. October 1985].

Stafford, Charlotte. "Easy Sleeveless Pullover." *Knitting World*, April 1986, pp. 32–33.

Stoddard, Maynard Good. "Knit 2, Purl 1, Hubby 0." *Saturday Evening Post*, April 1982, pp. 62–63.

"Susan Beebe's Sweaters Are Warm, but Can Cost a Cool $1,850 Each." *People*, November 16, 1981, p. 144.

"Sweaters." *Godey's Magazine*, September 1897, p. 442.

"Sweaters of the Future: Will They Be All Wool, Aralac, or Nylon?" *Consumers' Research Bulletin*, October 1942, pp. 24–25.

"Sweater Season Opens with Rush to Warm Bulky Wools." *Vogue*, October 21, 1940, pp. 62–64.

Tarbell, Ida M. "The American Woman." Part I: *American Magazine*, November 1909, pp. 3–17; Part II: *American Magazine*, December 1909, pp. 206–220.

———. "The Cost of Living and Household Management." *Annals of the American Academy of Political and Social Sciences*, July 1913, pp. 127–30.

"A Tea Party at Molly's." *The Gentlewoman*, May 1918, p. 33.

"Teen Agers Urged to Knit Ahead for School." *Calling All Girls*, June 1944, p. 44.

"They Make Sailors' Christmas Seasonal." *Modern Maturity*, December 1983–January 1984, pp. 60–61.

"To-day's Manners and Morals—the side of 'the girls.' " *Literary Digest*, July 9, 1921, pp. 34–42.

Treman, Irene Castle. "I Bobbed My Hair and Then—" *Ladies' Home Journal*, October 1921, p. 124.

"Triple Yarn Holder for Those Who Knit in Groups." *Popular Science Monthly*, May 1942, p. 193.

"Two Knitting Boxes . . . Timely Gifts for Red Cross Workers." *Popular Science Monthly*, December 1941, pp. 177–78.

"U.S. Knits Again." *Business Week*, February 22, 1941, pp. 49–51.

Upitis, Lizbeth. "Return of the Reticule." *Knitters*, Spring/Summer 1986, pp. 44–47.

Vivolva, Brett Harvey. "Pioneer Diaries: The Untold Story of the West." *Ms. Magazine*, May 1975, pp. 32–36.

"Vogue Covers Join the Ranks." *Vogue*, August 1, 1918, p. 29.

"A War Charity Established by a New York Woman." *Vogue*, April 15, 1918, p. 49.

"Warmth for the Orphans of Korea." *McCall's*, October 1953, pp. 16, 18.

Waterman, Nixon. "The New Woman and Her Grandam." *The Wheelwoman*, July 1897, p. 341.

Waterhouse, Alfred J. "Just Keep Knitting, Knitting, Knitting." *Stitches*, April 1903, p. 5.

"The Weaker Sex." *Woman Citizen*, October 19, 1918, p. 419.

Weaver, Polly. "What's Wrong with Ambition?" *Mademoiselle*, September 1956, pp. 113, 189–91.

Welter, Barbara. "The Cult of True Womanhood: 1820–1860." *American Quarterly*, XVIII (Summer 1966):151–74.

"What Can We Do to Help?" *Gentlewoman*, December 1917, p. 4.

"What the Smart English Sportswoman Wears for Golf." *Harper's Bazaar*, April 1923, p. 75.

"What War Has Done to Clothes." *Vogue*, October 15, 1918, p. 62.

"Wheel-Whirls." *Godey's Magazine*, October 1896, p. 446.

Wills, Helen. "Emancipated Legs Mean Better Sports." *Ladies' Home Journal*, April 1923, p. 33.

"Win a Red Cross Dog!" *The Delineator*, April 1918, p. 44.

"Woman of Civil War Times Now Instructs a Knitting Class." *Gentlewoman*, August 1918, p. 13.

"The Woman Who Saw." *Gentlewoman*, January 18, 1918, p. 7.

"The Woman's World." *Home Comfort*, March 1898, p. 9.

"Women's Clubs and War Work." *Vogue*, April 1, 1918, p. 128.

Woodbury, Helen. "The College Girl's Trunk." *Woman's Home Companion*, September 1921, pp. 66–67.

"Work in Far-off Alaska for the Junior Red Cross." *The Delineator*, May 1918, p. 59.

"Work of the Comforts Committee." *Sea Power*, May 1917–October 1919.

"Work! Work! Work! All Around America with War Activities." *The Delineator*, April 1918, p. 10.

"Work for Idle Hours." *Mme. Demorest's Semi-Annual What to Wear and How to Make it*, Spring and Summer 1880, pp. 44–47.

Xenakis, Alexander. "The Barbara Walker Mosaic." *Knitters*, Fall/Winter 1985, pp. 11–14.

———. "An Afternoon with Elizabeth." *Knitters* (premier issue), 1984, p. 12.

Young, Brigham. ["Discourse"]. *Journal History of the Church*, December 10, 1856, pp. 4–5.

———. ["Speech"]. *Journal History of the Church*, April 9, 1871, pp. 55–56.

——— and Kimball, Heber C. "The Fourteenth General Epistle to the Latter-day Saints." *Journal History of the Church*, December 10, 1856, pp. 1–44.

Zimmerman, Barbara Baker, and Carstonsen Vernon. "Pioneer Women in Southwestern Washington Territory: The Recollections of Susanna Marie Slover

McFarland Price Ede." *Pacific Northwestern Quarterly* (October, 1976), pp. 137–150.

Letters, Diaries, Journals and Memoirs

Andrews, Eliza Frances. *The War-Time Journal of a Georgia Girl, 1864–1865.* Edited by Spencer B. King. Atlanta: D. Appleton and Co., 1908. Reprint. Atlanta: Cherokee Publishing Co., 1976.

Ballard, Martha Moore. *Diary.* In Nash, Charles Elventon. *The History of Augusta* [Maine]. Augusta, Maine; Charles E. Nash and Co., 1904.

Beers, Fannie A. *Memories: A Record of Personal Experience and Adventure During the Four Years of the War.* Philadelphia: J. B. Lippincott, 1888.

Boquist, Laura Brewster. *Crossing the Plains with Ox Teams, 1862.* Privately published, 1932.

Bowne, Eliza Southgate. *A Girl's Life Eighty Years Ago.* New York: Scribner's, [c. 1887]. Reprint. New York: Arno Press, 1974.

Brown, Maria Foster. *Grandmother Brown's Hundred Years, 1827–1927.* Edited by Harriet Connor Brown. Boston: Little, Brown and Co., 1929.

Bryant, Blanche Brown and Bryant, Gertrude Elaine, eds. *The Diaries of Sally and Pamela Brown, 1832–1838.* Springfield, Vt.: William L. Bryant Foundation, 1970.

Bryant, Edwin. *Rocky Mountain Adventures.* New York: Hurst & Co., Publishers, [1846]. Reprint. *What I Saw in California, Journal of a Tour, 1846, 1847.* Minneapolis: Ross and Haines, Inc., 1867.

Butler, Jay Caldwell. *Letters Home.* Privately printed, 1930.

Carter, Kate B., comp. *Heart Throbs of the West* [a compilation of pamphlets of 1937–38]. 3 vols. in 1. Salt Lake City, Utah: Daughters of Utah Pioneers, 1939.

Chestnut, Mary Boykin. *Diary from Dixie.* Edited by Ben Ames Williams. Cambridge, Mass.: Harvard University Press, 1980.

Clappe, Louise Amelia Knapp Smith. *The Daily Letters from California Mines in 1851–1852.* San Francisco: Thomas C. Russell, Private Press, 1922.

Closz, Harriet Bonebright. *Reminiscences of Newcastle, Iowa, 1848.* Des Moines: Historical Department of Iowa, 1921.

Coco, Gregory A., comp. and ed. *Through Blood and Fire: The Civil War Letters of Major Charles J. Mills, 1862–1865.* 1st ed. Gettysburg, Pa.: n.p., 1982.

Colton, Jessie S. *The Civil War Correspondence of Matthias Baldwin Colton.* Philadelphia: Macrae-Smith Co., 1931.

Colt, Miriam Davis. *Went to Kansas.* Ann Arbor, Mich.: University Microfilms, Inc., 1966.

Cummins, Sarah J. *Autobiography and Reminiscences.* La Grande, Oreg.: La Grande Printing Co., 1914.

Davis, Mary Elizabeth [Maragne]. *The Neglected Thread: A Journal from the Calhoun*

Community, 1836–1840. Columbia, S.C.: University of South Carolina Press, 1951.

Dawson, Sarah Morgan. *A Confederate Girl's Diary.* Edited by James I. Robertson. Boston: Houghton Mifflin, 1913.

Duane, William, ed. *Extracts from the Diary of Christopher Marshall . . . During the American Revolution.* Albany, N.Y.: Joel Munsell, 1877.

Dye, Eva Emery. *The Soul of America: An Oregon Iliad.* New York: Press of the Pioneers, 1934.

Earle, Alice Morse, ed. *Diary of Anna Green Winslow.* Boston: Houghton Mifflin, 1894.

Emery, Sarah A. *Reminiscences of a Nonagenarian.* Newburyport, Mass.: William H. Huse and Co., 1879.

Ferris, Mrs. Benjamin. *The Mormons at Home* [Letters 1852–53]. n.p., 1856. Reprint. New York: Ames Press, 1971.

Finger, Maude Turner. "Some Womanly Recollections of the War Between the States." In *Carolina and the Southern Cross.* Kingston, N.C.: United Daughters of the Confederacy, February 1914.

Finley, Christine, ed. *Let Them Speak for Themselves: Women in the American West, 1849–1900.* Hamden, Conn.: Archon Books, 1977.

Fithian, Philip Vickers. *Journals and Letters, 1767–1774.* n.p., 1900. Reprint. Freeport, N.Y.: Books for Libraries Press, 1969.

Fitzpatrick, John C., ed. *The Writings of George Washington.* 39 vols. Boston: n.p., 1925. Reprint. Westport, Conn.: Greenwood Press, 1970.

Ford, Chauncy Worthington, ed. *Journals of the Continental Congress.* 34 vols. Washington, D.C.: U.S. Government Printing Office, 1904–1937. Reprint. New York: Johnson Reprint Corp., 1968.

Frizzell, Lodissa. *Across the Plains to California in 1852.* New York: New York Public Library, 1915.

Gay, Mary A. H. *Life in Dixie During the War.* DeKalb, Ga.: DeKalb Historical Society and Darby Printing Company, 1897.

The Garden of Memories: Stories of the Civil War as Told by the Veterans and Daughters of the Confederacy. United Daughters of the Confederacy, Arkansas Division. Mrs. M. A. Elliott, composer. Camden, Ark.: Brown Printing Co., 1911.

Gillespie, Elizabeth Duane. *A Book of Remembrance.* Philadelphia: J. B. Lippincott, 1901.

Gilman, Caroline Howard, ed. *Letters of Eliza Wilkinson.* New York: Samuel Coleman, 1839.

———— [Mrs. Clarissa Packard]. *Recollections of a Housekeeper.* New York: Harper and Brothers, 1834.

Greene, Jack P., ed. *The Diary of Landon Carter of Sabine Hall.* 2 vols. Charlottesville, Va.: University of Virginia Press, 1965.

Hague, Parthenia A. *A Blockaded Family.* 1888. Boston: Houghton Mifflin, Reprint. Freeport, N.Y.: Books for Libraries Press 1971.

Hall, Florence Marian Howe. *Memories Grave and Gray.* New York: Harper and Brothers, 1918.

Hampsten, Elizabeth. *Read This Only to Yourself: The Private Writings of Midwestern Women, 1880–1910.* Bloomington, Ind.: Indiana University Press, 1982.

Hancock, Cornelia. *The South After Gettysburg; Letters of Cornelia Hancock from the Army of the Potomac 1863–1865.* Philadelphia: University of Pennsylvania Press, 1937.

Hecox, Margaret. *California Caravans: The 1846 Overland Trail Memoir of Margaret M. Hecox.* San Jose, Calif.: Harlan-Young Press, 1966.

Herndon, Sarah Raymond. *Days on the Road Crossing the Plains in 1865.* New York: Burr Printing House, 1902.

Hitchcock, Ernest. *Memoirs of the Bloomsgrove Family.* n.p.: Literature House, 1790. Reprint. 2 vols. in 1. Upper Saddle River, N.J.: Gregg Press, 1970.

Hixon, Adrietta Applegate. *On to Oregon.* Fairfield, Wash.: Ye Galleon Press, 1973.

Holmes, Kenneth L., ed. and comp. *Covered Wagon Women: Diaries and Letters from the Western Trails 1840–1890.* 4 vols. Glendale, Calif.: Arthur H. Clark Company, 1985.

Holmes, Julia Archibald. *A Bloomer Girl on Pike's Peak, 1852.* Edited by Agnes Wright Spring. Western History Department, Denver Public Library, 1949.

Jones, Katharine M. *Heroines of Dixie: Confederate Women Tell the Story of the War.* Indianapolis: Bobbs-Merrill, 1955.

Larcom, Lucy. *A New England Girlhood.* Boston: Houghton Mifflin, 1889.

Le Conte, Emma. *When the World Ended: The Diary of Emma Le Conte.* Edited by Earl Schenck Miers. New York: Oxford University Press, 1957.

Lenroot Clara C. *Long, Long Ago.* Appleton, Wis.: Badger Printing Co., 1929.

Lockley, Fred. *The Lockley Files: Conversations with Pioneer Women.* Eugene, Oreg.: Rainy Day Press, 1981.

Lyman, Sarah Joiner. *Sarah Joiner Lyman: Her Own Story.* Compiled by Margaret Greer Martin. Hilo, Hawaii: Lyman House Memorial Museum, 1970.

Macon, Emma C. R. and Conway, Reuben. *Reminiscences of the Civil War.* Privately printed by K.C.M. Paulsen, 1896. Reprint. Cedar Rapids, Iowa: Torch Press, 1911.

McDonald, Mrs. Cornelia P. *A Diary with Reminiscences of War and Refugee Life in the Shenandoah Valley, 1860–1865.* Nashville, Tenn.: Cullom and Ghertner, 1934.

Meriwether, Elizabeth Avery. *Recollections of 92 Years, 1824–1916.* Nashville, Tenn.: Tennessee Historical Commission, 1958.

Mills, Charles J. *Through Blood and Fire: The Civil War Letters of Major Charles J. Mills, 1862–1865.* 1st ed. compiled and edited by Gregory A. Coco. Gettysburg, Pa.: Privately printed, 1982.

Morgan, Dale, ed. *Overland in 1846, Diaries and Letters of the California-Oregon Trail.* 4 vols. Georgetown, Calif.: Talisman Press, 1968.

Nelson, Amanda Wimpy. *My Sister and I.* Fairfield, Wash.: Ye Galleon Press, 1973.

Orr, Ellison. *Reminiscences of a Pioneer Boy*. Reprinted from *Annals of Iowa* (#7, Winter 1971, and #8, Spring 1971). n.p.: Iowa City, 1971.

Our Women in the War: The Lives They Lived and the Deaths They Died. Charleston, S.C.: News and Courier Books Presses, 1885.

Peddy, George W. and Peddy, Kate Featherstone. *Saddle Bag and Spinning Wheels, Being the Civil War Letters of George W. Peddy and His Wife, Kate Featherstone Peddy*. Macon, Ga.: Mercer University Press, 1981.

Personal Reminiscences and Experiences by Members of the 103rd Volunteer Infantry: Campaign Life in the Union Army 1862–1865. Sheffield Lake, Ohio: 103rd Ohio Volunteer Infantry Memorial Foundation, 1900.

Porter, Lavinia Honeyman. *By Ox Team to California: A Narrative of Crossing the Plains in 1860*. Oakland, Calif.: Oakland Enquirer Publishing Co., 1910.

Pringle, Elizabeth W. Allston. *Chronicles of "Chicora Wood."* Boston: The Christian Publishing House, 1940. Reprint. Atlanta: Cherokee Publishing Co., 1976.

Reminiscences of the Women of Missouri During the Sixties. Missouri Division, United Daughters of the Confederacy. Jefferson City, Mo.: Hugh Stephens Printing Co., 192[5?].

Roosevelt, Eleanor. *My Days*. New York: Dodge Publishing Co., 1938.

Royce, Sarah. *A Frontier Lady: Recollections of the Gold Rush and Early California*. New Haven, Conn.: Yale University Press, 1932.

Sanford, Mollie Dorsey. *The Journal of Mollie Dorsey Sanford in Nebraska and Colorado Territories, 1857–1866*. Lincoln Nebr.: University of Nebraska Press, 1959.

Schlissel, Lillian. *Women's Diaries of the Westward Journey*. New York: Schocken Books, 1982.

Smith, Sarah Bixby. *Adobe Days*. Cedar Rapids, Iowa: Torch Press, 1925. Reprint. Fresno, Calif.: Valley Publishers, 1974.

Smyth, Albert Henry. *The Writings of Franklin*. 10 vols. New York: Macmillan, 1905.

Society of California Pioneers. *Transactions, January 12–May 7th, 1863*, part 1, vol. 2. San Francisco: Alta California Book and Job Office, 1863.

Sod House Memories. Hastings. Nebr.: Sod House Society, 1963. Reprint. 3 vols. in 1. 1972.

Stewart, Helen Marnie. *Diary of Helen Stewart, 1853*. Eugene, Oreg.: Lane County Pioneer-Historical Society, 1961.

Tarbox, Increase S., ed. and ann. *Diary of Thomas Robbins, D.D.* 2 vols. Boston: Beacon Press, 1887.

Taylor, Mrs. Thomas and others, eds. *South Carolina Women of the Confederacy*. 2 vols. Columbia, S.C.: The State Company, 1903–1907.

Told by the Pioneers: Tales of Frontier Life and Tales Told by Those Who Remember the Days of the Territory and Early Statehood of Washington. [Olympia?], Wash.: U.S. Works Projects Administration, 1937–1938.

Ward, Harriet Sherrill. *Prairie Schooner Lady: The Journal of Harriet Sherrill Ward*. Los Angeles: Westernlore Press, 1959.

War Reminiscences of Columbus, Mississippi, and Elsewhere, 1861–1865. Compiled by the United Daughters of the Confederacy. West Point, Miss.: Sullivan's, 1961.

Wilson, Luzena Stanley. *Luzena Stanley Wilson, '49er*. Mills College, Calif.: Eucalyptus Press, 1937.

Michigan Women in the Civil War. Lansing, Mich.: Michigan Civil War Centennial Observance Commission, 1963.

Myres, Sandra L. *Westering Women and the Frontier Experience 1800–1915*. Albuquerque: University of New Mexico Press, 1982.

Pamphlets, Bulletins, Newsletters and Miscellaneous Publications

The Altruist Interchange. New York: The Altruist Society of the Needlework Guild of America, 1893.

American Fund for French Wounded. *Monthly Report*, September-October, 1917, vol. 2. Report of November 17, 1916, n.p.

American Red Cross publications:

> *Red Cross Courier*. Washington, D.C.: 1918–19
> Mid-American Chapter. *Bulletin*. Chicago: 1918.
> Northern Division. *Bulletin*. n.p., May 20, June 27, 1918.
> Northwestern Division. *Bulletin*. Seattle: 1917–19.
> Pennsylvania-Delaware Division. *Red Cross Clippings*. Philadelphia: 1917–19.
> Potomac Division. *Bulletin*. Washington, D.C.: 1918–19.
> Territorial, Insular, and Foreign Division. *Bulletin*. Hawaii: May 1918.
> War-time patterns from both World Wars in pamphlet form.

Brooklyn Institute of Arts and Sciences. *For Heads and Toes*. Brooklyn: 1974.

Brooklyn Museum Catalogue of Early American Handicraft. Brooklyn: February 2, 1924.

Bucilla Art Needlework Bulletin. Secaucus, N.J.: Bucilla Company, 1940–45.

Church World Service: A Tradition of Help . . . A Legacy of Hope. Elkhart, Ind.: Church World Service, 1986.

Cobello, Jo [words and music]. "Knittin' for Britain." Philadelphia: Song Association, Music Publishers, 1941.

Domestic Science: State Course of Study for the Public Schools of Indiana. Indianapolis, Ind.: Department of Public Instruction, Education Publications, September 1915.

Dry Goods Catalogue, Fall 1939. Chicago: Butler Bros., 1939.

Forget-Me-Knots. Elkhart, Ind.: Church World Service Clothing Appeal, n.d.

Frills, Flossy and Lorre, Ben [words and music]. "Knit One, Purl Two." New York: Music Products Co. Inc., 1942.

Great Western Sanitary Fair Catalogue of Large Collection of Autographs, Coins, Medals Etc. Cincinnati, Ohio: O. R. Charles and Co., 1864.

Highways of Service. Elkhart, Ind.: Church World Service, n.d.

How Can We Best Help Our Camps and Hospitals? New York: Women's Central Association—U.S. Sanitary Association, 1862.

Hubbard, Albert M. "The Knitting Song: Dedicated to the Patriotic Ladies of the North." Cincinnati, Ohio: John Church, 1863.

Industrial Home Work of Children. Bureau Publication #100, Children's Bureau of the U.S. Department of Labor. Washington, D.C.: U.S. Government Printing Office, 1922.

Griffith, Helen S. *The Knitting Club Meets, or Just Back from France.* Boston: Walter H. Baker and Co., 1918.

Macdonald, Anne L. *Documentary Case Studies in American History* [anti-suffrage pamphlets reprinted]. Washington, D.C.: National Cathedral School, 1980.

Needle and Bobbin Club. *Bulletin*, vol. 5. New York: Needlework Guild of America, 1921.

Oddie, Bill. "The Knitting Song." London: Noel Gay Music Co. Ltd., 1865.

Osgood, George L. "Knitting the Scarf" [song]. Boston: Oliver Ditson and Co., 1880.

Our Daily Fare. Philadelphia: [printed for the Philadelphia Sanitary Fair], 1863.

Our Drummer. Chicago: Butler Brothers Dry Goods Co., Fall 1939.

Proceedings of the First Annual School in Fair Management. Chicago: University of Chicago, May 12–17, 1924.

Quaife, Elise West. *The Knitting Girls Count One: A Patriotic Play in One Act.* New York: Samuel French, Publisher, 1918.

Risher, Anna Priscilla. "To the Soldier Girls at Home: Knitting" [song with words by Frank L. Armstrong]. Boston: Arthur P. Schmidt Co., 1917. Reprinted in *Part-Songs for Patriotic Occasions.* New York: Arthur P. Schmidt Co., 1918.

Scouting for Girls: Official Handbook of the Girl Scouts. New York: Girl Scouts Incorporated, 1920.

Seamen's Church Institute of New York and New Jersey: A Brief History. New York: Published by the Institute, n.d.

Sears Roebuck and Company Catalogue, no. 104. 1897. Reprint. New York: Chelsea House Publishers, 1968.

Sears Roebuck Catalogues of the Thirties. New York: Nostalgia, Inc., 1978.

The Sentiments of an American Woman [broadside]. [Philadelphia]: Printed by John Dunlop, 1780.

Smith, Samuel Abbot. *An Address Delivered in Behalf of the Soldiers of West Cambridge.* Boston: Alfred Mudge and Son, Printers, 1864.

Soldier's Relief Association. *To the Friends of the Southern Cause at Home.* Columbia, South Carolina: n.p., 1864.

Stoltfus, Amanda. *How to Organize and Conduct a School and Community Fair.* University of Texas Bulletin #2409. [Austin], Texas: March 1, 1924.

Teachers' College Bulletin: Tentative Course of Study in Household Arts for 7th and 8th Grades. New York: Public Teachers College, Columbia University, 1915.

The (Updated) Last Whole Earth Catalogue. New York: Penguin Books, 1975.

U.S. Sanitary Commission. *The Soldier's Friend.* Philadelphia: Perkenpine and Higgins, 1865.

Women's Centennial Committee. *New Century for Women.* Philadelphia: Woman's Building, International Exhibition, 1876.

Women's Central Association of Relief. *"How Can We Best Help Our Camps and Hospitals?"* New York: Wm. C. Bryant and Co., 1862.

Official Reports, Records, Speeches

Burnham, Elizabeth. *Address of Miss Elizabeth Burnham (of San Jose) on the Presentation of the Flag by the Pioneer Ladies to the Society of California Pioneers, September 9, 1853.* San Jose: n.p., 1850.

Circular and Constitution of the Salem Children's Friend Society. Salem, Mass.: Register Office, 1839.

The Constitution of the Ladies' Society of Columbia for the Encouragement of Industry Among the Female Poor and Especially for the Relief of Poor Widows with Small Children. Columbia, S.C.: Telescope Press, 1823.

Eagle, Mary Kavanaugh Oldham, ed. *The Congress of Women Held in the Women's Building, World's Columbian Exposition.* Chicago: American Publishing House, 1894. Reprint, New York: Arno Press, 1974.

Goodrich, Frank B. *The Tribute Book: A Record of the Munificence, Self-sacrifice, and Devotion of the American People During the War for the Union.* New York: Derby and Miller, 1865.

Greenville [SC] Ladies' Association in the Aid of Volunteers of the Confederate Army. *Minutes of the Proceedings.* Edited by James Welch Patton. Durham, N.C.: Duke University Press, 1937. Reprinted in *Historical Papers of Trinity College Historical Society,* Series XX.

Howe, G. J. *List of Contributions Received from Various Societies of Loyal Women, and from Individuals for the Use of Regimental and General Hospitals of the Army at the Boston Branch of the U.S. Sanitary Commission.* Boston: Tichnor and Fields, 1862.

Kansas Board of World's Fair Managers. *Report.* Topeka, Kans.: Press of Hamilton Printing Co., 1894.

Ladies' Association for Soldiers' Relief of Philadelphia. *Annual Report.* July 28, 1863.

Ladies' Hospital Relief Association [of Rochester, N.Y.]. *Report of the Christmas Bazaar, Held Under the Auspices of the Ladies' Hospital Relief Association.* Rochester, N.Y.: Benton and Andrews, 1864.

Ladies' Relief Association of the District of Columbia. *Proceedings on Opening of the Patent Office Fair Under the Auspices of the Ladies' Relief Association of the District of Columbia.* Washington, D.C.: "Printed for the benefit of the Fair," February 22, 1864.

Ladies' Relief Society of Passaic, N.J. *Report.* Passaic, N.J.: n.p., 1865.

Ladies' Southern Relief Association of Maryland. *Report.* Baltimore: Kelly and Piet, September 1, 1866.

Mussey, General Reuben D. "Response, [To] The Loyal Women of 1861–1865" [a response to a toast]. Cincinnati, Ohio: Army of the Cumberland Banquet in the Music Hall, October 25, 1887.

New England Women's Auxiliary Association Branch of the U.S. Sanitary Commission. *Annual Report.* Boston: Prentiss and Deland, 1863, 1864, 1865.

Oregon Pioneer Association. *Transactions of the 46th Annual Reunion in Portland of June 1918 and of the 47th Reunion of June 1919.* Portland, Oreg.: Chausse-Prudhomme Co., 1921, 1922.

Report Concerning the Special Relief Service of the U.S. Sanitary Commission. Boston: n.p., 1864.

Report for the Season Ending December 31st, 1893. n.p.: H. B. Claflin Co., 1893.

Seamen's Aid Society of the City of Boston. *Tenth Annual Report.* Boston: Eastburn's Press, 1843.

Soldiers' Aid Society of Northern Ohio. *First Annual Report to the United States Sanitary Commission.* Cleveland: Fairbanks, Benedict and Co., July 1, 1862.

Woman's Relief Association of the City of Brooklyn. *Report.* Brooklyn: [U.S. Sanitary Commission], 1863.

Women's Central Association of Relief. *Second Annual Report.* New York: William S. Dorr, Printer, 1863.

Women's Pennsylvania Branch of the U.S. Sanitary Commission. *Report of Special Relief Committee.* [Philadelphia], Pa.: n.p., March 1, 1864.

Fiction

Alcott, Louisa M. *Little Women.* Philadelphia, Pa.: John C. Winston Co., 1926.

Beatty, Jerome. *Bob Fulton's Amazing Soda-Pop Stretcher.* New York: William R. Scott., Inc., 1963.

Blanchard, Amy E. *A Girl Scout of Red Rose Troop.* Boston: W. A. Wilde Company, 1918.

Estes, Eleanor. *Rufus M.* New York: Harcourt, Brace and Co., 1943.

Montgomery, Lucy Maud. *Rilla of Ingleside.* Toronto, Canada: McClelland and Stewart, Ltd., 1920.

Unpublished Manuscript Sources

Cincinnati, Ohio. U.S. Sanitary Commission, Cincinnati Branch, Financial Records, Cincinnati Historical Society. Box 37; Folders 21, 24, 32; "Great Western Sanitary Fair Papers."

Hartford, Conn. Connecticut Historial Society Library, "Abigail Foote's Journal, June 2, 1775–September 17, 1775," pp. 1, 3.

Mount Vernon, Va. Mount Vernon Ladies' Association of the Union Library. "Mount Vernon Store Book," January 1, 1787–December 37, 1787; "Invoices and Letters," 1775–76.

Portland, Oreg. Oregon Historical Society. Arvazine Angeline Cooper Reminiscences, "Our Journey Across the Plains from Missouri to Oregon, 1863." In Manuscript Collection 1508, Overland Journeys to the Pacific.

Portland, Oreg. Oregon Historical Society. Sheba Hargreaves, "Pioneer Home-Makers of the 1840's." Sheba Manuscript Collection, Mss 375, p. 16.

Washington, D.C. National Archives. Office of the Quartermaster General, Record Group 92, Consolidated Correspondence Files, 1794–1915, Box 389, entry 225.

Cambridge, Mass. The Schlesinger Library, Radcliffe College. Fragment Society of Boston papers, MC 338 12V, Series II, Box 2; "Annual Report," December, 1862; MC 338, Box 3, Folder 15: "Minutes of the Annual Meeting," December 3, 1940; "Report of Meeting of February 2, 1941"; "Report of Meeting at the End of the Year, 1940–41"; Box 2: "Society Scrapbook," n.p.

Cambridge, Mass. The Schlesinger Library, Radcliffe College. North Bennet Street Industrial School papers, MC 269, Series II, Box 54, Folder 14. George C. Gruner, Director, "Report of the Director of the North Bennet Street Industrial School on the Industrial Work of the Special Class from the Hancock School," April 14, 1909, pp. 1, 3; "Afternoon Classes—Neighborhood Work: Knitting," [circa 1903–1910], single page; Series II, Box 57, Folder 48; "The North End Lantern," May 1917, p. 4; February 1919, p. 5; April 1919, p. 7; March 1920, p. 7.

Index

Illustration Sources
and Credits

vii. *The Young Ladies' Journal: Complete Guide to the Worktable,* London: E. Harrison, Merton House, 1885, p. 36.

CHAPTER 1. 4. "Old Method," after a copper engraving. The Bettmann Archive.

CHAPTER 3. 48. The Art Museum, Princeton University. Gift of Mrs. Frank Jewett Mather, Jr. 58. *Godey's Lady's Book and Magazine,* April 1858, p. 355.

CHAPTER 4. 70. William H. Fowler, *Women on the American Frontier,* Hartford, Conn: S.S. Scranton and Company, 1879, p. 172.

CHAPTER 5. 115. Sojourner Truth. Sophia Smith Collection, Smith College.

CHAPTER 6. 121. Jane Weaver, *Peterson's Magazine,* August 1864, p. 144.

CHAPTER 7. 137. *The Brown Family*; Eastman Johnson; National Gallery of Art, Washington; Gift of David Edward Finley and Margaret Eustis Finley. 138. Copyright © 1868. The Hearst Corporation, Courtesy of *Harper's Bazaar.* 145. Copyright © 1868. The Hearst Corporation. Courtesy of *Harper's Bazaar.* 147. Circa 1870. 148. Copyright © 1868. The Hearst Corporation. Courtesy of *Harper's Bazaar.* 150. "Heel and Toe," (Boston: Armstrong and Company, 1873). Library of Congress. 152. (left) Copyright © 1868. The Hearst Corporation. Courtesy of *Harper's Bazaar.* (right) Copyright © 1868. The Hearst Corporation. Courtesy of *Harper's Bazaar.* 158. Copyright © 1868. The Hearst Corporation. Courtesy of *Harper's Bazaar.*

CHAPTER 8. 161. Copyright © 1882. The Hearst Corporation. Courtesy of *Harper's Bazaar*. 162. (left) Mary Louise Kerzman, *Knitting: How to Knit and What to Knit*, Brooklyn: Henry Bristow, 1884, cover. (right) Jane C. Croly, *A Guide to the Use of the Needle and the Hook: The Jenny June Series of Manuals for Ladies*, New York: A. L. Burt, 1885, cover. 164. Copyright © 1887. The Hearst Corporation. Courtesy of *Harper's Bazaar*. 165. The Bettmann Archive. 166. (left) *Fancy and Practical Knitting*, Vol. III, #2 (New York: The Butterick Company, 1897), p. 175. (right) *Fancy and Practical Knitting*, Vol. III, #2 (New York: The Butterick Company, 1897), p. 167. 167. *The Self Instructor with Silk Knitting, Crocheting and Embroidery* (New York: Belding Bros. Co., 1891), p. 29. 169. Words by O. Schrage; Music by W. Potstock. Chicago: W. Potstock: 1894. Library of Congress. 171. Copyright © 1897. The Hearst Corporation. Courtesy of *Harper's Bazaar*.

CHAPTER 9. 178. Mary A. McCormack, *Spool Knitting* (New York: A. S. Barnes & Co., 1909), frontispiece. 179. Elsa S. Barsaloux, *The Utopia Yarn Book* (New York: Henry E. Frankenberg Co., Manufacturers of Utopia Yarns, 1916), p. 221. 184. (left) *Home Needlework Magazine*, July 1906, p. 288. Courtesy of the Bucilla Company. (right) Elsa Barsaloux, Designer, *Good Shepherd Fingering Yarns and Their Uses* (Newton, MA: Good Shepherd Worsted Mills, 1917), p. 221. 185. *Bear Brand Manual of Handiwork* (New York: Bernard Ulmann & Company, 1904), p. 31. Courtesy of the Bucilla Company. 187. (left) *Bear Brand Manual of Handiwork*, Vol. X (New York: Bear Brand Manufacturers, Bernard Ulmann Company, 1910), p. 56. Courtesy of the Bucilla Company. (right) *Bear Brand Manual of Handiwork*, (New York: Bernard Ulmann and Company, 1904), p. 28. Courtesy of the Bucilla Company. 188. (left) *Bear Brand Manual of Handiwork* (New York: Bernard Ulmann & Company, 1904), p. 38. Courtesy of the Bucilla Company. (right) Alice Maynard, ed., *What to Knit and Crochet and How to Do It*, The Lion Yarn Books (New York: Calhoun Robbins and Co., 1903), p. 51. 189. (left) *Bear Brand Manual of Handiwork*, Vol. X (New York: Bear Brand Manufacturers, Bernard Ulmann and Company, 1910), p. 75. Courtesy of the Bucilla Company. (right) *Bear Brand Manual of Handiwork*, Vol. X (New York: Bear Brand Manufacturers, Bernard Ulmann and Company, 1910), p. 41. Courtesy of the Bucilla Company. 190. (left) Adelaide J. Gray, ed., *The Sunlight Book of Knitting and Crocheting* (Chicago: W. G. Perry, 1912), p. 125. (right) Adelaide J. Gray, ed., *The Sunlight Book of Knitting and Crocheting* (Chicago: W. G. Perry, 1912), p. 118. 192. (left) Adelaide J. Gray, ed., *The Sunlight Book of Knitting and Crocheting* (Chicago: W. G. Perry, 1912), p. 103. (right) *Bear Brand Manual of Handiwork* (New York: Bernard Ulmann and Company, 1915), Vol. 13, p. 167. Courtesy of the Bucilla Company. 193. Elsa S. Barsaloux, *Good Shepherd Fingering Yarns and Their Uses: Infants' Wear* (Newton, MA: Shepherd Worsted Mills, 1917), p. 39.

CHAPTER 10. 200. Jane Eayre Fryer, *The Mary Frances Knitting and Crochet Book or Adventures Among the Knitting People* (Philadelphia: John C. Winston Company, 1918), p. 266. 201. *Sea Power*, August 1918, p. 137. Courtesy of *Sea Power* Magazine, The Navy League of the United States. 203. *Vogue*, August 1, 1918, p. 30. Courtesy

Vogue. Copyright © 1918 (renewed 1946, 1974) by the Condé Nast Publications Inc. 204. 1918. National Archives 205. 1918. National Archives 208. At the Bon Marche, one of Seattle's largest department stores, 1918. National Archives 209. August 1918. UPI/Bettmann Newsphotos 210. August, 1918. National Archives 211. August, 1918. National Archives. 212. (top) Brown Brothers. World War I. (bottom) Brown Brothers, 1918. 213. (top) Brown Brothers, 1917. (bottom) Brown Brothers. World War I. 219. (left) *Corticelli Lessons in Knit and Crochet* #8 (Florence, Mass: Nonotuck Silk Co., 1918), p. 10. (right) *Utopia Yarn Book,* 14th Ed., (New York: Henry E. Frankenberg Co., 1919), p. 71. 223. *Star Needlework Journal,* Vol. 3, #4, 1918, p. 10.

CHAPTER 11. 226. Department of Library, Archives and Public Records, State Capitol, Phoenix, Arizona. 227. (top) 1918. National Archives. (bottom) Universal Motion Picture Co., N.Y. 1917. National Archives. 228. National Archives. 231. Brown Brothers. 232. World War I, National Archives. 238. 1918. National Archives.

CHAPTER 12. 241. *Fleisher's Knitting and Crocheting Manual* (Philadelphia: S.B. and B.W. Fleisher, Inc., 1926). Courtesy of the Bucilla Company. 247. *Fleisher's Knitting and Crocheting Manual* (Philadelphia: S.B. and B.W. Fleisher, Inc., 1926), cover. Courtesy of the Bucilla Company. 249. *Fleisher's Knitting and Crocheting Manual* (Philadelphia: S.B. and B.W. Fleisher, Inc., 1926), p. 14. Courtesy of the Bucilla Company. 251. *Bear Brand Blue Book of Yarncraft,* #29 (New York: Bernard Ulmann Co., 1921), p. 41. Courtesy of the Bucilla Company. 253. Knights Templar Officers: Golf on Mississippi Gulf Coast. Library of Congress. 254. *Bear Brand Manual of Yarncraft* #29 (New York: Bernard Ulmann Co., 1920), p. 37. Courtesy of the Bucilla Company. 256. (top left) *Peace Dale Knitting Book,* Vol. 4 (New York: Peace Dale Mills, 1922), p. 43. (top right) *Utopia Yarn Book,* 14th Ed. (New York: Henry E. Frankenberg Co., 1919), p. 65. (bottom) *Corticelli Lessons in Knit and Crochet,* #15 (Florence, MA: Corticelli Silk Mills, 1920), p. 16. 257. *Fleisher's Knitting and Crocheting Manual* (Philadelphia: S.B. and B.W. Fleisher, Inc., 1921), p. 90. Courtesy of the Bucilla Company. 258. *Fleisher's Knitting and Crocheting Manual* (Philadelphia: S.B. and B.W. Fleisher, Inc., 1926), p. 59. Courtesy of the Bucilla Company.

CHAPTER 13. 261. Sarah Barnes, ed., *Styled Spring Hand Suits for Misses and Women* (Philadelphia: William H. Horstman Co., 1934), Vol. 34, p. 7. 262. *Minerva Men's Book* Vol. 37 (New York: James Lees and Sons, Co., 1934), Vol. 37, p. 5. 265. Sarah Barnes, ed. *Manual of Knitting and Crocheting: Infants' and Children's Wear* (Philadelphia: William H. Horstman Co., 1931), Vol. 34, p. 45. 266. (top left) *Motion Picture Movie Classic Hand-Knit Fashions* (New York: Bernard Ulmann Co., Inc., Fleisher Yarns, Motion Picture Publications, Inc., 1936, cover. Courtesy of the Bucilla Company. (top right) *Motion Picture Movie Classic Hand-Knit Fashions* (New York: Bernard Ulmann Co., Inc., Fleisher Yarns, Motion Picture Publications, Inc., 1936). Courtesy of the Bucilla Company. 267. (left) *Motion Picture Movie Classic Hand-Knit Fashions* (New York: Bernard Ulmann Co., Inc., Fleisher Yarns,

Motion Picture Publications, Inc.), 1936. Courtesy of the Bucilla Company. (right) *Motion Picture Movie Classic Hand-Knit Fashions* (New York: Bernard Ulmann Co., Inc., Fleisher Yarns, Motion Picture Publications, Inc.), 1936, p. 31. Courtesy of the Bucilla Company. 268. The Museum of Modern Art/Film Stills Archive 269. *Worth's Hand Knit Creations,* Mary Widdeke, collaborator (Los Angeles: Worth Brothers, Inc., 1936) Vol. 23, p. 21. 273. (left) Sarah Barnes, ed., *Columbia Book of Water Wear for Women,* Vol. 62 (Philadelphia: William H. Horstman Co., 1934), p. 16. (right) *Fleisher's New Showing of Handknits: Beachwear, Sweaters, Scarves and Vestees* (New York: Fleisher Yarns, Inc., 1935), #28, p. 2. Courtesy of the Bucilla Company. 274. Sarah Barnes, ed., *Columbia Book of Water Wear for Women,* Vol. 62 (Philadelphia: William H. Horstman Co., 1931), p. 16. 276. Sarah Barnes, ed. *Manual of Knitting and Crocheting: Infants' and Children's Wear* (Philadelphia: William H. Horstman Co., 1931), Vol. 34, p. 46. 279. *Angora Accessories for Day and Evening* (New York: Bernard Ulmann Co., Inc., 1938) Vol. 2, p. 8. Courtesy of the Bucilla Company. 285. August 13, 1936. The Bettmann Archive. 286. Nita-Nata-Nu Fraternity. The Bettmann Archive. 288. Underwood and Underwood. c. 1930, Herbert Hoover Presidential Library.

CHAPTER 14. 293 (left) *Minerva Hand-Knits for Men in the Service* (Bridgeport, Pa.: James Lees and Sons Co., 1941), Vol. 61, front cover. (right) *Minerva Hand-Knits for Men in the Service* (Bridgeport, Pa.: James Lees and Sons Co., 1941), Vol. 61, p. 21. 295. June 1940. Bettmann Newsphotos. 296. Mrs. George Blumental (national committee woman of the Citizen's Comittee for the Army and the Navy), Mrs. Franklin D. Roosevelt and Ilka Chase at "Knit for Defense Tea" at Waldorf-Astoria on September 30, 1941. UPI/Bettmann Newsphotos. 297. Gjon Mili, Life Magazine © 1941, Time Inc. 301. *Bernat Handicrafter: Baby Handknits* (Emil Bernat & Sons Co.: Jamaica Plain, Mass., 1951), #27, cover. Courtesy of Bernat Yarn & Craft Corp., Depot and Mendon Streets, Uxbridge, MA 01569. 303. Words and Music: Flossy Frills and Ben Lorre; edited by Glen Miller, New York: Music Products, Inc. Library of Congress. 306. (top left) *Movie Star Hand Knits for Men* (New York: Bernard Ulmann Co., Inc., 1940), Vol. 316, cover. Courtesy of the Bucilla Company. (top right) *Movie Star Hand Knits for Men* (New York: Bernard Ulmann Co. Inc., 1940), Vol. 316, p. 3. Courtesy of the Bucilla Company. (bottom) *Movie Star Hand Knits for Men* (New York: Bernard Ulmann Co. Inc., 1940), Vol. 316, p. 29. Courtesy of the Bucilla Company. 308. *Campus Classics for Knitters* (New York: Bernard Ulmann Co. Inc., 1940), Vol. 10, cover. Courtesy of the Bucilla Company. 317. *Bernat Handicrafter #19* (Emil Bernat & Sons Co.: Jamaica Plain, Mass.: 1949), p. 7. Courtesy of Bernat Yarn and Craft Corp., Depot and Mendon Streets, Uxbridge, MA 01569. 319. *Smart Knitting,* 4th edition, 1945. 320. © 1949. Courtesy of Elizabeth Zimmermann and Meg Swanson.

CHAPTER 15. 326. *Smart Knitting,* 9th edition, 1952, p. 39. 327. *Woman's Day,* cover. Copyright © 1950 by Diamandis Communications, Inc. 337. Summit, NJ, 1980. Courtesy of Elizabeth Zimmermann.

About the Author

ANNE L. MACDONALD was for fifteen years chairperson of the history department of the National Cathedral School in Washington, D.C. A lifelong knitter, she is now owner and president of Great Scot, a successful mail-order knitting business. She and her husband live in Bethesda, Maryland.